SuperStars of Baseball

SuperStars of Baseball
Their Lives, Their Loves,
Their Laughs, Their Laments

by BOB BROEG

Diamond Communications, Inc.
South Bend, Indiana
1994

SUPERSTARS OF BASEBALL

Manufactured in the United States of America

Diamond Communications, Inc.
Post Office Box 88
South Bend, Indiana 46624-0088
(219) 299-9278
FAX (219) 299-9296

Library of Congress Cataloging-in-Publication Data

Broeg, Bob, 1918-
    Superstars of baseball : their lives, their loves, their laughs,
their laments / by Bob Broeg.
      p.   cm.
    Originally published: Super stars of baseball. St. Louis :
Sporting News, 1971.
    ISBN 0-912083-61-1
    1. Baseball players--United States--Biography. 2. Baseball
players--United States--Records. I. Broeg, Bob, 1918- Super
stars of baseball. II. Title.
GV865.A1B66   1994
796.357'09--dc20
[B]
            93-36298
            CIP

CONTENTS

INTRODUCTION

Hopefully, the subtitle tells it—"Their Lives, Their Loves, Their Laughs, Their Laments." This book is meant to make these 55 giants of baseball come alive again as persons more than players, as flesh-and-blood humans, not merely athletic demi-gods.

I began this book nearly a quarter-century ago, inspired by the late Johnson Spink of *The Sporting News* to help celebrate the centennial of professional baseball. They began as lengthy features in the famed weekly, then were expanded into book form.

From a famed fabulous 40 of the printed period, circa 1969-71, updated to cover the careers and lives of original superstars, now dead, they've been expanded also to include 15 more modern "immortals," to use a purple-prosed passage from the past.

Writing as an obvious gee-whiz guy who still thinks he can call 'em as he sees 'em, I tried to record superstars' shortcomings as well as their long suits.

Weirdly, in effect becoming each man as I wrote about him, I found myself living their lives, like a Walter Mitty of jockstraps, glorifying and/or sorrowing with them, second-guessing them at times for having abused themselves physically off the field and wasting many of their great talents.

By nature, a happy fella, to whom the joys of life have been always half-full, not half-empty, I pushed away the typewriter more than once with a regretful sigh. And not only because players in the past embarrassingly were underpaid. Many just didn't have fairy-tale finishes.

But they were baseball greats, if occasional ingrates, and I tried to pursue them to the point, as the saying goes, where I could tell you what they ate or drank for breakfast—from the gastronomic garbage-can of Babe Ruth's gullet to the occasional catsup-on-cereal hijinks of Sandy Koufax to Grover Cleveland Alexander's tendency to mosey back into his hotel room for an extra booze bracer if the elevator to the breakfast level was tardy.

First time around—before updated and uplifted with a large assist from the Langfords of Diamond Communications—the book began with a jarring first-chapter sentence:

"Grover Cleveland Alexander was alcoholic, epileptic, and, above all, incredible, his own worst enemy and one of the best pitchers ever."

Now the leadoff superstar of the book is Hank Aaron, whom I've always respectfully called Henry ever since I saw him hit his first major-league home run off the Cardinals' Vic Raschi early in the 1954 season. Uh-huh, saw his 3,000th hit in 1970 at Cincinnati, Stan Musial's 3,000 in '48 at Chicago, and Paul Waner's No. 3-0-0-0 in '42 at Boston. That probably dates me a little.

From the time I was knee-high to one of Rogers Hornsby's line drives, I've read, heard, and watched baseball, covering probably 5,000 games, blessed with the big-city location that enabled me to see National and American league players as a boy.

I've always thought that youth helped in more than 20 years' service on the baseball Hall of Fames' Committee on Veterans. I'm just sorry that, personally, I didn't get to see all of the Fabulous 55 play—but, heck, just having Cy Young's signature probably would permit an autograph collector to cash in from the legendary old Ohio sudbuster's scrawl for more money than the winningest pitcher ever made.

Aware now of the card-collection bonanza for Hall of Famers, I thought a poignant point was raised by Cy Young a couple of years before he died in 1955, nearly 89 years old. At a reunion where they paid only for his fare from his scenic Tuscarawas County hideaway, the financially pinched old-timer grumbled, "You'd think they could give an old fella $75 or so."

The Hall of Fame does help now with the needy as, for instance, an old friend James (Cool Papa) Bell, whose biography is among many I wish I could have included here. Cool was class, off the field as well as on it, where I saw him play briefly just once.

The occasion seemed to sum up my life and many many others who witnessed the changing times by which the blacks got a better and earlier break on the athletic field than off it. As, for instance, the night the old St. Louis Stars installed lights as champions of the Negro National League in 1930.

Driving by the long-gone park with my dear also long-gone father, I was an excited 12-year-old kid at the sight of the unfamiliar lights. I urged Pop to stop. He did and I hurried to what really was a knothole in a wooden old fence, permitting me a chance to see wafer-thin speedster Bell at bat.

As I opted for a longer look, a big black policeman loomed behind me and growled, "What are you doing, boy?"

As fast as if I were Jack B. Robinson if not Jackie Robinson, I jumped back into my father's car. As we drove away, Pop put it in a sentence I've never forgotten.

"Now," he said, "now you know how the other half lives!"

Now, I hope you'll be interested in seeing how the exclusive half lives, the group of bronzed giants at Cooperstown, N.Y., where I gratefully received Hall of Fame writing recognition with the J.G. Taylor Spink award in 1980. There, I'd been annoyed and impatient that the honor roll of returned Hall of Fame players merely had been listed by name when introduced before induction of the new ceremonies.

Script in hand because I'm not that articulate off the cuff, I told the baseball pilgrims, "If every man has his idea of heaven, mine would be a ball game every day in the hereafter with the best players each playing in their prime."

Glancing at the appropriate polished diamonds of the diamond on the dais, I conjured up memories of several:

"I'd like to see Ted Williams sinking a line drive into right field like a blue dart…I'd like to see my old traveling companion, Stan Musial, running—as Fred Hutchingson like to put it—as a wounded turkey on a triple…or Joe Cronin, a couple of chins and many pounds lighter, jutting out that jaw and coming off the bench, swinging bats before belting one off the Green Monster at Boston…or Charley Gehringer gliding in front of a hot smash almost as effortlessly as the manner in which he hit hot smashes…

"Or Roy Campanella, hunkered down a little kid playing in the sand, scooping up a young, wild lefthanded Sandy Koufax's pitches or an old Preacher Roe's spitball…or Bob Feller lifting that left leg in his plow-jockey gait and pouring the coals past a hitter. These are some of the things I'd like to see again…"

Maybe I included some of your memories in my words then or in the pages that follow. Thanks for looking, and enjoy. As they say in the grand old game, keep your hopes high and the ball down.

God bless!

DEDICATED

With gratitude to *The Sporting News* for giving me another time at bat, to the Langfords of Diamond Communications for a chance to swing it and to literary alma mater St. Louis *Post-Dispatch* for permissions to use pictures, this effort is dedicated to a legendary baseball-publishing family: Terrible-Tempered Taylor, the Soft-Hearted Spink, and his gentle son, Johnson, the only guy who ever fired me!

755: Henry Aaron leads all the rest in home runs, four times matching in homers the uniform number he made famous—44.

HANK AARON

Just as Henry Aaron stood a wrist-snapping swing away from THE record, Babe Ruth's 714 home runs, which once seemed as safe as the fact that no one could prove the moon wasn't made of green cheese, The Hammer came to St. Louis to accept an award and clear his dinner plate rather than the bases.

It was early in 1974, the year IT happened, and the occasion was an annual Baseball Writers' chapter dinner of roasts and toasts, songs and skits. Jim Toomey, a reformed sportswriter occasionally hot-tempered as P.R. person for the Cardinals, prepared a Cole Porter parody of salute to Aaron.

To the tune of "You're the Top," it went, in part, as a show-stopper:

You're the top,
You're THE home-run hitter.
You're the top,
You're Gaylord's spitter.
You're a Bacharach tune, you gave Bowie
     Kuhn the pox,
You're the SEC,
The ITT,
You're Magnavox.

1

You're the top,
You're this baseball dinner.
You're the top,
You're a Series winner.
You're a center-fold that can't be told to strip,
You're an Egg-McMuffin,
You're turkey and stuffin',
You're skinny-dip.

You're the top,
You're Bob Gibson ripping.
You're the top,
You're Jabbar tipping.
The ghost of Ruth has gone, forsooth, ker-plop.
Though the Braves are near the bottom,
You're the top…"

So it went for three more amusing, lilting stanzas, the white teeth of The Hammer widening almost as much as when IT finally happened at 9:07 P.M. (Eastern Standard Time) on a Monday night, April 9, 1974 at Atlanta's Fulton County Stadium, where a sellout crowd of 52,870 saw Henry…er, Hank, if you prefer…connect in the fourth inning against Los Angeles lefthander Al Downing.

As the 1-0 pitch sailed over the inner left-field fence into the bullpen, where it was retrieved by Braves' reliever Tom House, Aaron trotted around the bases with characteristically short, choppy strides, not entirely unlike Babe Ruth's quick, mincing steps.

715.

The crowd rose to its feet as one, Aaron's teammates poured out of the dugout and bullpen to greet him at home plate, lifted him and carried him a few steps toward the bench before he broke away and trotted to a special box adjacent to the Atlanta dugout, where he embraced his wife, Billye, and his parents, Mr. and Mrs. Herbert Aaron of Mobile, Ala.

So at 40, as a reward for durability and consistency, strength and stamina, record consciousness

and a character that would withstand the slings, arrows and obscenities of the racially bigoted, the black man walking tall led not only the baseball alphabet. Aaron, like Abou Ben Adhem, led all the rest.

From that moment in early April of '74 at Atlanta until he finished up in late September of '76 at Milwaukee, a designated hitter no longer able to bat, run or field as before, it was all downhill on an uphill climb—if you'll forgive the uneven typographical terrain.

By the time he'd played largely two seasons as a designated hitter making $240,000 with the American League Brewers of Milwaukee BEFORE free agency lifted salary lids. In Sudsville's County Stadium where he'd also played the first 12 of his 23 years in the majors when the Braves were based there, Aaron had shredded the record book.

His home run total, though his last three-season total of 42 just about would match one of his typical years in his prolonged peak, had reached 755. His 3,771 base hits were second only to Ty Cobb's 4,191, prior to Pete Rose's subsequent record, and he'd collected the most long hits, 1,477, and total bases, 6,856, passing both the Babe and The Hammer's longtime National League rival, Stan Musial.

Of course, he'd also played the most big league ball games at that point, 3,298, and he'd gone to bat the most times, too, 12,364, because you can't get a base hit much less a long ball when bench warming. The rangy, rawhided righthanded hitter with the career average of .310, which went down as his home runs went up, must have been allergic to all wood except the kind he swung. He spent precious little time gathering splinters until he appeared in only 85 games his last year. Previously, favored by a 162-game schedule for 15 seasons, he'd played 150 or more contests 14 times.

For too many seasons, Aaron did his thing almost invisibly, chafing under lack of appreciation as an all-around ballplayer, truly one of the best, even more than failure to appreciate him as a hitter. Although he won a National League batting championship as far back as 1957, hitting .355 when he won his only Most Valuable Player award, he didn't arrive in many persons' eyes, nationally, until he achieved the 3,000-hit goal early in 1970, a year before he hit a career high of 47 home runs.

By then, he was 37 years old and, again, by then, he had hit 40 or more homers six times, including curiously, matching his uniform number—44—four times. It was when he rebounded with the high production in '71 that he began to think first of Ruth's Mt. Everest of hitting and Musial's National League hit high, 3,630, a figure he just missed because he went in a huff to the American League at Milwaukee.

For those who looked upon him as a phlegmatic automaton, Aaron's bolt back to the Brewers was not to return to baseball's equivalent of his athletic womb, but, rather, because he felt the Braves had capitalized fully on him as a hitter and planned only a token front office future. The financially shaky Atlanta operation obliged him by dealing him to Milwaukee for outfielder Dave May and pitcher Roger Alexander, hardly household words.

Aaron's reaction to the "hate" mail, which grew as figurative brown-shoed, white-socked, real-life Archie Bunker rednecks began to realize he really posed a threat to Ruth's career record, was one of dismay, then disgust, hurt and finally anger.

"I've always admired Jackie Robinson most because of what he did, but I didn't appreciate fully what he endured until now," said the black man to whom the "nigger" put-down had become only a part of the unpleasantness.

"I'm not trying to make anybody forget Ruth, but, instead, to remember Aaron," said Henry, who was born the year before the Babe hung it up, 1935. "It's just like the rest of my game. I never said I was Willie Mays defensively or that I threw as well as Roberto Clemente, but, until I hurt my arm late in

my career, nobody ran on me and I never threw to the wrong base and I could go get the ball."

For a fact, Aaron was underrated by many because he lacked the spectacular flair of Mays or the dynamic dash of Clemente, but he was all-all as a ballplayer, a point he proved when, at the urging of first Bobby Bragan and then Charley Dressen, he opened up as a base-stealer. One year, 1963, he joined that rare breed of 30-homer, 30-stolen base players, hitting 44 for four bases, and filching 31. Yeah, and he was thrown out only a couple of times.

The easy-does-it approach Aaron had, plus the fact that he put on no more than 10 pounds from the time he came up at 20 until he quit at 42, accounted in part for his knack of escaping pulled muscles. He hit with wrists that were exceptionally thick and which rolled over in his swing so that his right hand wound up on top of the left. Truth is, that's the way he'd batted as a kid—cross-handed—when he joined the Indianapolis Clowns of the vanishing Negro National League in 1952.

"If I'd had it to do over," said Aaron late in his career, "I'd have been a switch-hitter. After all, batting cross-handed from the right side, I was already part way there."

With his speed, as deceptive as his play in general, Henry would have legged out at least a few more in those 13,940 times he went to home plate from the time he first faced a big league pitcher, Cincinnati righthander Bud Podbielan, at Crosley Field on April 13, 1954. It was at the same park where he dribbled hit No. 3,000 over second base 16 years later.

Ingloriously, Aaron took the collar that opener in '54—"oh, oh for 5"—against Podbielan, Joe Nuxhall and Frank Smith in a slugfest won by the Reds, 9-8. Next day the first of those 3,771 hits came against St. Louis at Milwaukee, a double off the left-field fence at County Stadium.

The victim was a fast-firing veteran righthander, Vic Raschi, a veteran big name from the American

League and the New York Yankees. Little more than a week later, April 23, at St. Louis's Sportsman's Park, facing the same Raschi at a time Henry was getting along with .267, he got his first RBI and his first homer.

Who would have thought, then, that the kid Charley Grimm had picked to replace broken-legged Bobby Thomson in an outfield with Andy Pafko and Bill Bruton would hit one after another until he'd even passed the Babe by what amounted to a sizable season's total, 41 homers?

Sure, Henry went to bat almost 4,000 times more than Ruth did, so he's really the *greatest hitter of home runs rather than the greatest homerun hitter.* He bought that distinction from me one time, especially when I pointed out that it meant that the Babe was the most prodigious homerun hitter and that he (Aaron) was the most prolific. But for a guy who hit from 200 to 300 homers MORE than the likes of such muscle men as Ted Williams, Jimmy Foxx, Mel Ott, Ernie Banks, Ed Mathews, Musial, et al. it's a bit galling when suddenly someone starts counting the home runs Sadarahu Oh is hitting in Japan.

"Over here," said Aaron evenly even before Jim Rice at Boston had become the American League's Most Valuable Player in 1978, "I don't think anyone will break my records, but if anyone can or does, I'd suggest Rice as having the best chance."

Rice did have a beckoning target, the Green Monster, as Fenway Park's high, close barrier is called, but he fell far short. Aaron was favored with high altitude and a left-field fence pulled in for his benefit at Atlanta in the second half of his career. But Milwaukee was no piece of cake and, after the switch to Dixie in 1966, Henry didn't have Eddie Mathews, forming a tremendous tandem as they combined at Milwaukee.

The secret of Aaron's success was two-fold. For 20 years he averaged 120 games a year, an incredible number, and he hit home runs with almost monotonous consistency if not eye-popping quantity, to wit, en route to 715:

13… 27… 26… 44… 30… 39… 40… 34… 45… 44… 24… 32… 44… 39… 29… 44… 38… 47… 34… 40…

And after a winter's suspense before the 1974 season, with Commissioner Bower Kuhn disturbed that Mathews, then managing the Braves, hinted he'd like to keep The Hammer on the bench so that he could tie and break the record at home, Aaron answered the pressure by teeing off the Reds' Jack Billingham opening day at Cincinnati.

Belatedly, Atlanta had awakened to the significance at the tail end of the '73 season when, for instance, more than 40,000 came out for the final game, giving Aaron a warm, encouraging cheer when he popped up his last time up and trotted out to left field. So, as mentioned, not only was the park packed for the home opener on that magical Monday night in April 1974, but a national television audience watched a "Monday Night Game of the Week" that was far from routine.

If thousands say they saw the Babe hit No. 60 off Tom Zachary the last day of the 1927 season at Yankee Stadium, exaggerating, millions WILL be able to say they saw Aaron's No. 715—and mean it.

Yes, and through the marvel of television's instant replay, they saw it again and again. As customary, Aaron shuffled rather than walked into the batter's box, loose-limbed and relaxed until just before the ball was pitched. He had a habit of hitting off his front foot, dragging the tip of the right shoe so that he wore out more back-foot shoes than the front.

Over the years, I thought he'd been a better hitter at Milwaukee when he went to right field, the opposite field, more often to the point that the foe had to play him straight away. Now and then, he'd hit one out of there the other way, too. His nemesis then was herky-jerky St. Louis southpaw Curt Simmons, who changed-up beautifully on him, disdaining to throw the fastball, observing:

"Trying to throw a fastball past Aaron is like trying to sneak the sunrise past a rooster."

Well said, like The Hammer's remark the time Yogi Berra, catching in one of the many All-Star Games in which Aaron did not distinguish himself, showed both his powers of gabbiness and observation when, glancing up at the slugger's bat gripped with the trademark down, he said:

"Hey, Hank, you're holding your bat wrong."

Quote Mr. Aaron, "I don't read 'em, I just hit 'em."

He would agree, though, a bit wistfully, that he had been a better hitter at Milwaukee when he'd go to right-field or when, as in exasperation one time against Simmons in St. Louis, he guessed a change-up and, striding onto home plate, stepped into the ball and hit it onto the right-field roof. When The Hammer came around to "score," he found he'd been foiled again by Simmons. Umpire Chris Pelekoudas, working balls and strikes, declared Hank out for having stepped out of the batter's box (onto the plate) to hit the ball.

At Atlanta, becoming almost strictly a one-field hitter for whom the foe began to shift by placing three infielders on the left side, Aaron said he'd altered his stance and his swing.

"For one thing," he said, "Mathews left the lineup and Joe Adcock was gone. At Milwaukee, they were the power men for whom I could get on base. For another thing, in the move to Atlanta I felt the quickest way to win the hearts of the baseball fans in the Southeast would be to hit the long one."

Aaron also had heard, too, the old story that over the years the first sign of corrosion of coordination for a batter is decreased ability to pull the ball. In other words, an older player just can't get his bat around quickly enough on a good fastball and—.

The Hammer wouldn't accept the inevitable. "I adjusted my stance and my batting grip and swing," he said. "I brought my hands down somewhat and also held them closer into my body. The idea was to shorten my swing, to quicken it in reaction to the pitched ball."

Although he still took a king-sized swing, Aaron had what astute baseball judge Paul Richards called "the knack of adjusting to the pitch in mid-flight." And though aware Babe Ruth had been a great pitcher and had not benefited from airconditioning and other modern conveniences, Stan Musial noted that the Babe had profited from more small parks and the infrequent use of relief pitching specialists, which was still true through Musial's early years, too.

Furthermore, comparing or contrasting Aaron and Ruth, they were as different in their lifestyles almost as in the color of their skin and their physical appearances as well as habits. To the Babe, baseball merely was a pleasant interlude from an extra-inning evening of booze, broads and black cigars, from debauchery to devastating digestive mishmash.

Aaron would come to town, seek out the best Polynesian food, if possible, taxi there for dinner, and then return to his hotel to watch a television movie until past midnight. He drank hard liquor so seldom that, as he put it, smiling, his idea of something strong was an occasional bourbon with sweet soda used as mix. He smoked about half a pack of cigarettes a day and even when divorced, he regarded himself as conservative in his pursuit of all pleasures.

"I've found that I need my rest, lucky I wasn't hurt too often, and although I could eat anything, I'd eat only one meal a day so that my weight didn't fluctuate," said Henry, who would have a couple of beers after a night game, then rest until about 12:30 P.M. the next day. On the road he sent down for coffee and the newspapers. He'd watch an early afternoon soap opera or ancient movie on TV, catnap, then have an early dinner—often in his room—before going to the ballpark early.

"I wasn't anti-social," he said, "but I had goals to go and only one body with which to achieve them."

Smart boy, Henry Louis Aaron, middle child of seven who lived. He was born to Mobile folks who traced their ancestors back to slaves. Hank's father, Herbert, had a good job in Mobile as a boilermaker's helper at the Alabama Drydock and Shipbuilding Company. As a result, wife Estella and the kids had it a bit better than the average black in the suffering South of Depression Thirties. By young Aaron's own recollection, Henry hung pretty close to mom's apron strings. Younger brother, Tommy, later a fringe big leaguer, was just the opposite.

Born as a 10-pound Piscean, H. Aaron learned loyalty, love and how to take adversity from his family. When a brother accidentally belted open Henry's head with a broomstick and the boy wailed to his father, his father told him to stop bawling, as writer Al Stump recorded it, and to take it like a man.

He WAS a man among boys, so good as a 145-pound football player at Mobile's Central High School that, shrewdly, he finally quit. You see, Mom Aaron had it figured that he'd get a college athletic scholarship, probably from Florida A & M, and, by then, Henry had made up his mind that baseball was his dish of tea leaves. Sure enough, playing infielder for a kids' team, he caught the eye of the manager of a black semi-pro team.

Aaron soon was a "highly paid," $3-a-game semi-pro, but then he began to look so good for the Mobile Black Bears that the traveling secretary of the Indianapolis Clowns approached him. The black big leagues were disappearing as the top players and crowds had begun to flock to see Robinson, Roy Campanella, Don Newcombe, Willie Mays, Larry Doby, Monte Irvin and other black league graduates who had made the game better and the plight of their people.

A $200-a-month offer dazzled the boy, but his mother was firm. Bunny Downs and the Clowns would have to wait until Henry finished high school. Hank had done odd jobs such as cut weeds, trim hedges and pick berries, so he bought a new sports jacket and the two pair of pants he

owned when the rail ticket came to report to the spring training camp of the Clowns at Winston-Salem, N.C.

Aware that Aaron got up to nearly a quarter-million dollars to play ball even before the severing of baseball's umbilical cord, the reserve clause, made free agency possible is impressive, all right. So, too, is the $1,000,000 contract Hank signed with Magnavox for five years of promotion, including use of baseballs commemorating home runs No. 714 and 715 before they would go to the Hall of Fame at Cooperstown. Sensitively in his quiet way, Aaron always felt the Hall of Fame and the commissioner both were remiss in not making more of home run No. 700. Sorry, Hank, old friend, I'm with you in most instances, but not that milestone, incidental to IT.

If any would envy Aaron's subsequent financial success, please don't forget that this was the same willowy wanderer who left home with $2, two sandwiches, those extra pair of pants, a cardboard suitcase, and his family's well wishes. And in the segregation of the South on the Clowns' bus trips—the Supreme Court ruling striking down "seperate but equal" evasion of blacks' rights was still two years distant—the diet was baloney and crackers, grocery store cupcakes and cola. Restaurants wouldn't serve men of the different color then.

Even when the Braves paid $2,500 for a 30-day look-see option and a $7,500 follow-up, on the okay of their former manager, scout Billy Southworth, Aaron didn't get a penny of the price. It went to Sid Pollock, who owned the Clowns.

Paid $300 a month to play with Eau Claire, Wis., of the Class C Northern League in 1952, strictly on his own and only a so-so shortstop, the kid with the $5 suit, rag-tag glove and blazing .336 bat worked his way. Even though Aaron's average in the Class A Sally League with Jacksonville, Fla., a year later was .362, it was the RBI production (125) of the lad moved to second base that excited manager Ben Geraghty and general manager John

Quinn had as the Braves move from Boston to Milwaukee was the majors' first in a half century.

In Jacksonville as the season opened, Henry was wool-gathering on a street corner when he saw pretty Barbara Lucas, then attending Walker's Business College. Like John Smith of American heritage, Aaron found his John Alden in the team's clubhouse man who was well acquainted. Henry hustled T.C. Marlin, shy about girls, but not about his hitting:

"If you know the young lady, please introduce me to her as a great coming hitter."

Barbara had seen Henry take the collar opening night, but he promised that if she'd come again, he'd hit a home run for her. Indeed. A homer, double and a single.

Their marriage, which ended in divorce, produced two daughters and two sons. At the time their father broke Babe Ruth's record, Gaile was nearly 20 and Dorinda close to 12 and the boys, Hank, Jr., going on 17, and Larry at 16. Aaron wondered about the wisdom of having given his elder son, though himself a pretty good athlete, the handicap of the same name. Daughter Gaile, a student at Fisk University, delighted him then with a summer job as a newspaperwoman.

Later, Aaron would marry an attractive widow, Mrs. Billye Williams, a television talk show hostess whose first husband had been a civil rights' leader, Dr. Samuel Williams.

Aaron didn't know much about civil rights when he joined the Braves, but he found staunch allies, including little Donald Davidson, a Boston-transplanted dwarf who would be his long-time traveling companion as road secretary before finally bolting the Braves as Henry himself did. Another was the hand-wringing male Zasu Pitts, who was a Milwaukee favorite, Charley Grimm, former Chicago Cubs' first baseman and manager there and at Milwaukee.

When Thomson broke his ankle before the 1954 season—and, oddly Aaron would fracture his own ankle in September—Grimm had come to a couple of decisions. One, the kid as an infielder might make a helluva outfielder. Two, his bat was the best bet to replace Bobby's.

"You're my leftfielder, Hank," said Grimm, who, like other managers, would find Aaron even better in right, "and don't worry."

So it began there at Milwaukee in April 1954 and ended the same place in September 1976, though with the quixotic nature of people as well as places, when temperamental and colorful Ted Turner took over the Braves, he lured Aaron back to Atlanta as farm director or, to use the more glorified title of the day, in charge of minor league player development. Proving that professionals can remain pros, Henry's boss as general manager first became his former brother-in-law, the late Bill Lucas.

Although a horrendous .194 hitter for 24 All-Star Games, Aaron was an outstanding World Series performer, hitting .393 against the Yankees in the successful Braves' 1957 effort and .333 in defeat a year later. In 14 Series games he had 20 hits, including two doubles, a triple and three home runs, driving in nine runs.

The big moments for a man of dignity who lost his cool rarely, such as when he shoved a strawberry pie in a reporter's face or a brief scuffle with former friend and teammate Rico Carty, were man-bites-dog news. To me, his poise and cool under pressure of the assault on Ruth's record, with the lack of privacy for a private person and, especially, the villifying abuse, were admirable.

In a way, the final steps to the summit, No. 714 and No. 715, were the steepest, but, my, The Hammer had so many, including the one that meant so much to him and to Milwaukee. It was September 1957, and the Cardinals were making a fresh run at the Braves when, facing relief ace Billy Muffett who hadn't allowed a home run, Aaron belted one in extra innings over the center-field pennant to clinch the pennant.

"I'll always remember that one especially," Henry

would say, "because it meant so much to the ball club."

Nicely said and nicely done, but that's just about the way Henry Louis Aaron did things. Oh, now and then, he'd trip over his tongue or naturally strike out, but he was customarily as consistent personally as professionally. Other players liked him even if they felt—many, that is—that they didn't know him too well.

One who found out about him—the hard way—was Johnny Antonelli, Giants' lefthander off whom he'd just doubled. As The Hammer shuffled into the batter's box, next time up, Antonelli snarled:

"You can afford to lose some teeth, you bleep."

Easy-does-it Aaron answered easily, "But can you?"

Antonelli fired a fastball, head high, and Aaron hit it 450 feet. Oh, yes, aroused, the sleeping canine creamed the Giants for THREE home runs that day.

As Cole Porter put it and Jim Toomey parodied when Hank Aaron got the Dr. Robert F. Hyland award from St. Louis writers for meritorious service to sports, but not to Cardinals' pitchers:

You're the top,
You're a flag a-flapping.
You're a Countess Mara,
A tale by O'Hara.
You're Chanel 5, you're Mr. Clean, your schnapps.
You will never hit the bottom
'Cause you're the top.

HENRY LOUIS (HANK) AARON
Born February 5, 1934, at Mobile Ala.
Height 6-0 Weight 190
Threw and batted righthanded.
Named to Hall of Fame, 1982.

YEAR	CLUB	LEAGUE	POS.	G.	AB.	R.	H.	2B.	3B.	HR.	RBI.	B.A.	PO.	A.	E.	F.A.
1952	Eau Claire	North.	SS	87	345	79	116	19	4	9	61	.336	137	265	35	.920
1953	Jacksonville	Sally	2B	137	574	115	208	36	14	22	125	.362	330	310	36	.947
1954	Milwaukee	Nat.	OF	122	468	58	131	27	6	13	69	.280	223	5	7	.970
1955	Milwaukee	Nat.	OF-2B	153	602	105	189	37	9	27	106	.314	340	93	15	.967
1956	Milwaukee	Nat.	OF	153	609	106	200	34	14	26	92	.328	316	17	13	.962
1957	Milwaukee	Nat.	OF	151	615	118	198	27	6	44	132	.322	346	9	6	.983
1958	Milwaukee	Nat.	OF	153	601	109	196	34	4	30	95	.326	305	12	5	.984
1959	Milwaukee	Nat.	OF-3B	154	629	116	223	46	7	39	123	.355	263	22	5	.983
1960	Milwaukee	Nat.	OF-2B	153	590	102	172	20	11	40	126	.292	321	13	6	.982
1961	Milwaukee	Nat.	OF-3B	155	603	115	197	39	10	34	120	.327	379	15	7	.983
1962	Milwaukee	Nat.	OF-1B	156	592	127	191	28	6	45	128	.323	341	11	7	.981
1963	Milwaukee	Nat.	OF	161	631	121	201	29	4	44	130	.319	267	10	6	.979
1964	Milwaukee	Nat.	OF-2B	145	570	103	187	30	2	24	95	.328	284	28	6	.981
1965	Milwaukee	Nat.	OF	150	570	109	181	40	1	32	89	.318	298	9	4	.987
1966	Atlanta	Nat.	OF-2B	158	603	117	168	23	1	44	127	.279	315	12	4	.988
1967	Atlanta	Nat.	OF-2B	155	600	113	184	37	3	39	109	.307	322	12	7	.979
1968	Atlanta	Nat.	OF-1B	160	606	84	174	33	4	29	86	.287	418	20	5	.989
1969	Atlanta	Nat.	OF-1B	147	547	100	164	30	3	44	97	.300	299	13	5	.984
1970	Atlanta	Nat.	OF-1B	150	516	103	154	26	1	38	118	.298	319	10	7	.979
1971	Atlanta	Nat.	1B-OF	139	495	95	162	22	3	47	118	.327	733	40	5	.994
1972	Atlanta	Nat.	1B-OF	129	449	75	119	10	0	34	77	.265	996	70	17	.984
1973	Atlanta	Nat.	OF	120	392	84	118	12	1	40	96	.301	206	5	5	.977
1974	Atlanta (a)	Nat.	OF	112	340	47	91	16	0	20	69	.268	142	3	2	.986
1975	Milwaukee	Amer.	DH-OF	137	465	45	109	16	2	12	60	.234	2	0	0	1.000
1976	Milwaukee	Amer.	DH-OF	85	271	22	62	8	0	10	35	.229	1	0	0	1.000
American League Totals—2 Years				222	736	67	171	24	2	22	95	.232	3	0	0	1.000
National League Totals—21 Years				3076	11628	2107	3600	600	96	733	2202	.310	7433	429	144	.982
Major League Totals—23 Years				3298	12364	2174	3771	624	98	755	2297	.305	7436	429	144	.982

a Traded to Milwaukee Brewers for Outfielder Dave May and minor league Pitcher Roger Alexander, November 2, 1974.

CHAMPIONSHIP SERIES RECORD

YEAR	CLUB	LEAGUE	POS.	G.	AB.	R.	H.	2B.	3B.	HR.	RBI.	B.A.	PO.	A.	E.	F.A.
1969	Atlanta	Nat.	OF	3	14	3	5	2	0	3	7	.357	4	1	1	.833

WORLD SERIES RECORD

YEAR	CLUB	LEAGUE	POS.	G.	AB.	R.	H.	2B.	3B.	HR.	RBI.	B.A.	PO.	A.	E.	F.A.
1957	Milwaukee	Nat.	OF	7	28	5	11	0	1	3	7	.393	11	0	0	1.000
1958	Milwaukee	Nat.	OF	7	27	3	9	2	0	0	2	.333	14	0	0	1.000
World Series Totals—2 Years				14	55	8	20	2	1	3	9	.364	25	0	0	1.000

ALEX THE GREAT at 40. Ol' Pete Alexander still was a 21-game winner with the Cardinals in 1927.

GROVER ALEXANDER

Grover Cleveland Alexander was alcoholic, epileptic and, above all, incredible, his own worst enemy and one of the best pitchers ever.

Although he missed an early professional promotion by plunking in the ribs the minor league manager who insisted he'd be too wild, Alexander became a master of control. That is, ironically, of everything except himself and the unquenchable thirst that teamed with seizures of epilepsy after World War I to make his 20-season success as unbelievable as his ability to spot a ball.

When Alexander was pitching for the Cubs early in the Roaring Twenties, a decade in which he spent more time in the speakeasies than a federal agent, he agreed to a spring training stunt proposed by a Los Angeles newspaperman. With batterymate Bill Killefer squatting behind home plate with a tomato can rather than a catcher's mitt as the target, Alexander wound up and threw a strike into the open mouth of the can. With Killefer changing the position of the can, the incredible craftsman reportedly did it again and again.

Any study of superstars of the past will demonstrate it's not always easy to match the man with the legend, especially when the great were hero-worshipped by those who might be inclined to exaggerate a bit like, say, friend Thomas Clancy Sheehan, on the record one of the worst big league pitchers and, otherwise, one of the most astute baseball observers.

One year with the Philadelphia Athletics—1916—towering Tom won 32 fewer games than Alexander did for the neighboring Phillies. Alex was 33-12 that year with 16 shutouts, Sheehan was 1-16 with no excuses.

"And that's not all," said the florid, silver-haired Sheehan. "My roommate that year, Jack Nabors, was 1-20 (19 losses in succession). Man, you never saw two guys who had so much to celebrate when they won a game."

Clancy, as they called the jovial Irish giant who briefly managed the Giants and for years until his death had been their superscout, was as relaxed as when he gumshoed through a Chicago hotel lobby as a house detective. He was as relaxed then as Alexander sidewheeling with a short, effortless delivery. And Clancy was, at his best, in prolific praise of the pitcher who was known as Alec, Alex, Old Pete and, quite appropriately, Alexander the Great.

The double-chinned Sheehan, who had a deep bass voice and a perpetually surprised look, would puff up his ample cheeks, tongue packed firmly therein, and swear Alexander's control was so good that he once fired a game-ending third strike on a 3-and-2 pitch, with the bases loaded, as he fell off the mound in epileptic shock.

Far-fetched? Probably, though there is evidence that at least once Alexander did suffer an attack on the mound and managed to arch the ball up to the plate—for a strike!

Sheehan, who took his losing habits into the National League, remembered a time he was scheduled to oppose Old Pete on a bitter cold spring day in Chicago. Tall Tom took a lengthy warmup and

watched in amazement as Alexander waited until virtually game-time, walked out, threw a few pitches on the sidelines while conversing with a spectator, then flipped his glove to the mound.

"I say to myself, 'This time I got him,'" recalled Clancy, pausing for dramatic effect.

Well?

"He shuts me out," said the pop-eyed, pouting Sheehan, using the disappearing present-tense discourse of the diamond.

Another time, so help him Thomas Clancy Sheehan, Alexander wobbled into the Cubs' clubhouse 15 minutes before game time, roaring drunk. Happy, but soused.

Pete's old Philadelphia batterymate, Killefer, than managing the Cubs, ducked discreetly into the washroom to reach a decision, then came out and snapped angrily:

"You're still pitching."

"Who said I wasn't, Bill, old boy?" Sheehan quoted the gay inebriate, who hummed as he changed into uniform and weaved his way to the field.

What happened?

Clancy held up one finger with a haughty gesture.

So Alexander allowed one run?

"One run, hell, one hit," said superscout Sheehan, "and Alex got the game over so fast, he was still loaded when it ended."

As suggested, the jovial giant of the Giants might have been making a good story better, but it's true, as the famous pitcher's former wife told it, that Alexander would boast at times about the king-sized hangover with which he pitched. And Alex recalled, in an infrequent self-exploration shortly before his death in 1950, that he'd have a couple of belts of whiskey when he got up in the morning on his pitching days. He'd take a third shot after he brushed his teeth.

"And there were mornings I'd get to the elevator and turn back to my hotel room for a fourth before heading down to breakfast," he recalled.

If Alex ever was really under the influence of alcohol when he took the mound to start a game, it's almost believable that he still could have been under the effects of liquor when it ended. Not because he didn't have remarkable recuperative powers, which he did, but because he pitched so rapidly.

Alexander once reeled off a nine-inning victory in 58 minutes. Browsing through files of the *St. Louis Post-Dispatch*, trying to come up with the account of ceremonies in which Charles A. Lindbergh presented World Series rings to the Cardinals in 1927, I noted a game Alex had pitched against Boston a few days earlier. His pitching opponent, Dr. Hubert (Shucks) Pruett, troubled with an ailing arm, walked nine St. Louis batters, but Old Pete worked so quickly that he wrapped up a 6-1 Redbird victory in one hour, 33 minutes.

Alexander's former teammate, Jesse (Pop) Haines, who pitched 18 years for the Cardinals through 1937, explained that the foe long since had learned it didn't pay to try to wait out the corner-catching control artist.

"I called him Old Low-and-Away," Haines said, "because that's the way he pitched everybody, down at the knees and nicking the outside corner, with his good fastball or his short, sharp curve."

When Sheehan recalled that Alexander had squelched him by taking little warmup on a cold day and then shutting him out, it's unlikely that tall Tom was stretching his tall imagination. When Alex relieved Haines in the seventh game of the 1926 World Series, he took the mound without benefit of throwing in the bullpen and merely flipped five warmups.

Grover Cleveland Alexander won 373 games, a National League record he shares with Christy Mathewson. He won 30 or more in three successive seasons at Philadelphia, 1915-17.

He holds the league mark for most shutouts, 90 including the most in one season, 16, in the Baker Bowl bandbox. There, a righthanded pitcher had to be razor sharp because the right-field fence was so close that the second baseman and first baseman had to be careful they didn't get spiked by the right fielder on a short flyball.

Alex pitched four straight shutouts as a rookie in 1911. He pitched four one-hitters in 1915, a year he paced the Phillies to a pennant, and he had a 1.22 earned-run average, the league's low until Bob Gibson's 1.12 in 1968. Alexander was extremely strong and durable and twice, once each in 1916 and 1917, he won both ends of a doubleheader.

Despite all these achievements and other records, the man is remembered best, not for a game he won, but for a game he saved, the dramatic finale of the 1926 Series, one of the most exciting and eventful in the history of professional baseball's first 100 years.

This was the World Series in which farm-system baseball, Branch Rickey's brainchild by which the poor could compete with the rich, paid off in the first of 15 pennants and nine world championships for St. Louis, the long-time weak sister of the National League.

To balance and steady a young ball club and add experience to the pitching staff, Rickey added Alexander to the cast of the rag-tag Redbirds in June at the request of Rogers Hornsby, the hard-hitting second baseman who hit Alex hard, yet recognized that few others did.

By then, Alexander's reputation for drinking had become as prominent privately as his pitching prowess long had been publicly. But Hornsby, though a teetotaler, like Rickey, wanted Alex when Chicago's new manager, Joe McCarthy, became fed up. For $6,000 the fourth-place Redbirds exercised a waiver claim that enabled them to make history.

It helped that Hornsby had as a coach Alex' good friend and former catcher, Killefer, who had been fired as manager of the Cubs during the 1925 season. It was Reindeer Bill who hung on Alexander the nickname of Alkali Pete, later shortened to just plain Pete. The christening came after the pitcher slipped off a buckboard on a Texas hunting trip and landed flat on his kisser in a large pool of alkali and mud.

Killefer helped pick Old Pete out of the mud, figuratively, in 1926 when the rubber-armed righthander was 39 years old and saddled with a losing record and little to show for those years of stardom. The following Sunday, Alex made his first start in St. Louis, beat McCarthy and his old teammates, 3-2, and went on to win nine of 16 decisions.

The Cardinals, winning only 89 games, one of the lowest victory totals credited to a pennant club, were decided underdogs against the powerful Yankees in the World Series. Although Hornsby had three starters with better regular-season won-and-lost records, he chose Alexander to pitch the second game and the gaffer's 6-2 victory offset a St. Louis defeat in the opener. And in the sixth game of the Series, at New York, Alec evened it again winning, 10-2.

What happened then is subject to interpretation even after research. The purists would have it that Alexander lived like a Trappist monk the night before the last game, ready if he was needed. The other extremists would have it that he got roaring drunk and was still wobbling when Hornsby called on him in the tense moment of truth in the Series showdown.

The best indications are that Alex did celebrate his sixth-game victory and that he was hung over when he dozed in the left-field bullpen at Yankee Stadium, but, heck, that was par for the course for the pitcher with the iron constitution and asbestos-lined stomach.

After the Cardinals got three early tainted runs off Waite Hoyt, the Yankees rallied in the seventh inning against Haines, who had shut them out earlier in the Series. The St. Louis lead had been cut to one run, 3-2, the bases were loaded and two were out when Hornsby halted play, inspected the blistered right hand of the knuckleballing Haines and wig-wagged for a replacement.

Despite varied reports, Alexander was not among the Redbird pitchers warming up, but Hornsby, aware of both his ability to heat up hurriedly as well as his pitching-in-the-pinch reputation, wanted the old man to face Tony Lazzeri, hard-hitting rookie second baseman of the Yankees.

It was a raw, rainy day when the tall, knock-kneed figure with the cap perched characteristically on the top of his head, like a peanut shell, began his long, slow walk from the bullpen to the pitcher's mound.

He carried a red knit sweater, the high-collared windbreaker of the day, over his arm and, noting that Lazzeri nervously was pawing around outside the batter's box, he took his sweet old time.

On the edge of the grass, Hornsby, the second baseman, met him. What the hazel-eyed Hornsby saw was a long, seamy face mottled with freckles and the ravages of what he'd endured in World War I and had done to himself thereafter. His throat with the skin loose was wattled like a turkey's, but Hornsby was interested only in the sleepy gray eyes.

"There ain't no room, Pete," Hornsby said. "Yeah," Alex replied with his slow smile, "there's no place to put 'im, Rog. Guess I'll have to get 'im out."

The first pitch was a called strike, low and away, naturally. The second pitch got more of the plate than the pitching perfectionist intended. The righthanded-hitting Lazzeri lined it to deep left field and into the stands, a loud and frightening foul.

"A few feet more," Alexander would relate philosophically later, "and he'd have been a hero and I'd have been a bum."

Unruffled at the time, Old Pete missed with a pitch and then he broke off a sharp curve, low and away. Lazzeri swung, missed and struck out. A newsreel in the St. Louis Sports Hall of Fame captures on film the crisp pitch and the nonchalant manner in which Alex ambled to the dugout, flipping his glove with a gesture that seemed to symbolize the old man's haughty poise.

There still was a job to do, however, and Alexander did it. He retired the Yankees in order in the eighth. With two down in the ninth, he faced the mighty Babe Ruth, the slugger he limited to one home run and two hits in 10 official times at bat in the course of two World Series.

The old man pitched carefully to the foremost muscle man who was then at his power peak. The count went the limit.

Alexander, trying to avoid giving Ruth a shot at pulling the ball, fired for the outside corner. Hesitatingly, plate umpire George Hildebrand called it ball four.

Alexander, walking slowly toward the plate as he took catcher Bob O'Farrell's toss, inquired quietly, "Where was it?"

Hildebrand put the palms of his hands close together to indicate how far the pitch had been outside.

"If it was that close," said Old Pete quietly, "I think you might have given it to an old guy."

Unexpectedly, then, with righthanded-hitting Bob Meusel at bat and lefthanded Lou Gehrig on deck, the Babe tried to steal second. The surprise play, the only bad one, many believe, that Ruth ever pulled, did not find catcher O'Farrell unprepared. He gunned down the Babe with a perfect throw to Hornsby, who felt that the highlight of his career came when he tagged out Ruth to make his Cardinals the world champions.

For Alexander, too, the World Series in which he won two games and saved one at an age when most pitchers are through, was a moment to remember longest and the most fondly.

Curiously, the man Old Pete struck out, Lazzeri, though he became a clutch-hitting second baseman on several championship teams, is also remembered best for that dramatic showdown at Yankee Stadium. In fact, Push-'em Up Tony is mentioned on Alexander's plaque in baseball's Hall of Fame at Cooperstown, N.Y. Ironically, like Alex, Lazzeri also suffered epileptic attacks and was killed in a fall in 1946 when he was only 42 years old.

For Alexander, after fanning Lazzeri and saving the World Series, opportunities beckoned in the form of vaudeville and personal appearance tours, but the shy farm boy from Nebraska preferred to slip away for hunting and a little quiet drinking, armed with the best contract of his career, $17,500, for 1927.

The man who was named for a president of the United States was born into a family of 13 children, 12 of them boys, on a farm near St. Paul in the sandhills of Nebraska. Dode, as they called young Grover then, did his first hunting with stones and rocks. His mother marveled at the way he could bring down a chicken or a turkey on the run by plunking it with a rock.

That same awkward, funny, three-quarter delivery turned back the other kids in town ball games, to. At 19, Alex went to work as a lineman for the telephone company. One day he showed up late for work with a line gang because he'd been playing ball and the foreman fired him.

"You won't be any good to anybody until you get this ball playing out of your blood," the foreman said.

Alex went to Central City, pitched for $50 a month, drifted to a county fair at Burwell, Neb., where he pitched and beat a crack semi-pro team from Illinois. When Galesburg, Ill., heard about the kid who had tied up the tough semi-pros, the 22-year-old Nebraskan was on his way.

For $100 a month, he pitched in the Illinois-Missouri League in 1909, winning 15 games, but suffered an injury that might have accounted, in part, for his later physical difficulties. Trying to break up a double play, he charged into second base, standing, and was felled so hard by a strong-armed shortstop's throw that he was unconscious for 56 hours.

When he revived in a hospital bed, he saw two of everything and realized, sickeningly, that his eyesight had been affected by the blow to the head. He was told by the doctors, honestly if cruelly, as biographer Jack Sher put it, that he might suffer from double vision for the rest of his life.

Released from the hospital, Alex tried to pitch, but he kept seeing two batters, two catchers. The manager at Galesburg couldn't talk him into quitting and then, slyly, let his contract go to Indianapolis. There, the handicapped kid cracked three of manager Charley Carr's ribs with the first ball he pitched, and Carr would have nothing to do with him. Alex went back to the farm, the season over. And he didn't appear in a single game.

Throughout the winter, Alexander would go into town, day after day, to get someone to catch him. Still unable to focus correctly, he explained later that if he stopped throwing and gave up, he knew he'd "go to pieces."

He found it difficult to believe that he had been sent by Indianapolis to Syracuse in the New York State League. Fact is, needing a favor, Manager Carr had given the pitcher to Syracuse for nothing, explaining:

"He's wild as hell, but he's got plenty of speed."

Just before Alexander was scheduled to report to Syracuse, his vision cleared up miraculously. He was pitching to a friend in a schoolyard at St. Paul when, suddenly, everything became one or, as Sher said, clear and whole.

The sandy-haired pitcher with the brushback haircut and no sideburns pitched tremendously at Syracuse, winning 29 games, and was sold to the Philadelphia Phillies for the magnificent sum of $500. Club owner Horace Fogel promised him $250 a month in 1911—if he made good.

From the time he pitched five perfect innings against the world champion Athletics in the Philadelphia spring series, Alexander was sensational, probably the most spectacular rookie ever to burst across the big league scene. He led the National League with victories, 28.

Late in the season, young Alexander hooked up in a 12-inning duel and scored a 1-0 victory over a 44-year-old Boston pitcher making one of his last big league appearances. The victim was Denton (Cy) Young, author of the most major league victories, 511.

Young Alec took up where old Cy left off, posting seasons of 28-13, 19-17, 22-8, 27-15, then 31-10, 33-12 and 30-13 before the outbreak of World War I frightened the Phillies into unloading him, figuring that Chicago's William Wrigley could stand the financial loss better if the war lasted or if Alexander didn't come home from France.

By then, in the course of that brilliant three-season period of 94 victories and only 35 defeats, Pete had pitched Philadelphia to a pennant in 1915 and had pitched well in two low-score Series games against the Red Sox, winning one and losing one.

The only sore arm of his career—really a wrenched back—kept him from making a third start. He was, by the way, the first pitcher Babe Ruth faced in a World Series, pinch-hitting, and the Bambino grounded out sharply to first base.

Alex threw hard in those days, but he continued to win for years even when he no longer had a hummer. He not only could pinpoint the fastball and curve, low and away, but he also had the knack of taking something off his fast one by degrees and he came up with a screwball about which little has been written. He also threw deceptively.

The delivery was labeled as side-armed, but it really wasn't, as hitters who faced him remember, because he short-armed the ball, bringing it up across his chest and throwing out of his uniform front. The ball was especially difficult to pick up when it came out of his white home uniform.

By the time Alexander went off to war, at 31, he had married Aimee Arrants, a small, lively woman with titian hair and bright blue eyes. They'd had a courtship in Nebraska and were married at Camp Funston, Kan., just before he sailed for France.

He'd pitched three games in April 1918, winning two, before he left for service, relieved that the new club owner, Wrigley, would send Mrs. Alexander $500 every other month for three years.

Alex was gone from baseball only a year, but it was a costly year. He was up in the lines as an artillery sergeant with the 342nd Artillery Battalion of the famed 89th Infantry Division. The roar of the big guns deafened him in one ear and he first experienced the epileptic seizures that seemed to make him drink more often and more heavily.

When Mrs. Alexander worked with script writer Sher for *The Winning Team*, the movie in which Ronald Reagan, later president, portrayed Old Pete two years after the former pitcher's death, she explained that medical men weren't certain whether the war or the blow to the head several years earlier had caused the epilepsy. Certainly the war aggravated whatever weakness there was, including the fondness for alcohol.

"Sometimes the fit would strike him while he was out on the mound," Mrs. Alexander was quoted. "He always carried a bottle of spirits of ammonia with him. They would have to carry him off the field. Some thought he was drunk.

"They would take him into the locker room. Alec would whiff the ammonia, fight to get control of himself and then go right back out and pitch again."

So Aimee never blamed him when he drank. She couldn't endure it forever, understandably. They were twice married, twice divorced, yet never had an estrangement of the heart. Aimee couldn't live with Alec at his worst, but she could understand.

Astonishingly, though he had those twin monkeys of epilepsy and alcoholism on his back, Alexander twice put together 20-victory seasons in his seven full years at Chicago. In 1925, then 38, he pitched 19 innings against the White Sox in the annual fall city series. The game was called because of darkness, 2-2.

That was the same October afternoon that the two other of the three greatest pitchers of the 20th century also were involved in the news. Walter Johnson beat the Pirates in the World Series opener at Pittsburgh, 4-1, and Christy Mathewson died at the tuberculosis sanitarium at Lake Saranac, N.Y.

They told Alexander about Matty as, weary and worn, Old Pete sat in the clubhouse. A Chicago teammate reminded Alex that he had defeated Matty in two of three times they'd met head to head.

"He was past his best years when I beat him," Pete said, turning away.

A broken wrist handicapped Alexander one year. After he went to a sanitarium following the 1925 season to take the first of several drinking cures, which would help for a time, he broke an ankle in spring training at Catalina Island.

The new manager, Joe McCarthy, was the only teammate who never stopped at the hospital to see him, Mrs. Alexander related, and Old Pete was hurt further when he was required to make the trip from the island to the California mainland for exhibition games every day, cast and all.

Alexander was a kind, generous man, quiet and well respected by the men with whom he played. He made it a point, they say, never to drink with a young player and, in fact, did much of his imbibing alone.

Still, he made it tough for a manager, especially a new one like McCarthy, who was trying as a minor leaguer to establish much-needed discipline on a club that had finished last.

The end came one day when, red-eyed and unsteady, Alexander walked slowly—and late—into a meeting McCarthy was holding at a small banquet room at the Hotel Commodore in New York, the morning of the Cubs' first eastern swing in 1926. Alex took a seat in the back of the room and dozed off. Players tittered, but McCarthy chose to ignore the distraction.

His purpose, he advised his players, was to change the Cubs' signs because a former teammate, Rabbit Maranville, had been traded to Brooklyn, the first club to be met.

"The first time Rabbit gets to second base today, he'll have all our signs," said the manager.

16

Rousing himself, Alexander interrupted. "I wouldn't worry about Rabbit, Joe," Old Pete said. "He won't even reach second base."

The crack broke up the meeting, but it also led to Alex' date with destiny in St. Louis, where, by the way, he won 21 games in 1927 at the age of 40. He contributed 16 more victories in another pennant season, 1928, when, like everyone else on the Red-bird staff, the gallant gaffer was creamed by Ruth, Gehrig and Company in a four-game World Series sweep.

Conveniently, years later, Alex would forget that the Babe ever homered off him.

By then, Alexander's batterymate most of the time was John Barleycorn. He struggled and staggered through part of the 1929 season, a disappointing one for the Cardinals, whose club owner, Sam Breadon, patiently made Old Pete his personal reclamation project. He was just one victory shy of Mathewson's National League record, which then was recorded at 372 games.

When Bill McKechnie, who had managed the club to a pennant in 1928 and then had been demoted because of the shocking World Series rout, returned to take over as Redbird skipper again in July 1929, Alexander was just returning from a sanitarium.

"His eyes were clear and his face had a healthy look," McKechnie recalled shortly before his own death. "We were in Pittsburgh and Alec said, 'I'd like to pitch here.' I was a little skeptical because he hadn't pitched a ball in weeks, but I agreed and he pitched a shutout.

"Our next stop was Philadelphia, where he'd been so great and had so many intimate friends. We were tied after nine innings of a Saturday game and I sent Alec in, saying, 'Hold 'em until we can get that winning run for you.' He pitched five scoreless innings, we won in the 14th, and he had No. 373, breaking Matty's record."

McKechnie remembered that afterward Alexander had asked permission to go out with Philadelphia cronies, volunteering, "I won't take a drink."

"I don't care if you take a drink, so long as you report Monday morning, fit and ready to work." McKechnie said, shaking his head sorrowfully.

"When he did show up on Monday morning, he was a sad sight. I was sore and told him he'd let down his best friend, Sam Breadon, and that I was fed up. I had him down to pitch Wednesday at the Polo Grounds against the Giants and he promised to be ready. I even assigned one of my coaches, Gabby Street, to serve as his keeper. But, somehow, he escaped from Gabby and disappeared in New York."

When Alexander reported, shaky, and was hammered out of the box, McKechnie ordered Alexander back to St. Louis for disposition by Breadon, trying to cover up for the likable old cuss by saying he had arm trouble. The story leaked out, of course, and when Breadon couldn't get a positive response, he paid off the old pitcher in August, and sent him home for the rest of the season.

Alexander the Great went back to St. Paul in the belief he'd set a National League record for most victories, and, presumably the last incentive was gone and the last vestige of pitching pride. Cruelly, several years later, it was determined that back in 1902 Mathewson had been deprived of a victory in a clerical statistical error. So the top two were tied at No. 373, and it was much too late for Alexander to do anything about it.

Traded back to the Phillies in December 1929, he appeared in only nine games and 22 innings, losing three games and winning none, before he was released.

He pitched briefly and ineffectively at Dallas the same year, but mostly it was all downhill from then for Old Pete. Aimee did return to him and traveled with him and the bearded House of David, a team for which he barnstormed for a few years. With portable lights that belonged to the House of David, I saw Alex pitch against his old Redbird teammates one summer evening in 1932 at Sportsman's Park, three years before night ball would come to the majors and eight years before St. Louis had regular floodlights.

The crowd then was as warm and almost as large as in those couple of magical seasons immediately after the 1926 World Series when kids in the St. Louis Knothole Gang would give off a sing-song chant:

"We want Alex…we want Alex."

On the way down to the bottom of the bottle, Old Pete sank so low he even sat with the freaks in a flea circus on 42nd Street in Manhattan, getting to his feet on schedule to talk about baseball, to answer questions and to strike out Lazzeri again.

Baseball tried to help him, but he couldn't be helped. He was given a $100-a-month pension by Breadon through the National League, and a subsequent St. Louis club owner, Fred Saigh, also helped. A $60-a-month World War I pension also kept a roof over his head, but, despite hospitalization for cancer and removal of an ear, he steadfastly refused his former wife's pleas that he turn himself in to an old soldier's home.

The alcoholic monkey was on his back, and Old Pete Alexander wanted to be close enough to the next drink. He regarded the old home town of St. Paul, Neb., as extremely unfriendly when he went back there in the fall of 1950, miserable in body and spirit, and found the liquor supply cut off.

Just after he had tottered down the street to the post office, to mail his last letter to his beloved Aimee out there in Long Beach, Calif., hardly drawing a glance as he walked a street on which he'd been lionized in the past, Grover Cleveland Alexander walked heavily back to his rented room in the small Nebraska town. And far from the roaring crowd, Old Low and Away died on November 4, 1950, after 63 years that had been long and short, good and bad.

GROVER CLEVELAND (PETE) ALEXANDER
Born February 26, 1887, at St. Paul Neb.
Died November 4, 1950, at St. Paul Neb.
Height 6-1 Weight 185
Threw and batted righthanded.
Named to Hall of Fame, 1938.

YEAR	CLUB	LEAGUE	G.	IP.	W.	L.	Pct.	H.	R.	ER.	SO.	BB.	ERA.
1909	Galesburg	Ill.-Mo.	24	219	15	8	.652	124	49	-	198	42	-
1910	Syracuse	N.Y. State	43	245	29	14	.674	215	-	-	204	67	-
1911	Philadelphia	Nat.	48	367	28	13	.683	285	133	-	227	129	-
1912	Philadelphia	Nat.	46	310	19	17	.528	289	133	97	195	105	2.81
1913	Philadelphia	Nat.	47	306	22	8	.733	288	106	96	159	75	2.82
1914	Philadelphia	Nat.	46	354	27	15	.643	327	133	94	214	76	2.39
1915	Philadelphia	Nat.	49	376	31	10	.756	253	86	51	241	64	1.22
1916	Philadelphia	Nat.	48	390	33	12	.733	323	90	67	167	50	1.55
1917	Philadelphia (a)	Nat.	45	388	30	13	.698	336	107	79	200	56	1.83
1918	Chicago (b)	Nat.	3	26	2	1	.667	19	7	5	15	3	1.73
1919	Chicago	Nat.	30	235	16	11	.593	180	51	45	121	38	1.72
1920	Chicago	Nat.	46	363	27	14	.659	335	96	77	173	69	1.91
1921	Chicago	Nat.	31	252	15	13	.536	286	110	95	77	33	3.39
1922	Chicago	Nat.	33	246	16	13	.552	283	111	99	48	34	3.62
1923	Chicago	Nat.	39	305	22	12	.647	308	128	108	72	30	3.19
1924	Chicago	Nat.	21	169	12	5	.706	183	82	57	33	25	3.03
1925	Chicago	Nat.	32	236	15	11	.577	270	106	89	63	29	3.39
1926	Chicago (c)-St. Louis	Nat.	30	200	12	10	.545	191	83	68	47	31	3.06
1927	St. Louis	Nat.	37	268	21	10	.677	261	94	75	48	38	2.52
1928	St. Louis	Nat.	34	244	16	9	.640	262	106	91	59	37	3.36
1929	St. Louis (d)	Nat.	22	132	9	8	.529	149	65	57	33	23	3.89
1930	Philadelphia	Nat.	9	22	0	3	.000	40	24	22	6	6	9.00
1930	Dallas	Texas	5	24	1	2	.333	35	23	22	4	11	8.25
	Major League Totals—23 Years		696	5189	373	208	.642	4868	1851	†1372	2198	951	†2.56

† Does not include 1911 season when earned runs were not compiled.
a Traded with catcher William Killefer to Chicago Cubs for pitcher Mike Prendergast, catcher Dilhoefer and $60,000, November 11, 1917.
b In Military Service most of season.
c Waived to St. Louis Cardinals, June 22, 1926.
d Traded to Philadelphia Phillies with catcher Harry McCurdy for outfielder Homer Peel and pitcher Bob MGraw, December 11, 1929.

WORLD SERIES RECORD

YEAR	CLUB	LEAGUE	G.	IP.	W.	L.	Pct.	H.	R.	ER.	SO.	BB.	ERA.
1915	Philadelphia	National	2	172/3	1	1	.500	14	3	3	10	4	1.53
1926	St. Louis	National	3	201/3	2	0	1.000	12	4	3	17	4	1.33
1928	St. Louis	National	2	5	0	1	.000	10	11	11	2	4	19.80
World Series Totals			7	43	3	2	.600	36	18	17	29	12	3.56

"LET'S PLAY TWO:" Baseball's happy warrior, Ernie Banks, homer-hitting, shortstop-first baseman of the Cubs, twice National League MVP with second-division ball clubs.

ERNIE BANKS

If ever baseball perpetrated a hoax that would have titillated author hoax Clifford Irving and any other pipe-dreamer, serious or earnest, it was when the baseball commissioner's office awarded some years ago the first accolade ever given a player for all-around excellence, including cooperation with press and public, and gave the laurels to Willie Mays.

Now, even though he never seemed so satisfied in San Francisco as in New York, where as a wide-eyed rookie he had stopped en route home from the Polo Grounds to play stickball with the kids in the streets, it was the one-time Say Hey Kid, whose talent is unquestioned and who—when he chose—could be exuberant and charming.

But even though Ernie Banks, slower of foot and not so strong-armed, might have been unable to carry Willie's jock strap as a ballplayer—and Banks was p-l-e-n-t-y good—it was no-contest in Ernie's favor when it came to enthusiasm, evenness of disposition and sheer delight in playing the game and meeting people.

If there ever was a better ambassador of goodwill

for baseball than Banks, it would have had to be the game's Johnny Appleseed, the engineer named Alexander Cartwright, the man who laid out the diamond, put nine men on a side, nine innings on a scoreboard and then promoted the sport in a pre-Civil War trek that took him from Hoboken to Hawaii.

And no one ever has recorded Cartwright having smiled a toothpaste smile doing a happy black man's heel-kicking version of an Irish jig at the batting cage and suggesting shrilly:

"Let's play three today…"

For Chicago, the toddlin' town of song and sin, living down Capone and living up to Banks, Ernie was Billy Sunday without the evangelist ballplayer's fire, brimstone and crusade against Demon Rum. And for the hardest-hitting shortstop in history, one who was all but dead and buried in mid-career and then came back much of the way at bat and at first base, the serenity was, pun intended and only a nostaligic note of Bing Crosby's easy-does-it singing, "Sunday, Monday and Always."

"Welcome to Chicago, the toddlin' town, and to bea-u-ti-ful Wrigley Field," bullet-headed, bright-eyed Banks would greet an out-of-town player or writer once he'd overcome young shyness. And, dropping from a warbling canary's shrill to a pleasant sleep-in-the-deep bass, Ernie would spread his encomiums to other parks and other cities when he was wearing the Cubs' road blue-gray.

Enroute to his 512 home runs, most ever by a shortstop, the durable winner of two Most Valuable Player awards (1958-59) with second-division clubs, Ernie earned the "Mr. Cub" label penned on him by friend, admirer and former member of the Fourth Estate, the late, ample and affable Jim Enright, long-time baseball writer and Big Ten basketball official who collaborated with him on the autobiography of the same title.

Among other things, it was the often cavalier, occasionally cruel, treatment of Banks by an aging Leo Durocher, who was perhaps jealous of Ernie's standing with the fans and front office as well and Fourth Estate, that helped create the breach between The Lip and Enright and some other Chicago writers and broadcasters, too.

Even before Durocher backed down and then out, wearing out his welcome after stirring up things, including the sleepwalking ball club to which Philip K. Wrigley had entrusted him, The Lion ceased to roar about Banks and learned to purr, whether he meant it or not. Ernie, meanwhile, kept his cool like the man who deserves much and has received little in credit—or reward—for the discovery of the future star who was elected to baseball's Hall of Fame his first year eligible, 1977.

James (Cool Papa) Bell, also a black superstar who had been born too soon to go through the gates opened by Branch Rickey and Jackie Robinson, preceded Banks into the Hall of Fame four years earlier only because Cooperstown decided to give recognition to legendary Satchel Paige and at least some of the victims of insidious Jim Crow discrimination.

It was Paige who saluted two-legged greyhound Bell, a slick switch-hitting outfielder, by insisting that Cool Papa was "so fast that when he flipped the wall switch in a hotel room, he'd be in bed before the light went out."

Bell would smile at that exaggeration and chuckle over Ol' Satch's claim that the willowy wonder once had hit a slow grounder through Paige's long pipe-stem legs. "Yeah," Satchel would say, deadpanned, "only he was so fast that he outran the ball and was out when he slid into second base, hit in the butt by his own batted ball."

A long-time champion of the blacks as a man who is color blind, Bill Veeck, rated Bell as "an offensive magician, defensively on a par as a center fielder with Tris Speaker, Joe DiMaggio and Willie Mays."

As a sports senior citizen, pro basketball club-owning pioneer and a promoter of Negro National League ball games, Eddie Gottlieb went baseball Barnum Veeck even one better in summing up Bell, who followed the baseball sun from Canada to the Caribbean for nearly a quarter-century.

"If Bell had played in the major leagues," said Gottlieb, then a member of the Hall of Fame's former special committee on veteran black candidates, "he would have reminded fans of Willie Keeler as a bunt-and-run, hit-'em-where-they-ain't batter and of Ty Cobb as a baserunner. And he might have excelled both."

Cool Papa, rescued from anonymity of a long-time job as a night watchman in the St. Louis City Hall, was as modest as impeccable, but he took apologetic exception to what was listed as a base-circling 13.1-second clocking, two-fifths faster than Evar Swanson's accepted record with Cincinnati in 1932.

"The field was wet," Cool said. "On a dry field one time, I circled the bases in 12 seconds flat."

Proud of his own Hall of Fame election, Bell beamed over Banks' minimum-wait selection for induction, pleased to talk more about the kid he'd first fingered when Cool Papa was managing the Kansas City Monarchs' second unit in the late 1940s for a few seasons until the traveling team disbanded and the depleted black National and American Leagues, too.

Ernie Banks, second of 12 children sired by Eddie Banks, a one-time semi-pro catcher who later became a wholesale grocer, came along just at the right time. Born in Dallas on the last day of January in 1931, he was just about the right age—16—when Jackie Robinson's name first appeared in the lineup of the old Brooklyn Dodgers.

At the time, though, Eddie Banks picked cotton and then became a stock clerk with many mouths to feed. As a boy, Ernie shined shoes on the street, mowed lawns and tried cotton picking. But as a cotton picker, he was a heckuva athlete if a reluctant one.

"He never really learned how to pick it," the senior Banks would explain years later. "In fact, the only work Ernie did was at a hotel. He was supposed to carry out the garbage, but the cans were too heavy. After five days he quit and didn't even go back to collect his money."

The boy's interest in sports was limited to football, basketball, softball and track. "My dad bought me a glove for about $2.98 when I was a kid, but he had to bribe me with nickels and dimes to play catch," Ernie recalled merrily.

Still, he played softball so well that when he was 17, he got a chance to play with a semi-pro team, the Amarillo Colts, that barnstormed the South and the Midwest. And the paths led to San Antonio, where Cool Papa Bell was conducting a tryout camp for the Monarchs' No. 2 unit. Cool was captivated by a smooth-as-silk kid shortstop.

"When you get out of school, kid, we'll pick you up," said Bell, who then notified Tom Baird, the Monarchs' owner, that he had a kid for the Kansas City club's top unit, managed by John (Buck) O'Neill. Baird told him, in retort, that O'Neill said he already had a shortstop, Gene Baker, five years older.

"I've seen Baker," snapped Bell, "Banks is better."

So O'Neill took a look and liked what he saw, too.

The Monarchs signed Banks, who toured briefly before going into the Army for two years. When he came back, he hit .385 and 20 home runs, always moving, but getting nowhere financially.

"Five, ten, maybe 15,000 miles a year and our biggest payday was in Lincoln, Neb.—$20 for the night," Banks said ruefully.

By then, Veeck, running the lame-duck St. Louis Browns in 1953, heard about Banks from coach Bill Norman, whose opinion, positive and vocal, he valued. But by then Baird, like other black league owners, had a price on his players. Rickey had raided their ranks shamelessly without compensation. For Banks, Baird wanted $35,000.

Veeck, financially in the red, was red in the face,

too, after talking to his last-hope banker, and telling Baird the best he could do was $3,500 down and "the rest when you catch me." Baird liked the joke, but not that much. So Veeck pleaded, "All right, Tom, but do me a favor. Don't sell him to anyone in the American League."

Meanwhile, Veeck said he tipped off his old friend, Jim Gallagher, then general manager of Bill's boyhood favorites, the Cubs, and put the Chicago Nationals on Banks. In September, the Cubbies put up $35,000 for Banks and bought Baker, too, planning a new black double-play combination.

Cool Papa Bell, applauded, rubbed his hands together in glee. After too many years of $200-to-$400 baseball, he was going to get a good pay day. Baird and his partner, J.L. Wilkinson, had promised Cool 33 percent of the purchase price of any player he recommended who subsequently was sold to a big league club.

"When the Cubs bought Ernie, they gave O'Neill, who had taught him well, a lifetime scouting job, and, of course," said Bell, "Banks was on his way to well-deserved big money.

"Me?"

The Cool One, suffering with and from a nervous rash in his later years, smiled and said:

"The Monarchs suffered from a convenient lapse of memory. Instead of something close to $12,000, they sent me a gift—a basket of fruit."

Razzberries for Bell and huzzahs for Banks, who showed up at Wrigley Field without a glove and was given one by the club and a book called *How to Play Baseball*. He got into 10 late-season games, an unknown playing out the string with a bad ball club, and hit .314 with two home runs.

Did he remember the first one? Why, sure, it came off St. Louis' Gerry Staley, later sinkerball bullpen ace of the rival White Sox' 1959 pennant winners. And then Ernie began his love affair with the left-center field bleachers at the red brick, ivy-covered wall at Wrigley field, where he grooved his sweet swing to propel the ball just deep enough to

find eager Chicago hands to grab it as opposing outfielders look up helplessly.

Banks, chattering with opposing catchers and umpires as well as with teammates, would step into the batter's box comfortably, raise his bat and, like his friend and a rival for whom he shared mutual respect, Stan Musial, he would flex his fingers on the bat handle to avoid muscle constriction. At 6-1, 185, he seemed rangy and not at all powerful, but his forearms were like steel, as former Chicago manager Bob Scheffing noted. And though aided at times by the jet-stream to left-center and Waveland Avenue when the wind blew out at Wrigley Field, he hit enough when Jack Frost puffed his cheeks and blew in off Lake Michigan, and he didn't last19 years by doing nothing on the road except serve as a tour for local yokels as well as for fuzzy-cheeked Cubs.

In his first full season, 1954, Banks began to do what came naturally to the guy who grew up not caring a fig, Newton, about baseball and then wound up loving it as he did his wife and children. He was a deeply grieved man, this beautiful person, when brother Sam, then only 22 and an unsettled kid, was shot and killed apparently by accident after a dance back home in Dallas.

Ernie began, figuratively, to build his home in Chicago, where he became even more entrenched than the long-time mayor, Richard J. Daley, when he put in every game at shortstop in '54 and hit 19 homers, driving in 79 runs with a .275 average. Verily, the sunshine of the Southwest shone brightly on Boul Mich in '55 when he vaulted in 44 homers and 117 RBIs in a .295 season.

That year he did something no man before or after had achieved. He hit five grand slam homers. The fifth came off St. Louis' Lindy McDaniel, who would be a Chicago teammate some years ago. And in August of that year for the first of three times; Bingo-Bango, as they'd begun to call Banks, belted three homers in a game.

By now, though still not recognized generally for

his good nature and his generosity with the public in general and charitable works in particular, Ernie had established himself as a rarity, a long-ball-hitting shortstop and no liability defensively, either.

Assessments on the man afield are still mixed. As late as 1960 when he erred only 18 times and led shortstops defensively with a .977 percentage, *The Sporting News* had him on its All-Star field team. Even if he'd helped sway observers with his bat, the way good-hitting catchers somehow always seem better hunkering down behind the plate than they might actually be, Banks was steady and sure-handed at shortstop, meaning he got what he should have got. Whether he had sufficient range or strength of throwing arm is the question, but, regardless, the question wasn't serious enough to disturb his Hall of Fame chances. He breezed in with 288 votes cast out of 321.

So by 84 percent of the electorate, well in excess of the three-fourths necessary, Banks joined the elite of players selected their first time eligible: Bob Feller, Robinson, Ted Williams, Stan Musial, Warren Spahn, Sandy Koufax and Mickey Mantle. No such restrictions were in force when the famous First Five (Cobb, Babe Ruth, Honus Wagner, Christy Mathewson and Walter Johnson) were elected back in 1936. Subsequently, the long traditional five-year wait was waived for Lou Gehrig, fatally ill, in 1939 and for Roberto Clemente, who was killed in '73. Others since got their first time, too.

Banks' power-and-production peak undoubtedly was from 1957 through '60 when he homered in successive seasons 43, 47, 45 and 41 times, drove in 103, 129, 143 and 117 times, and batted .285, .313, .304 and .271.

It was in the middle two years, 1958-59, hitting .313 and .304, leading the league one year ('58) with his career-high homers, 47, and both seasons in RBIs, a two-year total of 272, that Ernie won the ultimate recognition: Back-to-back National League Most Valuable Player awards with a second-division ball club.

Summing up so well, cigar-puffing, sardonic Jimmy Dykes rasped, "Without Banks, the Cubs would have finished in Timbuktu."

Injuries and day-in, day-out play began to take their toll and Banks was shifted to first base—he quickly proved he couldn't play the outfield—and in 1963 he hit only 18 homers and dropped to 64 runs batted in and a .227 average.

For one, friend Musial, finishing that year his own career at nearly 43, 11 years older than Banks, shook his head.

"Ernie looks like he might be through," said The Man, "but he's too young."

Musial talked with Banks, as Ernie gratefully has acknowledged. Bingo-Bango always had waved a light (31-ounce) bat with big hands and willowy wrists. Musial suggested he go with a heavier bat up the middle, rather than try to pull, conceding that to start a swing earlier to rip to left field would mean less bat control.

After all, even Rogers Hornsby, a bigoted old-timer caught up by Banks' ability and personality, had said at Ernie's peak:

"Good eyes, timing and follow-through."

And Clyde McCullough, former Cubs' catcher, had likened Ernie's swing to a good heavyweight boxer's punch: "Short, sweet, without wasted motion or windup."

Now, taking Musial's advice and using his own hitting knowledge to make certain he didn't pull off the ball, the Banks, who in 1963 seemed through, as in well-done, lasted six more seasons as regular, then played part-time in 1970 and finished up briefly in '71 when he was 40.

As late as 1969 when the Cubs, wearying as Durocher kept his regulars on duty probably too long, faded and lost to Casey Stengel's amazin' Mets, old man Banks knocked in 106 runs with only 143 hits, though batting just .253. And one cold, raw afternoon at Wrigley Field, having played 12 seasons of 150 or more games, slammed one into his favorite bleachers of his favorite ballpark,

Wrigley Field, for home run No. 512, a figure that tied Eddie Mathews on the all-time Hit Parade.

If he'd wanted to manage the Cubs, it's double-mint to double pleasure that chewing-gum magnate P.K. Wrigley would have given the job to Ernie even against his better judgment. Banks was P.K.'s favorite player and, though seldom seen around the ball club that at long last had won for him in 1945, the late Mr. Wrigley was aware that managers are hired to be booed—and eventually fired. Why, even Phil's buddy of happier seasons on Chicago's North Side, Charley Grimm, his perpetual vice president, had been in and out of the manager's office out there at Clark and Addison streets as if Wrigley Field's foreman's cubbyhole had a revolving door.

Wrigley reveled in the good humor and good graces Banks had brought to the ballpark, along with those home runs, and Ernie sorrowed genuinely even more for the club owner than for himself that he'd never seen red-white-and-blue World Series bunting draped in "the friendly confines" of Wrigley Field.

The Edgar Guest of baseball, as someone once labeled the lovable shortstop-first baseman who finished first in the hearts of Cub fans, deserved the World Series chance, but, then, so did other superstars, including the great George Sisler and Napoleon Lajoie. And in the closest he ever came, the annual All-Star Game, Ernie hit .303.

A player-coach who played more than he coached under Durocher, Banks stayed in uniform the year after he returned, 1972, then went out to serve as an inspiration for the young players in the Chicago farm system, encouraging them, advising them and letting them know that baseball's Rebecca of Sunnybrook Farm was for real.

It wasn't until native Chicagoan, Kennedy, came back to the toddlin' town in 1977, the year Ernie went into the Hall of Fame, that Banks wound up back in the city he'd called home for more than two decades. Kennedy put him in group sales with the

logical belief that no one could best touch—or, in general, influence—Cubs' fans like Mr. Cub himself. Unfortunately, the second wedding didn't last.

Only thing Ernie hadn't been able to do was to get himself elected alderman, a post for which he ran in the face of the powerful Daley machine. But he accepted defeat gracefully, almost airily, and then was appointed by a Republican governor, Richard Oglevie, to the Chicago Transportation Authority.

Chances are that if Banks rode Chicago's subways, elevated trains or buses regularly, he'd be mobbed by autograph seekers. Chances are equal that, as always, he'd keep up a steady stream of happy small talk with them as patiently and methodically he filled their needs and wishes.

And if Ernie ever hawked public transportation the way he did baseball, the parking lots and garages in Chicago's storied Loop would look as empty as bubbling-over Banks' only wrong call: His annual prediction that the Cubs would win the pennant.

The man is something, all right, as probably described best by the talented typewriter of Bill Gleason, deep-dyed South Side fan of the White Sox and a columnist for the *Chicago Sun-Times*. Wrote Gleason, in part, when Banks was elected to the Hall of Fame:

"Certifiably famous now as a baseball player, Ernest Banks will be immortal for quite another reason. Ernie is an evangelist. Without pounding a Bible, shaking a tambourine, writing a homily, beating a drum or rattling a rosary. Ernie has spent a lifetime preaching love…

"Ernie Banks came among us as a young man and he made an entire city better. He came here, a battleground of racial hatred for 35 years and he helped the combatants to understand that there was a way better than the haters' way…

"This baseball player did what powerful white mayor and crusading black minister could not accomplish. This baseball player, by his every word and action, made us think about love as the way out…

"Ernie convinced everybody that a gentleman (also) could make it in professional sports. He didn't need to bolster his vocabulary with the vulgarisms and the street vernacular that are used by many athletes who had more education than he did.

"For Ernie, 'mother' is a sacred word, not a profane one...

"In a baseball player's funny uniform, instead of in flowing robes, Ernie Banks walked through the desert of racial hatred. He didn't need baseball. He doesn't need a Hall of Fame.

"He is an apostle of love."

Right on, and when that 163-ton abstract metal sculpture of Pablo Picasso was unveiled several years ago in the plaza of Chicago's Civic Center, an outraged alderman demanded that it be dismantled, labeling it a "rusting junk heap."

The Honorable John Hoellen had a better idea. Why not replace it with a 50-foot statue of that modern folk hero and living symbol of "a vibrant city," Ernie Banks?

Why not? What did Picasso ever hit? Besides, since old Fort Dearborn was a prairie town Mrs. O'Leary's cow kicked over with a lantern, who more than Ernie Banks has worked for the toddlin' town—and for baseball?

ERNEST (ERNIE) BANKS
Born January 31, 1931, at Dallas Tex.
Height 6-1 Weight 186
Threw and batted righthanded.
Named to Hall of Fame, 1977.

YEAR	CLUB	LEAGUE	POS.	G.	AB.	R.	H.	2B.	3B.	HR.	RBI.	B.A.	PO.	A.	E.	F.A.
1953	Chicago	Nat.	SS	10	35	3	11	1	1	2	6	.314	19	33	1	.981
1954	Chicago	Nat.	SS	154	593	70	163	19	7	19	79	.275	312	475	34	.959
1955	Chicago	Nat.	SS	154	596	98	176	29	9	44	117	.295	290	482	22	.972
1956	Chicago	Nat.	SS	139	538	82	160	25	8	28	85	.297	279	357	25	.962
1957	Chicago	Nat.	SS-3B	156	594	113	169	34	6	43	102	.285	241	348	14	.977
1958	Chicago	Nat.	SS	154	617	119	193	23	11	47	129	.313	292	468	32	.960
1959	Chicago	Nat.	SS	155	589	97	179	25	6	45	143	.304	271	519	12	.985
1960	Chicago	Nat.	SS	156	597	94	162	32	7	41	117	.271	283	488	18	.977
1961	Chicago	Nat.	SS-OF-1B	138	511	75	142	22	4	29	80	.278	273	370	21	.968
1962	Chicago	Nat.	1B-3B	154	610	87	164	20	6	37	104	.269	1462	107	11	.993
1963	Chicago	Nat.	1B	130	432	41	98	20	1	18	64	.227	1178	78	9	.993
1964	Chicago	Nat.	1B	157	591	67	156	29	6	23	95	.264	1565	132	10	.994
1965	Chicago	Nat.	1B	163	612	79	162	25	3	28	106	.265	1682	93	15	.992
1966	Chicago	Nat.	1B-3B	141	511	52	139	23	7	15	75	.272	1183	92	13	.990
1967	Chicago	Nat.	1B	151	573	68	158	26	4	23	95	.276	1383	91	10	.993
1968	Chicago	Nat.	1B	150	552	71	136	27	0	32	83	.246	1379	88	6	.996
1969	Chicago	Nat.	1B	155	565	60	143	19	2	23	106	.253	1419	87	4	.997
1970	Chicago	Nat.	1B	72	222	25	56	6	2	12	44	.252	528	35	4	.993
1971	Chicago	Nat.	1B	39	83	4	16	2	0	3	6	.193	167	12	0	1.000
Major League Totals—19 Years				2528	9421	1305	2583	407	90	512	1636	.274	14206	4355	261	.986

YOGI'S PAL JOEY: Joe Garagiola (right) poses with boyhood neighbor Yogi Berra in spring training, 1947.

YOGI BERRA

With Yankee teammates on second and third, righthander Skinny Brown pitching for Boston in a 1954 game at Fenway Park, Mickey Mantle moved toward the batter's box and New York's clean-up hitter, Yogi Berra, hurried to the batrack and on-deck circle the way he'd rush to the table for risotto, the Italian rice delicacy his mother served only on Sunday when he was a kid.

"Wait a minute, Berra," manager Casey Stengel called out pleasantly. "They're gonna walk Mantle. Take your time."

"Bet they don't," said Yogi.

"Bet they do," said Stengel. "I'm telling ya they will."

"Beer they don't," Berra defied the boss.

"Beer they do," said Stengel.

So when manager Lou Boudreau of the Red Sox ordered Mantle walked intentionally, to fill the bases, and then brought in southpaw Bill Wight from the bullpen to face the lefthanded-hitting Berra, Yogi harrumphed under his breath and said to Stengel: "Okay, you win the bet, but I'm gonna change my stance." "What stance you gonna use?" asked Stengel. "The home run stance with the bases loaded," answered Berra. "Watch it." Boom! Berra banged the second pitch over the right-field fence and Stengel cackled with joy, one beer, four runs and another victory richer.

It's hard to separate the myth from the man in the saga of Lawrence Peter Berra, who went from banana sandwiches with mustard on The Hill in St. Louis to top banana in baseball. If Yogi had been nearly as funny and as clever as an amused press made him, he would have put the wittiest Hollywood and television gag writers to shame and out of business. The sitdown catcher, let's make it plain, was no standup comic, but he was colorful, almost as colorful as he looked, which is going some because Yogi was built like an animated fireplug—"the bottom man on an unemployed acrobatic team," Larry MacPhail cracked after he'd seen him the first time—and he became the inspiration for a cartoon character almost as lovable as he is. Yogi Bear, no less.

But if he was never as quick with the quip or a crack as he was made to seem at times, he also never was as dumb as others portrayed him with stupid witticisms that were good for a laugh—at Yogi's expense.

Fact is, Berra not only was smart with quick reactions—the native instinct of a person as natural as seven-come-eleven on a dice table—but he was sensitive enough to be hurt at times by what he was supposed to have said, yet wise enough to keep his feelings to himself.

After all, as a guy who could add up a gin-rummy score lightning fast, Yogi added up the facts of life, the plusses and minuses, to find that he'd finished so far ahead of the game he could afford to be charitable to all and to laugh at everything, including himself.

From an apparent misfit to whom the Cardinals of his native St. Louis wouldn't even give the $500 bonus they gave his boyhood buddy, Joe Garagiola, and from a ninth-grade dropout to whom the clay mines and shoe factory would have been probably his only outlook in life, Berra went all the way to the top in his profession.

They said once that he had a frame like a fire hydrant and a face like a fallen souffle and that, when he walked, he looked as if his trousers were pinned together at the knees. In the unkindest cut of all, they said he didn't even look like a Yankee, but he wound up sharing more of the Yankees' glory directly than any player, past or present. To keep the record straight, his paisano, Frank Crosetti, was a coach for most of the years in which he rode the gravy train.

Berra, by contrast, played in 14 World Series in 17 seasons as a big league performer. He set Series records for most games (75), most hits (71) and with his 12 homers, including the first pinch-hit smash and a rare grandslam, he owned the second-best RBI total (39). Ten times he played on the winning side, and his reward for spending the first week or 10 days of every October playing golf or promoting Yoo-Hoo, a chocolate-drink company, was roughly $100,000 in Series money.

Moreover, the homely man who went from an awkward ugly duckling as a catcher to a Prince Charming behind the plate, certain to achieve eventual election to the Hall of Fame, won a milestone pennant for the Yankees in his one and only season as a big league manager. He managed the come-from-behind Mets to a division title in 1973, a pennant upset over Cincinnati and almost upset Oakland in the World Series. Later, 1984, he got a brief second chance with the Yankees. Dismissed early in '85 by trigger-happy George Steinbrenner, he boycotted his beloved Yankee Stadium. After four years coaching at Houston, he hung it up philosophically 44 years after he first put on a big league uniform.

If managers don't deserve credit for winning pennants, why do they get fired when they don't win or, even occasionally, as in Berra's case, when they do prevail? The pressbox pundits in Manhattan wove an involved web of interpretation and explanation when the Yankees shook up the baseball world by canning Berra hours after his 1964 team had lost the World Series to the Cardinals. In St. Louis, about the same time, there was an even greater shock when the man who had won the championship, Johnny Keane, due to be fired before his team's stretch run and distressed by dismissal of Bing Devine as general manager, walked away from a most attractive two-year contract.

If St. Louis, recognizing an injustice to Keane and eventually Devine, could offer a renewal to Keane, why couldn't the Yankees have rescinded what was said to have been a July decision to unload Berra? He couldn't communicate with the players, couldn't handle the men, seemed to be the reasons most frequently heard for sacking a fellow highly popular with the public. No, he couldn't compete with his old boss, Stengel, then with the Mets, as either a funny man or a box office attraction, but—.

But, managed by Yogi Berra, the New York Yankees came from six games back as late as August 22. They won 30 of their last 41 games despite these handicaps listed by a New York writer who, curiously, was trying to make a case against Berra, not for him:

". . . With Tony Kubek hurt on and off all year, with Whitey Ford lost for long periods, with no qualified relief pitchers, with three simultaneous sore arms in the bullpen, with Mickey Mantle semi-crippled, with Joe Pepitone 'not hustling' by his own admission, with Tom Tresh and Clete Boyer slumping endlessly, with Ralph Terry and others concealing injuries, not from the public, but from Berra."

With all these things, yes, the Yankees rallied for 99 victories and a pennant which would prove, indeed, to be one to remember. As professional baseball rolled into its second century, the proud New York Americans had gone longer without a pennant than at any time since they hoisted their first flag exactly 50 years earlier, 1921.

Berra, meanwhile, was doing what comes naturally to a natural winner—winning. Cut back as manager of the Yankees from his peak playing salary of about $60,000 to around $35,000 as skipper, he accepted a $25,000 settlement from the Yankees' profit-sharing plan and declined with thanks a supervisory job for $25,000 a year. Although there were none of the managerial offers he'd known before he became field foreman of the Yankees—then he'd turned down Boston and Baltimore—he found himself with three coaching jobs.

Washington was interesting and St. Louis more so, but the one that appealed to him most was with his old manager and friend, Stengel, who had gone from enforced retirement from the Yankees to a new career and life as pioneer skipper of the National League Mets, which they formed out of culls and kids, castoffs and rejects in 1962. Ol' Case, 72 years young then, delighted in doing in the Yankees at the box office and he scored again when he installed knock-kneed No. 8 as his first-base coach in 1965.

Berra, given as much for coaching the Mets as he had for managing the Yankees, seemed entirely happy in his new capacity. Patting a trimmed-down waistline, he said in spring training, 1969, at St. Petersburg, Fla., "I feel fine and I hope they (the Yankees) feel the same."

When the misfit Mets had a season as fantastic as the fairytale life of their first-base coach, Yogi dipped into the winner's share of another World Series. As always, he made sense, too, in one of his inimitable expressions when Ron (Rocky) Swoboda, the muscular and occasionally successful slugger, lamented that pitchers were jamming him inside.

"Then move back a bit from the plate," Berra advised.

"But Frank Robinson crowds the plate," Swoboda argued.

"If," said Yogi, "you can't imitate him, don't copy him."

This was a genuine Berraism, one of the kind

whose logic, if not language, couldn't be denied.

Now and then he'd come up with a dandy slip-of-the-tongue. Like the night early in his career when the Yankees were in St. Louis and he was honored by his friends and neighbors on The Hill. "Hill, hell, it's Dago Hill," said Yogi shocking the sensibilities of the ethnically prudish later but bringing down the crowd at the time when he said on the field:

"I want to thank all the baseball fans and everyone else who made this night necessary."

That could happen to anyone, of course. Some of the others, though, were pure Berraisms, meaning that they were amusing, yet meaningful, as, for instance, when he announced triumphantly that he was progressing as a catcher because Bill Dickey was "learning me his experience."

What else did you expect from a kid who, when asked what he liked best about school, said, "Closed." His favorite subject? "Recess."

As he became a celebrity, delightfully unchanged by it all, Berra was imposed on by St.Louis-area groups which sought to monopolize his off-season time by seeking him for talks, expecting (1) that he'd wow 'em with funny stories and (2) that he'd do it for zip. His good friend, Bob Burnes, executive sports editor of the old *St. Louis Globe-Democrat*, was among those who advised him that he'd be better off in New York, where friend and teammate Phil Rizzuto would see to it that Yogi would not be taken advantage of there.

Burnes, a good speaker who had made the rounds for years, was on programs with Berra in those early days and recalled one night when they were at a function at which orphans were brought as guests. Gifts, however, went only to the sons of the men who were sponsoring the party. Yogi, his sense of righteousness offended, left the head table, sat and talked with the orphans and declined to do anything except take a bow.

Berra was hurt again, in the climax to the imposition on his good nature, when he slipped and slid on an icy road one night to make an out-of-town talk for which payment had been implied. Afterward, timidly asking about his fee, he was told, haughtily, "If the great Yankees don't pay you enough, I guess we can scrape together a few dollars for gasoline."

So Yogi went to New York with his lovely wife, the former Carmen Short, to raise their children in suburban New Jersey and to go into the bowling alley-cocktail lounge business with Rizzuto for some years. Subsequently, too, he became vice president and then a goodwill representative for Yoo-Hoo, which still left him enough time to play golf—he drives righthanded and putts lefthanded—and to attend all sports events possible. Carmen has the business head in the family, Yogi will tell with a grin, and she reads the *Wall Street Journal.*

Yogi has graduated from comic books. "I like the ones about crooks best," he said back there in the image-making era when, for a fact, he roomed at Newark in 1946 with Bobby Brown, who was studying to be a doctor. As they turned out the lights one night and Berra put aside his comic book and Brown his medical textbook, Yogi asked, "How did your book come out, Bobby?"

One night at Toots Shor's restaurant in New York, the best-known saloonkeeper in the country introduced Berra to a sturdy, bearded man.

"Ernie," said Shor, "this is Yogi Berra. Yog, meet Ernest Hemingway."

The famed author conversed animatedly with the ballplayer for a time and then left. "You've read Hemingway, Yog?" Toots asked.

Berra frowned. "I don't think so," he said. "What paper's he with?"

Yogi had his own restaurant experience briefly in St. Louis when his old friend, the late Henry Ruggeri, coaxed him into a maitre d's starched shirt to showcase Ruggeri's well-known restaurant. Burnes was seated close by and caught it when two teenage couples came in, hesitatingly, and Yogi overheard one young swain whisper to the other, "Do you think we belong in here?"

"Sure," said Yogi, putting the kids at ease, "sit right down and enjoy yourselves. It's just like a hamburger joint."

Berraisms? How about the one about a famous restaurant? "Nobody goes there anymore because it's too crowded," said Yogi. At career's end, 1989, then 64 when he stepped out as a coach at Houston, he favored that one, but he'll probably be remembered best for having said profoundly, "It's not over until it's over…"

There were other goodies. For instance on a trip in 1961 to his parents' homeland, Italy—they came from Milano—Yogi took in the opera "Tosca" at LaScala. And how did Berra enjoy himself?

"It was pretty good," he said. "Even the music was nice."

Just like Yogi, actually, nice and more than pretty good from the time, as Joe Garagiola tells it, Berra was the best all-around athlete in their neighborhood until he became, with Roy Campanella, the best catcher of his generation.

The versatility Yogi demonstrated for the Stag A. C. back there in southwest St. Louis displayed itself in the majors, too, and toting up Berra's games played, he was at third base once, first base twice and in the outfield 260 times.

Better than anyone, Yogi explained the problem of picking up a flyball in Yankee Stadium in the autumnal haze when a combination of cigarette smoke, sunlight and shadows create a visual hazard.

"It gets late early out there," said Yogi. This was a profundity like it-ain't-over-until-it's-over.

As a catcher who once was so wild throwing that he hit a pitcher on the chest with his peg and another time beaned the second-base umpire, Berra became masterful. Dickey, brought back by Stengel as a coach in 1949 to work with the gifted goblin, taught him to move up closer behind the plate and to throw off his toes for better body balance.

The arm, always strong enough, became as potent as Yogi's bat and his ability to handle pitchers, run a ball game and, not just incidentally, run the bases. There was a tendency to accept Berra's box-like body and thick legs as automatic assurance that, like even more streamlined catchers, he was slow afoot. But he actually was fast.

"Mr. Berra," said Stengel, using the formal salutation he affected with "my assistant manager," as Ol' Case called him, "was second only to Joe DiMaggio in all-around ability among the players I managed."

Even when he just broke into the big leagues, unpolished and imperfect behind the plate, truly a diamond in the rough, Yogi could do incredible things. One day when the pennant-bound Yankees in 1947 were playing the Browns, St. Louis had a man on third when the batter bunted toward the right of the plate on a squeeze play. Berra leaped out from behind the plate toward first base, grabbed the ball, slapped it quickly on the batter and then dived back toward the plate to tag out the runner sliding in from third base.

Asked how in Hades he could complete such a dazzling unassisted double play, Yogi shrugged. "I just tagged everything in sight, including the umpire," he said.

Berra's agility with that short (5-8), blocky (190-pound) body combined with that strong, ultimately accurate throwing arm to execute two spectacular plays in succession in the opening game of the 1953 World Series at Yankee Stadium.

With the score tied in the seventh inning, 5-5, Brooklyn runners on first and second and none out, Billy Cox bunted toward third. Berra leaped out from behind the plate, pounced on the ball and fired a low strike to Gil McDougald at third, forcing Gil Hodges by a disputed fraction.

Next up, Clem Labine also bunted, again apparently good enough for a sacrifice, but once more Berra jumped from behind the plate in his cumbersome shinguards and chest protector—on Yogi they always seemed too large—and got the ball and then his man at third, Carl Furillo, with quick, clean fielding and a perfect peg.

After the Yankees' 9-5 victory in which Yogi contributed a home run and a single, the catcher wouldn't join in debating the call at third base on Hodges.

"I'll take the umpire's word for it," he said, "and you can take all that hollering from the Dodgers fans"—get this perfect slip—"with a grin of salt."

Actually, Yogi didn't always take the umpire's word, especially for balls and strikes when he squatted on his haunches behind the plate, talking to the hitter, to the pitcher and often to the man in blue. When the Yankees threw a day for him in 1959, American League umpires gave him an award for his help over the years, proving that they'd taken it—and him—in stride and good humor.

Yogi seemed to have his most trouble with Cal Hubbard, retired supervisor of umpires for the American League, and it was a sight, the short, sawed-off Berra standing there looking up, his chin practically buried in the belly button of the hulking Hubbard, a Hall of Fame football player and baseball Hall of Famer, too.

One time, Cal threw Berra out after this bit of dialogue which seemed to sum up the boyish enthusiasm with which Yogi played the game for those 17 seasons in which he averaged .285 and apparently hit more home runs than any catcher in history, 358.

"The umpire misses the third strike," said Berra in the archaic present tense of the diamond. "I know he misses it and he knows that I know it. So I argue and he tells me to get on with the game. I tell him I'll play when he admits he blew one. He says, 'Put on the mask,' and I say, 'I'll put it on when you tell me you missed it,' and he throws me out of the game."

Funny thing, when you laugh at that one, Berra can't understand it. Not that he doesn't have a sense of humor, but, you see, he's not really an entertainer like, say, his pal Joey, television personality Garagiola.

For years, Yogi has the perfect answer to their close relationship and mutual admiration society. "I'll talk if Joey will speak," says Yogi, drawing a fine line of semantics with one of the Berraisms. He and Garagiola were elected by Missouri sportswriters and sportscasters for induction into the state Sports Hall of Fame as practically an entry in October 1970. Berra was elected to Cooperstown's prestige Hall his second year eligible, '72.

As kids, born exactly across from each other on Elizabeth Avenue, St. Louis, Berra arrived first on May 12, 1925, nine months earlier than Garagiola. They were like talented twins. What would be the odds anywhere of two poor boys in one city block not only getting to the big leagues as catchers, but both also becoming wealthy and so prominent that they became practically household words?

As kids, they were subject to Old World discipline. For instance, at 4:30 when the quitting whistle blew at the nearby clay pits where their fathers worked, big Giovanni Garagiola and little Pietro Berra, the boys stopped right in the middle of a race to first base and skeedaddled home. They had to rush the growler, to get the old man's beer pail filled at the corner saloon—taverns, they called 'em after Repeal—before papa put his foot in the door.

Or else—whap, whap!—there would be someone belted like a ground-rule double. Like Yogi was by his father the time he laid out a diamond neatly on the brick street, but made the mistake of using Pietro's precious paint.

"Yogi was the organizer, the imaginative one, the leader," said Garagiola. "He could kick the ball the farthest in football, the hardest in soccer and he was the best hitter in baseball and the best in most of the sports we played with practically no equipment—corkball, basketball, roller hockey.

"I remember one time we scrimmaged some kids who had football helmets. Yogi butted heads with one helmeted kid who took off his headgear, crying, and went home. We had our own little club, the Stags. Dues were a dime a month and we'd buy 10-cent packs of Twenty Grand cigarettes and sell 'em for a penny apiece and we'd get wholesale boxes of candy bars, three cents each, and sell 'em for a nickel.

"I remember some older boys talked Yogi into boxing at a fight club and he won eight or nine, a couple by knockouts, and he got a few bucks, which he gave to his mother. Paulina—Mrs. Berra—was a fine woman and Yogi was always dutiful to her. When she was dying," said Joe, "he actually had a bad season because he couldn't keep his dear mom off his mind.

By the time he was 14, Lawdie, as his mother called him, trying in her limited English to say Larry, wanted desperately to quit school. A council was held with Papa Berra, the parish priest, handsome young Father Charles R. Koester, and the director of the South Side YMCA, "Uncle Joe" Causino, a man who aided many a youngster. They agreed, reluctantly, that Yogi could go to work.

Trouble was, he really didn't want to work, either. He just wanted to play ball. Oh, he worked in a coalyard and on a soft-drink truck and in a shoe factory, but he blew all the jobs because, wrapped in his lunch, invariably two large slices of Italian bread with a couple of bananas and a generous layer of mustard, was his baseball glove. He didn't mind working mornings, but by 3 P.M., about the time pal Joey and his other school-age friends were getting out to play ball, Yogi would duck.

The kids called him "Yogi" by then because one day they'd been to a movie and had seen a Hindu fakir sit motionless, arms and legs folded in the disciplined manner of a disciple of yoga. The folded arms and strong expression reminded one of the kids, Jack Maguire, of Berra seated on the bench between innings of their boyhood game.

So Maguire, who played briefly with the New York Giants, Pittsburgh Pirates and old Browns in the early '50s, was the first to call him "Yogi." The nickname stuck, but, curiously, when Berra first went up to the Yankees, neither he nor they seemed to like it. He'd autograph with his right name, and

the Yankees' public-address system elocutionist would intone daily the name of "Larry Berra."

But, as Mr. Lincoln said, you couldn't fool all of the public all of the time. The nickname fit and eventually Yogi began to wear it as a badge of honor. The Yankees used it and so did Yogi, but, of course, I have to be different, so I call him Lawrence Peter.

The only job for which Yogi probably ever gave a damn as a kid was one selling newspapers at the corner of Kingshighway and Southwest in St. Louis and then only because Joe Medwick, slugging left fielder of the Cardinals, stopped there en route home from old Sportsman's Park and bought the evening *Post-Dispatch* and maybe the old *Star-Times* from the shy Italian kid who hero-worshipped him in his own quiet way. When you wonder how and why Yogi became such a notorious and dangerous bad-ball hitter, you don't have to look any further than his admiration for Medwick. He'll tell you, grinning:

"Ducky was a bad-ball hitter, too, and it didn't keep him out of the Hall of Fame, did it?"

Berra, who gravitated with Garagiola to lefthanded batting just because they thought it was the thing to do, was a most unusual hitter in that even though he appeared to swing wildly, he seldom struck out. Didn't walk much, either, if you want the truth, but he prided himself on getting his full cut and yet fanning infrequently. Over his career, he drew 704 walks and struck out 415 times in 7,555 official trips.

Yogi's most walks, 65, came in 1956, and his fewest strikeouts, just 12 in 151 games and 597 times up, were in his best season, 1950. That year Yogi, then 25, hit .322 and had 28 homers and 124 RBIs, but he did NOT win one of his three American League Most Valuable Player awards that year. Friend Rizzuto was voted MVP in '50. Yogi was accorded the honor in 1951-54-55.

Except for a slight or oversight—call it what you will—Berra might have had to win those MVP awards in the National League with the hometown Cardinals. His three older brothers, Tony (Lefty), Mike and Johnny, all of whom had been compelled to turn down professional baseball chances to go to work to help support the family, joined the kid's plea that he be given a chance to try to salvage the family honor and name on the playing field. Pietro Berra, coaxed by Paulina, reluctantly agreed. Later on, Papa Berra, chest puffed out, would insist that it was Momma who almost cost Lawrence his chance.

When Yogi and pal Joey Garagiola worked out with the Cardinals, it was the neighbor's kid who got the attention and the money. Not much, but enough to hurt Berra's feelings and his family's. On their boyhood teams, Joe did the catching and Yogi usually played third base or the outfield—even pitched now and then—but, as Joe pointed out, Garagiola hit third and Berra fourth.

"Even then, he was something," Garagiola recalled. "We didn't have many signs, but any time our manager touched his nose—and what a major league schnozz he had—it meant we should bunt. 'Unless they're creeping in on you,' the manager said. 'Don't let 'em creep in on you.'

"There are men on first and second and we are trailing by a run. We look down at our Durante-looking coach and he's got an interlocking grip on his bugle. We say to ourselves, 'Bunt. He wants Yogi to bunt.'

"Here comes the pitch... Yogi swings... over the center fielder's head... one run in ... two runs in. Yogi's in.

"Our manager says to Yogi, 'I gave you the bunt sign. Why didn't you bunt?'

"Yogi answered, 'Because they were creeping in. They were creeping in on me.'

" ' Who was creeping in?'

" ' The center fielder. Didn't you see him move?' "
When the Cardinals gave Garagiola $500 to sign, enough to settle Giovanni's mortgage on his cottage, the Berras were looking for the same for Yogi, who hit even harder, even if he didn't look as handsome

or as smooth as that heavy-haired (ahem!) Garagiola kid. The best Branch Rickey would offer as general manager of the Cardinals was $250. So Berra walked out and went back to work, playing meanwhile for a powerful Junior American Legion team, the Stockhams, who were managed by Leo Browne, a prosperous oil distributor and Irish-born scrapper who had been a professional umpire. Browne, indignant, pestered the Yankees and his good friend, coach Johnny Schulte, to take a look at the gnome he had moved behind the plate.

After the Cardinals upset the Yankees in the 1942 World Series, Schulte, a St. Louisan and former catcher, liked what he saw and assured general manager George Weiss that Berra was worth the $500 he sought. So the Yankees signed him.

Here's the rub: They'd pulled a fast one on the naive kid. At Norfolk, Va., where he was getting $90 a month in the Piedmont League in 1943, Berra learned two painful facts—(1) he wouldn't get the $500 unless he lasted the season there and (2) he didn't have enough money to live on in the war-inflated economy of a military liberty town.

More than once Yogi wrote home to his mother to tell of his hunger and Mrs. Berra would slip off a small money order to him to help tide him over, cautioning not to let his father know because if Pietro knew his boy was hungry, he'd order him to come home. Once, Yogi went on a sitdown strike and told the Norfolk manager, Shaky Kain that he was too hungry to play. Kain fished out a couple of bucks. Yogi hurried out, gulped down three or four hamburgers and a couple of Cokes, burped a couple of times and was back in uniform, buoyed by enough to eat for a change.

If you're wondering why nice guy, naive Berra could prove to be so tough and obstinate a guy at contract time through the early seasons of his career with the Yankees, until he established himself in the big-salary bracket, it's because he was determined to get what was due him after treatment that was initially shabby.

At Norfolk, Yogi found a nice old feminine fan who recognized a hungry look when she saw one. Every Sunday, which, of course, was the big feast day back home, she'd bring him a real old-fashioned Italian hero sandwich, a whole loaf of bread filled with luncheon meat and cheese.

It was after one of those morale-boosting block-busters, Berra told Ed Fitzgerald in their delightful book entitled *Yogi*, that the Norfolk catcher became a two-day terror against Roanoke. In one game, he drove in 13 runs, one more than the major league RBI record set by Jim Bottomley with the Cardinals in 1924. He knocked in 23 runs in two days with six hits each time, including three homers, two triples and a double.

Although he batted only .253 in 111 games in his first professional season, Berra drove in 56 runs. His hopes for the future went with him into the Navy. In World War II, he volunteered to serve aboard a new kind of ship, a rocket launcher which later capsized off Omaha Beach in the invasion of Normandy. By 1945, after Naples and Bizerte, he was assigned to the submarine base at New London, Conn., where he was put on sports and recreation duty. He became maintenance man in the base movie theater and was supposed to be the bouncer in case of trouble. They'd read that boxing back-ground in his file.

The submarine base had a pretty good ball club and Berra kept pestering to get on it. The manager, Lt. Jimmy Gleeson, who had played in the outfield for Cincinnati and also for the Chicago Cubs, didn't believe that the squat figure had played pro-fessional baseball. Gleeson and an assistant, Ray Volpe, who had pitched for the Kansas City Blues, grilled him about the Yankee farm system and Pied-mont League personnel.

This was child's play for Berra, whose memory always had amazed Garagiola, Stengel and others, including Dr. Sidney Gaynor, the Yankee team sur-geon who remembers taking Berra to a hospital for X-rays of a bad thumb late in his career. They were

walking down a corridor of the hospital and met a doctor named Dick Ames, a Yale graduate who once pitched for the Yankee organization some years earlier.

"I nodded hello to Dr. Ames," said Dr. Gaynor, "and Yogi amazed me. 'I remember you,' he told Dr. Ames. 'I hit a home run off you on a change-up'—and he was referring to service ball 12 to 14 years before."

When Gleeson determined that Berra was no phony, he found himself a hitter who gratefully would name him as a Yankee coach when he be-came manager at a time Jimmy was in the New York organization. Yogi's big blast on the submarine base included three of four hits off the Giants' Ace Adams in an exhibition game.

Mel Ott, managing the Giants, was interested then, just as Branch Rickey really must have been more interested than that measly $250 bonus would indicate in 1942 when The Mahatma was lame-duck general manager of the Cardinals. The minute Rickey got to Brooklyn, he sent Yogi a wire, inviting him to report to the Dodgers' wartime base at Bear Mountain, N. Y., but by then Berra had signed with the Yankees.

Until Ott went to Larry MacPhail, who just had taken over as president of the Yankees, and offered $50,000 for Berra, the volatile redhaired baseball man didn't know the young paisano from a pizza, but he determined to find out. Physically, as mentioned, MacPhail was disappointed when he saw the stubby kid for the first time, but he reasoned wisely that if the Giants were willing to spend that kind of dough, Berra must have something that wasn't obvious.

The barrel-chested, long-armed lad, whose head sat squarely on his shoulders, shucked his Navy bell-bottoms and reported to Newark at Rochester in May 1946. In 77 games, he hit .314, with 15 hom-ers and 59 RBIs. When Newark was eliminated from the International League playoffs, the Yankees brought up Berra, third baseman Bobby Brown and pitcher Vic Raschi for the final week of the season.

Yogi hit a home run off Philadelphia's Jesse Flores in his first game in the majors and got another one the next day, hitting .364 in seven games.

The gifted goblin was on his way, but he encountered enough pressure that could have done in a lesser man especially one who, by nature, was as much a worrier as Yogi.

In spring training, 1947, veteran teammates put sand in his shoes and hot stuff in his jock strap, but that didn't bother Berra nearly as much as mastering the mechanics of catching. For one thing, his fingers were so short and stubby that pitchers couldn't pick up his signs.

"Why don't you get a pair of hands, Yogi?" needled Joe Page, the ace relief pitcher. When Berra attempted to help by painting his fingers with iodine, Page quipped, "It looks like your wrists are bleeding."

Discouraged at times, Yogi moped when playing the outfield. One day as he walked to his position in right field, Joe DiMaggio, trotting out to center field, veered over and admonished him. "Never walk to your position, kid. It looks as if you aren't hustling," said the class performer from whom a word would impress any young player, particularly an Italian kid who had admired him for years.

At bat, the 22-year-old Berra did well enough, hitting .280 with 11 homers and 54 RBIs in 83 games, but his catching was uncertain, especially his throwing. When the Dodgers won the National League pennant and announced they would run on the kid catcher, manager Bucky Harris winced. Jackie Robinson and Pee Wee Reese did steal in the first game, Reese again in the second game and Berra not only erred, but he was hitless in both contests.

The critical spotlight of the World Series could have caved in a man but, pinch-hitting the next day, Yogi began to show his championship class. He hit a home run.

The Yankees won that Series, but Berra remembers mainly that if he had thrown out Al Gionfriddo, trying to steal second with two out in the ninth inning of the fourth game, Floyd (Bill) Bevens would have had a no-hit victory. Instead, he suffered a 3-2 defeat on the Dodgers' only hit, Cookie Lavagetto's historic pinch-double.

In 1948, for the first of three times, Berra became a .300 hitter and the bashful ballplayer who had traveled the lonely road—he saw the Marx Brothers in every city one year in a movie, *A Night in Casablanca*—suddenly batted a perfect 1.000 in the Romance League.

One afternoon he walked into the Club 66, run by Julius (Biggie) Garagnani, who would become better known shortly as Stan Musial's partner in the highly successful St. Louis restaurant which bore their names. Biggie had a pretty new waitress.

"Fix me up with the gal, Big," said Berra, who was informed by Garagnani that the young lady, Carmen Short of Salem, Mo., was no pickup.

Hell, Yogi didn't want a pickup. With him, it was love at first blush—and it's pretty hard to blush through a swarthy complexion. With Garagiola along, he would haunt the restaurant, trying to get up nerve to ask for a date, puzzled and hurt to find that Miss Short, though polite, was quite cold. Why, Yogi even had pal Joey and Garagiola's girl friend, Audrie Ross, the pretty blonde Joe married, waiting in the wings for a double date—if only he could get to first base with Carmen.

"I don't date married men," Miss Short said tartly, as the horrible truth came out. Somehow, she'd thought Yogi was Terry Moore, center fielder and captain of the Cardinals. She knew Moore was married. So now the ice was broken and—.

Before Garagiola could get Miss Ross to the altar, Yogi was there with Carmen in January 1949. Pal Joey was Yogi's best man, just as Berra stood up for Garagiola a year later.

One of the supposed Berraisms that apparently isn't true involved Pete Reiser, another member of the large St. Louis baseball colony. Yogi, passing out invitations to his wedding and reception, was supposed to have asked Pete if he could come and Reiser said he was sorry, but he couldn't.

"Then I ain't wastin' any invitation," Yogi said. Or did he?

Lovely Carmen gave Yogi more confidence in himself. Any man who had been laughed at about his looks—"You don't hit a ball with your face," he'd said defensively—would be bound to feel bigger and better to have an attractive wife. With Carmen at his side, Casey Stengel prodding him and Bill Dickey polishing his playing as much as his wife did his manners, Yogi became a complete ballplayer as well as what he'd been, a kind and pleasant human being.

As a catcher, he hung up many records, among them one for going 148 games without an error. He probably also set a mark for mitt-and-mask durability when from 1950 to 1958 he was behind the plate for 151, 141, 142, 137, 151, 147, 140 and 134 games. No, check signals, in that period he did play an assortment of contests in the outfield, but not many. It's remarkable that, considering the bumps, bruises, aches and pains that are indigenous to the position, Berra could catch so often and still manage to put together his best years at bat.

In that eight-season stretch, he knocked in over 100 runs five times. He hit homers with great consistency—28, 27, 30, 27, 22, 27, 30 and 24—and batted .322 in '50 and .307 in '54.

In World Series play, too, Yogi got better and better. The first five Series in which he played, he hit four homers and had just 19 hits and eight RBIs in 27 games. But beginning in 1953, the year he pounced on those two bunts and gunned out Brooklyn runners in picture-book plays at third base, Berra was a powerful Series hitter.

"He worries us more than Mantle," said Jackie Robinson before one of the interborough battles between Brooklyn and The Bronx.

Yogi hit .429 in the '53 Series. In '55 he batted .417 and if Sandy Amoros hadn't made that brilliant, gloved catch of his high, slicing fly inside the left-field foul line at Yankee Stadium in the seventh game, Berra would have had another hit, a double, and the Dodgers' Johnny Podres wouldn't have had a Series-ending 2-0 victory.

Berra, in the '56 World Series, was devastating. Not only did he catch Don Larsen's perfect game and leap into the big pitcher's arms like a little kid greeting a returning father—Hall of Famer Ray Schalk always sent a congratulatory telegram to the catcher of a no-hit game—but Yogi also practically paralyzed big Don Newcombe and the Dodgers.

Big Newk, a 27-game winner, had won the Cy Young Award that year, but Berra treated him like a batting-practice pitcher. In the second game at Ebbets Field, Yogi unloaded a grandslam homer. In the seventh game Berra belted Newcombe for two home runs, the second one on a pitch low and away, one that neither Newcombe nor batterymate Campanella could understand how Yogi had hit.

"It wasn't your fault, Newk. It wasn't your fault," said Yogi, compassionately, as he circled the bases on the second one, a blow which really turned Newcombe from a topflight pitcher into just another performer.

A .360 hitter with three homers and 10 RBIs in '56, Berra batted .320 in '57 and then, after dipping to .222 in '58, he came back with .318 and eight RBIs in 1960. His three-run homer in the sixth inning of the final game gave New York a 5-4 lead, but Bill Mazeroski's famous homer in the ninth broke up the game and Series, 10-9.

In seven World Series between 1953 and '61, the Yog had 52 hits in 45 games, with eight doubles, eight homers and 31 RBIs.

Berra hung it up as a player when he became manager at the age of 39 after hitting .293 on part-time duty behind the fellow St. Louisan he highly regarded as his catching successor, Elston Howard. However, after the year on the bench as manager, he got into four games with the Mets as a player-coach in '65 when he was 40. All that did was to delay his entry to the Hall of Fame.

Some of the old gang were at Cooperstown to see him inducted, meaning the gang from back home, on The Hill—Yogi never did go high-hat—as well as the Garagiolas and other New York-area friends and, of course, Carmen and the three boys. Son Larry, then 21 taller and bigger, a right handed-hitting catcher, attended-Montclair (N. J.) St. College in his hometown. Brother Timmy, 19, played football at the University of Massachusetts. Dale, 14, at the time reached the big leaguers as a ballplayer but a drug problem betrayed him and saddened dear Carmen and Yogi.

Lawrence Peter (Yogi) Berra was a shrewd ballplayer with an elephantine memory. He rarely made a mistake and pitchers almost never shook him off because he seemed like a mindreader behind the batter. Still, there's so much to be said for formal education, and, as natural as always, Yogi said it when he was given that night by the Yankees in 1959 and he directed that the funds (nearly $10,000) collected be used for a scholarship at Columbia University.

See how it is when you've really got it? Berra wins again. Yogi didn't go to college, but his money did.

LAWRENCE PETER (YOGI) BERRA
Born May 12, 1925, at St. Louis, Mo.
Height 5-8 Weight 191
Threw right and batted lefthanded.
Named to Hall of Fame, 1972.

YEAR	CLUB	LEAGUE	POS.	G.	AB.	R.	H.	2B.	3B.	HR.	RBI.	B.A.	PO.	A.	E.	F.A.
1943	Norfolk	Pied.	C	111	376	52	95	17	8	7	56	.253	480	75	16	.972
1944-45	Kansas City	A.A.							(In Military Service)							
1946	Newark	Int.	C-OF	77	277	41	87	14	1	15	59	.314	344	45	11	.973
1946	New York	Amer.	C	7	22	3	8	1	0	2	4	.364	28	6	0	1.000
1947	New York	Amer.	C-OF	83	293	41	82	15	3	11	54	.280	307	18	9	.973
1948	New York	Amer.	C-OF	125	469	70	143	24	10	14	98	.305	390	40	9	.979
1949	New York	Amer.	C	116	415	59	115	20	2	20	91	.277	544	60	7	.989
1950	New York	Amer.	C	151	597	116	192	30	6	28	124	.322	777	64	13	.985
1951	New York	Amer.	C	141	547	92	161	19	4	27	88	.294	693	82	13	.984
1952	New York	Amer.	C	142	534	97	146	17	1	30	98	.273	700	73	6	.992
1953	New York	Amer.	C	137	503	80	149	23	5	27	108	.296	566	64	9	.986
1954	New York	Amer.	C-3B	151	584	88	179	28	6	22	125	.307	718	64	8	.990
1955	New York	Amer.	C	147	541	84	147	20	3	27	108	.272	721	54	13	.984
1956	New York	Amer.	C-OF	140	521	93	155	29	2	30	105	.298	733	57	11	.986
1957	New York	Amer.	C-OF	134	482	74	121	14	2	24	82	.251	707	61	4	.995
1958	New York	Amer.	C-OF-1B	122	433	60	115	17	3	22	90	.266	558	44	2	.997
1959	New York	Amer.	C-OF	131	472	64	134	25	1	19	69	.284	706	62	4	.995
1960	New York	Amer.	C-OF	120	359	46	99	14	1	15	62	.276	312	24	5	.985
1961	New York	Amer.	OF-C	119	395	62	107	11	0	22	61	.271	237	15	2	.992
1962	New York	Amer.	C-OF	86	232	25	52	8	0	10	35	.224	238	17	6	.977
1963	New York	Amer.	C	64	147	20	43	6	0	8	28	.293	244	13	3	.988
1964	New York (a)	Amer.							(Did not play—served as manager)							
1965	New York	Nat.	C	4	9	1	2	0	0	0	0	.222	15	1	1	.941
American League Totals				2116	7546	1174	2148	321	49	358	1430	.285	9179	918	124	.988
National League Totals				4	9	1	2	0	0	0	0	.222	15	1	1	.941
Major League Totals				2120	7555	1175	2150	321	49	358	1430	.285	9194	919	125	.988

a Released by New York Yankees, October 16, 1964.

WORLD SERIES RECORD

YEAR	CLUB	LEAGUE	POS.	G.	AB.	R.	H.	2B.	3B.	HR.	RBI.	B.A.	PO.	A.	E.	F.A.
1947	New York	Amer.	C-OF	6	19	2	3	0	0	1	2	.158	21	2	2	.920
1949	New York	Amer.	C	4	16	2	1	0	0	0	1	.063	37	3	0	1.000
1950	New York	Amer.	C	4	15	2	3	0	0	1	2	.200	30	1	0	1.000
1951	New York	Amer.	C	6	23	4	6	1	0	0	0	.261	27	3	1	.968
1952	New York	Amer.	C	7	28	2	6	1	0	2	3	.214	59	7	1	.985
1953	New York	Amer.	C	6	21	3	9	1	0	1	4	.429	36	3	0	1.000
1955	New York	Amer.	C	7	24	5	10	1	0	1	2	.417	40	4	0	1.000
1956	New York	Amer.	C	7	25	5	9	2	0	3	10	.360	50	3	0	1.000
1957	New York	Amer.	C	7	25	5	8	1	0	1	2	.320	44	2	1	.979
1958	New York	Amer.	C	7	27	3	6	3	0	0	2	.222	60	6	0	1.000
1960	New York	Amer.	C-OF-PH	7	22	6	7	0	0	1	8	.318	18	1	0	1.000
1961	New York	Amer.	OF	4	11	2	3	0	0	1	3	.273	11	0	1	.917
1962	New York	Amer.	C	2	2	0	0	0	0	0	0	.000	6	1	0	1.000
1963	New York	Amer.	PH	1	1	0	0	0	0	0	0	.000	0	0	0	.000
World Series Totals				75	259	41	71	10	0	12	39	.274	439	36	6	.988

A BOY'S GAME PLAYED BY MEN: Roy Campanella's cheerful definition of baseball. Three time MVP before a critical injury cut short his career.

ROY CAMPANELLA

When big league baseball moved west to the Pacific Palisades and to the Golden Gate in 1958, the game left behind in the broken-hearted boroughs of New York, especially Brooklyn, a breed of intensely critical, yet fiercely loyal fans. Left behind, too, was a veteran ballplayer who had even more reason to be broken-hearted.

After all, the National League faithful would know a day soon when a compromise franchise would return to Flushing Meadow in the form of the Mets, misfits who needed the blind devotion of mother's love and got it. New York took them to its metropolitan breast and damned if the ugly ducklings of the diamond didn't turn into a fairy-tale team of the last—and least likely—season of professional baseball's first century.

But things didn't turn out so well for the veteran ballplayer who had the most reason to be broken-hearted when the Dodgers and Giants fled to Los Angeles and San Francisco. Roy Campanella not only missed the salubrious climate of the West Coast, the kind that helps take the years off aging athletes, but he also missed a chance to attack the ridiculously close left-field target at the Coliseum, the famed football stadium where the Dodgers played their first four seasons on the West Coast.

Campanella, the joy guy of the Dodgers, was left behind as a virtual paraplegic, a result of an automobile accident in which his car skidded on an "S" curve near his fashionable suburban New York home shortly before he would have gone to spring training. Only the thick neck muscles of the coffee-colored catcher with the burly, bulging body of a displaced Buddha saved his life when the light, rented car he was driving in place of his handsome copper Cadillac skidded and wrapped itself around a telephone pole.

Pictures of Campanella confined to a wheelchair, barely able to move hands that once were so expressive as well as powerful, would be completely depressing except that Campanella, though almost physically helpless, never has lost the spirit that helped make him an animated athlete and field leader. Even deserted by his former wife, the mother of four of the six children he adored, Campy kept his chin up—both of 'em in fact—and managed from his wheelchair to operate his Harlem liquor store, conduct radio interviews and work with youth to help fight the juvenile delinquency that trapped a stepson. He was happily remarried, too. And, moved to the coast, he aids the Dodgers and has become a member of the baseball Hall of Fame's Veterans' Committee and board of directors. Sure, he was a Cooperstown electee, 1969.

When a Monte Stratton loses a leg, a Jackie Hayes his sight and a Campanella most physical functions, it's easy to get maudlin because few ballplayers suffer such complete impairment when still wearing baseball flannels. It's especially easy to get sentimental in Campanella's case because he was so entirely enthusiastic. Roy couldn't quite ever get over his good fortune in getting paid as a man to play a boy's game.

When he was inducted into baseball's Hall of Fame with Stan Musial, with whom he formed a mutual admiration society, the mustachioed Campanella sat before an attentive crowd at Cooperstown, and recalled an expression he'd used that received considerable mileage over the years and one which summed up his own attitude: "There's a bit of little boy in every good ballplayer…"

Uh-huh, and in Roy Campanella's case, at least, there was a lot of good ballplayer even when he was a little boy. Although some baseball men thought he was older because he began playing professionally so young—15—he was born on November 19, 1921, in Homestead, Pa., and grew up in a section of North Philadelphia known as Nicetown.

His mother was black, his father, John Campanella, a Sicilian fruit and vegetable huckster with five hungry kids to feed. Signor Campanella was a Roman Catholic but Roy's mother took him to a Baptist church and raised him on the precepts of the 23rd Psalm. Practicing ecumenism before most people ever heard the word, Roy Campanella sent his own oldest son to a Presbyterian Sunday school simply because it fielded a good Little League team.

That's how much baseball meant to the roly-poly Campanella kid who sold newspapers, cut grass and shined shoes to help the family. Mornings from the time he was nine or 10 years old, he recalled getting up at 2:30 to help older brother Lawrence deliver on his milk route. By 5:30 to 6, he'd jump back into bed before getting up at 8 o'clock to go to school.

"I got a quarter a day for the job," Campy would say later, smiling, when he became a $50,000 player in the big leagues.

Dutifully, Roy turned over the money he earned to his mother. His allowance was always spent on movies or a ball game. Shibe Park, the home of the American League Athletics, was within walking distance of the Campanella home, and Roy was there as often as he could scratch up the 25 cents necessary for an unofficial bleacher seat on the roof of one of the houses adjoining the place in right field.

Most kids on the narrow Nicetown streets played a form of stickball, but not Roy Campanella. His big hands felt awkward grasping a slim broomstick. He played sandlot baseball with the Nicetown Colored Athletic Club or the Nicetown Giants. Soon he was good enough for American Legion ball with Loudenslager Post No. 366.

Campy was not much of a hitter in those days, but was an earnest kid. In the spring of 1936, the baseball coach at Elizabeth Gillespie Junior High School put out a call for candidates. The best boys would be allowed to play for nearby Simon Gratz High School. Campy watched his buddies gather into separate groups, one for pitchers, one for infielders, a third for outfielders. No one stepped up to catch. Shrewdly, Campanella decided he'd take the lines of least resistance or of competition, anyway. He volunteered to put on the catcher's harness.

The next summer, when Roy was only 15, the manager of a Philadelphia black team known as the Bacharach Giants stopped by the house and asked his mother and father if they would be willing to let him go on a weekend trip with his team through Westchester County in New York, lower Connecticut and northern New Jersey. Mrs. Campanella was to be paid $25 in Roy's behalf. When Momma balked, the owner of the Bacharach ball club promised to see to it that the boy would get to church on Sunday.

This turned out to be a momentous journey. The Philly fellows were staying at the Woodside Hotel in New York when young Campanella was approached by the manager of the Baltimore Elite Giants of the Negro National League. Campy was as flattered as possible for a 15-year-old to be at a time when organized professional baseball was closed to his race.

The kid agreed to ride down to Norristown, Pa., for a workout with the Elite Giants. His potential impressed the professionals and he caught both ends of a doubleheader at Baltimore. The Elite Giants paid him $60 a month. Years later, when Ed Fitzgerald of *Sports* magazine wondered how he'd been able to get by on less than the equivalent of $15 a week, Campy grinned.

"I wasn't even gettin' that," he said in his high-pitched voice. "My mother was gettin' it."

Over the years, the agreeable Campanella hasn't worried what writers wrote about him, though usually he didn't have much to worry about because he was a great player, good copy and a pleasant person. Why, when Dick Young of the *New York Daily News* did a book on him shortly after he'd won the first of his three National League Most Valuable Player awards, Campy pulled what any writer would have to agree was the upset of the century. He refused to accept any part of the book royalties.

"You did the work," said Campanella, "and you deserve the money."

On one thing, however, Campanella was sensitive in his relations with the press. That involved his scholastic background. Not that he was trying to impress anyone. Far from it. He just didn't want his boys to know he quit high school. Like many other parents, he recognized that it wasn't enough to be able to tell his offspring, "Don't do as I did, but do as I say."

Before the major leagues began to siphon off their stars and interest in black baseball diminished, the Negro leagues had enough talent to fill American and National circuits, one primarily in the East, the other essentially in the West. From May to October, the bus leagues zig-zagged across the United States. Their buses were rolling dormitories. The young men used seats, aisles and luggage racks for beds at times. Often there was no time for a meal stop and sometimes no restaurant would serve a colored team. Then the players would carve up a big bologna and make sandwiches as they bounced along the highways and byways.

"Eating money? When I started out, it was 50 cents a day," said Campanella, who didn't complain then and still wasn't beefing.

When he was not catching, Campy played in the

outfield and even pitched. The trick, he told *Time* magazine one time, was to stay in the lineup at any cost.

"Since there was no trainer to tell us when we got hurt a man kept playing as long as he could stand up," Campanella remembered. "You had to. You got paid only if you played. There were no averages kept in those days. You couldn't go up to the boss and say, 'Look here, I'm hitting .350, so how about a raise? All you could do was make sure you played every day."

Campanella did and he established a resistance to pain that enabled him to catch 100 or more games for nine consecutive seasons in the National League—despite a proneness to injury—until he suffered the broken neck and crushed vertabrae that paralyzed him from the chest down and ended his career.

Even though only a boy playing against men when he broke in, Campy must have done all right. In 1938, his second season as a professional, his pay jumped to $90 a month. In 1939, he was paid $120 a month, a salary much less than that received by Satchel Paige and Josh Gibson, but pretty good to the wide-eyed kid who found he could follow the sun and play ball the year 'round.

He took to spending his winters playing Caribbean baseball, picking up as much as $45 a week, better money than he was making at home. Puerto Rican fans passed the hat for him when he hit a pair of home runs, and the good-natured humanitarian returned the kindness by distributing a 100-pound bag of potatoes in the slums.

"I guess I played about 200 ball games a year all told," Campanella toted it up one time. "I usually played ball all but two weeks of the year."

Doubleheaders were the rule rather than exception, and the squat, thick-thighed Campanella hunkered down behind the plate so often for two a day that he once did a double-double, catching four contests in one day. The Elite Giants played two one afternoon at Cincinnati's Crosley Field and the other that night at Middletown, O.

"I grabbed a sandwich on the bus," said Campanella in delightful understatement. "It wasn't so bad."

Campanella's team won the Negro League championship in 1939, with Roy getting five hits in five times up in one of the playoff games. As a reward, the kid was hiked to $150 a month in 1940. He needed the extra cash because he had married Ruthe Willis, a pretty New York girl whom he had met at the '39 World's Fair there.

Ruthe wouldn't be able to stand the gaff, unfortunately, after Roy's mishap in 1958 and five years later, estranged, she died unexpectedly at only 40 when she was talking on the telephone. But, as a couple of kids, they had a great time because Campy's wife went right along with him, whether he played in Puerto Rico, Mexico, Cuba or Venezuela—and he tried them all.

Winter ball was something. In Caracas one time, Campanella delighted in relating, Saul Rogovin, who later pitched in both the American and National Leagues, didn't want to work. The manager insisted. Annoyed, Rogovin, a control pitcher, walked the first four batters. Furious, the manager called the cops and Saul was marched off to the local jail.

As early as March 1941, when the Elite Giants were in Hot Springs, Ark., Campanella's draft board caught up with him, but it wasn't until a year later that the board decided to pass the father of two. Campy hurried to New Orleans, late for spring training, and arrived as the Baltimore Negro League team was about to play a doubleheader. Sure, he caught both games.

In mid-season, a Mexican League scout offered him $100 a week to finish out the season with the Monterrey club in the circuit bankrolled by Jorge Pasquel, who would make greater inroads against the Organized Baseball structure four years later. Campy left angry owner Tom Wilson and took Ruthe and the kids to Mexico until September and then to Havana for the winter.

In '43, Monterrey gave him $1,000 a month,

plus expenses, and he had a profitable winter in Puerto Rico before Wilson, his anger abated, offered the best contract Campanella ever had seen. Baltimore would pay him $3,000 for a six-month season.

To a 23-year-old an eight-season black league veteran who had reason to expect the baseball rainbow would stay lily white, this contract was generous. But better things were ahead.

After the 1945 season, Mrs. Effie Manley, owner of the Newark club in the Negro League, invited Campanella to play in a post-season series against a squad of barnstorming major leaguers. Curious to play against the major leaguers, Campy also welcomed the extra cash.

Black All-Stars lost the series, but one of their own gained important ground. Charley Dressen, managing the major leaguers, told Campanella that Branch Rickey wanted to see him at the Dodgers' offices on Montague Street in Brooklyn at 10 o'clock the next morning. Dressen had to tell Campy how to get there, but not when. Roy was 30 minutes early.

The first thing Rickey wanted to know was Campanella's correct age. B. R. believed Campy when he said he was 24, partly because Roy had such an earnest way about him. Partly, too, because Oscar Charleston, one of the deans of Negro League graduates, reminded Rickey's agents that Roy had started so young.

Rickey then went into his act. He scowled, whispered, thundered, gently praised and scathingly questioned the naive athlete of a different color.

"How much do you weigh?" he demanded.

"About 215," said the 5-9½ catcher.

"Judas Priest," roared Rickey, "you can't weigh that much and play ball."

Piped up Campanella, "All I know is I've been doin' it every day for years."

When Rickey got to his point, Roy said flatly he didn't want to take a chance with a new Negro league when he was doing all right with the one he was in, but he agreed, anyway, preparing to leave for winter ball in Venezuela, not to sign a 1946 contract with anyone until he saw Rickey again.

A few days later, Campy was playing gin rummy with Jackie Robinson when the former Army officer and ex-college halfback told Robinson that he'd signed to play with Montreal. The report was confirmed in a news story, October 23, 1945. Rickey had broken the color line in baseball and Campanella's heart sank for a moment. Perhaps, misunderstanding, he had missed his chance.

Obviously, Rickey already had made his choice when he talked to Campanella or else he would have disclosed more of his plan. To Campy, more flexible, the experience as the first Negro big leaguer of the century might have been less traumatic than it was for a man with Robinson's strong racial sensibilities. But it's possible, too, that Rickey questioned whether Campanella was far enough along to be as good a playing risk as Robinson, who also was better educated.

Anyway, one day a wire came for Campy in Venezuela from Rickey in Brooklyn. The team Roy managed already had clinched the pennant in Caracas, so he flew to New York, where B. R. offered him $185 a month, the Class B limit, to play at Nashua, N. H., in the New England League. To a player making $500 a month in the Negro League, this was an economic blow, but Campy gulped and decided to gamble. Besides, B. R. said he'd put Roy on the payroll to scout the Caribbean in the off-season.

Rickey and associates knew what they were getting behind the plate. Campanella would have to learn to throw off his right ear instead of drawing his arm back to wind up, but he had a powerful peg and, despite his girth, considerable agility. He believed in shifting to meet the pitch, rather than try to reach out for it, and the habit of hustle paid off in perfect body position. And he was like a warthog on low pitches. But would he hit?

They found out quickly at Nashua, where he and another black, a strapping young righthander named Don Newcombe, fell under the direction of two men they admired, Buzzie Bavasi, the general manager, and Walter Alston, the manager. Together, the four of them would have a date with destiny with the Dodgers.

Alston quickly recognized the take-charge qualities of the chattering catcher. "Roy," the manager said opening day, "you've got more experience than any of these fellows. If I ever get put out of the game, I want you to take over and run the team."

Pleased and proud, Campy got his chance to run the club one night at Lawrence, Mass., when Alston was ejected with Nashua trailing by a run. Roy Campanella's first move as a manager was classically successful. He beckoned Newcombe to pinch-hit and Big Newk knocked the ball into the Merrimack River for a game-winning home run.

Rickey had cautioned Campanella and Newcombe about how to conduct themselves in the face of insults and agitation, but they found New England natives extremely pleasant. Campy's only trouble came one game against Manchester when his rival catcher, Sal Yvars, later a big leaguer, stepped to bat and tossed a handful of dirt in Campy's face.

"Try that again," snarled the mild-mannered man, whipping off his catcher's mask, "and I'll beat you to a pulp."

Otherwise, Campy was the politest of players. "Good evening Mr. Corbitt. How are you tonight?" Campanella would sing out when, say, Claude Corbitt came to bat.

"The first time he did that," complained Corbitt, "I was so stunned that I could barely tap the ball back to the pitcher."

Campy began that pivotal '46 season with an opening-day home run and, batting .290 with 96 RBIs in 113 games, he hit 13 homers, a solid achievement at Nashua, where there was no outfield fence.

A local farmer offered 100 chickens for every home run. Campy sent his 1,300 prizes to his father, who raised them as a sideline to his vegetable business.

Chosen on the New England League All-Star team and selected as the league's Most Valuable Player, Campanella was promoted to Montreal in 1947, the year Robinson went from the Quebec metropolis to the majors. Once again, Roy's work drew rave notices and, when he again hit 13 homers and drove in 75 runs in a .273 season, he was hopeful Rickey would reward him with promotion to the Dodgers in 1948.

Well, he did and he didn't. Campy trained with the Dodgers and stayed with them until May, but Rickey confided to Roy that he wanted him to break the color line as the first black in the American Association. So he was shipped out to St. Paul, disappointed in a way, but determined not to rock the boat. Leo Durocher, managing the Dodgers after a year's suspension, didn't like the Mahatma's Machiavellian touch, either, but, hell, Leo had known B. R. too long to be surprised by anything.

Campanella broke in horribly at St. Paul on May 22 against Columbus, going hitless in four trips, fanning twice and making an error with a wild throw in a pickoff attempt. But Campy had been around too long and had waited too long to be bothered by a bad day. By the time the Saints rolled into Minneapolis to play their bitter Twin Cities' rivals, the Millers, he unloaded two homers in one day. When St. Paul came home the morning of Memorial Day for a traditional contest, Campy pounded a homer and triple against Minneapolis.

Durocher, watching the Dodgers skid to sixth place with inadequate punch, kept after Rickey without let-up as Campanella kept hitting. On June 30, Roy played a twilight twinbill at Toledo and collected a single, double and home run.

He was tired as he pulled off his uniform in the clubhouse, but he perked up as Alston, managing St. Paul by then, came up to him and said, "I've got news for you, Roy. Bad news for me, but good for you. The Dodgers want you back."

Everything happened fast. Campy grabbed his wife and children, who had been living in a St. Paul apartment, and hurried to Brooklyn. He arrived in the evening just before a night game against the bitter borough rivals, the Giants. Durocher said, "You're catching tonight," and advised clubhouse man John (Senator) Griffin to give him a uniform in a hurry.

The Senator sized up the squat figure, threw him a large uniform and then offered afterward to fit him out better, but Roy Campanella would have no part of any change. So No. 39 became famous because Campy had good fortune that first night before 33,104 at Ebbetts Field. The Dodgers lost, sinking into last place, but not because of what Campanella had done. Off righthanders Andy Hansen and Sheldon Jones, he produced a double and two singles.

They quickly came to love the peppery round man in Flatbush. The next night, he belted a triple and two singles and in a Sunday wrap-up of the series with the Giants, Campanella clobbered the first two of his 242 homers and also singled to knock in four runs.

With Campanella taking charge of Brooklyn's pitching staff and hitting .258 with nine homers and 45 RBIs in 83 games, the Dodgers rose from the cellar and almost won the '48 pennant before they were beaten back by the Boston Braves.

Roy was so well established by mid-season, 1949, that Billy Southworth, managing the National League All-Star team, picked him to catch most of the All-Star Game at Brooklyn even though Philadelphia's Andy Seminick had polled nearly 200,000 more votes from the fans. Campy began to star, despite a series of injuries.

At Pittsburgh in 1949, he was beaned with a pitch and carried to the hospital suffering from a severe concussion. Next day, he insisted on his release from the hospital and was ready to hit in batting practice, preparatory to catching, when Burt Shotton, then Dodger manager, got a good look at him.

"You all right?" Shotton asked in disbelief.

"Sure," said Campy.

"Then why," demanded Shotton, "is your left eye out of line?"

Benched a day to get his eye in focus, Campy came back and caught 130 games that pennant-winning season, hitting .287, cracking 22 homers and driving in 82 runs. Brooklyn's most sizable edge over St. Louis, beaten by just one game, was behind the plate. Campanella quickly had become the class of catchers in the National League and only the Yankees' Yogi Berra in the American League would come close to matching him throughout the years in which they competed against each other.

Campanella, appearing in five World Series, did not hit as well as Yogi did in the record 14 in which Berra participated. But Campy had his moments with four homers and five doubles among his 27 World Series hits. He drove in 12 runs in 32 Series contests and, truthfully, like many stars, didn't win his way into the Hall of Fame for what he did in the spotlight of baseball's blue-ribbon tournament.

There is, of course, more to the ancient game of rounders than just swinging a bat, as the Yankees discovered in the 1949 World Series, the first time they faced Campanella. Roy picked two of them off base, getting Tommy Henrich and Phil Rizzuto.

"That's the first time in my life I've ever been picked off third base," said Rizzuto, a superior baserunner.

"What an arm that Campanella has!"

Yes, a great arm and it was about the only thing that wasn't hurt over the next few years, seasons in which Campanella seldom caught without the miseries. In 1950, for instance, a year he hit 31 homers, including three in one game, he grabbed at a foul tip in September and suffered a dislocation of his right thumb.

That winter, he almost lost his sight when the hot water heater in his suburban New York home blew up in his face, blistering the cornea of his eyes. As the year wore on, Campy picked up a startling assortment of injuries: A split thumb from a foul ball in an exhibition game, a bruised hip sliding, a chipped elbow in a collision at home plate.

Despite these handicaps, he ripped eight hits in one two-game stretch against Boston at Brooklyn, including two homers and a double, and he finished with his best season to date. He batted .325 with 33 homers, 108 RBIs and, probably most important, he appeared in 143 games.

However, in the playoff that followed with the Giants, Campy reinjured his hip in the first game and, though he wanted to play, Manager Dressen reluctantly turned to Rube Walker. In the final game of the playoff, Campy repeatedly ducked into the toilet cubicle of the visitors' dugout at the Polo Grounds to pray.

When Bobby Thomson hit baseball's most unbelievable and dramatic home run Campy swore at the savage line drive. "Sink, you devil, sink," he kept muttering until the ball—and the pennant—disappeared.

Afterward, Campanella was on a barnstorming trip in Texas when he came back to his hotel from a shopping trip for his wife and family in downtown Houston. He found a long-distance call awaiting him from Dick Young. Young brought joyful tidings: Campy had been named the Most Valuable Player in the National League.

MVP awards followed in alternate years, 1953 and '55, enabling Roy to tie Stan Musial for most MVP laurels in National League history. In '53, Campy set a major league record for most homers by a catcher in a season, hitting 41 as he batted .312 and led the league in RBIs with 142 in 144 games.

The Yankees thought they could intimidate Campanella by pitching him high and tight and a delivery up and in by Chief Allie Reynolds badly bruised his left hand, which was aggravated in 1954 to the point he barely could grip the bat. He hit only .207 in 111 games and had just 19 homers and 51 runs batted in. It was no wonder the Dodgers lost their bid for a third straight pennant.

After a while, the hand was partially paralyzed and surgery was required. By spring of 1955, two

fingers of the left hand still were stiff, but Campy was confident. "I can curl them around a bat handle and that's what counts," he said.

Indeed. Campanella came back all the way with a .318 season in which he produced 32 homers and 107 RBIs in 123 games. The Dodgers breezed to a pennant and Campy delivered what he considered the most significant hit of his career when he doubled off the Yankees' Tommy Byrne in the fourth inning of a scoreless seventh-game duel with Johnny Podres. Roy then scored on a single by Gil Hodges and the Dodgers, adding another run, took the game, 2-0, and the world championship.

The title was Brooklyn's one and only and Campanella cherished it just as the Flatbush faithful did, but he reminisced later that he thought the '53 team was even better. That year, the Dodgers hit 208 home runs, 42 of them by Duke Snider, 41 by Campy himself, 31 by Gil Hodges, 21 by Carl Furillo and even 13 by Pee Wee Reese.

"We actually won in '55 with our best pitcher in service," Campanella said, referring to Don Newcombe. Big Newk, his friend and roomie, was not, however, the best he believed he ever caught.

"The best for ability and knowledge was Preacher Roe," he said, and the toughest hitter he ever caught behind in the big leagues was "easy," he said—Stan Musial.

Overall, however, counting those nine seasons in the Negro leagues, the best pitcher and the best hitter were the two legendary men Roy believes belong in the Hall of Fame. He referred to Satchel Paige and Josh Gibson. Paige received special-category recognition in 1971, Gibson less quickly in 1972.

"Everybody knows about Ol' Satch because he's still around, but Josh is gone"—Gibson died just about the time Campy got to the big leagues—"and it's too bad many white people and sportswriters didn't get to see him catch or hit. I couldn't carry his glove or bat."

Campanella estimated that he'd hit more than 500 home runs himself, counting those years in the Negro leagues when they played a whopping exhibition schedule, and he wondered just how many Gibson must have hit.

"You just couldn't fool him," said Campy, speaking from experience as a catcher who squatted behind the plate when Gibson was at it. "I never saw a home run hitter hit for such good average, and I once saw him hit a ball into the upper deck of the Polo Grounds way down beyond the bullpen in left field. Know somethin'? He was a slugger, but he seldom struck out."

The color line was broken too late for Gibson, who broke the seal off many a bottle in trying to drown his sorrows. Campanella, grateful for the opportunity, was generous with his family and himself. He bought a comfortable home in a prosperous shoreline section of Glen Cove, Long Island, N.Y. He tended the backyard rose garden, officiated at outdoor barbecues, played catch with his boys and found time, too, for his hobbies. A vast and valuable collection of toy trains cluttered the attic. Heck, they were Campy's, not the kids. So, too, were the carefully tended aquariums of expensive tropical fish. He also bought a sea cruiser which he named "Princess"—that was the family's, but it was Roy's pride and joy.

It was to this setting of super-suburban living that Campanella, proprietor of a prosperous Harlem liquor store, was headed home the fateful night when his rented Chevy skidded on a slick spot in the final turn of that "S" curve and careened into a telephone pole and overturned. The time was 3:34 A.M., Tuesday, January 28, 1958.

Campy was pinned in the car for a half an hour, his legs caught by a door and his body "twisted like a pretzel," according to Dr. W. S. Gurnee, a Manhattan gynecologist who lived nearby and was the first on the scene. The athlete had suffered fractures and dislocations of the fifth and sixth cervical vertebrae at the neck line, according to Dr. Robert W. Sengstaken, the neurosurgeon who performed an emergency operation at the Glen Cove Community Hospital.

"An inch or two higher (in the fourth cervical),

and he would have been dead," said Dr. Sengstaken.

Men of lesser moral fiber and mental determination would have wished they were dead when they found, as Campanella did, that he was paralyzed from the chest down. But Campy persevered, aided by his own courage and the goodwill and efforts of others.

At times, teammate Jackie Robinson, with whom he was not close, had considered him an "Uncle Tom" because he was such an agreeable black man in a white man's world, but Campanella couldn't help contrasting the little he'd known and the considerable he had achieved. More satisfied with his own progress and less a crusader than Robinson, Roy had achieved greater acceptance and recognition than any teammate—white or black.

When comedian Happy Felton began to conduct a pre-game television show every day before Dodger contests at Ebbets Field, he expected that young contest winners would want most to meet Robinson or Reese.

"Campy was way out in front," said Felton. "He just has a special way with kids. He gets along with them without even trying."

If Felton had made it "people" rather than "kids," he probably would have said it all. When Ty Cobb suggested in 1953 that Campanella would be remembered longer probably than any other catcher in baseball history, the one-time curmudgeon listed among his reasons one that seemed strange coming from Cobb—"disposition."

Campy still speaks with appreciation of the treatment accorded him by the late Walter F. O'Malley, owner of the Dodgers, who, as mentioned, had moved to Los Angeles a few months before Campy's career-ending accident. O'Malley not only paid Campanella an entire season's salary, $50,000, but also turned over another 50 grand to cover his hospital expenses after an exhibition at which more than 93,000 turned out at the Coliseum to see the Dodgers play Casey Stengel's New York Yankees.

Campanella's eyes gleamed when he saw that

beckoning, high screen fence in left field at the football stadium turned into an emergency ballpark. With his plate-crowding, open stance and the hoist to his swing, the uppercutting Campanella would have rebounded with another big season in 1958, everyone was certain, if—.

The "if" seems to bug many of us more than it did Campanella, who said when this article was being prepared, "I like to think I've accepted my fate as the Lord's will," he said, "and I'm lucky I've got so many who care."

Campy's parents lived in Philadelphia and he managed to get down to see them. By a seldom-mentioned first marriage, he is the proud father of two girls, Joyce and Beverly, both married and with children of their own in Philly.

Roy Campanella Jr., captain of his high school baseball team, graduated from Harvard in the spring of 1970 with a degree in anthropology and Campy beamed as he told how the No. 1 son had been invited to teach at Howard University and then in Africa. Tony and Ruth (Princess) were well educated.

Then, the Campanellas lived in Hartsdale, N.Y., close by White Plains, as a result of Roy's third marriage in 1965. Mrs. Campanella, the former Roxie Jones, lived in the apartment building that became Campy's home temporarily after his estrangement from his late wife, Ruthe. Roy had adopted Roxie's two children, Joni and John, both college graduates.

"He's a big catcher, 6-1, 200 pounds," Campy said as enthusiastically as if John really had the bloodlines of a baseball big leaguer.

When business still was pretty good in Campanella's liquor store in Harlem, getting around in an electric wheelchair, the former catcher was more wrapped up in his work for the New York Bank for Savings, an establishment that has 12 branches in the metropolitan area. Previously, Campy gave baseball clinics for the banks. More recently, he visited schools to talk to seventh, eighth and ninth graders.

"Those are the critical years," he said, then and now, "making certain that the junior high young-sters recognize the value of staying in school."

Roy Campanella spoke to young people as a stricken leader, a handicapped hero. Chances are, if he hadn't been hurt, Campy not only would have played until he was around 40, he most certainly would have become a coach and might have become the first black big league manager.

His picturesque language wouldn't have hurt his communications with his players. When Newcombe wasn't bringing the ball to him as rapidly as he once thought proper, Campy waddled out to the mound and shrilled, "You keep giving me the local, big boy, when I want the express."

Talking about the pitchers he hit the hardest, Roy remembered that he wore out soft-serving southpaws Al Brazle and Ken Raffensberger, who troubled many tough hitters, but he winced when he talked about side-wheeling righthander, fireballer Ewell Blackwell. "He gave me the blues," said colorful Campy.

Campanella shared mutual regard and respect with Walter Alston, long-time Dodger manager. Alston, the man who put him in charge when Walt was thrown out at Nashua back there in 1947, was delighted in Dodgers' spring training when the tireless, exuberant Campanella went out of his way to work with young Brooklyn pitchers.

"I just saw a big tall kid who impressed me, Skipper," Campy would say at Vero Beach, Fla. "Let me catch him for three innings against the Yankees next week and I'll give you a good line on him."

So Roy Campanella became one of the first on Don Drysdale's bandwagon, just as, years earlier when he joined Brooklyn, he recommended heartily a young Negro outfielder he'd seen at Birmingham.

"They sent Wid Matthews out to take a look at him, but Wid said the kid couldn't hit a curveball," said Campy, his voice rising with incredulity as he added, "Who ever heard of any 17-year-old hitting a curveball?"

Willie Mays was the name and when Willie came up with the Giants, Campanella would talk to him, chattering with the wily way that served to distract many a hitter. Flustered, tight-lipped, Mays finally beckoned to Leo Durocher, managing the Giants, and complained.

"The next time he talks to you, pick up a handful of dirt and throw it at him," snapped Durocher.

Campanella, hands on hips, feigned hurt feelings. "Willie's got better sense than that, ain't you, Willie? All I asked was, 'Are you married?'

"What's the matter, Willie? You mad at me? I keep talking to you, but you ain't never said a word to me. Ain't we friends?"

Of course they were, but Willie Mays, though as enthusiastic as Roy Campanella about baseball as a helluva fine way to make a living, must have recognized that No. 39 behind the plate was the No. 1 con man in a bird cage.

And until he died of a heart attack in early summer, 1993, shortly before former batterymate Drysdale also died of a heart attack, Campy had spent nearly half his 71 years in a wheelchair, a model to one and all.

ROY CAMPANELLA
Born November 19, 1921, at Philadelphia, Pa.
Died June 26, 1993, at Woodland Hills, Calif.
Height 5-9 1/2 Weight 205
Threw and batted righthanded.
Named to Hall of Fame, 1969.

YEAR	CLUB	LEAGUE	POS.	G.	AB.	R.	H.	2B.	3B.	HR.	RBI.	B.A.	PO.	A.	E.	F.A.
1946	Nashua	New Eng.	C	113	396	75	115	19	8	13	96	.290	687	64	15	.980
1947	Montreal	Int.	C	135	440	64	120	25	3	13	75	.273	642	83	9	.988
1948	St. Paul	A.A.	C-OF	35	123	31	40	5	2	13	39	.325	147	19	6	.965
1948	Brooklyn	Nat.	C	83	279	32	72	11	3	9	45	.258	413	45	9	.981
1949	Brooklyn	Nat.	C	130	436	65	125	22	2	22	82	.287	684	55	11	.985
1950	Brooklyn	Nat.	C	126	437	70	123	19	3	31	89	.281	683	54	11	.985
1951	Brooklyn	Nat.	C	143	505	90	164	33	1	33	108	.325	722	72	11	.986
1952	Brooklyn	Nat.	C	128	468	73	126	18	1	22	97	.269	662	55	4	.994
1953	Brooklyn	Nat.	C	144	519	103	162	26	3	41	142	.312	807	57	10	.989
1954	Brooklyn	Nat.	C	111	397	43	82	14	3	19	51	.207	600	58	7	.989
1955	Brooklyn	Nat.	C	123	446	81	142	20	1	32	107	.318	672	54	6	.992
1956	Brooklyn	Nat.	C	124	388	39	85	6	1	20	73	.219	659	49	11	.985
1957	Brooklyn (a)	Nat.	C	103	330	31	80	9	0	13	62	.242	618	51	5	.993
Major League Totals				1215	4205	627	1161	178	18	242	856	.276	6520	550	85	.988

a Incurred injuries in automobile accident, Janury 28, 1958, which ended his playing career.

WORLD SERIES RECORD

YEAR	CLUB	LEAGUE	POS.	G.	AB.	R.	H.	2B.	3B.	HR.	RBI.	B.A.	PO.	A.	E.	F.A.
1949	Brooklyn	Nat.	C	5	15	2	4	1	0	1	2	.267	32	2	0	1.000
1952	Brooklyn	Nat.	C	7	28	0	6	0	0	0	1	.214	39	5	0	1.000
1953	Brooklyn	Nat.	C	6	22	6	6	0	0	1	2	.273	47	9	0	1.000
1955	Brooklyn	Nat.	C	7	27	4	7	3	0	2	4	.259	42	3	1	.978
1956	Brooklyn	Nat.	C	7	22	2	4	1	0	0	3	.182	49	3	0	1.000
World Series Totals				32	114	14	27	5	0	4	12	.237	209	22	1	.996

CLASSIC: As classically majestic as when he stood on second base after the final hit of his career, his 3,000th, Roberto Clemente proudly poses for a photographer at the Pirates' dugout.

ROBERTO CLEMENTE

Roberto Clemente was one of a kind—as high-strung as a thoroughbred, sensitive, pleasant most of the time, bitter on occasion—but always proud. He was part insomniac, part hypochondriac and all ballplayer.

As one of the best ever, a superstar who had considerable self-esteem and yet even more consideration for others, the trim, wasp-waisted No. 21 in Pittsburgh's black-and-gold was accorded a special election to bypass the national baseball Hall of Fame's five-year wait for selection.

But the all-around athlete who had writhed sensitively too long—under-rated, under-appreciated and often misunderstood—would have commented in a high-pitched shrill that it took dramatic death on a mission of mercy to get him the attention and respect he craved as if it were an overwhelming addiction.

The truth is, recognition HAD come before Clemente went to a watery grave on New Year's Eve, 1972, the last day of the last year in which his last hit had been No. 3,000. Although for too long, the handsome ebony man who looked like a darker-skinned Harry Belafonte, the ballad singer, had played in the shadow of Willie Mays and then Henry Aaron and—until almost the end—the pitfalls of the Pirates' Forbes Field.

There, with beautiful Schenley Park a green backdrop for the red brick-walled ballpark of awesome playing dimensions, Clemente achieved stardom in what amounted to relative obscurity. And it rankled him as much as race, color, prejudice and his twitching rabbit-eared belief the skeptics felt that he complained too much of injury and wouldn't play hurt.

The fact is, Pittsburgh isn't New York, not by all its hills and valleys, nor even Chicago or Los Angeles, either, where the media and the best in show biz fawn over a fellow, making him feel bigger than life. And the king-sized playing field on which a no-hitter never was pitched from the time it opened in 1909 until it closed a couple of years before Roberto's life did, too, discouraged the long ball, the only department of play in which Clemente did not excel consistently.

Even so, the beautiful-bodied Puerto Rican hit not only 240 home runs, some of which were as long and as savage as you'd care to double-take, but he also twice hit three homers in a game. In addition, he homered once each in an All-Star Game and a National League championship series and—most important—twice teed off in the 1971 World Series.

It was that performance, naturally nationally televised with the day-to-day continuity and suspense only the Series can generate in baseball, that brought to Clemente his greatest acceptance and satisfaction. Now, EVERYONE knew that the mahogany-skinned marvel in No. 21 WAS one of the best ever. He hit .414, extending to 14 his streak of batting safely in every World Series game in which he ever played, and he lashed two doubles, a triple and two homers among his 11 hits against Baltimore. The second homer tipped the scales, 2-1, for Steve

Blass in the seventh game and, combined with Clemente's excellence in the field and a throwing arm beyond belief, it gave him parity with the best of his peers and of previous periods.

So he was a much more contented man, albeit one almost with premonition when he doubled for that precious on September 30, restless that he hadn't been given a hit on a questionable play earlier and determined to play no more so as to be rested for the playoffs against Cincinnati.

"I have a feeling I've got to get it now or maybe never," said Clemente in what amounted almost to weird prophecy. You see, the four hits he got in that third straight—and losing—championship series wouldn't have counted in the regular season total to the summit reached previously only by 10 players in baseball history.

So before that overloaded, creaky DC-7 crashed into the bay beyond San Juan shortly after takeoff, spilling some $150,000 of medical supplies of relief for earthquake victims at Nicaragua and closing the waters over the close-cropped head of Clemente and four other persons, Roberto had assured his own immortality.

Yes, and durability, too, because you don't get 3,000 hits moping in the dugout or moaning on the trainer's table when the ball is in play out there on the diamond. At 38, just shortly before he staked his own claim on batting's Mr. Everest, an 18-season veteran who had played more than 140 games in each of 10 years and over 150 three times, Clemente looked as if he'd go on to 40 and beyond. After all, in 102 games, he'd just hit .312, a mere five points below his career average, and then after .341, .352 and .345 the three previous seasons.

So it was with arm raised in triumph that Clemente stood at second base at Pittsburgh's Three Rivers Stadium, holding aloft the ball that would go to Cooperstown just before the man's Hall of Fame plaque itself. And though he had known rage and frustration, indignation and insecurity, he was triumphant and contrite.

"I felt kind of bashful," he said, "but I dedicate this hit to the Pittsburgh fans and to the people of Puerto Rico and to one man in particular," a reference to a teacher and baseball coach back home—Roberto Marin—who had driven kid Clemente back and forth across the island to play ball until the professionals were sufficiently impressed to sign him.

Clemente's reaction then, a 24-hour reversal from the keyed-up man who had shouted that he'd been robbed of a hit, was much like his compassionate message in Spanish to his parents from the championship-celebrating clubhouse the previous year.

Said religious Roberto with tender emotion, "On this, the proudest day in my life, I ask your blessing…"

P-r-i-d-e, it was the emotion that helped and hurt, the feeling of self-esteem aggravated by that gnawing lack of recognition for too long, that whipped him into the frenzy of a clutch-hitting, rapid-running, fence-challenging frenzy.

Over the years in which he was hurt often, if not so often as he would proclaim, they scraped that magnificent body off brick walls after incredible catches. And a clinical psychologist named Dr. Thomas Tutko, asked by former Pittsburgh general manager Joe L. Brown to analyze Pirate players, reported of Roberto:

"No one drives himself like Clemente. If he were a football player, he'd make Ray Nitschke (intense-playing Green Bay linebacker) look like a pussycat."

Clemente could have been the model for the wordmaster statesman, Sir Winston Churchill, when the knight of oratory described someone or something as, if memory serves, "an enigma wrapped in a riddle inside a mystery."

In this judgment, from one who respected the bittersweet ballplayer as much as a man as an athlete, the best description probably was given to Bill Christine, former Pittsburgh sports editor, by Clemente's close friend and confidante, Phil Dorsey.

Said Dorsey as Christine prepared a paperback book *Roberto!* for Stadia Sports Publishing, Inc., New York City, shortly after Clemente was killed:

"Don't make him a saint or a sinner. Roberto wasn't God and he wasn't the devil. But I'd like everybody to know that he was much closer to the one than the other."

Whether chauffering Clemente around in the ballplayer's Cadillac or listening to him laugh or lament, Dorsey knew the deep-feeling Latin as few others did. He knew, for instance, that Roberto admired swashbuckling Errol Flynn and matinee idol Tyrone Power most in the movies. Oddly, though grossly unalike in their conduct, the two silver-screen idols, like the lad from Puerto Rico who so much appreciated them, died too young.

Clemente played billiards, too, another oddity to a guy who over the years, watching him playing the tricky Forbes Field caroms in right field so adroitly that his deft defensive touch and rifle right arm held many a potential double or triple to a single, it was suggested he was Willie Hoppe without a cue.

Clemente's eating habits were as strange and as inconsistent as the Jekyll-and-Hyde in two-way stretch. For example, two of Roberto's favorite energizing drinks would defy an alchemist of gastronomy. He liked to mix milk, orange juice and ice cubes, stirred well. He also liked a concoction of grape juice and sugar, laced with three or four raw eggs.

Unusual? Sure, and that's not all.

At times Clemente, who advertised his ills as if he were indeed a hypochondriac, would moan and groan that he could eat nothing more substantial than oatmeal and soft-boiled eggs. It is a fact that in the 1972 stretch drive, his weight of 180 pounds fell to the point where he was wearing the extra baseball pants of 164-pound utility player Ronnie Stennett, later Pittsburgh second baseman.

When, however, his queasy stomach permitted,

Clemente not only would eat highly seasoned food native to Puerto Rico, but he also was so fond of Chinese food that he would eat chop suey a couple of times a week. Nothing pleased his taste buds more, Christine reported, than lobster Cantonese or sweet-and-sour shrimp.

It was after a walk for a late-night snack of bedtime fried chicken, to be taken back to his hotel room in San Diego for a snack while reading or watching television, that Clemente reported in 1970 of having been waylaid by four robbers. The men, he said, took his clothes, his money—everything—and prepared to gun him down, the way the athlete told it, until they wriggled off his 1961 All-Star Game ring and then believed what he'd been telling 'em. That is, who he was. Then, Roberto said, they gave it all back, including his sack of bedtime fried chicken.

Some implied that they thought Clemente embroidered that story, craving attention at the time, but it is true that he wore the 1961 All-Star ring in preference to the more customary world championship ring of 1960. You'll remember that unorthodox Series in which the New York Yankees outscored by Pirates lustily over seven games, two runs to every one, yet lost the title in a wild Forbes Field thriller, 10-9, on Bill Mazeroski's ninth-inning home run.

By the time the young Bucs celebrated with everybody else in the raucous release of recession-depressed Pittsburgh, Clemente had deserted the ship for his island paradise, aware he'd received insufficient credit for his part either in the regular season or Series. Hitting .310 in the October classic, he most certainly didn't begrudge Mazeroski the deserved glory—but Clemente burned over what had been written in the Pittsburgh press about Bucco Most Valuable Player candidates.

Sure enough, though he batted .314 with 16 homers, and 94 RBIs, establishing himself truly and firmly as a hitter as well as an all-around player, Clemente finished eighth in National MVP voting.

Dick Groat, the shortstop, won the award even though he'd been out nearly a month with a broken wrist, an absence during which benchwarmer Dick Schofield rose to the heights. Pittsburgh's colorful, noisy third baseman, Don (Tiger) Hoak, finished second.

If it wasn't obvious that Clemente felt both the articulate Groat and talkative Hoak were better politicians than a fellow American whose English was a chopped, chattering evenly delivered kind, it was as plain as manager Danny Murtaugh's broken nose that the excitable Puerto Rican and unflappable Irishman didn't understand each other fully.

Frankly, Clemente felt like part of a caste system in which, as he saw it, players were rated and recognized—accepted, at least—in order of (1) continental United States whites, (2) American blacks, (3) Caribbean whites and Latins of a darker hue. Roberto thought they segregated themselves, as noted, but he seemed to blame management more than either the front office or field command deserved.

Murtaugh, in turn, a tobacco-chewing, milk-sipping, ulcer-suffering victim, was a wry wit who said little, but thought much. And he thought, among other things, as he told Clemente, that players should be seen and not heard or, at least, not heard about injuries, either real or imagined. Although in the same breath, Murtaugh had told his right fielder he considered him No. 1, those sensitive feelings of the thoroughbred were hurt.

His career, therefore, took two turns and they were, indeed, for the better. He fought with the umpires, too, in that crusade for himself and black Latins. And in 1961 he was startled and impressed when a brother dying of cancer told him, "Quit fighting the umpires. You are too good a ballplayer to worry about them."

That year, Bob Clemente, as he liked to be called, yet seldom was, responded with his first of four batting championships, getting 200 hits for the first of four times, belting 29 homers and driving in

89 runs. His average was .351, but his critics would have their say. Why, even the Pirates' own year-book would use a cutting conjunction when, prais-ing him in photo cutlines, a stupid houseman wrote, "BUT he never has driven in 100 runs."

Hear that sizzle? It was Roberto burning.

Clemente, who had hit over .300 (.311) in his second big league season, 1956, became a .300 bats-man again in '60 and continued over that mark un-til the end except—by eight percentage points—in 1968. But he really came into his own as a leader, more self-certain, under Harry (The Hat) Walker in 1965 and '66, seasons in which, winning 90 games and then 92, the Buccos just missed pennants.

Early, there was the inevitable misunderstanding, but that's all it was, a misuse of a word by Walker, who was really trying to compliment Clemente and bring forth the latent leadership in the Latin. When they sat down, they shouted or soothed it out and, truth is, each became the other's champion.

Clemente would call Walker the best manager he ever played for, and The Hat, though labeling Stan Musial as the best with whom he had played and Terry Moore as the most inspirational, said of Clemente:

"By far, the best I ever managed. He could go into a fence all-out and get rid of the ball faster, stronger and more accurately than any outfielder I ever saw."

Walker, vaccinated with a needle, had been more than a pretty fair outfielder himself and, stepping down at age 60 in 1979 to coach the University of Alabama's Birmingham branch near his home at Leeds, the prosperous hitting instructor managed three teams for nine seasons—St. Louis, Pittsburgh and Houston—so his compliment wasn't an idle one. Besides, Dixie Walker's young brother—and both were batting champions—had had to over-come background of environment and heredity to give any black athlete full credit. The Hat did.

Like the great George Sisler before him, Walker would cringe when Clemente swung at bad balls, which he did with the regularity of a Joe Medwick or Yogi Berra. But both liked the results as much as they liked Clemente's versatility and class.

"A gentleman," said Sisler, then close to 80 when Clemente died, "a gentleman AND a great ballplayer."

Studious Gene Mauch, who writhed at Philadel-phia, Montreal and other points as a rival manager stung by No. 21's brilliance, probably put it best obliquely when he said:

"Clemente commits more of himself away from the ball than any hitter and still does more with it because of his tremendous hands."

As the *Philadelphia Daily News'* Stan Hochman suggested, that was "a polite way of saying how can that son-of-a-gun let his rear end fly south and still rap the ball 380 feet to right-center."

Roberto could do that, all right.

He'd stand in the batter's box, so far back that at times his back (right) foot was illegally a couple of inches outside the white line. Invariably, he'd taken a first pitch, often a fat strike down the middle by pitchers who would chance his cavalier treatment to-ward their first delivery. At times, Clemente would go back to the bench mumbling how he could be "mucho loco" to let such a pigeon pitch get by.

Just as invariably, Roberto would stride forward so that he seemed to balance like a stork on one (left) foot and, almost literally taking the ball out of the catcher's glove, he'd swing late and savagely, driving the ball to right-center or down the right field stripe. Oh, sure, he could pull to left field, but he always seemed his devastating best going the other way, which he couldn't do when he first came up to the majors in 1955.

A premier pitcher, Tom Seaver, reminiscing about Roberto, said:

"He had a weakness, yes. Because he stood so deep and far from the plate, if you could hum one across the black on the outside corner, but, my, if you missed—and how often can you thread a needle?—he'd leap into the ball the way he would a wall."

Defensively, Clemente was worth the price of admission even if, at bat, he didn't get the darned ball out of the infield. He'd make leaping, sliding, diving catches and come up throwing—at times underhanded—as quickly as when he would make a basket catch nonchalantly, crotch high, of a flyball and, unless someone was going, he'd flip it back with underhanded disdain.

When, however, the ball and a runner were in play, ah, then you'd see the master right fielder at his best, snatching the ball and sidearming accurately in one motion, powerfully and with pinpoint precision. At old Forbes Field, they swear he caught a ball at the old iron-gate in deep right-center and uncorked a tremendous throw 460 feet to the plate. And he certainly didn't lead the National League's outfielders five times in assists because they were testing his arm.

Gadzooks, they'd learned when Roberto was right out of Brooklyn's farm system that the Dodgers had come up with a right fielder even better and stronger-throwing than Carl Furillo, who used to make the foe play what amounted to girls' softball at Ebbets Field. That is, advance one cautious base at a time.

If the Dodgers hadn't outsmarted themselves, gambling they could hide Clemente away in their farm system and slip him through the draft by not playing him much at Montreal, Brooklyn—and Los Angeles—well might have wound up with the dangedest-throwing threesome ever: Clemente, Furillo and Duke Snider.

Or, looking at it another way, if the senior Clementes back home in Puerto Rico hadn't been people of principle more than of principal, declining a bonus offer ($40,000) four times larger from Milwaukee than their son orally had accepted from the Dodgers a few hours earlier, the Braves would have had an outfield two-thirds of which would include two Hall of Fame greats who well might be in the National League's mythical best outfield ever.

Right on. Roberto and Hank Aaron. With Willie Mays, the one Clemente envied because No. 24 got so much more acclaim than either Roberto or Hank did until Aaron neared Babe Ruth's career 714 homers, the trio of righthanded-hitting, all-purpose blacks make an utterly spectacular outfield. If they played together, you'd have to put the silk-smooth Aaron in left field if only because Henry's good throwing arm couldn't compare with Roberto's great one.

Roberto Walker Clemente—the middle name is ironic more because Bob so seldom walked than because it doesn't sound Spanish—was born to Puerto Rican parents in the Depression year of 1934. He was the youngest of six children, five of them boys. The sister and that younger brother who told him to get off umpires' backs died young.

Clemente's father was foreman of a sugar plantation so that, though not wealthy, the family lived well in a big wooden house—five bedrooms and, a luxury then, an indoor bathroom. Summers, the boy helped the father load sand for a small trucking business Mr. Clemente had on the side.

Roberto would wax lyrical about the love he learned from his parents and their indulgence so that he could play. In softball, he was shortstop. In baseball at Carolina, the Puerto Rican town in which he grew up, he played regularly and strengthened his hand and arm muscles by squeezing a hard rubber ball. To strengthen his arm, he threw the javelin. Good man in all phases of track, that Clemente muchacho. Threw the javelin 195 feet, high-jumped six feet, surpassed 45 feet in the triple jump and seemed certain to win a place on Puerto Rico's 1956 Olympic squad.

But baseball was too much in the picture of the boy who wanted to study engineering and briefly attended college. His first fan outside the family, high school history teacher Roberto Morin, touted him, unsuccessfully at first, but then Santurce's Pedro Zorilla listened, watched and was impressed. He offered $300 a month, but Roberto's parents said no.

Zorilla made it a $500 bonus and $60 a month. So the Clementes said "Si." Even so, Roberto really didn't envision playing in the States. "I thought you had to be a Superman to make it," he would recall, "but when (Minnie) Minoso and (Bobby) Avila made it big, I realized others could do it, too."

When Roberto was in high school, nine stateside big league clubs made an offer, but Señor Clemente insisted the son finish high school first. Latin players were offered peanuts, but the Dodgers finally offered $10,000. The same day the Braves made it 40 grand. That's when Señora Clemente said, sternly:

"If you give the word, you keep the word."

Although Roberto had studied English, he really couldn't speak it at all well then. Further, when Montreal's International League club went on the road, playing at Richmond, Va., he learned, shocked, what it meant not to be white. He couldn't stay with his teammates and found, he said, that white Latin players who might have helped because of a familiar tongue shied away from the Caribbean blacks for fear they'd be labeled "colored," too.

Montreal tried under orders from the big club to play Clemente as little as possible. A player then given a bonus of $4,000 or more had to be on a big league roster to avoid the draft and the Dodgers felt they needed every spot on their 25. A puzzled Clemente would find himself staying in the lineup if he struck out a couple of times, but jerked quickly, such as the day he hit three successive triples.

Then one pre-game, Pittsburgh scout Clyde Sukeforth, scouting another player, saw Clemente throw. Sukie, who had caught for the Dodgers and coached there, reported enthusiastically to Branch Rickey, a brilliant failure at Pittsburgh. B.R., a huge success in St. Louis and at Brooklyn, helped repay sportsman John Galbreath. He drafted Clemente.

The 20-year-old kid was bewildered. "I didn't even know where Pittsburgh was," he said.

When the homesick kid batted only .255 his first year, batting coach George Sisler corrected a bad head-bobbing habit and, though not even The Sizzler could do much with the Puerto Rican's prediliction for swinging at anything that wasn't rolled up to the plate, Roberto—or "Hershel," as pitcher Verne Law would call him for no good reason—jumped to .311.

He'd fall back, then, until 1960, but he was bothered more by injuries and that bric-a-brac tag he resented bitterly, vulnerable himself because he talked too darned much as if trying to come to the defense of Latin players, labeled generally as "lazy."

Clemente would bristle at the press and even fellow players. "They say 'jake,'" he'd struggle with the words until time made him handle words as well as he did enemy pitchers. "'Hot dog,' too, and 'goldbrick,' but I tried so hard to be ready. I slept so much."

To a friend, he would add, proving he was not humorless, which teammates also discovered over the years in back-and-forth banter when the clubhouse was closed to press and other visitors, "the more you rest, the prettier you become."

Clemente had had his troubles, no doubt of that. In the 1953 Puerto Rican winter league, trying to hit more home runs, he'd switched to a lighter bat, swung viciously, missed and hurt his back. Later, a drunk smashed his car into Clemente's, jarring loose three spinal discs.

On a desperate sidearmed throw in 1958, Roberto cracked his right elbow. The condition worsened three years later when Don Drysdale hit him with a pitch on the same spot, requiring surgery to remove a bone chip.

Colds, flu, nervous stomachs and even malaria and Clemente began to get the reputation: Malingerer or martyr. Take your choice.

I opt for neither, actually, seeing both sides of the dugout, but I do know that after learning in 1970 that Clemente said he'd almost quit in 1957 except for a chance visit to Logan College of Chiropractics in St. Louis, I became interested. Dr. Vinton

Logan, Roberto said, had relieved the pressure of a pinched nerve. Clemente had become a constant customer.

I gave Roberto oral tea and sympathy, especially honest interest, and offered to drive him out into the county the next day to the late Doc Logan's newer establishment so he wouldn't need a long cab ride. There, I found that the Pittsburgh superstar was the place's pet patient.

Doctors showed me X-rays of his arthritic spine, aggravated by the whiplash effects to the neck of that old automobile accident. Said Dr. Goodman of the Logan staff, smiling:

"Roberto is the best-known pain in the neck we've got. And he doesn't help his cervical condition by his neck-jerking habit in the batter's box."

Clemente didn't mind the rib or the scolding. He said, "All I know is that here they give me relief, which is more than I can say about the medical doctor whose remedy was to take out my tonsils and then tell me that my continuing neck discomfort was mental."

The best walking—or running—ad for Blue Cross resented most the raised brow or the patronizing tut-tut of the disbeliever. He was considerate and compassionate, honest and soft-hearted, other than with the three cute little boys he had with his lovely wife, Vera, the girl he'd met in a drugstore in Carolina and, uncharacteristically, to whom he'd introduced himself, saying the same night:

"That's the girl I'm going to marry."

Now, on a grassy slope in front of a lone pink stucco home in Rio Piedras, Puerto Rico, white stones form a baseball, a bat, a glove and Roberto's number—"21." Vera still is sad and somewhat bitter because courts have not upheld her suit of the company that owned the plane, officially labeled by the National Transportation Safety Board as "inadequately prepared for flight."

Clemente, a $140,000 performer concerned as always about the underprivileged and the underdog, which he had been, boiled to learn that profiteers were making theirs at the expense of the Nicaraguan earthquake victims. The popular hero of Puerto Rico raised the money, lined up and helped load the plane with the supplies. Then, with Vera driving him to the airport for the second attempt of the plane to take off, he left near midnight and the clock-striking in the New Year he never saw.

Since then, many have worked hard to fulfill Roberto Clemente's dream of a sports city for the kids in Puerto Rico. The government there donated a tract of more than 200 acres and more than $500,000 had been contributed even before a "Buck for Roberto's Dream" in 1977. Still, aside from the indoor arena named for him and the street on which he lived and the special election to the Hall of Fame in 1973, Roberto Walker Clemente lives mostly in the bodies of those three boys, the hearts of fans who remember and in the baseball record books.

Phil Dorsey, that close friend, said it all about Roberto Walker Clemente in the basement of that handsome house on the hill just after memorial services in Puerto Rico early in 1973 and a futile search for that beautiful, talented body which never was found. Dorsey looked at a pair of combat boots he'd given Clemente as a gift several years earlier. Just then, a mourner asked about the boots. Said Dorsey:

"They might as well leave those right where they are. There's nobody around who can come close to filling them."

Rest well, Roberto—and "Arriba!" (Charge!)

ROBERTO WALKER CLEMENTE
Born August 18, 1934, at Carolina, Puerto Rico.
Died December 31, 1972, at San Juan, Puerto Rico.
Height 5-11 Weight 185
Threw and batted righthanded.
Named to Hall of Fame, 1973.

YEAR	CLUB	LEAGUE	POS.	G.	AB.	R.	H.	2B.	3B.	HR.	RBI.	B.A.	PO.	A.	E.	F.A.
1954	Montreal (a)	Int.	OF-3B	87	148	27	38	5	3	2	12	.257	81	1	1	.988
1955	Pittsburgh	National	OF	124	474	48	121	23	11	5	47	.255	253	18	6	.978
1956	Pittsburgh	Nat.	OF-2B-3B	147	543	66	169	30	7	7	60	.311	275	20	15	.952
1957	Pittsburgh	Nat.	OF	111	451	42	114	17	7	4	30	.253	272	9	6	.979
1958	Pittsburgh	Nat.	OF	140	519	69	150	24	10	6	50	.289	312	22	6	.982
1959	Pittsburgh	Nat.	OF	105	432	60	128	17	7	4	50	.296	229	10	13	.948
1960	Pittsburgh	Nat.	OF	144	570	89	179	22	6	16	94	.314	246	19	8	.971
1961	Pittsburgh	Nat.	OF	146	572	100	201	30	10	23	89	.351	256	27	9	.969
1962	Pittsburgh	Nat.	OF	144	538	95	168	28	9	10	74	.312	269	19	8	.973
1963	Pittsburgh	Nat.	OF	152	600	77	192	23	8	17	76	.320	239	11	11	.958
1964	Pittsburgh	Nat.	OF	155	622	95	211	40	7	12	87	.339	289	13	10	.968
1965	Pittsburgh	Nat.	OF	152	589	91	194	21	14	10	65	.329	288	16	10	.968
1966	Pittsburgh	Nat.	OF	154	638	105	202	31	11	29	119	.317	318	17	12	.965
1967	Pittsburgh	Nat.	OF	147	585	103	209	26	10	23	110	.357	273	17	9	.970
1968	Pittsburgh	Nat.	OF	132	502	74	146	18	12	18	57	.291	297	9	5	.984
1969	Pittsburgh	Nat.	OF	138	507	87	175	20	12	19	91	.345	226	14	5	.980
1970	Pittsburgh	Nat.	OF	108	412	65	145	22	10	14	60	.352	189	12	7	.966
1971	Pittsburgh	Nat.	OF	132	522	82	178	29	8	13	86	.341	267	11	2	.993
1972	Pittsburgh	Nat.	OF	102	378	68	118	19	7	10	60	.312	199	5	0	1.000
Major League Totals—18 Years				2433	9454	1416	3000	440	166	240	1305	.317	4697	269	142	.972

a Drafted by Pittsburgh Pirates from Brooklyn Dodgers' organization, November 22, 1954.

CHAMPIONSHIP SERIES RECORD

YEAR	CLUB	LEAGUE	POS.	G.	AB.	R.	H.	2B.	3B.	HR.	RBI.	B.A.	PO.	A.	E.	F.A.
1970	Pittsburgh	National	OF	3	14	1	3	0	0	0	1	.214	7	0	0	1.000
1971	Pittsburgh	National	OF	4	18	2	6	0	0	0	4	.333	12	0	0	1.000
1972	Pittsburgh	National	OF	5	17	1	4	1	0	1	2	.235	10	0	0	1.000
Championship Series Totals—3 Years				12	49	4	13	1	0	1	7	.265	29	0	0	1.000

WORLD SERIES RECORD

YEAR	CLUB	LEAGUE	POS.	G.	AB.	R.	H.	2B.	3B.	HR.	RBI.	B.A.	PO.	A.	E.	F.A.
1960	Pittsburgh	National	OF	7	29	1	9	0	0	0	3	.310	19	0	0	1.000
1971	Pittsburgh	National	OF	7	29	3	12	2	1	2	4	.414	15	0	0	1.000
World Series Totals—2 Years				14	58	4	21	2	1	2	7	.362	34	0	0	1.000

.367: The majesty of Ty Cobb's fabulous seasons are embodied in that remarkable overall career batting average.

TY COBB

Ty Cobb, a tall, balding man with a drooping bow tie and a rumpled suit that made him look as though he was down to his last buck rather than his last 12 million, sat sipping drinks with Frank Frisch and a rabbit-eared baseball writer in the light of a silvery moon at Cooperstown's Lake Otsego.

This was the picturesque upper New York village the night before baseball dedicated a new wing on the Hall of Fame in 1958. Till nearly midnight, his southern drawl soft and syrupy, Cobb purred like a kitten as Frisch praised his all-out play and slashing base-running. "Isn't that so, Tyrus?" the 60-year-old former Flash would say, rolling around the 70-year-old Cobb's full first name as he tried to tease baseball's famed Georgia Peach. "Come on, Tyrus, tell 'em about the time you undressed the third baseman with your spikes."

Almost like a school girl fluttering her lids, Cobb coyly demurred and—it was amusing to hear a man long in the tooth use the diminutive in referring to another past middle age—Ty would say sweetly, "Oh, now, Frankie, I wasn't nearly as rough as everyone said."

Gradually, though, as the bubbling grape and the persuasion eroded the veneer of the dignified elder statesman, the light blue eyes began to lose their watery warmth. They glinted with the fire of recollection, and the voice no longer was sugary and soft.

Frisch, grinning, retreated into silence. This was the Cobb he had come to hear, the cold and calculating competitor who had slashed his way into baseball history. And now the 40-year-old baseball writer could believe the incredible event experienced one time by Cobb's good friend, Grantland Rice, the dean of American sportswriters.

Several years earlier, Rice and Cobb had been tilting the bowl that cheers with a former American League catcher, Nig Clarke, who in the midst of merry recollection of their playing days, recalled that he'd been especially adept in fooling umpires with a quick fake tag at the plate.

"Why, Ty, I can remember at least five times an umpire called you out when I didn't tag you," Clarke said, gaily. Cobb clouded up and rained all over the surprised Clarke, until pulled away by the startled Rice. "You so-and-so," Ty stormed, "you cost me five runs."

The amazing depth of inner compulsion that drove Cobb to the heights in 23-plus tempestuous American League seasons might have astonished many, but not George (Nap) Rucker, later a mighty good Brooklyn pitcher, who could remember an episode when he and the 19-year-old outfielder were South Atlantic League teammates at Augusta, Ga., in 1905.

Rucker, knocked out of a game, returned to his hotel room he shared with Cobb and took a bath. The outfielder, arriving later, grumbled that he should have taken his bath first. There were, you see, no showers anywhere at the time, much less in a rinky-dink minor league ballpark.

"You mean," said Rucker, amiably, trying to es-tablish a ground rule of companionship, "that you wanted to be first today?"

"I mean, Nap," said Cobb, firmly, "that I've got to be first all of the time—first in everything."

He was, too, including the first into the Hall of Fame in 1936 when he polled 222 of 226 votes to lead the first super five tapped for induction at Cooperstown. Fourteen years later in a rundown of accomplishments from 1900 to 1950, the Associated Press would find in a broader poll that Babe Ruth, only recently dead, had nosed out Cobb as the No. 1 baseball figure of the half-century. But they'll never settle that one.

After all, how can you compare fully the slide-rule scientist and the abstract painter? The dotted-i rigidity of the legal eagle and the will-o'-the-wisp intangibles of the philosopher? The toe-to-toe puncher and the boxing master of the prize ring? The brain that was Cobb and the brawn that was Ruth?

Cobb always insisted that others had more talent than he, but just not as much determination or dedication. Although in his later years he drank excessively, he was a paragon of virtue throughout his career by comparison, taking care of his body with a passion that enabled him to hit .323 when he was nearly 42 years old.

By then, when he finished 23-plus seasons in the majors, the insatiable Cobb had put together a remarkable record, most of which will be more certain to withstand the pressure of time than even Ruth's 714 home runs. It's possible, if the resiliency of the ball and distance to the fences are altered appreciably, to see the Bambino's mark jeopardized. But no one could expect even to approach Cobb's 4,191 career hits or extraordinary .367 lifetime average. Yet, Pete Rose passed the hit total by going to bat the equivalent of more than four full seasons batting only .026 (65 hits in 2.623 more at-bats).

Cobb was, however, even prouder of his .367 lifetime average, nine large points higher than Rogers Hornsby's .358, than he was of his 12

American League batting championships, his three .400-and-higher seasons and his 892 stolen bases. Ty hit .420 in 1911 and stole 96 bases in 1915.

Maury Wills broke the Georgia Peach's single-season record for stolen bases with 104 in 1962, but Cobb's ability to find safe territory at bat was so far superior to any other that consider this:

Typically, Cobb created a stir in 1952 when, writing for *Life* magazine, he singled out only Musial, the versatile star of the St. Louis Cardinals, and Phil Rizzuto, the slick little shortstop of the New York Yankees, as capable of full-fledged recognition during his long day in the sun, 1905-28.

But he appeared to have given the matter less than complete concentration. When he visited *The Sporting News* publisher J. G. Taylor Spink in St. Louis that hot summer, he was asked to take a long, hard look at hustling Enos Slaughter, veteran Redbird outfielder whose all-out effort was reminiscent of Cobb's. Ty did and amended his opinion.

Fact is, though he jawed with Williams at times and publicly chided the rangy Red Sox slugger for failure to hit to all fields, Cobb had admiration for the Boston clouter and wrote him long, helpful notes, which batting student Williams gratefuly acknowledged.

No one, though, ever put more into the study of baseball as a business, profession and, the way Cobb approached it, an art form.

A slender, light-complexioned kid with handsome hawk features and reddish brown hair which receded with the seasons, Tyrus Raymond Cobb came up to the majors a growing boy, 5-10 and 155 pounds. He stayed to play at 6-1 and eventually 190 pounds of sinew and muscle.

Through experiment, he adopted a closed batting stance, feet together, bat choked slightly, hands held apart for better bat control, he explained. He was able, therefore, to slide the top (left) hand down to the right, to swing away, or to bring the bottom hand up to bunt or push the ball.

For a time, H. Guy (Doc) White, Chicago

White Sox southpaw whose consecutive scoreless-inning record was knocked out of the box by Los Angeles' Don Drysdale in 1968, used to bother the young lefthanded-hitting Cobb. But Ty tackled the problem with the intensity that was so typical and finally decided to drop deeper in the box, to give himself a longer look at the curveball, so that he could hit the pitch to the opposite field after it broke. Before long, Ty called Doc "cousin" as he did almost every pitcher he faced.

The greatest pitcher, in his estimation, was Washington's Walter Johnson, who was truly overpowering. The flame-throwing righthander could handcuff even the great Cobb, who customarily slashed at the ball and punched or poked it more than he pulled for power.

Cobb detected one flaw in Johnson's makeup, his basic gentleness. Like a coldblooded riverboat gambler, Ty began to crowd the plate with his toes and to lean over, showing physical courage himself and confidence in his fellow man, the immortal Johnson. Rather than cave in Cobb's ribs or spin his cap around, the Big Train would try to avoid hitting him, the Detroit batting champion reasoned.

As usual, he was right. Johnson would pitch away, fall behind on the ball-and-strike count, then come in with a delivery that didn't have the most mustard. Cobb, stepping away, would get good wood on the ball and line it out for another base hit.

"I took advantage of Walter's good nature," Ty would say later, smiling, "and I hit him better than any man had a right to."

Cobb would practice bunting by the hour, spreading a blanket along the first or third-base line, for instance, to see if he could dump a ball dead. He'd slide until his hips and thighs were raw. He'd hunt with heavy boots all winter to keep his legs in shape and in spring training he'd wear lead weights in his spiked shoes so that when he removed them on opening day, he felt frisky as a feather on the breeze—and just as light.

But, ah, much more forceful and ferocious. Cobb

ran the bases as if they belonged to him, which they did. A sizable man, especially for his day, he ran fast and slid hard, sharpened spikes high, but he created an intimidation more than a physical threat because he acquired early the new hook slide and improved on it, learning to catch the corner of a bag with just a toe.

He also mastered the fallaway slide in which he'd sweep wide of a bag and then reach back with an outstretched arm to latch onto a corner of the cushion, meanwhile avoiding a tag.

Cobb said he'd never had any nervous habit, but the Detroit writer contradicted him, reminding Ty that every time he reached first base he absentmindedly kicked the bag a couple of times.

Cobb granted his old associate a patronizing smile.

"I wanted the other side to think as you did, but that wasn't an absentminded habit at all," he said. "It was really a percentage trick. With my long lead and pitchers trying to pick me off, I needed every advantage. By kicking the sack a couple of inches closer to second base, I got the edge at times when a good, quick pickoff move almost got me going back into first base."

Even if time has exaggerated feats of the Peach's flying feet and the derring-do of the daring young man on the flying trapeze, it's apparent from documentation that he coaxed or coerced his way into some tremendous achievements.

Like scoring from first base on an infield out, for instance, because he'd been off and running with a pitch; and when first baseman Hal Chase threw across the diamond to get him at third base, he reasoned that the third baseman, head down, would straddle the bag so that he'd have to pivot completely around to throw home.

So, instead of sliding, Cobb came into third, standing up, toed the inside corner of the bag, catapulting himself directly toward the plate. And, running straight up to create a screening problem for the surprised third baseman, who reached down

and felt nothing before wheeling around, he hit the dirt and beat the delayed, high throw home.

A former St. Louis catcher, Lou Criger, boasted one time that if Cobb ran on him, Ty would be a "dead pigeon." That was Criger's first mistake. His second occurred when a St. Louis newspaper printed the brag. That afternoon Cobb stole five bases. And one time, holding up the game at first base to tell Criger exactly what he would do, Ty stole second, third and home.

Wasn't that really taking a long chance, though, predicting what he'd do in retaliation for the challenge?

"Not," said Cobb, "when you knew you could run on the pitcher that day as well as I did."

The thin-skinned superstar's revenge wasn't always so well-conceived. A former Yankee catcher, Fred (Bootnose) Hofmann, would take proudly to his grave, like a medal of honor, the humiliation heaped on him by Cobb the first time the chattering rookie caught against Detroit.

As the scourge of the league for a dozen seasons stepped into the batter's box, Hofmann cracked, sarcastically: "So this is the great Georgia Peach?"

Cobb, taken aback, stepped out of the batter's box and surveyed the rookie. "Listen, busher," he said, coldly, "I'm going to get on and when I do, I'm coming around." Ty singled, stole and then tried to score from second on a grounder to deep short. The throw from first had him beaten by so much, however, that Hofmann determined to retire Cobb with a hard bare-handed tag Ty would remember.

Just as Bootnose opened up to let Cobb have it, the fury in flannels took off at him through the air, feet first. One spike caught the catcher's chest protector and ripped it to one side, another cut his thigh and tore one shinguard away. They went down, Cobb one way, Hofmann another, the ball a third way.

Let Hofmann tell it as he would over the years:

"Cobb got up, stepped over me onto the plate,

brushed his dust off on me, looked down and said, 'Yes, you fresh busher, that WAS the great Georgia Peach.' "

Cobb would insist many times years later, including the night he lapped the sauce with Frisch under the light of the silvery moon at Cooperstown, that he really only cut up two or three guys deliberately, and none of 'em was Hofmann, whose feelings were hurt that the great man didn't remember.

Hotly, Cobb always insisted that one of his intentional victims decidedly was not Frank (Home Run) Baker, Philadelphia's hard-hitting third baseman whose arm he slashed deeply in a slide in a tense and important late-season game in 1909.

"Pictures show I couldn't have done it deliberately and Baker didn't lose an inning," Cobb protested, "but I got 13 Black Hand letters and one of the nuts threatened to shoot me from a window outside the park."

Cobb could be cruel, no matter how much he protested. Cruel and courageous, even more when he played after the threat at Philadelphia or again when he went into the stands and fought an obscene fan in New York, drawing a suspension that brought objections from teammates who didn't even like him.

Their one-day strike in 1912 caused the Tigers to field a team of sandlot Philadelphians, major leaguers for a day, to avoid paying a $5,000 forfeit. A crowd of 20,000 was attracted by curiosity and saw the hometown pickup team trounced by the hometown major league Athletics, 25-2.

Baseball greybeards could remember with awe, as Grantland Rice did, when Ty played under painful handicap.

"I recall," Rice once reminisced, "when Cobb played a series with each leg a mass of raw flesh. He had a temperature of 103 and the doctors ordered him to bed for several days, but he got three hits, stole three bases and won the game. Afterward, he collapsed at the bench and was revived by a hypodermic injection of strychnine."

Cobb was sadistic. He brawled in a hotel room with Buck Herzog of the New York Giants, fought under the stands with American League umpire Billy Evans and waded into others, fists and feet flying. But he must have been a masochist, too.

How else could anyone explain a fight he had early in his career with gentle Charley (Boss) Schmidt, a tremendously powerful Detroit catcher? Schmidt, who could drive a spike into the clubhouse floor with his bare fist, tried to roll good-naturedly with oral punches. He took comments from Cobb even more cutting than Ty himself must have received when he came out of Georgia as a young gentleman whose idealism was blunted by the abuse he received from rowdy, older players.

When Schmidt refused to fight him, Cobb finally tore into the strong man, 50 pounds heavier, took a fearful beating, got up and tried again, lamely and gamely, before even teammates who hated his insides took pity and pulled Schmidt off him.

Was there a connection between this mean streak and the unkind treatment he insisted he'd received before and after he doubled off New York's Jack Chesbro in his first big league time at bat in 1905?

Or, psychologically, would there be something deeper, the release of the painful hurt he'd suffered when the father to whom he was devoted was shot accidentally and killed by the faithful wife for whom he'd set a trap?

Tyrus Raymond Cobb, born in the tall pine and red clay country in Narrows, Ga., near Royston, couldn't agree with Prof. W. H. Cobb, his schoolmaster-state senator father, who wanted him to study law or try for West Point. Ty would have preferred medicine, but he was partial to baseball. And there's no doubt he lost something dear to him in the shattering experience of having his father wiped out by his mother. The senior Cobb, returning home through a window unexpectedly in the dark, thought he'd find Mrs. Cobb with another man. Her only companion was the shotgun most rural women left alone at that time kept for their protection.

Ty, just breaking into the big leagues then, had owed a debt of gratitude to his father and to one other for guidance. Even though Prof. Cobb was opposed to baseball as a professional future, when young Ty was released by Augusta in his first trial in 1904, the father came through with a boost and a challenge.

Over the phone, haltingly, Ty told his father he'd been released and. . .

"Well, if that's the case, what are you going to do?" Prof. Cobb asked.

Haltingly, Ty said he'd like to try out for a team at Anniston.

"Go after it," his father ordered, "and I want to tell you one other thing—don't come home a failure."

The second time around at Augusta—and this will be hard to believe in view of the almost insane singleness of purpose with which Cobb later played—he dropped a flyball because he was trying to play the position one-handed. No foolin', he was eating popcorn with the other hand.

A man of considerable compassion and understanding, a minor league manager named George Leidy took him in tow, explained the gravity of his complacency and painted a picture of a promising career.

Leidy not only taught the polite kid a strong lesson of life, but he supplemented it with intensive private practice on bunting, place-hitting, baserunning and the other fine points at which the demoniacal Detroit star eventually would excel.

When Leidy was in need later, Cobb took care of him gratefully and royally. Ty was a man of incongruities—mean and kind, stingy and generous.

Years later, he set up a medical center in Royston in his father's name and also established an educational foundation he endowed. Characteristically, Cobb insisted that kids seeking a college education show the ingenuity and fortitude to manage their way through the freshman year before becoming eligible for Cobb assistance.

Unfortunately, he wasn't so successful as a husband or parent. Twice divorced, he had five children, three of whom preceded him in death. A son who became a doctor, as Ty might have been, was not at all close to him. Another son, James, became a Hall of Fame perennial into the 1990s.

Old Tyrus gave up the ghost to cancer and other debilities one July day in 1961 at Cornelia, Ga., close by Chenocetah Mountain, where he'd talked about building a home. Before his death, he'd flitted restlessly from northern California to Nevada's Lake Tahoe and back to the tall pine country. He appeared even more lonely than he'd been as a loner in baseball.

Through wise early investments in General Motors and Coca Cola, Cobb was extremely wealthy. Money, however, can't buy the kind of enduring companionship that seemed to elude the great old superstar as exasperatingly as he could avoid a frantic baseman's tag.

Although he considered former Detroit club owner Frank Navin a pinchpenny, Cobb battled his way up to $50,000 a year as player-manager of the Tigers. He resented the fact that his club was always just short in his six seasons as manager. And he had good reason to resent a couple of other things.

In 1910, some members of the old St. Louis Browns conspired to let Cleveland's popular Napoleon Lajoie beat out Cobb for the batting title by directing rookie third baseman John (Red) Corriden to play so deep for Lajoie that Nap beat out seven bunts among eight hits on the last day of the season.

Investigation made other suspicious actions of that disgraceful day so obvious that manager Jack O'Connor and pitcher-coach Harry Howell of the Browns were dropped at the end of the season. Cobb still won the batting title with a .385 average, a fraction better than Lajoie, and took the new car offered by the Chalmers automobile company, the car the bitter rivals didn't want him to have.

Cobb was considerably more bitter himself after the 1926 season when he and Tris Speaker, the famous Cleveland center fielder, were eased out as player-managers. Then a bombshell hit. A former pitcher, Hubert (Dutch) Leonard, not to be confused with Emil (Dutch) Leonard of a later generation, had written American League President Ban Johnson of a "fix." Leonard, though refusing to face Cobb or Speaker, said he'd heard the two great players agree to throw an end-of-the-season game to Detroit seven seasons earlier so they could wager a few hundred dollars each on the inconsequential contest.

In the game, won by Detroit, 9-5, Cobb, whose side was supposed to win, singled once in five trips. Speaker, whose side was supposed to lose, hit two triples and a single, a most damaging blow to Leonard's gossamer case.

Baseball botched it. Rather, Johnson botched it and Judge K. M. Landis, the commissioner who didn't like the American League founder, let Johnson stew in his own juice.

The accusation, which had led to the surreptitious dismissal of Speaker and Cobb, was made public in October. Johnson was forced to resign as American League president early in January. Later that month, with public indignation mounting, Landis cleared Cobb and Speaker.

Not soon enough. An understandably incensed Cobb wanted to retire, to rest his aching legs, but he wanted vindication even more. A lawsuit hung over baseball's head as club owners sought Cobb's services. Not until the man he admired, Philadelphia's Connie Mack, asked him to join the Athletics did Ty relent. His price for 1927 was $70,000 in salary and bonuses.

It was at Philadelphia, incidentally, hitting a game-tying two-run homer in the ninth inning of a crucial game in 1907, that young Cobb experienced his greatest thrill as a player. Detroit went on to win the first of the three straight—and only—pennants the Tigers' greatest player ever enjoyed.

Cobb was a good outfielder, not a great one, though he made some great plays, including throwing three men out at first base in one game. His arm was only fair, which of course, would give Ruth an edge on him there, but old Ty managed to hoodwink young Babe a few times.

Once, managing from center field, Cobb whistled to a Detroit pitcher to give the Babe an intentional pass. Ruth relaxed and the pitcher fired a strike down the middle. Cobb rushed in from the outfield, chewed out the pitcher and returned to his position. Instead of lobbing the ball wide of the plate, the pitcher again poured a strike in there.

Like a wild man, Ty dashed in from the outfield a second time, called both pitcher and catcher to the mound, loudly fined them $100 each and brought in a new pitcher and catcher. When play was resumed and everyone expected completion of the intentional walk, the second pitcher slipped the first one right past the surprised Ruth for a called third strike. Cobb, cackling with glee, had set up the entire act to fool Ruth.

But could the boxer slug with the puncher, the singles batter match power with the long-ball hitter?

In late May 1925, the Tigers were playing the Browns at old Sportsman's Park in St. Louis. Before the game, a St. Louis writer had been talking about Ruth and home runs he'd hit at the park with its beckoning right-field pavilion. And Harry Heilmann, Cobb's hard-hitting right fielder, even teased the 38-year-old manager about his going to left field with so many pitches.

"Watch me today, smart guy," Ty snapped.

With a wind blowing to right field—and it's mentioned only because the sharp-featured figure with the sharp look of an eagle wasn't missing anything—Ty Cobb lashed a double, two singles and three homers. Six for six and good for 16 bases. And the next day, he hit two home runs and just missed another pair, almost giving him seven in two games, with doubles high off the wall.

With Tyrus Raymond Cobb, you see, the impossible merely took a little bit longer.

TYRUS RAYMOND (GEORGIA PEACH) COBB
Born December 18, 1886, at Narrows, Banks County, Ga.
Died July 17, 1961, at Atlanta, Ga.
Height 6-0 3/4 Weight 175
Threw right and batted lefthanded.
Named to Hall of Fame, 1936.

YEAR	CLUB	LEAGUE	POS.	G.	AB.	R.	H.	2B.	3B.	HR.	RBI.	B.A.	PO.	A.	E.	F.A.
1904	Augusta	Sally	OF	37	135	14	32	6	0	1	-	.237	62	9	4	.946
1904	Anniston (a)	S.E.	OF	22	-	-	-	-	-	-	-	.370	-	-	-	-
1905	Augusta	Sally	OF	104	411	60	134	-	-	-	-	.326	149	15	13	.927
1905	Detroit	Amer.	OF	41	150	19	36	6	0	1	12	.240	85	6	4	.958
1906	Detroit	Amer.	OF	97	350	44	112	13	7	1	41	.320	107	14	9	.931
1907	Detroit	Amer.	OF	150	605	97	212	29	15	5	116	.350	238	30	11	.961
1908	Detroit	Amer.	OF	150	581	88	188	36	20	4	101	.324	212	23	14	.944
1909	Detroit	Amer.	OF	156	573	116	216	33	10	9	115	.377	222	24	14	.946
1910	Detroit	Amer.	OF	140	509	106	196	36	13	8	88	.385	305	18	14	.958
1911	Detroit	Amer.	OF	146	591	147	248	47	24	8	144	.420	376	24	18	.957
1912	Detroit	Amer.	OF	140	553	119	227	30	23	7	90	.410	324	21	22	.940
1913	Detroit	Amer.	OF	122	428	70	167	18	16	4	65	.390	262	22	16	.947
1914	Detroit	Amer.	OF	97	345	69	127	22	11	2	57	.368	117	8	10	.949
1915	Detroit	Amer.	OF	156	563	144	208	31	13	3	95	.369	328	22	18	.951
1916	Detroit	Amer.	OF	145	542	113	201	31	10	5	67	.371	325	18	17	.953
1917	Detroit	Amer.	OF	152	588	107	225	44	23	7	108	.383	373	27	11	.973
1918	Detroit	Amer.	OF-1B	111	421	83	161	19	14	3	64	.382	359	26	9	.977
1919	Detroit	Amer.	OF	124	497	92	191	36	13	1	69	.384	272	19	8	.973
1920	Detroit	Amer.	OF	112	428	86	143	28	8	2	63	.334	246	8	9	.966
1921	Detroit	Amer.	OF	128	507	124	197	37	16	12	101	.389	301	27	10	.970
1922	Detroit	Amer.	OF	137	526	99	211	42	16	4	99	.401	330	14	7	.980
1923	Detroit	Amer.	OF	145	556	103	189	40	7	6	88	.340	362	14	12	.969
1924	Detroit	Amer.	OF	155	625	115	211	38	10	4	74	.338	417	12	6	.986
1925	Detroit	Amer.	OF	121	415	97	157	31	12	12	102	.378	267	9	15	.948
1926	Detroit (b)	Amer.	OF	79	233	48	79	18	5	4	62	.339	109	4	6	.950
1927	Philadelphia	Amer.	OF	134	490	104	175	32	7	5	93	.357	243	9	8	.969
1928	Philadelphia	Amer.	OF	95	353	54	114	27	4	1	40	.323	154	7	6	.964
Major League Totals				3033	11429	2244	4191	724	297	118	1954	.367	6394	406	274	.961

a League not in Organized Ball.
b Released by Detroit Tigers November 2, 1926, and signed with Philadelphia Athletics, February, 1927.

WORLD SERIES RECORD

YEAR	CLUB	LEAGUE	POS.	G.	AB.	R.	H.	2B.	3B.	HR.	RBI.	B.A.	PO.	A.	E.	F.A.
1907	Detroit	Amer.	OF	5	20	1	4	0	1	0	0	.200	9	0	0	1.000
1908	Detroit	Amer.	OF	5	19	3	7	1	0	0	4	.368	3	0	2	.600
1909	Detroit	Amer.	OF	7	26	3	6	3	0	0	6	.231	8	0	1	.889
World Series Totals				17	65	7	17	4	1	0	10	.262	20	0	3	.870

100%: If ever a cameraman caught the spirit and fury of a major league player, it was in this photo of Mickey Cochrane charging out of the dugout as player-manager of Detroit's champion Tigers in the '30s.

MICKEY COCHRANE

One day back in 1928 when the New York Yankees were whaling the what-for out of the Philadelphia Athletics, who seemed to have accepted the inevitable with annoying complacency, the A's florid-faced catcher came snarling back to the dugout in a red rage, ripping off his mask, flinging aside his chest protector and kicking away his shinguards.

"You yellow-bellied buzzards," screamed Mickey Cochrane, reaching into the bat rack to lead off the inning. "You're quitting like the yellow dogs you are."

Turning his back on his teammates who were shaken up by his denunciation, Cochrane stepped into the batter's box and lined a base hit between the outfielders. Al Simmons followed with a hit. So did Jimmie Foxx and Bing Miller and Jimmy Dykes and—.

And suddenly the Athletics not only won a ball game that seemed lost, but they made a race of what appeared another Yankee runaway and, though he batted only .293, Cochrane was voted winner of the

American League's Most Valuable Player award, which then carried with it a $1,000 bag of gold.

More important, Philadelphia went on from there to win three consecutive pennants and two world championships, providing two of the few instances since 1915-16 when any American League team other than the Yankees had succeeded itself as pennant winner. At least until the dizzing dynasty was blunted after 1965 and interrupted again from 1979 on.

One of the other early exceptions came in 1934-35 when Detroit, after ending a quarter-century drought, achieved first a pennant and then a world championship. And there is absolutely no coincidence to the fact that the player-manager of the Tigers then was the same jug-eared, raven-haired catcher who had ranted and raved at the Athletics several seasons earlier.

Black Mike Cochrane, the Boston-area Irishman, was that kind of an influence on a ball club, as well as a helluva fine hitter and a good catcher. When you put it all together, it spells leadership and recognition, too, as perhaps the finest all-around mask-and-mitt man in baseball history. At least, that's the way most veteran observers see it when they attempt to pick an All-Star team for baseball's first century.

The fact is, no matter whether you prefer Buck Ewing, Roger Bresnahan, Bill Dickey, Gabby Hartnett or any other, including more recently Yogi Berra, Roy Campanella and Johnny Bench, you've got to face up to appreciation of what Cochrane accomplished from the time he stepped up as a pinch-hitter for Ralph (Cy) Perkins in 1925 until he lay in the dust at home plate at Yankee Stadium in 1937, his skull fractured in three places and his life in almost as great a danger as his career.

In those 12-plus seasons, he not only led two teams to five pennants, but he also batted a lifetime .320, topped by a .357 season in 1930. Even though fast enough to lead off, if necessary, he was powerful enough to hit 23 homers one season, 1932, and productive enough to knock in 112 runs the same year.

Cochrane's intangibles tell even more than the talent that took him into the Hall of Fame in 1947. Take, for instance, his rundown condition in the 1934 World Series when he spent every night at Detroit in a hospital bed, rather than in his apartment, making certain that he'd be able to drag himself out there another day.

As if he didn't have enough to do, Cochrane reportedly had to wet-nurse one of his infielders through the rough-and-tumble World Series in which the Tigers were outmatched against the cutthroats of the St. Louis Cardinals' Gashouse Gang.

Black Mike found defeat intolerable as Roger (Doc) Cramer, fleet Philadelphia outfielder, learned when he joined the Athletics and beat Mickey by a yard in a match race.

"We started at 5 o'clock, to run just one sprint before dinner," Cramer recalled, "but Cochrane kept insisting on just 'one more' and, so help me, we were still out there at 11 P. M."

The burning obsession with victory played a shrieking tune on the fiery fellow's taut nerve strings. His wife and hometown sweetheart, the former Mary Hohr, learned to give him a wide berth after a particularly tough defeat, even stopping off to visit teammates' wives until Black Mike would fall asleep.

Cochrane brooded when the stock market crash of the depression wiped him out financially, but he brooded even more when he was tabbed as the World Series goat in 1931, even though the Cardinals' Pepper Martin ran wild at the expense of Philadelphia pitchers who hadn't faced a basestealing daredevil.

The emotional peaks and valleys experienced by Cochrane in the heat of a pennant race exhausted him to the point that he suffered a nervous breakdown in 1936 and was limited to only 44 games, the first time he'd played fewer than 115. The Tigers fell short and lost to the Yankees in a bid for a third straight pennant.

Still, at 34, he was batting .306 in late May

1937, when he homered off New York's Irving (Bump) Hadley and then, with a teammate on first base, crowded the plate the next time up so that he'd be certain to pull the ball behind the runner. When Hadley fired a 3-and-1 pitch that sailed up and in, Cochrane lost sight of the ball about six feet in front of the plate.

The ball hit him with a sickening sound near the right temple, an inch or two above the right eyebrow. Dickey, catching for the Yankees that day, remembered with detailed horror:

"The ball dropped in front of the plate and Mike fell almost on top of it, right on his face. Then he rolled over and said, 'Good God Almighty.' "

Cochrane, who didn't recall having said anything, remembered reviving briefly in the clubhouse, where he gamely asked that the game be held up until he could return to the field. Then he lapsed into unconsciousness and was out for the better part of 10 days.

"The only time I came to was when they were tapping my spine," Cochrane reminisced years later with Dickey when Mickey was scouting for the Yankees and Bill was coaching for his old team.

When Mrs. Cochrane, who had maintained a bedside vigil, wondered if there was anything she could do for her husband as he rejoined the living, Mickey showed his Irish humor. Smiling, he said "Yeah, get me a new head."

There was, unfortunately, nothing that could remove the effects of the severe injury—the skull was fractured in three places—and Detroit owner Walter O. Briggs, presumably acting with the advice of medical counsel, rejected Cochrane's plea that he be allowed to go behind the plate again.

So the exciting, productive playing career of an exciting, colorful player ended abruptly.

As a benchwarmer, Cochrane was a caged-up tiger, nervously prowling the dugout and unable to set an example with the kind of leadership that made him and another fierce competitor, Frank Frisch, considerably more successful as playing managers than bench bosses.

When Briggs relieved him as manager in August, 1938, New York sports columnist Jimmy Powers summed up the feeling of many when he cracked, "Sentiment is fine, but only when it's good business."

Cochrane, however, found no fault with Briggs and even reportedly turned down the second season of a $36,000-a-year contract. The generous gesture was sporting, but expensive, because by the time he died at the age of 59 in 1962, Mickey's resources had been pared by illness and reverses to the point he'd wondered why baseball at least didn't pension Hall of Fame members among its old-timers.

Writing this book of profiles of players from the past for *The Sporting News*, a guy, especially when he's half-Irish, found himself tending either to become maudlin in what he wrote or just sad as he sat at the typewriter. In so many instances, the superstars not only are dead, but they died either young or broke or unhappy.

It's possible that Cochrane qualified on all counts and the temptation is to wallow in pity, but that wouldn't be right. Not, at least, when you know that better than most men who play the game of life, Gordon Stanley Cochrane called his shot—and put it in the side pocket.

Born of Scotch-Irish parents, the Mickey who was Gordon only to his mother, was the son of John Cochrane, a coachman and caretaker for a wealthy suburban Boston family. Pop saved up enough money to buy a small place outside of Bridgewater, Mass. Mickey was born there, about 50 miles south of Boston, on April 6, 1903.

At the age of 10, toting a baseball glove, the Cochrane kid already had an ambition that seemed to typify the take-charge aggressiveness that made him a man to watch, to listen to and to follow.

"Lots of kids wanted to be a big league player," he explained years later to New York writer Frank Graham, "but I wanted even then to become a manager. What makes a kid think like that? Maybe I just had to be boss."

Better still, the leader, which Cochrane proved himself to be at Boston University, where he was even better than the late, ill-starred Harry Agganis as undoubtedly the finest all-around athlete B. U. ever had.

Greybeards at old Braves Field, where the Terriers later played, can tell with awe of Cochrane's prowess on the ball field, the football field, the cinder track, the basketball court and in the boxing ring. Then only 160 pounds, 20 fewer than his peak playing weight, Mickey mixed it good and was impressed most with a campus light heavyweight who became a good friend.

Ever hear of Charles Farrell, who made a movie classic with Janet Gaynor called *Seventh Heaven* and another, *Sunny Side Up*? Farrell later starred with Gale Storm in an early television series, "My Little Margie."

Cochrane was especially outstanding as a halfback in football. Included in his feats of gridiron derring-do for old B. U. at a time when Boston University didn't have a home field to its name was the time he went in to punt against Brown. Mickey took a look at the goalposts, 52 yards away, and accepted a sudden challenge. To heck with the punt, he'd dropkick and did—for three points.

Working his way through college, "The Kid," which was his nickname in New England before Ted Williams, played a saxophone in dance bands and also washed dishes at a campus establishment close by a hotel where he'd see Babe Ruth and other big leaguers stay, including the college outfielder's boyhood favorite, Ty Cobb.

"Someday," Mickey promised his fellow pearl divers, "I'll be sitting over there watching jokers like us swab the dishes."

When he went out to play professionally with Dover of the Eastern Shore League in 1923, Cochrane used the name "Frank King" he'd adopted when he was playing summer semi-pro ball to protect his amateur status. Now, though graduated, he called himself King to protect his reputation.

"If I was a flop," he said, "nobody would know who I was, and I could start all over again some place else."

Dover needed a catcher more than it did an infielder or outfielder, so Cochrane recognized an opportunity when he saw one and put on the tools of ignorance.

One day, with Tom Turner, owner of the Portland club in the stands, Mickey got four hits, but dropped a couple of foul flies and threw wildly to second base twice. Obliquely, Turner suggested to the Dover manager, one E. A. Donohue, "You've got a great pitcher on your ball club and I'd like to buy him."

Donohue grinned. "Uh-huh," he said, "that great pitcher is behind the plate."

If Turner thought the wily Donahue was asking too much for a kid who'd hit .322, Cochrane's robust .333 season for Portland in the Pacific Coast League in 1924 gave Turner similar ideas of financial grandeur. In fact, the asking price for Cochrane was so high that the Philadelphia Shibes, at the suggestion of Connie Mack, bought controlling interest in the club.

The public price announced for Cochrane was $50,000 and five players but, actually, Mack said years later to Ed Pollock, veteran Philadelphia sports editor, the price was considerably higher. The A's, you see, dropped between $200,000 and $300,000 in operating the Portland club before selling it back to Turner.

But was Cochrane worth it? Pollock wondered.

"Worth it!" exclaimed Mr. Mack. "He was worth 10 times that much. More than any other player, he was responsible for the three pennants we won in 1929, 1930 and 1931."

But Tom and John Shibe, who'd seen Connie blow a bundle for another Coast league phenom named Paul Strand, a bigger bust than Mae West or Dolly Parton, sweated through spring training in 1925 at Fort Myers, Fla., almost as much as Cochrane did.

The solidly built kid with the matted black hair, dark whiskers, ruddy cheeks and blazing blue eyes was completely hopeless on foul lines. At Mack's request, No. 1 catcher Ralph (Cy) Perkins worked tirelessly with Cochrane, who never asked for relief, but doggedly worked on popups and other mystifying phases of his profession.

Mack had made up his mind that, no matter how crude, the hard-hitting, fast-running, strong-armed kid held the future of the Athletics in his eager, unsmooth hands. But Perkins was behind the plate on opening day.

"Only until about the eighth inning," Cy would tell later, "when we came up a couple of runs down with a couple of men on and my time at bat. The kid hit for me and doubled off the scoreboard in right-center, and I knew I'd lost my job."

Improving daily with Perkins helping him, Cochrane was outstanding in 134 games that first year, batting .331, and eventually he became skilled on pop flies, too.

"It's no wonder Mike didn't know how to catch," Perkins said later. "He didn't know how to stand or to shift, but he hadn't been at it very long. He was too high behind the plate, an easier stance from which to throw, but not a good enough target for pitchers who want to keep the ball down.

"It's tougher throwing from back there when the ball is low and especially if the catcher's knee is down, but Mike worked on throwing them out from down low until he was blue in that tomato face instead of red. He was great at it."

Cochrane began to assert himself as a leader, too. One time when Rube Walberg hit a wild spell, walking the bases loaded and forcing in a run, Black Mike called time, stormed out to the mound, grabbed the pitcher by the shoulders and spun him around. To Walberg's surprise, Cochrane kicked him right in the seat of the pants and said, "Damnit, Rube, settle down."

Walberg, though startled, chuckled at the direct parental approach and did settle down to win the game.

When Lefty Grove was at his terrible-tempered best—and Cochrane went to his grave praising the fireball pitcher—the catcher wouldn't back down from his long-armed, short-fused batterymate.

In fact, one time when Cochrane fired the ball back to Grove and Lefty cussed him out, only the quick intervention of Foxx and Dykes kept Black Mike from tangling right on the mound with his own pitcher.

In the Athletics' three pennant-winning seasons, Cochrane, promoted to the No. 3 spot in the batting order, hit .331, .357 and .349, averaging 129 games a season and 90 RBIs. He batted .400 in the five-game Series rout of the Cubs, including the remarkable 10-run inning that overcame an eight-run deficit in the fourth game.

The language used by both the A's and Cubs became so sulphuric that even Commissioner K. M. Landis, who had heard all the words and used most of them, was shocked. He issued a cease-and-desist order.

Late in the final game, when one of the Cubs dawdled going up to hit, Cochrane affected a feminine falsetto and said, "Hurry up, sweetheart. Tea will be served at 4 o'clock."

Afterward, when the champions were being congratulated, Judge Landis walked over to Cochrane. Eyes twinkling, the Judge told him, "I heard what you said—'sweetheart.'"

The way Black Mike was playing then, it seemed as if the world were his private preserve, but he'd lost heavily in the Black Tuesday of the stock market crash in October 1929. And there was another sharp drop and a call from his brokers for margin he couldn't provide to protect his vanishing investments at the time of the '31 Series. Worse, he was hampered by sinus trouble, leg bruises—and Pepper Martin.

When the Wild Horse of the Osage stole five bases, batting .500, Cochrane seethed not only because the Athletics had missed a rare third straight championship, but also because he knew that Martin had run on Grove and George Earnshaw. Only

Waite Hoyt of the Philadelphia pitchers had been able to hold Martin close to base.

It didn't help Cochrane's state of mind, either, when he left immediately after the seventh game in St. Louis for a trip to Japan with an All-Star team that included the Cardinals' captain and second baseman, Frank Frisch, who needled Mickey until Fred Lieb, a writer making the trip, begged the Flash to lay off.

Three years later, Cochrane and Frisch were at it again, but the backdrop was different for the No. 1 backstop. The financially pinched Athletics had sold Black Mike to Detroit for $100,000 and catcher John Pasek.

The principal stockholder, Frank Navin, wanted Babe Ruth as manager because the Yankees, eager to get out from under the aged Bambino, had offered Ruth's contract free. Navin missed connections with the Babe on the West Coast, however, and H. G. Salsinger, sports editor of the *Detroit News*, urged him to deal for the Cochrane contract so that he'd get a star player in his prime as well as a manager.

Trouble was, Navin had the financial shorts, a common malady in those troubled economic times, and that's when Briggs, an avid fan who would take over the club shortly, advanced him the money and said, "Go get Cochrane."

So the kid who at 10 had dreamed that one day he'd manage a big league ball club took over the fifth-place Tigers and, with other future Hall of Famers Charley Gehringer, Hank Greenberg and Goose Goslin, Detroit won its first pennant since 1909. Cochrane, though he felt the strain of driving his team as hard as he did himself, still managed to equal his lifetime average—.320.

Proud to have caught the last two 16-game winning streaks in the American League—Grove in 1931 at Philadelphia and Schoolboy Rowe in '34 at Detroit—Cochrane found himself galled by the audacity of the Gashouse Gang.

Frisch had told the Redbirds to lay off the rough stuff in the field, but the cut-ups had heard Rowe say

on the radio to his bride, "How am I doin', Edna?" And the Cardinals took it from there.

When Cochrane was hospitalized overnight, a Detroit newspaper carried Black Mike's photo with the caption, "Our Stricken Leader." Oh, my, how the Redbird bench jockeys enjoyed themselves with that one.

So the Tigers began to go at the Cardinals on the basepaths, roughing up the Redbirds, to whom this was second nature. The Tigers came off second best, all-around, and Frisch rubbed it in when Cochrane made the tactical error of ordering a semi-intentional pass to load the bases for his rival field foreman in the third inning of the seventh game. Frisch rapped a three-run double that led to a seven-run inning and an 11-0 cakewalk for Dizzy Dean, who laughed it up at the finish.

Cochrane, bothered again by Pepper Martin, too, had batted under .200 in three composite Series against St. Louis and he proved he didn't forget or forgive either. The following spring when Babe Ruth, released by the Yankees, went over to the Boston Braves of the National League and posed for pictures with Dean in the spring, Mike chewed out the Babe.

"What the hell you doing being so friendly with Dean?" Cochrane crabbed. "You've been an American Leaguer all your life. I can't see it, not after what those guys did last year and what they said about our league."

Although he was beginning to create his own pressure, the kind that helped unseat and unnerve him, the marvelous Mickey still had a big climax season in front of him. He'd brought Detroit its first pennant since 1909 and now, in 1935, he gave the Tigers their first world championship—ever.

Cochrane hit .319 in the regular season and .292 in the World Series, in which he experienced the greatest thrill of his career, a sixth game almost as exciting as the peppery catcher himself.

Although he'd lost slugger Greenberg with a broken wrist in the second game of the Series, Cochrane came down to the sixth contest with a 3-2 lead, but defeat leered at the Tigers, with the score tied, when Stan Hack opened the ninth inning for the Cubs with a triple.

Cochrane bounded out to talk to his pitcher, Tommy Bridges, a brilliant curveball pitcher, and told him, "Breaking balls, nothing except breaking stuff."

Trouble was, the second pitch got away from Bridges, a low curve that bounced two feet in front of the plate. "Judas, here goes the Series on one pitch," Cochrane moaned to himself.

But the old master of the mask and mitt still was equal to the challenge. He skidded forward on one knee, blocked the ball and scrambled forward to retrieve it so that Hack, who had started for the plate, was forced to retreat to third base.

Bridges, reprieved by his great batterymate, struck out Bill Jurges, retired Larry French on a tap back to the mound and got Augie Galan on an outfield fly. The score was still tied.

Cochrane, who had singled to set up Detroit's first run in the opening inning, batted in the No. 2 spot, just ahead of Gehringer, and the boss man began the home ninth with a base hit. Gehringer, also a lefthanded hitter, followed with a savage shot over first base, but the Cubs' young first baseman, Phil Cavarretta, dived to his left, blocked the ball, picked it up, stepped on the bag and then threw to second, where his throw struck the sliding Cochrane in the back.

"I don't see how they could have criticized the kid for that difficult throw," Mickey said later, "not after he'd made such a great play.

"I think I might have been safe, anyway, because they had to tag me."

The veteran Goslin, another lefthanded hitter against southpaw French, proved himself once more to be a tough codger in a clutch. The Goose lined a 2-and-2 pitch over Billy Herman's head into right-center; and Cochrane, digging around third, reached home plate and jumped on it again and again and again, to cap the moment of great glory for Detroit and for the man who as a boy had wanted to be a manager.

Down in Commerce, Okla., a wiry miner beamed at the radio report. He knew he'd picked the right player for whom to name his towheaded son—Mickey Mantle.

For the other Mickey, meaning Gordon Stanley Cochrane, stormy sessions with Briggs preceded his resignation as manager, vice president and a member of the board of directors. Thereafter, Cochrane's happiest years probably would be in World War II when he was an officer in the Navy's fitness program, running the athletic program at Great Lakes Naval Training Station and coaching a baseball team that had more talent than most wartime big league clubs.

The war, however, was as costly for Cochrane as for many fathers. He lost his son, Gordon, Jr., and the old spirit sagged. When Mickey died, he was survived by his wife and two daughters, Mrs. John Cobb of Denver and Mrs. Kenneth Bollman of Allentown, Pa.

Cochrane represented a Detroit-to-Chicago trucking line for a time. He operated a dude ranch in Wyoming. He came back to baseball briefly with Connie Mack at Philadelphia in 1950, Mr. Mack's last year as manager, and served the feuding family for just one season as general manager.

George Weiss hired him as a scout for the Yankees one year, 1955, and after he had been in and out of hospitals, bothered by a respiratory ailment, Detroit put him back on the payroll in 1960, to scout at the major league level and to work with Tiger catchers in spring training.

It just wasn't the same. Mickey Cochrane had been born to lead, not to follow. In the game of life to which he gave so much of himself, eating himself up inside in an effort to excel, he lost too much when they took the bat out of his hands and the mitt away from him.

From the time he lay at home plate at Yankee Stadium in 1937, 25 years before his death, the great Mickey Cochrane became just another guy named Gordon.

GORDON STANLEY (MICKEY) COCHRANE

Born April 6, 1903, at Bridgewater, Mass.
Died June 28, 1962, at Lake Forest, Ill.
Height 5-10 1/2 Weight 180
Threw right and batted lefthanded.
Named to Hall of Fame, 1947.

YEAR	CLUB	LEAGUE	POS.	G.	AB.	R.	H.	2B.	3B.	HR.	RBI.	B.A.	PO.	A.	E.	F.A.
1923	Dover (a)	East.	C	65	245	56	79	12	6	5	-	.322	222	70	13	.957
1924	Portland	Sh.	C	99	300	43	100	8	5	7	56	.333	278	49	14	.959
1925	Philadelphia	P.C.	C	134	420	69	139	21	5	6	55	.331	419	79	8	.984
1926	Philadelphia	Amer.	C	120	370	50	101	8	9	8	47	.273	502	90	15	.975
1927	Philadelphia	Amer.	C	126	432	80	146	20	6	12	80	.338	559	85	9	.986
1928	Philadelphia	Amer.	C	131	468	92	137	26	12	10	57	.293	645	71	25	.966
1929	Philadelphia	Amer.	C	135	514	113	170	37	8	7	95	.331	659	77	13	.983
1930	Philadelphia	Amer.	C	130	487	110	174	42	5	10	85	.357	654	69	5	.993
1931	Philadelphia	Amer.	C	122	459	87	160	31	6	17	89	.349	560	63	9	.986
1932	Philadelphia	Amer.	C	139	518	118	152	35	4	23	112	.293	652	94	5	.993
1933	Philadelphia (b)	Amer.	C	130	429	104	138	30	4	15	60	.322	476	67	6	.989
1934	Detroit	Amer.	C	129	437	74	140	32	1	2	76	.320	517	69	7	.988
1935	Detroit	Amer.	C	115	411	93	131	33	3	5	47	.319	504	50	6	.989
1936	Detroit	Amer.	C	44	126	24	34	8	0	2	17	.270	159	13	3	.983
1937	Detroit (c)	Amer.	C	27	98	27	30	10	1	2	12	.306	103	13	0	1.000
		Amer.														
Major League Totals				1482	5169	1041	1652	333	64	119	832	.320	6409	840	111	.985

a Played under name of Frank King.
b Sold to Detroit Tigers for $100,000 and catcher John Pasek, December 1933.
c Suffered fractured skull when hit by pitched ball by pitcher Irving (Bump) Hadley of New York, May 25, 1937, ending career as active player.

WORLD SERIES RECORD

YEAR	CLUB	LEAGUE	POS.	G.	AB.	R.	H.	2B.	3B.	HR.	RBI.	B.A.	PO.	A.	E.	F.A.
1929	Philadelphia	Amer.	C	5	15	5	6	1	0	0	0	.400	59	2	0	1.000
1930	Philadelphia	Amer.	C	6	18	5	4	1	0	2	3	.222	39	1	1	.976
1931	Philadelphia	Amer.	C	7	25	2	4	0	0	0	1	.160	40	4	1	.978
1934	Detroit	Amer.	C	7	28	2	6	1	0	0	1	.214	36	5	0	1.000
1935	Detroit	Amer.	C	6	24	3	7	1	0	0	1	.292	32	3	1	.972
World Series Totals				31	110	17	27	4	0	2	6	.245	206	15	3	.987

CONGRATULATIONS—AGAIN! *Long after Eddie Collins scored the run that beat John McGraw's New York Giants in the 1916 World Series, Mr. McGraw shakes hands with Collins, then player coach of Philadelphia's White Elephants.*

EDDIE COLLINS

The experienced, educated cells in Edward Trowbridge Collins' nimble baseball brain began to react the instant teammate Hap Felsch hit back to the pitcher with Collins on third base and Joe Jackson on first in the sixth game of the 1917 World Series at New York.

Collins, the 30-year-old superlative second baseman of the White Sox, sensed at once he'd have to draw a throw from the New York Giants' pitcher, Rube Benton, to prevent Benton from wheeling to start a double play.

With Collins breaking for the plate, Benton threw to his catcher, Bill Rariden. Collins stopped and started back toward the bag, with third baseman Heinie Zimmerman behind him and Rariden coming up the line with arm cocked.

Dancing along the line, seeking to avoid a putout until Jackson could go from first to third and the batter, Felsch, from home to second, Collins saw something that made his sleepy-looking brown eyes sparkle. Neither Benton nor the Giants' first baseman, Walter Holke, was backing up Rariden.

When the catcher finally stopped to feed the ball to Zimmerman, close behind Collins, Eddie quickly halted his retreat, reversed stride with the skill and coordination of a great baserunner. He broke for the plate, which was uncovered, and the crowd of 33,969 was treated to quite a sight.

Zimmerman chased Collins all the way across the plate with a run that helped provide the margin of victory, 4-2, as the White Sox clinched the world championship.

Zimmerman emerged from the Series as the butt of jokes because of that Keystone Kop chase. Manager John McGraw exonerated him, of course, pointing out that Holke, the first baseman, should have been covering the plate. Heinie the Zim came to his own defense, too, with a classic question:

"Who the hell was I supposed to throw the ball to? Klem?"

Not even the famed umpire, if he had traded the blue serge of neutrality for his National League allegiance, could have halted Cocky Collins, as they called him, when the jug-eared, long-nosed, thick-lipped champion of the American League's cause was on a rampage.

Connie Mack regarded him as "the greatest second baseman who ever lived," an especially interesting evaluation because Mr. Mack also had Napoleon Lajoie. When Collins died in 1951 at 63, Frank Frisch, himself one of the finest, said:

"Eddie Collins was the greatest infielder I ever saw. He could do everything."

He played 25 years, the record this century for most playing seasons. He held membership in the exclusive 3,000-hit Club with a lifetime average of .333, not to mention a .328 mark for six World Series.

Twice, he stole six bases in a game en route to basestealing highs of 67 in 1909, 81 in 1910 and 63 in 1912. In 1914, he received the Chalmers Award as the Most Valuable Player in the American League.

A brusque, honest man, Collins was revolted by the Black Sox scandal in which eight of his Chicago teammates conspired to throw the 1919 World Series to the Cincinnati Reds.

He found it difficult the rest of his life to talk about the episode that infuriated him. When he did, it's worth noting that he showed no compassion for the third baseman, George (Buck) Weaver, who went to a bitter grave contending that he had not participated in the fix and hadn't received a cent, but merely hadn't ratted on the conspirators.

Collins, his own ethical standards too high for him to believe what his eyes told was happening, couldn't forgive Weaver, but he still could rate the unfortunate teammate as the best American League third baseman he'd ever seen.

Collins rated Ty Cobb, George Sisler, Honus Wagner and, reluctantly it seemed, Babe Ruth, as the best players he ever saw. And, in a reminiscence shortly before his death and with a touch of the old self-confidence that earned his nickname, Cocky Collins said he felt he would have received additional recognition himself if it hadn't been for the overwhelming presence of Cobb.

Curiously, they wound up together at Philadelphia in the greatest collection of future Hall of Fame players ever assembled. The 1928 Athletics had Cobb, Collins, Tris Speaker, Mickey Cochrane, Lefty Grove, Jimmie Foxx and Al Simmons, all of them now in the Hall of Fame with old Connie, but they didn't win the pennant in '28. The rub, of course, was that Cobb, Speaker and Collins all were at the end or so close to it that their greatness was in the past tense.

Collins coached third base those last few years for his dear friend and mentor, Mr. Mack, who had earmarked him as his successor if Eddie had had the patience and constitution to wait that long. Old Connie didn't step down as manager until 1950, when he was almost 88 years old, and Collins, by then, had only a few months to live.

As a player-manager at Chicago in 1925-26, Eddie batted .346 and .344, not far from his career high of .369 at Chicago in 1920. He boosted a cellar club to fifth place in '25 and, though again finishing fifth, put together a good 81-72 record in '26, yet, surprisingly, he drew his release Armistice Day.

Collins, a graduate of Columbia University, was so highly regarded as a smart baseball man that when Miller Huggins died near the end of the 1929 season, owner Jacob Ruppert offered him what would have seemed then a plum—the chance to manage the mighty Yankees.

Collins, who earlier had turned down an offer to manage the St. Louis Browns, rejected the Yankees' offer because he said, he had been assured by Mack and the Shibe brothers, John and Tom, who owned the Athletics, that he would succeed old Connie. But when?

Eddie lived in suburban Philadelphia and was happy there. He and his wife, the former Mabel Doane, a Philadelphian by birth, were rearing two sons who would make them proud. Paul became an Episcopalian minister and Eddie, Jr., a good enough ballplayer to perform for the Athletics in 1939, '41, '42, became assistant general manager of the Phillies.

Married to the former Jane Pennock, daughter of Eddie's closest friend, Herb Pennock, Eddie, Jr. stepped out of professional baseball to teach and coach baseball at Episcopal Academy in Philadelphia.

The Collins-Pennock merger gave their children the unusual distinction of having both their grandfathers in baseball's Hall of Fame. Collins was elected to Cooperstown in 1939. Pennock, a lefthanded pitcher with Philadelphia, Boston and New York in the American League from 1912 through '34, was tapped for the honor in 1948.

By then, Pennock was dying at 53 after having served as general manager of the Phillies for five seasons. He laid the groundwork for the Whiz Kids, the young team that in 1950 gave Philadelphia its first National League pennant in 35 years.

The senior Collins, though he disliked the National League intensely until his death three years later, was extremely proud of Pennock's accomplishment. Eddie merited a bow of his own at Boston, if not for finally having given sportsman Tom Yawkey a pennant winner in 1946, for the results of the only scouting trip he ever made as general manager of the Red Sox.

Cocky Collins went out in 1936 to scout a journeyman infielder who became a good big league coach, George (Stud) Myatt, and wound up buying a second baseman named Bobby Doerr. Eddie also won the right of first refusal on a tall skinny kid who impressed him. You've heard of Ted Williams.

How did Collins get into the executive end of baseball? In 1928, Cobb took him to dinner to meet a young friend keenly interested in baseball, Tom Yawkey, whose father had been part-owner of the Detroit Tigers when Ty was there. Young Yawkey and the veteran Collins learned they were bound by an old school tie. They were fellow alumni of Irving School in Tarrytown, N. Y.

Three years later, Collins learned that Bob Quinn, running the rundown Red Sox, would sell if he could find the right party. Eddie thought of friend Tom and arranged for a luncheon meeting with Quinn and American League President Will Harridge.

By February 1933, Yawkey was ready to enter baseball—a red-letter day for the Red Sox and the game—but only if Collins would quit as coach at Philadelphia to join him as vice president, treasurer and general manager.

Despite the attractiveness of the offer, the decision to get out of uniform and to leave a man (Connie Mack), a club (the A's) and city (Philadelphia) for which he had great affection was not easy for Collins.

"By all means, take it," Mr. Mack said. "You figure prominently in our future plans, but this is an opportunity you can't afford to pass up."

Only once thereafter did the man who had been

in big league baseball uniform for a quarter-century put on the old monkey suit. Collins was highly flattered, he said, to be asked by Connie Mack to coach for the American League team in the first All-Star Game that summer of 1933 at Chicago, where, to Eddie's delight, his side won, 4-2, on a homer by Ruth.

At Boston, Collins inherited a monumental job because after the sale of Ruth and other stars to the Yankees, Harry Frazee, the theatrical magnate who emasculated the club, the Boston Americans had fallen on times as lean as a sheet of facial tissue. From 1922 through '32, for instance, they had finished this way: 8-8-7-8-8-8-8-8-6-8.

They became the Gold Sox, as Collins spent Yawkey's money in an effort to build a quick winner, but, meanwhile, he also built a farm system that proved productive. Frustratingly to a man who had played on six pennant winners and coached for three more, dipping into the winners' share of six World Series, the six second-place finishes and the pennant (1946) the Red Sox knew the last 13 years of his life couldn't compensate for not winning in 1950.

In the fall of 1950, when the sands of time were running out for him, Collins looked down from the Bosox offices at Fenway Park into Jersey Street as he talked to Jim Leonard, a Boston editor with whom he only recently had collaborated on a series of articles for *The Sporting News*. Eddie said in anguish:

"This was the year they had to do it. This was the year the Red Sox should have won the pennant . . . not next year . . . or the year after. This was the year . . . and they failed in the clutch."

To a fierce competitor like Cocky Collins, aggressive and confident, jam wasn't merely something you spread on bread. It was a tense moment to be relished.

Afield, he could relax until he seemed to droop. At times he even seemed to loaf when a ball was hit to him. But though never as graceful as, say, Lajoie or Charley Gehringer, two other outstanding second basemen, he always seemed to be in front of the ball.

For one thing, he played hitters both wisely and well with his massive hands.

A medium-sized man with little batting power, as such—he stood 5-9 and weighed only 160 pounds until late in his career—he was a choke-gripped lefthanded hitter who could drag-bunt expertly and spray the ball to all fields.

His tenacity was never more evident than when he batted. In an era when tobacco chewing was a mark of manliness, Collins preferred gum. When he stepped in to hit, he'd remove the gum from his mouth and stick it onto the button atop his cap.

If the opposing pitcher got two strikes on him, he'd reach up, pluck the gum off its jaunty perch, pop it back into his mouth and knead it vigorously as he redoubled his efforts to get a piece of the ball.

Collins, looking back on his career as a heart ailment brought him to an untimely end, said he had no regrets. "I could have been a doctor, lawyer or teacher," he said with quiet, characteristic self-assurance, "and I'm sure I could have done well in industry or finance, but I became a professional baseball player and loved it."

Born on May 2, 1887, in Millerton, N. Y., Eddie Collins played ball as early as he could remember after the family moved to Tarrytown. But when he enrolled at Columbia University in 1903 as a 16-year-old freshman, football was his favorite game. He was a 140-pound varsity quarterback.

Playing summer semi-pro ball for the extra money he needed before his senior year at Columbia, he caught the eye of a Philadelphia scout who arranged for him to meet Connie Mack. Mack offered him a contract and Collins, though he had another year to go in college, couldn't resist.

When he walked into Mack's office at the Philadelphia ballpark, the tall manager was talking to a former ballplayer, Tim Murnane, who became a Boston sportswriter. Connie spotted the kid.

"Hello, Sullivan," he addressed the perplexed rookie, pushing him out of the door. "Glad to see you."

81

The explanation was that Connie felt that Murnane, a writer from an Ivy League city, might have seen Collins play against Harvard. He advised Eddie to remain Sullivan and to stay out of uniform until the Red Sox left town.

So Collins was Sullivan until he rejoined the Athletics a year later. Then, with Philadelphia teammates still stubbornly calling him Sully, a St. Louis newspaper commented, "The A's have a new rookie infielder listed under the name of Collins. Actually Collins is Sullivan. He played briefly with them last September."

The 19-year-old Collins played his first big league ball game at Chicago in September 1906. He was at shortstop behind the eccentric southpaw, Rube Waddell, who had completely subdued him in batting practice the first day he reported. Then Rube put his arm around the crushed rookie's shoulders, saying loudly:

"Don't mind that, kid. I do that to them all."

The first pitcher Collins faced was big Ed Walsh, famous iron-man righthander of the pennant-winning White Sox. Years later, Connie Mack would remember, fuzzily, that Eddie had tripled off Walter Johnson in his first time up in the big leagues, but it was really a single off big Ed Walsh, the man of whom it first was said that he could strut sitting down. And that wasn't bad.

Walsh won in 11 innings, 5-4, but Sullivan—or Collins— handled six chances without an error. Mr. Mack decided later that Collins wasn't a shortstop and, as Eddie ruefully recalled after another experiment, that "I'd be killed if I played the outfield."

So a great second baseman was made, but not before Collins returned to Columbia. There, he was deprived of his eligibility, not because he'd become Sullivan of the Athletics, but because earlier that summer he'd accepted pay for semi-pro ball under his own name in New England. Unable to play for Columbia in the spring of 1907, Collins became the coach.

"I believe," he would recall proudly, "it was the

first time in any school that an undergraduate was paid to coach."

In 1909, 22-year-old Collins hit .346, reaching instant stardom that aided considerably in four Philadelphia pennants over a five-year period.

When the A's won in 1910, Eddie remembered later, with amusement, someone had begun to eat pineapple, superstitiously, and soon the entire club was eating "the wonder fruit," as they called it, even during their five-game World Series upset over the favored Chicago Cubs.

Collins batted .429 with nine hits in the 1910 Series and stole four bases, but his winner's share was only $2,062.79. By 1914, a winning team had paled on the Philadelphia fans and perhaps the habit had jaded the players, too. Boston's "miracle" Braves, the team that came from last-to-first after the Fourth of July, swept the A's in four straight in the World Series. Even the brilliant Collins batted just .214 in the embarrassing Series.

For financial reasons, Connie Mack tore up his championship team and Collins was crushed to learn in December that he had been sold to Chicago for $50,000, a sizable sum then.

To stay in the East, he asked permission to make a deal with Joe Lannin, owner of the Red Sox, but he said later he was certain that Ban Johnson, founder and president of the American League, blocked any efforts to keep Collins from Chicago.

The White Sox faced stern Federal League competition with Joe Tinker managing the Feds, and both Johnson and Charles A. Comiskey wanted a strong team there.

The Old Roman apparently paid pinch-penny salaries which, in part, contributed to the Black Sox scandal, if there ever can be any justification for bartering away personal integrity. But Collins, with star status and a disinclination to make the move, bargained well with Comiskey.

Reportedly, Eddie drew around $15,000, twice as much as other members of the Sox. Some of them resented him, his ways and his salary. He was college-educated, proper and even aloof. He formed a great admiration for the spunky little catching master, Ray Schalk, but neither Swede Risberg, the shortstop, nor Chick Gandil, the first baseman, spoke to him.

A rough play at second base when Collins was with the Athletics had made Gandil a bitter enemy. Risberg was a stooge for Gandil.

Gandil, Risberg, Buck Weaver and a fourth in-fielder, Fred McMullin, were adjudged conspirators in 1919, along with pitchers Eddie Cicotte and Claude (Lefty) Williams and outfielders Joe Jackson and Happy Felsch. Baseball's first commissioner, Judge Landis, barred them from baseball for life.

Collins starred in the 1917 World Series, climaxed by Zimmerman's comic-opera chase, and in August 1918, he enlisted in the Marines. Troubled by the times, he had batted only .276 in 97 games.

Before he could get overseas, World War I ended, but Cocky Collins retained one champion's admiration for another thereafter. He was honored, even briefly, to have been a Marine.

Collins said shortly before his death that he regarded the 1917 and 1919 White Sox teams as the greatest he ever saw because, in part, they won despite widening dissension.

"That was the amazing thing about that team," Eddie reminisced reluctantly. "It was torn by discord and hatred during much of the '19 season. From the very moment I arrived at training camp from service, I could see that something was amiss.

"We may have had our troubles in other years, but in 1919 we were a club that pulled apart rather than together. There were frequent arguments and open hostility.

"All the things you think—and are taught to believe—are vital to the success of any athletic organization were missing from it, and yet it was the greatest collection of players ever assembled, I would say.

"The wonderful Athletic teams I played for believed in teamwork and cooperation. I always thought you couldn't win without those virtues until I joined the White Sox. Players would even double-cross each other on the field and yet, despite these things, we still managed to win the pennant."

Did the honest players on the team ever suspect the conspirators?

"That's an interesting question," Collins said. "There has been much written about the Black Sox and in almost every account, it has been stated that the sellout was clumsily arranged. I don't agree.

"Once the fact of misdeed was established and the way the players involved contrived to look good while not giving their best, 'funny' plays suddenly became significant. Like Risberg taking my throw on a double-play pivot, reaching back with his foot to tag second base, then missing again and losing a play both there and at first base.

"But I'd say, even today, no one realizes how subtly conceived and executed the whole thing was."

The point is, you see, that the heavily favored White Sox, losing the best-of-nine Series to Cincinnati, didn't go out in five or even six games. They carried it to eight. Little lefthander Dickie Kerr, a knight in shining armor, won two games and Cicotte even won one. Moreover, Jackson batted .375 and, in fact, other players involved hit for higher average than, for instance, Collins. He batted just .226.

"Sure, I heard that the fix was on," said Eddie in one of his rare references to the episode he preferred to forget, "but I looked on it as just idle gossip and completely preposterous. I hadn't been close to some of the fellows, but, still, they were my teammates. Why shouldn't I defend them?"

Eddie's teammates didn't always defend him. Back in 1912, the only year in a stretch of five that the Athletics didn't win the pennant, a couple of Philadelphia players blamed Collins for having accepted $2,000 from *American Magazine* to do a series of 10 articles on inside baseball.

In one, he explained how opposing pitchers had been tipping off their deliveries. The unhappiest A's argued that, alerted, the foe had corrected the give-away weaknesses.

Collins, though extremely loyal to baseball and relieved that the sport had rebounded so robustly from the Black Sox scandal, sounded like a typical old-time player rather than an executive with vested interests when he expressed himself in *The Sporting News* series published shortly after his death.

"Pitching," he said, "is a problem that baseball must study and solve if the other departments of play are not to outdistance this important part of the game. I suggest that something be done to help the pitcher instead of hindering him."

Collins complained, too, about the lack of base-running in 1950. Two decades later, the concern would be that pitching had become too dominant in baseball again. And baserunning, thanks to the flying feet of Maury Wills Lou Brock, Bert Campaneris, Rickey Henderson, Vince Coleman and others, was recording, at the time, the base-stealing totals of the days of Cobb, Collins and Max Carey.

Collins grumbled also about the "high salaries" in 1950, unaware that the players' big bonanza was still to come. He referred also to the celebrated in-field in which he'd played at Philadelphia in 1913-14 (Stuffy McInnis, 1b; Collins, 2b; Jack Barry, ss, and Frank (Home Run) Baker, 3b).

"They called that a '$100,000 infield,' " said Collins. "Now it would be worth $2,000,000."

If old Cocky has been made to seem humorless here, it's not this intention. He could tell stories, including the one about the funniest play he'd ever seen.

This was when he was back at Philadelphia the joyous second time around. In a game at St. Louis, the Browns had a runner on second when the batter grounded a single to center field. Bing Miller, play-ing center for the A's, cut loose a wild throw to the plate.

The ball went over catcher Wally Schang's head and the runner scored. Schang, retrieving the ball

with the batter headed for second, threw wild over Collins' head, and the ball rolled into center field, where Miller juggled it and fired to the plate again, once more over Schang's head.

"Finally," said Collins, merrily, "one of the Browns' coaches got the ball and held it under the ice water spigot, pretending he was cooling it off."

It was in a World Series atmosphere at St. Louis that old World Series hero Eddie Collins almost won another for the Athletics—from the coaching box.

In 1931, the year after Collins had quit at 43 by getting one hit in two times at bat, he was coaching third base as the A's sought a third straight world championship. They might have prevailed despite Pepper Martin's pyrotechnics if they had been able to take advantage of Eddie's alertness in the second game of the '31 Series.

With the Cardinals leading in the ninth inning, 2-0, two on, two out, the runners were in motion when St. Louis southpaw Bill Hallahan broke off a jagged overhanded curve to pinch-hitter Jimmy Moore. When Moore swung and missed the pitch into the dirt for an apparent game-ending third strike, the Cardinals started off the field and the crowd started onto the diamond. But both plate umpire Dick Nallin and the sharp-eyed Collins had seen something.

The low-dipping pitch had touched the ground and Moore had to be tagged out or thrown out. The Cardinals' smart catcher, Jimmy Wilson, goofed. Instead of tagging the batter or throwing to Jim Bottomley at first before Bottomley started off the field, he lobbed the ball down to third base, where Jake Flowers said with a shudder later that he almost tossed the ball to a relative seated in a nearby box seat.

Collins, charging down from the third-base coaching line, practically grabbed Moore by the arm as the unhappy young pinch-hitter retreated toward the first-base dugout and shooed him to first base. When Flowers suddenly became aware the game wasn't over, there was no one at first base to receive the ball.

So the bases were loaded. When the field finally was cleared of fans who were more puzzled than angry, Hallahan, a hard-throwing lefthander with spotty control, rose to the heights. He retired Philadelphia's leadoff man, Max Bishop, on a foul ball Bottomley caught as he fell into temporary seats behind first base.

If Bishop had hit safely and the Athletics had won the game that inning when they were given four outs, Edward Trowbridge Collins would have made Jimmy Wilson feel considerably more foolish—and with far better reason—than Heinie Zimmerman felt chasing cool Cocky across the plate in the spotlight of an earlier World Series.

EDWARD TROWBRIDGE (COCKY) COLLINS
Born May 2, 1887, at Millerton, N.Y.
Died March 25, 1951, at Boston, Mass.
Height 5-9 Weight 175
Threw right and batted lefthanded.
Named to Hall of Fame, 1939.

YEAR	CLUB	LEAGUE	POS.	G.	AB.	R.	H.	2B.	3B.	HR.	RBI.	B.A.	PO.	A.	E.	F.A.
1906	Philadelphia (a)	Amer.	3B	6	17	1	4	0	0	0	-	..235	8	12	2	.909
1907	Philadelphia	Amer.	SS	14	20	0	5	0	0	0	3	.250	11	10	3	.875
1907	Newark	East.	2B-SS	4	16	6	7	0	0	0	-	.438	5	12	4	.810
1908	Philadelphia	Amer.	2B-SS	102	330	39	90	18	7	1	37	.273	190	189	24	.940
1909	Philadelphia	Amer.	2B	153	572	104	198	30	10	3	69	.346	373	406	27	.967
1910	Philadelphia	Amer.	2B	153	583	81	188	16	15	3	80	.322	402	451	25	.972
1911	Philadelphia	Amer.	2B	132	493	92	180	22	13	3	71	.365	348	349	24	.967
1912	Philadelphia	Amer.	2B	153	543	137	189	25	11	0	66	.348	387	426	38	.955
1913	Philadelphia	Amer.	2B	148	534	125	184	23	13	3	75	.345	315	448	41	949
1914	Philadelphia (b)	Amer.	2B	152	526	122	181	23	14	2	81	.344	354	387	23	.970
1915	Chicago	Amer.	2B	155	521	118	173	22	10	4	78	.332	344	487	22	.974
1916	Chicago	Amer.	2B	155	545	87	168	14	17	0	56	.308	346	415	19	.976
1917	Chicago	Amer.	2B	156	564	91	163	18	12	0	67	.289	353	388	24	.969
1918	Chicago (c)	Amer.	2B	97	330	51	91	8	2	2	32	.276	231	285	14	.974
1919	Chicago	Amer.	2B	140	518	87	165	19	7	4	73	.319	347	401	20	.974
1920	Chicago	Amer.	2B	153	601	115	222	37	13	3	75	.369	449	471	23	.976
1921	Chicago	Amer.	2B	139	526	79	177	20	10	2	58	.337	376	458	28	.968
1922	Chicago	Amer.	2B	154	598	92	194	20	12	1	69	.324	406	451	21	.976
1923	Chicago	Amer.	2B	145	505	89	182	22	5	5	67	.360	347	430	20	.975
1924	Chicago	Amer.	2B	152	556	108	194	27	7	6	86	.349	396	446	20	.977
1925	Chicago	Amer.	2B	118	425	80	147	26	3	3	80	.346	290	346	20	.970
1926	Chicago (d)	Amer.	2B	106	375	66	129	32	4	1	62	.344	228	307	15	.973
1927	Philadelphia	Amer.	2B	95	225	50	76	12	1	1	15	.338	124	150	10	.965
1928	Philadelphia	Amer.	SS	36	33	3	10	3	0	0	7	.303	0	1	0	1.000
1929	Philadelphia	Amer.	PH	9	7	0	0	0	0	0	0	.000	0	0	0	.000
1930	Philadelphia	Amer.	PH	3	2	1	1	0	0	0	0	.500	0	0	0	.000
Major League Totals				2826	9949	1818	3311	437	186	47	1307	.333	6625	7714	463	.969

a Played under name of Sullivan.
b Sold to Chicago White Sox for $50,000, December 8, 1914.
c In Military Service most of season.
d Released by Chicago White Sox, November 11, 1926; signed with Philadelphia Athletics, December 23, 1926.

WORLD SERIES RECORD

YEAR	CLUB	LEAGUE	POS.	G.	AB.	R.	H.	2B.	3B.	HR.	RBI.	B.A.	PO.	A.	E.	F.A.
1910	Philadelphia	Amer.	2B	5	21	5	9	4	0	0	3	.429	17	17	1	.971
1911	Philadelphia	Amer.	2B	6	21	4	6	1	0	0	0	.286	12	22	4	.895
1913	Philadelphia	Amer.	2B	5	19	5	8	0	2	0	3	.421	16	18	1	.971
1914	Philadelpia	Amer.	2B	4	14	0	3	0	0	0	1	.214	9	12	0	1.000
1917	Chicago	Amer.	2B	6	22	4	9	1	0	0	2	.409	11	22	0	1.000
1919	Chicago	Amer.	2B	8	31	2	7	1	0	0	1	.226	21	31	2	.963
World Series Totals				34	128	20	42	7	2	0	10	.328	86	122	8	.963

NEVER STOPPED SHORT: Clutch-hitting shortstop Joe Cronin poses with Hank Greenberg (left), who reached the Hall of Fame with him in same election, 1956.

JOE CRONIN

The kid coaching on crutches at first base hobbled to the dugout, threw away the crutches, grabbed a bat and limped to home plate. The time was 1924, the place was San Francisco, the occasion was the Catholic high school league championship baseball game and the batter with the bum wheel was the wounded hero of the trailing team.

Down through the years there have been ballplayers who could come through in the clutch like some fictional hero fresh off the pen of Burt L. Standish, who was writing about the derring-do of

Frank Merriwell and brother Dick for pulp magazines when Joseph Edward Cronin was growing up in the Bay area.

Not even Standish, in whose imagination little was improbable and nothing impossible, had the gall to suggest that his hero would wind up as president of Yale, even if baseball fan A. Bartlett Giamatti went from Yale to the commissioner's seat in fictional fancy.

But Joe Cronin, the teamster's son, wound up not only leading the team but running the league, meaning the American League. And he came pretty close to making the incredible climb from player to commissioner. Giamatti would have preferred Cronin's route to prominence.

Joe was a Merriwell in the fleshy flesh, a pink-cheeked, jut-jawed, good-looking kid with sandy hair and sand in his craw when he hobbled up there to hit for Sacred Heart against St. Ignatius in the Catholic prep final in Frisco in '24. Without their star shortstop's bat, Sacred Heart trailed, 1-0, but there were two on, two out when Cronin did what came naturally to him throughout his major league career. He accepted and met the challenge with a two-run pinch-double that won the game and championship.

Cronin's climb from the sandlots of San Francisco to the presidency of the American League is almost as unlikely as his physical growth. Tall and skinny when he broke into the big leagues, the boy who went from the Far West to the East spread out North and South, physically, after he won his fame and fortune.

For a younger generation watching the jowly, cigar-puffing American League president with the aldermanic paunch, it must have been hard to envision the same man as probably the best all around shortstop ever developed by the league he headed since 1959. Not the best-fielding shortstop, but a pretty good one and a .302 lifetime hitter who must have hit .402 with men on base.

Cronin's accomplishments as top administrator for his league must be questioned, as his motives were suspect when he fired as "incompetent" two umpires, Bill Valentine and Al Salerno, just after they had led a drive to organize American League umpires who had seen their National League counterparts win higher salaries and better benefits.

The truth is, Cronin succeeded his good friend, starchy Will Harridge, at a time when the National League that Joe had helped bury as a player came to life to dominate All-Star and World Series play and, for that matter, expansion and most other areas of progress. Although Cronin was the first to give the Negro a major league chance as an umpire, hiring Emmett Ashford from the Pacific Coast League, the American League lagged early and lost in the race to acquire the best black playing talent.

As far back as 1945, when Cronin was manager, the Red Sox, under pressure to give Negro players a tryout in exchange for legislative repeal of a state Sunday curfew, took a look at Jackie Robinson and Sam Jethroe, both of whom reached the majors quickly with other clubs after Branch Rickey signed Robinson to a Brooklyn contract in '47.

A decade after taking that cursory glance at Robinson, the Red Sox still hadn't found a black player worthy of wearing their colors. If Cronin really had any prejudice in his nearly quarter-century with the Red Sox, it was one Irishman's soft spot for another, plus the hardheaded good business sense that if there was one thing better for the box office in Boston than a good Italian player, it would be a great Irish star—someone the quality of Cronin himself.

The Bosox came up with a dandy second-generation son of Italy in Dom DiMaggio, the Little Professor, in center field and a star of the 1946 pennant-winning team Cronin managed. Over the years, though, when Joe's Bosox teams usually ran second to the great Yankees, it was Dom's older brother, the classical Joe DiMaggio, who was on Cronin's mind the most.

"He has made the difference in so many races," said Cronin, who went from Washington to Boston as player-manager in 1935, a year before DiMag came out of the same Bay area that has spawned so many major league stars.

Cronin was right. Before DiMaggio, his own Washington club had defeated New York for the 1933 pennant and the Yankees trailed Detroit in both '34 and '35. From the time DiMag broke in a year later, however, the Yankees won four straight world championships and seven pennants until Cronin led his Bosox in '46 to their first pennant in 28 years.

Four times when he was still playing, Cronin finished second to DiMaggio and the Yankees. One of the highlights of his career, however, was a five-game sweep over the Bronx Bombers at Fenway Park in 1939.

Other highlights, naturally, include leading Washington to a pennant at the age of 27; winning the American League's Most Valuable Player award in 1930; seven times over a nine-year period earning recognition by *The Sporting News* as major league All-Star shortstop, and setting an American League record by hitting five pinch-homers in a season.

Cronin, in a pinch, was Capt. Blood, a swashbuckler. In the era of the playing managers, a period of considerable color, charm and drama, Joe would put himself on the spot with a flair and courage that would make lesser men gulp.

"I pulled rank and waited until the wind blew out," he commented modestly at the time this article was being prepared. Fact is, he always was extremely modest, though you just wouldn't believe it if you walked into a game situation when the field foreman of the Red Sox decided that it was time to take a hand himself.

Time would be called and there would be a suspenseful pause. Cronin, if not coaching at third base, would wait momentarily in the dugout and then come out carrying several bats. The Fenway faithful would set up a roar at the sight of their leader with the determined chin, hitching the pants he wore short.

Outside the batter's box, he'd whirl the bats over his head, put them down, select one and then prepare to step in as the field announcer made it official:

"For the Red Sawks"—remember the New England pronunciation, please—"Cronin batting for…"

Someone wrote once about Joe's "Tony Lazzeri" batting stance. Actually, by his own recollection, he used innumerable stances, including one in which he felt like trying to get down on his knees to get a better look at Carl Hubbell's poof pitch. That was Hubbell's low-fading screwball which Cronin faced in the 1933 World Series and in All-Star Games.

At times, I had the impression that pitchers attempted to drive Cronin out of there by throwing at his knees, because he was fearless against head-high intimidation. Joe couldn't remember unusual sensitivity to the knee-high pitch inside or that he'd been pitched down and in more than high and tight.

"I do remember that Ted Lyons would make you skip rope at times, throwing at your feet," one Hall of Famer said of another. "At times, you know—and you don't see this much anymore—I'd walk up into a pitch, the way I'd seen Fred Lindstrom do over in the National League. If you hit the ball, fine, but if you didn't, the pitchers, understandably, didn't like it and they'd drive you back with the next pitch."

The righthanded-hitting Cronin, wagging his bat in a jam, was a menacing figure. The long chin would thrust out more determinedly than ever. The handsome features would flush with excitement and the cords on his neck would stand out. And, cousin, whether wading into the ball or just striding into it, ripping the ball to all fields, Mr. Cronin was Mr. Clutch.

By 1943, close to 37, Joe would have preferred to hang it up as a player. The year before, for instance, he'd played in only 45 games, hitting .304 with 24 RBIs on 24 hits, but with the war on, he was forced to stay on the active list. Again, in '43, he got 24 hits, batting .312, and this time he drove in all of 29 runs, clubbing four doubles and five homers.

As a pinch-hitter that year, Cronin was peerless. He went to bat 49 times as a substitute and came through with seven walks, nine singles, four doubles and those five record homers. (Johnny Frederick set the major league high of six at Brooklyn in 1932). Pinch-batting, Joe batted .429, but, wait, that's not all.

At the time he hit those five pinch-homers in one season, the career high in the American League was five, as set by Goose Goslin from 1928 through '38.

Moreover, Cronin batted in 14 runs with those five swings of his bat this way:

June 15—Off Luman Harris, Philadelphia Athletics, two on.

June 17 (first game)—Off Everett Fagan, Athletics, two on.

June 17 (second game)—Off Don Black, Athletics, two on.

July 9—Off Bob Muncrief, St. Louis Browns, one on.

August 12—Off Lee Ross, Chicago White Sox, two on.

Connie Mack had reason to be both prejudiced and impressed, of course, because rival manager Cronin's pinch-hitting produced five hits in seven trips, including three homers and a double good for 10 runs. As mentioned, he homered in both ends of a doubleheader against Mack's Athletics in June 1943.

"Oh, my, yes, Joe is the best there is in the clutch," Connie said. "With a man on third and one out, I'd rather have Cronin hitting for me than anybody I've ever seen, and that includes Cobb, Simmons and the rest of them."

It's no accident or coincidence that Joe Cronin, batting .300 or better 11 times in the big leagues, knocked in 100 or more runs eight times. No, that short fence at Fenway Park didn't hurt, but, fact is, Cronin topped 100 RBIs five times at Washington, where the fences at old Griffith Stadium were an overnight ride from home plate.

The wonder of it all is that he ever hit. Pittsburgh found him wanting and the Old Fox, Clark Griffith, snapped when scout Joe Engel bought Cronin and brought him from Kansas City in 1928. Joe was an infielder batting only .245 and looked so unimpressive that Kaycee was about to ship him farther down.

The dedication that drove him to self-made heights as a hitter and player came out of the ashes and shambles of the San Francisco earthquake and fire in 1906. Joseph Edward Cronin was born six months after his parents had been left with nothing

except an old rocking chair. His father, Jeremiah Cronin, an Irish immigrant, drove a team of horses, and Joe had two older brothers. Ray became a postal worker, Jim a truck driver.

Young Joe, the only athlete in the family, worked and played at a furious pace. Prescott Sullivan, *San Francisco Examiner* columnist, remembered his boyhood friend buying his first long-trousered suit out of his own savings for $11.98 at Prager's department store.

"Joe had a fine future in the banking business had he cared to follow it," Sullivan wrote some years ago for the *Christian Brothers'* magazine. "He was good at counting money and more than sufficiently Irish to be trusted by the widows O'Flynn, O'Connell and O'Brien, who made up a considerable part of the depositors at the Hibernia Bank, where Joe was employed as a junior clerk."

At 14, Joe won the junior tennis championship of San Francisco, but from the time he wore knee-length britches with long, black, cotton stockings at Excelsior Playground in the outer Mission district, he was fascinated by baseball.

Cronin could rattle off the names of San Francisco heroes, players a bit older who went up to make it…Willie Kamm…Babe Pinelli…Lefty O'Doul…Lew Fonseca…Sammy Bohne…Ping Bodie.

He recalled another for a different reason from rival Jackson Playground at the foot of Russian Hill. Whenever it looked as if the Excelsior kids would win, the Jackson instructor would send for a big Italian kid, a couple of years older, who'd take time out from helping in his father's grape-pressing business to pitch in a jam or deliver a big hit. That would be Tony Lazzeri.

At Mission High School, Joe played in the same infield with Wally Berger, who was to go on to hit 38 home runs in his rookie season with the Boston Braves. When Mission burned down, Joe transferred to Sacred Heart and starred in basketball and soccer as well as baseball.

After graduating from Sacred Heart, he was offered a basketball-baseball scholarship at St. Mary's College. He didn't take it because he knew his family needed whatever money he could bring in. Instead, he became an alternate instructor in the playground system, filling in whenever a regular took sick or went on a vacation. He worked with kids who would follow him to the majors—Eddie Joost, Dario Lodigiani and Frank Crosetti.

Years afterward, when Crosetti was playing third base for the Yankees, he pulled the hidden-ball trick on Cronin. The mortified manager of the Red Sox screamed at the grinning Crosetti, "You Dago so-and-so, this is the thanks I get for teaching you this game."

To satisfy his hunger for baseball—how would he know he'd wind up in a position to see a ball game every day into his 60s?—Joe began to play semi-pro ball for Napa, a small city across San Francisco Bay. He would get up Sundays at 6 A.M. to attend Mass, grab a street car to the Bay, catch a ferry for the long trip across and then take a train to Napa.

One day his mother made the long trip to see him play. When he got home that evening, Mrs. Cronin met him at the door with a large safety pin.

"If you have all that trouble keeping up your pants, Joe, you had better use this pin," she said. Mom hadn't seen him play previously and didn't know that he had a nervous habit of hitching his britches from time to time.

Pleased at his mother's interest, Cronin invited her to another game. Afterward, he said, "Let's go have an ice-cream soda, Mother."

Mrs. Cronin wondered whether he had enough money. Joe produced three $5 bills he'd received for playing shortstop. The Irish mother was most impressed.

"Fifteen dollars for playing baseball and enjoying yourself!" she said. "The next time you come here, I'll bring Ray and Jim, and we'll get $45."

Before she died in 1936, Mrs. Cronin long since had learned that it wasn't simply a case of putting on a uniform to get paid for playing baseball—not even for the star's brothers.

In 1925, the 18-year-old Cronin received an offer to play ball from Charley Graham of the hometown San Francisco Seals. Thinking it over, he was flattered to be approached by Joe Devine, West Coast scout for the Pirates. Joe leaped before he looked. Pittsburgh had a helluva shortstop, hard-hitting, strong-armed Glenn Wright.

Optioned to Johnstown, Pa., in the Mid-Atlantic League, the stringy West Coast kid—he carried only 152 pounds on a six-foot frame—batted .313 in 99 games, but he was the wrong man in the wrong place at the wrong time. Although he trained three times with the Pirates at Paso Robles, Calif., Cronin couldn't displace either Wright or the Hall of Fame third baseman, Pie Traynor.

Cronin played in 38 games with the Pirates in 1926, then was sent down to George Weiss' New Haven club in the Eastern League. In '27, as the Buccos won the pennant, Joe rode the bench for all except 12 games and 22 times at bat.

Pittsburgh and the National League represented a big zero in the life of the man who became a star and then president of the American League. Still, typically for a person who has a way with people, Joe developed lifelong loyalties and friendships. Wright helped him. So did a hardworking little clubhouse man named Socko McCarey, who pitched morning batting practice for the eager kid.

Characteristically, Joe never forgot. Wright became a Red Sox scout when Cronin was general manager. Socko scouted the Pittsburgh area for the Red Sox long after he was hired by a man whose faults most certainly do not include ingratitude. On the contrary, some have suggested that Joe was too good to too many.

For himself, however, he didn't appear good enough when the Pirates sold him to Kansas City in 1928 and, rusty from inactivity, the 21-year-old infielder struggled at both third base and shortstop with the independently owned Blues of the American Association. He was batting only .245 and was ticketed for Wichita when Washington's one-man scouting staff, Joe Engel, came to town.

The Senators had a problem. Owner Clark Griffith was smitten with a young shortstop, Bobby Reeves, only a couple of years older than Cronin, but Reeves was worn down for good reason. The Senators' hard-hitting left fielder, Goose Goslin, had hurt his arm in spring training, foolishly putting the shot. Washington needed the Goose's bat and manager Bucky Harris had instructed Reeves to hurry out to left field to relay Goslin's feeble throws.

Griffith wanted an infielder to spell the overworked, underweight Reeves, not replace him. Engel, finding that Kansas City would expect considerable for the return of Topper Rigney, a former Washington infielder, learned that young Cronin was about to be demoted. The scout had watched the kid take infield practice in the 1927 World Series and liked him. The price should be cheap, Engel reasoned, but it wasn't. Not by those (1928) standards, anyway. George Muehlebach, who owned the Blues, insisted on $7,500.

Engel sweated, but—on one of his happiest hunches—committed Griffith to the deal and then wondered how he'd face the old man. He bought Cronin a new suit of clothes—the kid was sending his money home—and then dispatched a note to Griffith's niece and secretary, Mildred Robertson.

Attractive Mildred Robertson Cronin still has the letter, which informed her:

"Am bringing home to you a real sweetie, Joe Cronin. So be dolled up about Wednesday or Thursday to meet him. Tall and handsome. Hold all our mail. Don't show this to anyone."

Griff wasn't nearly as impressed as his niece when he met the tall, skinny shortstop, whom he felt lacked power.

Engel talked fast to placate the boss. Actually, manager Bucky Harris at second base, and veteran Joe Judge, playing first, liked Cronin better than Reeves at the outset.

"This kid, Cronin, may be a little way off right now, but he's a cinch to make a great player," Judge told a Washington sportswriter after the first week. "He's smart. He handles himself well, has a great arm and he'll start hitting one of these days. This is a boy with great determination."

No one ever worked harder than the hungry Mick from Mission. Al Schacht, the pitcher-coach better known as the Clown Prince of Baseball, pitched tirelessly to him and one of the kids who shagged flyballs for him every morning was Mildred Robertson's brother, Calvin Griffith, the Old Fox' adopted son who became president of the same ball club, the rechristened and relocated Minnesota Twins.

In 63 games with Washington, Cronin batted .242 in 1928 and almost went to Boston as a throw-in in a trade that winter. Six seasons later, he went to the Red Sox for a startling sum, $250,000, which, considering the difference in the value of the dollar during that Depression period and now, must rate as the greatest cash purchase in the history of baseball. Current equivalent for the economic impact would be somewhere between $750,000 and $1,000,000.

Back in the fall of '28, Harris and Schacht persuaded Griffith not to give up Cronin, but to let Reeves go in the multiple-player deal by which Buddy Myer was reacquired from the Red Sox. Reluctantly, Griff went along with his advisers. Reeves went to Boston, then one stop from baseball oblivion.

Cronin found himself established at shortstop at the time a new manager was appointed. Walter Johnson, the great pitcher, was in charge in 1929, a year in which Cronin boosted his average to .283.

Then a dramatic thing happened. Working hard over the winter, running four to five miles daily and wielding an ax to help fell trees in a forest, Cronin developed himself across the chest and shoulders. He boosted his weight to 180 pounds, en route to the 194 at which he finished his career and the unmentionable figure afterward. In 1930, not yet 24 years old, Joe Cronin had quite a year.

He rapped 203 hits, including 41 doubles, eight triples and 14 homers, for a .346 average and 126 RBIs, lifting the Senators from fifth place to second and winning the American League's Most Valuable Player award. He'd drive in the same number of runs again in '31, but never again, though hitting consistently well, would he post so high an average.

By the time the Senators dropped to third place in 1932, Griffith was thinking shrewdly about how to solve two problems. The Old Fox was disenchanted, regretfully, with Johnson as a manager. Back in 1924, he'd taken a 27-year-old second baseman, Bucky Harris, and had seen him become a Boy Wonder, a pennant-winning manager his first year. Maybe if he turned now to his 26-year-old shortstop, Cronin, with times tough, it would be one way to combine salaries.

Cronin asked Griffith to let him sleep on the surprising offer, and then couldn't sleep. In the morning, he phoned Johnson. Sir Walter told him, by all means, to take the extra money and the extra responsibility.

Griffith, pleased that Cronin would accept the job as manager and the challenge, suggested the old man and young one sit down and decide which obtainable players might help them. On this subject, Cronin had definite ideas because he felt that not only were the defending world champion Yankees the team to beat, but that the one way to finish ahead of New York was to acquire players who did well against the Yanks.

Together, Griffith and Cronin listed six players they hoped to get, aware they might be fortunate just to get one. From the St. Louis Browns, the Senators wanted back lefthanded-hitting outfielder Goose Goslin, righthanded-hitting center fielder Fred Schulte and southpaw pitcher Walter Stewart. From Detroit, they sought lefthander Earl Whitehill and reliever Jack Russell. From Cleveland they wanted catcher Luke Sewell. Astonishingly, the Senators got all six of the players and on terms with

which they could live. Not only that, but every deal worked out better than Cronin could have hoped.

As starting pitchers, Whitehill had a 22-8 record and Stewart 15-6. Russell came out of the bullpen 50 times and posted a 12-6 mark. Sewell, a master receiver, also hit .264. Goslin, like Cronin, tough in a pinch, hit .297 and the slick-fielding Schulte was only two points behind. Moreover, Washington beat New York decisively on the season's series, 14 games to eight.

Legend has it that to gain respect, young Cronin gathered his team in the clubhouse and challenged anybody who wanted to find out whether he was a punk kid or a grown man to step outside with him. It didn't happen that way, said Cronin, long before his death in 1984 at 78, and probably it didn't, though Joe was too pleasant a man, too self-effacing, to beat his chest. Joe did remember the Senators' first visit to Yankee Stadium in 1933. Stewart beat George Pipgras, 4-3, in the first game of the series and a crowd of 35,000 was out for the second game, April 29. With Washington ahead, 6-3, two on and nobody out in the eighth inning, Tony Lazzeri hit a long drive to deep right-center. Lou Gehrig tagged up at second and, as a result, when the ball hit the wall and rebounded directly to Goslin, who fed the ball to Cronin, the Senators' manager wheeled to find a delightful prospect.

Instead of at least one run in and probably two, Joe found Gehrig rounding third followed by Dixie Walker whom third-base coach Art Fletcher hadn't been able to hold up for fear of causing Gehrig to stop, too. Cronin put his muscle behind his throw and gunned the ball on line to Sewell at the plate. Gehrig barreled into Sewell tagging himself out, and bumped the Washington catcher into Walker, trying to evade a tag at the other side of the plate. Double play on a double!

"That's where we won it," said Cronin. "When things are breaking for you, you get breaks like that. The team begins to feel it's going to keep on getting 'em and then nothing can beat 'em."

Nothing did, at least not until the World Series

in which, despite Cronin's .318 average, the Senators lost a low-scoring, five-game Series to King Carl Hubbell and the Giants.

In 1934, hit by massive injuries in which Cronin himself was included, breaking an arm in September as he collided at first base with pitcher Wes Ferrell of Boston, the Senators skidded to seventh place. Cronin, who had hit .309 in the championship season, dipped to .284, but he still drove in 101 runs in just 127 games.

For Joe, the highlight of the season—and one of his greatest thrills—was managing the array of talent the American League put into the All-Star Game at New York's Polo Grounds. To the team man, it didn't matter that he had been among five men in succession Hubbell had fanned in one of baseball's historic moments.

The significance, to Joe, was that he was running the team that included those illustrious fellow victims—Babe Ruth, Lou Gehrig, Jimmie Foxx and Al Simmons—and the rest of a lineup that had Charley Gehringer, Bill Dickey and Heinie Manush in it.

For Cronin, too, the thrill was in the American League's come-from-behind, 9-7 victory. "And I got a kick when Mel Harder pitched so well," Cronin said, referring to the Cleveland righthander he had named to the All-Star staff. Harder held the National League scoreless the last five innings.

The Irish are traditionally slow to marry. Cronin early had caught the heart of Griff's niece, Mildred, but Miss Robertson didn't catch Cronin until the end of the '34 season, just before his 28th birthday. They honeymooned with a sea voyage and docked at San Francisco to find a message for Cronin to call Griffith.

"Unk"—that's what the young adopted Griffiths and the Robertsons called the Old Fox. To the older players, Griff was "Teach." Cronin, like one of the family, called him "Unk" and "Unk" had a problem.

The Boston Red Sox' new owner, sportsman

Tom Yawkey, and Yawkey's general manager, Eddie Collins, had made it known that they wanted Cronin. Griffith didn't want to trade or sell his star shortstop and manager, much less Mildred's husband and a member of the family.

Finally, the Red Sox came up with the staggering $250,000 offer, one which would ease the old man's financial problems. Griff stalled, bargaining. He needed a shortstop, that Broadway fellow, Lyn Lary. He bargained more. They'd have to give Cronin a five-year contract at $50,000 a year as player-manager. The Red Sox, meaning Yawkey, would do it all.

"I've got to talk to Cronin first," Griffith pleaded. Cronin, when he found out on his call from the West Coast what was in the air, actually was pleased. He'd been concerned about the new relationship with Griffith because of his marriage to Mildred. Now, he was relieved.

"Go ahead and make the deal, Unk," Joe said. And in his home, Cronin kept the yellowed scrap of paper, reportedly wrapping paper from around a bundle of laundry, that was used for the informal memo in which Yawkey agreed in writing to pay a fortune for Clark Griffith's talented young son-in-law.

Informally or officially, the transaction packed a sock that rocked baseball and dazzled Boston, as Frank (Buck) O'Neill related lyrically later for *The Sporting News*:

"There are as many Irish in Boston as there are in Dublin. Maybe there are more, but it was, and it is, in such an environment that Cronin belongs. His smile and his speech and his manner place him rightfully in the midst of the blood royal of the Fighting Race."

Under Cronin, the Gold Sox, as the expensively assembled team was known, were called just as often the Red Flops. But, to be fair about it, whether agreeing with Cronin's handling of pitchers or his strategy, who else was beating the Yankees in those days?

Besides, Cronin's personal charm and clutch play, which carried him into the Hall of Fame in 1956, won him the eternal affection and admiration of Yawkey and enough support from the rest of New England. Although still a very good player, Joe never really was as great at Boston as he had been at Washington, partly because he had to control temperamental talent that included Wes Ferrell...Lefty Grove...Bill Werber...Footsy Marcum...Ted Williams.

Only at the beginning at Boston did Cronin really falter under the pressure. In his third game at Fenway Park in 1935, he made three errors. The next day, he made another error and as Ed Linn wrote in a study in depth for *Sport* magazine some years ago, "A Ladies Day crowd started to work him over in the immemorial manner of women who believe the merchandise is overpriced."

The day after that, the Red Sox went into the ninth inning leading behind Wes Ferrell, 3-1. Cronin booted two grounders, the Sox lost, 5-3, "and the voice of the rabble arose in the land."

As Linn pointed out, things got so bad that for a time Joe developed a complex about groundballs, and the fans were treated to the unlikely sight of the major leagues' All-Star shortstop for the five preceding years dropping down on one knee to field balls hit directly at him.

"The $250,000 squat," his players called it among themselves. Finally, after a ball squirted past Cronin's bent knee, his sure-fielding second baseman, Oscar Melillo, gave him the best possible advice.

"If you're going to miss 'em, Joe," Melillo called over, "miss 'em like a big leaguer."

That was the only time the man who wound up with too large a gut didn't have more than enough guts. For a man who might have been, as some suggested, as lucky as he was good, there is positively no question that he had courage.

He had compassion, too, and he still did as professional baseball began its second century. By then,

Cronin long since had become a man of baseball distinction. How many managers, after all, work 15 years without getting fired?

Cronin, finally bringing Boston a pennant in 1946, the year after he quit as a player, stepped down following the 1947 season or, rather, stepped up to become general manager. Eleven years later, the youngest manager ever to win a big league pennant became only the second big league ballplayer ever to ascend to a major league presidency. And John K. Tener, president of the National League just before World War I, had been only a journeyman pitcher for three seasons.

Cronin could roll with a punch. He refused to become agitated when a story persisted that as player-manager of the Red Sox he had recommended that Boston sell a young Louisville shortstop for whom the Bosox had spent considerable. You've heard of Pee Wee Reese?

Cronin, typically, wouldn't involve others in the organization's decision by which Reese, the reason the Red Sox had bought the Louisville American Association club in 1938 for $175,000, went to Brooklyn a year later for $150,000 and five players—and stayed to star with the Dodgers until 1958.

"As a manager," Cronin merely said, evenly, "you don't move players because of personal feelings. Above all, as a manager, my job depended on how many games I could win, much more than it could on whether I played or used someone else."

Undoubtedly, the four Cronin children, of whom Joe and Mildred can be proud, would adjudge the old shortstop as a fair and just man.

The senior Cronins, meaning Joe and Mildred, made a decision after his mother died, 34 years ago. (Pop Cronin died in '49.) Although loyal to the Bay Area, they would make their home in Boston, to raise a family without moving twice a year, and the years in suburban Newton Center were as happy as that decision. Later Mildred and Joe set up a winter villa near the home of the Senators/Twins so that he was close to baseball even during his final battles with cancer.

Back in 1938, Boston first honored its adopted son with a "day" at Fenway Park. A crowd of 13,000 turned out in September to watch the Sox beat the Yankees and to present Joe with a $1,250 silver service and an Irish terrier.

When he was elected to the Hall of Fame in 1956, they did it again. This time, close to 30,000 turned out and the great shortstop of the past was given a Cadillac with the appropriate license plate, "HF-56." He also was presented with plaques and checks. Joe turned the money over to charity and then brought tears to many eyes when he asked the crowd to stand with him in silence to the memory of baseball men who had helped him make good.

Included were prominent baseball men like Clark Griffith, Connie Mack, Eddie Collins and Walter Johnson, but, characteristically, Joseph Edward Cronin remembered others not quite so well known to whom he felt indebted—players, coaches, trainers, umpires, even sportswriters and radio men.

To steal one of the old clutch-hitting Sacred Heart kid's own favorite lines, "Isn't he a sweetheart?" He was.

JOSEPH EDWARD CRONIN
Born October 12, 1906, at San Francisco, Calif.
Height 6-0 Weight 187
Threw and batted righthanded.
Named to Hall of Fame, 1956.

YEAR	CLUB	LEAGUE	POS.	G.	AB.	R.	H.	2B.	3B.	HR.	RBI.	B.A.	PO.	A.	E.	F.A.
1925	Johnstown	Mid.-At.	2-S	99	352	64	110	18	11	3	-	.313	-	-	-	-
1926	Pittsburgh	Nat.	2B-SS	38	83	9	22	2	2	0	11	.265	74	92	6	.965
1926	New Haven	East.	SS	66	244	61	78	11	8	2	-	.320	136	222	27	.930
1927	Pittsburgh	Nat.	SS	12	22	2	5	1	0	0	3	.227	28	31	3	.952
1928	Kansas City	A.A.	SS	74	241	34	59	10	6	2	32	.245	87	146	14	.943
1928	Washington	Amer.	SS	63	227	23	55	10	4	0	25	.242	133	190	16	.953
1929	Washington	Amer.	SS	145	492	72	139	29	8	8	60	.283	285	459	62	.923
1930	Washington	Amer.	SS	154	587	127	203	41	8	14	126	.346	336	509	35	.960
1931	Washington	Amer.	SS	156	611	103	187	44	13	12	126	.306	323	488	43	.950
1932	Washington	Amer.	SS	143	557	95	177	43	18	6	116	.318	306	448	32	.959
1933	Washington	Amer.	SS	152	602	89	186	45	11	5	118	.309	297	528	34	.960
1934	Washington (a)	Amer.	SS	127	504	68	143	30	9	7	101	.284	246	486	38	.951
1935	Boston	Amer.	1B-SS	144	556	70	164	37	14	9	95	.295	277	435	37	.951
1936	Boston	Amer.	SS-3B	81	295	36	83	22	4	2	43	.281	133	229	26	.933
1937	Boston	Amer.	SS	148	570	102	175	40	4	18	110	.307	300	414	31	.958
1938	Boston	Amer.	SS	143	530	98	172	51	5	17	94	.325	304	449	36	.954
1939	Boston	Amer.	SS	143	520	97	160	33	3	19	107	.308	306	437	32	.959
1940	Boston	Amer.	SS-3B	149	548	104	156	35	6	24	111	.285	253	445	38	.948
1941	Boston	Amer.	1-S-3-O	143	518	98	161	38	8	6	95	.311	247	362	27	.958
1942	Boston	Amer.	1-SS-3B	45	79	7	24	3	0	4	24	.304	47	28	6	.926
1943	Boston	Amer.	3B	59	77	8	24	4	0	5	29	.312	12	18	1	.968
1944	Boston	Amer.	1B	76	191	24	46	7	0	5	28	.241	428	27	9	.981
1945	Boston (b)	Amer.	3B	3	8	1	3	0	0	0	1	.375	2	8	0	1.000
American League Totals				2074	7472	1222	2258	512	115	171	1409	.302	4235	5960	503	.953
National League Totals				50	105	11	27	3	2	0	14	.257	102	123	9	.962
Major League Totals				2124	7577	1233	2285	515	117	171	1423	.302	4337	6083	512	.953

a Traded to Boston Red Sox for shortstop Lyn Lary and $250,000, October 1934.
b Suffered fractured right leg, April 19, 1945, and out of action remainder of season.

WORLD SERIES RECORD

YEAR	CLUB	LEAGUE	POS.	G.	AB.	R.	H.	2B.	3B.	HR.	RBI.	B.A.	PO.	A.	E.	F.A.
1933	Washington	Amer.	SS	5	22	1	7	0	0	0	2	.318	7	15	1	.957

OL' DIZ: Which is what Dizzy Dean called himself at only 23 when he was a rangy, rawboned, smooth-working master of the mound.

DIZZY DEAN

Jay Hanna (Dizzy) Dean warmed up for the first time in the major leagues on the last day of the 1930 season, a lean, lanky, long-armed righthander with a smooth, flowing delivery. Standing nearby at a box, next to the St. Louis Cardinals' dugout at old Sportsman's Park, manager Charles E. (Gabby) Street talked to the St. Louis mayor, Victor J. Miller, who had come out to congratulate Street on a spectacular fourth-to-first, down-the-stretch drive to the National League pennant.

The mayor nodded toward the high cheekboned pitcher, then only 19 years old, if you could believe anything about Dizzy, including his birth certificate.

"How about that Dean, Gabby?" His Honor asked. "Is he going to be as good as they say?"

Street smiled. "I think he's going to be a great one, Mr. Mayor," said Gabby in one of the most prophetic double-barreled pronouncements ever, "but I'm afraid we'll never know from one minute to the next what he's going to do or say."

Street should have gone into the Hall of Fame with Dean for putting that one in the side pocket. Ol' Diz, as the gangling guy called himself from the outset, did become a great pitcher, his career cut short by arm injury when he should have been just reaching his peak.

And from the time he threw a three-hitter at Pittsburgh that first game, 3-1, helping himself with a hit, until he ballooned into a living legend as a baseball broadcaster, Dean fulfilled the second half of Street's prophecy, too.

Never has anyone, including the Great One, ever been sure what he'd say or do.

Ol' Diz helped thin the sparse gray thatch of Frank Frisch, manager of the Gashouse Gang, a colorful Depression-era ball club of which Dean was the most colorful member. And he never ceased to amaze, amuse—or anger—Frisch.

Like the time at Boston when an East St. Louis night-club comic, Johnny Perkins, as corpulent then as Dizzy became later, accompanied the Cardinals on a trip and heard Dean insist that he'd strike out Vince DiMaggio every time at bat the next day. The eldest ballplaying DiMaggio brother, a brilliant outfielder with power, struck out frequently and couldn't carry brother Joe's bat—or Dominic's, either.

Still, to fan any hitter four times isn't easy, as Perkins knew, and he offered a friendly bet that Dean couldn't do it. It was a small thing, no doubt, though later Ol' Diz would play golf for high stakes and was called in for some embarrassing questions in a Detroit gambling probe. The pitcher remembered the Boston bet with Perkins as only a nickel, to be redoubled, etc., if he kept striking out Vince, so that maybe no more than 80 cents cash was involved.

But for money, marbles or fried channel cat with hush puppies, Dean was a deep-dyed-in-Dixie competitor. He whiffed DiMaggio three times and then quickly fired across two strikes as he faced the Boston outfielder a fourth time in the ninth inning with two out and the tying run on second base.

Suddenly, Vince got a piece of the ball, lifting a high foul behind the plate and toward the visitors' dugout. Young Bruce Ogrodowski, rookie Redbird catcher, ripped off his mask and headed for the ball, fist thumping his glove, a confident sign that he'd make a game-ending catch.

To Frisch's consternation in the dugout, Dean thundered down off the hill toward Ogrodowski, hands cupped to his mouth, screaming:

"Drop it ... drop it...."

Startled, Ogrodowski looked at Dean.

"Damn it, if you want to catch me again, drop it," Dizzy demanded.

Ogrodowski permitted the ball to fall, and Frisch, leaping to his feet, cracked his head on the concrete roof of the dugout. Before the dazed manager could recover, Dean calmly had gone back to the mound and fired—no, "fogged" is the word he always used—a third strike past DiMaggio. Thus Diz protected, in order, his pride, that 80 cents or whatever it was and, oh, yes, the ball game.

Dizzy was capable of the unexpected from the time he was choppin' cotton as the son of a poor sharecropper in Arkansas and Oklahoma. When a neighbor friend lost a son and grieved deeply over his loss, young Jay Hanna was quite comforting. He allowed as how it would be neighborly to change his name to that of the man's dead youth.

So Jay Hanna became Jerome Herman and if that doesn't throw you, you must be as perceptive as the Army sergeant who nicknamed him Dizzy at Fort Sam Houston when the skinny, big-footed country kid was pulling a peacetime hitch for Uncle Sam. These were—understand!—roots of an obscure background at least before author Bob Gregory in Tulsa promised to rearrange if not destroy Deans image in an interesting book.

Dean's predilection for the unexpected never was more evident than in the 1934 World Series, the one in which he and brother Paul—Me 'n' Paul, as Dizzy called 'em—scored two victories each over the Detroit Tigers, a club that had four future Hall of Famers as did the Cardinals.

Catcher Mickey Cochrane, first baseman Hank Greenberg, second baseman Charley Gehringer and left fielder Goose Goslin of the Tigers were on their way to Cooperstown. So, too, were Cardinals' second baseman Frank Frisch, left fielder Joe Medwick, pitcher Jesse Haines and, naturally, Dean himself.

Ol' Diz had a ball for himself from the time the Cardinals arrived at Navin Field for a pre-Series look and found the Tigers working out. Dean, in street clothes, took a bat out of a surprised Tiger's hands, stepped into the batting cage, hit a pitch into the left-field seats and said, "That's the way to do it, fellas."

Dean, the National League's last 30-game winner that year, won the Series opener, 8-3, and apologized for pitching poorly. He served as a pinch-runner in the fourth game and, leaping to break up a double play, was hit smack on the head by Billy Rogell, Detroit's shortstop, and was carried off the field.

You couldn't hurt Ol' Diz by hitting him on the head. Not seriously, anyway. Shucks, I saw him react slowly on a hot, steaming day, pitching against the Giants, when former teammate Burgess Whitehead caromed a line drive off Dean's head and into the left-field bullpen—on the fly—for a double.

So when newspaper headlines told the story— "X-Rays of Dean's Head Show Nothing"—Dizzy came out of the hospital and pitched the next day in the fifth game of the '34 Series, losing a tough one to Tommy Bridges, 3-1.

The Tigers, therefore, took a 3-2 lead in the Series, but Dizzy's brother, Paul, a 21-year-old rookie, battled to his second victory, 4-3, sending the Series to a seventh and final game.

There was no open date for Series travel after the second and fifth games, as now, so that Dizzy Dean would have to come back for the seventh game with just one day's rest. Besides, he'd pitched 11 times in the tense month of September, winning seven

games and helping save three. In the final nine National League games, when the Cardinals caught and then passed the slumping New York Giants, he'd pitched four complete-game victories, three of them shutouts, including one on the final day.

So the rangy righthander really had worked too often, Manager Frisch told the press after the sixth game, suggesting that lefthander Bill Hallahan would be the Cardinals' pitcher in the windup. A steaming Dean charged into the showers, where Frisch slipped in for the showdown the manager slyly sought.

"Dawgonnit, Frank," Dean protested, "I don't see how you can even think of pitching Hallahan tomorrow when I've brought you this far."

The Dutchman, as Dizzy ordinarily called Frisch, let the 23-year-old pitcher plead for the assignment and then promise to get a good night's sleep, which is what the manager wanted most. Then Frisch said the job was Dean's.

"And remember, Jerome," Frisch said, "if you win that ball game tomorrow, it can be worth $50,000 to you now and more over the years."

For a pitcher earning only $7,500—remember, this was deep in the Depression—50 grand had to sound, well, just grand.

Which is the way Dizzy felt for game No. 7. He posed for pictures with his good friend, Will Rogers, the cowboy humorist who spoke his same twang of the Southwest. He didn't horse around as he did in earlier games at Detroit, where he'd draped a tiger skin over himself and played a tuba for the first time, predicting he would "twist the tail of the pussy cats." But he still had time for the gamemanship that made him deadly in later life on the golf links.

Walking behind Elden Auker, submarine-throwing righthander who was warming up to start the blue-chip ball game for Detroit, Dean paused, shook his head and then said airily, as Auker glowered:

"You don't expect to get anyone out with that stuff, do you, podnuh?"

The game, however, was scoreless until the third inning when Ol' Diz, leading off, hit what amounted to a routine single to left field. Years later, justifiably, the Great One was proud because of the Pandora's Box he opened with his hitting and his hustle.

Always a good athlete, a loping runner who could let out, Dean watched Goslin in left field handle the ball casually. Rounding first base, Diz took off unexpectedly for second base and beat the startled Goslin's weak, late throw with a hook slide that, viewed today in films, is a classic.

The double meant far more than one base. When Pepper Martin, next up, grounded to Greenberg at the first baseman's right, Hank would have had an easy play at second if Dean had been on first. But now, required to make the stop backhanded, then wheel and throw across his body to Auker covering first, Greenberg couldn't retire Martin on a bang-bang play that went for an infield hit.

So instead of a man on first, one out, St. Louis had runners on first and third, none down. And when Martin quickly stole second, both runners were in scoring position, creating a problem for Detroit and leading to questionable strategy by Manager Mickey Cochran.

The great catcher ordered Jack Rothrock passed carefully to fill the bases, setting up a double play situation. But Frisch, even in his athletic dotage a money player, slugged a bases-clearing double, leading to a decisive seven-run inning, which had been set up by Dizzy Dean's derring-do. The Great One tied a Series record with two hits that inning.

As the score mounted, so did Dean's enjoyment. When he began to cut up and laugh as he turned back the Tigers, taking particular delight in teasing Greenberg, Frisch stormed in from second base and threatened to remove him from the game.

"Aw, c'mon, Frank, you wouldn't dare take out Ol' Diz when he's pitching a shutout," Dean said.

"The hell I wouldn't," said Frisch. "Just try me. Just lose Greenberg."

Dizzy struck him out, the ninth time Hank had fanned in the Series. Despite the interruption for a barrage aimed at Medwick after a baseline incident with Marvin Owen, the Detroit third baseman, Dean breezed to a laughable 11-0 climax to an exciting World Series. And with personal appearances, endorsements and other benefits of that season, the Dizzy who wasn't so Dizzy earned about $40,000.

As a pitcher with the Cardinals, for whom he won 82 games and lost just 32 over one three-year stretch, 1934 through '36, Dean got up to $25,500, the highest salary paid a National League pitcher until better times and a big bonus paid to young Johnny Antonelli prompted Johnny Sain of the Boston Braves to stage a brief sitdown strike at the All-Star break in 1948.

So Ol' Diz was off base and merely trying to stick the needle in his former boss, Sam Breadon, when he would tell how little he was paid the year he won 30. He was annoyed, for one thing, because Breadon forever removed competition from the Redbirds' radio broadcasts when he gave exclusive rights in 1947 to establishment of a network. Dean, then airing both the Cardinals' and Browns' games, was with the wrong beer sponsor and with the wrong station.

The gregarious, good-natured big guy with the blue eyes, wide grin and western white hat could be spiteful at times, just as he could be difficult when he was a skinny kid wearing No. 17 and mowing down batters in a manner that brought him a 150-83 record, a good one that would have been great if he hadn't been hurt.

Even giving or taking a year in his age, Ol' Diz had won 133 big league ball games before he was 27. And if he'd followed his inclination—and his suitcase—as he wanted to at the All-Star interval in 1937, he might have escaped the unfortunate early end to what well might have been one of the greatest pitching careers.

In addition to supreme confidence, Dean had developed excellent control and a good curve and change-up to go with his high hard one, but when he was unable to "rare back and fog 'er through," as he used to put it, he became just another pitcher.

Even so, sore arm or not, forced to lob the ball side-armed rather than crank up and let fly with a fluid three-quarter delivery, Ol' Diz still managed to contribute a 7-1 record to the Cubs in 1938, after he had been sold to the Wrigleys for three players and $185,000. He walked just eight batters in 75 innings and posted a 1.80 earned-run average.

Dean had been in drydock for a considerable time when the surging Cubs collared sagging Pittsburgh in late September at Wrigley Field. Even the highly competitive Dean did a double-take when manager Gabby Hartnett asked him to pitch the pivotal middle contest of the decisive three-game series. But using cunning, control and changing speeds, Ol' Diz blanked the Pirates into the ninth, 2-0, before giving way to wheelhorse Bill Lee, who wild-pitched home a run, then preserved the victory that put the Cubs in first place to stay.

Hartnett, playing a hunch, started Dean in the second game of the 1938 World Series at Chicago. Dizzy's nuthin' ball was painfully apparent, but his soft curves and off-stride pitches were so well directed that he held the slugging Yankees at bay until the eighth inning. By then, actually, he should have been 3-0 if, weirdly, third baseman Stan Hack and shortstop Bill Jurges hadn't bumped heads on a slow second-inning grounder that trickled into leftfield with—of all people—the pitcher in pursuit of the ball.

Still, Diz led by a run into the eighth when he thought he'd slipped a third strike past Frank Crosetti, the Yankee shortstop and leadoff man. Crosetti then rapped a full-count pitch over the left field wall for a two-run homer.

As Crosetti trotted around the bases, Dean circled the pitcher's mound, cussing and fussing at the batter all the way. Finally, as Frank stepped on home plate with the run that put the Yankees ahead to stay, Dean said:

"And, furthermore, if I'd had my old fast ball, you wouldn't have seen the ball."

To which Crosetti replied graciously, "Darned if I don't think you're right, Diz."

In the clubhouse later, a downcast Dean was startled—and pleased—to look up and see Connie Mack. The baseball institution patted Dizzy on the back and said, "My boy, you've given me one of the greatest thrills I ever had. It was magnificent, but it must have hurt you terribly...."

As late as the last day of the 1947s season, when he was six years out of baseball and already beginning to bulge at the seams, Dean was given permission generously by the Cubs' Phil Wrigley, a man he respected highly, to pitch the final game of the season for the Browns. After all, he still was on Chicago's voluntarily retired list.

Broadcasting for the bumbling Browns, Ol' Diz hadn't been able to resist a remark here or there about the quality of what he was watching, which was pretty horrible. So, shrewdly, club president Bill DeWitt challenged him to try to do better himself, aware that the magic name of the popular pitcher and play-by-play announcer would draw a crowd.

Ol' Diz worked out a few times with the Browns and then toed the rubber for them in the season windup against the White Sox, still unable to throw hard, but still able to catch the corners with the changing speeds and curves. The overweight Great One worked four innings, yielding three hits and one walk, but not a run.

He'd have kept going, too, if he hadn't been too good at bat for his own good. In the fourth inning, he hit safely to leftfield, delighting the crowd and, sliding into second base, the out-of-shape pitcher pulled a leg muscle. He got up, limping, and his wife, Pat, seated in a box next to the Browns' dugout, leaned over and yelled to manager Muddy Ruel:

"Get him out of there before he kills himself."

Pat Dean, the former Patricia Nash of Bond, Miss., a Houston sales girl when Dizzy met and married her in 1931, frequently had the last word in matters dealing with Ol' Diz. At times it even had been profane, but, usually, it had been for the former pitcher's own good.

No wife probably ever acted in her husband's best interests more conscientiously than Pat Dean, who can be even more outspoken and direct than Jay, which is what she called Dean. Back in 1935, for instance, when Diz was holding out in Bradenton, Fla., Branch Rickey dropped by impolitely late one night and awakened the young couple.

"I'm not here to talk contract, Jerome," said Rickey pontifically, "but just to find out why Mrs. Dean doesn't like me."

Diz started to apologize, as Rickey shrewdly anticipated. "Now, Mr. Rickey, she really is fond of you," Dean began, but he never finished.

Pat interrupted. "He's a stinker," she said.

The former Patricia Nash, childless, babied Ol' Diz over the years when, after he had weathered cataract operations, she suffered heart attacks that prompted Jay to give her the attention she'd always shown him. As a good-hearted guy, by nature a gambler who had won as much as $8,000 on a round of golf, Dizzy could have lived life in constant jeopardy of easy-come, easy-go. But Pat insisted that they save $1,200 out of the $3,000 he earned the year they were married and, though they were quietly generous, she saw to it with even occasional hardboiled protectiveness that no one took advantage of her man, financially or otherwise.

The affluent Deans, whose wealth was made largely after Dizzy's playing days, divided their time between a farm in Bond, Miss., and a home in Arizona. They once had a handsome ranch-style bungalow in Phoenix, then later spent the winter months at a fashionable hotel so that Pat could take it easy and Ol' Diz could skin someone on the golf course. He was invariably just good enough to win the day's play.

In Mississippi, they thought so highly of Pat Dean's husband that they wanted Dizzy to run for governor at one time. Wisely, though flattered, Dizzy bowed out. Even though he could afford a pay cut from Falstaff Brewing Corp. to take the governor's salary in Mississippi, it just wouldn't do to keep him from the "darndest catfishin' you ever seen."

The fried "eat" sweet corn and hush puppies he favored contributed to the 6-3 Dean's bulk, which at times was uncomfortably close to 300 pounds, more than 100 greater than in his playing career.

On the golf course one time, President Dwight D. Eisenhower asked, "Dizzy, for a man who plays golf so well, how can you permit yourself to get so overweight?"

Dean had a ready answer. "Mr. President," he said, "I was on a diet for 25 years. Now that I'm makin' some money, I'm makin' sure I eat good to make up for the lean years."

They were lean, all right, leaner than Jay Hanna Dean grew into after he was born in Lucas, Ark., in 1911. Sure, he told three reporters one day that he was born in two other states and on two other dates, too, but as he confided to his favorite chronicler, J. Roy Stockton of the *St. Louis Post-Dispatch*:

"I give 'em each a scoop, Roy, so that their bosses can't bawl the three of 'em out for gettin' the same story."

If at times reading "The Gashouse Gang and a Couple of Other Guys," you wonder which is the more amusing, Dean or Stockton, meaning the one and only Jay Hanna or the Dizzy as seen, heard—and helped—by the talented, puckish baseball writer, don't look at me. I find 'em both funny. They represented one of the happiest of coincidences by which a fresh, colorful character came along to be covered by an extremely able writer who not only wouldn't stand in the way of a good story, but even might be willing now and then to make it just a bit better.

Except, however, for the time that brother Elmer (Goober) Dean was left behind a string of cars at a railroad crossing and not seen for years when the family was scratching a pitiful living out of the land, there wasn't much funny in Dizzy's boyhood. His mother died when he was three years old and Paul was an infant. Pa—Albert Dean—drove 'em from job to job in Arkansas, Oklahoma and Texas in a sputtering jalopy. More than one community like Holdenville, Okla., can claim proudly, "Didya know that Dizzy Dean chopped cotton here?"

Jay left the school books behind after the fourth grade. At the tender age of 10, he was getting up at five in the morning and picking as much as 400 pounds of cotton a day. No wonder the Army was tempting with a three-year hitch when he was only 16. After all, Uncle Sam offered new shoes, clothes, three squares a day—and a chance to play baseball.

Shortly before his Army enlistment was to end, with his father's encouragement and $120 they'd scratched up, the brilliant pitcher that wise Army sergeant had called "Dizzy" bought himself out of service, a practice in those peace-time days. He took a job with the public service company in San Antonio so that he could pitch for the company baseball team. And that's where Don Curtis, a scout for the Cardinals' Texas League farm club at Houston, signed him in the fall of 1929.

At St. Joseph, Mo., in 1930, Dizzy topped the Western League in pitching, I. O. U.'s and wild stunts. Man, imagine getting paid to pitch! He rented rooms at three addresses, asked hitters what they wanted thrown to them and where—and then poured the ball past them.

When he was 17-8, the eccentric kid was transferred to Houston, where he pitched a night game, won by a 12-1 score and then walked into club President Fred Ankenman's office the next day and apologized.

"I'm awfully sorry," he said. "I promise if you'll give me another chance, it'll never happen again. Can you imagine them bums getting a run off me?"

A few nights later, arriving in the hotel past curfew, the 19-year-old pitcher met the club president in the lobby.

"Well, I guess me and you will get the devil for this, Mr. Ankenman," the boy said, reassuringly, "but I won't say nuthin' about it if you don't."

After his major league debut in the final game of the 1930 season, Dizzy swaggered through spring training in '31, reporting later for practice than the sportswriters. When Gabby Street rebuked him, the hurt kid would strike out Al Simmons, Jimmie Foxx and Mickey Cochrane of the world champion Athletics in one inning and then threaten to go back to Houston.

A pennant-winning ball club didn't need to put up with insubordination. When the cocky kid was optioned back to Houston, relief pitcher Jim Lindsey cracked, "A world's record—it's the first time a ball club ever lost 30 games in one day."

Without Dean, the 1931 Cardinals won 101 games, took the pennant by 13 games and upset the Athletics in a bid for their third straight world championship. With Dizzy, that veteran, well-balanced team might have been the best ever.

So Dizzy cost himself a probable World Series share in '31, but by returning to Houston, where he won 26 games and struck out 303 batters, he met Pat Nash, who declined in a whirlwind romance to be married at home plate. Dizzy borrowed two bucks from a friend for the marriage license. And Pat took over the finances for a happy-go-lucky lad who'd been so irresponsible that in spring training the Cardinals had put him on a dollar-a-day allowance. Pat fortunately didn't reform or remake her Jay, but she helped to moderate him. And they had a happy, profitable marriage.

As a rookie in 1932, when a poorly conditioned championship club collapsed to a tie for sixth and seventh place, the bony, uncombed Dean was wild, but effective with a high-kicking fastball. He won 18, lost 15 and led the National League in strikeouts.

A year later, another second-division season, he was 20-18, again first in strikeouts. He began to skip exhibition games, collect fines and became a "name" overnight. On July 30, 1933, he struck out 17 Chicago Cubs, which existed as a major league record until Bob Feller, Sandy Koufax, Don Wilson, Steve Carlton and Tom Seaver came along.

Dean enjoyed horseplay with Pepper Martin, Rip Collins and other fun-loving members of the Gashouse Gang, but he had a loose lip, too, and he found himself overmatched whenever he'd criticize the fielding of the smaller, but muscular, left fielder, Joe Medwick.

"Dawgonnit, that Medwick don't fight fair," Dizzy complained. "You argue with him and he whops you even before you've had a chance to speak your piece."

When brother Paul came up from Columbus in 1934, observers tried to tab 'em as Dizzy and Daffy, but the alliteration wasn't apt. If Dizzy wasn't really dizzy, certainly Paul was not at all daffy, though queasy would have fit after he'd watched the Redbirds' batboy, Kayo Brown, a boxing protege of Pepper Martin, get his block knocked off in a prize ring. P. Dean suffered an upset stomach.

He was quiet and poker-faced then, though he has become articulate, and considerably more affable in recent years, running his own baseball school in suburban Dallas and also serving as athletic director at the University of Plano, an institution designed to help young men who need remedial reading.

Paul got his lumps early in the 1934 season, but manager Frisch stuck with him, and brother Dizzy, bragging more about his brother's speed than his own pitching stuff, forecast reassuringly that "Me'n Paul will win 45 games."

For once, Ol' Diz was a piker. P. Dean chipped in with 19 victories, J. Dean with 30, despite two sitdown strikes. One was for more money for Paul, then getting only $3,000 a season, and the other for back pay after a fine and suspension for failing to show up for an exhibition game train trip to Detroit.

It was mid-August and the Cardinals were a half-dozen games behind the league-leading Giants.

Dizzy didn't think Frisch could afford to set down his best pitchers.

"The hell I can't," snapped Frisch. "I'll pitch Hallahan, Carleton, Walker and the two old men (Haines and Vance) and we'll win."

They did, too, seven out of eight at a critical period when Dizzy was balking at paying for uniforms he'd torn up. After a hearing with the baseball commissioner, Judge Landis, the costs to Dizzy were $100 for missing the exhibition game, $350 for seven days' salary and $36 for two torn uniforms. Paul was fined $100.

The Deans were miffed at Frisch, momentarily, but they took out their spite on the foe and they came down the stretch like gangbusters. At Brooklyn in September, Dizzy pitched a three-hitter in the first game of a doubleheader and Paul a no-hitter in the second contest.

"Gee, if I'd known Paul was gonna do it, I'd done it, too," said Dizzy, who had held the Dodgers hitless until the eighth inning.

A victory by Paul the next-to-last day of the season put the Cardinals into first place and Dizzy shut out Cincinnati in the clincher, 9-0.

Setting the tone for the raucous, rowdy, rough-sliding, knockdown pitching of the 1934 World Series, Dizzy apologized after throwing a home run ball to Hank Greenberg his 8-3 opening game victory.

"Why, that Greenberg hit a curve that hung up there so that a kid could have hit it. I could bring four National League teams over here and win the American League."

In the next couple of seasons, Dizzy was as good as in 1934, on the strength of 28-12 and 24-13 seasons and working in and out of turn. The Cardinals were just a bit short both seasons, however, losing in 1935 to the incredible 21-game winning streak of the Cubs and in 1936 to the Giants.

The Giants' great lefthander, Carl Hubbell, bested Dizzy often in their famous duels of the mid-'30s, but Hubbell would say, "For a few years, Diz was as great as any pitcher."

In 1937, after umpire George Barr had called a critical balk on him in a game at St. Louis, Dizzy spoke at a church supper in nearby Belleville, Ill., and was quoted as labeling Barr and National League President Ford Frick as "the two biggest crooks in baseball."

Frick suspended him, pending an apology, but Dizzy came up with one of the best-remembered quotes of his career. "I ain't signin' nuthin'," he said, and he didn't, winning a newspaper decision when the National League president lifted the suspension.

So he was 12-7 with a fourth-place ball club, a likable braggart, the popoff who would make good most of his boasts and the last gasp of gas in the Gashouse Gang when he tried to take French leave and pass up the 1937 All-Star Game in Washington.

When he showed up in St. Louis, even wife Pat advised him that he owed it to baseball, and when he flew to Washington, then a six-hour flight away, owner Sam Breadon accompanied him.

A shutout pitcher for three innings in the All-Star Game the year before, Dizzy started for the National League in '37 and was one out away from a three-inning runless stint. Then he shook off his catcher, Gabby Hartnett, and insisted on a fastball on a full-count pitch to Lou Gehrig, who hammered a two-run homer.

The next batter, Earl Averill of Cleveland, hit a hot smash back through the box. Dean, despite the full free follow-through of a hard-throwing pitcher with a smooth delivery, ordinarily was quick enough to recover his fielding position because he not only was a pretty good hitter and baserunner, but also a fifth infielder, defensively. Averill, however, had a unique habit of knocking pitchers off the mound with line shots through the middle, and his hummer cracked the big toe of Dean's firmly planted left foot.

Dizzy was hurt, painfully, and the toe was put in a splint. The Cardinals' surgeon, Dr. Robert F. Hyland, cautioned him not to pitch too soon. But for a guy who ducked an exhibition at the drop of a railroad schedule—he preferred trains to planes—

Dean was highly competitive and a team man who prided himself on showing up rather than showing off when it counted.

Frisch needed him, and Dizzy volunteered to pitch in Boston, where the perceptive and gentlemanly manager of the Braves, Bill McKechnie, coaching third base, counselled him:

"Don't, Jerome, don't. You'll hurt your arm by favoring that foot with an unnatural stride and delivery."

Late in the game when Diz was pitching to shortstop Bill Urbanski in a tight game, he felt something pop and his arm dangled at his side.

"You've done it, Jerome. You've done it," said McKechnie in prophetic anguish that Dizzy Dean never forgot.

Gone was the fastball that once was so good that in the same ballpark where it left him forever—Braves Field—Ol' Diz once had faced the Boston players and, grinning, taunted 'em this way:

"Tell you what I'm going to do, fellas. We won't use no signs today, and I'll throw nuthin' except fastballs—honest!"

They knew what was coming and he still shut 'em out.

When the bottom dropped out of his playing career, the loquacious, lively-larynxed Dean found himself in front of a microphone, as you'd know if only because you'd seen movie actor Dan Dailey play Dizzy in a so-so film of his life.

Pride of St. Louis, as they called it most uninspiringly, was good for $50,000 for Ol' Diz, but it was good for fewer laughs than the Great One himself could generate.

As a radio announcer, he mangled the language so badly in St. Louis that school teachers protested the syntax-fracturing. Kids were talking how a guy "slud" into second base and the runners returned to their "respectable" bases.

Dean won 'em over, of course, just as he did most of the nation's baseball fans, especially the rural folks who talked his twang and homespun humor. New generations discovered him nationally, through television, just as St. Louis had in radio during the weather-enforced censorship of World War II when he explained a rain delay at the old ballpark by saying:

"I can't tell you what it's doin', folks, but if you'll stick your head out the window, you'll find out."

By his own modest self-evaluation, Dean wasn't the greatest pitcher, but he was "amongst 'em," as he put it. And whether squatting on the field in 100-degree weather, building a fire when seated with a blanket over his head or bursting into song on one of his broadcasts to yodel the ballad of the "Wabash Cannonball," Ol' Diz dedicated a lifetime to fulfilling Gabby Street's prophecy the day he broke into the big leagues:

Before he died in 1974 at only 63, no one ever knew from one minute to the next what Jay Hanna (Dizzy) Dean would say or do.

JAY HANNA (DIZZY) DEAN
Born January 16, 1911, at Lucas Ark.
Died July 17, 1974, at Reno, Nev.
Height 6-3 Weight 202
Threw and batted righthanded.
Named to Hall of Fame, 1953

YEAR	CLUB	LEAGUE	G.	IP.	W.	L.	Pct.	H.	R.	ER.	SO.	BB.	ERA.
1930	St. Joseph	Western	32	217	17	8	.680	204	118	89	134	77	3.69
1930	Houston	Texas	14	85	8	2	.800	62	31	27	95	49	2.86
1930	St. Louis	National	1	9	1	0	1.000	3	1	1	5	3	1.00
1931	Houston	Texas	41	304	26	10	.722	210	71	52	303	90	1.57
1932	St. Louis	National	46	286	18	15	.545	280	122	105	191	102	3.30
1933	St. Louis	National	48	293	20	18	.526	279	113	99	199	64	3.04
1934	St. Louis	National	50	312	30	7	.811	288	110	92	195	75	2.65
1935	St. Louis	National	50	324	28	12	.700	326	128	112	182	82	3.11
1936	St. Louis	National	51	315	24	13	.649	310	128	111	195	53	3.17
1937	St. Louis (a)	National	27	197	13	10	.565	200	76	59	120	33	2.70
1938	Chicago	National	13	75	7	1	.875	63	20	15	22	8	1.80
1939	Chicago	National	19	96	6	4	.600	98	40	36	27	17	3.38
1940	Chicago	National	10	54	3	3	.500	68	35	31	18	20	5.17
1940	Tulsa	Texas	21	142	8	8	.500	149	69	50	51	19	3.17
1941	Chicago (b)	National	1	1	0	0	.000	3	3	2	1	0	18.00
1947	St. Louis (c) (d)	American	1	4	0	0	.000	3	0	0	0	1	0.00
American League Totals			1	4	0	0	.000	3	0	0	0	1	0.00
National League Totals			316	1962	150	83	.644	1918	776	663	1155	457	3.04
Major League Totals			317	1966	150	83	.644	1921	776	663	1155	458	3.04

a Traded to Chicago Cubs for pitchers Curt Davis and Clyde Shoun, outfielder Tuck Stainback and $185,000, April 16, 1938.
b Released as player and signed as coach with Chicago Cubs, May 14, 1941; retired as coach to accept baseball broadcasting job in St. Louis, July 12, 1941.
c Signed by St. Louis Browns to pitch final game as gate attraction.
d Made promotional appearances with Sioux Falls and Denver in Western League and Fargo-Moorehead in Northern in 1941; with Clovis in West Texas-New Mexico in 1949.

WORLD SERIES RECORD

YEAR	CLUB	LEAGUE	G.	IP.	W.	L.	Pct.	H.	R.	ER.	SO.	BB.	ERA.
1934	St. Louis	National	3	26	2	1	.667	20	6	5	17	5	1.73
1938	Chicago	National	2	8 1/3	0	1	.000	8	6	6	2	1	6.48
World Series Totals			5	34 1/3	2	2	.500	28	12	11	19	6	2.88

EASY DOES IT: Bill Dickey was a smooth, graceful catcher but a hard hitter for the Yankees in his Hall of Fame career.

BILL DICKEY

Bill Dickey, whose home run had wrapped up the 1943 World Series for the New York Yankees, was in the warm haze of happy celebration when he stepped into an elevator hours later at the Chase Hotel in St. Louis. He was addressed by a soldier whose face was familiar.

"I'll bet you don't remember me," said the grinning G. I., a former journeyman ballplayer.

"I can't place the name," said Dickey, smiling, "but I know how we pitched to you."

One of the sharpest, smoothest and best catchers ever, the tall, knock-kneed Dickey might not remember a name, but he wouldn't forget any facet or phase of a job at which he excelled for the Yankees for 16 years, until he himself followed the baseball journeyman and many other big league ballplayers into military service.

Just before he went into the Navy, where he became a lieutenant commander with service in the Pacific, the ruddy, rangy receiver with the brown hair, high cheekbones and gray eyes proved that at 36 he still was outstanding at the plate and behind it.

In 1943, for only the second time in his illustrious career as Mickey Cochrane's competitor for No. 1 catching honors, Dickey did not strap on the harness of his trade for 100 or more games. But he hit a robust .351 and then capped his last full playing season by teeing off on the Cardinals' Mort Cooper for a homer that gave Spud Chandler and the Yankees a 2-0 wrap-up in the fifth and final game of the World Series.

Watching Dickey do so well at an advanced baseball age, it must have seemed hard to believe he'd ever been better. But in a career in which he averaged .313, he'd actually been so consistently good that it's harder to believe he never won the Most Valuable Player award.

Bill was a hit from the time he batted .324 in 1929, his first full season and, except for 1935, he never finished below .300 until he began to tail off in 1940. Then, he still was good enough to spread the frosting on the cake in '43 when he played in his eighth World Series with the Yankees.

A rookie who watched with awe and admiration in the 1928 World Series as Babe Ruth, Lou Gehrig and associates decimated the Cardinals in four straight games, Dickey went on with good friend and roommate Gehrig to become the link between the Yankees' pennant winners of the '20s and their championship clubs of the '30s and early '40s. As a coach, he stayed on until 1960, just before the Yankees' dynasty began to crumble.

In Dickey's admittedly prejudiced opinion, Gehrig was the greatest Yankee of them all, but he also had affection and respect for Ruth, whose stature as the most prominent player he understood and appreciated.

Smiling, Dickey could relate in his Arkansas twang the tale of how he hit two triples against Washington, each time just after manager Walter Johnson of the Senators had moved his center fielder.

When Johnson again shifted the center fielder,

shading him farther to the right, and Bill hit the ball to left-center for an apparent record-tying third triple, the Yankee catcher laughed so hard rounding the bases that he was thrown out at third.

When Dickey returned to the Yankees' dugout, Ruth needled him. "Pittridge," said the Babe, "I can outrun you."

The veteran Bambino called the young catcher "Pittridge" because, as Dickey remembered, some of the old Yankees spoke of partridge when they meant quail. And outdoorsman Dickey always was talking about bird hunting.

One rib led to another and finally Dickey was insisting he could outrun Ruth and the Babe was betting he couldn't. Bill gulped when Ruth set the stakes at 100 bucks, a sizable sum to a young player, but he couldn't back down.

The match race was set for the next day before the game, across the outfield grass. Dickey wanted to make it for 100 yards, but the aging Bambino insisted on 75. To Dickey's relief, he caught the veteran outfielder about two-thirds of the way along the makeshift course, which was lined with teammates who had made side bets.

"The old-timers bet on the Babe and the young ones on me," said Dickey. "I couldn't have beat him when he was younger, but I was happy the way it came out."

In the pranks of the Yankee clubhouse—and some of the hijinks were pretty low down—Dickey once got the best of the Babe by breaking a raw egg into one of Ruth's baseball shoes. The Babe, who liked to play rough, didn't think the yolk was a joke, son, and for a few hairy minutes the embarrassed young Dickey thought he would have to fight the menacing, growing superstar.

But then the Babe laughed, changed his sanitary understockings and the prank was forgiven and, presumably, forgotten.

The Babe, who liked a good laugh, must have been amused in 1934, his last year with the Yankees, when Dickey, by then an accepted master of the mitt, suddenly found himself trying—unsuccessfully—to catch Burleigh Grimes' spitball.

With a runner on first base, a spitter dipped below Dickey's glove for a passed ball. When another spitter again eluded the clever catcher, the runner advanced to third, and the redfaced Dickey called time and walked to the mound.

"What do you want me to throw now?" purred Grimes, sarcastically.

"The damned spitter again," said Bill, "but be ready to cover home plate."

This was, of course, merely an amusing interlude in the artistry of the 6-1½, 185-pound Dickey, whose height was regarded early as a handicap, yet eventually became an asset.

"At least they wouldn't throw the ball over my head," quipped the drawling Dickey, who really had few passed balls. One year he had none at all.

Learning how to handle low pitches, Bill became a master of quick movement behind the plate finding body balance so rapidly that he became in later years the tutor for his most eminent Yankee successor, Yogi Berra. "Bill learned me his experience," said the inimitable Berra.

Dickey catching, had a quick, strong arm, which wasn't too accurate at first, but he began to throw strikes, and he revolutionized play at his position by discarding the bedpillow-sized mitt for a lightweight catcher's glove which seemed no larger than a first baseman's and proved just as maneuverable.

Dickey caught four Yankee Hall of Fame pitchers—Herb Pennock, WaiteHoyt, Red Ruffing and Lefty Gomez.

Of the pitchers Dickey saw, Lefty Grove had the most speed and Bob Feller the most all around stuff, but Ruffing and Gomez were his favorite Yankee pitchers, even though Bill never knew from one minute to the next what Lefty might do or say.

One day with the bases loaded, Gomez beckoned him to the mound for a conference. Knowing that the cool Castillian never got rattled and didn't need calming down, a puzzled Dickey quickly analyzed the next hitter in his mind as he strode out to meet Gomez.

"Yes?" he said, giving it the rising inflection.

"Hey, Bill," said the unpredictable pitcher. "Do you have any extra bird dogs?"

"Criminy," Dickey exploded, "why do you ask a question like that at a time like this?"

Gomez shrugged his shoulders.

"I dunno," he said. "I ran into a guy last night who wanted to buy some bird dogs and I told him about you. So he said to ask you about it if I ever thought of it. Well, I just happened to think of it."

Yankee pitchers rarely shook off the suggestion of their thinking man's catcher, but one day Gomez crossed up Dickey, who stormed out from behind the plate.

"I signaled for a fastball and you threw me a curve," the catcher snapped.

"How are your bird dogs?" asked Lefty, trying to change the subject.

Dickey solved the problem of catching the fast-firing, nearsighted Gomez.

"I quit giving him signs," Bill said. "I'd set myself for the fastball and figure I could adjust to the curve. That was a helluva lot safer than being set for the curve and have that high, hard one of his smash against my mask."

Catchers must be careful, when giving a target for the pitcher, not to tip off the delivery with their hands, Dickey said, explaining:

"There's a tendency to hold the hands high for a fastball, low for a curve. A hitter taking a peek can see what you're doing. I'd coach our pitchers to throw at my knee for breaking pitches so that I could cross up the batter at times by keeping my hands high when a curve was coming."

William Malcolm Dickey was born at Bastrop, La., June 6, 1907, Scotch-Irish by descent, American by birth and an Arkansan as quick as his father, John Hardy Dickey, a Missouri Pacific Railroad man, could move to Kensett, Ark. The senior Dickey had seven children, four of them boys.

Bill's father pitched and caught at Memphis before the big leaguer was born. Bill's older brother, Gus, played second base and pitched in the East Arkansas Semi-pro League and would have been the best player in the family if he hadn't hurt his arm, Bill insisted. Younger brother, George, called Skeets, caught for the Boston Red Sox and Chicago White Sox, on and off, between 1935 and '47.

"Skeeter is my boss now and a good one," Bill said proudly at a Hall of Fame reunion in St. Louis baseball's centennial season. The Dickeys sold securities in Little Rock. Bill was crushed when Skeets died unexpectedly in 1972 at 61.

As a boy, Bill went through grade school at Kensett and spent his high school years at Searcy, Ark., four miles away. He pitched and played second base on the Kensett town team and when he entered Little Rock College, he developed a unique baseball partnership with one Jimmy Foley. They'd take turns pitching and then catching each other.

Foley also had a job catching for a team in Hot Springs, Ark., and, unable to make it one weekend, he urged Dickey to take his place. Bill didn't like the idea. Neither, for that matter, did the Hot Springs manager, Roy Gillenwater. But Gillenwater appreciated talent when he saw it—even in a larger package than usual for a catcher.

Lena Blackburne, manager of Little Rock's Southern Association ball club, came scouting a Hot Springs outfielder named Paul Phillips, but he saw tall, willowy catcher Dickey make one strong, powerful wild throw—and he shifted his attention.

On the back of his Elks membership card, Blackburne signed the 18-year-old Dickey to a Little Rock contract in 1925, much to the disgust of the Fort Smith club president, Blake Harper, who got a flat tire en route to Hot Springs to sign Dickey.

Harper, close to Branch Rickey, ultimately became concessionaire for the Cardinals and Browns in St. Louis.

He lamented how he might have had Dickey. But Blackburne wasn't much happier three years later when he was managing the Chicago White Sox, finding that Dickey would play against him, not for him.

The White Sox had a working agreement with Little Rock which farmed out the home-area athlete to Muskogee, Okla. and then to Jackson, Miss. Other big league clubs took for granted Chicago's interest in Dickey, but the Yankees didn't, which might explain why for many years through World War II St. Louis in the National League and New York in the American had far and away the best farm systems.

Chicago, it developed, would pass. Johnny Nee, a Yankee scout, wired Edward G. Barrow, prime minister of the New York baseball empire: "I will quit scouting if this boy does not make good."

Dickey, en route to a date with a cute chick and a chicken dinner, brushed off the man who approached him outside the ballpark at Jackson until he heard what he thought he heard.

"Did you say, 'New York YANKEES?'" inquired the young son of Dixie. He'd heard right, Nee assured him. Dickey forgot the chick and chicken dinner and spent time with Nee. He was delighted at the end of the 1927 season to read that his contract had been sold to New York. The stipulation was that he would spend the '28 season in Little Rock, where he hit .300 before getting to New York in time to catch a few games in September for the pennant-bound Yankees.

As Murderers' Row ripped through the foe in '27 and '28, zipping both Pittsburgh and St. Louis in one-sided World Series, there was only one position of uncertainty—behind the plate. John Grabowski, Benny Bengough and Pat Collins divided the catching.

By 1929, Dickey had become so entrenched as a rookie that manager Miller Huggins, who would die before the season's end, could observe:

"I made a mistake letting Muddy Ruel get away because I thought he was too small. Wally Schang did all right for us, but I can see now why Clark Griffith wanted to relieve us of Dickey when he was still at Little Rock. He's going to be a great one."

By Dickey's own severe self-analysis, the big boy

from Little Rock didn't come into his own until about 1934, which would be the year he boxed Burleigh Grimes' spitter. Evidence points strongly to the fact that Bill learned rapidly. He moved closer to the batter, crouched lower and, using the smaller mitt, became more flexible behind the plate and extremely dangerous at it.

By 1932, when the Yankees celebrated a return to the championship under Joe McCarthy, a man for whom Dickey had high regard, Bill was en route to what would be the first of several seasons of more than 20 homers and 100 RBIs. Even though limited to 108 games, he had 15 homers and 84 runs batted in, and his .310 average was the lowest of his first four full seasons.

The reason Dickey caught fewer games that year was an almost incomprehensible black mark in the career of a quiet man whose ability to keep his cool was almost as noteworthy as his overall accomplishments.

In the midst of a rough series with Washington, Carl Reynolds, a big outfielder of the Senators, slid hard and high into Dickey, upsetting the Yankees' catcher in more ways than one. When Reynolds started back to the plate, merely to touch it, Bill thought Carl meant to fight, and the Yankee catcher got in the first lick.

It was good, hard and expensive. Dickey broke Reynolds' jaw and was suspended 30 days. He also was fined $1,000 when his salary was about $14,000.

"I felt terrible about what I'd done and I deserved the punishment, which was considerable," Bill would say years later, at a loss to explain the blowup fully himself.

In the rough-language World Series of 1932 with the Chicago Cubs, whose niggardly treatment of former Yankee Mark Koenig had led to bitter bench-jockeying, Dickey stuck to his job. He did it splendidly, too, batting .438 in a four-game sweep for the Bronx Bombers.

Against the same club in 1938 he had 4-for-4 off Bill Lee in a 3-1 Series victory for batterymate Ruffing and batted .400. For eight Series, Dickey hit .255, driving in 24 runs in 38 games. His five home runs included the one that broke up the scoreless duel between Chandler and the Cardinals' Cooper in 1943.

The only losing Series of eight in which Dickey played was 1942, a five-game upset at the hands of the swift young Cardinals. So the blow in '43 represented sweet revenge.

"I doubt, though, that while playing I ever got quite the thrill I did out of the first Series game in 1949 when I was coaching," Dickey said one time in reminiscing with Dan Daniel for *The Sporting News.*

Brought back to the Bombers by Casey Stengel and George Weiss in Casey's first season as manager, Dickey worked to smooth out the wrinkles in the catching and throwing technique of Berra, a student who eventually crowded the teacher for accomplishments in the Yankee pinstripes.

The Cardinals, training in St. Petersburg, Fla., with the Yankees, also asked Dr. Dickey, the catching physician, to take a hand with their own young catcher, Joe Garagiola. And years later Dickey learned, to his amusement, that Brooklyn's brilliant new catcher, Roy Campanella, also profited by watching Bill work with both Berra and Garagiola.

In 1949, however, to get back to the thrill old team man Dickey described as his biggest, the Yankees didn't win the pennant until the final day of the regular season. They caught and then passed Boston in a decisive two-game series at Yankee Stadium. The World Series then began there with a duel between Allie Reynolds of the Yankees and Don Newcombe of the Brooklyn Dodgers.

"The situation was so tense into the bottom of the ninth," Dickey said, "and then Tommy Henrich hit one for a great 1-0 victory for us."

It's worth noting that Dickey's span of World Series experience extends from 1928, when Babe Ruth made a brilliant Series-ending catch of a foul off Frank Frisch's bat in St. Louis to the moment of truth in 1960 at Pittsburgh when the Pirates' Bill Mazeroski hit the ninth-inning, seventh-game homer that won the championship.

"And don't forget," Dickey quipped, "that I even stole a base in a (1938) World Series game."

Dickey's return to the Yankees for a string of several more pennants and world championships under Stengel was heartwarming after the last link of the Ruthian era had been cut off the payroll in September 1946.

Returning from service with other war veterans of a ball club that just couldn't find itself, Dickey caught infrequently in '46, his last playing season in the majors. In late May, he was as startled as the rest of baseball when it was announced that Joe McCarthy, ill and apparently feuding with Larry MacPhail, had resigned as manager. To Bill Dickey, the big man from Little Rock, went the honor—and challenge—of succeeding the highly successful field foreman for whom he'd played.

The appointment made sense because Dickey was a smart player and a respected performer, a vital figure in the Yankee tradition. He'd turned down chances to manage the Phillies for Bill Cox and the Braves for Bob Quinn at Boston. Don Barnes, operating the old St. Louis Browns, had approached the Yankees about him, too.

"I'd like to manage like Joe McCarthy, the greatest I ever saw," said Dickey the day he took over in 1946. But he was relieved of the job in favor of Johnny Neun on September 12.

"I had no hard feelings," Dickey said looking back, "and no bad feeling about not managing. I didn't enjoy it."

Back home in Little Rock, Bill managed the Travelers to a rousing last-place finish with an horrendous 51-103 record and finished up as a player at age 40. He went to bat 12 times and—what else?—got four hits for a .333 average.

His big league peak season had come exactly 10 years earlier when he hit .332 in 140 games, collecting 29 homers and driving in 133 runs.

Nervous exhaustion forced him out in 1957 when he was coaching for the Yankees, but selling securities Dickey never seemed more relaxed or happy. Until brother Skeets' death, he tremendously widened his personal contacts in Arkansas. Until age threw him a Grimes' spitter, he liked to hunt, and he played a good game of golf, but he no longer flew his private plane.

Dickey's wife was the former Violet Arnold, an attractive woman who performed on the New York stage in Earl Carroll's *Vanities* and also sang and danced in Florenz Ziegfeld's *Showboat*.

Dickey always did have good taste. Showman Carroll described Miss Arnold's hair as "a garment of gold" and referred to her eyes as "fountains of blue and white moonlight." When Yankee teammate Sam Byrd introduced the catcher from Dixie to the showgirl from Passaic, N. J., in 1932, the big man from Little Rock fell hard.

Bill and Vi were married after the 1932 season and Mrs. Dickey gave up her career. She and Bill had one daughter, Vickey, a widow. Dickey's grandson, Billy Stafford, learned the joy of fishing from the gray-thatched old catcher who looked trim enough to step up and hit one, if not to catch nine.

Dickey, scouting for the Yankees in the period when ill health kept him off the coaching lines, worked hard to sign a widely sought young Memphis catcher for the Bombers. He promised the boy a catcher's mitt. And when Tim McCarver signed instead with the St. Louis Cardinals, he was flabbergasted to find that Dickey still would make him the present of the mitt.

Why?

"I'd given my word," explained Dickey. "Besides, I liked the boy. And maybe I've been brainwashed so much down here in 'Cardinal territory' that I feel like I'm almost a member of the family."

When old friend Casey Stengel managed the Mets back when the expansion team was an amusing also-ran, Dickey took off from his job of selling stocks and municipal and corporate bonds for

Stevens, Inc., a Little Rock investment-banking firm. He accepted a summons from Stengel to spend a week working with the Mets' young catchers.

One of Stengel's veteran players interrogated the Hall of Fame catcher even more intently than the young men he'd been asked to tutor.

The inquisitive ballplayer wanted to know what position a catcher should be in to throw after receiving a pitch low and inside to a lefthanded batter.

"Balance is the thing, no matter where the ball is pitched," said Dickey. "The right foot must be properly balanced at all times or it is impossible to make a good throw."

Bill recognized a good and appreciative audience when he had one and continued:

"When Yogi Berra first broke in, he used to throw high and the ball often would sail over second base. The reason was that Yogi was stepping back before making the throw. He was not in balance. Once Yogi learned to move in, the ball went down and right to the bag, and he became one of the better throwers in the league."

Gil Hodges nodded. As a former catcher briefly himself and a man who had ambitions to become a manager, the one-time first-base master recognized the voice of authority when he heard it.

William Malcolm Dickey always said Mickey Cochrane was the best catcher he'd ever seen and Cy Perkins the smartest, but the big man from Little Rock, who died late in 1993, never saw one outstanding mask-and-mitt man—himself.

WILLIAM MALCOLM DICKEY
Born June 6, 1907, at Bastrop, La.
Died November 12, 1993, at Little Rock, Ark.
Height 6-1 1/2 Weight 185
Threw right and batted lefthanded.
Named to Hall of Fame, 1954.

YEAR	CLUB	LEAGUE	POS.	G.	AB.	R.	H.	2B.	3B.	HR.	RBI.	B.A.	PO.	A.	E.	F.A.
1925	Little Rock	South.	C	3	10	1	3	0	0	0	-	.300	8	2	0	1.000
1926	Muskogee	W.A.	C	61	212	27	60	6	2	7	-	.283	300	58	13	.965
1926	Little Rock	South.	C	21	46	6	18	1	5	0	8	.391	36	4	2	.952
1927	Jackson	Cot. St.	C	101	364	46	108	31	3	3	-	.297	457	84	9	.984
1928	Little Rock	South.	C	60	203	22	61	12	6	4	32	.300	151	52	8	.962
1928	Buffalo	Int.	C	3	8	0	1	0	1	0	0	.125	12	4	2	.889
1928	New York	Amer.	C	10	15	1	3	1	1	1	2	.200	7	2	0	1.000
1929	New York	Amer.	C	130	447	60	145	30	6	10	65	.324	476	95	12	.979
1930	New York	Amer.	C	109	366	55	124	25	7	5	65	.339	318	51	11	.971
1931	New York	Amer.	C	130	477	65	156	17	10	6	78	.327	670	78	3	.996
1932	New York	Amer.	C	108	423	66	131	20	4	15	84	.310	639	53	9	.987
1933	New York	Amer.	C	130	478	58	152	24	8	14	97	.318	721	82	6	.993
1934	New York	Amer.	C	104	395	56	127	24	4	12	72	.322	527	49	8	.986
1935	New York	Amer.	C	120	448	54	125	26	6	14	81	.279	536	62	3	.995
1936	New York	Amer.	C	112	423	99	153	26	8	22	107	.362	499	61	14	.976
1937	New York	Amer.	C	140	530	87	176	35	2	29	133	.332	692	80	7	.991
1938	New York	Amer.	C	132	454	84	142	27	4	27	115	.313	518	74	8	.987
1939	New York	Amer.	C	128	480	98	145	23	3	24	105	.302	571	57	7	.989
1940	New York	Amer.	C	106	372	45	92	11	1	9	54	.247	425	55	3	.994
1941	New York	Amer.	C	109	348	35	99	15	5	7	71	.284	422	45	3	.994
1942	New York	Amer.	C	82	268	28	79	13	1	2	37	.295	322	44	9	.976
1943	New York	Amer.	C	85	242	29	85	18	2	4	33	.351	322	37	2	.994
1944-45	New York	Amer.							(In Military Service)							
1946	New York	Amer.	C	54	134	10	35	8	0	2	10	.261	201	29	3	.987
1947	Litltle Rock	South.	C	8	12	2	4	2	0	1	2	.333	13	2	0	1.000
Major League Totals				1789	6300	930	1969	343	72	202	1209	.313	7866	954	108	.988

WORLD SERIES RECORD

YEAR	CLUB	LEAGUE	POS.	G.	AB.	R.	H.	2B.	3B.	HR.	RBI.	B.A.	PO.	A.	E.	F.A.
1932	New York	Amer.	C	4	16	2	7	0	0	0	4	.438	25	1	0	1.000
1936	New York	Amer.	C	6	25	5	3	0	0	1	5	.120	38	4	1	.977
1937	New York	Amer.	C	5	19	3	4	0	1	0	3	.211	26	1	0	1.000
1938	New York	Amer.	C	4	15	2	6	0	0	1	2	.400	31	5	0	1.000
1939	New York	Amer.	C	4	15	2	4	0	0	2	5	.267	27	2	0	1.000
1941	New York	Amer.	C	5	18	3	3	1	0	0	1	.167	24	2	0	1.000
1942	New York	Amer.	C	5	19	1	5	0	0	0	0	.263	25	1	1	.963
1943	New York	Amer.	C	5	18	1	5	0	0	1	4	.278	28	3	0	1.000
World Series Totals				38	145	19	37	1	1	5	24	.255	224	19	2	.992

THE YANKEE CLIPPER: Joe DiMaggio, a flawless player whose memory and mystique grows with the years. He set a remarkable and romantic record with his 56-game hitting streak in 1941.

JOE DIMAGGIO

Joe DiMaggio was so good that he actually was slipping in 1941 when he put together his famous 56-game hitting streak, one of the most formidable accomplishments in baseball history. Why, when he was just 18 years old, playing his first full season of pro ball for his native San Francisco in the Pacific Coast League, the poor foreign-born fisherman's son hit safely in 61 consecutive contests.

At baseball's centennial celebration, an unforgettable dinner held in Washington in connection with the 1969 All-Star Game, DiMaggio was named the game's No. 1 living player or, putting it another way, the top former performer still inhaling and exhaling. The honor as foremost, living or dead, had gone to DiMag's colorful Yankee predecessor, Babe Ruth, who quit the Bombers two years before Joe joined them in 1936.

Whether one opted for Willie Mays, Stan Musial, Ted Williams, George Sisler, Pie Traynor, Henry Aaron, Roberto Clemente, Frank Frisch,

Bob Feller, Charley Gehringer, Jackie Robinson, Mickey Mantle, Sandy Koufax, Bob Gibson or any other as the outstanding player or past performer still breathing as the big leagues turned into their second 100 years, he couldn't really argue too strenuously against the choice of DiMaggio as the living symbol of the game's first century.

For one thing, Babe Ruth himself had paid DiMag the highest accolade as a highly publicized rookie, the day in early May the New York newcomer had hit the first of his 361 home runs, a shot into the right-center field bleachers in the Stadium, the House That Ruth Built.

The Bambino, though miffed at the Yankees' management, walked into the clubhouse, went up to DiMaggio, shook hands and said, "Hello, Joe."

Veteran Yankees did a double-take, and Lefty Gomez, DiMaggio's roommate, put it in proper perspective for the shy, blushing young man from the Bay.

"With the Babe, veterans are 'Doc' and rookies 'Kid,'" said Gomez. "You're the first guy I ever heard him call by name."

In addition to DiMaggio's brilliance as an all-around player—a power hitter who hit for average, ran well, threw even better and fielded perhaps best of all—there would be another reason for his recognition as the ranking baseball man this side of a grave. It would be the lure and the lore of his name, the mystique of a man who seemed aloof, yet one who married the most glamorous motion picture actress of the generation, Marilyn Monroe.

DiMaggio, up close and in tight, if he'll permit you to penetrate that far, is a powerful personality, one who prompted Paul Simon of the Simon-and-Garfunkel songwriting team to inquire in the enchanting *Mrs. Robinson* number in the smash movie, *The Graduate*:

"Where have you gone, Joe DiMaggio?
A nation turns its lonely eyes on you
(Ooo ooo ooo)
What's that you say, Mrs. Robinson?
Joltin' Joe has left and gone away
(Hey, hey hey, hey hey hey.)"

DiMaggio, they say, couldn't quite understand that one because, hell, he knew where he'd been all along and, besides, at about the time Mrs. Robinson was giving the young college graduate a cinematic short course in one national pastime, the Yankee Clipper was returning to the other as a vice president and coach for the Oakland Athletics.

DiMaggio, no doubt, for all his pride and privacy, probably could see himself as no more than, as one writer had years before, "a tall, thin Italian youth equipped with slick black hair, shoebutton eyes, squirrel teeth and a receding chin."

What he didn't see, perhaps not even when he looked in a mirror, was a lean, long-legged, heavy-thighed man with black curly hair that had turned gray at the temples. Although he rationed his smiles as he did his conversation, his eyes shone from behind one of the great noses, a fine sharp tip above big nostrils and tiny bones built out from the bridge.

Joe Dee or the Clipper as most players and close acquaintances call him, is a good-looking man with a handsome schnozz, as more than one woman discovered before DiMaggio met Miss Monroe. Their marriage lasted only nine months, but before the mixed-up beauty died unexpectedly eight years later, Joe and Marilyn had become close friends. Obviously still carrying a torch for her, the former athlete was deeply distressed by her death.

To DiMaggio, as he told his close friend, sports columnist Jimmy Cannon, the sexpot symbol of the silver screen was plain and simple, in the most pleasant and tender connotation of the expression, and so honest that she charmed him by insisting when they first met, a blind date as a dinner threesome, that she never had heard his name before.

If that one makes Marilyn sound like the beautiful dumb blonde she portrayed on the screen, it's merely hard to believe that anyone hadn't heard of Joltin' Joe, a 13 season center-field star with the New York Yankees, three-time winner of the American League Most Valuable Player award and, as mentioned, author in 1941 of the fabulous 56-game hitting streak.

At a time when war was raging over Europe and

when America was only a sneak-attack away from involvement, daily bulletins of DiMaggio's streak were the sports pages' good-news equivalent—or contrast, rather—of the news page disaster overseas.

Why, the two-month assault that flattened all previous records for batting consistency even produced a song "Joltin' Joe DiMaggio," by Alan Courtney and Ben Homer, recorded by Les Brown's band. And when the streak ended at 56, a dozen games longer than the previous best by Wee Willie Keeler back in the gaslight '90s, a St. Louis sports editor not given to sophomoric nonsense made a pretty good suggestion. John Edward Wray of the *Post-Dispatch* proposed that a "6" be added to DiMaggio's uniform number, the since-retired No. "5," so that Joe would wear a meaningful "56" for the rest of his career.

Mr. Wray's idea was too daring for the stuffed shirts of baseball, none of whom was more starchy than the Yankees before they lost patronage supremacy in the Big Town to the upstart, amusin', amazing Mets. Bushy-browed Ed Barrow, who then bossed the Bronx Bombers as general manager, was a tough old bird. Cousin Ed even suggested that it was DiMaggio's patriotic duty, or something like that, to take a pay cut after he batted .357 with 30 homers and a league-leading 125 RBIs in the season his inspirational streak brought another pennant and increased box office business to the Yankees.

The Yankees conveniently had put Joe Dee in the position previously of appearing greedy. Barrow wasn't above leaking a little salary information to a writer friendly to the club's cause. One year the fans even had booed DiMaggio because they'd thought he had indeed tried to come up too far and too fast financially, but by '41 all he heard was cheers.

It's too bad Miss Monroe didn't know him then. Not that, at 25, Joe was as graceful off the field as he'd always been on it. Probably by then he hadn't acquired all of the poise and polish that travel and life with a big league ball club, particularly with a man of Gomez' wit and warmth, eventually meant

to him. But Marilyn could have better appreciated the hold the Clipper had on so many people, large and small, big and little.

When they married at a time he was closing in on 40, an ex-ballplayer playing in the other party's ballpark Hollywood, rather than San Francisco or New York, the 27-year-old bride was considerably busier than he was. She was hot property at the time they honeymooned in Tokyo. An American general introduced himself and asked if, as a patriotic gesture, Marilyn would visit the troops in Korea. Why the brass didn't ask DiMag, too, to give the G.I.s a doubleheader of what they missed most—girls and baseball—seems even now a silly omission or oversight.

Marilyn looked hesitatingly at Joe. "It's your honeymoon," he said, shrugging. "Go ahead if you want to." The blonde beauty appeared 10 times before service crowds estimated at 100,000. When she returned, she said, "It was so wonderful, Joe. You never heard such cheering."

"Yes, I have," said DiMaggio, softly, significantly. And quite young, too, he could have added.

Giuseppe Paolo DeMaggio, Jr.—the surname became DiMaggio through a newspaper error in San Francisco—was born across the bay at Martinez on November 25, 1914, the eighth child and fourth son in a family of four girls and five boys. His parents, Giuseppe and Rosalle, had migrated from Isolda delle Femmine on the Sicilian coast, living briefly in New York before moving to California.

When Joe was an infant, the family moved to the bottom flat of a three-story frame and plaster building on Russian Hill, just above Fisherman's Wharf, where the DiMaggio family boat tied up with the other fishermen of the Bay. A block and a half away was the asphalt and tar North Beach playground where all the DiMaggio boys—Tom, Mike, Vince, Joe and Dom—played as kids.

The family lived in close quarters in the $25-a-month house, the girls in one room, the boys in another, spilling out into the living room and dining room where sofa beds were kept. Joe's father would leave at 4 A.M. and cast off for the fishing grounds where he went after salmon, herring, smelt and crabs.

In *Joe DiMaggio, the Golden Year, 1941*, published in 1970 by Prentice-Hall, author Al Silverman's thorough job included the observation that Ernest Hemingway drew inspiration from the DiMaggios, father and son, when he wrote the novel, *The Old Man and the Sea*. One passage reads:

"I would like to take the great DiMaggio fishing," the old man said.

"They say his father was a fisherman. Maybe he was as poor as we are and would understand."

As poor, no doubt, but it was a source of annoyance to the senior DiMaggio for years that young Giuseppe neither had the stomach nor the heart for fishing or the smell of it, including the chore of cleaning the boat his father and older brothers worked. Joe's idea of fish was sauteed with onions as delightfully prepared by his mother.

The way Joe tells it, brother Tom, who later ran the DiMaggio family restaurant on Fisherman's Wharf, would have been the best ballplayer if he hadn't adhered to the family-comes-first loyalty of the old-line Italians. Joe sold newspapers on a corner with younger brother Dom, who was a better hustler by Joe's evaluation, but Joe loved most to play softball at the North Beach playground, sliding recklessly on the tar and asphalt surface. His father would mutter considerably more than his mother about the wear and tear on shoes and clothes.

A bit older, young Joe moved into baseball competition and to a horse lot at the corner of Bay and Taylor streets. "The lot belonged to a milk company," Joe told Silverman, "and they let us use it provided we rounded up all the dozen milk-wagon horses resting on it before every game and tied them up in one corner. We had to stage a roundup before we could play."

The bases were chunks of concrete, home plate was a flattened-out oil can and the catcher had the only glove. An economic crisis would be the nickel necessary for a roll of black friction tape to cover a weary old ball.

DiMaggio played first base then because he was tall for his age, "Long Legs," the other kids called him in Italian. Joe's big disappointment, he has reflected to Cannon and others, was in not having just the modest admission price necessary to see movies like Al Jolson's *The Jazz Singer*, *All Quiet on the Western Front* and *The Patent Leather Kid*.

Joe's playing favorite in a town that sent so many players to the majors was Joe Cronin, the jut-jawed shortstop who once passed along infield tips to him at a playground visit, but he was fascinated most by Babe Ruth. When the Babe came into San Francisco barnstorming, Joe recalled hanging around the ballpark all day in a futile effort to get in to see the home run king.

The DiMaggio brothers helped each other and that's one reason why, in Joe's judgment, three reached the majors. Vince, two years older, was an outstanding defensive outfielder with a strikeout flaw in a power swing. He played with several National League clubs from 1937 to 1946. Dom, bespectacled and nicknamed the Little Professor, was a smaller edition of Joe—enough said, right?—as a member of the Boston Red Sox from 1940 to '53.

"We used to play catch out in front of the house after dinner and we were always correcting each others' mistakes," Joe explained. "If one of us picked up a new trick, like shading the eyes for a flyball, we'd pass it along to the other. And like most kids, we always tried to outdo each other. We'd throw high flies to each other and try to make impossible catches—over the shoulder backhanded, shoestring, etc. Or maybe we'd have some kind of contest on throwing—like how far or accurately we could fire the ball—and we used to hit by the hour."

First, Vince quit school over his parents' protest to take a fruit-produce job so that he could play semi-pro ball as a springboard to the pros. Joe, temporarily distracted by the tennis bug because Little

Bill Johnston was from the San Francisco area, looked around him, saw unemployment and decided tennis wouldn't pay like baseball might.

Joe finished junior high school, but went only one year to Galileo High School because, unable to take physical education, he didn't like the alternative, ROTC. Crating oranges and picking crabmeat in a cannery—three dollars a day if and when he worked—Joe began to play with a semi-pro ball club, the Rossis. As shortstop, he hit two home runs and won two baseballs and a pair of gift certificates good for $15, a considerable prize in the depths of the Depression (1931).

Next, he hit .633 in 18 games for Sunset Produce, a fast semi-pro club, earned himself a pair of baseball shoes and moved on to join the Mission Red A's, backed by the San Francisco Missions of the Pacific Coast League. Former Yankee catcher Fred Hofmann, managing the PCL club caught Joe's act and invited him to work out with the grown-up Missions. Two months later Hofmann said to him, "Sign a contract with us and I'll give you $150 a month."

The price, $25 over scale, excited both Joe and brother Tom, but just then brother Vince, hitting hard at Tucson, was called up by San Francisco's other Coast League club, the Seals. So Joe stood outside the left-field fence, the story goes, watching through a knothole, when Seals' scout Spike Hennessey, who had seen Joe play, tapped him on the shoulder.

"You're Vince's kid brother, aren't you?" he said. Joe nodded and Hennessey said, "What the devil are you doing here? Never stand on the outside looking in unless it's a jail. Come with me."

Hennessey introduced the bashful DiMaggio boy to the Seals' owner, Charley Graham, who said he'd arrange a tryout. With three days to go of a sad sixth-place season, Augie Galan, the Seals' shortstop, begged off early because of a chance to barnstorm profitably in Hawaii with Henry Oana, an Islander who played in the outfield for the Seals.

Manager Ike Caveney was agreeable, but who would play shortstop Saturday and in the Sunday season-ending doubleheader?

"I got a kid brother who can play shortstop," Vince DiMaggio spoke up, and Caveney, who had heard Hennessey speak of the kid, invited Vince to bring Joe over.

So a couple of months short of his 18th birthday, Joe DiMaggio stepped into a top minor league club's lineup nervously, throwing too softly to first base on the first grounder he fielded and then, jabbed by the third baseman's rebuke, firing the second one so hard that he threw the ball well up into the seats for his lone error.

At bat, though, he broke in, well, like the DiMaggio the majors would come to know, He banged a curve thrown by Ted Pilette for a triple off the left-field fence. For the three games, he had two hits in nine trips. The other blow was a double."

Uncertain, unsigned and unpaid, DiMag reported for training the next spring. Graham watched him work out in the infield, then signed him for $250 a month.

"Joe," the veteran baseball man said to a kid who would be remembered as one of the most graceful outfielders ever, "you're the clumsiest ballplayer I ever saw, but you can hit."

Unable to beat out Galan at shortstop, DiMaggio rode the bench for a couple of weeks and then pinch-hit, drawing a walk. When the inning was over, he went back to the bench, got his glove and started for the clubhouse.

"Hold it," said Manager Caveney. "You play right field."

Joe thought the skipper was kidding and started for the clubhouse again. Brother Vince ran after him.

"He means it. Go out to right field."

"I never played right field in my life," Joe said.

"I know you didn't," said Vince, "but you're going to start now."

So all the 18-year-old kid did, as mentioned, was

to put together a brow-raising, 61-game hitting streak, one that drew so much attention even Papa DiMaggio became a baseball fan. The day the boy hit in his 50th straight game, breaking the old record, San Francisco mayor Angelo Rossi came out and presented Joe with a gold watch and presented his mother and young sister Marie with flowers. Joe's old boys' club team, the Jolly Knights of North Beach, gave him a traveling bag and his San Francisco teammates presented him with a check.

Pressure? Sure, but the hometown kid with the faint flicker of a smile, didn't know what it meant to choke. First off, in a three-run first inning for Los Angeles, Joe made a great throw from right field to double a runner at the plate. Next, batting fourth, he stepped up to the plate against boastful Buck Newsom, the Coast league pitching kingpin who had vowed to stop him, and drilled a two-run single over second base, bringing a five-minute ovation.

A .340 hitter with 45 doubles, 13 triples, 259 hits, 28 homers and a league-leading 169 RBIs, he was off to an even better season in 1934 when he suffered the knee injury that threatened to end his career and probably affected the manner in which he was sold and to whom. Certainly the price wasn't as right as it would have been if DiMaggio hadn't worn thereafter the label of damaged goods.

Curiously, Dutch Ruether, then managing Seattle, bugged DiMaggio with a question of why he dragged his left leg at a time when Joe insisted he wasn't hurt. But then in June 1934, after a long doubleheader and then dinner at a married sister's, he rode home in a cramped taxi and his left leg became numb. When he put the foot on the pavement, he heard something pop.

Diagnosis at a hospital, where he received emergency treatment, was that he'd sprained knee tendons, but a couple of days later when he hit a home run and could only walk around the bases, Caveney knew something was seriously wrong. New examination showed torn knee tendons.

DiMaggio's left leg, from ankle to thigh, was encased in an aluminum splint for three weeks. A brooding man by nature, Joe wallowed in self-pity as he heard that big league scouts no longer were interested in him.

The Boston Red Sox, even though spending Tom Yawkey's money as if he had his own printing press, backed off. Pittsburgh manager Pie Traynor was interested, but his front office wasn't. Only Joe Devine and Bill Essick, Yankee scouts, had the vision to recommend an adequate outlay for the handicapped player who had batted .341 in 101 games.

Devine appealed to Barrow that now was the time to get DiMaggio cheap. Barrow offered $20,000. Graham, recognizing he had lost some of his bull market, wanted $40,000. The Yankees' owner, Jake Ruppert, had been bearish about big cash outlays since the Bombers had paid more than $100,000 for an Oakland double-play combination, Lyn Lary and Jimmy Reese, a few years earlier.

Barrow finally sold Graham on taking $25,000 and five players from the Yankees' farm system. When a San Francisco orthopedic man said the knee would be okay, Barrow made another enjoyable concession for Graham. The Seals could use the kid again in 1935 and he could receive regular knee treatments in San Francisco.

The rest of baseball winced in '35 when the mighty Yankees, the team that just had lost Babe Ruth, came up with the Bambino's successor from outside the organization. DiMag hit .398 with 34 homers, 270 hits and 154 RBIs in 172 games of the expanded Coast schedule. The only thing the immigrant's son couldn't do was make a speech when he was given a Frisco farewell. Heck, he was too scared even to read one that had been written for him by Seals' trainer, Bobby Johnson.

At 21, Joe was a greenpea, all right. The next spring, he rode to training camp at St. Petersburg, Fla., with two fellow Bay area Italians who were Yankee stalwarts, Tony Lazzeri and Frank Crosetti.

Somewhere in Texas, weary of taking turns behind the wheel, Lazzeri and Crosetti wanted DiMaggio to drive, but found—to their disgust—that he didn't know how.

The "kid," as Tony and Cro called him, didn't learn his social graces or any lessons in elocution from the taciturn pair. A New York writer swore that he watched quietly one time that season in the lobby of the Chase Hotel in St. Louis as Lazzeri, Crosetti and DiMaggio sat silently for 80 minutes. Finally, Joe cleared his throat.

"What did you say?" asked Crosetti.

"He didn't say a damn thing," said Lazzeri. "Shut up."

The talking was done by other veterans who would needle the highly publicized newcomer. His first day in camp, Red Ruffing, ace of the pitching staff, chided him that if he hit .398 in the Coast, he certainly could hit .400—no, make it .450—against the new white baseballs used in the American League.

Manager Joe McCarthy, who had gone three seasons without a winner after his first pennant as Yankee skipper, talked to him about how his future would be in center field, though he might have to play left, too. McCarthy told him about what it meant to be a Yankee. In those days that meant, among other things, dressing neatly and not using the clubhouse to do anything except to talk baseball. No card-playing, not even shaving.

Boss Barrow wanted to say a word, too. "I don't want all this advance praise to spoil your playing," said the general manager who had put Babe Ruth in his place.

"Don't worry, Mr. Barrow," said DiMaggio, speaking up for the first time, "I never feel excited."

Actually, DiMag said later, as a rookie, he was self-confident, actually cocky, but he tried not to let it show. He made a career of keeping things inside himself—even when he became more outgoing—and if you wonder why the man never got an ulcer, the truth is that he did. Although a heavy cigarette

smoker, he eventually had to ease up on his favorite Italian dishes and, though never a heavy drinker, he had to forego beer. He switched to tea and an occasional hard drink, usually vodka.

His first time up for the Yankees in an exhibition game, DiMaggio tripled against the St. Louis Cardinals. Within three days, veteran New York baseball writer Dan Daniel had called him "the replacement for Babe Ruth," but then, just when everyone was so impressed by his grace and skill, he suffered a severe setback.

Undergoing diathermy treatment for the first time in his life—he had twisted an ankle—DiMaggio stayed under the lamp too long and suffered a badly burned instep, which was slow to heal. Daniel, rushing to the defense of trainer Doc Painter, wrote:

"How was Doc to know that DiMaggio's blood chemistry ran a little high in sugar? DiMaggio's foot burned just like a cake with too much sugar frosting would have burned if left in the oven . . ."

Daniel, hard to please, had been impressed considerably by DiMaggio in more ways than one. Asked by his paper to arrange a series of articles containing the hot-copy kid's life story, Dan sat with the rookie for several hours and prepared for the series.

Then another New York newspaper offered $3,000 for exclusive syndication. To a player making $8,000, the sum was large, and DiMag wondered what to do.

"I can offer you no compensation, Joe," Daniel said. "We have advertised the series, but we have no hold on you."

DiMaggio showed championship class. "You got there first and you are entitled to the story," he said. "Make out a release and I'll sign it."

When DiMaggio was slow to heal in the spring of '36, even Ed Barrow grumbled. "All I can say now is that I have a young man with half an ankle who cost us a lot of money. Maybe he will look good when he gets to play. But when will that be?"

Cousin Ed should have lived so long as to worry

about DiMaggio. Joe rode the bench with his ailment until May 3. Then, putting the pressure on the 6-2, 187-pound rookie, the Yankee Stadium field announcer informed the crowd with an old-fashioned megaphone that DiMag would make his major league debut the next afternoon.

A crowd of 25,000 came out, many of them waving Italian flags, for a game against the St. Louis Browns, who were hardly box office. What the fans saw was a ritual, stance and results that would become pleasantly familiar over his career. The period would have been 16 years or longer if World War II hadn't taken the center-cut out of DiMaggio's career, three choice seasons, and if injuries hadn't taken further physical toll.

Before moving up to the plate, DiMaggio stood in the on-deck circle, swinging two bats, discarding one and ambling to the plate. Before he stepped in, he went into his pre-bat ritual, the one bit of witchcraft he practiced throughout his career, as Al Silverman put it in his book about DiMag. Joe would stub his right toe in the dirt behind his left heel. Almost a dance step, it was indeed a pure DiMaggio trademark.

DiMaggio would make himself comfortable in the batter's box. He picked up dirt and rubbed his hands together. He tapped his bat on the plate and planted his feet, shoe size 9½-E, wide apart, about four feet wide, his left leg stiff and still. He stood more erect than in normal posture, his right elbow fairly close to his side, the bat held at the end and at port arm's position on his right shoulder, cocked and ready. He did little preliminary bat-wiggling.

Tom Meany once wrote, "If Joe were to take the same stance, discard his bat and extend his left arm straight out, he would look like an old boxing print of John L. Sullivan with the right hand cocked close to his breast."

From his widened stance, deep in the batter's box and close to the plate because he wanted to pull for the close left-field corner at Yankee Stadium, DiMaggio merely slid his left foot forward in a short stride of four to five inches. He seemed nonchalant, perfectly relaxed, despite the fact that the Stadium is a tough park for a righthanded power hitter.

His 1935 manager at San Francisco, the fabled Lefty O'Doul, a heckuva hitter (.349 lifetime) who would become his golf partner in later life, had tried to school him to pull for the corner, only 301 feet from the plate. Left field in the lopsided stadium then flares out to 415 feet quickly, 444 in the left-center field power alley and 461 feet in dead center.

No righthanded slugger really had been effective there over a long haul before DiMaggio, who grounded out his first time up against the Browns. Typically of his previous debuts, he then tripled off lefthander Elon (Chief) Hogsett. He singled twice, too, and the Yankees won, 14-5.

The next day, DiMag had three more hits and, in the third one, he hit safely twice against Detroit and showed his fielding class. Playing left field, with the tying run on third and the leading run tagging up at first to take a scoring position, he went to the foul-line near the fence for lefthanded-hitting Charley Gehringer's long fly. Making his decision in a split second to play it boldly rather than cautiously, he then cut loose a tremendous on-the-fly peg to the plate, retiring Pete Fox to end the game in a 6-5 New York victory.

"What are you trying to do, Joe, show me how strong you are?" mockingly said McCarthy, who had ordered Yankee outfielders to throw the ball on a bounce to the plate. To Barrow that night, a pleased McCarthy said, "The kid can field—and he's got guts."

DiMaggio hit so hard that, at the June 15 trading deadline, the Yankees traded Ben Chapman to Washington for Jake Powell and put Joe Dee where he would win his rich reputation—in center field.

Selected to start as a rookie in the 1936 All-Star Game at Boston's Braves Field, DiMaggio laid an ostrich egg in a 4-3 loss to the National League. He went hitless in five trips, but, worse, he misplayed three balls hit to him. He permitted a single to go for extra bases, let a sinking line drive get past him for a triple and misjudged another flyball.

"Don't let it get you down," said McCarthy.

"I won't," said Joe Dee, "but I won't forget it, either."

Although missing 16 games, DiMaggio was a remarkable rookie, tying for the league lead in triples with 15 and also collecting 44 doubles and 29 homers among 206 hits. He drove in 125 runs and batted .323.

DiMag would play in 10 World Series, but he'd really never do better—or enjoy one more—than the first in 1936 when the Yankees and their New York rivals, the Giants, renewed a confrontation of the Roaring Twenties. The Jolter, as John Drebinger and a few others called The Clipper, hit .346 with nine hits, three of them doubles, and drove in three runs.

In the second game when the Bombers bombed the Giants, 18-4, DiMaggio had two singles and a double, then ended the game with a flourish and one of the finest catches ever pulled off in the horseshoe-shaped Polo Grounds. The quick-breaking, long-striding DiMag, racing back for a long smash by Hank Leiber, outran the 475-foot smash toward the center-field clubhouse, caught the ball over his shoulder and, without breaking stride, went up the stairs into the visitors' dressing room.

Joe got his biggest kick, however, out of a play in the sixth game when the Yankees led only by a run in the ninth inning. DiMaggio, first up, singled and took third on a hit by Lou Gehrig. Bill Dickey followed with a slowly hit grounder to Bill Terry at first base.

DiMaggio stopped, waiting to see what move Terry would make, figuring the Giants' player-manager would run right at him and force Joe to break for the plate or back for the bag. Instead, Terry cocked his arm to throw to the third baseman, who was closing in behind DiMaggio.

In that instant, the rookie broke for home. The Giants' big catcher, Harry Danning, had the plate

blocked and DiMag knew he couldn't make it feet first. Recklessly, he dived headlong over the crouched catcher, landed behind the plate, but reached back with his hand to score the run. A big Series-clinching inning followed.

Painfully shy to the point some thought he was sullen, DiMaggio would duck crowds over the years. In New York, before and between marriages, Toots Shor's restaurant was his second home and the big, bluff restaurateur whose bark was worse than his bite, was an unofficial bodyguard as well as good friend.

McCarthy's judgment to room him on the road with the witty, urbane Gomez was wise. Lefty advanced the little-educated Italian lad beyond the comic-book phase, interested him in show business and other activities, including casino. Gehrig was championship bridge, Gomez casino.

DiMaggio liked movies, not only because he'd missed so many as a poor boy, but because the shadows permitted him to watch without the hero worship he enjoyed inwardly, yet outwardly didn't know how to handle. He began to wear conservative, well-tailored $125 suits when a buck went more than quadruple the distance of the '80s.

The hero-worship, you see, was in full bloom by the time Joe made the sophomore jinx a joke when he led the American League in homers with 46, driving in 167 runs with a .346 season in 1937. The Yankees really were window-breakers then. Gehrig knocked in 159 runs that year and Dickey 133.

After bombing a tremendous home run off the Giants' Cliff Melton in the World Series, won by the Yankees in five games, DiMaggio faced his annual contract hassle with Barrow more resolutely. Cousin Ed had glowered him down to $15,000 when he asked for $25,000 after his rookie season. Now, he asked for $45,000.

Barrow did a slow burn. "Young man," he said, "do you know how long Lou Gehrig has been with this club? Well, I'll tell you—13 years—and do you know how much he gets? $41,000. What have you got to say to that?"

"Mr. Barrow," said DiMaggio, "Gehrig is badly underpaid and . . ."

Barrow literally blew him out of the office, the way Silverman phrased it, and, getting nowhere with Jake Ruppert, either, Joe found himself stuck with a $25,000 ceiling in a holdout that carried two weeks into the season. Fans don't like it when their heroes don't answer the bell on time. Joe was docked his pay until he was ready to play and then ran into boos everywhere. In a period when the country still was suffering from the financial shorts, those reactions were more understandable to others than DiMaggio.

Joe didn't let the hurt feelings hurt his play, too much, however, as witness a .324 season with 32 homers and 140 RBIs. And with a token hike to $27,500, he finally made an opening-day lineup for the first time in 1939. In the first fortnight, however, he tore muscles in his right leg above the ankle, trying to make a quick turn for a difficult catch, and missed 33 games.

Returning to the lineup, he hit savagely to become the first player to play on four successive world championship teams in his first four seasons in the majors. En route, he made probably the greatest catch of his career. Racing back to deep center field in the cavernous Stadium, he got behind the flagpole at the 461-foot mark, turned, leaped and gloved the ball hit by Detroit's Hank Greenberg, an instant before he hit the fence.

Head characteristically cocked shyly to one side, DiMag loped back toward the infield, unmindful that the catch hadn't retired the side and that his teammates were calling for the ball, trying to double off a runner who was trying to retrace his steps from first to third. Joe Dee, after all, merely was human, as he proved as late as his final season, 1951, when at nearly 37, the master outfielder also forgot the number of men out and carried in a ball he should have thrown in. That time, of course, he

just hadn't stunned everyone with an eye-popping catch.

In '39, DiMag stunned 'em, too, with his hitting. In fact, with only three weeks left in the season, he was batting .412. Then a nerve in his eyelid began giving him trouble and made him blink at the plate. The Yankees had clinched the pennant, but McCarthy was reluctant to remove DiMaggio from the lineup.

"If I take you out," he explained, "they'll say I did it to make you a .400 hitter and they'll call you a cheese champion."

Maybe. The truth is, his vision bothered, DiMaggio played and finished with a league-leading .381 and the first of his three Most Valuable Player awards.

That fall, he married blonde actress Dorothy Arnold in a big San Francisco wedding. The marriage broke up when Joe was away in service in World War II, but the union produced a son, Joe Jr., born in 1941. Father and son always have been extremely close. Joe, a grandfather, is proud of his college-educated, Marine-trained youngster who works for his uncle, Dom DiMaggio, a prosperous industrialist in New England.

For the first time, the Yankee Clipper learned what the players of the other clubs did at World Series time when the Yanks finished third, despite his second straight batting championship, .352, 31 homers and 133 RBIs.

A holdout again until a week after spring training started, squeezing out a $5,500 raise to $37,500, DiMaggio got off with one of his good-omen triples opening day at Washington, but by mid-May he was slumping and so were the Yankees. They had lost four in a row and were at .500, 14 and 14, in fourth place and five and a half games behind league-leading Cleveland. On May 15, the Yankees were beaten again, drubbed by the Chicago White Sox, but Joe DiMaggio hit a run-scoring single off Edgar Smith, chunky Chicago southpaw.

The hit and date were significant only because,

for two months and 56 games, DiMaggio would get at least one hit in each game, an accomplishment that many regard as the most amazing offensive achievement in big league baseball's first century.

Along the way, as DiMag would remember proudly, there were only a couple of hits on the infield, only a couple of times when the crowd and players would strain to see what the official scorer had ruled. DiMag could run well enough circling the bases, letting out with long legs that could turn the corners without wasted motion, but he was no fast man getting down to first base.

Interest began to mount with each passing day. The Yankees' club record fell at 30 straight games. At 36, a Browns' rookie righthander, Bob Muncrief, blanked DiMag until the eighth, aided by a good catch by Roy Cullenbine on one long smash. When DiMaggio singled his last time up, the St. Louis manager, Luke Sewell, wondered why Muncrief hadn't walked him.

"Because," said the pitcher, "that wouldn't have been fair—to him or to me. Hell, he's the greatest ballplayer I ever saw."

As tension mounted and crowds grew, DiMaggio's favorite bat was stolen out of the rack at Washington and then finally returned after a mysterious phone call, but not before Joe had begun to use one of Tommy Henrich's models. There was all kind of drama.

In game No. 38, St. Louis' submarining righthander, Elden Auker, had DiMaggio blanked into the eighth inning. Six times Joe Dee faced that last-time pressure in the streak. This time, leading 3-1, with one out, team man Tommy Henrich asked McCarthy, "If Red (Rolfe) gets on, do you mind if I bunt?"

Henrich didn't want to rap into a double play to kill DiMaggio's last chance. McCarthy, a devotee of big-inning baseball, ordinarily would have answered negatively, just as he knew Henrich wouldn't have asked. Someone once asked Marse Joe how well DiMaggio bunted and McCarthy replied, "I'll never know."

Now, realizing Henrich's intent, McCarthy said casually, "That'll be all right."

Henrich sacrificed perfectly and, stepping in to face a hushed crowd, DiMaggio was confident Auker wouldn't walk him for spite. He didn't. Joe ripped Auker's first pitch over third base for a double that brought a loud roar from the crowd and the Yankees pounding bats on the dugout steps and dancing in delight.

To DiMaggio, the most satisfying hit of the 91 in his streak came in game No. 40 against Philadelphia's Johnny Babich, a former Yankee farmhand who had beaten his old club five times the year before. Babich retired DiMaggio the first time after Joe had lashed a long drive, barely foul, and Joe was angered next time up when Babich missed with three straight pitches, far outside, and he became annoyed, convinced the pitcher intended to walk him.

With the hit sign on 3-and-0, DiMaggio reached out for a pitch that was too wide and smashed it on a line through the box. Babich, unprepared, barely fell to the ground in time to avoid the ball. He was white-faced, a smiling DiMag remembered years later.

On June 29 at Washington, a crowd of 31,000 came out to see whether Joe Dee could tie and break George Sisler's record of 41 games set in 1922. DiMaggio doubled off knuckleballer Emil (Dutch) Leonard in the sixth inning of the first game and then, after sipping coffee and puffing a cigarette between contests, the Yankee Clipper went out and waited dramatically until the seventh inning of the second contest before he lined out a hit off Washington reliever Arnold Anderson.

Sisler sent off a congratulatory wire to DiMaggio and I then commented, "I'd rather see DiMaggio break it than anybody I can think of. The guy is a natural in everything he does and is a great hitter. His streak is no lucky fluke, believe me."

A couple of days later, DiMaggio broke Wee Willie Keeler's old major league mark of 44 consecutive games set back in 1897. The blow came off righthander Heber (Dick) Newsome and was a home run.

For years, a story has persisted that Dom DiMaggio jeopardized his older brother's streak with a great catch on an afternoon when he was scheduled to have dinner with Joe. Didn't happen quite that way, but time and again Dom did deprive Joe of hits, including about six RBIs one day when he was to be Joe's guest.

At dinner, Dom apologized. "Joe," he said, "if you had hit those two smashes just one inch farther, I never could have caught either of them!"

On July 17 at Cleveland, "it" happened. The record pressure had been relieved, but the streak still was the talk of baseball and good box office. A crowd of 40,000 came out at Cleveland. When a gabby cabby told DiMaggio he was sorry but that he had a "feeling" the streak would end that night, Joe was philosophical, but Gomez was incensed.

"Well, if it is, it is," said DiMag with a shrug, tipping the driver well.

"What'd you tip him for?" Gomez hollered. "The guy was trying to jinx you."

That night off lefty Al Smith, DiMaggio hit two hot smashes that were fielded brilliantly by Ken Keltner, the Cleveland third baseman. Once, Joe walked. Then in the eighth, facing righthander Jim Bagby, Joe hit one of the hottest grounders of his career, he would reflect later, but the ball was within shortstop Lou Boudreau's range and, though it bad-hopped at the last second, the quick-reacting Boudreau grabbed the ball and started a double play that ended the streak.

DiMaggio was so shaken up that he immediately went out and hit in 17 more consecutive contests!

In the 56 games the Yankees came alive, winning 41 and tying two for a .759 percentage, to take a six-game lead over Cleveland. Ted Williams would recall later in his autobiography that he hit four points higher than DiMaggio over the same period, but Ted's .412 wouldn't be remembered and Joe's

.408 would be recalled as the sum total of his grand 56-game effort of 91 hits, which included 16 doubles, four triples and 15 homers, for 160 total bases. He drove in 55 runs, walked 21 times and struck out just seven of 223 trips.

DiMaggio's Yankee teammates threw a private surprise party for him shortly thereafter at Washington so that they could present to him a handsome engraved silver cigarette humidor, one with his batting likeness on it, the record and the signatures of his appreciative comrades.

Hurt in mid-August, DiMaggio returned to the lineup in early September and, with the Yankees breezing to another easy pennant, the Clipper had a .357 season of 30 homers, a league-leading 125 RBIs and the most excitement of his career.

Never thrown out of a game, a master of self-control, keeping his churning emotions under check, DiMaggio bridled and exchanged words with Whitlow Wyatt, then advanced on the veteran Brooklyn righthander he thought had thrown at him in the 1941 World Series. Nothing came of it. The Dodgers already were done from Mickey Owen's mishap the day before, missing reliever Hughie Casey's spitball for what would have been a game-ending third strike on Henrich. DiMaggio, Charley Keller and Joe Gordon quickly followed with hits that turned a 4-3 defeat into an unforgettable 7-4 victory.

For all DiMaggio's contribution to the Yankees' financial coffers that season, Cousin Ed Barrow suggested a paycut of "only" $2,500—the war, y'know, old boy—but DiMag muscled a hike to $43,750 and then had his tamest season to that point, batting just .305 with 21 homers and 114 RBIs in 154 games—the first time he had played a full schedule.

The Cardinals upset the Yankees in a five-game World Series in which DiMaggio batted .333 with seven singles and then he was off, at age 28, in what should have been his peak seasons, for three years in the Army. He played service ball in this country and in the Pacific, waiting for the war to be over.

"I thought it would never end," he told Al Silverman in reflection for the book on his career. "Those years never seemed to move at all."

DiMaggio had a difficult time getting into shape and had personal problems in 1946, a bad year for the Yankees. With the first silver threads among the coal black, DiMag batted only .290 in 132 games. He had 25 homers and—for the first time—fewer than 100 RBIs (95).

A gnawing bone spur on his left heel pained him physically and mentally all year. The one-eighth inch bone growth was removed the following February and he didn't get into the lineup until the fifth game of the season, but he batted .315 with 20 homers and 97 RBIs. The figures were minnows by his old standards, but they won the fisherman's son his third MVP award and the Yankees won another pennant.

In '48 a bone spur developed on the right heel. "There were days," he said, "when every step on the field was like someone driving an ice pick into my heel. I tried various cushions and padding devices, but none helped. I tried running and walking on my toes, but this only strained the leg muscles and sometimes gave me a charley horse in the thighs. I think I overworked every nerve in my body making it to that last game."

Giuseppe DiMaggio was there to root for brother Dom, whose Red Sox were locked in a three-way fight with the Yankees and Indians. On the next-to-last day at Boston, Joe got three hits, including a home run.

"What's Joe doing?" Giuseppe asked the players' sister, Frances. "Why's he hitting so good?'

The Red Sox won the game, however, eliminating the Yankees, and Poppa DiMaggio was happier. On the last day of a painful season in which he missed only one game, hitting .320 with a league-leading 39 homers and 155 RBIs, 33-year-old Joe DiMaggio felt it was a matter of honor that he play.

Quite obviously the man preferred to see his brother's team win, the Red Sox who were managed by his old manager and friend, Joe McCarthy, rather than Cleveland. Yet he got four hits in five times up and when he hit one off the left-field wall in the ninth inning and limped to first base, manager Bucky Harris lifted him for a pinch-runner.

Boston, winning the game and a shot at the playoff could afford to be particularly magnanimous. Joe was given, as he put it, "one of the greatest ovations and thrills of my baseball life."

Another heel operation followed, and it was a failure. DiMaggio was in and out of the hospital with the heel and other illnesses. In early May 1949, his father died. Although by now an articulate man, Joe became a recluse. People were saying he was through.

Then one morning he put his foot out of bed and for the first time the heel wasn't hot or painful, but cool and Joe felt no pain. DiMaggio, whose salary had been hiked to $70,000 in the post-war boom and then to $100,000 by a grateful new ownership, wanted so much to deliver.

On June 14, he took batting practice to begin toughening tender hands. A week later he played nine innings in an exhibition against the Giants, preparing himself hopefully for a crucial three-game series at Boston against the menacing Red Sox. He flew into Boston with a special high orthopedic shoe, built up at the heel without spikes, and the new manager, Casey Stengel, was delighted.

That mid-season series has to rate as the crowning glory for one of the greatest ever. The first night DiMaggio singled and hit a two-run homer off southpaw Mickey McDermott as the Yankees gained a 5-4 victory. Wildly cheered by the Red Sox fans, Joe Dee responded by removing his cap, with a wide smile on his ordinarily solemn features.

The next day, the Yankees were trailing by six runs, 7-1, when DiMaggio came up with two men on and homered. Later in the game, with the score tied, he hit another two-run homer for a 9-7 New York victory.

Off Boston lefthanded ace Mel Parnell in the

third game, DiMag hit a tremendous three-run homer as the Yankees swept the series—"the greatest of my career," the Yankee Clipper would say.

"Those three days in Boston," he said many years later, "were the most satisfying of my life and they taught me about faith and people. Letters and telegrams poured in by the thousands cheering my comeback . . ."

Two weeks before the end of the season, DiMaggio caught viral pneumonia. He was desperately ill with a temperature of 104 and it looked as if he would not make a "day" scheduled for him the next-to-last afternoon at Yankee Stadium. Advised not to leave his sickbed, 18 pounds underweight and still feverish, DiMaggio insisted, "If the Yankees are going down, I'll go down with them."

Joe's mother, dying of cancer, had come to New York to be with her ailing son. When Joe received fine gifts like a Cadillac, speedboat, television set, radio, watches, jewelry and a bicycle for little Joe, his mother also was given an automobile. At the field microphone, DiMaggio cried for the second time of his adult life. He'd cried last at Lou Gehrig's farewell in 1939.

Now all he could say was, "Thank the good Lord for making me a Yankee."

So the old shadow went out and, unable to pull the ball, singled and doubled to right field as the Yankees caught the league-leading Red Sox in the standings, 5-4. And the Bombers then beat the Bosox in the final game, 5-3, for the pennant that would lead to a record of five straight world championships under Stengel.

DiMaggio, hitting .346 for 76 games in '49, struggled through 139 contests in 1950, batting .301, hitting 32 homers and driving in 122 runs, but that's what it was—a struggle. He hit .308 with one decisive homer in a four-game Series sweep over Philadelphia. But the end was near.

In '51, batting just .263 in 116 games, hitting only 12 homers with 71 RBIs, he shook his head. "The old boy can't be that bad," he said, but not

even a farewell homer off Sal Maglie in the fourth game of the World Series could make a proud man like Joe DiMaggio stay on just to pull down another paycheck. He couldn't run, throw, field or hit as he had in the past.

"When baseball is no longer fun, it's no longer a game," he said when he announced his retirement at 37, four years before he went into the Hall of Fame. "So I've played my last game of ball."

Not really. Now and then he'd put on his uniform for an old-timers' game. And years later when a younger generation listening to Simon and Garfunkel might have thought he was merely a legend, Joe Dee suited up as vice president and coach of the Oakland Athletics. Seeing the famous No. 5 in the wedding-gown white, with the kelly-green undershirt and gold-striped sox, was about as shocking as having Santa Claus appear in a purple bikini.

But, know something? The distinguished-looking, ruddy-complexioned, graying DiMaggio did almost as much for the vest-style softball uniform of the A's as he did for the neat, conservative pin-striped blue and gray of the Yankees.

It's almost impossible to hide C-L-A-S-S.

JOSEPH PAUL (YANKEE CLIPPER) DI MAGGIO
Born November 25, 1914, at Martinez, Calif.
Height 6-2 Weight 193
Threw and batted righthanded.
Named to Hall of Fame, 1955

YEAR	CLUB	LEAGUE	POS.	G.	AB.	R.	H.	2B.	3B.	HR.	RBI.	B.A.	PO.	A.	E.	F.A.
1932	San Francisco	P.C.	OF	3	9	2	2	1	1	0	2	.222	4	7	1	.917
1933	San Francisco	P.C.	OF	187	762	129	259	45	13	28	169	.340	407	32	17	.963
1934	San Francisco	P.C.	OF	101	375	58	128	18	6	12	69	.341	236	11	8	.969
1935	San Francisco	P.C.	OF	172	679	173	270	48	18	34	154	.398	430	32	21	.957
1936	New York	Amer.	OF	138	637	132	206	44	15	29	125	.323	339	22	8	.978
1937	New York	Amer.	OF	151	621	151	215	35	15	46	167	.346	413	21	17	.962
1938	New York	Amer.	OF	145	599	129	194	32	13	32	140	.324	366	20	15	.963
1939	New York	Amer.	OF	120	462	108	176	32	6	30	126	.381	328	13	5	.986
1940	New York	Amer.	OF	132	508	93	179	28	9	31	133	.352	359	5	8	.978
1941	New York	Amer.	OF	139	541	122	193	43	11	30	125	.357	385	16	9	.978
1942	New York	Amer.	OF	154	610	123	186	29	13	21	114	.305	409	10	8	.981
1943-44-45	New York	Amer.							(In Military Service)							
1946	New York	Amer.	OF	132	503	81	146	20	8	25	95	.290	314	15	6	.982
1947	New York	Amer.	OF	141	534	97	168	31	10	20	97	.315	316	2	1	.997
1948	New York	Amer.	OF	153	594	110	190	26	11	39	155	.320	441	8	13	.972
1949	New York	Amer.	OF	76	272	58	94	14	6	14	67	.346	195	1	3	.985
1950	New York	Amer.	OF	139	525	114	158	33	10	32	122	.301	376	9	9	.977
1951	New York	Amer.	OF	116	415	72	109	22	4	12	71	.263	288	11	3	.990
Major League Totals				1736	6821	1390	2214	389	131	361	1537	.325	4529	153	105	.978

WORLD SERIES RECORD

YEAR	CLUB	LEAGUE	POS.	G.	AB.	R.	H.	2B.	3B.	HR.	RBI.	B.A.	PO.	A.	E.	F.A.
1936	New York	Amer.	OF	6	26	3	9	3	0	0	3	.346	18	0	1	.947
1937	New York	Amer.	OF	5	22	2	6	0	0	1	4	.273	18	0	0	1.000
1938	New York	Amer.	OF	4	15	4	4	0	0	1	2	.267	10	0	0	1.000
1939	New York	Amer.	OF	4	16	3	5	0	0	1	3	.313	11	0	0	1.000
1941	New York	Amer.	OF	5	19	1	5	0	0	0	1	.263	19	0	0	1.000
1942	New York	Amer.	OF	5	21	3	7	0	0	0	3	.333	20	0	0	1.000
1947	New York	Amer.	OF	7	26	4	6	0	0	2	5	.231	22	0	0	1.000
1949	New York	Amer.	OF	5	18	2	2	0	0	1	2	.111	7	0	0	1.000
1950	New York	Amer.	OF	4	13	2	4	1	0	1	2	.308	8	0	0	1.000
1951	New York	Amer.	OF	6	23	3	6	2	0	1	5	.261	17	0	0	1.000
World Series Totals				51	199	27	54	6	0	8	30	.271	150	0	1	.993

SCHOOLBOY WONDER: Bob Feller, an Iowa farm boy, was just 17 when he struck out 15 at the outset of his big league career. If he hadn't spent four-plus years in the Navy, he would have breezed past 300 victories.

BOB FELLER

At the ripe old age of seven, a second-grade farm boy at Van Meter, Iowa, fulfilling an essay-writing assignment, chose to tell his "life story," a pithy paragraph that prophesied the preparation and dedication by which Robert William Andrew Feller became one of the greatest pitchers ever to swish a third strike past a hitter.

"My Life," young Master Feller called the composition that went like this:

"When I was a tree, with my brothers and sisters there was many of us, but there is not many of us now. Many of us have been cut down and made into lumber and it came my turn and they cut me down and made me into a big board and Mister Struck's manuel training boys got me and made me into a home plate on the baseball diamond, and that's the end."

But, no, it was just the beginning for the kid who was groomed from the age of five for a baseball career, a spectacular success from the moment he fanned 17 big league batters when he was only 17 years old until he breezed into the Hall of Fame before he was 44.

Many a father has dreamed that one day his son would succeed where the old man has failed as a ballplayer, held back by injury or family responsibility or, as is generally the case, simply by lack of ability. Most men find it hard to admit they just had two left feet, ran like molasses in mid-winter and threw the ball as daintily as if they'd been taught by Lady Chatterley.

But few of the Walter Mittys of the baseball mitt ever gave their sons the time and attention that Bill Feller, Iowa farmer, devoted to his son, Bob. Why, Bill went so far out of his way to see to it that he could play ball daily with his boy that he didn't even plant corn and oats, generally the best crops in his part of Iowa. He planted wheat, which didn't require so much attention, leaving more time to play catch with his eager lad.

Bob Feller was a wunderkind long before he fanned eight members of St. Louis' famed Gashouse Gang in three innings of an exhibition game when he was 17. At nine, the boy could throw a baseball 275 feet. At 13, by his father's tape measure, he could peg the ball even farther. By the time he was full grown, throwing for speed instead of distance, his fastball was timed at 98.6 miles per hour.

"And I really wasn't letting all out," Feller apologized afterward, "because I wasn't really warmed up and I was throwing into a narrow device, an inverted wooden pyramid only about three feet wide. I was afraid of breaking it, which I finally did when I hit one of the supports.

"I'm sure when I'm opened up in about the third or fourth inning of a ball game, my fastball would be well over 100 miles an hour."

Even when he was a shy boy, long before he became a businessman-ballplayer and a player's spokesman quick to comment on injustices, real or imagined, Feller had confidence.

Shortly before he became 16—by then he was

playing on his father's own team on the family's own field, Oak View Park, hacked and hewed out of the Fellers' 360 acres—he went to the 1934 World Series with his father. They drove to St. Louis, stayed at a motor court outside of town so they could play catch in the evenings and then stood in line early for bleacher tickets to two games.

Young Bobby watched with interest as Paul Dean bested Tommy Bridges in one game, 4-1, but then as he saw St. Louis parade Tex Carleton, Dazzy Vance, Bill Walker, Jesse Haines and Jim Mooney to the mound in a rout the next day, 10-4, the junior Feller nudged the senior.

"I can do better than that," he said, and he probably was right. Less than two years later he first faced big league hitters and, as he would do for the better part of 20 years, he stood 'em on their ears.

Thirty years afterward—July 6, 1966—the Cleveland Indians presented Feller with a gold commemorative medal and gave every spectator a polished aluminum replica. Few of the fans probably had been there that Monday in '36 when the Gashouse Gang, leading the National League, stopped off in Cleveland to play what amounted to a meaningless, yet significant exhibition against the fifth-place Indians.

Stout Steve O'Neill, 45-year-old bench manager of the Indians, planned to catch the 17-year-old schoolboy himself to determine how much seasoning the kid would need. Steve started pitching coach George Uhle against the Cardinals, but Frank Frisch, 38-year-old player-manager of the Gashouse Gang, caught a glimpse of Feller warming up. The Old Flash watched a white blur crash against the backstop.

"Have you ever played second base?" Frisch asked Lynn King, young St. Louis outfielder. King hadn't.

"Well, you are today," said Frisch. "The Flash is too old to get killed in the line of duty."

Mind you, Bobby Feller, the kid from the farm, hadn't played anything more advanced or more serious than a semi-pro game for which he'd been paid $30 to $40. A man named Pat Donovan wrote three letters to Billy Evans, then general manager of the Indians, and Evans dispatched scout Cy Slapnicka to look over the lad from Iowa's Raccoon River country.

Slapnicka got there first and, in July 1935, signed Feller in a fashion that was then illegal, yet popularly evasive. Under a regulation at the time, major league clubs had agreed not to sign free agents other than college players. Minor league teams were supposed to sign high school talent and sandlot players and then sell them to big league clubs.

Slapnicka, though representing Cleveland, signed Feller to a contract with Fargo-Moorhead of the Northern League. So that he could finish high school first, Feller was invited to seek voluntary retirement in 1936 and his contract was transferred from Fargo-Moorhead to New Orleans, another Cleveland farm club.

Between the time Bob bound himself to the Indians, with parental consent, and public disclosure that he belonged to Cleveland, he pitched so brilliantly for Des Moines in a national semi-pro tournament that scouts flocked to see him. Detroit reportedly was willing to offer $9,000, a handsome bonus sum for the Depression, and a free trip to the World Series for all the Fellers—Bill, Bob, his mother and his younger sister.

When Bill Feller wondered whether such a trip would obligate him, scout Steve O'Rourke of the Tigers smelled an undercover deal. A check with baseball's minor league offices, then administered by William G. Bramham, the Judge Landis of the minor leagues, showed a young feller named Feller already listed as the property of the Cleveland club.

Ultimately, Lee Keyser, who operated the Des Moines club of the Western League, lodged a complaint with Commissioner Landis, claiming violation of the major-minor league agreement. Landis, recognizing the legitimacy of the claim and yet the utter impracticality of the rule, ordered Cleveland to

pay Des Moines $7,500 and moved to eliminate the restrictive clause that theoretically kept the bigs from competing with the minors for free agents.

All this happened, by the way, AFTER the schoolboy phenom from I-o-way had made perhaps the most dazzling debut of any kid fresh off the farm, meaning the agricultural kind, not the baseball variety.

At the time, it was suggested that if Judge Landis had declared Feller a free agent, Bob could have received as much as $100,000, a staggering sum when the country was still dusting itself off from the dustbowl drought of the Depression Thirties.

It's interesting, in view of Feller's outspoken views in later years, including resistance to the reserve clause in a 1957 appearance before Congress, that the Fellers—father and son—stoutly expressed satisfaction with his Cleveland negotiations and contract.

The reason Feller became such a hot and valuable, as well as disputed, baseball property was obvious from the minute he first toed a major league mound that July day in '36 at old League Park, Cleveland.

What the Cardinals saw that day was a dimple-chinned, pouty-lipped kid, an apple-cheeked 4-H boy with wide shoulders and strong arms and legs, made powerful from toting 2,000 gallons of water a day. It had been, after all, some work as well as much play back home on the farm.

Brown-eyed with dark brown hair, the 6-0, 180-pound Feller was extremely splay-footed with a plow-jockey gait and leg-hiking delivery he'd never lose. He strutted around the mound as if he knew just exactly how good he was. And he wound up fiercely in his pitching delivery and followed through as earnestly as Bill Feller had told him. Those private father-son sessions paid off from the minute Bruce Ogrodowski, first big leaguer to face him, bunted and was thrown out.

Next up was Leo Durocher, brassy, gutty shortstop of the Gashouse Gang. Leo struck out. So did

Art Garibaldi, third baseman for the 1936 Cardinals.

In the Redbirds' next inning, the fifth pitcher Les Munns fanned. Center fielder Terry Moore singled to left and stole second. Stu Martin, then playing second base, walked, and facing a green, young pitcher, Feller, and a fat, old catcher, O'Neill, Martin and Moore promptly executed a double steal.

Pepper Martin, playing right field for St. Louis, struck out. Slugger Joe Medwick, the left fielder, walked to fill the bases. On a passed ball—O'Neill just couldn't handle his young hoss—Moore scored and S. Martin took third. Switch-hitting Rip Collins, the first baseman, struck out.

In the St. Louis sixth, Joe Becker went behind the plate, to replace O'Neill, who knew he'd seen enough to want Feller, right now and to heck with the future.

Ogrodowski blooped a double to short right, but Charley Gelbert, batting for Durocher, struck out. Garibaldi again fanned. Ditto for Munns.

Feller was through, but only for the day. O'Neill made tracks to make certain Cleveland would reimburse its New Orleans farm club for Feller ($1,500) and then arrange for him to request reinstatement from the voluntarily retired list. He'd been working that summer in Cleveland's concessions department when he wasn't working out with the Indians, whose realization about the size of their prize was heightened by the evaluation of umpire Emmett (Red) Ormsby.

The veteran Ormsby, who'd called balls and strikes the first time the big leagues ever saw Bob Feller, was lavish in his praise.

"He's the best pitcher I have seen come into the American League," said Red. "I don't care if he is only 17. He showed me more speed than any I have ever seen from an American League pitcher, and I don't except Walter Johnson."

Whether Feller was as fast as Johnson—or as good—is beside the point, which is that Rapid Robert went rapidly from letting out some of the gas in the Gashouse Gang to become immediately, as a boy, a man among men.

In mid-August, after a couple of tuneup relief performances, he made his first American League start against Rogers Hornsby's old St. Louis Browns. He fanned 15 in a 4-1 victory.

A month later, he set an American League record and matched Dizzy Dean's major league mark by striking out 17 Philadelphia Athletics. Incongruously, the strikeout king of the majors then went back to Iowa to finish high school.

Feller went on from there to smash pitching records, some of which were, in turn, toppled by Sandy Koufax. Bob became the first pitcher since Cy Young to hurl three no-hitters, a figure exceeded by Koufax. He also set a record with 18 strikeouts against Detroit on the final day of the 1938 season. Koufax twice equaled that record, which fell in September 1969, when St. Louis' Steve Carlton whiffed 19 of the pennant-bound Mets. In 1970 the Mets' Tom Seaver tied that figure.

Koufax also wiped out Feller's single-season strikeout record by fanning 382 in 1965. Bob broke Rube Waddell's old standard with 348 in 1946, one of the greatest seasons any pitcher ever experienced.

In '46, after nearly four seasons away in World War II duty with the Navy, the 27-year-old Feller came back to Cleveland with conquering class. Working 48 games and 371 innings, he posted a 26-15 record and a handsome 2.18 earned-run average.

Overall, fireballer Feller won 266 games and lost 162, a .621 percentage, but he missed more baseball at his peak than any other player. He was away, winning eight battle stars in the Navy, just 72 innings short of four full seasons. He left baseball just after having won 24, 27 and 25 games in consecutive seasons. Among other fantastic statistics, he showed 12 one-hitters and 2,581 strikeouts.

If he hadn't been called to the colors, Feller, at his own winning rate, would have wound up with about 360 victories, a total reached only by Cy Young, Walter Johnson, Grover Cleveland Alexander, Christy Mathewson, Warren Spahn, Pud Galvin and Kid Nichols.

As researchers have suggested, Feller might have

set a record for most years leading either major league in games won. He tied Johnson and Alexander with six, but Spahn led eight times.

At his strikeout rate Feller probably would have passed 3,500, nipping Johnson's total of 3,508.

"Yeah," Bob will quip, appreciating the flattery, "but I'd have set a base-on-balls record that would have been out of sight, too." He walked 1,764.

Feller's moods carry him from modesty to chestiness, but he had something when he suggested a few years ago that he'd like to be pitching now because of the increased emphasis on long-ball hitters.

"I liked to go against guys who swung for the fences," he said. "The strikeouts came easier."

When Bob broke in with that 5-3 record and 3.34 ERA for 62 innings as a 17-year-old in 1936, the American League was in a savage hitting mood. The league batting average was .289 and even though Cleveland finished fifth, the Indians led with a .304 team mark.

Luke Appling, White Sox shortstop, led in hitting with a .388 average, and 46 players, appearing in 10 or more games, batted .300 or better. Cleveland's first baseman Hal Trosky, drove in 162 runs and the Yankees' Lou Gehrig belted 49 homers.

Looking back, years later, Feller would remember Gehrig as extremely tough and he would pay tribute, too, to Joe DiMaggio and to Ted Williams. Although Williams hit only .270 against him, Bob remembered that Ted beat him with some big blows.

"But the toughest hitter was Tommy Henrich," he would say, mentioning the Yankees' Old Reliable, their lefthanded-hitting right fielder, a clutch performer.

The span of Feller's career can be appreciated best when he mentioned the two best righthanded hitters he'd faced as Rogers Hornsby and Al Simmons.

"But you didn't pitch against Hornsby," said Feller's first wife, the former Virginia Winther of Waukegan, Ill., aware that the Rajah belonged to an earlier baseball generation.

"Yes, I did, my first couple of years up," said the

pitcher, absolutely correct in his recollection. "Hornsby was old, but he impressed me the way he could stand back here deep in the batter's box and stride into the ball."

The young man, more than 20 years his junior, impressed Hornsby, too. "Sure, he's green," said the Rajah, "but with a fastball like that, you can be so green that the cows chase you to the train. And don't forget, the kid's got a helluva curve, too."

Aboard ship, as a gun-crew chief on the U.S.S. *Alabama* in World War II, Rapid Robert developed a slider, the third pitch that some baseball men, like Stan Musial, think contributed to his spectacular 1946 season.

The big season was produced for the right man, Bill Veeck, a generous executive whose hoopla and a new winning way transformed Cleveland into the immediate box-office wonder of postwar baseball. When The Sportshirt got through negotiating with Feller for '47, he pointed out to the playing field at Cleveland's mammoth stadium and cracked, "Feller now owns everything to the left of first base."

From an Iowa hayseed, Bob Feller became completely urbane and baseball's first incorporated athlete, Ro-Fel, Inc. To most athletes, he must have epitomized success as the businessman-ballplayer, one able to devote considerable time to a myriad of outside activities and endorsements, yet able to maintain physical condition and mental concentration for his primary pursuit—pitching.

In Ro-Fel's playing days, it worked that way, too, because no matter how much he participated in other activities, his performance couldn't be said to suffer. In '47, he slipped on a follow-through, twisted a knee and, continuing to pitch, hurt his arm. But he still was quite a feller, upper or lower case, and won 20 games.

He was estimated that year to have earned $150,000, counting endorsements for sporting goods, ice cream, peanut butter, breakfast food and shaving cream, plus magazine articles, book royalties and radio appearances.

A magazine article, incidentally, showed that

Feller's whopping income still couldn't be compared with the approximate $130,000 Babe Ruth took down in 1930, a Depression year when the Bambino was paid $80,000. After all, the 1930 dollar was worth $1.40 in terms of 1947 purchasing power, the story said, and, of course, the big difference was in taxes. Ruth, it was said, was taxed only $33,250 on $130,000. Feller, on the other hand, reportedly would keep only $47,000 except for the legal maneuver of being incorporated under the laws of Ohio.

Bob was president of Ro-Fel Inc., wife Virginia was secretary and his father-in-law, W. M. Winther, a wealthy man, was vice president and treasurer.

Feller, too, was presumed wealthy over the years that followed, but it was shattering to hear late in baseball's centennial season, 1969, that one of the shiniest examples of business acumen had encountered financial difficulties. At that point, it seemed that the practical joker, whose penchant for visual gags was fanned at Great Lakes by the football coach, Paul Brown, needed to pull a financial rabbit out of the hat he wore at a jaunty angle.

He'd learn to live well, Bob and his wife and the three sons on whom he doted. For a time, Feller owned a 27-foot cabin cruiser, a boat that slept four. He drove a fast, maroon Cadillac with long, loud twin horns, and, of course, his wife had a car. He traveled with three bags when he was on the road with the Indians, including one for his business files, magazines, books and gadgets, and for years he flew his own plane.

It's possible that Feller just wasn't a good businessman or, more specifically, a good insurance salesman. He has given considerable time to working with juveniles and aiding the conservation program. He has been quick to make a talk and a sucker for clinics. Maybe that's not the way to run a railroad or an insurance business.

To put aside further speculation about how or why Feller would feel the pinch, unless he was tied too tightly in annuities that hadn't been paid off, it's

enough to say that he made himself a name and gave other big league ballplayers big ideas.

Immediately after the 1946 World Series, Feller took on tour by chartered plane, traveling first class all the way, an array of talent that included Stan Musial, Mickey Vernon, Spud Chandler, Johnny Sain, Charley Keller, Ken Keltner, Dutch Leonard, Johnny Berardino, Sam Chapman, Rollie Hemsley, Frankie Hayes, Jim Hegan, Jeff Heath, Bob Lemon and, of course, Ro-Fel himself.

Bob Feller's Major League All-Stars won 29 of 35 games against assorted opposition. Eighteen of those contests were against Satchel Paige's All-Stars, a team of the best Negro players who traveled in another plane chartered by Feller.

The pace was gruelling—Feller himself pitched from two to five innings in all but one of the games—but the trip was rewarding to ballplayers whose salaries had not yet profited either from the pressure of threatened contract-jumping to Mexico or from baseball's post-war box office boom. The individual payoff ranged from $1,700 to $6,000. Musial, the National League's batting champion and Most Valuable Player, earned considerably more from the barnstorming tour than from a skimpy World Series return in which each winning share was around $3,500.

Resultant baseball legislation, forcing a larger guaranteed Series pool, probably didn't endear Feller to the owners, who passed a restriction prohibiting barnstorming until after the completion of the Series. Reports were that Feller, who had profited handsomely from his first king-sized expedition, lost heavily the second time around.

A vigorous spokesman for the players at times and yet critical of their stand on other occasions, Feller remained a chesty, articulate, positive—and frequently controversial—person.

Incongruously, he could champion players' rights and then beg off from the All-Star Game that benefited them. He could risk criticism by southern sports followers more than 40 years ago for playing against Negroes in exhibitions and then damage his popularity among black fans by predicting that Jackie Robinson never would make the big leagues.

The feud with Robinson, apparently stemming from financial unpleasantries that harked back to the barnstorming days, broke out at baseball's centennial celebration in Washington in 1969. When Robinson spoke out against the baseball establishment for alleged discrimination against black men in managerial or executive capacities, Feller rushed to baseball's defense and drew further charges of prejudice. It's a fact, however, supported by a *Saturday Evening Post* story, that Feller was among the first, if not actually the first, to go to bat for Satchel Paige as deserving election to the Hall of Fame.

Bill Feller, who died when Bob was serving in World War II, certainly didn't bring up a coward. When his Cleveland teammates clammed up after a famed insurrection against manager Oscar Vitt in 1940, the year they blew the pennant to Detroit, only Feller said what he thought.

"Oscar makes us nervous," he told reporters then, lifting his eyebrows in a characteristic nervous gesture. "I wouldn't want to play for him next year."

However, no manager apparently ever found Feller wanting, either in his willingness to work or in his devotion to physical conditioning. From the time he employed arm-and-back-strengthening exercises with a chair in the Feller farm kitchen at Van Meter until he labored alone with stretching exercises in the outfield of major league parks, Rapid Robert was a physical faddist. As in business hookups, he merely was ahead of his day.

Just as he usually was ahead of the hitters even when he was behind them with occasional errant pitches of high velocity, the kind that could turn a hitter's hair white when the ball whistled across the nape of his neck.

The reason Cleveland paid him better than $80,000 a year at his peak was partly because of the obvious, his ability to win, and partly because he had compelling presence in baseball flannels. The

cocky-looking guy with No. 19 on his back was the best toe-plated attraction from Dizzy Dean to Sandy Koufax and the best pitcher, too.

When he fanned 18 Tigers the final day of the 1938 season, he crabbed Hank Greenberg's chances of catching Ruth's 60-homer record. Greenberg went into a last-day doubleheader needing two homers and was stopped cold, but not so completely as Chet Laabs. Feller fired a third strike past the stubby outfield slugger five times. The same Laabs won the 1944 pennant for the St. Louis Browns with two final-game homers.

Feller's first no-hitter was unusual. It came on opening day, 1940, at Chicago and was the first hitless opener ever pitched in the American League. Bob fanned eight and walked five in his 1-0 conquest of the Chisox.

His third hitless game also was unusual because Detroit scored a run without benefit of a hit in the July 1, 1951, contest he won, 2-1, walking three men. "That one," he reminisced, "kinda snuck up on me."

Feller pitched in five All-Star Games and allowed just five hits and one run in 12⅓ innings, passing four batters and striking out 13. And in his first World Series game in 1948, allowing just two hits at Boston, he lost a heartbreaker to Johnny Sain, 1-0. Umpire Bill Stewart obviously blew a play on which Feller and shortstop-manager Lou Boudreau teamed to pick off Phil Masi, who then scored the game's only run on a single by Tommy Holmes.

Knocked out in another start in '48 as Cleveland beat Boston in six games, Feller didn't get a chance in 1954 when the pitching-rich Indians, who had won 111 regular-season games, were upset in four straight by the New York Giants. A 13-3 spot pitcher, three seasons removed from his sixth and last 20-game season, Rapid Robert understood manager Al Lopez' problem.

"I received a lot of mail afterward telling me it was a 'shame' I hadn't pitched, and I appreciated the well-meant sympathy," said Feller, who was close to bowing out, which he did after the 1956 season. Just short of 38 that season, he lost four decisions and won none.

"Baseball," Bob insisted at the time and would repeat later, "owes me nothing and I owe everything to baseball."

If this summary of Feller's career has seemed to emphasize his disaffection with the game just because he has been critical at times of persons or situations, it has been an unintentional distortion. The man comes across to some of us as complex, confusing and, at times, contradictory, but he is, above all, with that big grin and his availability, a goodwill ambassador of baseball.

He's one of the real superstars, a player elected to the Hall of Fame with a whopping 93 percent endorsement after the minimum five-year wait. In the two previous elections, then held every other year among 10-year active-writing members of the Baseball Writers' Association of America, no player had been given the 75 percent approval necessary.

Writers could remember many things about Feller, just as the fans did. Many games, too. Bob's own favorite was the second of his three no-hitters, the 1-0 game he won at Yankee Stadium on April 30, 1946.

Feller, back that season from that long service layoff, had started slowly and there were stories in the New York press that maybe Robert wasn't so rapid any more.

"They thought," the fireballer said afterward, making his usual direct assault on a touchy situation, "that I was washed up."

After Boudreau came in fast behind the mound for an acrobatic play on a slow-hit ball by swift Snuffy Stirnweiss in the first inning, Feller was supreme. He walked five and Boudreau kicked a leadoff groundball in the ninth, but by then batterymate Frank Hayes had hit a home run off Floyd Bevens. And the high-kicking Feller striking out 11, retired the side.

"It was," he said, "my most satisfying victory."

His toughest defeat, other than the one he lost in the '48 Series when he gave up only two hits, was in a duel of one-hitters with the St. Louis Browns' Bobby Cain early in 1952. A misjudged fly off the bat of leadoff man Bobby Young fell for a first-inning triple, and Al Rosen, playing third base, then kicked a grounder hit by Marty Marion.

Feller could forgive and forget, but he also could remember if he cared to. In 1937, when Cleveland and the New York Giants began their long annual Pullman grind a profitable barnstorming train trip home from spring training, New York's National League writers were eager to get a look at the 18-year-old. So, too, were members of the Giants, en route to a second straight pennant.

The first time Feller faced the Giants was at Vicksburg, Miss. He pitched the first three innings, held the Giants hitless and struck out six men, four of them in succession. Everyone was impressed except peppery Dick Bartell, feisty, raspy-voiced Giants' shortstop.

Bartell, who had popped out, shook his head and popped off. "We've got several guys in our league who can throw just as hard. I know he isn't as fast as Mungo."

The Giants saw a great deal more of Feller that spring, for the tour with the Indians carried them through many stops, including New Orleans, Tyler, Tex., Shawnee, Okla., Thomaston, Ga., Decatur, Ala., Pine Bluff, Ark., and Little Rock, just to name a few.

Feller, continuing to strike out the Giants, zeroed in on the talkative Bartell. As Tom Meany recalled, he fanned Dick something like 16 times in 19 turns at bat. Bill Slocum wrote, "Bartell went all the way to Fort Smith before he got so much as a loud foul against Feller."

The more often Feller struck him out, the louder Bartell would proclaim that Fireball Bob wasn't as fast as Brooklyn's Van Lingle Mungo. A couple of years later, the National League played a dirty trick on Dick, trading him to Detroit, where he had to face Feller more often.

The same thing happened: Bob, bearing down extra hard against his detractor, would strike out Bartell even more than he did other hitters, and the irascible little infielder would continue to insist, "Not as fast as Mungo, not as fast…"

Years later, reminded of the one-sided vendetta, Robert William Andrew Feller flashed his crooked grin.

"Oh, yeah, Bartell," he said. "Sure was stubborn, wasn't he?"

ROBERT WILLIAM ANDREW FELLER
Born November 3, 1918, at Van Meter, Ia.
Height 6-0 Weight 185
Threw and batted righthanded.
Named to Hall of Fame, 1962.

YEAR	CLUB	LEAGUE	G.	IP.	W.	L.	Pct.	H.	R.	ER.	SO.	BB.	ERA.
1936	Cleveland	Amer.	14	62	5	3	.625	52	29	23	76	47	3.34
1937	Cleveland	Amer.	26	149	9	7	.563	116	68	56	150	106	3.38
1938	Cleveland	Amer.	39	278	17	11	.607	225	136	126	240	208	4.08
1939	Cleveland	Amer.	39	297	24	9	.727	227	105	94	246	142	2.85
1940	Cleveland	Amer.	43	320	27	11	.711	245	102	93	261	118	2.62
1941	Cleveland	Amer.	44	343	25	13	.658	284	129	120	260	194	3.15
1942-43-44	Cleveland	Amer.					(In Military Service)						
1945	Cleveland	Amer.	9	72	5	3	.625	50	21	20	59	35	2.50
1946	Cleveland	Amer.	48	371	26	15	.634	277	101	90	348	153	2.18
1947	Cleveland	Amer.	42	299	20	11	.645	230	97	89	196	127	2.68
1948	Cleveland	Amer.	44	280	19	15	.559	255	123	111	164	116	3.57
1949	Cleveland	Amer.	36	211	15	14	.517	198	104	88	108	84	3.75
1950	Cleveland	Amer.	35	247	16	11	.593	230	105	94	119	103	3.43
1951	Cleveland	Amer.	33	250	22	8	.733	239	105	97	111	95	3.49
1952	Cleveland	Amer.	30	192	9	13	.409	219	124	101	81	83	4.73
1953	Cleveland	Amer.	25	176	10	7	.588	168	78	70	60	60	3.58
1954	Cleveland	Amer.	19	140	13	3	.813	127	53	48	59	39	3.09
1955	Cleveland	Amer.	25	83	4	4	.500	71	43	32	25	31	3.47
1956	Cleveland	Amer.	19	58	0	4	.000	63	34	32	18	23	4.97
Major League Totals			570	3828	266	162	.621	3271	1557	1384	2581	1764	3.25

WORLD SERIES RECORD

YEAR	CLUB	LEAGUE	G.	IP.	W.	L.	Pct.	H.	R.	ER.	SO.	BB.	Ave.
1948	Cleveland	Amer.	2	14 1/3	0	2	.000	10	8	8	7	5	5.02

CRAFTY AND CAPABLE: Whitey Ford, slick southpaw off the sidewalks of New York, was an annual big game winner. He and his pal Mickey Mantle entered the Hall of Fame together.

WHITEY FORD

In Damon Runyon's delightful *Guys and Dolls*, set to bright, tuneful music by Frank Loesser's talent, Sky Masterson—or was it another colorful dark-shirted, white-tied gambling sharpie from Manhattan, Nathan Detroit?—told the take-an-edge gambling sharpies at Mindy's that his old daddy had told him to be aware the slick guy.

"If," said the Runyonesque character, as sage as Thanksgiving turkey dressing, "a fella wants to bet he can squirt cider out of his ear, don't bet.

Chances are, you'll wind up with an earful of cider yourself."

Yeah, you know, just like the old admonition of never eating at a place called "Mom's" or of playing cards with a guy addressed as "Doc." It's poison to the pocketbook and to the personal vanity to try to match wits or dollars and wits with a man named "Slick."

"Slick," that's what old sly guy Casey Stengel and the New York Yankees called Edward Charles

(Whitey) Ford, the winningest percentage pitcher among 200-game victors ever. And after he was safely ensconced in the baseball Hall of Fame, the good-looking strawberry blond from the sidewalks of New York let the rest of us know just how slick he was.

Clever enough to qualify almost overnight as a customer's man for a stock brokerage in which Donald M. Grant, board chairman of the New York Mets, was a partner. But proving that high school graduate Ford was more than a quick mathematical study, he boldly admitted that he had cheated to help further and to prolong his career.

Sitting down with *The New York Times'* gifted Joe Durso to put out *Whitey and Mickey*, an autobiography for Viking Press with playmate Mantle, Whitey raised the *Times'* man's brows by insisting on including a detailed discourse on the tricks he had used, doctoring of the ball that officially was outlawed in 1920, eight years before the Ford who became the Cadillac of pitchers first wisecracked his way out of the womb.

The purists will blush for the pitcher because of the gimmicks, about which more will be said later in this profile, but, suffice to say, *The New York Times'* Sunday magazine summed it up pretty well with an excerpt from the Ford-Mantle book in a piece entitled: "Confessions of a Gunkball Artist."

So the Snow White-complexioned son of Irish-Swedish parentage was not nearly so pure as that schoolgirl complexion, either in cavorting into the beer drinker's Hall of Fame, which the city slicker and country boy Mantle did vulgarly for television suds' commercials after their election to Cooperstown, or in throwing a baseball with both consummate skill and deceitful guile.

The temptation, therefore, is to censure more than to cheer Ford, but the lefthander's frankness, though almost painfully refreshing, does bring up a point other than Slick's obvious ingenuity. To wit, how MANY pitchers since 1920 have cheated, other than Whitey and his skinny Brooklyn south-

paw rival, Preacher Roe, who confessed for financial consideration after his career that he indeed had, as the saying goes, loaded 'em up.

The spitter, according to Ford, is one illegal pitch Whitey used rarely. The most notable example, he related, was in the first of the two 1961 All-Star Games. The scene was San Francisco, then a new playground for Ford, Mantle and other American Leaguers, and Slick and Mick made the most out of the schedule hiatus, including taking advantage of sportsman Horace Stoneham's invitation to use his country club for golf and a visit to the 19th hole.

Well, sir, like kids let loose in a candy store, the two famous Yankees decided they needed sticks and shoes, etc., and by the time they'd wet their whistle and wandered away, they'd built up a $400 tab, pretty hefty back there in a recession period. Dutifully, they offered to reimburse Stoneham, but the Giants' club president prankishly offered a sporting proposition, forgetting friend Runyon's story about the cider in the ear and the fact that one of the two parties with whom he was wagering had the nickname of "Slick."

Aware that Willie Mays hit Ford as if Whitey were Willie's honky cousin, Horace said he'd tear up the tab if the pitcher struck out the great San Francisco slugger on the morrow. Agreed.

The next day in the first inning, the crafty lefty got two strikes on the menacing righthanded hitter and then did what he would deadpanned say his mother told him never to do: Put his fingers in his mouth. He loaded up a beaut, a spitter that, he told Durso for the peach of the pinstriped pair's book, started at Mays' chest and plopped abruptly down to Willie's knees and, most importantly, beneath his flailing bat.

That's why, as Whitey told it, amusedly, even though the All-Star Game was only an inning old, Mantle came charging in from center field, clapping his hands with glee, a couple of hundred bucks ahead.

Probably when Whitey was knee high to one of those chickens his father plucked over there in

Astoria, Queens' Borough, N.Y., before his Irish Pop ran a pub that was like mother's milk to Ford and friends, the future star learned competitively how to take an edge. Heck, then only 5-9, 145 pounds, he had to turn from first base to pitching just to prove to Paul Krichell, the famous Yankee scout, that he belonged in a baseball uniform rather than in the bleachers.

By the time he signed for a $7,000 bonus—the New York-based Giants were outbid and Brooklyn Dodgers simply blew it—Ford moved almost as fast as the flim-flam man who conned him out of 40 bucks at a carnival at Binghamton, N.Y., where he pitched brilliantly (16-5, 1.61 earned-run average) in 1949. Manager Lefty Gomez, whose Yankee southpaw supremacy he would surpass, hung on him the nickname of "Whitey." The "Slick," as mentioned, came later at a time when Ford was so prominent that batterymate Elston Howard described him with awe as the "Chairman of the Board."

As a con man of the mound himself, Ford was impressed that any sideshow hawker could hook him in a game of chance. You know, it was like the guy who invented the old Army game, the shell game of three pods and a pea, finding that the reuben he was taking had substituted a second pea. Whitey never forgot that he had been suckered.

Nineteen years he wore the famous flannels of the Yankees, beginning in the era of Joe DiMaggio and winding up with an ailing wing in the sundown of Mantle, the man with whom he shared many a sunrise. When he stepped down—11 pennants, eight championships and 10 World Series victories after he came up—the urbane, smiling, affable Chairman of the Board had to blow his nose and brush away the tears in May 1967.

Not because of the pain, though he'd had more than his share, as he battled his way through the gout and two operations to relieve arterial blockage that impaired his circulation. A bone spur on the left elbow was excruciating and, at 38, Ford not only frowned on a third operation, but he found the Yankees' long-time team surgeon, Dr. Sidney Gaynor, agreeing with him. So Slick said farewell with—and not to—arms, particularly the over-developed left one that hung an inch lower except when he pitched. Then it would contract for hours to become two inches shorter than the right.

Even though only 2-and-4 in seven games in 1967 when he hung up his glove and his gimmicks, the gifted guy of gab and guts had an ERA of only 1.64 for 40 innings. Overall, winning 203 and losing just 106 for the best-of-the-century percentage, .690, he compiled a handsome 2.74 ERA.

Ford not only had tied a major league record with two consecutive one-hit games in 1955 and owned the most Series victories ever, 10, but the Cy Young winner of '61 broke Babe Ruth's priceless blue-ribbon perfection by not allowing a run in $33\frac{2}{3}$ consecutive World Series innings from 1960 to '62, meaning against Pittsburgh, Cincinnati and San Francisco.

With all due respect to Mantle, the shy introvert the slick Big Town towhead took as a running mate, what an entry of 1 and 1-A Whitey would have made with the Babe!

For the big-game winner, like the big-game hitter, it was a Coney Island world of wit and whoopee, of camaraderie if not cotton candy, and even when blinking back the tears at the going-away press conference, the masterful southpaw was the master of the situation.

"I came here in 1950 wearing $50 suits and I'm leaving wearing $200 suits, so I guess I'm doing all right," said Slick Ford, smiling with a cut-rate crack:

"And I'm getting 'em for $80."

Whitey left 'em laughing, which is the way he came in. Although Stengel always insisted it was the pitcher himself who had phoned long-distance in 1949 and said, "Why don't you bring up this kid Ford?" Eddie said he'd never gone that far.

But when he came up in 1950 at a time the Yankees were hurting for pitchers and reeled off a 9-1 record, his eighth straight was a pivotal production at Detroit, where Taters Frank Lary and the Tigers were making things troublesome for the Yanks. En route on the train to St. Louis, writers asked whether the victory at Detroit had been the most exciting and significant of his youthful career.

The impish 21-year-old's blue eyes twinkled. "I wouldn't say so," he deadpanned. "I remember pitching the Maspeth Ramblers to a 17-11 victory over the old Astoria Indians. That was a big one, too."

The same season when the Yankees bowled over the Philadelphia Phillies four straight in the World Series, Ford sat in the clubhouse preparing to go out for his 15-minute warmup of some 80 pitches. In came portly, cowboy-hatted Dizzy Dean, then doing Yankee broadcasts.

"Hey, Diz," said Whitey, out-Deaning Dean, "no wonder you won 30 games in that league. I could win 40."

Ford delighted in annoying the Yankee front office or so it seemed, anyway. Exasperated, starchy general manager George Weiss said one time, "He's just one of those typically fresh, aggressive New York kids. He holds out just to aggravate me and then signs at the last minute."

Another Yankee official said back in 1956, "I don't believe Whitey ever met—or went to—a party he didn't like. If there's not enough life, Ford will organize a songfest and get everybody into it except the waiters."

"F" stands for Ford and fun. Whitey had it. He had fun when he was a kid playing for the Thirty-Fourth Avenue Boys Club of Astoria. He had fun with the Army (1951-52) as a corporal and he had fun, barrels of it, with the Yankees. First, with Billy Martin and Mantle in a group called Mirth, Inc., before Weiss exiled future manager Martin to Kansas City after a fracas at the Copacabana night club.

Then, later, the fun was the tremendous twosome of Durso's book duo, Whitey and Mickey. They missed a train to Detroit once, and another

time they blew a plane from Boston, but, oh, how they delivered. Why, Ford was so relaxed that even as a rookie he overslept and reached Chicago's Comiskey Park just a half-hour before he pitched a three-hit shutout, one of his 45.

A pitching whiz as a coach, taciturn Jim Turner said that Ford, who filled out to about 180 pounds, was better-developed physically than it seemed and threw harder than generally believed, setting him apart from another clever lefthander of the overlapping era, Eddie Lopat.

"But, mainly," said Turner of Ford, "he's completely relaxed in even the most competitive situations."

Take, for instance, the time Whitey was leading the Boston Red Sox in the ninth inning at Yankee Stadium, 3-2, bases loaded, two out and dangerous Jackie Jensen at bat. Whitey stood on the mound, leaning over to take the battery sign, lips characteristically pressed against his teeth in a beardown situation.

Suddenly, as the crowd and a television audience watched, puzzled, Ford backed off the rubber, stooped over, made a minute examination of the dirt in front of the mound. Cradling the ball from his bare hand to his glove, he picked up something off the ground and then put it in his hip pocket.

Getting back to the business at hand—oh, yes, that chap Jensen—Whitey threw a game-ending, swinging strike past the Boston slugger and then, gleefully, greeted his interrogators in the clubhouse, holding up a two-dollar bill.

"My secret weapon," he shouted. "I found the two bucks before that last pitch."

When, really, did Ford come up with his real secret weapon, the gadgetry by which he tampered illegally with the ball?

Mixing his motion from overhanded to three-quarter overhanded to sidearmed, he blended a fastball, sinker, curve and, finally, it was said, an effective slider to go with pinpoint control, a perfect pickoff motion and an ability to help himself with his fielding, bunting and even hitting, too. But when, actually, did Slick begin to cheat?

Under Stengel, he'd been the Yankees' money man of the mound with such seasons from 1953 as 18-6, 16-8, 18-7 and 19-6 through 1956, but then he developed shoulder trouble in '57, a year he was 11-5, and was 14-7, 16-10 before capping—for him—a mediocre season of 12-9 in 1960 with two shutout victories over Pittsburgh in the World Series.

The Pirates, you'll recall, won that wild Series, though widely outscored, and both Stengel and Weiss were eased into retirement, at which point Ford was rumored to be dealt to St. Louis. Whitey reportedly nixed the trade by hinting to a St. Louis writer close to the Cardinals that his arm was so sore that he couldn't comb his hair.

Under Stengel, Slick often had missed a turn or at least a day to pitch a pivotal game and, as a result, never had won 20. He hit his peak when Ralph Houk took over in '61. The Major suggested a regular four-day rotation.

Stengel would bristle that he'd merely tried to protect the delicate piece of merchandise, i.e., Ford's left arm, especially as Allie Reynolds, Vic Raschi and Lopat reached the end of the line.

Ol' Case would discourse, obliquely, how Ford, by holding runners close to first base and then throwing low-breaking stuff hit onto the ground, had been rewarded with many rally-killing double plays because the baserunners couldn't get to second base in time to break up the two-for-one rhythm of the middle infield.

But there's no doubt, just as Ford demonstrated when he later coached for the Yankees, that Whitey was a Houk man. With 25-4, 17-8, 24-7 and 17-6 through 1964, he was a spectacular 83-25 over a four-year period. Great for a guy 35, indeed, but arm trouble limited Whitey to one ineffectual appearance against the Cardinals in the 1964 World Series.

With Mantle and Howard and Roger Maris showing telltale signs of wear and tear, and Yogi Berra a one-year manager instead of hard-hitting catcher, a dynasty was done. The Yankees didn't get into the winner's circle again until George Steinbrenner bought the store from CBS and re-stocked it.

By then, at 50, Edward Charles Ford still was married to Joan Foran, whom he had met and taken as his bride in 1951 before giving Uncle Sam two years. They had a daughter and a son, Eddie, who was good enough to win a professional chance as an infielder with the Boston Red Sox. The father spoke proudly of the son when, in 1975, virtually arm in arm with buddy Mickey Mantle, Slick and Mick went into the Hall of Fame.

Mantle, deservedly, was a rare first-time-eligible choice. Ford got to Cooperstown on his second try, an impressive tribute considering that, for instance, both Early Wynn and Robin Roberts, winners of more games, needed four elections each to achieve approval of 75 percent of the Baseball Writers' Association of America and Juan Marichal also required two rounds of ballots.

Whether Whitey would have been chosen so quickly if he "confessed" before publication of the book by Durso is a question—at least in this opinion.

You see, even though maintaining he had practiced his mischief only "a few times, mostly late in my career when I could use a little help," Ford related how he had practiced his black magic of the mound as early as 1961, the year he burst forth a 25-game winner. To combat the opening-day cold, well, let's hear Whitey as he tape-recorded it for his book:

"What I did was to make a sticky stuff from a few well-selected ingredients. I took some turpentine, some baby oil and some resin and mixed them all together in a jar. It turned out like Elmer's Glue.

"It was white stuff, not black, so you couldn't spot it on my fingers. I'd put it on both hands, on my uniform shirt, on as many places as I could, and I'd do it between innings in the dugout when nobody was watching me—least of all, the other club and the umpires…

"I even found a sophisticated way to keep the stuff stashed away: I bought a roll-on deodorant, took out the roll-on ball, emptied out the deodorant stuff, poured my sticky stuff in, and shoved the little can in the pocket of my warm-up jacket. Between innings, I'd just ooze some of it out onto my hands and fingers, and now I was getting a good grip on the ball, cold weather or no cold weather. We won the game, all right…"

Ford was quoted further:

"Look, they didn't call me Slick for nothing, but I wasn't the only pitcher in baseball who gave himself a little edge. The other clubs were always watching me like hawks, but some guys made a living by doing tricks with the balls…

"Eddie Lopat and I used pine tar a few times, but it was black and it would cake on your fingers. Between innings you'd have to wash it off with alcohol. Not so good."

Here, Whitey suggested that the psychological helped even when he wasn't doctoring the ball, writing:

"…Like when I was (merely) warming my fingers on a hot-water bottle or something, managers like Charlie Dressen would be screaming to the umpires about me, anyway."

Recalling that he and Pedro Ramos were the only Yankee pitchers to draw opposing protests, Ford explained:

"Timing is important when you're working with tricks. Sometimes I wouldn't use a loaded pitch at all in a game, whether it was a mud ball or a cut ball or a sticky ball. Sometimes I'd throw it to get a strikeout or a groundball. You could usually get a groundball because the pitch was sinking, and a groundball could get you out of an inning."

A year after he quit, 1968, he was coaching for Houk when the Yankees played their New York rivals, the Mets, in the annual mid-summer Mayor's Trophy game for charity, and Ford remembered Houk suggesting, "You want to have some fun? Pitch an inning tonight."

Whitey said he "rubbed hell out of the ball" in bullpen cement and, phoning Mantle from the bullpen, told the outfield star, then playing first base, to use the game ball for infield practice that inning so Whitey could spirit his scuffed up ball into action. The Mets went down feebly, 1-2-3.

"It would take a pitcher to suspect something right away," Durso quoted Ford, "like it takes a thief to catch one. So Dick Selma came running over from the Mets' dugout demanding to inspect the ball. I just laughed and walked off the mound. But after the game, Selma came over again holding my bullpen ball in his hand—all cut and almost bleeding, it was cut so bad—and asked me to autograph it for him. Like Willie Sutton autographing a bank vault."

In the 1963 World Series, going from the ridiculousness of an exhibition to the sublime of the big-money spotlight, Ford said he "threw mostly mud balls or cut balls the whole game" and held the Dodgers to two hits, but still lost to Sandy Koufax, 2-1, on giant Frank Howard's second hit, a homer.

"I guess I didn't cut the ball enough," Ford lamented.

Other than the $400 tab-saving strikeout pitch to Willie Mays in the '61 All-Star Game at San Francisco, Whitey said he'd thrown one other spitter—to Kansas City's Manny Jiminez three years later—but he acknowledged that batterymate Elston Howard "sometimes would cut the ball on his shinguards for me…but it was hard for him to cut it good on the little metal rivet…"

Ford labeled the foregoing "tricks"as "child's play compared with the main event—the RING. I always figure that'd be a secret forever, but since I'm laying it all on the line, I might as well go all the way…"

Late in his career, Whitey disclosed he'd used his "street-smart overtime" and had a jeweler friend make up for him a ring to specifications—"a half-inch by quarter-inch piece of rasp, all nice and scratchy like a file…"

Whitey would wear the stainless steel "hunk of rasp" on his glove (right) hand, then during the game, he'd just stand behind the mound like any other pitcher rubbing up a new ball and—.

"I'd take the glove off and rub up the ball. That rasp would do some job on it, too. Whenever I needed a groundball, I'd cut it good. It was as though I had my own tool bench out there with me.

"To hide it, I even got a skin-colored Band-Aid and wrapped it around the ring to match my finger. Camouflage and all. I also worked out some signs with Elston to warn him which way the ball was going to break…"

The secret weapon, withheld from Yankee teammates, lasted until one day at Cleveland when pitching rival Jim (Mudcat) Grant picked up the cut ball and showed it to umpire Hank Soar. Then Alvin Dark, managing the Indians, retrieved a few foul balls hit into the Cleveland dugout and showed them to Soar. The umpire came over to Ford and asked, "How are you cutting the ball?"

"Then," said Whitey, "he spotted my ring and got to the point. 'What's that?' he asked me. "And—Joannie forgive me—I said, 'My wedding ring.'"

Whitey Ford reluctantly got rid of that $100 piece of metal aid to pitching mettle, but, somehow, like the naive guy who got cider squirted into his ear, I wish you'd kept your smarts to yourself, Slick.

EDWARD CHARLES (WHITEY) FORD
Born October 21, 1928, at New York, N.Y.
Height 5-10 Weight 181
Threw and batted lefthanded.
Named to Hall of Fame, 1974.

YEAR	CLUB	LEAGUE	G.	IP.	W.	L.	Pct.	H.	R.	ER.	SO.	BB.	ERA.
1947	Butler	Mid. Atl.	24	157	13	4	.765	151	86	67	114	58	3.84
1948	Norfolk	Pied.	30	216	16	8	.667	182	83	62	171	113	2.58
1949	Binghamton	East.	26	168	16	5	.762	118	38	30	151	54	1.61
1950	Kansas City	A.A.	12	95	6	3	.667	81	39	34	80	48	3.22
1950	New York	Amer.	20	112	9	1	.900	87	39	35	59	52	2.81
1951-52	New York	Amer.					(In Military Service)						
1953	New York	Amer.	32	207	18	6	.750	187	77	69	110	110	3.00
1954	New York	Amer.	34	211	16	8	.667	170	72	66	125	101	2.82
1955	New York	Amer.	39	254	18	7	.720	188	83	74	137	113	2.62
1956	New York	Amer.	31	226	19	6	.760	187	70	62	141	84	2.47
1957	New York	Amer.	24	129	11	5	.688	114	46	37	84	53	2.58
1958	New York	Amer.	30	219	14	7	.667	174	62	49	145	62	2.01
1959	New York	Amer.	35	204	16	10	.615	194	82	69	114	89	3.04
1960	New York	Amer.	33	193	12	9	.571	168	76	66	85	65	3.08
1961	New York	Amer.	39	283	25	4	.862	242	108	101	209	92	3.21
1962	New York	Amer.	38	258	17	8	.680	243	90	83	160	69	2.90
1963	New York	Amer.	38	269	24	7	.774	240	94	82	189	56	2.74
1964	New York	Amer.	39	245	17	6	.739	212	67	58	172	57	2.13
1965	New York	Amer.	37	244	16	13	.552	241	97	88	162	50	3.25
1966	New York	Amer.	22	73	2	5	.286	79	33	20	43	24	2.47
1967	New York	Amer.	7	44	2	4	.333	40	11	8	21	9	1.64
Major League Totals—16 Years			498	3171	236	106	.690	2766	1107	967	1956	1086	2.74

WORLD SERIES RECORD

Holds records for most series by pitcher (11); most games by pitcher (22), games started (22), games won (10), games lost (8), innings pitched (146), bases on balls (34), strikeouts (94) and consecutive scoreless innings (33), total series.

YEAR	CLUB	LEAGUE	G.	IP.	W.	L.	Pct.	H.	R.	ER.	SO.	BB.	ERA.
1950	New York	Amer.	1	82/3	1	0	1.000	7	2	0	7	1	0.00
1953	New York	Amer.	2	8	0	1	.000	9	4	4	7	2	4.50
1955	New York	Amer.	2	17	2	0	1.000	13	6	4	10	8	2.12
1956	New York	Amer.	2	12	1	1	.500	14	8	7	8	2	5.25
1957	New York	Amer.	2	16	1	1	.500	11	2	2	7	5	1.13
1958	New York	Amer.	3	151/3	0	1	.000	19	8	7	16	5	4.11
1960	New York	Amer.	2	18	2	0	1.000	11	0	0	8	2	0.00
1961	New York	Amer.	2	14	2	0	1.000	6	0	0	7	1	0.00
1962	New York	Amer.	3	192/3	1	1	.500	24	9	9	12	4	4.12
1963	New York	Amer.	2	12	0	2	.000	10	7	6	8	3	4.50
1964	New York	Amer.	1	51/3	0	1	.000	8	5	5	4	1	8.44
World Series Totals—11 Years			22	146	10	8	.556	132	51	44	94	34	2.71

BESTIAL BELTER: Jimmy Foxx was called "The Beast" because he lived as hard a life off the field as he did on it, but Double-X was one of the most powerful hitters ever.

JIMMIE FOXX

Heading home by automobile for Kansas City after the fifth game of the 1930 World Series, a Jackson County judge stopped on the outskirts of St. Louis and a passerby yelled to the judge's party and asked the score.

"Jimmie Foxx 2, St. Louis 0," was the quick, clear comeback by the western district jurist, a man who would prove again later his ability to get across a point— Harry S. Truman.

Foxx' ninth-inning home run off the Cardinals'

Burleigh Grimes just had broken up the decisive game of the Series won by the Philadelphia Athletics, one of two American League clubs for whom the powerful slugger performed most of his nearly 20 years in the big leagues.

For more than another 20 years after he finished, Foxx stood second only to Babe Ruth in career home runs and was, in fact, the only righthanded hitter to have achieved 500 or more homers. But even though Hank Aaron and others have now exceeded Jimmie's 534, the pumpkin-faced Maryland Strongboy still must be regarded as one of the most menacing hitters ever.

One time when deadpanned Vernon (Lefty) Gomez, the happy Hidalgo of the New York Yankees, had decided with lefthanded logic that he might recover his famed fastball if he began to wear bifocals, the experiment had a sudden and shocking end.

"My God!" said Gomez, returning to the bench and removing the glasses, "I just took a look at Foxx through these, and he's more frightening than ever."

Although Foxx was a friendly, smiling fellow who said he was born to die broke, which he did, a victim of constant check-grabbing, unfortunate investments and plain bad luck, he cast quite an awesome shadow at home plate. With bare, bronzed biceps bulging from beneath sleeves cut deliberately short, he was broadbacked, square-jawed and presented an almost vengeful appearance from his straddle stance.

"He could hit me at midnight with the lights out," moaned Gomez over the years, and, grinning, Foxx never tut-tutted the compliment.

"If I could have hit only against lefthanders, I would have batted .500," said the vicious-swinging Philadelphia and Boston blockbuster who averaged .325 even though he was always well up in strikeouts as well as home runs.

They called him Foxxie—"Fawksie," as Connie Mack pronounced it with his New England accent— and Double X and The Beast. No matter what they called him, Jimmie was an impressive sight, especially if his huge physical proportions were magnified by glasses like the leg-pulling Gomez wore.

Lefty faced Foxxie in a jam one time as batterymate Bill Dickey riffled through the signal semaphore, forward and backward, trying to settle on a sign that would please the Yankee pitcher. Finally, taking off his mask, Dickey walked to the mound and said:

"Well, you've got to throw something."

"Not necessarily," Gomez replied. "Maybe if I stand here long enough, he'll go away."

Double X didn't go away. One time against Gomez, he hit a ball that probably was hit harder and farther than Mickey Mantle's shot against the facade at the top of the triple-tiered roof in right field at Yankee Stadium.

Yankee Stadium is considerably deeper in left field than in right. Foxx hit one five or six rows back into the third deck, just next to the bullpen runway. Despite the distance, the ball still had enough force to break a seat.

"I thought it was a fastball when I threw it," said Gomez ruefully, "but it was going a lot faster after Foxx hit it. Afterward, it took me 20 minutes to walk up into the stands and out there to the spot where he'd hit it in a split second."

An exaggeration, yes, but you didn't have to embroider the truth when Double X really dug into a pitch. He hit one clear out of Chicago's double-decked Comiskey Park into a playground, and the groundskeeper offered to bet that the ball went 600 feet.

"But he had no takers," Foxx would recall, smiling, in those later years when all he had left were his memories.

The *Philadelphia Bulletin*'s Sandy Grady put it so well when he wrote after Jimmie's death in 1967 that he knew something of those monstrous home runs "only by echo."

When a Richie Allen, Henry Aaron or Orlando Cepeda hit a moonshot over the high, double-deck left-field stands at Connie Mack Stadium, Grady made the trip outside the park known in Foxx' day as Shibe Park, seeking to discover where the ball landed.

"Oh, 'bout here," an old geezer would say, unimpressed. Then he'd point to the darkness in the parking lot beyond. "But Foxx hit several 'way back there."

The longest ball The Beast ever belted at Philly, he always said, was one which went to the left of the flagpole in center field, landing past the corner of Twentieth and Somerset streets.

For hitting homers far and often, as well as hitting

for average, Foxx played for as little as $2,000 in the big leagues and, with attendance bonus, got no higher than $32,000 briefly at Boston, before sinus flareups and high living seemed to take too much out of him at the age of 34. His name appeared in big league box scores for parts of the next four seasons, but 1941 was actually his last season of consequence.

Batting .300 with 105 runs batted in for just 135 games, Foxx finished that season with 19 homers after having hit 30 or more for 12 consecutive years, a record. Only 15 big league homers remained in the bat of the man who led the American League twice in batting, three times in RBIs and four times in homers.

Foxx, three times Most Valuable Player, 1932-33-38, probably would have to be considered the finest handyman in baseball history. Although primarily a first baseman, he caught and played third base enough to be remembered at those positions and, actually, performed for the Athletics briefly every place except on the mound. He pitched one inning as a gag with the Red Sox and retired all three batters.

Then, at the finish with the rival Phillies in the wartime season of 1945, when manager Ben Chapman was strapped, Jimmie even pitched. He would remember proudly that in what he recalled as his last big league game, he pitched five scoreless innings before he weakened and still wound up a winner.

The fact that Foxx played at all at Philadelphia was the result of a story that went back almost as far as 1907, when he was born in Sudlersville, Md., the same Eastern Shore area from which Frank (Home Run) Baker had gone to World Series fame.

James Emory Foxx was the son of Sam Dell Foxx, a Protestant Irish farmer. Jimmie walked from town to school, plowed, milked and did the usual chores of the country boy until 1917. At 10, he decided to run away and join the Army as a drummer boy. His paternal grandfather, Joseph Emory Foxx, was a

Confederate veteran who had filled his head about stories of courageous drummer boys in the Civil War.

Uncle Sam, though grateful, couldn't use the lad in World War I and Jimmie turned his attention to sports. Amazingly, when you consider that he was built like a small tank, he ran so well that his first love was track.

"I dreamed of becoming faster even than Charley Paddock, then the world's fastest human," Foxx would recall, insisting that he could break 10 seconds in the 100-yard dash.

Playing ball on the Sudlersville High School team and country teams, Jimmie first began to demonstrate the position-by-position versatility that later would prove so helpful. Then came demonstrations of power which attracted Home Run Baker, managing Easton in the Eastern Shore League. One morning, Foxx walked down to the RFD mailbox and found a penny postcard on which Baker had penciled an invitation for him to try out.

Jimmie went to Easton with the idea that he was a third baseman or maybe a pitcher, but Baker was short of catchers and wondered if the kid would go behind the bat.

"Just so I get a chance to hit," said Foxx, who impressed Baker so much that Home Run—a nickname he'd earned for two key World Series homers in 1911—wondered if the kid had brought his clothes with him. Heck, Jimmie didn't own much more than the overalls in which he'd tried out.

Happy to be asked, the lad, who was only 16 years old, went home, talked to his father and quit school with the understanding he'd finish in the fall. In May 1924, the powerful farmboy broke into professional baseball and, batting .296 in 76 games, showed so much power and promise that late in the season Baker came to him and said:

"I have a chance to make a deal for you with either New York (Yankees) or Philadelphia (Athletics). Mr. Mack is a wonderful man. I'd advise you to take the A's."

Baker was repaying a debt. When he quit the Athletics in 1915 at a time Mack was breaking up his championship club, the third baseman still belonged to Philadelphia. When the Yankees approached him, Baker could only refer them to Mack. Connie called in Baker and said he'd sell his contract to the New York club, which could afford to pay a larger salary.

"You'll never regret this," said Baker. "Someday I'll do something for you."

The "something" was Foxx, but Mr. Mack, with young Mickey Cochrane and the veteran Cy Perkins as catchers, wondered what he'd do with another mask-and-mitt man.

" I don't know," said Baker, "but the way he can hit, you'll find somewhere for him to play."

Baker told Foxx he would report to the Athletics in the spring of 1925. In late August, the Maryland Strongboy was playing in an all-star game against the Blue Ridge League. He was sitting in the dugout at Martinsville, W. Va., when he told Connie Mack was phoning from Philly.

Jimmie thought he was being ribbed and reluctantly answered the phone. It was THE Mr. Mack! "Get up here after tomorrow's game," Connie told him.

"Gosh, I've only got a handbag," the boy protested. "I'll have to go home to get some clothes."

Mack chuckled. "Pick up nothing," he said. "We'll buy them for you."

So two months short of his 17th birthday in 1924, Jimmie Foxx rode the bench for the Athletics, catching in batting practice and sitting at Mr. Mack's side, learning. On a western swing in an exhibition game against Cincinnati, he pinch-hit against the Redlegs' fine old lefthander, Eppa Rixey, and tripled to win the game.

The following year, on May Day, 1925, the Athletics were at Griffith Stadium in Washington when the announcement was given a crowd of 17,000:

"Foxx batting for Grove."

The kid they'd know as Double X stepped up to face Vean Gregg, a veteran who had pitched his first pro game when Jimmie was only a few months old. The count ran to 2-and-2 and then Foxx unloaded his first of 2,646 major league hits, a blue darter to left field for a single.

Although young Foxxie had six hits in nine trips, he was optioned to Providence, where he played 41 games, hitting .327. In 1926, he also sat by as his roommate, the illustrious Cochrane, did the A's catching. He got into only 26 games, most of them as a pinch-hitter, batting .313.

By 1927, Mack had begun to use him behind the plate often enough against lefthanded pitching for Foxx to participate in 61 games and go to the plate 130 times. As a result., hitting .323, at close to 20 years old, he hit his first three big league homers.

A year later, Foxx began to play third base, first base and to continue to catch on occasion, getting in 118 games, raising his homers to 13 and his average to .328. Now, Connie would have to find a regular place for him and, after Foxx played every game at third base in spring training, 1929, the athlete thought he knew where it would be. He was wrong.

Opening day, the venerable manager, who had waited 15 years for a pennant, asked if Jimmie had a first baseman's glove. No, he didn't.

"Well, get one," said Mr. Mack, "because you're the first baseman today."

Yes, today and almost every day thereafter and, though he never would be brilliant defensively, the greatest utility regular of them all wouldn't have to be. He began that year a reign of terror against American League pitching.

For 13 straight seasons, Double X drove in 100 or more runs, reaching a high of 175 at Boston in 1938. His career total of 1,921 was fifth only to Babe Ruth, Lou Gehrig, Ty Cobb and Stan Musial. His highest batting average, .364, was achieved with the A's in '32. He hit 50 homers in Boston in '38 and won his third MVP award.

But The Beast was at his battering best, unfortunately, in the depths of the Depression and, consequently, didn't profit as he might have. For instance, in 1929, when the A's won their first of three straight pennants, Foxx was paid only $5,000 as he contributed a .354 average, 33 homers and 117 RBIs.

When he tore the league apart in 1932, he was working on a three-year contract for $50,000 total. That season he hit .364, drove in 169 runs and slammed 58 homers, the most hit by any player other than Ruth and Roger Maris' 61 in 1961. Hank Greenberg matched the 58 in 1938.

Historians have calculated that except for a couple of ballpark alterations, Foxx would have hit more than 60 homers the year he hurt a wrist in August and had a cool spell before finishing briskly in September. Five times he hit the right-field screen at St. Louis' Sportsman's Park, where the screen had not been erected until 1930, three years after Ruth's 60. Furthermore, in 1932, they say, a screen was installed in front of the left-field bleachers at Cleveland's League Park and Foxx reportedly hit it "at least" three times.

When Foxx followed in the last year (1933) of his three-season contract with a Triple Crown season—.356 average, 48 homers and 163 RBIs—for a second successive MVP award, Mack asked him to take a pay cut from $16,333 to $12,000 because of the hard times.

"I had a helluva time settling for $16,000," Double X would explain in later years, smiling at a time when he was financially embarrassed and embarrassed that his problems had become common knowledge.

Mr. Mack, unloading his stars one by one to salvage the franchise, saved Fawksie for last. The Maryland Strongboy went to Boston's Gold Sox after the 1935 season with pitcher John (Footsie) Marcum for a battery of Gordon Rhodes and George Savino and (ahem!) $150,000 of Tom Yawkey's treasure chest.

Boston was a break for Foxx, financially as well as

artistically, because the high, green left-field wall at Fenway was a target and Double X tattooed it until the sinus and living habits closed him out sooner than really should have been necessary. Not, however, until he followed his big '38 season with a 1939 performance—.360, 35 homers and 105 RBIs—that impressed a tall, willowy rookie named Ted Williams.

"Foxx was getting toward the end of his career then," said Williams, "but he had switched to a lighter bat, maybe 35 or 36 ounces, and he was hanging in, getting a lot of blunk hits and every now and then really crashing one. I remember on a road trip that year Jimmie hit four balls like I never had seen before.

"The first one was a real ripper in Chicago, over the left-field stands, and in Cleveland I was on second and Mel Harder was pitching when Foxx hit one over the 435-foot sign. Then in Detroit, right after that, he hit the longest ball I'd ever seen—way up into the bleachers in left-center. Just hard to believe.

"I truly admired Foxx," Williams told biographer John Underwood. "He was older, of course, and he and I were a generation apart, but he was such a good-natured guy. Always a giggle and a 'Yeah, sure, sure.'

"He never made any bones about his love for Scotch. He used to say he could drink 15 of those little bottles of Scotch, those miniatures, and not be affected. Of course, nobody could do that and stay healthy, and it got to Jimmie later on."

By then, unfortunately, the good, late paydays were gone, along with the money Foxxie had lost in the stock market crash. Later he blew close to $100,000 on an ill-timed golf course venture at St. Petersburg, Fla., just before Pearl Harbor.

"You'd have thought, the way folks fled Florida, that they thought the Nazi U-boats were coming up the Gulf," the old slugger reminisced in later years.

Foxx was waived by the Red Sox to the Chicago Cubs in June 1942. He stayed out of baseball in

'43, but came back in '44 at the invitation of Jim Gallagher, then general manager of the Cubs. When it was obvious he'd lost it, Gallagher lined up for him a managerial job at Portsmouth, Va. A year later, in 1945, he wound up the season even pitching for the Phillies. He finished at age 37 by batting .268 with seven homers and 38 RBIs in 89 games.

Just one more season and Foxx would have qualified for the player pension plan, which embraced all players on big league rosters after September 1946. A season's difference could have made the last 21 of his 59 years more pleasant. Or would it just have provided more opportunity for a hail-fellow-well-met to grab more checks?

From 1946, except for brief managerial and coaching stints in the lower minors, until Yawkey brought him back for a season as a coach at Minneapolis in 1958, just after disclosure of his dire financial straits, Foxx was out of baseball. He did manage to coach the University of Miami ball team one year, but a bad back limited the amount of physical work he could do. Then another bad business venture forced him into bankruptcy.

Older-looking than his years, his blue eyes watery and the thick, dark, brown hair turned gray, he couldn't hold a job fronting a steak house with his name at Galesburg, Ill. He suffered a heart attack, then was hospitalized in 1963 when he came to St. Louis as guest of a Columbus sportsman for Stan Musial's retirement dinner. Musial visited Foxxie.

Married a second time and with three grown children, Foxx was at his brother's place in Miami in July 1967, a couple of days before the annual reunion at Cooperstown, where he had been inducted in 1951 when he was only 44 years old.

Eating dinner with his brother Sam, Jimmie choked to death, the Miami medical examiner reported, when a piece of meat lodged in his throat. The death was as depressing as the old slugger's lean years had been.

Somehow, though, like the little boy who never really grew up, Jimmie could slip back gracefully into the comfortable world of make-believe and relive those salad seasons of the past. The cold reality of the present would be forgotten except when he'd slip as, for instance, when he talked about Williams.

"He's the greatest student of hitting I ever saw, the best hitter, a great all around guy and, besides," he'd say, winking, "I owe him money."

Foxx thought Walter Johnson even late in his career, threw harder than former Philadelphia teammate Lefty Grove did in his prime, indicating that perhaps Double X had felt the sting of Grove's churlishness. Jimmie thought Bob Feller's curve was even better than his fastball, and he praised two National League righthanders he'd seen briefly, Grover Cleveland Alexander when Foxxie was young and Dizzy Dean when Double X was at his peak.

"Alexander threw with such an easy motion," Double X recalled. "You fought to get up there and take some swings at him and then Alex would strike you out on three pitches at three different speeds.

"I remember the first time I batted against Dean. It was a night exhibition in Houston and Dizzy was a youngster. He threw one past my ear and I could only hear it. I tell you, I was ready to concede that night that one strike was out."

The toughest pitchers for Foxx, actually, were Johnny Allen of Cleveland and New York and the nomadic Louis Norman (Buck) Newsom. "But I finally caught up with Bobo," Double X said proudly, when he talked about his career as he lay hospitalized in St. Louis a few years before his death.

"The biggest homer I ever hit, not the longest, but the biggest, was the one here in the 1930 World Series," Foxxie said, remembering the one that Harry Truman also had recalled at the White House.

The World Series was tied in games, two apiece, and the fifth contest was scoreless when the husky Philadelphia first baseman faced veteran spitball righthander Burleigh Grimes in the ninth with one on and one out. "Earlier in the Series, Burleigh had surprised me with a curve, which I really didn't think he had," said Foxx, "and when I came up there in that spot I thought to myself, 'Maybe he'll throw it again.'

"He did, a change-of-pace curve, and I hit it way up in the left-center field bleachers, almost out of the ballpark, for a 2-0 victory and we won the Series the next day."

Foxx' smile widened. "Every time since that I've seen Grimes, the first thing he says is, 'One too many, Jim, one too many.' And he's talking about curves, not drinks."

Too many drinks, too, but that's water over the Scotch. Besides, and habits aside, Foxx still managed to distinguish himself by hitting .344 for three World Series, belting three doubles, a triple and four homers among 22 Series hits. His Series averages were characteristic of his consistency—.350, .333 and .348 and he drove in 11 runs in 18 games.

Foxxie also hit .316 in All-Star competition, featured by a gigantic clout that won the 1935 game for the American League at Cleveland. On the field at the 1963 game in the huge lakefront park, Foxx delighted in pointing out to younger writers the far-flung point in left field where he'd teed off for two runs that held up for a 4-1 A. L. victory.

The Cleveland playing field was so big originally that, as author Tom Meany recalled, Babe Ruth took a look at it the first time the Yankees went into the new stadium and cracked, "How would you like to see Smead Jolley, Fat Fothergill and me playing the outfield here—on polo ponies!"

Although Foxx regarded his first-base rival Lou Gehrig as even "more dangerous" a hitter than Ruth, he was resigned, like Gehrig, to playing in the shadow of the Bambino, whom he regarded as "a fantastic hitter."

Nobody could top the Babe, but James Emory Foxx gave it a helluva try, on and off the field.

The only trouble was, as John Lardner once wrote, "The only press agent Jimmie Foxx had was his bat."

Or, as Joe DiMaggio told him once, "You made only one mistake, Jimmie. You were born 25 years too soon."

Double X smiled the smile that lasted longer than the insufficient funds and almost, but not quite, as long as the glory.

"I guess," he said, "I was born to be broke . . ."

JAMES EMORY (JIMMIE) FOXX

Born October 22, 1907, at Sudlersville, Md.
Died July 21, 1967, at Miami, Fla.
Height 5-11½ Weight 190
Threw and batted righthanded.
Named to Hall of Fame, 1951

YEAR	CLUB	LEAGUE	POS.	G.	AB.	R.	H.	2B.	3B.	HR.	RBI.	B.A.	PO.	A.	E.	F.A.
1924	Easton	East. Sh.	C	76	260	33	77	11	2	10	-	.296	379	73	16	.966
1925	Philadelphia	Amer.	C	10	9	2	6	1	0	0	0	.667	0	0	0	.000
1925	Providence	Int.	C	41	101	12	33	6	3	1	15	.327	75	9	4	.955
1926	Philadelphia	Amer.	C	26	32	8	10	2	1	0	5	.313	19	5	0	1.000
1927	Philadelphia	Amer.	1B	61	130	23	42	6	5	3	20	.323	263	15	7	.975
1928	Philadelphia	Amer.	1B-3B-C	118	400	85	131	29	10	13	79	.328	416	155	17	.971
1929	Philadelphia	Amer.	1B	149	517	123	183	23	9	33	117	.354	1226	74	6	.995
1930	Philadelphia	Amer.	1B	153	562	127	188	33	13	37	156	.335	1362	79	14	.990
1931	Philadelphia	Amer.	1B-3B	139	515	93	150	32	10	30	120	.291	988	104	15	.986
1932	Philadelphia	Amer.	1B-3B	154	585	151	213	33	9	58	169	.364	1338	97	11	.992
1933	Philadelphia	Amer.	1B	149	573	125	204	37	9	48	163	.356	1402	93	15	.990
1934	Philadelphia	Amer.	1B	150	539	120	180	28	6	44	130	.334	1378	85	10	.993
1935	Philadelphia (a)	Amer.	1B-3B-C	147	535	118	185	33	7	36	115	.346	1226	93	4	.997
1936	Boston	Amer.	1B-OF	155	585	130	198	32	8	41	143	.338	1253	76	13	.990
1937	Boston	Amer.	1B	150	569	111	162	24	6	36	127	.285	1287	106	8	.994
1938	Boston	Amer.	1B	149	565	139	197	33	9	50	175	.349	1282	116	19	.987
1939	Boston	Amer.	1B	124	467	130	168	31	10	35	105	.360	1101	91	10	.992
1940	Boston	Amer.	1B-3B-C	144	515	106	153	30	4	36	119	.297	1023	100	10	.991
1941	Boston	Amer.	1B-3B-C	135	487	87	146	27	8	19	105	.300	1162	118	14	.989
1942	Boston (b)	Amer.	1B	30	100	18	27	4	0	5	14	.270	231	34	1	.996
1942	Chicago	Nat.	1B-C	70	205	25	42	8	0	3	19	.205	491	24	9	.983
1943	Chicago	Nat.							(Did not play)							
1944	Chicago (c)	Nat.	C-3B	15	20	0	1	1	0	0	2	.050	9	6	0	1.000
1944	Portsmouth (d)	Pied.	PH-1B	5	2	0	0	0	0	0	0	.000	0	1	0	1.000
1945	Philadelphia	Nat.	1B-3B	89	224	30	60	11	1	7	38	.268	304	54	8	.978
1946	-	-							(Out of Organized Ball)							
1947	St. Petersburg	Fla. Int.	PH	6	6	0	1	-	-	-	-	.167	-	-	-	-
	American League Totals			2134	7685	1696	2543	438	124	524	1862	.331	16957	1441	173	.991
	National League Totals			174	449	55	103	20	1	10	59	.229	804	84	17	.981
	Major League Totals			2317	8134	1751	2646	458	125	534	1921	.325	17761	1525	190	.990

a Traded with pitcher John Marcum to Boston Red Sox for pitcher Gordon Rhodes, catcher George Savino and $150,000 December 10, 1935.
b Released on waivers to Chicago Cubs, June 1, 1942.
c Released as player and signed as coach, July 6, 1944; released to Portsmouth as manager, August 25, 1944.
d Released by Portsmouth, December, 1944, and signed by Philadelphia Phillies, February 10, 1945.

PITCHING RECORD

YEAR	CLUB	LEAGUE	G.	IP.	W.	L.	Pct.	H.	R.	ER.	SO.	BB.	ERA.
1939	Boston	Amer.	1	1	0	0	.000	0	0	0	0	0	0.00
1945	Philadelphia	Nat.	9	23	1	0	1.000	13	4	4	10	14	1.57
	Major League Totals		10	24	1	0	1.000	13	4	4	10	14	1.50

WORLD SERIES RECORD

YEAR	CLUB	LEAGUE	POS.	G.	AB.	R.	H.	2B.	3B.	HR.	RBI.	B.A.	PO.	A.	E.	F.A.
1929	Philadelphia	Amer.	1B	5	20	5	7	1	0	2	5	.350	38	1	0	1.000
1930	Philadelphia	Amer.	1B	6	21	3	7	2	1	1	3	.333	53	3	0	1.000
1931	Philadelphia	Amer.	1B	7	23	3	8	0	0	1	3	.348	69	2	1	.986
	World Series Totals			18	64	11	22	3	1	4	11	.344	160	6	1	.994

MONEY PLAYER: Frank Frisch performed on more World Series teams (8) than any National Leaguer. His fire spread to the whole Gashouse Gang, including Peper Martin (right).

FRANK FRISCH

The Browns, playing their N. L. neighbors, the world champion Cardinals, filled the bases in the first inning of the spring city series in 1927. George Sisler, the Browns' famed first baseman, hit a sharp double-play grounder to the Redbirds' new second baseman, who reached down and, as the saying goes, felt nothing.

Frank Frisch, already figuratively hopping from one foot to the other on the hot spot marked "X," lowered his head as the ball went through him for a two-run error and cringed as the most vociferous in the crowd yelled:

"We want Hornsby!"

Although Frisch had played eight seasons at New York most of them spectacularly, he found himself in 1927 in probably the most impossible situation ever to confront a ballplayer traded from one city to another. Hornsby, the man for whom he'd been dealt, not only was the greatest righthanded hitter in baseball history, but he had just managed the Cardinals to St. Louis' first pennant and world championship in 38 years.

The shock had been so great in St. Louis over the loss of Hornsby that the Chamber of Commerce, in extraordinary resolution, had condemned the Cardinals' owner, Sam Breadon, and black crepe had been draped on the door of Breadon's home and his Pierce Arrow automobile agency. One St. Louis sports editor wrote huffily that he'd never cover another Redbird game.

The man in the middle of this emotional muddle was Frisch. He was like the innocent bystander who got punched in the puss. And when Sisler's groundball slid through his stocky legs, obvious—and odious—comparison of Hornsby and his St. Louis successor had moved from the white paper of winter conjecture to the green grass of direct summer competition.

That first-play fumble might have symbolized the choke-up reaction of a lesser man, but, as he proved through 19 sparkling National League seasons and in eight World Series, Frank Francis Frisch reacted positively to competition and to tense situations. The excitement of a blue-ribbon moment brought out the best in the Fordham Flash, a money player and a winner.

In the eighth inning of that spring series game with the Browns back there in '27, Frisch hit a home run that wiped out the error and the Browns. And he went on from there, not to make St. Louis forget Hornsby, but to remember Frisch fondly as one of the greatest and most colorful players ever to wear the Cardinals' uniform. Or, for that matter, any other ball club's colors.

Now, more than a half-century after he last ran out from his cap to catch a pop fly or to dive into base headfirst, showing his bald crown, Frisch is recalled as the pilot light of the old Gashouse Gang and as an umpire baiter, summa cum laude. Later, he was regarded as a hairshirt because of his speeches and writings in which, for instance, he referred to present-day spring training as "a country club with-

out dues" and the modern plastic batting helmet as "an inverted garbage can."

To anyone who missed the broad strokes of exaggeration in elder statesman Frisch's commentary, to those who saw red at what he said and missed the twinkle in his heavy-lidded brown eyes, it must be explained that at times the Old Flash didn't know the difference between humor and sarcasm.

But he was a funny man, full of overstuffed German gemuetlichkeit into his early 70s and full of even richer memories than of rich food, good books, symphonic music and the horticultural hangover of a man blessed with a green thumb and an appreciation of the good life.

To one for whom Frisch was his boyhood favorite, the laughs and laments, the amazing achievements and amusing anecdotes made this idol of youth like a smorgasbord. There was so much of the multi-sided, many-splendored Flash that was difficult to know where to start and when to quit.

Although he played as if he had grown up cutting his teeth on a brass cuspidor, Frankie was born with a silver spoon in his mouth, the son of a wealthy lace-linen manufacturer who never could quite understand how such a bright student of chemistry could be so fascinated by boys' games.

Young Frisch grew up in the Bronx on 206th Street, five miles north of New York's Polo Grounds, where he achieved his early baseball reputation. Professional, that is, because, by the time he graduated from Fordham University in 1919, he'd already earned an athletic reputation.

Reflecting his qualities of leadership, he captained the football, basketball and baseball teams at Fordham. Jake Weber, long-time trainer of the Rams, regarded him as the most gifted athlete ever to matriculate on Rose Hill. The gutsiest, too. Catching one day, Frisch continued to play with a middle finger broken so badly on his right hand that it became permanently deformed and made it remarkable that the Dutchman, as they called him, could grip the ball well enough to throw so hard.

The great John McGraw, then master of all he surveyed in New York and the National League, signed the swift 21-year-old shortstop, who had been a second team All-America halfback in football and had a quick, aggressive, almost gridiron approach to baseball. He dived dangerously, recklessly and was a switch-hitter who batted cross-handed from the right side.

McGraw preferred to option him out, but Frisch, who could afford to take baseball or leave it because Herr Frisch wanted Frankie to join him and two older brothers in the linen business, balked at going to the minor leagues. This decision would make the Flash unique because in nearly 50 years as a player, manager, coach and broadcaster, he never left the big leagues.

McGraw worked with him mornings, teaching him how to slide and how to get that right hand on top of the left when he batted righthanded. At Pittsburgh early in June, he stepped up as a pinch-hitter and was safe on an error. At Chicago, he went into the game as a pinch-runner, and Charley Dryden, the wit who wrote baseball brilliantly there, asked a New York writer to spell the name.

"F-r-i-s-c-h."

"Hmmm," cracked Dryden, "sounds like something frying."

Uh-huh, and ready to sizzle, too, when unexpectedly in September as pennant-bound Cincinnati came to the Polo Grounds for three successive doubleheaders, McGraw boldly pulled the disbelieving rookie off the bench and started him at second base in place of aging, ailing Larry Doyle.

By then, McGraw had decided that Frisch wasn't a shortstop, because he didn't have sure enough hands and, though extremely quick, he didn't have the range to the right desirable for a shortstop. The Fordham Flash, McGraw reasoned most astutely, would be good at third base, great at second base. And he said that he became convinced he was right after the first Cincinnati batter, Morris Rath, smashed a hot grounder at Frisch.

The ball bad-hopped off the kid's chest and bounced away but, like a crooked-nosed cat, Frisch pursued it, pounced on it and strong-armed a throw that retired Rath.

"That was all I had to see," McGraw would say later.

"The average youngster, nervous anyway at starting his first game in a pennant situation like that, would have given up on the play or lost it."

By the time the Giants won their first of four straight pennants in 1921, Frisch was tremendous, a whirling dervish of the diamond, knocking down hot smashes with his chest, diving for others that seemed out of reach, ranging far and wide for pop flies, pawing at the dirt to get a long lead and then stealing bases, but always losing his cap.

Friendly rival Beans Reardon, the umpire, once cracked, "How do you expect a round cap to stay on a square head?"

Frisch would contend that he did, too, have a round head because another rival, bitter foe Burleigh Grimes, who became a pennant-winning teammate in St. Louis, "rounded it off, inch by inch, pitch by pitch."

The Old Flash, as he referred to himself in later times, wondered what it would have been like to wear a batting helmet. "I know a guy like Grimes or Dizzy Dean would have delighted in playing a tune on it," he concluded, grinning.

Frisch, a fresh, sassy rookie, in Grimes' judgment when Burleigh was pitching for Brooklyn retaliated for repeated knockdown pitches by dragging a bunt. His spikes nearly severing Grimes' Achilles tendon as the Dodger righthander covered first base.

That did it. Every time up, Burleigh would deck him. But a good lowball hitter lefthanded, a highball hitter righthanded and pretty good with a highball in either hand, Frisch would cream Grimes' quick-dipping spitter.

"The only time I was really scared in my life," Frisch explained years later, "was when Burleigh threw at me one time on a 3-and-0 count."

"The count," Grimes corrected him dryly, "was 3-and-1."

Frisch knew the supreme excitement, if not fear, of a World Series first in '21 when, after batting .341 and driving in 100 runs, he faced the fierce Yankee submarine righthander, Carl Mays, who had killed Cleveland's Ray Chapman with a pitch the previous year. Mays shut out the Giants in the opener on five hits. Frisch got four of them.

For four World Series in his hometown, Frisch batted a gaudy .300, .471, .400 and .333. He wasn't nearly so outstanding in four Series at St. Louis, though, as usual, he got his share of big ones, including the biggest of his career. But even at the advanced baseball age of 37, he found the excitement of the Series undiminished.

When the Fordham Flash batted .348 in 1923, leading the league in hits and total bases, plus driving in 111 runs, the Giants headed west on a train with a stranger who gave a lecture on snakes and displayed a wriggling, tan specimen about three feet long.

"This," he said, "is the North American coach whip, the fastest snake on this continent. I know you are famous athletes, but if I were to release him in that field outside the train, not one of you could catch him."

Outfielder Ross Youngs, himself a fast man, interrupted quietly. "Frank Frisch could."

Observers could see in the fleet, fiery, fighting Frisch the image of the man for whom he played, McGraw. "McGraw's boy," they called him, and maybe there was too much of the Old Man in him. By 1926, he was field captain of the Giants and, as such, he was the whipping boy. McGraw traditionally berated his captains for mistakes of others.

Frisch couldn't take it, not indefinitely, anyway. One day in St. Louis, he packed his bags and took a train to New York. A breach had been created with the man who had earmarked him as his probable successor. Frisch hit the September home run that knocked Cincinnati out of the race and gave St.

Louis its first National League pennant. Three months later, traded for Hornsby, he was a Redbird.

Frisch didn't want to go to St. Louis. He didn't want to leave New York, but he recognized that a trade had become inevitable and he recalled all too clearly that he was, indeed, on the spot marked "X." Hornsby was the better and harder hitter, a fast man, too, though not a basestealer. Despite astonishing difficulty in handling pop flies, he was a good second baseman and an outstanding pivot man on double plays.

Frisch, reacting to the challenge, took his wife, the former Ada Lucy, the childhood sweetheart he'd married four years earlier, to Lake Placid for the winter to skate, ski, tramp the woods and even bobsled. When he was tired, he would just sit out in the snow with his dogs and read.

Except to meet St. Louis general manager Branch Rickey at Syracuse for a pep talk, the Flash stayed in the rugged winter-resort country until spring training. The Cardinals were cool to him, but not for long. You can't dislike a guy who is putting money in your pocket, especially when he's a warm personable character like the Flash. He only seemed cocky and arrogant.

Frisch, in 1927 was the greatest single-season player Sam Breadon had in the nearly 30 years the club owner was connected with the Cardinals. They spoke each other's language and, in fact, used it. Both pronounced the ball club "Cawd'nals" with a New York accent, and Frank saved Sam's baseball bacon.

Although Hornsby hit .361 at New York, Frisch had the more spectacular year, batting .337, stealing 48 bases and fielding so sensationally that he set a record for chances accepted (1,037) that never has been approached by a second baseman. When shortstop Tommy Thevenow suffered a broken leg and the Cardinals brought up Heinie Schuble, a kid who was woefully unprepared, the Flash began making plays on both sides of second base.

More than once after Schuble would boot one,

Frisch would put his arm around the rookie's shoulder as they left the field. The Cardinals, though crippled, lost the pennant by only a game and a half to Pittsburgh. Paul Waner nipped Frisch by a point for the Most Valuable Player award he probably deserved more than the one he was given in 1931.

Breadon, his box office up even after abuse he'd received for trading Hornsby, acknowledged his debt to Frisch and said, "Just as I was sure night baseball would make every day Sunday, I was convinced after the 1927 season that it's the ball club that counts, not the player. The way the fans reacted to Frisch and to another good pennant race, I never again feared trading anyone."

Frisch, the boss' pet, fell into temporary disfavor in St. Louis in 1932, the season after he'd made a trip around the Orient following an All-Star baseball tour of Japan. The world champion Cardinals fizzled, and Frisch, batting .292, dropped below .300 for the first time in 12 seasons. He jogged on infield grounders he used to run out. Was this the same Flash who would fling himself head first into first base to beat out a grounder?

The crowds booed in protest, and J. Roy Stockton, baseball writer for the *St. Louis Post-Dispatch* and a Frisch admirer, buttonholed him one day in a hotel lobby in Pittsburgh and said, "Frank, they're saying some harsh things about you. They say you're dogging it, lying down on Gabby Street, trying to get his job."

Frisch was taken aback. "Hasn't the Sarge told you what's wrong with me?" he asked. Stockton shook his head, so Frisch invited the writer up to his room. There, he unbuckled his trousers and dropped them to show that both of his thick thighs were taped. "I'm riding the worst charley horses I've ever had," his nasal voice rising shrilly in anger and indignation as it did when he yak-yakked with an umpire. "We're going lousy, but I'm playing because, even hurt, I'm better than anybody Street's got. I try to let it all out only when it really counts.

"I don't want the old man's job. But I'll tell you

this: If or when I manage this club or any other and I've got to use a man who's under par, I'll certainly let the press know his condition, in all fairness to the player."

He did, too, Stockton pointed out, after Breadon asked Frisch to take over the ball club at mid-season a year later.

The truth is, totally unaccustomed by habit or instinct to losing or second division, the same player who drove himself fiercely when the stakes were high, did seem to lose interest when the chips weren't on the table. Teammates would snicker or mutter about his convenient lumbago, which would give him a few days off here and there in the dog days of summer in St. Louis and around the league.

But if the club was in the running, and if the Flash could smell the lettuce, he'd return to the lineup, refreshed, and play like a demon down the stretch, a one-man gang of whom Lou Gehrig once said, "Don't get Frisch mad because he'll beat you by himself."

It's too bad that statistics weren't kept then on game-tying hits or plays because Frisch would have been front and center among clutch players. Big crowds and big moments drove him to the heights.

In the first All-Star Game in 1933 at Chicago's Comiskey Park the veteran St. Louis second baseman singled and then batting lefthanded, belted a home run off righthander Alvin Crowder.

"Everybody remembers the homer Babe Ruth hit, but nobody remembers that the Old Flash hit one, too." Frisch would lament in later years, delightfully blending self-pity and self-deprecation when he'd tell in the next minute how he'd been the only player in history "to take three pitches from each side of the plate."

Batting righthanded, he'd been thrown three straight balls one day by Brooklyn lefthander Watson Clark, at which time the Dodgers made a pitching change and brought in righthander Hollis Thurston. Frisch drooled because he hit Thurston regularly like a cousin, but . . .

"But he threw three fat curves, each fatter than the other, and I took 'em all for called strikes," said the most prominent switch-hitter until Mickey Mantle.

Frisch stood only 5-9, but he weighed 175 pounds or more as the years went on. In addition to those heavy lids, which made him squint, he had a hooked nose that dog-legged to the right, a thick chest, strong arms, powerful legs and extremely small feet, which he gave priority treatment. He would wear a torn-sleeved sweatshirt at times and a dirty uniform, but he always wore sanitary understockings and bought several new pairs of shoes a season. A generous clubhouse tipper, he had them polished constantly and he helped keep the gloss on them by stepping into the batter's box and habitually rubbing the toe of each shoe on the back of each stockinged calf.

Batting lefthanded with a slightly choked grip, Frisch would pump the bat up and down a couple of times, then wiggle it at the pitcher almost to the point you'd think he'd be caught off stride. He could drag bunt or, flatfooted, push a bunt toward third base and often beat it out. He hit to all fields, but he was especially adept at punching an outside pitch into left field. He'd be off in a gallop toward second base, trying to stretch a single into a double.

With power behind him—he batted third, the same as the uniform number he wore—Frisch stole less frequently than he might have, though his 48 thefts in 1927 rated as a St. Louis high until Lou Brock surged forth nearly 40 years later. The Flash could score from first on a single now and then and from second on an infield out.

Batting righthanded Frisch had more power, but he didn't pull too well and wasn't as good. He spread out more at the plate so that if the count worked to the limit, he had reduced the strike zone considerably. Although this was defensive hitting, Frisch could be aggressive from the right side, too, as he proved to Stockton when they traveled together to New York for the 1934 All-Star Game at the Polo Grounds.

"I see where I'm leading off tomorrow," Frisch said, "and Lefty Gomez is going to start for the American League. Lefty likes to throw the smoke in there on the first pitch. If he does, I'll hit a home run."

No one ever hit the bull's-eye better. Frisch, batting righthanded, lined Gomez' first delivery over the beckoning right-field wall. The same year, Frisch's Cawd'nals came from behind to win the pennant when the Giants faltered. This was the fabulous Gashouse Gang, not a great ball club, but a team of one-of-a-kind characters featuring Dizzy and Paul Dean, Pepper Martin, Leo Durocher, Joe Medwick, Rip Collins and, of course, the manager himself.

A stormy 1934 World Series with Detroit, a slashing series of rough talk and rougher play, got down to the seventh game there. And an aging Frisch's reputation as a money player—his professional pride—was at stake in the third inning of a scoreless showdown. With runners on second and third, none out, the Tigers' manager, catcher Mickey Cochrane, ordered right fielder Jack Rothrock passed carefully to fill the bases for Frisch. Questionable strategy and a decided affront.

The Flash, hitting lefthanded, faced submarine righthander Eldon Auker and, working the count to the limit, he fouled off pitch after pitch, bulldog determinedly hanging on. When Frisch finally belted a curve into the right-field corner, clearing the bases and setting up a seven-run inning, he broke up the Series.

"I tripled into a double," he would reminisce. "I became so fascinated by watching the runners score, I slowed and stopped at second when I should have reached third. If one of my men had done that I'd have fined him."

That blow, the biggest of his career, came as time was beginning to run out on the leg-scarred old war horse. He almost pulled out another pennant for his team down the stretch in 1935 when the oldest Redbird (Frisch) and youngest (Terry

Moore) had a hot hand in September. But Moore broke his leg and the Cubs, winning 21 in a row, surged past the St. Louis team that once again had overtaken New York.

A severe spike wound reduced Frisch's action to 103 games that season, and his average dropped to .274 in 1936 when he played in just 93 contests. The last home run of his career gave Paul Dean a 3-2 victory over the Cubs' Bill Lee early in the '36 season. St. Louis and Chicago tied for second behind New York.

By 1937, when the Gashouse Gang began to run out of gas, Frisch had become virtually a bench manager. But early in the season, when the Cardinals floundered at Philadelphia, the Old Flash benched Jimmy Brown and Stu Martin, returning Durocher to shortstop and himself to second base.

The Cardinal bats boomed and won a game. The next day, hitting well again, Frisch was on second, Moore on first when Medwick pickled one into the right-field corner at old Baker Bowl, which had an extremely close right-field fence. By the time the greybearded Frisch reached third, Moore had rounded second, and Mike Gonzalez, coaching for the Cardinals, warbled in his cracked-ice English:

"He come, Fronhk, you go. He come, you go."

Just as Frisch stepped on home plate, Moore slid in under him, upsetting the embarrassed manager, who got to his feet, dusted himself off and, reaching the bench, said:

"Any time they can run down the Flash, it's time to quit. You, Brown, go to second base."

Frank Frisch never returned to second base and, in fact, didn't get into a ball game again until considerably later when the Cardinals were struggling home in fourth place. One day, before a small midweek crowd at Sportsman's Park, Frisch, coaching at third base, looked at his bench for a pinch-hitter for his young catcher, Mickey Owen. The bases were loaded, two were out in the ninth inning and the Cardinals trailed by a run.

"Why don't you hit, Grandma?" a falsetto voice suggested from the shadows of the dugout.

Frisch bristled and reddened. He walked to the bench, picked up a bat and stepped in to face the Braves' star righthander, Jim Turner. Frisch bounced the first pitch over first baseman Elbie Fletcher for a two-run single. And as the winning run scored, Redbirds poured out of the dugout as if they'd won a pennant. Powerfully, playfully, Pepper Martin tried to hoist the embarrassed Frisch onto his shoulders.

It would be nice to say that the old favorite wound up his career with that game-winning hit, the kind that characterized his clutch play, but he went up a day later in a similar, though not identical, situation against righthander Danny MacFayden. For an instant, it looked as if the Flash had done it again because he spanked a pitch back up the middle, but, playing him perfectly, shortstop Rabbit Warstler grabbed the ball behind the bag, stepped on second and fired to first for a double play. Frisch, trying to step up his pace, pulled up lame—and that was it.

As far back as 1931, when St. Louis savored a fourth pennant in six years and a World Series upset of the powerful Philadelphia Athletics, Branch Rickey had sat glumly at a victory party. Why so thoughtful?

"Because," said B. R., the father of the farm system, "I'm wondering what we're going to do when we have to replace Frisch."

By the time Frisch's career, .316 lifetime average, ended officially at the age of 40—the Flash always had been a year older than listed—he was expendable. Not because the Cardinals had come up with another Frisch. They wouldn't, in fact, come up with a solid replacement until Red Schoendienst, several seasons away. But because, as a player, the Flash no longer could do it for them and, as a manager, well . . .

"I was a better manager with a good ball club than with a bad one," Frisch said in honest self-analysis years later on one of his joyful visits to St. Louis after he had managed at Pittsburgh and Chicago through 1951.

"I always wanted to win so badly and couldn't stand defeat and couldn't stand the bad baseball.

Those Cubs nearly killed me. Seems to me I put on the squeeze play seven times before one of my guys even fouled a ball. I guess I should have given him a box of cigars."

See the good-natured sarcasm? Smiling, Frisch then summed himself up better than even his warmest friend or severest critic could:

"I think managing shortened my playing career, but I was a better manager when I was playing, when I could lead like a platoon sergeant in the field rather than as a general sitting back on his duff in a command post.

"But," he emphasized, the introspection turning to self defense, "I won't apologize for having wanted my players to be as good as I was supposed to be. If intolerance of mediocrity is a crime, I plead guilty."

Frisch's bouts with the umpires were delightful. He'd jaw with Reardon, for instance, cheek to jowl, and wind up getting thrown out of the game. Then they'd drink beer together and listen to Max Steindel of the St. Louis Symphony pick out on a cello the kind of music the incongruous Frisch liked.

Reardon called him "Happy" or "Hap" because the hypochondriac moaned about his health when he wasn't groaning about his players. One night, Reardon borrowed Frisch's car, insisted Frank fill it with gas—and then threw him out of the game the next day and recommended a fine and suspension.

Frisch could forget one day's insults overnight and expected the men in blue to do the same. They caught on to a hot-weather device in New York, where he loved to stay at his restful New Rochelle home when the Cardinals were there. He'd tend fondly to his roses, rhododendron, laurel, azalea, yew and American holly. The Flash would get thrown out of the game early, risking a $50 fine, so he could spend a peaceful day in the garden or on his veranda.

"Listen, Frisch," an umpire finally told him, "it's as hot as blazes out here for me, too. I'm staying and so are you."

The Flash was Bill Klem's pet, probably because he was such a National League blue-chip performer in World Series and All-Star play. Frisch could get by with more in salty exchanges with the Old Arbitrator than other managers could. But he overdid it, managing at Pittsburgh, when he feigned a faint at an adverse decision and keeled over backward in the coach's box.

Klem rushed to him, leaned over and yelled, "If you ain't dead, Frisch, you're out of the game."

The portly pixy was thrown out of another game for going out to home plate carrying an umbrella, a suggestion too slapstick that a game being played in the rain should be called. And he was photographed giving a mocking, sweeping bow to glaring George Magerkurth after Maje had cleared the bench at Pittsburgh.

With the Pirates, a club he managed seven seasons after a year (1939) as play-by-play broadcaster for the Braves in Boston, Frisch was at his funniest. Maybe it was the only way he could keep from crying, though he did bring the Pirates home second in 1944.

Frisch was coaching third base for the Pirates one day at Chicago when a weak-hitting Pittsburgh shortstop named Frankie Zak, trying to score on an extra-base hit by Jim Russell, was hipped by Eddie Stanky, the Cubs' third baseman, as Zak rounded the base. The runner almost went headlong into the third-base dugout and the umpire, Jocko Conlan, awarded Zak a run because of defensive obstruction.

An excited Frisch determined to fix Stanky himself. As Russell came around to third base with a triple, the batter slid into the bag from one side and Frisch slid into the bag from the coach's box. Stanky tagged Frisch and missed Russell.

"He's safe," snapped Conlan, pointing to Russell and then to Frisch, "and you're out—outta the game."

Although the umpires appreciated Frisch for his ability to bury yesterday's bitter argument in a pregame smile, they respected him for something considerably more personal.

One time when the Pirates protested a mixup on

the field and appealed to National League President Ford Frick for a hearing, Frisch walked into Frick's office just in time to hear the league president say that the situation was so serious that it could cost the involved umpire his job.

"No ball game is worth an umpire's job," said Frisch, turning and said walking out, "Good day, gentlemen."

Frick liked Frisch for that, too, and was amused by Frank's antics. Like the time Flash had been fined and called him collect and talked on and on until, suddenly, the league president realized that he'd accepted the charges. Another time when Frisch was fined, Ford got wind of the fact that Frank planned to pay the $100 fine with a large sack of pennies he would trundle out to home plate.

Frisch got the message from Frick in a wire which read, simply, "DON'T, DUTCHMAN."

The Dutchman did play-by-play baseball broadcasting in New York and then pre-game and post-game television commentary, before and after his final managerial fling at Chicago in 1949-51. Despite his high-pitched voice and lack of training, he did all right. Neighborhood kids would delight him by walking or riding by his place in New Rochelle, imitating his radio lament when they'd yell:

"Hey, Flash: 'Oh, those bases on balls.'"

After a heart attack in 1956, well-fixed as a player who had been paid well and had invested wisely, the Hall of Famer limited himself to commercials and infrequent speaking appearances for a lecture bureau and brewery. His timing and his inflection made it extremely difficult to catch in print the full flavor of this animated, articulate man, part ham actor, who was at his best when he was with his good friend, former teammate and ex-managerial rival, Casey Stengel.

When Stengel fell and broke his hip after an old-timers' reunion that went extra innings in New York, Ol' Case was hospitalized in the maternity ward. Frisch sent him roses and diaper pins.

Back in 1943, when a cab struck down Stengel on a cold, rainy night in Boston, where he managed a bad ball club, Frisch sent a cheerful telegram:

"Your attempt at suicide fully understood. Deepest sympathy you didn't succeed."

Stengel reciprocated often, including the time an apparent game-winning, two-run homer by Russell at Pittsburgh had been nullified because Zak, on base, just had called time to tie a shoe lace.

Stengel wired: "AM RUSHING PAIR OF BUTTON SHOES FOR ZAK."

When Frisch was bedded down at his Pittsburgh hotel, immobilized by the flareup of an old spike wound, Stengel walked into the suite just as room service was delivering a steak dinner.

"Put it right over here, young man," said Casey, gaily eating a cussing Frisch's dinner, just out of the Flash's reach.

In a home-and-home series of check-grabbing between the two gregarious Dutchmen, Frisch was the harder loser, the more difficult to get out to play when he'd been beaten. But Stengel had his way, including the time his lowly Braves had taken a doubleheader from the lofty Cards.

Frisch curtly broke a dinner engagement with Stengel and walked back to his hotel, steaming. Until, that is, Casey kept driving around the block in a taxicab, alternately taunting and tempting him. Frisch relented finally and hopped in for another night on the town with his fellow bon vivant of baseball.

Except to break out now and then for a baseball reunion somewhere or to make an occasional talk, Frisch moved from New York City to a five-acre place at Quonochontaug, a village of about 450 in little Rhode Island. Quonochontaug, near Bradford, is Indian for Big Black Fish, rather appropriate for a guy whose name sounded like something frying. His dear Ada died early in 1971.

Reading by the seashore, visiting with friend Eugene Istomin, the concert pianist who is a good baseball fan or listening to Istomin's recorded music or others whose works he admired, squire Frisch was a gentleman farmer and far from the maddening crowd. But who had richer memories?

Who else was paid the rarest of tributes by Joe McCarthy, the great Yankee manager? A young reporter, approaching McCarthy, said he was getting ideas of "the makeup of a perfect composite player" and . . .

McCarthy interrupted him. "What are you going to all that trouble for?" asked Marse Joe. "What couldn't Frank Frisch do?"

When Frisch's young friend, Red Schoendienst, took over at St. Louis, Frisch counselled him about managing. "Just stay away from firearms, Red, and don't room higher than the second floor. You might want to jump."

Years before he died at 75 in 1973, a result of a heart attack after recovering from a motor mishap, the Old Flash struck a blow for all managers, past and present, when he was field foreman at Forbes Field, Pittsburgh. There where he listened patiently as a heckling boxseat occupant second-guessed him loudly.

Going back and forth from the coaching box, wearing a disarming smile, Frisch began to solicit suggestions. What would the patron prefer? The pleased customer asked for a bunt here, a hit-and-run there and . . .

Politely, the manager asked where the fan worked. The man gave him a downtown business address, but wondered why the famous Old Flash would want to know about little old him.

"Because," blazed fire-eating Frank Francis Frisch, the funny Fordham Flash, "I'm going to be down at your office tomorrow morning, flannelmouth, and tell you how to run your blanketyblank business."

FRANK FRANCIS (FORDHAM FLASH) FRISCH
Born September 9, 1898, at New York, N.Y.
Height 5-10 Weight 185
Threw right and batted right and lefthanded.
Named to Hall of Fame, 1947.

YEAR	CLUB	LEAGUE	POS.	G.	AB.	R.	H.	2B.	3B.	HR.	RBI.	B.A.	PO.	A.	E.	F.A.
1919	New York	Nat.	2B-3B	54	190	21	43	3	2	2	22	.226	100	130	6	.975
1920	New York	Nat.	3B	110	440	57	123	10	10	4	77	.280	104	251	12	.967
1921	New York	Nat.	2B-3B	153	618	121	211	31	17	8	100	.341	226	418	33	.951
1922	New York	Nat.	2B-3B	132	514	101	168	16	13	5	51	.327	228	405	22	.966
1923	New York	Nat.	2B-3B	151	641	116	223	32	10	12	111	.348	327	493	22	.974
1924	New York	Nat.	2B	145	603	121	198	33	15	7	69	.328	391	537	27	.972
1925	New York	Nat.	2B-3B-SS	120	502	89	166	26	6	11	48	.331	215	393	37	.943
1926	New York (a)	Nat.	2B	135	545	75	171	29	4	5	44	.314	261	471	19	.975
1927	St. Louis	Nat.	2B	153	617	112	208	31	11	10	78	.337	396	641	22	.979
1928	St. Louis	Nat.	2B	141	547	107	164	29	9	10	86	.300	383	474	21	.976
1929	St. Louis	Nat.	2B-3B	138	527	93	176	40	12	5	74	.334	304	407	22	.970
1930	St. Louis	Nat.	2B-3B	133	540	121	187	46	9	10	114	.346	315	493	27	.968
1931	St. Louis	Nat.	2B	131	518	96	161	24	4	4	82	.311	290	424	19	.974
1932	St. Louis	Nat.	2B-3B	115	486	59	142	26	2	3	60	.292	252	309	14	.976
1933	St. Louis	Nat.	2B-SS	147	585	74	177	32	6	4	66	.303	395	413	18	.978
1934	St. Louis	Nat.	2B-3B	140	550	74	168	30	6	3	75	.305	325	388	20	.973
1935	St. Louis	Nat.	2B	103	354	52	104	16	2	1	55	.294	193	252	8	.982
1936	St. Louis	Nat.	2B-3B	93	303	40	83	10	0	1	26	.274	159	192	14	.962
1937	St. Louis	Nat.	2B	17	32	3	7	2	0	0	4	.219	12	14	0	1.000
Major League Totals				2311	9112	1532	2880	466	138	105	1242	.316	4876	7105	363	.971

a Traded with pitcher Jimmy Ring to St. Louis Cardinals for second baseman Rogers Hornsby, December 20, 1926.

WORLD SERIES RECORD

YEAR	CLUB	LEAGUE	POS.	G.	AB.	R.	H.	2B.	3B.	HR.	RBI.	B.A.	PO.	A.	E.	F.A.
1921	New York	Nat.	3B	8	30	5	9	0	1	0	1	.300	13	24	2	.949
1922	New York	Nat.	2B	5	17	3	8	1	0	0	2	.471	10	20	1	.968
1923	New York	Nat.	3B	6	25	2	10	0	1	0	1	.400	17	18	1	.972
1924	New York	Nat.	2B-3B	7	30	1	10	4	1	0	0	.333	17	25	0	1.000
1928	St. Louis	Nat.	2B	4	13	1	3	0	0	0	1	.231	8	13	0	1.000
1930	St. Louis	Nat.	2B	6	24	0	5	2	0	0	0	.208	13	14	3	.900
1931	St. Louis	Nat.	2B	7	27	2	7	2	0	0	1	.259	23	19	0	1.000
1934	St. Louis	Nat.	2B	7	31	2	6	1	0	0	4	.194	16	26	2	.955
World Series Totals				50	197	16	58	10	3	0	10	.294	117	159	9	.968

The IRON HORSE: Lou Gehrig is remembered even more for his hitting savagery than for his record 2,130 consecutive games. Sadly, his career and his life came to a tragically early end.

LOU GEHRIG

Lou Gehrig stood up there formidably in the blue-trimmed, pearl-gray road uniform of the New York Yankees and simply devastated a good pitcher, righthander George (Moose) Earnshaw. The bulging-bottomed, piano legged lefthanded slugger lined three consecutive home runs over the right-field fence at Philadelphia's Shibe Park.

The Athletics' manager, Connie Mack, whose team just had won three straight pennants with Earnshaw, second only to Lefty Grove for pitching effectiveness, relieved his starting pitcher with an-

other righthander, Leroy Mahaffey, and advised Earnshaw not to go directly to the clubhouse.

"Sit beside me, George," said the old gentleman. "You've been pitching wrong to Gehrig and I want you to watch how Mahaffey does it."

So Gehrig hit his fourth straight home run, this one a blast to the opposite field, and the steaming Earnshaw said tartly:

"Now I understand, Mr. Mack. Mahaffey made him change direction."

As only the third player ever to hit four homers

in a big league game and the first in the 20th century, Gehrig merited the nation's sports headlines that red-letter June afternoon in 1932, but he didn't get them. John McGraw chose the same day to resign after 30 years as the famed manager of the New York Giants.

Gehrig, who played Avis to Babe Ruth's Hertz for most of his career, understood and accepted the unique nature of a situation in which one of baseball's most productive players did not receive proper attention until the tragedy of his shocking fatal illness and the noble manner in which he met death.

When Babe Ruth was struggling with the Yankees in 1934, a New York baseball writer, Tom Meany, talked to Gehrig, captain and first baseman of the Yankees, but junior partner in baseball's version of Murder, Inc. Tom wasn't trying to be a meanie when he suggested that the weary Babe wouldn't be back in '35.

"No, and it's a shame," Gehrig said at a time when a definite coolness existed between him and Ruth. "The big fellow did a lot for this ball club and for all baseball. He'll be missed all over."

Meany suggested that with Ruth gone, Gehrig would get more headlines. Lou laughed.

"I'm not a headline guy and we may as well face it," he said. "I'm just the guy who's in there every day, the fellow who follows Babe in the batting order. When Babe's turn at bat is over, whether he strikes out or belts a home run, the fans are still talking about him when I come up. If I stood on my head at the plate, nobody'd pay any attention."

Maybe not, but only because everyone expects the sun to come up in the East, July to be warmer than January and Bob Hope to quip about the man in the White House. Or, back there in the mid-'30s, old maestro Ben Bernie was expected to exchange insults, yowsah, with keyhole columnist and radio prattler Walter Winchell.

Gehrig was indeed taken for granted or, at least, for granite. He was the Iron Horse, the indestructible, the most durable ballplayer ever, and perhaps the most consistent. A guy could wind his watch and keep time just through watching the Yankees' lineup and seeing what Gehrig did day-in and day-out for 14 full seasons.

And then one day the quiet hero, the uncomplaining star without temperament or first-person complex, was not only out of the lineup, but, despite bulging biceps and a body that looked as strong as ever, almost out of life, too.

Now, the man had bitten the dog. Czechoslovakia had invaded Germany. Dimitri Shostakovich had written the Hut-sut Song. Amos 'n Andy had acquired British accents and Shirley Temple had been cast as the Wicked Witch of the West. Everything, in other words, was wrong—all wrong. All wrong with Gehrig and a sports world that had come to expect everything from the man who wasn't the greatest hitter in baseball history, but probably the most productive.

Look at it this way: Cut down by amyotrophic lateral sclerosis, a hardening and disintegration of the spinal cord, Gehrig played only 14 full seasons, which means that more than 50 players participated in more major league games than he did. Yet only 17 ever outhit him for average, just four scored more runs, only six got more total bases, only four delivered more extra-base blows, and just two, twin home run kings Henry Aaron and Ruth, who else?—drove in more runs.

My, how that Gehrig could fetch runs home and only, in part, because he hit 493 homers. For 13 straight years, he drove in 100 or more a season, topped by an American League record 184 in 1931. That season, for the first and only time until Ruth almost tripped over his beard and beer belly, Lou almost nudged out the Babe in home runs.

That is, Lou would have if he hadn't been destined always to play the Crown Prince to the King of Swat, as they were called in a period of purple-prose journalism. In '31 at Washington, Gehrig hit one so hard and so fast into the far reaches of Griffith Stadium that the ball crashed into the center-field stands and rebounded out into the hands of an outfielder.

As a result, teammate Lyn Lary, jogging around the bases ahead of the Iron Horse, looked up just in time to see the outfielder with the ball and, assuming it had been caught, Lary left the baseline between third base and the plate. The modest Gehrig, trotting around with his head down, didn't notice the mistake and, consequently, passed the spot at which Lary strayed.

Out for passing the previous runner, Gehrig was credited only with a triple, not a homer. So he finished with 46 home runs, the same total as Ruth's.

Lou led the league in homers with 49 in 1934, the Babe's last year with the Yanks, and again with 49 in 1936, just before the ravages of the fatal disease began to eat into his remarkable body. At 33 then, a clean-living athlete who hadn't missed a day in the lineup from the time he'd taken over as a regular 12 years ago, he hit .354 and had 152 RBIs. In 1934 he had topped the league in RBIs with 165 and batting with a .363 mark.

Named in 1936 to an unprecedented fourth Most Valuable Player award—he'd been honored previously in 1927, 1931 and 1934—Gehrig appeared likely to break all kinds of records in '37, just as he had for most grandslam homers, 23, and for consecutive games played, a figure that would reach 2,130. But he held even at .351, 159 RBIs and 200 hits.

Even when he tailed off in 1938, dropping to 29 homers, 114 RBIs and a .295 average, figures which a generation later would seem more robust than they did at the time, there was no reason to believe he'd experienced anything except an off-season or, at the worst, the first hint of advanced baseball age.

But, as evidenced later, the Gehrig of 1938 had begun to feel the clutches of the disease that eventually turned his 6-1, 212-pound body into a hollow, halting shell. Mystified by his condition, berating himself for not having walked more in the off-season, he stumbled through spring training of 1939, weak and uncoordinated.

He started the season at first base for the world champions, seeking a fourth straight title and their eighth pennant in the years he wore the Yankee pinstripes. But after playing eight games in which he collected only four hits and drove in just one run, he took himself out of the lineup, a decision his good friend and silent admirer, Joe McCarthy, would have found most difficult.

The end came when the Iron Horse struggled to make what his intellect told him was a routine play covering first base to take a throw from pitcher Johnny Murphy. When he came to the bench, teammates chirped, "Nice play, Lou."

Gehrig groaned to himself, "Heavens, has it been that bad?"

That was April 30, 1939. After an open date, the Yankees played at Detroit and Gehrig told McCarthy that he felt he ought to step out for the good of the ball club. The manager concurred. It's doubtful that either man realized the Hall of Fame player never would play again.

The nation that had taken Gehrig for granted was shocked then. The country was stunned about six weeks later when after a visit to Mayo Brothers' clinic in Rochester, Minn., the lethal diagnosis was made. Anyone with access to informed medical advice soon learned that the good-looking, blue-eyed, dimpled giant with the gray flecking his thick, wavy hair was doomed. The timetable? Two years.

Baseball moved swiftly to honor the Iron Horse. On July 4, 1939, a crowd of 61,808 gathered at Yankee Stadium to shower him with gifts and admiration and, if he could master his emotions, to hear a dying man speak.

With head bowed, his big strong back already beginning to waste from the insidious tentacles of the disease that had whittled more than 20 pounds off his sturdy Teuton frame, Gehrig stood with old teammates and new, listening to his virtues extolled by New York's Mayor Fiorello H. LaGuardia, Postmaster General James A. Farley and others.

McCarthy, who'd never let him know that he'd

been the manager's favorite player, presented Gehrig with a trophy from the players. And Babe Ruth, awkwardly, affectionately, tears filling his eyes, threw an arm around his shoulders in the kind of hug that was unnatural for two men's men.

Then, head bowed, choked with tears and prodded gently by McCarthy, Gehrig made remarks of acknowledgment that captured the courage, humility and sincerity of a man of grace.

"Fans," he said, his voice carrying extremely well under the circumstances, "for the past two weeks you have been reading about a bad break I got. Yet today I consider myself the luckiest man on the face of the earth. I have been in ballparks for 17 years and have never received anything but kindness and encouragement from you fans.

"Look at these grand men (the 1927 and '39 Yankees). Which of you wouldn't consider it the highlight of his career just to associate with them for even one day?

"Sure, I'm lucky. Who wouldn't consider it an honor to have known Jacob Ruppert; also the builder of baseball's greatest empire, Ed Barrow; to have spent six years with that wonderful little fellow, Miller Huggins; then to have spent the next nine years with that outstanding leader, that smart student of psychology, the best manager in baseball today, Joe McCarthy.

"Who wouldn't feel honored to have roomed with such a grand guy as Bill Dickey?

"Sure, I'm lucky. When the New York Giants, a team you would give your right arm to beat, and vice-versa, sends you a gift, that's something. When everybody down to the groundskeepers and those boys in white coats remember you with trophies, that's something.

"When you have a wonderful mother-in-law who takes sides with you in squabbles against her own daughter, that's something. When you have a father and mother who work all their lives so that you can have an education and build your body, it's a blessing. When you have a wife who has been a

tower of strength and shown more courage than you dreamed existed, that's the finest I know.

"So I close in saying that I might have had a tough break, but I have an awful lot to live for."

He did indeed, but Henry Louis Gehrig died on June 2, 1941, 16 years to the day that he got his chance at first base with the Yankees when Wally Pipp came up with the most expensive headache in baseball history. Pipp sat down on the bench one day and wound up the next year in Cincinnati.

What could you call Gehrig except great? Well, he was known as Columbia Lou and Larrupin' Lou and, because of his boxcar build and the full cut of baseball bloomers in those days, Biscuit Pants. Iron Horse, of course, and one more nickname that Babe Ruth hung on him when he was young and a powerful kid hitting cleanup behind the Bambino— Buster.

Buster Gehrig. I always liked that because it had the double connotation of what Lou was, a clean-living chap with bow tie and pipe and, indubitably, a helluva hard hitter.

They called him "Fat" when he grew up in the tenement district of New York's upper East Side, son of German immigrants who had come to America just three years before he was born in 1903. Little Looie was the only one of four children who survived as Henry and Christina Gehrig struggled to make a living.

Herr Gehrig was an artisan, an ironworker who made ornamental grilles when he could get work at his trade. Mama was a hausfrau who was forced to take to helping earn a living when she wanted Looie to go to college. By then, Papa was an ailing janitor.

Lou had so little as a boy that he went to school on cold winter days with a khaki shirt, khaki pants and heavy brown shoes, but no hat or overcoat. Years later, his wife found it hard to get him to wear a coat.

Working after school in butcher shops, grocery stores and at other odd jobs, he still found time to play soccer, football and the sport he liked best, baseball. He was bigger than most kids, good-natured, but slow-witted and they called him "Chicken."

It was tough enough being a lefthanded catcher, but he was labeled as the Heinie janitor's son in World War I, by which time his mother, to whom he was devoted, had gone to serving as a cook and housekeeper for a fraternity on the Columbia University campus. Mama scrimped and saved so that Looie could go to college.

By then, he was enrolled at Columbia University and waiting tables at the Phi Delta Theta fraternity, which pledged him. The Phi Delts in more recent years established in Gehrig's memory an award that has been made to a list of distinguished players most closely matching the humble and honorable man, on and off the field. But as an undergraduate, the shy and sensitive Gehrig writhed at the caste system by which some brothers who couldn't carry his morals or ethics made him feel as poor as he was.

When both his parents became ill, Lou seized on the opportunity to flex his baseball muscles for a living. He'd played summer ball professionally under an assumed name in 1921, causing Columbia no end of embarrassment. But the Lions and their Ivy League opponents were understanding because of the extreme financial need. When the Yankees offered a $1,500 bonus, Gehrig left college for good.

By then, he'd already shown enough power as a high school boy to hit a home run out of the park in an interleague all-star game at Chicago's Wrigley Field. And years later, he could recount in painful detail how he trained with the Yankees in '23 at New Orleans with just $12 in his pocket for tips and incidentals. He was quietly looking for a dishwashing job when the Yankees put up meal money for the barnstorming trip north.

If Gehrig was frugal later, a pinchpenny as some thought, though generous with his parents and his wife, he wouldn't have been the first poor boy to

play it close to the vest. Besides, as Joe DiMaggio would suggest years later, smiling, Lou wasn't the hardest bargainer at contract time.

His peak salary apparently was $39,000 in 1938, a figure which, though it would make him close to a half-million player under present economic conditions and tax laws, wasn't as robust as his batting.

When young DiMaggio soared to stardom and sought pay increases, general manager Ed Barrow would remind him that Joe Dee certainly didn't expect to make more than Gehrig had earned. Barrow didn't like to be reminded that Ruth had been paid more than twice as much.

Lou batted .423 with the Yankees in 13 games in 1923, a year he spent most of the season at Hartford. Again in '24, batting 12 times, he hit .500 in the major league uniform before batting a lusty .369 at Hartford.

Day after day, early in 1925, Huggins sat the kid next to him on the bench, giving Gehrig the benefit of his baseball wisdom. Finally there came the morning when Wally Pipp reported with the splitting headache and, in the understatement of the ages, Huggins suggested, "Why don't you take the day off?"

Gehrig, whose unforgettable streak had begun with a pinch-hit performance the day before, stepped into the lineup that June afternoon with a wide stance, spread-eagling the plate. He took a short stride with those thick, powerful legs and swung blacksmith arms. He was an immediate hit and played the last 126 games of the 1925 season to hit 20 homers and bat .295.

From the time he drove in 107 runs in his first full season, 1926, a year the Yankees won the pennant and lost the only World Series of the seven in which he played from 1927, Gehrig cleaned up behind Ruth, creating an amazing 1-2 punch as the 3-4 men in the Yankees' batting order.

When Ruth hit his 60 homers in '27, Babe actually had more home runs than any club in the American League except his own. Yet young Gehrig was close at hand with 47 and, moreover, he boomed 117 extra-base hits out of the 218 he had, leading the league in doubles with 52 and hitting 18 triples. He batted .373, slugged in 175 runs and it was the shy young first baseman, not the gregarious and glamorous outfielder, who was awarded the American League's Most Valuable Player award.

The unhappy foe had learned it no longer paid to pitch around Ruth by walking the Babe, because a base on balls merely put one more man on base for Buster Gehrig to drive in.

Larrupin' Lou had some handsome hitting figures in the years that followed, but the productive consistency is best reflected in his RBIs, 1926 through '38:

107... 175... 142... 126... 174... 184... 151... 139... 165... 119... 152... 159... 114.

Over that period, too, Gehrig was a blue-ribbon ballplayer in World Series play. Why, even in 1938, when heavens knows how much the fatal illness had gnawed into him, he still managed a respectable .286 with four hits in 14 trips of a four-game sweep over the Cubs.

There were two big differences. Gehrig didn't get an extra-base hit or drive in a run that last Series, but he still finished with 10 homers and 35 RBIs in 34 World Series games.

In 1928, a fierce four-game sweep over St. Louis, Biscuit Pants hit a blistering .545 with a double and four homers among six hits good for nine RBIs. But—wouldn't you know it!—the Babe even out-did him with three homers in one game and 10 hits for a .625 average. However, with Ruth on base so often, Gehrig reaped a harvest with the nine RBIs in four games.

Curiously, even though he batted .361 in World Series competition, Gehrig reminisced at the end of his career that his greatest thrill had come in a Series in which he'd hit just .292. He referred to the 1936 Series in which he smashed a two-run homer off the Giants' great lefthander, Carl Hubbell.

"Hub had already beat us once," Gehrig ex-plained, "and if we hadn't beaten him in the fourth game, it's a cinch we'd have had to meet again if it had gone seven. The way he was pitching at that time, we might not have beaten him a second time."

Lou's second greatest thrill, he said, had come a year later in the All-Star Game at Washington, where Dizzy Dean, then at the peak of his short and meteoric success shook off catcher Gabby Hartnett, who wig-wagged for a curve with a full count on Gehrig in the third inning. Ol' Diz tried to smoke his fastball past him, and Buster—no, by then, the Iron Horse—busted it over the right-field fence.

Thrill No. 3 were those four homers in a game five years previously, an accomplishment that es-caped even Ruth.

The basis for the strained relations between the most destructive duo is obscure. Back in 1929, Gehrig praised Ruth highly in an interview with Harry Brundidge of the old *St. Louis Star-Times*, not only for his ability, but for his friendship and his hitting help. At that time Lou said his biggest "kick" had been seeing his more prominent teammate get his 60th homer in 1927.

In early years, Buster was almost an errand boy for the Babe, not because Ruth necessarily was de-manding, but because Gehrig was just obliging. Some have suggested that in later years, the older man became jealous of the younger one's vitality and ability. Others have suggested that their wives created a breach.

Gehrig was momma's boy for years, displaying to both his parents a respect and affection that was laudatory. In 1928, he bought a home for them in suburban New Rochelle, with the flower garden, lawn and trees they'd missed in the asphalt jungle of New York. And he lived with them until he met and married Eleanor Twitchell five years later.

Biographers picture Columbia Lou as shy, self-conscious and lonely until then, a good-natured guy who didn't like to drink and, except for an occasional date, spent hours riding amusement park rollercoasters alone. But when Lou met Eleanor, his mother no longer was his best girl.

Miss Twitchell, reared to wealth in Chicago, had gone to work after the stock market crash of 1929. She had a secretarial job at Chicago's World Fair of 1933 when she met Gehrig and several other ballplayers at a party. She and Lou were married in New York late that September and lived happily together, though, unfortunately, for only too few years.

And even though the movie of Gehrig's life, *Pride of the Yankees*, filmed in 1942 with Gary Cooper in the starring role, was several cuts above other baseball biographies, all of them bad, there still is too much uncertainty about the courtship by which momma's boy became Eleanor's husband.

As previously mentioned, there's similar uncertainty about the Ruth-Gehrig coolness, which Stanley Frank discovered as a young writer when he joined the Yankees in 1932. He sat in with urbane Richards Vidmer, another New York writer, as partners against the two great home-run hitters in a rainy day bridge game.

As predicted by Vidmer, Ruth and Gehrig lost their good card sense and bid wildly, especially the Babe, laughing off losses as he belted a bottle of Prohibition Scotch.

Frank, happily pocketing $16.50, which was more than a half-week's pay and quite a haul at a quarter-cent a point, recalled that Vidmer had commiserated with Lou later for the bad beating he had taken on the Babe's wild bidding.

"Yeah, the big guy has a big, loose mouth," Gehrig said. He brooded for a minute and then blurted, "He pops off too damn much about a lot of things."

Lou was referring, Frank realized, to a crack Ruth made after he had been set five tricks on one hand. "Jeez, I sure loused that one," he'd boomed. "I butchered it, like McCarthy handles the pitchers."

Team man Gehrig was furious with the Babe for having ridiculed the manager in the presence of two reporters, a breach of confidence that offended his sense of propriety.

Good guy Gehrig, who got loaded early in his career one time, to break a slump, and then swore off the stuff, participated in the clowning that goes on in every clubhouse, but if a group of Yankees were making themselves conspicuous off the field with rowdy behavior, Lou would glare at them impatiently, veteran observers recall, and the raucous conduct stopped abruptly.

His wife might have had to help him in areas of self-confidence and in an appreciation of the arts, but he WAS the pride of the Yankees, and Stanley Frank summed it up well when he wrote:

"Lou was not the best ball player the Yankees ever had. Ruth was No. 1 by every yardstick. DiMaggio was a more accomplished performer in every department except hitting. Mickey Mantle was endowed with much more natural ability. Bill Dickey, a catcher without a peer, gave the Yankees a big edge over all rivals in the most difficult position to fill and might have been as indispensable to the team as Lou.

"Yet Lou was the most valuable player the Yankees ever had because he was the prime source of their greatest asset—an implicit confidence in themselves and every man on the club. Lou's pride as a big leaguer brushed off on everyone who played with him....

"The Yankees had that intangible quality called class. It was a tradition perpetuated by guys such as Dickey, DiMaggio, Gordon, Henrich, Rolfe, Keller, Gomez and Ruffing, but it stemmed from Lou, and it was the decisive factor in forging their remarkable chain of successes. It is significant that the Yankees never were involved in nightclub brawls or drew adverse publicity from clashes between managers and players until DiMaggio and Henrich, the last men who had been exposed to Lou's influence, left the club.

"Polishing the Yankees' public image was Lou's full-time job. This may seem a trivial point, but he never appeared in a restaurant, hotel lobby or any other public place without a coat and tie. There was no air conditioning in those days and Lou, a big man, was as uncomfortable as a polar bear—and sometimes as grouchy—when the temperature hit the 90s. No matter how hot it was, he always was dressed properly in conservative clothes. A Yankee who showed up in a dining room wearing a garish sports shirt without a coat seldom did it more than once.

"'You're a big leaguer,' Lou would tell him sharply. 'Look like one.'"

A lifetime .340 hitter, Gehrig played with injuries and ailments that would have floored lesser men. Working around Sportsman's Park in St. Louis as a kid, I recall the scuttlebutt one steaming summer day of the dust-bowl drought in the Depression. Unable to sleep, Gehrig reportedly had wrapped himself in ice-soaked sheets and slept under an electric fan all night.

The next morning he had lumbago so bad that he barely could get out of bed and to the ballpark, where he was listed as leadoff, batting in the shortstop's spot. He singled and then retired for pinch-runner Lyn Lary to have that aching back worked on.

Could such extreme abuses, if not exaggerated, have led to or, at least, contributed to the disease that attacked the spinal cord? No matter the difficult answer. One day the indestructible Iron Horse just broke down.

Until in that awful illness he no longer could walk, Lou served, conscientiously, as a New York city parole commissioner for Mayor LaGuardia. The Baseball Writers' Association of America voted Gehrig into the Hall of Fame by acclamation in 1939. The Yankees retired his uniform number—4—and, after his death in '41, they erected a monument to him in center field at Yankee Stadium. Twelve years later, a plaque to his memory was unveiled by his mother, dedicated by the city at his birthplace, 309 E. 94th street, a four-story apartment that had become a six-story laundry.

A monument even more enduring to Henry Louis Gehrig, the man they took for granted and granite, is that incredible line in the record book for most consecutive games played—2,130.

HENRY LOUIS (LOU or IRON HORSE) GEHRIG
Born June 19, 1903, at New York, N.Y.
Died June 2, 1941, at Riverdale, N.Y.
Height 6-1 Weight 212
Threw and batted lefthanded.
Named to Hall of Fame, 1939.

YEAR	CLUB	LEAGUE	POS.	G.	AB.	R.	H.	2B.	3B.	HR.	RBI.	B.A.	PO.	A.	E.	F.A.
1921	Hartford *	East	1B	12	46	5	12	1	2	0	-	.261	130	4	2	.985
1922	-	-	-						(Not in Organized Ball)							
1923	New York	Amer.	1B-PH	13	26	6	11	4	1	1	9	.423	53	3	4	.933
1923	Hartford	East.	1B	59	227	54	69	13	8	24	-	.304	623	23	6	.991
1924	New York	Amer.	PH-1-O	10	12	2	6	1	0	0	6	.500	10	1	0	1.000
1924	Hartford	East.	1B	134	504	111	186	40	13	37	-	.369	1391	66	23	.984
1925	New York	Amer.	1B-OF	126	437	73	129	23	10	20	68	.295	1126	53	13	.989
1926	New York	Amer.	1B	155	572	135	179	47	20	16	107	.313	1565	73	15	.991
1927	New York	Amer.	1B	155	584	149	218	52	18	47	175	.373	1662	88	15	.992
1928	New York	Amer.	1B	154	562	139	210	47	13	27	142	.374	1488	79	18	.989
1929	New York	Amer.	1B	154	553	127	166	33	9	35	126	.300	1458	82	9	.994
1930	New York	Amer.	1B-OF	154	581	143	220	42	17	41	174	.379	1298	89	15	.989
1931	New York	Amer.	1B-OF	155	619	163	211	31	15	46	184	.341	1352	58	13	.991
1932	New York	Amer.	1B	156	596	138	208	42	9	34	151	.349	1293	75	18	.987
1933	New York	Amer.	1B	152	593	138	198	41	12	32	139	.334	1290	64	9	.993
1934	New York	Amer.	1B-SS	154	579	128	210	40	6	49	165	.363	1284	80	8	.994
1935	New York	Amer.	1B	149	535	125	176	26	10	30	119	.329	1337	82	15	.990
1936	New York	Amer.	1B	155	579	167	205	37	7	49	152	.354	1377	82	9	.994
1937	New York	Amer.	1B	157	569	138	200	37	9	37	159	.351	1370	74	16	.989
1938	New York	Amer.	1B	157	576	115	170	32	6	29	114	.295	1483	100	14	.991
1939	New York	Amer.	1B	8	28	2	4	0	0	0	1	.143	64	4	2	.971
Major League Totals				2164	8001	1888	2721	535	162	493	1991	.340	19511	1087	193	.991

* Played under name of Lewis with Hartford in 1921.

WORLD SERIES RECORD

YEAR	CLUB	LEAGUE	POS.	G.	AB.	R.	H.	2B.	3B.	HR.	RBI.	B.A.	PO.	A.	E.	F.A.
1926	New York	Amer.	1B	7	23	1	8	2	0	0	3	.348	78	1	0	1.000
1927	New York	Amer.	1B	4	13	2	4	2	2	0	5	.308	41	3	0	1.000
1928	New York	Amer.	1B	4	11	5	6	1	0	4	9	.545	33	0	0	1.000
1932	New York	Amer.	1B	4	17	9	9	1	0	3	8	.529	37	2	1	.975
1936	New York	Amer.	1B	6	24	5	7	1	0	2	7	.292	45	2	0	1.000
1937	New York	Amer.	1B	5	17	4	5	1	1	1	3	.294	50	1	0	1.000
1938	New York	Amer.	1B	4	14	4	4	0	0	0	0	.286	25	3	0	1.000
World Series Totals				34	119	30	43	8	3	10	35	.361	309	12	1	.997

SOLEMN AS A JUDGE: A great judge of a pitched ball as a line-drive hitter and a great, graceful fielder—Charlie Gehringer.

CHARLIE GEHRINGER

Charlie Gehringer played baseball so effortlessly that it was the foe which should have looked like it was ready to cry, not the sad-faced Detroit second baseman who was a ballplayer's ballplayer, a craftsman so skilled and polished that it's doubtful the public ever appreciated fully how really great he was.

A highly respected, long-time Detroit sports editor, the late H. G. Salsinger, attempted one time to assess the ability of the handsome, poker-faced Gehringer. Although emphasizing at once that the quiet, graceful Gehringer was as different from con-

troversial Ty Cobb "as Niagara Falls from the Dead Sea," Salsinger noted that the so called Mechanical Man was like the flamboyant Georgia Peach in one precious respect.

"He, too, has the distinct qualities that are appreciated only by the schooled members of his profession," Salsinger wrote, explaining that he'd always regarded Christy Mathewson as superior to Walter Johnson because the Big Train simply overpowered hitters and Matty outwitted them.

"You find the same situation on the theater stage

or under the canvas of a circus," Salsinger commented. "There are actors' actors. There are trapeze performers and acrobats who get their true appreciation not from the audiences that watch them, but from their fellow performers.

"The crowds like the bizarre. They are taken in by the flashy acrobatics. It is twice as difficult to turn a front somersault than a back somersault, but, between the two, the back somersault will always get the major portion of the applause.

"The performers who execute the most difficult tricks under canvas earn their reputation mostly among their professional brothers and sisters who, having tried the trick or having studied the rare technique involved in its execution, appreciate it. But the performer, so skillful that he makes the most difficult turn look simple, does not impress the audience. A veteran in the show business may say that he lacks showmanship, and that is probably true."

And that brought Salsinger to Gehringer and, drawing on experience which would span a half-century as a baseball writer until his death in 1958, the *Detroit News'* authority said flatly and firmly:

"He lacks showmanship, but he has polish that no other second baseman, with the exception of the great Napoleon Lajoie, ever carried. He has so well schooled himself in the technique of his position that he makes the most difficult plays look easy."

In Salsinger's judgment, evaluating the three greatest second basemen in the history of the American League, Eddie Collins was the best baserunner, Lajoie the best hitter and Gehringer the best fielder, though obviously all could do everything well.

Gehringer was indeed a ballplayer's ballplayer, as was evident in research done for *The Sporting News* for this book on former superstars. Hall of Fame players spoke of Charlie with unfailing respect that borders on awe. But it can't be said that his talent for doing the right thing with the least amount of effort was lost on the press.

Gehringer not only was elected to the Hall of Fame in 1949, just seven years after his retirement,

but a special committee of baseball writers named him the game's greatest living second baseman at the time of the sport's centennial celebration in 1969.

If the public didn't fully appreciate him over the nearly 17 seasons he played second base at Detroit, finishing with a .321 career average, it's only because he was so stylish and so silent.

At a dinner honoring Detroit's world champions in 1935, Mickey Cochrane, the fiery catcher who managed the ball club, used about Gehringer the expression that would be heard most often over the years.

"He says 'hello' opening day, 'goodbye' closing day and, in between, hits .350," Black Mike said.

Another Detroit teammate, Roger (Doc) Cramer, was credited with another one about Gehringer that has endured. "You wind him up opening day and forget him," said an admiring Cramer.

If research is right, however, it was Broadway Lyn Lary, flashy-dressing former American League shortstop, who hung the Mechanical Man nickname on the Great Robot, as someone else called Gehringer (pronounced with a hard second "g," not a soft "j.") Actually, the thing became a bit nauseating when the alliterative effort was stretched into extra innings to make it the Mechanical Man from the Motor City.

The truth is, there was exaggeration throughout because Charlie had a dry sense of humor as well as his share of opinions, but he spoke as conservatively as he dressed, and he was as impeccable personally as in his playing, for which there really is only one word—stylish.

Afield, Gehringer glided gracefully, ranging far afield with more speed than seemed apparent. At just under six feet, weighing close to 190, with big hands that were strong and sure, he had trim legs, slightly bowed, which permitted him to make hard plays look easy.

He'd ease back for pop flies or glide behind second to backhand the ball. He'd move smoothly to his left to provide aid and comfort to his first baseman, usually Hank Greenberg, and he was without a peer at making the second baseman's toughest play, coming in quickly to make the bending pickup of a slow roller or drag bunt, following with an off-balance throw.

Ironically, it was one of his patented plays he didn't make that hastened the end of his playing career, which came officially at the age of 39 in 1942, more than two years after he'd felt like calling it a career.

After the 1940 World Series, which Detroit lost in a seventh game, veteran reporters found him slumped unhappily before his locker in Crosley Field's old visitors' clubhouse with the cramped quarters and potbellied stove.

"I'll never go through another season like this one," said Gehringer, who had struggled physically through 139 games and batted .313, but then had batted just .214 in the World Series. Previously, in Series play against St. Louis in 1934 and Chicago in '35, he'd hit .379 and .375.

"Playing ball was a torture for me," Charlie went on quietly, light blue eyes sadder than ever behind dark brows and a bronzed complexion. He ran his fingers through black hair matted with perspiration.

"On most days I couldn't get out of bed until noon. Any time I tried to field a ball off to either side, especially to my left, I felt as if my insides were being torn loose. Often I couldn't stoop over to pick up a ball after blocking it. I've had so many heat treatments that I feel like a boiled lobster and so many massages that I must look like a hunk of well-kneaded dough. At times I didn't think I could move two steps or get the bat off my shoulder."

For years, a story persisted that Gehringer had injured his back shoveling snow in a Michigan winter, but in one of the centennial reunions the distinguished-looking 66-year-old businessman said he'd been hurt making one of those patented pickups on the run in spring training.

"I came in, scooped up the ball, started to fire and saw a kid had run out into my range," he explained.

"In motion and off-balance, I checked my throw at the last instant, lurched, and had misery thereafter."

Despite the threat to quit after the 1940 season, Gehringer got just enough relief to try again in '41, but he wasn't the same, either at bat or afield. And a crowd of more than 40,000 must have done a double-take of disbelief on the Fourth of July when manager Del Baker made a change.

"Perry now playing second base for Detroit," came the field announcement, which was like sending up a hitter for Babe Ruth, the mighty one who had called Gehringer the greatest player in the game.

Boyd Perry never made it, so Gehringer, tailing off to .220 in 127 games, agreed to come back in '42 as a player-coach only because of the threat of what World War II would do to the manpower. Pinch-hitting, he got in only 45 games and batted .267.

"I won't be back," said Gehringer that fall when he accepted a commission in the Navy as a lieutenant. The 39-year-old bachelor wound up as a lieutenant commander in the Navy's fitness program before he returned to Detroit at the end of the war, but not as a ballplayer.

Next to Ty Cobb, Charlie had put in more seasons in a Detroit uniform than any player until Al Kaline. A farm boy who had attended the University of Michigan for a year, Gehringer had reasoned that a ballplayer ought to make some kind of business connection, preferably in the city in which he played.

He'd made good money, but had not been overpaid. The first Detroit club owner for whom he played, Frank Navin, was a tough man with a buck. Players would find themselves battling for $500 or $1,000 raises after big seasons.

With Walter O. Briggs, who bought out Navin in the mid-30s, things were different. Gehringer got up to $40,000 and was grateful.

Still, he'd quit a year too soon to qualify for the players' pension plan. (He received service credit for the three years in the Navy.) But he'd come up with a good thing after having worked off-seasons early in his career as a sporting goods clerk in a Detroit department store, as a wholesale coal salesman and then as a gas station operator with hired help.

One day after he'd played a couple of years with the Tigers, he walked into the sales room of a car dealer and bought a Hupmobile from a salesman named Ray Forsyth, a rabid sports fan. Gehringer bought two more Hupmobiles from Forsyth and then switched to Buicks when his friend changed brands.

In 1938, Gehringer and Forsyth went into partnership. A New York woman named Ann Friedolph had a patent on a new upholstery button. Patent attorney J. M. Misselle was a friend of Charlie and Ray. When the woman wanted to sell the button to the automotive companies, the Gehringer-Forsyth partnership decided to take a shot at it.

As Charlie explained it, upholstery buttons used in automobile interiors never had seemed to hold tight. A metal stay that looked like a paper clip would poke through and scratch motorists or tear their clothes. The button the partners sold was pushed through the material and released with a long needle.

Chrysler and Ford were the first customers. Later, General Motors bought the buttons. "We sold them by the jillion," said Gehringer.

The firm, Gehringer and Forsyth, added alloys for heat-treating furnaces as the second item. Then came upholstery material, leather vinyl, carpeting and a variety of manmade fibers in the manufacturers' agent category.

As Watson Spoelstra, *Detroit News'* baseball writer, put it, "Look about in the car you own. Chances are that Gehringer and Forsyth sold the auto company some of the interior materials."

From his colonial-styled office 10 miles from downtown Detroit to his red-brick early American home on a five-acre wooded area in suburban Birmingham, Mich., the affluent former second baseman needed baseball "like a hole in my head," as he put it when he was thrust suddenly back into the game in 1951.

Living with his mother in the house he'd built for her—she died in 1946—the most eligible bachelor hadn't married until the year he went into the Hall of Fame, 1949. His wife was the former Josephine Stillen. They'd go into town now and then to watch the Tigers, but Charlie preferred to play golf, shooting from 75 to 80, and he enjoyed feeding the pheasants and other birds in the wooded area of his suburban property.

Then Mr. Briggs—W. O., as Charlie called him—summoned his former star in the summer of 1951 with a flattering, but stunning offer. The veteran Billy Evans would step down as general manager and Briggs wanted Gehringer.

Away from baseball for nearly nine seasons and without front office experience, Charlie didn't want the job and tried to unsell the man for whom he felt affection as well as gratitude. Suddenly, though, Briggs stuck out his hand.

"It seemed like an eternity until I took it," Gehringer related. "What could I say?"

Taking over a team that in an exciting near-miss under Red Rolfe almost had won a pennant in 1950, Gehringer found that the payroll was up, the attendance down as the Tigers fell back in '51. He retained Rolfe as manager but traded name players like George Kell, Hoot Evers, Dizzy Trout, Virgil Trucks and Vic Wertz.

A year later, Briggs was dead and his son, Spike, was running the club. Rolfe was fired. Ted Lyons turned down the job as manager, and Gehringer and young Briggs talked of naming a player to become manager. Spike mentioned Pat Mullin, the outfielder. Gehringer persuaded him that Fred Hutchinson, the pitcher, might prove a more enduring leader.

Hutch quit a couple of years later, shortly after Gehringer himself went back to his business, but Charlie called the turn on Hutchinson when he learned that Hutch had taken a minor league managerial job at Seattle.

"That's the way to get back," said Gehringer before Hutchinson returned at St. Louis and then went on to win a pennant at Cincinnati before suffering an untimely death.

"I know Mickey Cochrane was provoked when he lost his job at Detroit in 1938 and he wouldn't go back to the minors," Gehringer said. "But if he had, he would have managed in the majors again."

Gehringer, preparing the way for his own early departure after W. O. Briggs' death by hiring Herold (Muddy) Ruel for the Tigers' front office, said he'd frankly not enjoyed the general manager's job because of lack of preparation. However, he delighted later in Detroit's world championship seasons, 1968 and 1974. Retired from business, he and dear Jo wintered in Florida. By 1993, closing in on 90 and still a good golfer before a fatal stroke, he only recently had relinquished duties with baseball's Hall of Fame and its old-timers committee.

He did, after all, express considerable appreciation for the game that took him off a farm near Fowlerville, Mich., some 60 miles up the highway from Detroit to East Lansing.

Some years later, driving through Fowlerville, a Detroit newspaperman asked a man leaning against a lamp post, "Is Charlie Gehringer's home on this route?"

"Don't know," said the man. "Don't know a family named—what did you say the name was?"

"Gehringer," said the Detroit writer, beginning to burn.

"Never heard of them," said the lamp pole propper-upper.

"Don't tell me," the writer sizzled, "that you never heard of Charlie Gehringer?"

"Oh," said the man, "you mean the ballplayer. Did he say he comes from Fowlerville?" The writer nodded, afraid to trust himself to speak.

"Aw, he's just bragging," said the man. "He lives in the suburbs."

Fowlerville is so small that its suburbs are—or were— farmhouses, lush fields, horses, cows, chickens and pigs, all of which Charlie tended.

They're sensitive about the size of the place. Even the guy who didn't really live there, Gehringer.

Years later an annoyed Cobb, miffed because of implications he'd given up on Charlie as a rookie, tried to straighten out the record about the time he'd helped "the kid from that little town of 400."

Said Gehringer, solemnly, "Ty did help me, just as I know he helped Heinie Manush, Harry Heilmann and others, but somebody tell him, please, that Fowlerville has nearly 1,000 population."

So it was in large part pride in his environs that produced the biggest thrill in a career that must have had many more than the modest Gehringer can remember.

Why, one time in 1929 he hit three triples in a game. The same year he led the American League in stolen bases. In 1939, he hit for the cycle in a game. You know, single, double, triple and homer. Even after going hitless in the first All-Star Game at Chicago's Comiskey Park in 1933, he hit a sizzling .500 for six appearances in the mid-summer classic, 10-for-20.

Seven seasons he had more than 200 hits, with a five-year streak from 1933 through 1937. He led the league in batting with a .371 average in 1937, the year he won the Most Valuable Player award. Over one four-year stretch, he hit .356, .330, .354 and .371 and, in fact, playing 150 or more games nine times in a period of 11 seasons, he was below .300 just once.

"That," he explained, "was the year I was going to be like Babe Ruth. I think I had eight home runs before he had any and I began going for the fences. I wound up getting not many homers or many hits, either."

The .298 average, with 19 homers and 107 RBIs, was a bad one in 1932 for Gehringer, who prided himself on his bat control. A lefthanded hitter with a picture-book batting stance and smooth, level swing, he invariably spotted the pitcher a strike.

"I liked to look around up there," he said, "but I didn't do much taking with men on base."

Quiet and motionless at the plate, Gehringer needed only one swing before stroking an outside pitch to left, driving one up the middle or pulling sharply. He had a remarkable reputation as a two-strike hitter.

"I honestly believe," said his old boss, Del Baker, "that Charlie could spot a pitcher two strikes all season and still hit within 15 points of his regular average."

For this man of many accomplishments, who delighted in stealing third base because he figured it was the easiest to swipe, the No. 1 thrill came when about 500 persons from Fowlerville came to Detroit to give him a "day."

By then, his father was dead, but his mother, brother and sister were at Navin Field for a game with the New York Yankees and Gehringer fretted privately that, as so often happens when a player is honored, he would have a bad day with the bat or glove.

After all, for all his skill, he could remember having made three errors in a game. He honestly thought he should have been charged with six. And he could remember, too, the mortification of becoming so dejected that after striking out once against the old St. Louis Browns, he trotted to his position, head down only to be met by his rival second baseman, Oscar Melillo, who was grinning.

"Hey, Charlie," said Melillo, "did you come out to help me get the third out?"

Against the Yankees, however, on the day he most wanted to play well for his friends, neighbors and especially the proud Gehringer family, Charlie really showed his class. And, friends, with this man class began with a capital C.

Off George Pipgras, Yankee righthander who later became an American League umpire, he hit a home run his first time at bat. The next three times at bat, he hit safely, too. Then, with Wilcy Moore pitching for New York, Gehringer stole home.

"And to make the day perfect," he recalled, "we beat the Yankees."

Gehringer was so happy that he never uttered a word when the folks from home gave him a set of righthanded golf sticks, even though he was a lefthanded hitter. Politely, he learned to play golf righthanded, though his good friend, Horton Smith, the professional, wondered if he really hadn't given up something by losing the stiffer elbow of his dominant arm, the right one.

That good right arm, which stood him in good stead as a slick pivot man on the double play, betrayed him only—and quite mysteriously—in 1931 when he was laid up for considerable time, unable to throw. If the injury—which left as quickly as it had come—had been suffered when he was hit by Lefty Grove's blazer, Charlie wouldn't have been puzzled.

Asked about the fastest pitcher he'd ever seen, talking to Lowell Reidenbaugh of *The Sporting News* at a Hall of Fame reunion in St. Louis, Gehringer permitted a light smile to turn up the corners of his lips.

"Grove, I'd have to say," he said, "and painfully. Lefty hit me just above the right elbow one time, and it felt as if the ball burrowed in there and stuck. I didn't rub it, but when I got down there to first base, tears were running down my cheeks."

Tears were running down Charlie's mother's cheeks, too, back in 1924 when the 20-year-old son, who had put in a year on the campus at Ann Arbor, said he preferred baseball to farming. Charlie's father, though a German immigrant, understood. Years later, his mother would smile and say, "And to think I tried to have Charlie miss all of this."

On the farm three miles from Fowlerville, Charlie and brother Al laid out a diamond behind the barn, using a rock for home plate, a pump handle for first base, the door of an outdoor cellar for third base and a rain barrel for second.

Charlie played third for his high school team and for the Fowlerville town team. He also pitched before going to Michigan, where he played both football and baseball.

A hunting friend of Bobby Veach, one Floyd Smith, told the long-time Detroit outfielder about

Gehringer, and Veach, seeing that seeing really was believing, arranged with Navin for a tryout for the farm boy.

Although there would be a story that Cobb didn't think the kid would hit, it apparently was spurious. Ty always insisted that after one look at Gehringer he didn't even bother to take off his spike shoes before clomping into the Detroit owner's office to tell Navin to sign Charlie.

Gehringer, delighted to sign for a few dollars more than his expenses, was farmed out to London in the old Michigan-Ontario League, where he batted .292, and then was called up by the Tigers at the end of the season.

"In my first big league game, I had a tough day," he remembered. "Seems to me I booted two or three balls and didn't get any hits. On my last trip to the plate, I thought I had one. I smashed the ball to left field, but somebody jumped up in front of the scoreboard and made a great catch.

"After that game, we went to Chicago, and I loosened up away from home."

Indeed. In 11 times at bat that fall, the kid got six hits for a .545 average. In 1925, he was optioned to Toronto, where he hit .325 with 206 hits, 25 homers and 108 runs batted in.

Gehringer had reported to the Tigers as a third baseman, but at the time they had Bobby Jones and Fred Haney. So Cobb converted him into a second baseman before sending him to London. By the time the Tigers trained at Augusta, Ga., in 1926, which would be Gehringer's first full season with the club and Cobb's last, Charlie's hopes were high that he would open the season at second base.

"I had every assurance I was going to play, but at the last minute I was benched for Frank O'Rourke," said Gehringer. "I never got my chance until O'Rourke came down with measles and the advice on batting I got from Cobb, a tough taskmaster."

Cobb's viewpoint, for what it's worth, is that he didn't want to pressure the rookie at the start of the season. "I worked with his stance and how to hold

his hands and arms," Ty said, "because his potential excited me."

After the rookie batted .277 in 1926, the Tigers released Cobb, who was succeeded as manager by George Moriarty. The new manager immediately made a deal with St. Louis for a fiery second baseman, Marty McManus. Moriarty told Gehringer to work out at third base behind Jackie Warner.

"When we came north to open the '27 season, I was still the utility infielder," Gehringer said, "but then I got a good break and McManus a bad one. Marty became ill and I went to second base. I didn't miss a game until my arm went bad in St. Louis four years later."

By that time, Charlie was firmly entrenched, a result of successive seasons in which he hit .317, .320, .339, .330 and, even when limited to 101 games by the temporary arm trouble, .311.

Only once in that time did anyone attempt to move the virtuoso of the keystone from the position he played with such grace and greatness.

At the time Bucky Harris became manager in 1929, the Tigers badly needed a shortstop, and Harris figured he might solve two problems by moving Gehringer to shortstop and by playing second base himself. Trouble was, Bucky was rusty and didn't look too hot and, worse, Gehringer, the marvelous second baseman, seemed completely miscast at shortstop. The experiment lasted one day at Shreveport, La.

Gehringer, whose World Series average exactly matched his career mark, .321, waited a long time to get into the battle for baseball's blue ribbon. But even though the Tigers lost to the Cardinals' Gashouse Gang in the rude, rough and rowdy 1934 Series, Charlie wasn't found wanting. Although he committed three errors, which was unlike him, he belted 11 hits, including a homer off Dizzy Dean and a double off brother Paul.

A year later, when the Tigers defeated the Chicago Cubs, Gehringer faced lefthanded Larry

French in the ninth inning of the sixth game with Cochrane on first base, where young Phil Cavarretta was holding the runner. Gehringer, whose nine hits included three doubles, bid for another two-base blow or a game-winning triple when he hit a torrid shot over the bag, but right at Cavarretta.

Phil knocked down the smash and stepped on the bag, retiring Charlie, as Cochrane moved to second base, from where he scored on Goose Goslin's single for the run that gave Detroit its first world championship.

It could have been at this precise moment that Bucky Harris, himself a pretty good hand in the clutch in his day, summed up Charles Leonard Gehringer, the professionals' professional.

"I've never seen one man hit in so much hard luck, consistently," said Harris. "Year after year, he leads the league in line drives right at somebody. No wonder he looks so sad."

CHARLES LEONARD (MECHANICAL MAN) GEHRINGER
Born May 11, 1903, at Fowlerville, Mich.
Died January 29, 1993, at Birmingham, Mich.
Height 5-11 1/2 Weight 185
Threw right and batted lefthanded.
Named to Hall of Fame, 1949.

YEAR	CLUB	LEAGUE	POS.	G.	AB.	R.	H.	2B.	3B.	HR.	RBI.	B.A.	PO.	A.	E.	F.A.
1924	London	Mich.-Ont.	2B	112	401	60	117	19	18	3	60	.292	309	335	23	.966
1924	Detroit	Amer.	2B	5	11	2	6	0	0	0	1	.545	12	17	1	.966
1925	Toronto	Int.	2B	155	633	128	206	38	9	25	108	.325	403	471	31	.966
1925	Detroit	Amer.	2B	8	18	3	3	0	0	0	0	.167	8	20	0	1.000
1926	Detroit	Amer.	2B	123	459	62	127	19	17	1	48	.277	255	323	16	.973
1927	Detroit	Amer.	2B	133	508	110	161	29	11	4	61	.317	304	438	27	.965
1928	Detroit	Amer.	2B	154	603	108	193	29	16	6	74	.320	377	507	35	.962
1929	Detroit	Amer.	2B	155	634	131	215	45	19	13	106	.339	404	501	23	.975
1930	Detroit	Amer.	2B	154	610	143	201	47	15	16	98	.330	399	501	19	.979
1931	Detroit	Amer.	2B	101	383	67	119	24	5	4	53	.311	224	236	10	.979
1932	Detroit	Amer.	2B	152	618	112	184	44	11	19	107	.298	396	495	30	.967
1933	Detroit	Amer.	2B	155	628	103	204	42	6	12	105	.325	358	542	17	.981
1934	Detroit	Amer.	2B	154	601	134	214	50	7	11	127	.356	355	516	17	.981
1935	Detroit	Amer.	2B	150	610	123	201	32	8	19	108	.330	349	489	13	.985
1936	Detroit	Amer.	2B	154	641	144	227	60	12	15	116	.354	397	524	25	.974
1937	Detroit	Amer.	2B	144	564	133	209	40	1	14	96	.371	331	485	12	.986
1938	Detroit	Amer.	2B	152	568	133	174	32	5	20	107	.306	393	455	21	.976
1939	Detroit	Amer.	2B	118	406	86	132	29	6	16	86	.325	245	312	13	.977
1940	Detroit	Amer.	2B	139	515	108	161	33	3	10	81	.313	276	374	19	.972
1941	Detroit	Amer.	2B	127	436	65	96	19	4	3	46	.220	279	324	11	.982
1942	Detroit	Amer.	2B	45	45	6	12	0	0	1	7	.267	7	9	0	1.000
Major League Totals				2323	8858	1773	2839	574	146	184	1427	.321	5369	7068	309	.976

WORLD SERIES RECORD

YEAR	CLUB	LEAGUE	POS.	G.	AB.	R.	H.	2B.	3B.	HR.	RBI.	B.A.	PO.	A.	E.	F.A.
1934	Detroit	Amer.	2B	7	29	5	11	1	0	1	2	.309	19	26	3	.938
1935	Detroit	Amer.	2B	6	24	4	9	3	0	0	4	.375	14	25	0	1.000
1940	Detroit	Amer.	2B	7	28	3	6	0	0	0	1	.214	18	20	0	1.000
World Series Totals				20	81	12	26	4	0	1	7	.321	51	71	3	.976

APTLY NUMBERED: Bob ("45") Gibson possessor of an arm like a gun as well as incredible competitive courage.

BOB GIBSON

The rat that bit little Bobby Gibson's ear when the five year-old boy lived in an Omaha ghetto must have wound up with a frozen rodent's lip. Competitive fire surged through Gibson's veins and burned at his vitals. He was one cool customer in a clutch, unafraid and darn near unbeatable.

For a guy who once in the distant past had an undeserved reputation of fading at the finish, Gibby became the personification of the blue-chip, big-game winner. If, somehow, the pennant label or World Series spotlight had been focused on every game, would the long-legged, wide-shouldered, wasp-waisted righthander EVER would have lost?

When the going got tough or when the prize pressure almost equalled his pride of performance, Bob Gibson would become glassy-eyed with concentration and competition. Said Red Schoendienst, his manager for the last 10 of his 17 seasons in the major leagues, "I never saw Gibby smile the days he worked."

Many an opposing player thought he was a mean so-and-so, an intimidating pitcher who threw a fastball that had a blue-flame tail and perhaps the best hard slider ever to dart savagely across the outside corner. The truth is, Gibson did NOT talk to enemy players, so when a fella wound up in that same red-trimmed uniform with the double-Cardinal insignia trademark across his letters, he was surprised to find that No. 45 didn't actually carry a .45 like a Clint Eastwood in cleats.

In the clubhouse, on planes or on buses that carried the Cards from ballpark to airport, city to city, Gibson was articulate and amusing, the life of the party, but even then his humor was barbed. He was THE master needler as well as THE master.

When Gibson was given a goodbye day by the ball club in September 1975, shortly before he quit in disgust because he had been figured as through, which he really was, the Cardinals gave away to an S.R.O.-50,000 crowd a handsome slick souvenir program that included numerous pictures and capsules of highlights from the 40-year-old superstar's career.

Included, too, were comments from the likes of Stan Musial, Henry Aaron, Ken Boyer, Ernie Banks, Lou Brock, Willie Stargell, Bobby Bonds, Pete Rose, Johnny Bench, Willie McCovey, Richie Allen and others.

They were different, their comments, but they were the same, too, or, rather, they wound up with the same thought. To a man, each friend and foe, teammate and rival, regarded Gibson as the most fierce competitor he—and they—ever had seen.

With more intensity than most, Joe Torre, the dark-visaged, ominous-appearing major league manager with the warm heart and clever dialogue, would emphasize how Gibby scared the living bejabbers out of him until Torre joined the Cardinals from Atlanta, including the throne room of the king of the hill.

"To describe Bob Gibson," said Torre, "try pride, intensity, talent, respect, dedication. You need them all…"

Indeed. The record books tell the eloquence of the man's efforts out there 60 feet 6 inches from home plate, including his phenomenal 1.12 earned-run average in 1968, the lowest ERA ever for a 300-inning pitcher; his record seven consecutive complete-game wins in World Series play and his becoming the first National League pitcher ever to achieve 3,000 or more strikeouts.

Sure, the records list five 20-game seasons for a pitcher who almost always worked with four days' rest, and *The Sporting News'* Baseball Register lists his two Cy Young awards (1968 and '70), his National League Most Valuable Player award ('68) and his nine consecutive seasons as the Rawlings Gold Glove pitcher of the NL.

But neither statistics alone, nor even awards, can capture the things Torre mentioned, plus the anger and resentment that welled within Gibson, an impatient man who writhed more silently over racial injustices and such slights as minimal commercials and endorsements when he was, in fact, well-spoken and a handsome man, but a black one.

So THE moment came, but not when Gibson pitched at age 36 the 1971 no-hitter he figured a high-hard-one hurler never would accomplish. It really wasn't in the Series-clinching victories in 1964 and '67, either. Gibby's fury came in the 1968 World Series, sensed by none other than the only pitcher to whom the fair-minded Gibson really would doff a cap as superior—Sandy Koufax.

In a taxicab en route to St. Louis' Busch Memorial Stadium, then serving briefly as the television color commentator that Gibby later also would hold for a time, Koufax noted that the '68 Series opener had been hailed as a classic duel between Gibson and Detroit's dimpled darling Denny McLain, a 31-game winner.

Koufax, the overpowering Los Angeles' left-hander who had yielded to an excruciating arthritic elbow and retired after the '66 World Series, was aware that even though Gibson had posted a 22-9 record and that unbelievable 1.12 earned-run average, McLain inferentially had overshadowed him.

Denny was charming. His organ-entertaining and honor of having become the majors' first 30-game winner since Dizzy Dean 34 years earlier had trumped the more qualitative if not quantitative St. Louis pitcher's season.

"You know," said Koufax, "four years Gibson has had the same kind of elbow I had, but you didn't hear as much about it. Now, he's had a fabulous season, but you've heard more about McLain's. If I know Gibby—and I think I do—he'll eat McLain alive today."

Lefty Sandy was right on. Considering that the game was played in daylight, where strikeouts come harder, and considering further the significance of the World Series, I wonder if Robert Gibson's 17 strikeout performance on October 2, 1968 wasn't the greatest ever?

Working rapidly as he always did, as though eager to get on with strumming his baritone ukelele or rebuilding his toy antique automobiles, Gibby fired strikes past the hard-hitting American League Tigers.

In the fourth inning the Cardinals got to McLain. Roger Maris and Tim McCarver walked, and hits by Mike Shannon and Julian Javier helped produce three runs. A fourth St. Louis score came in the seventh when Lou Brock, always a hot Series hitter, homered off reliever Pat Dobson.

Gibson, meanwhile, giving up only five hits and one walk, was threatened only in the sixth when Dick McAuliffe singled and Series hero Al Kaline, another gallant gaffer, doubled in Detroit's second baseman.

Here, old No. 45 reared back and fired an inning-ending third strike past Norm Cash. Inning after inning, the strikeouts piled up. Kaline and Cash fanned twice each before the ninth, and McAuliffe, Jim Northrup and Bill Freehan, too. Mickey Stanley, Don Wert, Eddie Mathews and McLain also had gone down on strikes.

By the time Detroit batted last time up, a partisan crown of 54,692 knew that Gibson was only one strikeout shy of Koufax' Series record of 15.

When Gibson whiffed Kaline a third time, the crowd roared and batteryman McCarver pointed out to the center-field message board, whose bright neon lights carried the information Tim wanted Gib to see.

McCarver started out to the mound to give Gibson a pep talk. Gibby waved him back. "Give me the damn ball," he snarled.

Swish, swish, swish! Reaching back for all he had, Gibson fanned Cash for a third time and—for good measure—he blazed a game-ending third strike past Horton to achieve a 4-0 shutout of 17 strikeouts and a standing ovation.

Said Kaline afterward, shaking his head, "I've never seen such overpowering pitching."

Gibson said he preferred to pitch to free swingers such as Detroit sent up the plate rather than choked-grip singles hitters.

"But I can't understand these guys," said Gibson, who had used 141 pitches, of which 91 were fastballs. "They were swinging at my breaking ball"—that hellacious hard slider—as if I didn't have one."

If you'll recall, Gibson's seventh straight start-and-finish Series victory was one that was begun and allowed to continue for the benefit of a Sunday audience and national television. Twice, after his initial warmup, the often slow-starting Gibson had to heat up after rain delays, but he won and yet maybe lost just a trifle as he then came back for the seventh game with short rest and with a stiff, weary arm.

For Detroit, pot-bellied Mickey Lolich was magnificent, but Gibson matched the sinkerball southpaw inning after inning and, in fact, he turned to head for the home dugout in the seventh, certain he was still scoreless, when Northrup hit a line drive to center field with two on and two out. After all, the St. Louis center fielder was suck-'em-up Curt Flood, the player Gibson ranked with second baseman Julian Javier as the best two defensive performers who regularly played behind him.

Lo, in this instance, Flood misjudged the ball, losing it momentarily in the white shirts of the bright shiny afternoon in downtown St. Louis. He started in quickly rather than casually to move back a step or two. As Curt detected his misjudgment, he turned quickly to his right. Unfortunately, freshly sodded turf gave way under him, throwing Flood off balance and farther to his right.

The ball he could have caught if he barely had moved a muscle sailed over Flood's head and hit the ground several yards short of the center-field wall, a tainted two-run triple. Suddenly, a hush fell over the crowd. Gibson's shoulders sagged an instant and another run-scoring base-hit followed to make it a three-run inning, enough for Lolich to snap Gibby's personal streak and the Cardinals' proud double World Series record. Not only had the St. Louis Nationals won eight of 11 previous Series, by far the best in the NL, but six previous times they'd been forced to a seventh and deciding game—and never before had lost one.

Afterward, as the Cardinals dressed silently in their clubhouse, preparing to hurry immediately to Japan for a post-Series tour, little Flood adamantly refused to be a big man about his misplay, declining to discuss it or to say he was "sorry."

Gibson, who often could be cutting with the press when circumstances were much more pleasant, proved a champion in adversity. Asked about the error of omission that maybe kept him and Lolich from pitching out there all winter, he shrugged those big shoulders.

"He," said Gibby, referring to Flood, "has won many a game for me with his glove."

Ten years later when Anheuser-Busch celebrated a quarter-century of brewery ownership of the Cardinals and brought back several selected stars for the occasion, the Big Eagle—August A. Busch, Jr.—showed class by including Flood, who had been exiled by baseball after his infamous, losing assault on the baseball reserve clause after St. Louis traded him to Philadelphia following the 1969 season.

Gibson, who hadn't been to town since he drove off after the 1975 season in a $30,000-plus Elegzana mobile home given him by Busch as a going-away present, also was at the ballpark. Affectionately, which he rarely was in public, the big pitcher threw his arms around the little outfielder who'd had a tough time of it since he protested "peonage" too soon.

Gibby had had his own troubles. Not only had knee surgery cost the Cardinals at least a division title and himself probably a couple of more years of pitching, but lovely wife Charline had walked out. He'd loved that militant woman, all right, and, his weight down from anguish and worry, he'd come to camp near the end, father-and-mother both to two frisky, teen-aged daughters and reportedly some $250,000 lighter in alimony.

When Gibson quit in disgust just before the end of the 1975 season, in which a woeful 3-and-10 won-and-lost record and horrendous 5.04 ERA tell the story of the ineptness of a "one-legged" champion who was down, but not out, he had taken a token salary cut from $160,000 to $150,000. Gibby's amicable salary negotiations over the years with Bing Devine, the general manager with whom he shared mutual regard, had been a quiet, dignified meeting of two intelligent minds.

When the last ball was over—and the last one Gibby threw was a grandslam by Chicago's Pete LaCock, who can tell his grandchildren about that one—Gibson busied himself back in Omaha with a bank and radio station, black-oriented, in which he had financial interests. At one time he'd done a bit of television back there in the Nebraska metropolis, but then he'd been for a time on one of American Broadcasting Company's Monday night string of baseball telecasts.

On championship series radio, Gibson had done extremely well, speaking clearly and with a refreshing frankness that showed, as St. Louis and baseball already knew, that he was really no company man. But then after Pittsburgh's John Candeleria pitched a no-hitter on national television and Gibson was rushed down to interview the giant lefthander, the knowledgeable ex-pitcher asked the Candy Man as many inane, innocuous questions as the kind for which Gibby used to sneer at the press.

As a result, Bob was blasted by the media, particularly the television critics. Others just smiled as if to say, "C'est le guerre, Gib!"

As his own man, a Ted Williams of the toeplate, Robert Gibson—the Cardinals nicknamed him "Hoot" after the pioneer movie cowboy—Gibson could vaccilate from individual kindness and thoughtfulness to the handicapped or underprivileged to rapier-like rudeness or more amusing insults to those he wanted to brush off.

For instance, autographing when it pleased him, Gibson didn't like to be accosted by strangers for his signature or to pass the time of the day when eating, especially when the person persisted with asking baseball questions. That cold shoulder from the bespectacled pitcher wasn't at all funny to his fans, but, to many, Gibson was so good out there between the foul lines that they endured his aloofness without anger or acrimony.

As for his acidulous sense of humor, one of Gibson's best came after he'd suffered a broken ankle, his second such to ricketts-weakened legs, in the 1967 season. As he returned on crutches, chafing to get back into the harness and tired of answering the same questions over and over, he finally hung a sandwich-board type of sign around his neck. It read:

"Yes, it's off (the cast). No, it doesn't hurt. I'm not supposed to walk on it for one week. I don't know how much longer. Ask Doc Bauman (trainer). Ask Dr. Middleman (team surgeon)."

From ghetto to glory, from rat bites to rickets, from boyhood asthma to adult arthritis in his pitching arm, from abject poverty to affluence, Bob Gibson has run the gamut like that rat, which bit him as a boy and affected the outlook and attitude of the child who was born three months after his father died.

When Pack Gibson, a millworker, left wife Victoria with seven children, the youngest sickly little Robert, the woman worked valiantly in a laundry and as a house cleaner. His mother and eldest brother Leroy, a Creighton University graduate and social worker nicknamed "Josh" after the great black catcher, were the two people to whom Bob was—and IS—most indebted.

At seven, Bob and a few other ghetto kids broke into an old barn and stole a keg of rusty nails, winning a couple of hours lockup in jail and a box to the ears from Josh, who had carried him as a coughing, wheezing child expected to die when, encouragingly, the big brother promised him a ball and bat to make it.

In *Bob Gibson, Pitching Ace*, published by G.P. Putnam's Sons, two *St. Louis Post-Dispatch* writers, David Lipman and the late Ed Wilks, dug up many nuggets about the pitcher whose aching arm was gold, such as:

1) Gibson was a switch-hitting catcher and shortstop on an Omaha YMCA team; 2) he tinkered with jalopies as a hobby; 3) he grew so fast overnight in high school that he needed a doctor's permission to compete in sports because of a heart murmer; 4) he was the first black to play basketball for Creighton;5) he could leap so high to rebound that he could "almost" put his elbow on the rim of a basket; 6) he became the first member of Creighton's athletic Hall of Fame, where his college and professional numbers were retired and—.

Gibby went to Creighton instead of Indiana because—signs of the times—the Hoosiers said they had their "quota" of black athletes. Bob was all for taking a $3,000 bonus offer from veteran Redbird scout C.A. (Runt) Marr, but Josh said no, college first. A couple of subjects short of graduation in philosophy, Gibby did sign with Omaha Cardinals' general manager Bill Bergesch in 1957 for $4,000.

There, encountering for the first time the influence of Johnny Keane as a manager, the versatile Gibson—the best all-around athlete NEVER to be invited to Rotonda, Fla., for the televised Super Stars' competition—was 2-and-1 the rest of the 1957 season in the American Association. He played off-season that first winter with the Harlem Globetrotters until Bing Devine asked him to desist and avoid injury. Gibby put in a couple of years of winter ball.

By now, he was 6-1½, 195 pounds and some man. When he went out to alma mater Creighton to work out, Paul Silas, who was a good five inches taller and would become an outstanding rebounder in professional basketball, was the Creighton star. Silas laughed in retrospect.

"That Gibson, what a competitor!" exclaimed Silas. "Here I was bigger and a great rebounder and, scrimmaging, Gibson forgot it was for fun. He outrebounded me and beat me bloody. No wonder he became great."

By 1959, Gibson had been promoted to the St. Louis varsity, managed then by Solly Hemus. He didn't get a good start. The first batter he faced, Los Angeles's Jim Baxes, hit a home run. Hemus, not duly impressed, called him "Bridges," meaning lefthanded Marshall Bridges, and a special insult to blacks, who writhe under that old sick joke that "they all look alike."

By the time Gibby was 3-5 that year and 3-6 in 1960, sent down and regarded as a weak-kneed guy who didn't have the stomach in the late innings, all he needed was a little more control and a little more confidence in him by the other guy. He got both, most especially the confidence from Keane, who replaced Hemus as manager the Fourth of July weekend in 1961.

Keane handed Gibby the ball at Los Angeles and said, "Here, yo're pitching." (An in-and-out-of-the-lineup kid named Flood also returned to center field). Gibson celebrated with a shutout and a home run, and everything was fair and warmer as, for instance, his victory total:

13... 15... 18... 19... 20... 21...

Six straight seasons of improved figures were halted just after the All-Star break in 1967 when a screaming line drive off Roberto Clemente's bat felled Gibson, who gamely got to his feet and tried to continue pitching—with a broken ankle. He'd broken a leg at the tail end of the 1962 season when his spikes caught in the batter's box in batting practice. And he'd lost his bid for a first 20-game season in 1963 when he'd been ejected from a cakewalk Cardinal victory before the five-inning minimum required.

In 1964, reaching 20 for the first time, Gibson won nine of his last 11 starts, among them a 1-0 duel lost to the New York Mets' Al Jackson on the Friday night before the season closed. The race was as close as one second to another. Into the final Sunday, St. Louis and Cincinnati were tied and Philadelphia, which had lost 10 straight, was one game behind when the Phils batted at Crosley Field as the Cardinals entertained the Mets.

In relief, Gibson clinched the pennant on a high pop fly clutched by Dal Maxvill, then the club's utility man. And in the World Series after Gibby lost his game and composure when a curveball was adjudged to have nicked Joe Pepitone in the second game, the good-hitting, great-fielding, fast-running, hard-throwing pitcher proved his versatility in a pivotal fifth.

The Series was tied at Yankee Stadium, two victories each, but Gibson led into the ninth, 2-0, when, as he followed through on his left foot, right hip spun around to the plate, Pepitone lined a pitch off the buttock. The ball scooted toward the third-base line as Gibson, recoiling from his left to his right, gave rapid chase, corralled the ball and gunned out Pepitone in a play so spectacular that neither the batter nor manager Yogi Berra believed umpire Al Smith's call. But slow-motion films confirmed Smith's decision.

Gibson's pluperfect play saved the game, for, angrily, Gibby grooved a fast one to Tom Tresh, who hit a home run that, though it tied the score, would have won the game if Pepitone had been as safe as everyone figured the New York first baseman would be.

A three-run homer in the 10th by batterymate McCarver gave Gibson a 5-2 victory that began his brilliant string of complete-game World Series records, breaking Red Ruffing's mark just as Gibson's single-game strikeouts against Detroit and total against the Tigers (35) would stand as Series' highs.

In the 1964 showdown at old Busch Stadium, near Sportsman's Park, a tiring Gibson faltered near the finish. Keane visited the mound once and saw the fire still burned in the big brown eyes. Barely had the Redbird manager resumed his seat on the bench when another home run reduced the Cardinals' lead to 7-5. Should he...?

"No," Keane said he told himself, folding his arms defiantly, "Gibby has brought me this far. Win or lose, I'm going all the way with him."

Until, as mentioned, friend Curt Flood misjudged that ball in the 1968 showdown, Bob Gibson just didn't know the meaning of defeat in a World Series game. In that pitching peak with Koufax stepping down, the San Francisco Giants' great Juan Marichal seemed repeatedly to duck matchups that would have been modern Mathewson-Brown, Dean-Hubbell, Feller-Newhouser, Spahn-Roberts duels. And until near the end, Gibby would win many shootouts with young Tom Terrific Seaver.

When Gibson crumbled in 1967, Nelson Briles came out of the St. Louis bullpen to win nine straight games, a considerable help that eased up the race. But Red Schoendienst, who had succeeded Keane as manager, already had his Series blueprint. If only he could get Gibby off those crutches and onto the mound just a couple of times in September...

Red did and so did the red-fused righthander, who, though only 13-7 in that bobtailed regular season, knocked off the Boston Sox three times in a row in the World Series.

The last one brought to the fore a characteristic Gibson as a cool cat working himself up. At breakfast at a nearby Quincy (Mass.) motel, the pitcher had been snubbed, perhaps accidentally on purpose, and they called an all-aboard bus trip for Fenway Park.

So the grousing ace hadn't had a morsel as he grumped aboard. As an alarmed St. Louis writer, aware that my own ulcer acted up if he didn't get three meals five times a day, hopped off at a corner near the ballpark, rushed into a cafeteria for two ham-and-egg sandwiches and cabbed it to Jersey Street.

Gibson ate one sandwich before the game, then afterward nibbled smilingly on the other, washing it down with champagne, after having put the Sox away with a swinging strikeout over giant George Scott, who'd said—silly boy—that Gibby wouldn't go five that day.

The smug St. Louis writer hemmed to himself that, by gosh, Gibson might have done it for seven innings, but that the ink-stained wretch's egg had helped him from the eighth and that slice of fried ham through the ninth. S-o-o...

A couple of three years later, off to his traditionally slow start—he was an early-inning and early-season patsy—Gibby talked before a warm Sunday afternoon game against the hard-hitting Cincinnati Reds. He'd left the park before the Saturday night game, he said, had had a bit of wine and a Caesar salad about 8:30.

No meat?

The veteran pitcher shook his head. "No," he said no breakfast this morning—just coffee and prune juice.

But how could he go since mid-afternoon the day before with only a salad and—.

"Don't worry," said Gibson. That afternoon he struck out 15 Reds and struck out the writer's theory that I'd helped win the 1967 World Series.

Over the course of his career—251 victories, 174 defeats—Gibson was not exactly cushioned with offensive support. Even before his abortive final season, a St. Louis fan had figured that the pitcher had lost 28 times to shutouts and, with a career ERA of

2.91—certainly some or many of the 57 games in which his teammates scored only one run for him, of the 56 in which they'd got him two runs and some of the 79 games he'd been backed with just three.

Not, however, in 1968 when, allowing just 198 hits in 305 innings, he struck out 268, walked only 62 and permitted a mere 38 earned runs. Ergo, that 1.12 ERA in a 1.12 season. Thirteen times he shut out the opposition.

When after that Year of the Pitcher, as it was appropriately called, rules makers lowered the mound and reduced the strike zone, Gibson bitched that they were plotting against his profession. So all he did was go 20-13 with a 2.18 ERA in 1969 and 23-7 with 3.12 efficiency in '70.

Only the Great Scorer above knows just how far or long Robert Gibson might have gone effectively if, in early August 1973, one of the Cardinals' noblest seasons, he hadn't suffered torn knee ligaments diving back into first base at New York.

It was Hall of Fame weekend upstate at Cooperstown as the Cardinals played the Mets at New York's Flushing Meadow. A team that was way last with 5-and-20 had surged 11 games over .500 to take a five-length lead when Gibson was hurt and surgery sidelined him until the end of the season.

By then, deprived of their stopper and leader, with the pitching staff having crumbled the way Gibson physically did when hurt, the Cardinals had lost out to the Mets, who won with only an 82-79 record. The last day, just to see if the knee was as sound as it felt, Gibson worked several scoring innings to beat ex-teammate Steve Carlson.

But the knee didn't rehabilitate over the winter as strongly as hoped for. Additionally, Gibson, who ordinarily had disdained winter work, didn't give it his best shot. Also, his familial difficulties prevented proper attention. At any rate, in 1974, the year Lou Brock ran wild with 118 stolen bases and the Cardinals played well, Gibson was only 11 and 13.

Better than his record, yes, but this would best illustrate the point:

Just a game behind Pittsburgh with two to go, Gibson got the assignment and ball, naturally, from Schoendienst, relying on his old reliable, and on that cold early-autumn night in Montreal, the old master was—well, the old master until the home eighth.

With two out, a man on second and lefthanded-hitting Mike Jorgenson at bat, first base open, relief ace Al Hrabosky—the Mad Hungarian—heated up in the bullpen. Sound judgment, as broadcaster Jack Buck noted, indicated a call to the No. 1 game-saver.

But Schoendienst could remember many of those 3,117 career strikeouts by Gibson, many of them in clutch situations. He could remember that the rat who'd bitten five-year-old Bobby Gibson back there in the Omaha ghetto must have gotten a frozen lip because this was THE competitor. So Red stuck with Bob, as Johnny Keane had done 10 years earlier—and Jorgenson ripped a two-strike game-winning, division-killing home run over the right-field fence.

Second guess Schoendienst? Naw, not for sticking with the grand geezer of the mound even if that gimpy knee kept him from jumping around the infield between starts, making so many dazzling plays, that an old critic of the newer breed, Frank Frisch, had said pitcher Gibby would have made one helluva good shortstop. Right on, Uncle Frank.

The difference, you see, was not in the man's strong arm or stronger heart, but in his weaker knee. He couldn't shove off as forcefully as before and when he pivoted, shifting weight onto that left leg to put the oomph behind his delivery and follow-through, too often those vitamin-deficient legs just didn't hold up.

So, like the legendary immortals, the great one had his Achilles' heel—or knee, too—and he was vulnerable, as Gibby proved again in 1975 when, after announcing beforehand that it would be his last year, the greatest Redbird pitcher of them all no longer could make the kind of play he'd demonstrated on national TV just a couple of years earlier.

Beating St. Louis nemesis Jim Barr, 3-2, in a fast-moving, well-played game against the San Francisco Giants, Gibson had ranged back halfway to second base for a high-chopped grounder. Back to the plate, he'd snared the ball over his shoulder and like a football pass catcher. Still headed toward second, he flung the ball backhanded like a blind basketball pass to get his man.

"Podnuhs," crowed guest announcer Dizzy Dean, "that Gibson's the best since Ol' Diz. We ain't the best pitchers ever, but we're amongst 'em and that play—that one's the best I EVER saw."

And when Gibson struggled on one leg in 1975, seldom seen and rarely used, it brought to mind an observation quietly made by home run king Henry Aaron.

"I remember," said Aaron, "when one of our kid players hit one pretty good off Gibby and the ball was caught. The kid called him 'lucky.' I seldom say much, but that time I couldn't resist.

"'Son,' I said, 'if that had been the Gibson of old instead of an old Gibson, you'd have been lucky to get a loud foul.'"

ROBERT (BOB) GIBSON
Born November 9, 1935, at Omaha, Neb.
Height 6-1 Weight 193
Threw and batted righthanded.
Named to Hall of Fame, 1981.

YEAR	CLUB	LEAGUE	G.	IP.	W.	L.	Pct.	H.	R.	ER.	SO.	BB.	ERA.
1957	Omaha	Amer. Assoc.	10	42	2	1	.667	46	26	20	25	27	4.29
1957	Columbus	Sally	8	43	4	3	.571	36	26	18	24	34	3.77
1958	Omaha	Amer. Assoc.	13	87	3	4	.429	79	45	32	47	39	3.31
1958	Rochester	International	20	103	5	5	.500	88	35	28	75	54	2.45
1959	Omaha	Amer. Assoc.	24	135	9	9	.500	128	59	46	98	70	3.07
1959	St. Louis	Nat.	13	76	3	5	.375	77	35	28	48	39	3.32
1960	St. Louis	Nat.	27	87	3	6	.333	97	61	54	69	48	5.59
1960	Rochester	International	6	41	2	3	.400	33	15	13	36	17	2.85
1961	St. Louis	Nat.	35	211	13	12	.520	186	91	76	166	119	3.24
1962	St. Louis	Nat.	32	234	15	13	.536	174	84	74	208	95	2.85
1963	St. Louis	Nat.	36	255	18	9	.667	224	110	96	204	96	3.39
1964	St. Louis	Nat.	40	287	19	12	.613	250	106	96	245	86	3.01
1965	St. Louis	Nat.	38	299	20	12	.625	243	110	102	270	103	3.07
1966	St. Louis	Nat.	35	280	21	12	.636	210	90	76	225	78	2.44
1967	St. Louis	Nat.	24	175	13	7	.650	151	62	58	147	40	2.98
1968	St. Louis	Nat.	34	305	22	9	.710	198	49	38	268	62	1.12
1969	St. Louis	Nat.	35	314	20	13	.606	251	84	76	269	95	2.18
1970	St. Louis	Nat.	34	294	23	7	.767	262	111	102	274	88	3.12
1971	St. Louis	Nat.	31	246	16	13	.552	215	96	83	185	76	3.04
1972	St. Louis	Nat.	34	278	19	11	.633	226	83	76	208	88	2.46
1973	St. Louis	Nat.	25	195	12	10	.545	159	71	60	142	57	2.77
1974	St. Louis	Nat.	33	240	11	13	.458	236	111	102	129	104	3.83
1975	St. Louis	Nat.	22	109	3	10	.231	120	66	61	60	62	5.04
Major League Totals—17 Years			528	3885	251	174	.591	3279	1420	1258	3117	1336	2.91

WORLD SERIES RECORD

Holds records for most consecutive games won, lifetime (7); most strikeouts, game (17), October 2, 1968; most strikeouts, series (35), 1968.
Shares record for most games won, series (3), 1967.

YEAR	CLUB	LEAGUE	G.	IP.	W.	L.	Pct.	H.	R.	ER.	SO.	BB.	ERA.
1964	St. Louis	Nat.	3	27	2	1	.667	23	11	9	31	8	3.00
1967	St. Louis	Nat.	3	27	3	0	1.000	14	3	3	26	5	1.00
1968	St. Louis	Nat.	3	27	2	1	.667	18	5	5	35	4	1.67
World Series Totals			9	81	7	2	.778	55	19	17	92	17	1.89

HOMER HANK: Tiger Hank Greenberg was a most productive slugger and an independent thinker, on and off the field, during and after his career.

HANK GREENBERG

David Greenberg, a Romanian immigrant whose hobbies were fishing and gardening, came home one day in the late '20s at the Crotona Park area of the Bronx in New York to find, horrified, that the pride-and-joy emerald of his life—his well-kept, tenderly manicured backyard lawn —was covered with ugly yellow sawdust.

Mystified and angry, Mr. Greenberg learned that his second son, Henry, a tall, gangling kid, had bought the sawdust at the butcher shop and had covered the lawn so that he could learn to slide like his favorites on John McGraw's aggressive New York Giants.

Pappa didn't mind Henry playing baseball, because one of the reasons men migrated from the Old World was to give their families more freedom and a better life in the new one, but this was too much. An enterprising, hard-working man who had earned a good living for his family with his own cloth-shrinking business in Manhattan's textile center, the elder Greenberg didn't ask much for himself. Just a chance to fish now and then and, especially, to putter around in his garden and to tend to that beautiful lawn.

Forthwith, son Henry was ordered to get the sawdust the hell off Pappa's lawn and to keep it off. Years later, reminiscing about his son's baseball success, David Greenberg would smile and offer that sawdust episode as an insight into his boy's perseverance and determination.

You see, though he loved his father, Henry Benjamin Greenberg wouldn't take no for an answer. To placate his parent, and yet continue the practice he felt he needed, he would put the sawdust on the lawn every morning and then painstakingly remove it every afternoon, before the old man got home from work.

As Mr. Greenberg said, "That, I believe, tells you a lot about the boy. He always was a hard, persistent worker. And when he was in high school, playing baseball, football, basketball, soccer and handball, he would be up at 6 o'clock in the morning, studying."

If ever there was a self-made ballplayer, it was Greenberg, who went on to become a Hall of Fame hitter, a first baseman-outfielder who shared into professional baseball's second century the distinction for the most home runs hit in a season by a righthanded batter.

Philadelphia's Jimmie Foxx hit 58 home runs in 1932, five years after Babe Ruth reached the 60 that became the most-glamorous single-season standard in the game. Double-X needed a cluster of homers in his last few games to get close to Ruth's record, but six years later, when the Babe's mark had gained even greater stature, Greenberg threatened the record more seriously.

Strange thing about 1938, as Hank remembered it. The Detroit slugger, a lifetime .313 hitter who just had averaged close to .340 for four consecutive seasons, just couldn't get hits. Home runs now and then, yes, but hits, no.

"There was one nine-game stretch when I made only five hits, but all were home runs," Greenberg recalled.

By the All-Star break, still not hitting consis-

tently, depressed by a low batting average and miffed because the New York Yankees' Joe McCarthy hadn't played him the year before, the 27-year-old Greenberg went to the Detroit front office and made a request that he be withdrawn from the All-Star squad.

This wasn't the sporting thing to do, but at least there was no tie-up between the All-Star Game and pension plan in those days, because there was no fund for player pensions. Greenberg used the three-day layoff to rest—and the upper-case Tiger came out hitting like one.

Singles, doubles and, ah, more homers sprang off the big bludgeon of the tall (6-3½) and powerful (215-pound) Greenberg. Before the All-Star break, he hit two homers in a game three times. Now, as his average soared to what would be a satisfactory if not spectacular .315, Hankus-Pankus began spanking 'em in pairs.

No fewer than eight times the second half of the '38 season, Greenberg teed off with twin homers, including four in September, to give him a record 11 two-homer games in a season. And so it came to pass that with five games to go, Hank already had tied Foxx. Five games to get two to tie Babe, three to beat him! "I think I can do it," Greenberg told himself.

The schedule called for two games at Detroit's Briggs Stadium with the old St. Louis Browns and then the final three at Cleveland. The race, as usual, already belonged to the Yankees. So the only interest in the American League was in whether Greenberg could bring down the Bambino.

Facing an erratic, wild St. Louis lefthander named Howard Mills in the first of the final five, the big guy got a bad break. Mills walked him four times.

Next, he had to face a personal nemesis, the colorful, strutting Buck Newsom, who would be a teammate when the Tigers won a pennant two years hence. Old Bobo limited Hank to one single in four times at bat.

So now came the showdown, the final series at Cleveland, where Greenberg went up against a crafty righthander, Denny Galehouse, at old League Park. Galehouse blanked him. Now, the Indians dealt the visiting slugger another blow. They called off the Saturday game, not because of rain, but because they sought to create a box-office atmosphere for the final day—a doubleheader at mammoth lakefront Municipal Stadium.

In 1960, a year before Roger Maris' spectacular 61-homer season brought excitement and controversy, Greenberg kibitzed about '38. Then vice president of the White Sox, after having served as general manager at Cleveland, Hank could talk about baseball from all sides. As usual, he spoke authoritatively and argumentatively but—this time—from management's viewpoint.

In this era, he said, front office executives were constantly trying to "build up" their players in the hope of turning them into box-office attractions.

"Just think," he said, "of what it would mean today if someone came along and had a good chance to break Ruth's record. The front office would bend over backwards and see that he got every possible advantage. But, in the old days, they just didn't think of it that way. They were more concerned—or at least that's the way it seemed to me—that if a player had a big year and broke any records, there might be a subsequent salary dispute about next year's contract."

With 19-year-old Bob Feller facing homer-hitter Greenberg, it seemed that the Indians had more than a casual eye on the gate appeal when they turned an otherwise routine windup into a most attractive double-dip. Unfortunately, the shift to the lakefront stadium, with the deep power alley in left-center at the time, did serve as a handicap to Greenberg. So, too, did the dark, dismal weather.

In the doubleheader opener, probably many timid Tigers were thinking about home as much as about the intimidating wildness of Rapid Robert. In that game, Feller became the first big league pitcher to record 18 strikeouts. Included was Greenberg—twice.

So now High Henry, as they would know him later at Cleveland when he was rechristened by Bill Veeck, was down to just one game. It was getting darker and darker after Hank doubled twice off Johnny Humphries, another hard-throwing righthander, hitting the distant fence with one 420-foot drive.

Sympathetically, veteran umpire George Moriarty let the game continue as far as he could. In the sixth inning, however, the umpire said to Greenberg, "I'm sorry, Hank. This is as far as I can go."

"That's all right, George," said Greenberg, weary and discouraged. "This is far as I can go, too!"

Although disappointed that he didn't exceed 58, a figure of which he can be forever proud, Greenberg never wavered in his regard for Ruth as the king of home run hitters. Nor did he fail to express enthusiasm for Maris when Rog came up with 61 in '61.

Down the stretch that year, with both Maris and Mickey Mantle hitting homers at a record pace, Hank told Arthur Daley of *The New York Times*:

"Naturally, I've been following Maris and Mantle with intense interest. I have a proprietary feeling toward Roger—a pride of authorship, you may call it—because I was the one who brought him into baseball (at Cleveland).

"What I've grown to resent is a great inclination on the part of many to deprecate the feat even before it is accomplished. They speak of the lively ball, expansion, dilution of pitching strength, smaller ball parks and all that nonsense.

"As much as I revered the Babe, I still feel that he was not subjected to the strains of day-and-night baseball, the constant travel and the frantic publicity commotion that has to be unsettling to these two young men. I'm convinced that the accomplishment of breaking the record is greater now than it ever was."

Greenberg, though he made big money in baseball and earned a fortune in the stock market, was not obsequious, as he proved once more when he testified on behalf of Curt Flood in the outfielder's suit challenging the validity of the reserve clause, the first major challenge of baseball's second century.

"I've come out in the past for Bill Veeck as commissioner because I thought baseball could use showmanship and I've favored interleague play, too," said Greenberg at the time this book was first written. "But I don't like to be categorized as either a hair shirt or as a disinterested old-timer. I still go to the game and like it, but I think it has become too steeped in tradition. And in the face of increased competition from football, basketball and hockey, all fast-action sports, I think baseball needs to speed up where possible. I always did believe fans were more interested in offense over defense. They appreciate good plays and good pitching, but they want to see runs."

As a hitter, High Henry certainly gave them what he believed they wanted. Although losing some 4½ seasons of his career to military service, and virtually another full season to injury, he still slugged 331 homers and 1,276 RBIs in the equivalent of about 10 playing seasons.

At Detroit, where he broke in with a .301 season in 1933 when he was just 22, he hammered home 170 runs in 1935. And after playing only 12 games in '36, when he went out with a recurrent wrist injury, he bounced back in 1937 with 183 RBIs. He drove in 146 the year he hit 58 homers and in 1940, his last full pre-war season, the 29-year-old Greenberg blasted in 150 runs with 41 homers and a .340 average.

First baseman Greenberg's second Most Valuable Player award came that year as an outfielder, proving that for all his alleged sensitivity to boos and to embarrassment, the good-looking ugly duckling of the diamond could prove once again that his determination and dedication would overcome shortcomings. Not many players, superstars much less journeymen, could improve at bat at the same time they were learning and conquering the defensive challenges of a new position.

For a kid who was born into a family of means,

Henry Benjamin Greenberg was as determined and as hungry for success as the underprivileged to whom sports were open sesame. He never was fast afoot, never a great first baseman or a great outfielder, but not because he didn't try. And if he hadn't tried so hard, David and Sarah Greenberg might have had their way that their No. 2 son would become a college graduate like the rest of their children.

The senior Greenbergs migrated from Bucharest, David when he was 16 and Sarah when she was 18. They met in New York, where David worked hard in the textile industry, specializing in the examination and processing of cloth. He and Sarah had three boys and a girl. Hank, the third born, arrived on New Year's Day, 1911, when the family lived in Greenwich Village.

By the time Hank was seven years old, his frugal father had prospered to the point he was able to move his family to Crotona Park, North. The Greenbergs had a 16-room house later sandwiched between tall apartment buildings. Summers, they moved to a pleasant cottage in Atlantic Highlands, N. J., out by the Twin Lights of Navesink, from where Hank, as a little kid in the summer of 1920, watched the trials for the America's Cup. The late Sir Thomas Lipton and his Shamrock IV were over here, yachting bent, and laying ground for a sympathetic market for his tea.

Bruggy, as neighborhood kids called Hank then, took advantage of that park across the street. He played on his first organized baseball team when he was going to grammar school, P. S. 44 in the Bronx. He was big and slow and awkward, so they put him at first base. Even then he could hit for power and distance. Even then, too, he approached the game with what Ed Fitzgerald described years later in *Sport* magazine as "loving reverence and iron determination."

Fitzgerald looked up Hank's high school coach, Irwin Dickstein, who put it so well. "Hank Greenberg never played games," said the coach. "He worked at them."

He was so big for his age and so graceless that he was painfully self-conscious, but, Dickstein pointed out, the constant fear of being made to look foolish had an important effect on his development. It made him try twice as hard as anybody else. It drove him to practice prodigiously in a stupendous effort to be the greatest on the team. Remember the laborious laying down and sweeping up of the sawdust on Pop's lawn every day, so Hank could practice sliding?

Greenberg's father became part owner and then owner of the cloth-shrinking plant in New York, where Hank helped on a delivery truck during summer months. At James Monroe High School, where he was even better in basketball than baseball, Hank first attracted the attention of Paul Krichell, the renowned Yankee scout who was the first to encourage the big boy from the Bronx by telling him that he might be able to play the game professionally.

The Yankees' general manager, Ed Barrow, ultimately called in the reluctant father, spoke first of $1,000 and then got up to $7,500. Mr. Greenberg wasn't interested. He wanted Hank to go to college. Barrow warned of the pitfalls of permitting the boy to go with an out-of-town team. Mr. Greenberg nodded. He trusted Henry.

Joe Engel of the Washington Senators came along and offered $12,000. Jean Dubuc of the Detroit Tigers said he could pay $9,000. The senior Greenberg still wanted the boy to go to college, but Papa decided he'd get the opinion of a master about his boy's possibilities. He asked a banker friend to ask John McGraw about Hank's chances.

For years, McGraw drooled over the thought of landing a Jewish player who would attract New York's Jewish population. He'd just missed with Andy Cohen, a young second baseman who had started like a combination of Rogers Hornsby and Frank Frisch, the great ones he'd succeeded, but then had been wined and dined right out of the league.

Now, with the chance of a big-office lifetime because big Bruggy Greenberg certainly would have been a home run threat in the cozy Polo Grounds, McGraw told David Greenberg's banker friend that the boy was too big and awkward. He'd never make it. Mr. Greenberg's pride was hurt. Why, Henry had hit three home runs in one game for the Bay Parkways, a fast semi-pro team in Brooklyn, against the touring House of David club.

When Dubuc came back with an altered bid by which Detroit would split its $9,000 offer and permit the boy to go to college first, the elder Greenberg relented. Hank didn't want to go with the Yankees because the formidable presence of Lou Gehrig made it highly unlikely he'd get much chance with a big-name ball club in the Bronx.

Actually, Hank enrolled at New York University on an athletic scholarship in the fall of 1929, intending to stick it out, but by spring he realized he was kidding himself and his parents. He couldn't wait four years for a chance to play ball. Reluctantly, his disappointed parents gave him permission to report to Detroit.

Optioned out, Greenberg played only 17 games at Hartford in the Eastern League, then hit 19 homers with 93 RBIs and a .314 average at Raleigh, N. C., in the Piedmont League. He even got up to Detroit for one time at bat at the end of the 1930 season, before going out to Evansville, Ind., where he hit .318 in the Three-I League in '31. In 1932, he proved he was ready by belting 39 homers and driving in 131 runs in a .290 season for Beaumont in the Texas League.

Manager Bucky Harris, with slick-fielding first baseman Harry Davis, for whom the Tigers had paid $75,000 the previous year at Harris' suggestion, was dubious when he saw the still-awkward Greenberg in spring training. But Bucky knew potential power when he saw it.

Greenberg moved in to play regularly and he really had only one difference with the manager, a difference for which Hank couldn't blame Harris. Seeking a day off when the Tigers were scheduled for an exhibition game at Albany, N. Y.—he wanted to visit his family—the rookie made the mistake of asking for permission after the Tigers had suffered a tough defeat. Sourly, Harris said no, but Hank took off anyway, and it cost him 50 bucks.

By the time Mickey Cochrane came to Detroit as player-manager in 1934, Greenberg was ready to break loose with a season that helped immeasurably toward a pennant, long-awaited by Detroit since Ty Cobb was a stripling. Hank hit cleanup for "The G-Men," as they were called—Gehringer, Greenberg and Goslin.

Greenberg was so vital to the cause with his 26 homers, 139 RBIs and .339 average that pennant-hungry fans howled in dissent when he said he wouldn't be in the lineup on Rosh Hashana, a high Jewish holiday. A rabbinical ruling enabled Greenberg to play and the troubled kid, fearful of hurting his parents, delivered two home runs that beat the Red Sox, 2-1. But on Yom Kippur, the Day of Atonement, Hank flatly refused to play. The Tigers lost without him, but he emerged a bigger man and was saluted by Edgar Guest, the folk poet whose offerings were a daily newspaper feature in that era.

Greenberg battled bigotry in those days when, head high and dark hair longer than other players wore at the time, he played with a nose-in-the-air attitude that gave him an appearance of insufferable superiority. When a photographer wanted to pose him with a prominent actor, High Henry snapped, "He's got no business down here on the field."

The Cardinals' Gashouse Gang, razor-tongued, called him "Moe" and razzed him about his demotion from fourth to sixth in the batting order when Cochrane dropped the slump-shackled young slugger after the third game of the World Series. The Jews long since have proved that, even if they don't like it, they can take it. Greenberg came out in the fourth game with a record-tying four hits, including two doubles.

The inclination, remembering that Greenberg struck out nine times in the '34 Series and had trouble hitting with men on, is to conclude that the big kid was a total flop against Dizzy and Paul Dean and associates. Fact is, he wound up hitting .321 with four extra-base hits and, for that matter, batted .300 or better in three of the four World Series in which he played. His Series average, .318, just about matched his American League consistency. Moreover, he hit five homers and drove in 22 runs in 23 Series games.

The one Series in which Greenberg really didn't hit was one in which he barely batted. In 1935, just 24, Hankus-Pankus earned his first MVP award by knocking in 170 runs and batting .328. The giant hit 46 doubles and ran well enough to get 16 triples. He hit 36 homers, a figure he would top four times in four of the five full seasons he would play over the next 11 seasons.

In the Series against the Cubs—and this one was just about as rowdy as the '34 set with St. Louis—Greenberg hit a two-run homer in the first inning of the second game. In the seventh inning, pitcher Fabian Kowalik of the Cubs hit Hank on the left wrist with an inside pitch the Detroit star couldn't duck.

Greenberg took his base with the arm hurting. Coming around to score, he aggravated the injury in a collision with the Cubs' rugged catcher, Gabby Hartnett. Overnight, the wrist swelled alarmingly, and X-rays produced the bad news that it was broken.

The Tigers went on to win the World Series without Greenberg, but they weren't so fortunate in 1936. Over the first 12 games, Hank was hitting .348 when Jake Powell, aggressive Washington outfielder, ran into High Henry at first base. The weak wrist was broken again and put in a cast. He never got back into the game all season.

Throughout the off-season, word was passed around that Greenberg was through, that his wrist was chronically weak. That his power was gone. All he did in '37 was miss Lou Gehrig's American League RBI record of 184 by just one and, as detailed, he followed in '38 with his 58-homer season.

Greenberg's 1939 season—33 homers, 112 RBIs, .312 average—was mighty good, but general manager Jack Zeller told him the only way he could escape a $10,000 cut was to move to left field.

"We've got to make room for Rudy York," said Zeller.

"Let him play the outfield," shot back Greenberg, aware how hard he'd worked to establish himself as a decent hand defensively at first base and aware, too, how vulnerable he'd be in a new position.

York couldn't play the outfield any more than he could catch or play third base adequately, Zeller pointed out. "First base is the only place we can use him and we need his bat."

The wheels were spinning in Greenberg's cerebrum. "I'm naturally suspicious," he said, years later. "I tried to figure Zeller's angle. Was he trying to get me out there where I'd look bad, so he could justify trading me? So I decided to try him.

" 'I'm the one that's taking the risk,' I told him. 'I ought to get paid for it. Give me a $10,000 raise, and I'll try it.' "

The agreement was reached that if Greenberg was in left field on opening day, the $40,000 salary that had started out being cut to $30,000 would go up to $50,000.

At Lakeland, Fla., the following spring, Hank Greenberg, the self-made first baseman, became an outfielder, helped by the tireless fungo bat of coach Bing Miller. Opening day he was in left field and a $10,000 check was his. A share of the World Series money, too, and the MVP award, because the Tigers won the pennant with York's bat added to Greenberg's. Hank drilled 50 doubles to go with his 41 homers in that .340 season of 150 RBIs.

Except for Ted Williams, no hitter of prominence lost as much time to military service as did Greenberg. With a low draft number drawn out of the fishbowl which launched Selective Service in the fall of 1940, bachelor Greenberg was highly vulnerable.

A short-lived furor existed over his draft status when a doctor in Florida declared him unfit for military service because of flat feet, but he was re-examined in Detroit and, in early May 1941, after hitting two home runs that beat the Yankees, 7-4, Bruggy Greenberg got up at 6:30 the next morning and walked into an old corset factory in downtown Detroit. Along with 300 other draftees, he became a private in the Army of the United States.

At 30, the career of the highest-paid player in the majors was in jeopardy. Things looked up in December, however, when a new provision permitted discharge of men over 28. Sergeant Greenberg stepped out of khaki two days before Pearl Harbor. When the Japanese attacked the United States fleet there, he quietly re-enlisted, this time as an officer candidate in the Army Air Corps.

Eventually a captain, Hank served with distinction. For 11 months in China, he was administrative commanding officer of the first B-29 Super-fortress base established on foreign soil. He flew the Hump and took part in the first land-based bombing of Japan in June 1944.

Of all people perhaps, a former championship basketball coach Ken Loeffler, a wartime associate of Greenberg and later a professor of business law at the University of Nevada, captured best the mood, manner and accomplishment of soldier Greenberg in a column he wrote 20 years back for newspapers in Red Bank and Asbury Park, N. J.

"Most everyone who has followed sports wonders what happens to some of the famous figures after they leave the headlines," wrote Loeffler, a sharp-witted, often cynical man. "Sometimes, it is better to remember them as they were, but other times, the news about them is pleasant, as it was the other day when Dorothy Kilgallen reported that Hank Greenberg had made a million dollars in the stock market.

"Just about 23 years ago, Hank was hitting homers for the Detroit professional team and threatening Babe Ruth's record. He was big, handsome and single, and the world was his oyster. But Hitler and his purge were in the offing and before long Hank, of Jewish faith, was in the service as a private and on maneuvers in the swampy southland. All sporting eyes were upon him and his performance in this new and exciting life, far from the comfort and the fun of the roaring crowds.

"Shortly thereafter, he was in officers' training and emerged a second lieutenant to become finally a captain… I often encountered him at various bases where he led the admiring cadets through the obstacle course. Then he was in China with combat, the enemy and malaria.

"I received a letter from him, written August 15, 1944, telling of Tokyo Rose and her broadcasts warning them they could be strafed if they ran down to the river to hide in the bushes during the raid. All of this was, indeed, a far cry from Fort Worth and rooming with Bill Holden, the movie star.

"This was long, long ago and much aqua has flowed over the terra, but if there is one person in the world tonight who will understand the helpless feeling of some of our boys in Vietnam, it will be Hank Greenberg, now living comfortably as an investor in New York City…"

When Capt. Henry Greenberg returned to baseball with four battle stars on July 1, 1945, there were nearly 48,000 cheering, yelling spectators at Briggs Stadium, eager to welcome back a hero and to see whether the 34-year-old veteran still could hit that ball. The pennant-contending Tigers needed help.

When Greenberg homered in his first big league ball game in four years, helping the Tigers to a 9-5 victory over the Philadelphia Athletics, the crowd roared nearly as loudly as… well, nearly as loudly as when Detroit celebrated a pennant at the end of the season.

Knocked out of the race on the final day in 1944, Detroit teetered close to a playoff with Washington in '45 when the Tigers played the previous season's champions, the Browns, in a rain-soaked finale in St. Louis.

The Browns led into the ninth, 3-2. Hub Walker, pinch-hitting for Hal Newhouser, singled off Nelson Potter. Skeeter Webb bunted for a sacrifice and Walker beat first baseman George McQuinn's throw to second. Eddie Mayo bunted the runners to second and third, opening first base, which manager Luke Sewell of St. Louis promptly filled by ordering an intentional pass to Doc Cramer.

The ex-G. I., Greenberg, came up in the pressure cooker and exploded a grandslam homer that won the pennant dramatically for Detroit. In a half-season he had 13 homers, 60 RBIs, .311 average. As a climax he hit .304 in the World Series, with three doubles, two homers and seven runs batted in. Detroit won the world championship.

A grateful owner, Walter Briggs, kicked up his salary in 1946 to $75,000, and when York was traded to Boston, Greenberg heeded manager Steve O'Neill's request to go back to first base. By then, he felt the quick stops and starts at first base were tougher than the longer, loping strides of an outfielder, but he played the bag for the good of the club. In 142 games, though slowed and his average dipping to .277, old Hankus-Pankus still hit a league-leading 44 homers and a top RBI total, 127.

So, he was positively shocked in January to learn on a car radio that he had been waived out of the American League to Pittsburgh. If baseball wants to know now why Greenberg, subsequently part owner of a ball club, would be so disloyal as to oppose the reserve clause in its strictest sense, there was a clue as far back as nearly 20 years ago when he told Fitzgerald:

"I just felt that if they were going to let me go, they could at least have brought me into the office and talked to me about it. If they didn't do that, they could have given me my unconditional release. The decision not to keep me in Detroit was theirs to make. I have no quarrel with that. I just didn't like the way they went about it."

At first, High Henry thought he would quit. He

had saved some money and the previous spring he'd married beautiful, raven-haired Caral Gimbel, daughter of New York merchant prince, Bernard Gimbel. But the new owners of the Pirates—Frank McKinney, John Galbreath and Bing Crosby—coaxed him into uniform by waving so much money in his face that Hank couldn't possibly think up a good reason for turning it—or them—down.

"They paid me $100,000," said Greenberg flatly, dispelling the long-held belief that Stan Musial's $100,000 in 1958 was the first in National League history. Actually, it was only because part of Hank's "hundred" was bonus.

Musial, playing first base himself in 1947, Greenberg's only season in the National League, summed up the feeling about—and for—High Henry that year.

"He was hurting," Stan said. "His feet were killing him and when he ran the bases, he snorted like a broken-down racehorse."

Despite obvious evidence that he was over the hill, Greenberg contributed to Pittsburgh's attendance and to National League glamor that '47 season. With Greenberg Gardens established in Forbes Field—an artificial fence from the left-field line to left-center, to cut down the home run distance—Hank hit 25 homers. In 125 games, he drove in 74 runs, but batted only .249.

His greatest contribution was in the time, teaching and attention he gave to Pittsburgh's young slugger, baby-faced Ralph Kiner, who became his protégé and remained a close friend. Until he met Greenberg, who could be as tough on Ralph as he had been on himself, Kiner thought an open date meant a day of rest. To Greenberg, it meant an opportunity for Kiner to groove the home run swing that made him a man of means and prominence in the National League.

Expecting and welcoming his release from Pittsburgh at the end of a last-place season, Greenberg bumped into Bill Veeck at Toots Shor's in New York. The sports-shirted executive and the well-groomed former star found themselves kindred souls in many respects. A friendship and association was formed.

Hank joined Bill at Cleveland in 1948, ostensibly a potential pinch-hitter and coach, but primarily as a vice president who wanted no part of the playing field. He gave it a halfhearted try in spring training and then gave up, retiring upstairs to learn from Veeck and the late Harry Grabiner the intricacies of front office operation.

Serving first as farm director, as the Indians won their first pennant in 28 years, the season of Lou Boudreau's magic as a player and manager, Greenberg finally succeeded to the general manager's job two years later when friend Veeck was bought out by Ellis Ryan. An early decision brought down the Cleveland wrath on the big bloke from Detroit. He dealt the popular Boudreau to Boston to make room for a new manager, a man with whom he had been smitten at Pittsburgh—Al Lopez.

Greenberg, rewarded with a pennant from Lopez at Cleveland in 1954, saw the Señor win again five years later at Chicago when Hank rejoined Veeck as vice president, this time with a piece of the action. He had been unable to pry loose stock at Cleveland, where he couldn't possibly achieve the popularity either of Boudreau or of his front office friend and mentor, the colorful Veeck.

Never particularly diplomatic, High Henry seemed a bit highhanded in an early interview when, asked about booing by the fans, he said:

"As a player, I thoroughly disliked it. As general manager, I plan to do something about it. I'm referring only to the two or three obnoxious fans in every ballpark. If I can, I'm going to get these abusive popoffs thrown out of the stadium. Not only is the vicious fan a thorn to the player, he also irritates the other fans. That's the primary reason I want to have him barred…"

What was Greenberg's attitude toward the players? One of sympathy, said the general manager out of the ranks, explaining that he felt paychecks should be based partly on performance and potential, but also on personality and years of service.

"I don't believe in the old baseball theory, 'Never cut a player, trade him instead,'" Greenberg told Hal Lebovitz in an interview for *The Sporting News* more than 20 years ago.

"I want our players satisfied, but not oversatisfied. Too much money too soon hurts many players, but I don't agree with the St. Louis Cardinals' former theory, 'Keep the players hungry.'"

Hank Greenberg never had a hungry day in his life, unless it was in service, but he played as if he were starved. Presumably, he hit Wall Street with the same burning desire to succeed, a profitable venture that permitted him to devote considerable time to improving his backhand on the tennis court once he left the White Sox in 1963, a couple of years after Veeck departed.

Hank's marriage to Caral Gimbel went on the rocks, unfortunately, and the Manhattan cliff-dweller was married four years later to the former Mary Jo Tarola. He spoke with great pride of his three children by his first marriage.

One, Steve, would have gladdened the old gladiator's heart. Hank, battling cancer, lost a fight against the clock when dictating his biography in 1986 at 75. Son Steve, a former Yale captain and minor leaguer, became assistant commissioner in 1989. Like father, like son—Steve quit in '93, disillusioned, discontented or both.

Hank, of course, would be forgiving, understanding. Big Bruggy Greenberg, just 10 pounds over his playing weight worked at keeping fit, mindful that his father was a robust 86 when he died in 1969.

David Greenberg, who learned to appreciate success because he worked for it so hard himself, long since had forgiven his famous son for passing up college in favor of sawdust and sawbucks.

HENRY BENJAMIN (HANK) GREENBERG
Born January 1, 1911, at New York, N.Y.
Height 6-3 1/2 Weight 215
Threw and batted righthanded.
Named to Hall of Fame, 1956.

YEAR	CLUB	LEAGUE	POS.	G.	AB.	R.	H.	2B.	3B.	HR.	RBI.	B.A.	PO.	A.	E.	F.A.
1930	Hartford	East.	1B	17	56	10	12	1	2	2	6	.214	157	13	2	.988
1930	Raleigh	Pied.	1B	122	452	88	142	26	14	19	93	.314	1052	78	23	.980
1930	Detroit	Amer.	1B	1	1	0	0	0	0	0	0	.000	0	0	0	.000
1931	Evansville	I.I.I.	1B	126	487	88	155	41	10	15	85	.318	1248	84	25	.982
1931	Beaumont	Texas	PH	3	2	0	0	0	0	0	0	.000	0	0	0	.000
1932	Beaumont	Texas	1B	154	600	123	174	31	11	39	131	.290	1437	103	17	.989
1933	Detroit	Amer.	1B	117	449	59	135	33	3	12	87	.301	1133	63	14	.988
1934	Detroit	Amer.	1B	153	593	118	201	63	7	26	139	.339	1454	84	16	.990
1935	Detroit	Amer.	1B	152	619	121	203	46	16	36	170	.328	1437	99	13	.992
1936	Detroit	Amer.	1B	12	46	10	16	6	2	1	16	.348	119	9	1	.992
1937	Detroit	Amer.	1B	154	594	137	200	49	14	40	183	.337	1477	102	13	.992
1938	Detroit	Amer.	1B	155	556	144	175	23	4	58	146	.315	1484	120	14	.991
1939	Detroit	Amer.	1B	138	500	112	156	42	7	33	112	.312	1205	75	9	.993
1940	Detroit	Amer.	OF	148	573	129	195	50	8	41	150	.340	298	14	15	.954
1941	Detroit	Amer.	OF	19	67	12	18	5	1	2	12	.269	32	0	3	.914
1942-43-44	Detroit	Amer.						(In Military Service)								
1945	Detroit	Amer.	OF	78	270	47	84	20	2	13	60	.311	129	3	0	1.000
1946	Detroit (a)	Amer.	1B	142	523	91	145	29	5	44	127	.277	1272	93	15	.989
1947	Pittsburgh (b)	Nat.	1B	125	402	71	100	13	2	25	74	.249	983	79	9	.992
American League Totals				1269	4791	980	1528	366	69	306	1202	.319	10040	662	133	.990
National League Totals				125	402	71	100	13	2	25	74	.249	983	79	9	.992
Major League Totals				1394	5193	1051	1628	379	71	331	1276	.313	11023	741	122	.990

a Sold to Pittsburgh Pirates for undisclosed sum, January 8, 1947.
b Released unconditionally by Pittsburgh Pirates, September 27, 1947, and joined Cleveland Indians' front office, March 27, 1948.

WORLD SERIES RECORD

YEAR	CLUB	LEAGUE	POS.	G.	AB.	R.	H.	2B.	3B.	HR.	RBI.	B.A.	PO.	A.	E.	F.A.
1934	Detroit	Amer.	1B	7	28	4	9	2	1	1	7	.321	60	4	1	.985
1935	Detroit	Amer.	1B	2	6	1	1	0	0	1	2	.167	17	2	3	.864
1940	Detroit	Amer.	OF	7	28	5	10	2	1	1	6	.357	12	0	0	1.000
1945	Detroit	Amer.	OF	7	23	7	7	3	0	2	7	.304	8	1	0	1.000
World Series Totals				23	85	17	27	7	2	5	22	.318	97	7	4	.963

THE LION OF LONACONING: Great, grumpy, hot-tempered Lefty Grove, maybe the most overpowering lefthander of all time.

LEFTY GROVE

Patriarchal Connie Mack chose a Sunday in late August 1931, as his pennant-bound Philadelphia Athletics played the moribund Browns, to tell the *St. Louis Post-Dispatch* that his star lefthander of the moment, Robert Moses (Lefty) Grove, was indeed greater than two top southpaws he'd had previously, legendary Rube Waddell and stylish Eddie Plank.

Grove was going that day for his 17th consecutive victory, seeking to break the American League record. His chances were fair and warmer, even hotter than the weather in St. Louis, because the Browns were 35½ games behind the Athletics, who were breezing to a third straight championship.

Moreover, the Browns' pitcher in the opening game of the Sunday doubleheader was a righthander, Dick Coffman, on whom they'd asked waivers three weeks earlier.

The A's were hurting physically because Mule Haas, the center fielder, had suffered a fractured wrist, and both the shortstop and third baseman, Joe Boley and Jimmie Dykes, were sidelined with charley horses. And the slugging left fielder, Al

Simmons, with an infected toe, had begged off a few days to go home to Milwaukee.

Still, there was power and class in the Philadelphia lineup, with powerful Jimmie Foxx at first base, Max Bishop at second, Bing Miller in right field, the incomparable Mickey Cochrane behind the plate and, of course, Grove himself pitching.

Why, the Athletics were so formidable that more than 20,000, a staggering crowd for a St. Louis American League team that was starving at the box office, turned out to see the locals fed to the lions. Instead, they stayed to watch the incredible.

In the third inning, Fred Schulte of the Browns singled to left field. Then Oscar Melillo sent a line drive to left, which was played in Simmons' absence by a rookie named Jimmy Moore. The kid misjudged the ball, raced in, completely fooled, and the ball fell where he had been standing, rolling to the fence. Schulte scored.

On the mound, tall, thin-faced, thick-lipped, squinty-eyed Bob Grove slapped his leg disgustedly. That big guy—what's his name, Simmons?—would have caught that one, he knew.

In those days, Lefty had almost as much trouble remembering names as the opposition did hitting him, and he owned a 25-2 record at the moment.

Yeah, 25-2, and after he'd opened the season with 11 straight victories, he'd lost a tainted game and had ripped up a low-ceilinged clubhouse in high dudgeon.

He was a churlish character who referred to one player, for instance, as "the big guy with the big feet" and another as "that lug with the ugly kisser." Considering Lefty wouldn't win any beauty prizes himself, he had a lot of nerve mentally caricaturing others, but that's the way he was.

He was, you see, a fireball pitcher with a temper to match and when, inning after inning, that one stinkin' St. Louis run held up in August 1931, his blood pressure began to rise.

"We'll get 'im, Mose," the embarrassed Mackmen shouted encouragingly to their red-faced,

jug-eared terror of the toeplate, but now it was the ninth inning. And Coffman, completing a startling three-hitter in which he walked just one batter, walked off the field with a 1-0 victory.

Grove, who also would have been unscored on except for that misjudged fly, burned fiercely at the thought that a chance for that record-breaking 17th straight victory had gone down the shower-room drain because Simmons had taken the day off. Worse yet, the A's had suffered their first shutout defeat.

The powerful 31-year-old pitcher, 6-3 and 205 pounds, charged into the rickety visitors' clubhouse at old Sportsman's Park. He tried to pull the door off its hinges. He splintered locker panels. He tore his uniform off, threw it on the floor and jumped on it.

Venting his spleen on the shower itself, he wasn't helped either, to realize that behind Waite Hoyt, the Athletics were back on the field, belaboring the Browns in the second game, 10-0.

Mose was mad at Moore, yes, but not nearly so much as he was enraged at Simmons for taking the day off, and at Mack, for giving it to him. Old Connie wasn't in the clubhouse to listen to the diatribe, but later he tried the soothing salve of logic on the pitcher he'd just called his greatest.

"Robert," he said, "that boy (Coffman) pitched a great game, too, and if we had played all night, we probably still wouldn't have scored."

Grove grunted. He didn't talk to anybody for a few days. After all, he HAD learned to control himself somewhat from that one losing major league season as a rookie back in 1925.

The fury within that helped drive him to greatness, to the remarkable career won-and-lost percentage of .682, a result of 300 victories and only 140 defeats, made him difficult to live with for a time.

He'd lock himself in his hotel room after he'd lost and would refuse to talk to the kindly Mack. He'd ignore the manager's pleadings to learn how to hold men on base. He'd argue with old Connie about intentional passes when he didn't flatly refuse to put a man on. And often he'd chew out veterans who had made errors behind him.

Once when he was relieving and Mule Haas misplayed a drive in the outfield, permitting two runs to score, Grove came off the field, threw his glove against the dugout wall and shouted, "That's the last blinking relief pitching I'll ever do for this blankety-blank ball club."

Quietly, Mack told him not to talk like that.

"Don't tell me how to talk!" yelled Grove, throwing his jacket on the floor and kicking it.

Mack, actually driven to rare profanity by his terrible-tempered pitcher, jumped up, walked over to the jacket and kicked it himself.

"I'll tell you how to talk," he said, turning to another lefthanded pitcher, Rube Walberg, and adding:

"Go down and warm up, Walberg, and we'll get a real pitcher in this game."

As Walberg hurriedly started away, Grove yelled, "Yah, yah, go ahead and get your whole staff ready. You'll need 'em all to get anybody out."

But Lefty picked up his glove, sullenly, and went out and won the game, which was what he usually did. The lug with the ugly kisser, to use old man Mose's language, won 20 or more games for seven straight seasons. During those seven years, he led the American League in winning percentage four seasons and had the lowest ERA four times.

He saved numerous games in relief, including many for LeRoy Mahaffey, a pitcher who had a habit of running out of gas.

"Old Popeye was the greatest seven-inning pitcher I ever saw," Grove recalled one time. "I saved plenty for him, yes, sir."

No one ever had to save many for Grove, who posted a remarkable 128-33 record for a sizzling .795 pace over a five-year period, 1928 through '32, and then posted a 24-8 record just before he was dealt to the Red Sox.

In 1930-31, the last two American League pennants ever won by Mr. Mack and Philadelphia,

Lefty was almost always right. He won 59 games and lost only nine. And in '31, when he was 31-4, the year that misjudged flyball cost him a shot at a league record for consecutive victories, he might have been 3-1 because his four defeats were 2-1, 7-5, 1-0 and 4-3.

Much wiser than better-educated teammates who blew a bundle in the stock market—he carefully invested in government bonds—the great Grove might have been a grouchy guy in his pitching prime, but, at his own expense, he quietly equipped and outfitted kids' teams in Philadelphia.

He didn't believe in waste or overindulgence, but he permitted himself the luxury of 25-cent cigars when he won. When he lost, he punished himself with 10-cent stogies, as former teammate Dykes explained, but he seldom had to endure a cheap smoke.

He mellowed with the years, but he never completely overcame the red neck. At Boston, after suffering arm trouble in 1934, he adjusted from a blow-'em-down fastball pitcher just wild enough to keep hitters loose, to a veteran of cunning, control, a better curveball and a forkball he used as a change-up.

He bounced back with his eighth 20-win season in 1935 and as late as 1939, when he was 39 years old, he posted a 15-4 mark and league-leading 2.54 ERA.

Pitching for Boston, Lefty lost a game to the White Sox at Chicago, 4-2, and stormed into the clubhouse, yelling,

"You think Grove is going to pitch his arm off for you hitless wonders?"

He refused to ride with the players the rest of the series, walking some five miles to Comiskey Park by way of Michigan Boulevard.

As slick-fielding second baseman Oscar Melillo recalled—yes the same Melillo whose misjudged double beat him in 1931—the pressure mounted for infielders playing behind him in the late innings of a close game.

Melillo, obtained by the Red Sox, too, in that

period when Tom Yawkey's wealth couldn't make winners out of the Gold Sox, found himself hoping the foe would hit the ball to someone else.

One day late in Lefty's career, someone hit a sharp grounder to Boston's player-manager, Joe Cronin, the Hall of Fame shortstop who became president of the American League. Cronin, as was his cautious custom in his later years, dropped to one knee to block the ball, but it skipped off his leg, permitting the tying and winning runs to score.

As soon as the game ended, Cronin hurried into his semi-private clubhouse office, but he couldn't escape Grove's wrath. Lefty rushed into the clubhouse, pushed a stool against the covered wire screen of Cronin's cubbyhole, climbing it so he could glower down at the manager.

"Why, you sophomore blankety-blank, don't you field the ball like a man?" he snapped. "You couldn't even play with my high school club."

Which was pretty good, considering that Robert Moses Grove quit school in the eighth grade. Lefty's father, John Grove, a coal miner who lived to be 92, had four sons he put to work in the Georges Creek coal mines at Lonaconing, Md.

"Pop, I didn't put the coal in here and I don't see why I should have to dig it out," son Bob declared, after working for 50 cents a day.

He went to a glass works as an apprentice glass blower before a strike came along. He then journeyed to Cumberland to work in the railroad shops.

Until he was 17, Grove never played in an organized baseball game and then was at first base at Midland, Md., when the manager thought it was ridiculous to have the first baseman throw harder than his pitcher.

He was 20 in 1920 when he was signed to play for Martinsburg in the old Blue Ridge League for $125 a month, and the same year, Jack Dunn, longtime operator of Baltimore's International League franchise, paid $2,000 for his contract.

"Dunn must have thought he picked a real stiff," Grove recalled, "because the first hitter I faced at Jersey City tripled."

Uh-huh, but Lefty won the game, as was to become his habit. He was 12-2 for that part-season. When the Orioles won the Little World Series, which for years was a traditional climax between the International League and American Association champions, he went home with $2,000 in his pocket and married his hometown sweetheart, Ethel Gardner.

The Groves had two children, a son and a daughter. After his wife died in 1959, Lefty moved to Norwalk, O., to live with his son, Robert, a former college pitcher who had done well in business.

By then, white-haired and bespectacled, old man Mose could look back with pride over the fact that he'd won his 300 games even though he hadn't reached the major leagues until he was 25. Why did it take that long for a pitcher who won 109 games at Baltimore in five seasons and lost only 36?

Because Dunn paid big league salaries. Walking almost as many as he struck out—or so it seemed, anyway—the overpowering Grove was drawing down $7,500 a season in 1924 when Connie Mack called to make another purchase from an old friend.

They agreed to a $100,000 tag on the long-armed lefthander who would be known proudly as the Lion of Lonaconing. Then Dunn had an afterthought.

"Hey, Connie," he said, "let's make this an historic occasion. Add another $600. That will be more than the Yankees paid for Babe Ruth. It'll be baseball's biggest deal."

Grove liked that because he reacted competitively to classic clashes of his strong arm and Ruth's big bat.

Lefty could tell proudly that he'd limited the Babe to nine homers in 10 years and had more trouble with a blankety-blank little New York infielder, Joe Sewell, who twice struck out only four times in 150 games a season.

Mack tried to slow down his delivery to help

him harness his high hard one, which was faster than Bob Feller's if you'll take the word of Charlie Gehringer, a great hitter who batted against both of them.

"Count to ten before you pitch, Robert," said old Connie, and the opposition—even the fans—caught on and would count with the great lefthander, who wasn't rabbit-eared enough to let the distraction bother him.

When he was boiling on the field, though, only his good friend, Dykes, the third baseman he called Pudgy, could calm him down.

Dykes would get the ball, hold it and walk toward the mound. Near it, but not too near, Jimmie would explain.

Grove would yell, "Gimme me the blankety-blank ball." Dykes would step back and say, "Now, wait a minute, Mose."

"Gimme the damned ball," Lefty would insist.

"Relax, Mose, this is your old buddy, Jimmie. Just relax."

"Gimme the blinking ball," Grove would repeat. And the instant Dykes got close enough to the mound, Lefty would grab it.

He knew what to do with it, all right, even though he'd had precious little schooling on the mound. That long, sinewy body was as tough and as fibrous as the mountain pines of his native lair, and the long-armed lefthanded Lion of Lonaconing was tremendous.

He lost to Herb Pennock and the Yankees in the heyday of Babe Ruth and Lou Gehrig, 1-0, even though he struck out 15 in 15 innings.

Joe Judge, former Washington first baseman, remembered the rubber-armed Grove beat Washington one day, 2-1, then came out the next afternoon and tried to knock down coach Earle Mack in a 30-minute warmup. After that, he relieved in an eighth-inning jam, throwing just three or four pitches before striking out the batter and fanning the side in the ninth.

Maybe you prefer the time he was leading the

Yankees in the ninth inning, 1-0. The first batter tripled and Grove wound up striking out three in a row, including Ruth and Gehrig. Or how about the time a company wanted to demonstrate an unbreakable glass and decided it would be great advertising to have Lefty throw his hummer at it?

"He whistled one at the glass and nobody ever heard any more about the experiment," Dykes would explain, eyes bulging in amused emphasis. "The ball went clean through. Made a perfect circle."

Anti-social, a lobby sitter, the tall, taciturn pitcher was difficult for even the most famous writers of his day to interview, but he didn't care.

"If I owned a ball club, I'd want a ball club with 25 guys as eager to win as I am," he said. "They don't have to be too educated, you understand. Sometimes I think the smart guys are too smart."

Lefty outsmarted—and outlasted—most of the smart ones, pitching until he was 41 years old when he was gray-templed and wide-hipped. As he struggled for a 300th victory, he became crankier than in his crabby youth.

Finally, on July 25, 1941, the Red Sox beat Cleveland, 10-6. It wasn't neat or gaudy, but it was No. 300. And old man Mose threw a party, to which, as I recall it, he either didn't invite manager Joe Cronin and Ted Williams, or maybe the veteran shortstop and fresh young left fielder just thought better about attending.

It was a long-cherished celebration, anyway, and the Hall of Fame, to which he won election six years later, wanted the baseball he'd kept for the last out.

He'd preserved the 299 other victory balls, too, and had them neatly inscribed back home at Lonaconing, but there came a day when the gray had turned to silver that the old Lion decided that the balls would do the kids in town more good to play with than for him to look at.

The glory of his times didn't mean that much to Grove but he died a bit too hard as a pitcher, struggling through a few more pastings after he scored

No. 300, which was the last one. Finally, given a silver service set by the Boston fans, he went home.

A few months later, he was turkey shooting in South Carolina with his good friend, Tom Yawkey, owner of the Red Sox. Lefty said he felt, reluctantly, that he'd had it.

The date, December 7, 1941, is remembered for an event more explosive than the pitcher's temper.

Back home in Lonaconing, he bought a building which housed three bowling alleys and the Republican Club. He hunted and fished, saw his son and daughter grow up, leave and get married. He worked with a half-dozen Little League teams before Mrs. Grove's death took the Lion out of Lonaconing. He died at 75 in 1975 with little left except memories of rich pitching.

Despite arm trouble in 1934 and again in 1938, despite his late start, Robert Moses Grove won his 300 games in just 17 major league seasons.

Mind you, his career was spent in an era of the lively ball, including the jackrabbit of 1929-30, seasons in which there were some 50 hitters batting better than .300 in each major league.

"I never threw at a hitter, no sir," old man Mose would say later with his firm politeness. "If I ever hit a guy on the head with my fastball, he'd be through. I knew it and the hitters knew it."

Grove grinned. "Course," he said slyly, "I was just wild enough to give 'em something to think about. Yes, sir." Yes, sir!

ROBERT MOSES (LEFTY) GROVE
Born March 6, 1900, at Lonaconing, Md.
Died May 22, 1975, at Norwalk, Conn.
Height 6-3 Weight 204
Threw and batted lefthanded.
Named to Hall of Fame, 1947.

YEAR	CLUB	LEAGUE	G.	IP.	W.	L.	Pct.	H.	R.	ER.	SO.	BB.	ERA.
1920	Martinsburg	Blue Ridge	6	59	3	3	.500	30	16	-	60	24	-
1920	Baltimore	International	19	123	12	2	.857	120	69	52	88	71	3.80
1921	Baltimore	International	47	313	25	10	.714	237	131	89	254	179	2.56
1922	Baltimore	International	41	209	18	8	.692	146	90	65	205	152	2.80
1923	Baltimore	International	52	303	27	10	.730	223	128	105	330	186	3.12
1924	Baltimore	International	47	236	27	6	.813	196	95	79	231	108	3.01
1925	Philadelphia	Amer.	45	197	10	12	.455	207	120	104	116	131	4.75
1926	Philadelphia	Amer.	45	258	13	13	.500	227	97	72	194	101	2.51
1927	Philadelphia	Amer.	51	262	20	12	.625	251	116	93	174	79	3.19
1928	Philadelphia	Amer.	39	262	24	8	.750	228	93	75	183	64	2.58
1929	Philadelphia	Amer.	42	275	20	6	.769	278	104	86	170	81	2.81
1930	Philadelphia	Amer.	50	291	28	5	.848	273	101	82	209	60	2.54
1931	Philadelphia	Amer.	41	289	31	4	.886	249	84	66	175	62	2.06
1932	Philadelphia	Amer.	44	292	25	10	.714	269	101	92	188	79	2.84
1933	Philadelphia (a)	Amer.	45	275	24	8	.750	280	113	98	114	83	3.21
1934	Boston	Amer.	22	109	8	8	.500	149	84	79	43	32	6.52
1935	Boston	Amer.	35	273	20	12	.625	269	105	82	121	65	2.70
1936	Boston	Amer.	35	253	17	12	.586	237	90	79	130	65	2.81
1937	Boston	Amer.	32	262	17	9	.654	269	101	88	153	83	3.02
1938	Boston	Amer.	24	164	14	4	.778	169	65	56	99	52	3.07
1939	Boston	Amer.	23	191	15	4	.789	180	63	54	81	58	2.54
1940	Boston	Amer.	22	153	7	6	.538	159	73	68	62	50	4.00
1941	Boston	Amer.	21	134	7	7	.500	155	84	65	54	42	4.37
Major League Totals			616	3940	300	140	.682	3849	1594	1339	2266	1187	3.06

a Traded to Boston with second baseman Max Bishop and pitcher George Walberg for infielder Harold Warstler, pitcher Bob Kline and $125,000, December 12, 1933.

WORLD SERIES RECORD

YEAR	CLUB	LEAGUE	G.	IP.	W.	L.	Pct.	H.	R.	ER.	SO.	BB.	ERA.
1929	Philadelphia	Amer.	2	6 1/3	0	0	.000	3	0	0	10	1	0.00
1930	Philadelphia	Amer.	3	19	2	1	.667	15	5	3	10	3	1.42
1931	Philadelphia	Amer.	3	26	2	1	.667	28	7	7	16	2	2.42
World Series Totals			8	51 1/3	4	2	.667	46	12	10	36	6	1.75

OLD TOMATO FACE: Strong-armed and power-hitting Charles Leo (Gabby) Hartnett. Joe McCarthy rated him ahead of Mickey Cochrane and Bill Dickey as a catcher, all-around.

GABBY HARTNETT

Jesse (Crab) Burkett, a little cuss with a big bat, hit over .400 three times in the gaslight '90s. But as a scout for the New York Giants, well, Burkett was the kind of forward observer who would have told General Custer that there wasn't an Indian in sight.

Back in 1921, the 51-year-old New England resident, who had coached at Holy Cross, was asked by John McGraw to evaluate a kid playing ball for a wire company team close to Burkett's home in Worcester, Mass.

"Take a look at him and let me know if he can

be a big league catcher," asked McGraw, an old former St. Louis teammate for whom Burkett also coached briefly at New York.

By the time Burkett ran the kid down, the prospect already was catching for the Worcester Club of the Eastern League. He'd been a second-stringer for three days, then had taken over as No. 1. So scout Burkett had a chance to get a good look at him.

"HARTNETT WILL NEVER BE BIG LEAGUE CATCHER, " Burkett wired McGraw. "HIS HANDS ARE TOO SMALL."

A year later, at only 21, Charles Leo Hartnett was catching the great Grover Cleveland Alexander for the Chicago Cubs, beginning a distinguished career of nearly 20 National League seasons as a hard-hitting, topflight catcher, probably the best in his league's history and perhaps as good as any in professional baseball's first century.

When Bill Dickey went into the Hall of Fame in 1954, veteran sportswriter Joe Cashman of the *Boston Record* reported an interview of several years previous in which he had asked Joe McCarthy to pick the best catcher he ever had seen. McCarthy's credentials were notable because he'd managed both Hartnett and Dickey and also had seen much of Mickey Cochrane in the period from the mid-'20s through the late '30s, when all three were at their peak.

"I must take Hartnett," Cashman quoted McCarthy. "Dickey was wonderful, but during the years he and Cochrane were rivals, I never heard anybody in the American League argue that Mickey wasn't the better of the two. Mickey's superior speed and spark gave him the edge.

"But Cochrane, as great as he was, didn't impress me as much as Hartnett. I rated Gabby the perfect catcher, a manager's dream. He had everything except speed and, though few realized it, he was far from slow. He was super smart. Nobody ever had more hustle. Nobody could throw with him. There have been few great clutch hitters. I must take Hartnett as the best."

Even if Cashman was gilding the lily or overstating the case for Hartnett at the conservative McCarthy's expense—and Cashman was the kind of writer who drew even press critic Ted Williams to his retirement party in 1970 after 53 years covering the baseball beat—it's apparent that one Joe had caught the other Joe's general appraisal of master catchers and, particularly, of Hartnett.

A year after Cashman's recollection of his baseball bull-session with McCarthy, Hartnett joined both Cochrane and Dickey in baseball's Hall of Fame.

If comparisons are odious as well as controversial,

so be it. The intention here merely is to put in perspective, figuratively, the stature of a man who, literally, was imposing.

Hartnett was a big man physically at 6-1 and about 215 pounds during his golden years. He had an erect posture, head high and chest out like an Irishman in a St. Patrick's Day parade. He wore a dimpled, engaging, vote-getting smile and an air of confidence.

He talked it up behind the plate and, at least until he hurt his arm and became more cautious, peppered the ball around the infield and back to the mound with a zest and strength that made some of the foe label him as a showoff. When an enemy struck out, the bare right fist of the hands that scout Jesse Burkett thought were too small would clench the ball and raise it in triumph.

Even though conversationally he never came off as a sparkling wit, his appearance provided the kind of magnetism that would make a politician drool with envy. Why, he even added an aldermanic paunch, nothing like Babe Ruth's, but still enough of a bulge that made his belt sag toward his hips.

"Puffy," teammate Pat Malone called him, bringing a merry rebuttal from Hartnett. Said Gabby, "He's got a gut," which Malone did have. Pat, a pitcher, and Hack Wilson, an outfielder, were a couple of colorful characters who led the Cubs in elbow-bending in a period when Chicago often led the National League in everything including attendance and victories.

To most teammates, Hartnett was known by his middle name, Leo. To the general public, forever after a Chicago sportswriter nicknamed him when he was a rookie, he was "Gabby." But there was another nickname that was most apt—"Old Tomato Face."

They said Hartnett was rabbit-eared, that he could hear everything in the ballpark. With his grinning, florid Irish puss, head up, the big guy was a natural for comments, the catcalls and the wisecracks as well as the good wishes and shouts of encouragement.

For years in St. Louis, for instance, a strong-voiced, rabid woman fan, Mrs. Mary Ott, sat in a box behind the visitors' dugout. Using a whinny that would have made a Derby horse envious, the famous fan got under many skins with her horse-laugh. But Gabby would grin at her, greet her cheerfully by her first name and, as a result, Hartnett and Mel Ott, no relation of Mary, wound up as Mrs. Ott's favorites among the foe.

Old Tomato Face never beamed more than in the dusk of autumnal gloom in late September 1938, at vine-covered Wrigley Field when he delivered one of the most dramatic blows in baseball history, the shot in the shadows or, as it is more popularly known, the "homer in the gloaming" that won the pennant.

Into every player's life, the busher as well as the superstar, there comes a moment, molecular or monumental, that must stand out. Hartnett, with six seasons of .300 or better, one year (1930) with 37 homers and another (1935) when he was named Most Valuable Player in the National League, had numerous high spots in his career. The highest had to be the climax to the 1938 season when he took over as manager of the Cubs in late July and led them down the stretch in pursuit of the Pirates.

Pittsburgh was so sure of a pennant in early September that the management even went to the expense of constructing a new rooftop pressbox at Forbes Field. Chicago had enjoyed a pattern of a pennant every three years—1929, 1932 and 1935—but 1938 seemed to be an exception. In third place, 6½ games down when Charley Grimm recommended to owner Phil Wrigley that Hartnett take over, the Cubs still were 3½ games back after they lost and tied in a doubleheader at Brooklyn on Sunday, September 17.

Here, Hartnett wrestled with a difficult decision—and won.

The second game at Ebbets Field had gone only five innings when it was halted by darkness, 5-5. The Dodgers had an open date Monday, but the Cubs didn't. They were scheduled at Philadelphia. The Brooklyn club president, flamboyant Larry MacPhail, saw potential gate receipts in a replay. The Cubs had an open date at the end of the Philadelphia series. MacPhail invited them to return to Ebbets Field, and the Chicago players wanted to play, too.

"They knew we had to win to gain on the Pirates and so did I," Hartnett recalled, years later. "They felt they could beat Brooklyn and I had confidence in them. But still I hesitated. I asked MacPhail for 24 hours in which to think it over. I had an idea in the back of my mind and I wanted to sleep on it."

Hartnett's thought was an upcoming three-game series with Pittsburgh, 10 days hence at Chicago. The Cubs would have to sweep the series, Gabby reasoned. Their pitchers already were weary.

"I always felt a manager had to think of his pitchers," said Harnett, exposing a bit of his baseball philosophy. "My players argued with me, but I stuck my neck out and turned down MacPhail's offer."

This was before the recently enacted rule requiring a playoff the day after the season's end of any game that might affect the outcome of a division or pennant race. Then, however, it was possible to win a pennant by a half-game, or lose one.

For three straight days, the Cubs were rained out in Philadelphia and the Pirates were idled in Brooklyn. On Thursday, the Cubs played and won a doubleheader, 4-0 and 2-1, with big Bill Lee, the staff workhorse, scoring his 20th victory and fourth straight shutout in the first game. Annoyingly, however, Pittsburgh also won two at Brooklyn.

But, by the time Pittsburgh watched on an open date from the stands at Wrigley Field as the Cubs beat St. Louis on the eve of their showdown series, the Pirates' lead had been cut to 1½ games. Trouble was, though, using workhorse Lee as often as possible in his shortened rotation, Hartnett just had used his ace in the 6-3 conquest of the Cardinals.

Here, Gabby gambled again. For the series opener with Pittsburgh, he picked the expensive damaged goods, Dizzy Dean, for whom the Cubs had given the Cardinals three players and $185,000 in April. Ol' Diz, though just 27 years old or so, had suffered arm trouble after throwing unnaturally following a foot injury in the 1937 All-Star Game at Washington.

Hartnett, the last to catch Dean at his fast-firing best, knew that the smooth three-quarter delivery had dropped almost to side-arm. He knew that the blazing fastball was gone and that in its place were only slow curves and pinpoint control—Dizzy walked just eight men in 75 innings that year—but he knew something else, too.

"I banked on his heart," said Hartnett, reminiscing as he approached his own 70th birthday in 1970. "I knew nobody would scare him."

Dean, with a 6-1 record, hadn't pitched for two weeks and hadn't started for more than a month when Hartnett squatted down behind the plate and flashed him his first sign for the series opener at Chicago. Incredibly, the cunning competitor held the hard-hitting Pirates scoreless into the ninth—hitters the caliber of the Waner brothers and Arky Vaughan—and then in the last inning, with two on and two out, Hartnett wig-wagged for Lee. Big Bill wild-pitched a run across, but then Al Todd, the bulky catcher who'd always hit Dean pretty good, with his bat or his fists, struck out and the Cubs won, 2-1.

So the Pirates' lead was shaved to one-half game September 28, a date to remember. Still, in a seesaw game, Pittsburgh led into the eighth, 5-3, but even when the Cubs tied it up, as a result of key blows by Rip Collins, pinch-hitter Tony Lazzeri and Billy Herman, Pittsburgh appeared to have escaped. After all, Paul Waner's fine throw retired pinch-runner Joe Marty at the plate on Herman's hit, and darkness was falling fast into the ninth.

A tie seemed likely as the umpires huddled, but they decided to try to make it a full nine innings, anyway. A doubleheader would be necessary the next day. Greybeard Charley Root relieved in the

first of the ninth and got through quickly. In the home half, Mace Brown, the remarkable Pittsburgh relief pitcher who had kept a staff of questionable pitching quality on top, was on the mound.

Phil Cavarretta, first up, flied deep to Lloyd Waner. Carl Reynolds grounded out, and now it was Gabby's turn as the last man, and a crowd of 34,465 Chicago faithful, aware that a twilight tie seemed inevitable, greeted the big skipper with a hopeful roar as he stepped into the batter's box and pounded his bat on the plate. Old Tomato Face closing in on 38, definitely was past even a peak he had reached late.

Hartnett, who had singled and knocked in one of Chicago's five runs, was a curveball catcher, meaning he placed considerable faith in the breaking ball when he squatted down behind a hitter. He knew, too, that Brown was a curveball pitcher. Although the darkness might have favored a fastball, Mace stuck with his best pitch, the old No. 2.

Hartnett swung at the first curveball and missed. The crowd groaned. Brown broke off another deuce and this time Gabby got just a piece of it and fouled it back. A waste pitch might have been in order and pitchers have been fined for letting a batter make contact on a two-strike delivery, but Brown just made the third curve too good.

"I wanted to make it low and outside, but I put it over the plate between his belt and knees," said Brown.

Gabby swung and made contact. Many in the crowd couldn't follow the flight of the ball because of the failing visibility, but Charles Leo (Gabby) Hartnett, who hit 236 major league runs, knew the feeling of exhilaration the minute the biggest of his career blows was struck.

"I got the kind of feeling you get when the blood rushes to your head and you get dizzy," Hartnett said. "I knew it was gone."

The ball landed in the left-field seats for the "homer in the gloaming" that gave the Cubs a 6-5 victory and first place. Before Hartnett reached second base, the whooping, hollering throng was on the field. And there's a famous photo of hilarious fans and ushers following Hartnett around the bases. Even Pat Pieper, the Chicago institution as field announcer, is shown smiling as he trots along to accompany Old Tomato Face as, head up as usual and his grin wider than ever, the player-manager completes what had to be the happiest round trip he ever took, regardless of the mode of transportation.

"And when I got to the plate," said Hartnett, "there was George Barr, the umpire, still hanging around to make sure I touched it."

A generation later, judging by what happened at New York's Shea Stadium when the Mets won the unbelievable pennant and world championship in 1969, there might have been no home plate left to touch by the time the hero of the hour got around the bases.

The job wasn't done, back there in '38, but the Pirates were. They succumbed the next day to Lee, 10-1. The day before the season ended, as Pittsburgh lost at Cincinnati, the Cubs clinched the pennant at St. Louis. And I can still see Hartnett sitting there in the dugout at old Sportsman's Park the last day of the pennant race, hung over but happy after a pennant-clinching celebration. He sat, grinning, accepting congratulations, pumping up and down a giant, bat-shaped gourd a well-wisher had sent him from out West.

Gabby Hartnett would manage the Cubs for two more seasons and he'd play part-time in the big leagues through 1941 when, as a player-coach with the New York Giants and almost 41 years old, he'd still hit .300. But this was the zenith, 1938, a once-in-a-lifetime event. Check signals, make that once in very few lifetimes.

Except for one brief and happy interlude with Charlie Finley's Kansas City Athletics, Hartnett was out of baseball after he managed Buffalo in 1946. Even though he did well for some 20 years in a suburban Chicago bowling alley, he seemed more perplexed and hurt that baseball hadn't had a place for him.

Unless he was more flannel-mouthed than an outsider would know, more critical of the Cubs' ownership and management, you wonder why he wouldn't have qualified, for instance, as a coach with the Cubs.

"I would have like to share in that pension plan," said Hartnett, who finished just before baseball's coverage of players began. Finley kindly qualified him for the pension. But, golfing again after a close call with a bleeding ulcer in 1969, Gabby really wasn't complaining. Until death followed cancer in 1972 when he was 72. Until then he first ran a bowling alley, then eased up. How nice it was to get out of the mills and into baseball in the first place.

Born in Woonsocket, R.I., Gabby grew up in Millville, Mass., a town of some 2,500 population. His father, Fred, was a streetcar conductor and later a bus driver in Worcester. Charles Leo was the first of 14 children. The kids called him "Dowdy" because, in a reverse twist on the meaning of the word, Leo's old man was a pretty sharp dresser and father Fred was the first to be called Dowdy Hartnett.

At 13, young Dowdy won 55,000 marbles at "pooning," a game in which a marbles' contestant seeks to hit an adversary's taw with his own, using an overhand flick at 35 paces. The 55,000 marbles that Gabby won were enough to fill three 25-pound sugar sacks. Once he put them all on the floor of the sitting room and they more than covered a 9x12 rug.

When his own son, Buddy—Charles Leo Hartnett, Jr.—became about six years old, Gabby stopped off in Millville to pick up his marbles, figuring he'd overwhelm his young man with a king-sized present. Trouble was, over the years Dowdy's brothers had done him in by losing his marbles.

At 14, chesty Master Hartnett claimed the blueberry-picking championship of his county. "I not only was a fast blueberry picker," Gabby once told Ed Burns of the *Chicago Tribune*, "but I was clean. I sold all the berries I picked. Folks knew they never got any hay or sand when they got a Hartnett-plucked berry."

At 16, Gabby went to his first formal dance, dressed to kill in a tuxedo rented in Worcester, only to discover after the grand march was over that he had on different colored socks, one black and the other tan.

When Gabby played semi-pro ball, his father invariably was there, arranging his streetcar run so that he could perch in a tree at Millville to holler instructions to the young catcher. When Gabby was up in a pinch, Pop would shout, "It's no beans for you tonight, my lad, if you don't sock one."

Baked beans were almost a staple in New England. Young Hartnett began to bring home the bacon, too. To work at the American Steel and Wire mill at Worcester 26 miles from his home, he had to get up at 5:30 in the morning and he didn't get home for supper until 7:30 P.M.

One morning, in 1921, it was 20 degrees below zero when Leo Hartnett hustled off to work. By the time he got into the warmth of the plant, he discovered that both his ears had been frozen. The pain was excruciating.

"The situation startled and angered me," Hartnett told Burns years later. "Right then and there I denounced work in all its branches."

Curiously, in research for this chapter I found that Hartnett couldn't recall an episode stated so positively back in the late '40s by a high school classmate, E. Clifton Moore, a Utica man who had been a young baseball reporter for the *Worcester Telegram* when Dowdy Hartnett got his chance in 1921.

The manager at Worcester, Michael J. McMahon, better known as Jack Mack, issued a call to Hartnett to report for a trial in the spring of 1921. Gabby left his home for Boulevard Park, but, the way Moore remembered it and Hartnett didn't, the young player failed to show up for three days. Moore said he found him in a burlesque house.

Hartnett reportedly told the reporter friend that he was hesitant about reporting, fearful he wouldn't make the grade. That doesn't sound like the chesty Hartnett the National League came to know, but it's set down here as perhaps part of Hartnett's personal history.

The fact is, after hitting .264 at Worcester, Hartnett was sold to the Cubs for $2,500 and, as mentioned, made his major league debut at the age of 21 in 1922, catching the great Alexander.

"Alex was the greatest I ever caught throwing at three different speeds," he said. "Yes, he did throw a screwball by the time I broke in and it was a good one. I don't know why you haven't heard or read more about it."

For 12 seasons, Hartnett caught 100 or more games for the Cubs, quickly establishing himself at the plate and behind it. Early in 1929, after a courtship of about four years, he married the former Martha Henrietta Marshall of Chicago and they had two children, Buddy, in the chemical business in Chicago, and daughter Sheila, who married and lived in suburban St. Louis.

Each of Gabby's children has four youngsters. Two of Sheila's, Tim and Tom Hornof were bowl linebackers at the University of Missouri.

By the time Hartnett was married, he had become a .300 hitter. As early as 1925, in his third season as a regular, he'd hit 24 home runs. By '29, the first of two seasons of savage hitting with a juiced-up ball in both major leagues, Gabby was ready for the biggest season of his career. Yet the career itself became jeopardized.

Hartnett loved to use that powerful throwing arm. Funny thing, those hands Jesse Burkett talked about eight years earlier were small, but not small enough to keep Gabby from developing the great reputation for throwing or for snaring foul flies. New York columnist Jimmy Powers noted years later that Hartnett had missed only three foul flies in some 1,900 games behind the plate. And Gabby prided himself that his meat hand was not gnarled or broken like those of most former catchers.

But enthusiasm for the Cubs' outlook in 1929, after Bill Veeck, Sr., had obtained Rogers Hornsby to play second base, carried Hartnett away the second day of spring training at Catalina Island. He threw too hard, something snapped and it's a bitter fact that Gabby not only didn't catch that season, but the Cubs won the pennant without him.

"Zack Taylor did a good job," said Hartnett. "That '29 club had as much power as any I ever saw." Yeah, but not behind the plate.

The season in which hitters fattened up on overmatched pitchers probably cost Hartnett a career average of .300. It's not that his 6-for-22 (.273) really cost him any of his career .297, but if he had hit in '29 what he did in '30, he'd have made it a .300 lifetime average.

In 1930, happy to be healthy and whole again, Hartnett was in 141 games and hit for power and average. He batted .339 with 31 doubles, three triples and 37 home runs among 172 hits. He also drove in 122 runs.

With Kiki Cuyler, Hornsby, Hack Wilson, Riggs Stephenson, Hartnett and Grimm hitting hard and often, the Cubs had a remarkable batting order, up and down the lineup. That was the season Wilson hit 56 homers and drove in the fabulous record high of 190 runs. But the Cubs lost to the Cardinals, their chances hurt by injury and their pitchers unequal to the challenge. The entire National League batted .303 in 1930.

McCarthy left as manager during the 1930 season to begin a championship reign with the New York Yankees. Hornsby took over in late September 1930, and was succeeded in August 1932, by the first baseman, Grimm. Jolly Cholly's gang came on to win a pennant and Hartnett, who had been limited to pinch-hitting appearances in the five-game loss to the Philadelphia Athletics in the 1929 Series, caught his first full-fledged World Series in '32.

Old boss McCarthy's Yankees were the foe, and it was a Series of bitterness. Although former Yankee shortstop Mark Koenig had come up to spark the Cubs to a pennant down the stretch, hitting .353 in 33 games, Chicago players had voted him only a half-share of their Series money. This action was harder to understand than their failure to vote anything to Hornsby, the inveterate horseplayer who had borrowed from some of his players.

When the Series opened, booming-voiced Babe Ruth yelled greetings to old teammate Koenig and asked, "Who are the cheapskates you're with, kid?"

The bench-riding was rough as the Yankees won four straight. If Hartnett's ears twitched, he didn't let the sarcasm bother him personally, for he contributed five hits in the four games, including two doubles and a home run, batting .313. But he flatly denied the claim that Babe Ruth pointed to center field and called his shot on a homer mentioned even more than Gabby's 1938 pennant winner.

"I don't want to take anything away from the Babe because he helped all of us get good salaries," Gabby reminisced, "but he didn't call the shot. He resented the Koenig thing and he didn't like it, either, because our trainer, Andy Lotshaw, was riding him.

"Charley Root was pitching, you know, I was catching and the Babe had two strikes on him with our bench on his back. Looking at our dugout and not at center field, he held up the index finger of his left hand, though pointing to the outfield. This is what he said:

"'It only takes one to hit.'"

That's all it took Hartnett, too, as he seemed to get better with age. Five straight years he caught in the All-Star Game, which began at Chicago's Comiskey Park in 1933, and Gabby seemed to be getting better all the time. He treasured having caught Carl Hubbell in King Carl's famed strikeout streak in the '34 All-Star Game at New York's Polo Grounds as one of his finest moments.

"Yeah," Gabby acknowledged, answering a question, "after the first two batters got on base in the first inning, I called time and went out to Hub and said, 'Why don't you throw the "thing?" It always gets me out.'"

The "thing," of course, was Hubbell's screwball.

"Hubbell was the best lefthander I caught," said Hartnett, "and next to Alexander, the Dean I caught in those All-Star Games when he was at St. Louis was the best righthander. If a couple of our infielders (Stan Hack and Billy Jurges) hadn't collided on a groundball for a fluke two-run hit early in the '38 World Series game in which Frank Crosetti and Joe DiMaggio finally homered off him late, I believe Diz might have beaten the Yankees in the World Series when he had nothing."

Hartnett hit .344 in 1935 and won the MVP award as Grimm's Cubs put together their unforgettable 21-game winning streak in September. Gabby hit .292 in the six-game World Series loss to the Tigers and had one home run.

In '36, he batted .307 and a year later, closing in on his 37th birthday, Old Tomato Face was in 110 games and batted .354. He didn't begin to show his age until he became manager and then, of course, he still had the biggest blow up his sleeve.

When Hartnett took over as manager in '38, friends and Chicago observers wondered if he'd be tough enough on troops with whom he'd played. Intimates knew he could be solemn and that his temper could sizzle, that he was subject to moods of silent suffering that the public and even the rest of the National League didn't realize. Gabby wasn't worried about it, but, truth is, as it came out later, he issued only two fines in his two-plus seasons as manager, both of them to—you guessed it—Dizzy Dean. And Hartnett's fondness for Dean is obvious throughout the tale of the talented New England Irishman.

Hartnett's 1939 team finished fourth with an 84-70 record, 13 games behind pennant-winning Cincinnati. When the Cubs dropped to fifth in 1940, the first time they had been out of the first division in 15 seasons, they were 25½ out with their 75-79 mark. Attendance was down to 534,878, the lowest since 1921, the year Gabby Hartnett turned professional back home at Worcester.

So in mid-November, the Cubs released their manager, a man whose name had appeared in their box scores for parts or all of 19 seasons. Just a month short of 40, he'd appeared in only 37 games that year and batted just .266, the lowest since those 31 games in '22 when he'd been a kid fresh up from the Eastern League.

Hartnett had been in camp only a few days at Catalina Island that spring when manager Bill Killefer, himself a former catcher, had lauded the husky target for his pitchers and told Chicago writers, "Boys, there's a real catcher."

Joe McCarthy saw Gabby catch a game at Buffalo in 1946 when he was bench manager of the Bisons after two seasons as part-time player and pilot at Indianapolis and Jersey City. McCarthy saw Hartnett, almost 46, catch against a team of sportswriters, throw out two scribes stealing and hit a home run in his only time at bat.

"Gabby quit playing five years too soon," said McCarthy. "His arm is strong and he can play 36 holes of golf without tiring. His legs are still sound."

Indeed. Back there at Catalina when he was a kid Killefer had been a stern taskmaster. He'd send the Cubs through the hills for five-mile runs almost every day and over the years Hartnett stayed on his feet.

A 190-average bowler those years when he was running that bowling center and sporting goods store in suburban Lincolnwood with partner Lou Frantini, Gabby was even more devoted to golf. Twice he shot 68 and he averaged in the 70s. Even after nearly losing his life with the bleeding ulcer in 1969, he was back out on the links regularly the following spring, still able to shoot in the low 80s.

Frantini was a hunting partner for pheasants in South Dakota back in those playing days when Gabby Hartnett lived up to his promise the day of those frostbitten ears as a kid to avoid work as much as possible. To him, baseball, like golf and bowling and hunting, wasn't work. And though he couldn't play a banjo or fry the best hamburgers or crack wise as well as his old teammate and managerial predecessor, Grimm, Gabby Hartnett was not without charm in those idle off-the-field hours.

He did tricks with cards, matches and mechanical gadgets—ever see a man put a half dollar into a beer bottle?—and he even gave the illusion once of singing. After the 1929 World Series, Gabby teamed with Hack Wilson, Kiki Cuyler and Cliff Heathcote, all now gone, to do a vaudeville act in which they were supposed to sing. Behind a drop curtain, professional crooners warbled the notes that actually reached the ears of the hero-worshipping audience.

Not exactly honest, but, heck, no one ever questioned the integrity of the good-natured guy with the infectious smile, not even when the fellas needled him about being the best peeper at cards on the ball club. In a split second the old sign-stealing catcher, they said, could case a 13-card hand and list every card from left to right. No one guffawed louder at himself than Hartnett.

Although he wasn't smart enough, if that's the right word, to get a job in baseball until Finley brought him back, silver-haired, to coach for the A's in 1965, shortly after Gabby had sold out his bowling interests, Hartnett was smart enough to recognize a reasonable (ahem!) request when he saw one.

One day at Wrigley Field at the end of the Roaring Twenties, in which Chicago seemed at times to be a giant shooting gallery, Hartnett was called over to a front row box by a man he recognized. Who'n hell didn't know Scarface Al Capone everywhere, much less in the toddlin' town?

Capone, accompanied by a young nephew and his bodyguard, wanted an autograph for the boy. Hartnett, pleasant even to the mild and meek, chatted with the underworld king. A photographer snapped the scene, and the baseball commissioner, Judge Kenesaw Mountain Landis, didn't like the published picture. He issued a non-fraternizing ban for all major league players, and it was a bitter pill for Old Tomato Face, who had a cheery hello for everyone.

I always liked the version that when Landis supposedly reprimanded Hartnett, Gabby's reported retort was, "If you don't want anybody to talk to the Big Guy, Judge, you tell him."

Hartnett, smart enough to pitch out on ball four so he could pick a runner off third base, was wise enough not to cross Capone when the Big Guy wanted only his signature, not his life. Chances are, when Capone was the guest of the government in federal prison, the gang leader cheered along with the rest of Gabby Hartnett's fans the day Old Tomato Face beat Mace Brown with the storybook home run that put Hartnett's uniform in the Chicago Historical Society. The homer in the gloamin' certainly didn't deter the inevitable—the great catcher's trip to Cooperstown.

CHARLES LEO (GABBY) HARTNETT
Born December 20, 1900, at Woonsocket, R.I.
Height 6-1 Weight 218
Threw and batted righthanded.
Named to Hall of Fame, 1955.

YEAR	CLUB	LEAGUE	POS.	G.	AB.	R.	H.	2B.	3B.	HR.	RBI.	B.A.	PO.	A.	E.	F.A.
1921	Worcester	East.	C	100	345	38	91	21	7	3	-	.264	447	104	19	.967
1922	Chicago	Nat.	C	31	72	4	14	1	1	0	4	.194	79	29	2	.982
1923	Chicago	Nat.	C-1B	85	231	28	62	12	2	8	39	.268	413	39	5	.989
1924	Chicago	Nat.	C	111	354	56	106	17	7	16	67	.299	369	97	18	.963
1925	Chicago	Nat.	C	117	398	61	115	28	3	24	67	.289	409	114	23	.958
1926	Chicago	Nat.	C	93	284	35	78	25	3	8	41	.275	307	86	9	.978
1927	Chicago	Nat.	C	127	449	56	132	32	5	10	80	.294	479	99	16	.973
1928	Chicago	Nat.	C	120	388	61	117	26	9	14	57	.302	455	103	6	.989
1929	Chicago (a)	Nat.	PH-C	25	22	2	6	2	1	1	9	.273	4	0	0	1.000
1930	Chicago	Nat.	C	141	508	84	172	31	3	37	122	.339	646	68	8	.989
1931	Chicago	Nat.	C	116	380	53	107	32	1	8	70	.282	444	68	10	.981
1932	Chicago	Nat.	C	121	406	52	110	25	3	12	52	.271	484	75	10	.982
1933	Chicago	Nat.	C	140	490	55	135	21	4	16	88	.276	550	77	7	.989
1934	Chicago	Nat.	C	130	438	58	131	21	1	22	90	.299	605	86	3	.996
1935	Chicago	Nat.	C	116	413	67	142	32	6	13	91	.344	477	77	9	.984
1936	Chicago	Nat.	C	121	424	49	130	25	6	7	64	.307	504	75	5	.991
1937	Chicago	Nat.	C	110	356	47	126	21	6	12	82	.354	436	65	2	.996
1938	Chicago	Nat.	C	88	299	40	82	19	1	10	59	.274	358	40	2	.995
1939	Chicago	Nat.	C	97	306	36	85	18	2	12	59	.278	336	47	3	.992
1940	Chicago (b)	Nat.	C	37	64	3	17	3	0	1	12	.266	69	9	4	.951
1941	New York	Nat.	C	64	150	20	45	5	0	5	26	.300	138	15	1	.994
1942	Indianapolis	A.A.	C	72	186	17	41	12	2	4	24	.220	190	36	7	.970
1943	Jersey City	Int.	C	16	16	0	4	1	0	0	5	.250	9	4	1	.929
1944	Jersey City	Int.	C	13	11	1	2	1	0	0	6	.182	0	0	0	.000
Major League Totals				1990	6432	867	1912	396	64	236	1179	.297	7562	1269	143	.984

a Had sore arm and was used as pinch-hitter.
b Unconditionally released by Chicago Cubs, November 13, 1940; signed as player-coach, New York Giants, December 2, 1940.

WORLD SERIES RECORD

YEAR	CLUB	LEAGUE	POS.	G.	AB.	R.	H.	2B.	3B.	HR.	RBI.	B.A.	PO.	A.	E.	F.A.
1929	Chicago	Nat.	PH	3	3	0	0	0	0	0	0	.000	0	0	0	.000
1932	Chicago	Nat.	C	4	16	2	5	2	0	1	1	.313	31	5	1	.973
1935	Chicago	Nat.	C	6	24	1	7	0	0	1	2	.292	33	6	0	1.000
1938	Chicago	Nat.	C	3	11	0	1	0	1	0	0	.091	14	3	0	1.000
World Series Totals				16	54	3	13	2	1	2	3	.241	78	14	1	.989

MR. BLUNT: A tough-talking Texan, Rogers Hornsby, greatest righthanded hitter, felt sorry for the pitchers he faced.

ROGERS HORNSBY

Rogers Hornsby, baseball's Mr. Blunt, must have thought that diplomacy was a respiratory disease.

One night when he was playing second base for the New York Giants in 1927, he was eating with Eddie (Doc) Farrell, the team's young shortstop. A New York writer stopped by the table and asked Rog if he thought the Giants could win the pennant.

"Not with Farrell playing shortstop," replied Hornsby, who qualified as baseball's most rugged individual as well as its greatest righthanded hitter.

Hornsby averaged .358 for nearly 23 seasons in the major leagues. Averaging better than .400 over one remarkable five-year stretch, he put together in 1924 the greatest season of any batter in this century—.424.

They called him the Rajah, and the lofty nickname fit him quite well and only partly because he was handsome and hazel-eyed, dimple-cheeked and with a glowing complexion. He also was majestically aloof and taciturn, independent and a loner.

He was, however, too rough-cut in speech, manner and background to be truly regal, but the image of majesty was there. In fact, to be as honest as Hornsby, he was a petty and prejudiced person, though a frank, outspoken man who hated hypocrisy almost as much as he did baseball general managers.

As one who managed ball clubs often, if never long in the same place, he resented questions about his strategy, but he could second-guess other managers royally. The trait wasn't admirable, but it typified hard-headed Hornsby, who often said what others merely thought.

To know and to like Hornsby and be liked by him was to understand him, make allowances for his shortcomings and appreciate his baseball skills, his earnestness and his interest in children. Hardboiled Hornsby was a pushover for kids.

As the champion lounge lizard of any era, the lobby-sitting athlete loved to talk baseball, especially to young big league players and even more so to small fry for whom he would happily demonstrate a pointer. It's no coincidence that the Rajah spent his most productive years after he put down his blazing bat conducting schools for the *Chicago Daily News* and in instructing Chicago youngsters as part of Mayor Richard J. Daley's youth program.

Chances are he'd still be talking to the kids and trying to show 'em—probably hitting line drives, too—if he hadn't suffered a fatal heart attack in January 1963, when he was in a hospital after surgery, ironically, for removal of cataracts.

Ironically, yes, because no baseball player ever guarded his eyesight more than Hornsby, who passed up the movies, read little and even left the small racetrack agate of the Daily Racing Form to his favorite handicapper. Rog was so obsessed about eye care that when he preached to the old St. Louis Browns in 1952 on the dangers of watching movies, rookie Jim Rivera interrupted brashly:

"Oh, come on now, Rog, the movies don't flicker anymore."

If he liked you, you could tease him, as Rivera

did and as I did in a discussion of his astonishing .424 season of 1924 and Stan Musial's greatest year, .376 in 1948.

I'd been fascinated by Hornsby's considerable edge despite Stan's spectacular year. Thanks to the late James M. Gould's scorebook, I'd learned that whereas Musial had put together four record-tying five-hit games and six four-hit contests, he had been held hitless in 33 games. Hornsby had been horsecollared in just 22 contests and had collected one hit in 46 games, two hits in 47, three hits in 25 and four hits in three.

"And, besides, Rog," I said, intending a compliment to him, "Stan beat out a few hits."

"But I could run, too," bristled the Rajah, who once had offered to bet $500 that he could beat his swift St. Louis successor, Frank Frisch, in a foot race.

"Oh, then you also got a few leg hits," I said with a gentle needle that reddened the old slugger's neck.

Actually, for all his seldom-mentioned straight-away speed, Hornsby was at a competitive disadvantage against any fast lefthanded hitter, getting down to first base. But no one, lefthanded or righthanded, ever hit the ball consistently harder than Hornsby, who stood at the extreme rear corner of the batter's box, away from the plate, and then strode into the ball.

"They all thought I was a sucker for the pitch low and away, but not the way I stepped into the ball," he said, explaining with a wink:

"The pitch I didn't like was high and tight, but by going into the ball and then pulling away from it when it was up and in, I often got a break from the umpires."

No great player, especially one so generally quick to speak his piece, ever accorded the men in blue more respectful silence than did Hornsby. Rog hurt himself with more than one club owner for whom he managed by refusing to storm the umpires or at least to make a fighting show of it.

"Hell, they're human beings with a job to do and

they don't beat you," he would say with a shrug. "The only thing I hated to see 'em ever do was miss the third strike on me so I didn't get a chance to swing."

The umpires respected Hornsby and especially that sharp batting eye. One time a pitcher thought he had slipped across a called third strike on the Rajah, but the umpire—Bill Klem, I believe—shook his head.

Hornsby hit the next pitch out of sight and the umpire said to the pitcher, sweetly, "You see, Mr. Hornsby will tell you when it's close enough to be called a strike."

The way Rog recalled it, he was thrown out of a game only once—by a young umpire, Cy Pfirman. Then he was allowed to remain in the game because Klem interceded with his colleague on the basis of Hornsby's impeccable behavior.

"I made a mistake, kicking the bag as much in disgust at myself as at the umpire," Hornsby related. "I learned a lesson."

He apparently learned another lesson early in his career when there was an argument at home plate with Art Fletcher, then managing the Phillies. Suddenly at a loss for words, Hornsby hit Fletcher on his jutting jaw and dropped him. Dejected, but not ejected, Hornsby let his bat do his hitting thereafter.

That is, until he was managing the Browns for the first time in the depression '30s, when relief pitcher Dick Coffman got on a train the worse for wear. Hornsby slugged him and sent him home.

Coffman was lucky the Rajah wasn't swinging a bat. The Hall of Fame second baseman hit line drives so regularly, to all fields, but especially to right-center, that a long-time friend, J. Roy Stockton of the *St. Louis Post-Dispatch*, had a wry explanation for the excellent pivot man's weakness at going back for pop flies.

"Hornsby," wrote Stockton, "was unfamiliar with pop flies because he hit so few of them himself."

When Casey Stengel managed the Boston Braves just before World War II and a player would complain about the wind blowing off the Charles River, Stengel would sniff.

"Yes, I know it's terrible," he'd say with his most pungent sarcasm. "Mr. Hornsby played here one year and hit only .387 against the wind."

Hornsby, who came up as a 140-pound weakling in 1915, became a six-foot, 200-pounder who played in the big leagues until he was 41 years old in 1937. But he was handicapped first by a broken leg suffered at Chicago in 1930 and then by a painful heel spur. He regretted the surgery he underwent on the spur and, though never a braggart, honestly felt he could have played a few more years.

Certainly he still could swing a bat. In 1944, by then a baseball vagabond, he managed briefly for Jorge Pasquel in Mexico before the colorful eccentric went on his famed raiding spree for American talent.

Hornsby's Veracruz Blues won a Friday game and when they trailed Saturday in the second of a lucrative three-game weekend series, Pasquel urged the 48-year-old Hornsby to pinch-hit in the ninth inning with the bases loaded, the Blues trailing by three runs.

Hornsby obliged and hit the ball over the right-field fence for a game-winning homer. The Rajah trundled around the bases characteristically and the sombrero-waving señors cheered. Pasquel, strangely, was unhappy. "Meester Hornsby," he complained, "now there will be no interest in the third game of the series."

"Then you got the wrong damn boy," snapped Hornsby, recommending to Pasquel, as Stockton put it so adroitly, an utterly impossible disposition of a job in which it was a crime at times to hit home runs.

Mr. Blunt lost the best job he ever had by offending a club owner. The kid from Winters, Tex., bought by the Cardinals for $500 from a Class D club in 1915, was a shortstop who needed beefing up, in the judgment of manager Miller Huggins.

Rog worked hard and ate heartily on an uncle's farm that winter, boosted his weight to 160 and began his incredible assault on the pitchers in 1916.

Asked one time if he ever feared any pitcher, Hornsby said with no effort to be egotistical, "No, I felt sorry for them."

By coincidence, the rival St. Louis Browns came up at the same time with a graceful first baseman named George Sisler. For the next 11 seasons, until Hornsby was traded to New York and Sisler to Washington, they provided a competitive batting rivalry the likes of which no city has ever seen.

Sisler, twice hitting over .400, batted .420 in 1922, two years after he set the major league mark of 257 hits.

Hornsby, in a five-year stretch, 1921-25, hit .397, .401, .384, .424 and .403, topped by the .424 in '24. As historian Lee Allen calculated, Rog's average that year would have been .506 if walks had counted as hits as they had in 1887 when Tip O'Neill of the Browns was credited with .492.

Over Hornsby's protests, Rog was named playing manager of the Cardinals on Memorial Day, 1925, after Sam Breadon wearied of Branch Rickey's experiments. Miffed, Rickey disposed of his stock, which Breadon made available to Hornsby.

The Rajah, though annoyed at times by Rickey's polysyllabics, was impressed by the farm-system innovator's baseball know-how. But the first thing he did when reluctantly taking over as manager was to throw out Rickey's clubhouse blackboard.

"You don't win ball games in here," he told the Redbirds in his first clubhouse meeting, "and if you don't know how to make the plays by now, you're not going to stay."

Mr. Blunt's simplified approach paid off a year later when the Cardinals won their first pennant. Hornsby's mother, the former Mary Dallas Rogers, whose last name had become his first name, predicted beforehand that St. Louis would win. Mrs. Hornsby died the day the Cardinals clinched the pennant, urging with her last breath that Rog stay with his ball club until after the World Series. The funeral was accordingly delayed.

The 1926 World Series was a classic because, for one thing, it marked the first appearance of a perennial have-not, the rag-tag Redbirds, a team that would become the National League's best standard-bearer in the blue-ribbon competition.

For another, the Series marked the return of 39-year-old Grover Cleveland Alexander, one of the game's greatest. Alex had not been in a World Series since 1915.

Alexander, with a drinking problem, had been put on waivers in June by Joe McCarthy, managing the Chicago Cubs. Hornsby didn't smoke and he didn't drink, but he wanted Alexander. Old Pete was the sentimental star of the Series, winning two games and saving a third, the dramatic seventh contest, when Hornsby called on him in the seventh inning. Alexander struck out Tony Lazzeri with the bases loaded and the Cards prevailed, 3-2.

Hornsby won seven batting championships, six of them in succession, and earned two Most Valuable Player awards, but he never tired of recounting the 1926 season and Series as his favorite moment, which was climaxed—surprisingly, as he saw it—when Babe Ruth tried to steal second for the Yankees and was tagged out by Rog on a perfect throw from catcher Bob O'Farrell.

Hornsby could have become a baseball club owner if he hadn't frittered away too much money on slow horses, though he would lamely insist that he lost more in an untrustworthy stock market. He might have stayed on indefinitely in St. Louis, where he was a tremendous favorite, if he hadn't recommended to Breadon that utterly impossible disposition of an exhibition game the club owner couldn't cancel during the tiring stretch run.

Breadon, a proud man, was hurt and when he offered Hornsby only a one-year contract at $50,000 for 1927, he knew the terms would not be acceptable to the positive Rajah, who insisted on a three-year package.

The trade that followed—Hornsby to the Giants for another second baseman, Frisch, and a throw-in pitcher, Jimmy Ring—brought the wrath of St. Louis fans on Breadon. Sam's baseball bacon was saved by Frisch's brilliance and the Cardinals' continued pennant contention.

Hornsby, coldly infuriated, determined to make Breadon pay for the more than 1,000 shares of Rickey stock he'd acquired for $45 a share. A St. Louis broker advised Rog that, as a result of the Redbirds' world championship, the value of a share had increased to $120.

The tightfisted Breadon, just as stubborn as Hornsby when aroused, refused to meet the price. Dramatically, so that the National League wouldn't lose a box office attraction—after all, as Judge Landis put it, how could a man play second base for New York and own stock in the St. Louis club?—the commissioner called a meeting of N. L. club owners.

The owners anted up $5,000 apiece to meet the difference between what the unmovable Breadon had offered and the unflappable Hornsby had demanded.

Hornsby hit .361 for the Giants in 1927, belted 26 homers and drove in 125 runs. When John McGraw was away because of real estate problems in Florida, the newly appointed captain ran the ball club—his way.

He objected one day to the make-sure-of-one care with which third baseman Fred Lindstrom started a double play.

"But that's the way the Old Man wants it made," protested Lindstrom.

"When he's here, make it the way he wants," ordered Hornsby coldly, "but I'm in charge now and I want it done my way."

The Rajah had a high regard for Mr. McGraw, as he called him, and for his first major league manager, Huggins. He respected Rickey, too, as a former player who had gone to the top. He liked William Wrigley, who then owned the Cubs.

Hornsby also had considerable affection for Judge Emil Fuchs, a kindly man who ran the Boston Braves, to whom Rog was traded after only one season in New York.

Hornsby was coldly aloof to Charley Stoneham, the Giants' owner, who had panted for his big bat for some seasons. Rogers brushed off the big boss at least once in a hotel lobby at Pittsburgh when Stoneham inquired politely about a strategy move. Rog forgot that one, typically, but chose to remember only years later that he felt traveling secretary Jim Tierney had poisoned the management against him.

"We lost a tough one on excusable errors by a fine shortstop, Travis Jackson," Hornsby would explain, "and when Tierney complained to me about Jackson, I told him to mind his own blankety-blank business and to take care of the railroad tickets and hotel rooms and leave the shortstopping to Jackson and the managing to me."

That was Hornsby, all right, but he hit if off immensely well with Fuchs, an admirer for whom Rog had the big year at Braves Field that Stengel always mentioned. There was some unpleasantness as Rog succeeded Jack Slattery, a popular Boston College coach who had been miscast temporarily as the Braves' manager.

The Braves were a bad ball club and worse off financially. When a tearful Fuchs came to Hornsby after the 1928 season and hesitated before taking a Chicago offer of five players and $200,000 for the batting champion, the Rajah scolded him gently.

"Come now, Judge," he said, "you can't afford not to take that kind of offer."

William Veeck, Sr., the former sports columnist then serving as general manager of the Cubs, shared manager Joe McCarthy's view that with Hornsby, Chicago could win the 1929 National League pennant. The Cubs did, thanks in large measure to Rog's .380 average, 40 homers and 149 RBIs.

A year later, after McCarthy was dismissed, leading to his remarkable success in New York with the

Yankees, the hobbling Hornsby was named manager of the Cubs. But he ran into front office trouble and was canned in August 1932.

The senior Veeck claimed the well-paid manager was borrowing money from his players to cover gambling losses. Hornsby charged that he'd been fired because he'd used promising rookie Frank Demaree in a pinch-hitting jam that Veeck felt Hornsby should have filled himself.

"These second-guessing general managers,"he snarled. "They get a young player, want you to use him, but then complain when you try to find out what he can do in a jam. Demaree didn't that time, but he will."

Hornsby accused both first baseman Charlie Grimm, his successor, and catcher Gabby Hartnett, another long-time Chicago favorite, with having run to the front office. McCarthy also had no love for Rog, either, for years.

Although the Rajah had been with them until August, the second-place Cubs, rallying to the 1932 pennant, coldly cut him completely out of their World Series money. Hornsby also was called in for an accounting of his betting activities by Judge Landis, the first baseball commissioner, to whom betting on horses was a grievous sin.

Before the craggy, scowling jurist who had the vocabulary of a stevedore and unlimited authority, sinners quaked and quavered, but not Mr. Blunt. Back in 1926, when the Judge had said that the New York Central Railroad would haul the World Series traffic, Hornsby flatly refused to comply. The Cardinals, he said loyally had traveled all season to New York on the Pennsylvania Railroad and it would be the Pennsy in the Series, too, period.

When Landis hauled him into baseball's court of last resort in '32 to explain his gambling, Hornsby tartly told the Judge that he didn't consider betting on the horses any more of a gamble than losing in the stock market.

Rog not only was sensitive about having lost $100,000 in the '29 crash, irrationally arguing that he'd never had a run for the money, but he hit Landis where the Judge also was thinskinned. The commissioner had invested some of baseball's money in the pie-in-the-sky utilities empire of Samuel Insull that collapsed.

Friend Rickey had to talk fast to persuade Landis to permit free-agent Hornsby to rejoin the Cardinals as a utility infielder and pinch-hitter in 1933.

At 37, virtually broke, in and out of lawsuits, divorced and dogged by that bad heel that slowed him, Rog still managed five consecutive pinch-hits and a .325 average before Rickey came up with a better thing for him in June.

And, by the way, if anyone doubts that Hornsby and Frisch ever played together, remind 'em that Ty Cobb and Tris Speaker also were teammates at the end of their illustrious careers.

Named manager of the rival Browns in June 1933, Hornsby worked for a plain-spoken, tough-minded sportsman he liked, Phil Ball. The wealthy ice man had to like what I recall, perhaps mistakenly, as the Rajah's first time at bat in the American League.

Against the Yankees, he came down off the third-base coaching line to pinch-hit in a late-inning jam at old Sportsman's Park. Lefty Gomez was the pitcher, I recall, as the chesty world champions crowed:

"So here's the great National League hitter, Mr. Hornsby."

The Rajah hit the first pitch onto the pavilion roof in right-center. He trotted around the bases, stepped on home plate and faced the visitors' bench before wheeling toward the home dugout. Said the Rajah:

"Yes, you____, that WAS the great National League hitter, Mr. Hornsby."

The death of Ball brought onto the scene a new club owner, Donald L. Barnes, head of a small loan firm, and a new general manager, Bill DeWitt. Hornsby always longed for the days when a manager could run the club on the field, make the trades and be accountable only to the club owner. Ball clubs, he insisted in an outdated way, needed only a business manager, not a general manager.

When DeWitt learned that Hornsby again was playing the horses, he reported the information to Barnes. As Rog laid before Barnes a certified check to pay for stock that had been available to him in the small loan company, the club owner demanded to know whether this was money that had been won on horses.

Hornsby didn't lie. One word led to another, the second more pleasant than the first, as always seemed to be the case when Hornsby was challenged. And Rog said the magic words to small loan exec. Barnes.

"I don't see," he said, "where playing the horses is as bad as charging exorbitant interest rates to widows and orphans."

Rogers Hornsby didn't get back to the big leagues for 15 years, then got there only because Bill Veeck, son of the man who had fired him at Chicago, was impressed sufficiently by the job he had done with winning clubs at Beaumont in the Texas League and Seattle in the Pacific Coast League.

Veeck hired him to manage the Browns in 1952, but the Rajah didn't last long. He didn't last at Cincinnati, either, where Gabe Paul finally paid him not to manage the Reds after the 1953 season.

The parade, as Paul suggested unhappily, had passed Hornsby by. He was too professional, too impersonal in an era when athletes demanded more consideration.

Hornsby helped a few of them get farther as ballplayers than they ever would have without him because, for one thing, he was precisely what he figured every ball club needed and few have even today. That is, a highly competent batting coach.

He would defend his general position this way:

"I'm not asking them to do anything for me. I'd say the manager comes fifth—after themselves, their families, the ball club and the fans."

But the players resented the little things that to them were big. For instance, Hornsby's halting play by standing on the top of the dugout steps, jerking a thumb to a pitcher he wanted to leave the mound and then wig-wagging to a reliever to come up the foul line. The walk to the showers is long enough without having to make it alone.

Old Sweet Talk was what they used to call the amusingly profane Rajah those last several years around the press room at Wrigley Field or Comiskey Park—whenever the bangtails weren't running in Chicago. He had a passion for ice cream until he died at nearly 67, twice divorced, three times married and the father of two sons, one of whom, Billy, played minor league ball briefly.

When they buried the Rajah down there at Hornsby Bend, Tex., he left behind countless memories, including the appreciation of one reporter he'd come across years before in a gaming room. Hornsby wondered how much the kid had lost and the young writer told him.

Rog peeled off that amount, gave it to the reporter and advised him, "All right, now you've seen what it's like. Stay away from it."

Next to base hits, a long shot at the track and a thick milk shake, Hornsby liked a thick steak. Al Spohrer, catching for the Braves, figured a way to distract him at a time he knew Boston's feeble pitchers couldn't stop Rog.

"Say, Rog," said Spohrer, squatting behind the plate when Hornsby went to bat in a tense moment, "my wife has discovered a butcher who sells the finest steaks."

"That so?" remarked Hornsby with polite interest.

"Strike one," the umpire intoned.

"Not only that, Rog," continued Spohrer, "but my wife can cook steaks better than anyone I know. Grace really can broil 'em."

"Strike two," said the umpire.

"What Grace and I thought," Spohrer went on, "was that the next time you're in Boston, you might come out to the house and have a steak with us."

Crack! Hornsby smashed the ball over the fence and then jogged around the bases. As he crossed the plate, he turned to a crestfallen Spohrer:

"What night shall we make it, Al?"

ROGERS (RAJAH) HORNSBY
Born April 27, 1896, at Winters, Tex.
Died January 5, 1963, at Chicago, Ill.
Height 5-11½ Weight 200
Threw and batted righthanded.
Named to Hall of Fame, 1942.

YEAR	CLUB	LEAGUE	POS.	G.	AB.	R.	H.	2B.	3B.	HR.	RBI.	B.A.	PO.	A.	E.	F.A.
1914	Hugo-Denison	Tex.-Ok	SS	113	393	47	91	12	3	3	-	.232	208	285	45	.916
1915	Denison	W.A.	SS	119	429	75	119	26	2	4	-	.277	267	354	58	.915
1915	St. Louis	Nat.	SS	18	57	5	14	2	0	0	4	.246	48	46	8	.922
1916	St. Louis	Nat.	INF	139	495	63	155	17	15	6	60	.313	325	315	45	.934
1917	St. Louis	Nat.	SS	145	523	86	171	24	17	8	70	.327	268	527	52	.939
1918	St. Louis	Nat.	SS-OF	115	416	51	117	19	11	5	59	.281	211	434	46	.933
1919	St. Louis	Nat.	INF	138	512	68	163	15	9	8	68	.318	185	367	34	.942
1920	St. Louis	Nat.	2B	149	589	96	218	44	20	9	94	.370	343	524	34	.962
1921	St. Louis	Nat.	INF-OF	154	592	131	235	44	18	21	126	.397	305	477	25	.969
1922	St. Louis	Nat.	2B	154	623	141	250	46	14	42	152	.401	398	473	30	.967
1923	St. Louis	Nat.	2B	107	424	89	163	32	10	17	83	.384	192	283	19	.962
1924	St. Louis	Nat.	2B	143	536	121	227	43	14	25	94	.424	301	517	30	.965
1925	St. Louis	Nat.	2B	138	504	133	203	41	10	39	143	.403	287	416	34	.954
1926	St. Louis (a)	Nat.	2B	134	527	96	167	34	5	11	93	.317	245	433	27	.962
1927	New York (b)	Nat.	2B	155	568	133	205	32	9	26	125	.361	299	582	25	.972
1928	Boston (c)	Nat.	2B	140	486	99	188	42	7	21	94	.387	295	450	21	.973
1929	Chicago	Nat.	2B	156	602	156	229	47	7	40	149	.380	286	547	23	.973
1930	Chicago	Nat.	2B	42	104	15	32	5	1	2	18	.308	44	76	11	.916
1931	Chicago	Nat.	2B-3B	100	357	64	118	37	1	16	90	.331	128	255	22	.946
1932	Chicago (d)	Nat.	3B-OF	19	58	10	13	2	0	1	7	.224	17	10	4	.871
1933	St. Louis	Nat.	2B	46	83	9	27	6	0	2	21	.325	24	35	2	.967
1933	St. Louis	Amer.	PH	11	9	2	3	1	0	1	2	.333	0	0	0	.000
1934	St. Louis	Amer.	3B-OF	24	23	2	7	2	0	1	11	.304	2	3	0	1.000
1935	St. Louis	Amer.	INF	10	24	1	5	3	0	0	3	.208	38	5	0	1.000
1936	St. Louis	Amer.	1B	2	5	1	2	0	0	0	2	.400	10	0	0	1.000
1937	St. Louis	Amer.	2B	20	56	7	18	3	0	1	11	.321	30	41	4	.947
1938	Baltimore	Int.	2-1B-OF	16	27	2	2	0	0	0	0	.074	22	2	0	1.000
1939	Chattanooga	South	2B	3	3	1	2	0	0	1	2	.667	0	0	0	.000
1940	Oklahoma City	Tex.	PH	1	1	0	1	0	0	0	0	1.000	0	0	0	.000
1942	Ft. Worth	Tex.	2B	1	4	0	1	0	0	0	2	.250	2	2	0	1.000
National League Totals				2192	8056	1566	2895	532	168	299	1550	.359	4201	6767	492	.957
American League Totals				67	117	13	35	9	0	3	29	.299	80	49	4	.970
Major League Totals				2259	8173	1579	2930	541	168	302	1579	.358	4281	6816	496	.957

a Traded to New York Giants for infielder Frank Frisch and pitcher Jimmy Ring, December 20, 1926.
b Traded to Boston Braves for outfielder Jimmy Welsh and catcher Francis Hogan, January 10, 1928.
c Traded to Chicago Cubs for infielder Fred Maguire, catcher Doc Leggett, pitchers Percy Jones, Harry Seibold and Bruce Cunningham and $200,000, November 7, 1928.
d Signed with St. Louis Cardinals, October 24, 1932.

WORLD SERIES RECORD

YEAR	CLUB	LEAGUE	POS.	G.	AB.	R.	H.	2B.	3B.	HR.	RBI.	B.A.	PO.	A.	E.	F.A.
1926	St. Louis	Nat.	2B	7	28	2	7	1	0	0	4	.250	15	21	0	1.000
1929	Chicago	Nat.	2B	5	21	4	5	1	1	0	1	.238	9	11	1	.952
World Series Totals				12	49	6	12	2	1	0	5	.245	24	32	1	.982

MEAL TICKET: That's what they called Carl Hubbell when his famed screwball pitched Bill Terry's Giants to three pennants in five years, 1933-37.

CARL HUBBELL

They said Carl Hubbell wasn't colorful. The heck he wasn't—even though he didn't pop off, chew out umpires, sit down temperamentally for more dough or stand up aggressively for the rights of lefthanded pitchers to be recognized as human beings.

When Hub beat the Boston Braves in a key game for the New York Giants down the stretch in 1933, the first of two years in which he won the Most Valuable Player award and the first of his five successive 20-game seasons, columnist Heywood Broun took humorous note of the event.

"There must be a skeleton in Hubbell's closet somewhere, such as a righthanded maternal grandmother," quipped Broun, impressed by Hubbell's incredible control.

King Carl did have astonishing control, not only for a southpaw, but for any kind of pitcher in any period of play of baseball's first century. Why, he once pitched an 18-inning shutout and didn't walk a man. But, above all, the man had control of himself, creating the quiet impression that he wasn't colorful.

But physically he indeed stood out as different, a

basic ingredient of the intangible called color. Awkwardly angular, gaunt, lean-visaged and almost Lincolnesque in appearance, the tall, leathery-looking lefthander had no hips, less derriere and the longest shinbones in captivity.

Present-day players who think they popularized the obnoxious fad of wearing baseball pantaloons extremely low are reminded that it ain't necessarily so. Although Hubbell's flannels weren't tailored indecently skin tight and the stirrups of his baseball socks weren't stretched to show too much of the white understockings, the former pecan farmer and cotton chopper from Meeker, Okla., wore the uniform knickers long.

"I just couldn't keep 'em up," Hubbell said years later, smiling. "You gotta have a better anchor than I did. I didn't have any behind."

Even more unusual was Hubbell's left hand, which looked as if it were waiting for a baton or a surreptitious payoff.

Seeing Hubbell walk by once, the left palm turned outward, Pepper Martin of St. Louis' Gashouse Gang nudged New York writer Tom Meany and said:

"Look at the crooked-arm son of a gun. His left hand turns the wrong way. No wonder he's such a good pitcher. He's a freak."

Martin, the Wild Horse of the Osage, spoke as one of three fellow Oklahomans—the Waner brothers, Paul and Lloyd, were the others—who could brag that they hit reasonably well against Hubbell from 1928 until he turned in his spikes 15 years later. Hub always included Gabby Hartnett, Chick Hafey, Joe Medwick, Billy Herman and Ernie Lombardi among the hitters toughest for him.

Except for the Waners, the hitters mentioned were righthanded, a bit of a surprise in view of the general belief that lefthanded batters fared better against the puzzling southpaw because his money pitch, the screwball, faded down and away from righthanded hitters. Frustrated, switch-hitting Frank Frisch batted lefthanded against Hub, the

National League's winningest lefthander until Warren Spahn.

The screwball, meaning the pitch he threw and not the pitcher who threw it, was the delivery that combined with Hubbell's pinpoint control to make him King Carl, a craftsman capable of 253 victories against only 154 defeats. He once (1933) pitched 10 shutouts in a season, hurled 46 consecutive scoreless innings and owned 16 consecutive league victories in one season and 24 over a two-year period. He had an earned-run low of 1.66 in '33 and a victory high of 26 in '36.

Back in Christy Mathewson's day, the screwball was called the fadeaway. In Hubbell's era, it became known as the butterfly. Now it's referred to most often, though still seldom seen, as the screwjie. The rose, by any other name, is exactly what pedantic Branch Rickey called it—the reverse curve.

To throw a curveball, a lefthander twists his wrist to the right clockwise, or, if you will, inward. The ball breaks down and away from a righthanded batter. To throw the screwball which Hubbell did extremely well, partly because he had an exceptionally long and supple wrist, is to defy nature, so to speak, by turning the left wrist to the right. The ball breaks down and to the left, away from the righthanded hitter. The strain on the elbow is considerable.

Hubbell, warned not to throw the screwball, finally faced the consequences—elbow surgery for removal of bone chips—but not before he'd pitched the Giants to three pennants and a world championship and had established himself indelibly with those 115 victories over the five-year peak in which he lost only 50 games and was named four times to *The Sporting News'* All-Star team.

Over the years as he served as farm director for the Giants, first in New York and then in San Francisco, the thick, black hair lightened and the lines of the gaunt, sober face deepened. But the badge of Hub's profession—or, rather, his peculiar proficiency at it—remained that famous left arm. Clever columnist Jim Murray summed it up well with his well-turned amusingly outrageous exaggeration.

"The only eccentric thing about him is his left arm," Murray wrote in 1968 when Hubbell was honored by the Sportsmen's Club of the City of Hope at a dinner in Las Vegas. "He looks as if he put it on in the dark.

"The palm turns out instead of in. He used to get dirty looks in subways from young ladies and guys would shift their wallets when they got a load of the position of his hand. He almost always looked as if he was trying to slip you something behind his back. The arm looked like a cruller. From the looks of the arm, they should have called the pitch the 'corkscrew' ball."

The corkscrew, which is just about as apt and certainly more descriptive than "screwball," was something special in the palm of Hubbell's outgoing hand because of King Carl's pitching savvy. He wasn't content to throw the screwjie one way and at the same speed. Heck, he threw the pitch at three different speeds and could break it away from a righthanded hitter or more rapidly down and away as if it were falling off the table, like a well-defined sinker.

Head to head, Hub beat Dizzy Dean six of 11 times in a pitching rivalry that brightened the Depression Thirties. Averaging 298 innings a year for those five peak seasons when he and Dean were far and away the best, King Carl qualified as Bill Terry's Meal Ticket, a nickname which reportedly didn't sit too well with the Giants' playing manager at the time.

Working in turn and at times out, Hubbell darn near pitched the light-hitting, slick-fielding Giants to five consecutive pennants in a three-way fight for supremacy with St. Louis and Chicago.

The mild man from Meeker wasn't really a one-pitch performer, of course, and it's a fact that he struck out nearly two and one-half men for every one he walked and more importantly, issued a pass just about every five innings. He could sneak a fastball across for a strike, and his curve improved with

the practice for perfection that was characteristic of his pitching. But let's face it, as Hub did: Without the screwball, he wouldn't have made it big. And with it, he'd have reached the big leagues earlier.

Born in Carthage, Mo., on June 22, 1903, Carl Owen Hubbell grew up on an Oklahoma pecan farm. When he graduated from high school, he went to work for an oil company. In August of the same year, 1923, he was signed by Cushing of the Oklahoma State League, which collapsed the following year. He pitched briefly that season with Ardmore and Oklahoma City.

By 1925, when he won 17 and lost 13 in the Western League the 22-year-old lefthander already had begun to throw the screwball, which he'd developed when seeking to turn the ball over to make it sink. Jack Holland, operating the Oklahoma City club, sold him to Detroit for a reported $20,000.

Hubbell's first spring training with a big league club in 1926 was a bitter experience. First, George McBride, a coach for the Tigers, advised him not to throw the screwball and then none other than Ty Cobb himself, still player-manager, cautioned that he could hurt his arm as Hub Pruett had done.

Pruett, fresh off the University of Missouri campus, had bamboozled Babe Ruth and the New York Yankees as the St. Louis Browns just missed a pennant by a game in 1922. But the young lefthander hurt his arm, and everyone blamed it on the screwball that baffled the Babe. As a postscript, everyone should do as poorly as late Dr. Hubert Pruett, an eminent St. Louis physician and collector of ragtime music.

So Hubbell, deprived of his pet pitch, wasn't even permitted to pitch an inning of an intrasquad game and was shipped to Toronto, where orders had been received that he was to forget the screwball. With Toronto, he was only 7-7 with a 3.77 ERA.

The following spring, ebullient George Moriarty, former third baseman and umpire, was managing the Tigers and there's one report that at San Antonio, Tex., where the Tigers trained, the fire-eating Moriarty even called the cadaverous-looking kid "yellow" because he didn't get the ball over the plate in a camp game. No matter whether he did or didn't, Moriarty did take a dim view of the screwball, too, and a shocked Hubbell was shipped down to Decatur, Ill., of the Three I League. Not even a 14-7 record preserved confidence in his baseball future.

Detroit, giving up on him, sold Hubbell to Beaumont Tex., where the relieved lefthander reported in the spring of 1928, happy to find that the manager, Claude Robertson, a catcher, had no objections to Carl's use of the screwball.

After two years in drydock, the screwball wouldn't behave at first and Hubbell lost several games. But then the delivery began to fall in place, meaning the strike zone, down around the knees, and Hubbell began to win.

A Giants' scout, Dick Kinsella, was a delegate from Illinois to the Democratic national convention that nominated Alfred E. Smith for the presidency in 1928. He became bored with the political proceedings at Houston and took in a Texas League game. He saw a brilliant 11-inning duel between lefthanded pitchers. Houston's Bill Hallahan property of the St. Louis Cardinals, lost to Beaumont's Hubbell, 1-0.

Back at the Rice Hotel, Kinsella phoned John J. McGraw in New York. McGraw, whose Giants were short of pitching in a pennant fight with St. Louis, listened intently as the scout said:

"Mac, I think I saw another Art Nehf today."

What Kinsella had seen was not another Nehf, though Artie had been a classy little lefthander for the Giants' four pennant-winners of the early '20s. He'd seen a pitcher who would rank with Mathewson and Juan Marichal as the Giants' greatest ever.

There are conflicting reports that McGraw told Kinsella to send Hubbell along immediately or to take another look. The former is the more dramatic, the latter more practical. Stories gather gloss along the way.

When secretary Jim Tierney of the Giants finally called Rube Stewart, president of the Beaumont club, they haggled over terms before another voice, exasperated, got on the line at New York and bellowed, "To hell with the price, I want that pitcher."

That, the way Hubbell heard it, is the way—for about $30,000—the Giants got a pitcher who would prove such a bargain. Hub remembers, too, how martinet McGraw showed him kindness and patience.

"I got fined by Mac a couple of times later for mistakes I made on the field," Hubbell recalled, "but I remember more that when I was young and needed understanding, he gave it to me."

In Hub's first start against Pittsburgh, he was knocked out with seven runs in the second inning. Worse, the Giants rallied before losing to Burleigh Grimes and the Pirates, 7-5.

Dejected, Hubbell told his roommate, Bill Walker, another young lefthander, "I guess this is the finish."

The next day, McGraw called Hub into his office in the Polo Grounds. "Sit down," said baseball's Little Napoleon and Carl sat, fearing the worst.

"They hit you," said McGraw, "but the club played poorly behind you, too. I liked your stuff, your control and the way you pitched, if not the results. When you get to know the hitters, you're going to be all right. Don't let those seven runs bother you. You're going to be a great pitcher for us."

Heady with emotion, Hubbell staggered out of the office. Seven hits and seven runs in an inning and a third, and McGraw had said, "You're going to be a great pitcher!"

In the next eight days, McGraw twice used Hubbell as a relief pitcher. Then came a series with St. Louis. The Cardinals knocked out starter Jim Faulkner in the third inning, and McGraw beckoned for the lanky, long-legged lefthander in whom he'd created self-confidence. Hub held the Redbirds until the 15th before losing.

A star had been born in defeat. Although he didn't score his first big league victory until July 31, 1928, at Chicago, Hubbell won 10 games for a ball club which narrowly missed the pennant that went to St. Louis.

Timidly, Hub hadn't thrown the screwball in the majors until he faced a jam in that long relief effort against the Cardinals.

When slugging Chick Hafey came to bat with the winning runs on base and the count went to 3-and-1, Hubbell broke off a screwjie. Hafey swung and missed. Again came the fadeaway. Again, Hafey, not expecting the ball to break down and away, swung and struck out.

The Giants' giant catcher, jovial Frank (Shanty) Hogan, shook his head. "I don't know what the hell that pitch is, kid," Hogan told his rookie battery-mate, "but keep throwing it."

A year later against Pittsburgh, a lineup which included the Waner boys and Pie Traynor among other accomplished hitters, Hubbell hurled a no-hitter on May 8. He polished it off proudly, too. In the ninth, after New York errors had put two men on base, Hubbell threw a called third strike past Lloyd Waner and then induced brother Paul to slap sharply back to the mound. Even though stumbling, Hubbell worked fast with shortstop Travis Jackson, pivoting, and Bill Terry at first base, to complete a game-ending double play on the fleet Waner.

No-hit games weren't quite so frequent then in a period of higher batting averages. For example, Hubbell's no-hitter was the first thrown in the majors by a lefthander since Hub Leonard of the Boston Red Sox 11 years earlier. It also was the first in the majors since Ted Lyons of the Chicago White Sox had hurled a hitless game in 1926.

Hubbell, however, was just beginning to do the extra-ordinary. By July 1933, there was excitement in Harlem. The Giants were bidding for a pennant in Terry's first season as manager. And nearly 50,000 turned out for a Sunday doubleheader with the Cardinals. They saw a classic.

The first game took three minutes longer than four hours. The reason? Eighteen innings, that's why. Eighteen innings in which, facing the likes of Martin, Frisch, Medwick, Rip Collins, Jimmy Wilson and even Rogers Hornsby as a pinch-hitter, Hubbell allowed only six hits. He struck out 12 and walked NONE.

In the inning in which he completed the equivalent of a second nine-inning shutout, Hubbell hurried to first to avoid a double play on a force-out grounder. And New York's little second baseman, Hughie Critz, then delivered a two-out-game-winning single off Jesse Haines, veteran Redbird righthander who had replaced Tex Carleton in the 17th.

As a P. S. to that 1-0 game, the Giants then won the second game, too, and again by 1-0, a result of a fourth-inning home run by third baseman Johnny Vergez off Dizzy Dean. Diz was hooked up in a hard-throwing battle against wild young Leroy (Tarzan) Parmelee in the diminishing daylight. It was so discouraging to try to hit that Leo Durocher once started away from the plate after a second strike.

"You've got another one coming," said plate umpire Cy Pfirman to Durocher, turning away.

"You take it," said The Lip, who screwed up enough courage to hit well enough in the pinch, yet had no taste for trying to avoid Parmelee's blue darts in the gloaming.

Hubbell, reminiscing about his marathon masterpiece, said, "It wasn't the most important game I ever pitched or won, but it was probably the best. I remember that Frisch hit a couple of long fouls that were almost home runs because of the short fences and Medwick just missed one, too.

"I didn't notice the physical strain even though it was a gray, muggy day. I guess all the tension builds up nervous energy. But I sure was happy to see Critz' groundball go through because I thought it would never end. And about an hour after the game ended, I was completely washed out."

The 1933 Giants, long on pitching and defense and short on punch, brought New York its first National League pennant in nine years. Hubbell, as mentioned, was superb and a deserving MVP with his 23-12 record and 1.66 ERA.

In the World Series against Washington that fall, King Carl beat the Senators twice, topping lefty Walter Stewart in the opener, 4-2, and then outdueling Monte Weaver in the fourth contest, 2-1, in 11 innings.

When Washington threatened in the last of the 11th, putting runners on first and third with one out, the Giants huddled to plan their defensive strategy as a lefthanded-hitting rookie, catcher Cliff Bolton came out of the Senators' dugout. A New York reserve infielder, the veteran Charley Dressen, hurried out with intelligence for Manager Terry.

"I played against this kid in the Southern League," said Dressen. "He's slow and can be doubled up."

If the infield played back, of course, the challenge would be to keep the ball down so that Bolton would hit it on the ground. Would Hubbell want to try?

"Play 'em back," the Meal Ticket of the Mound told Manager Terry, and, lo, Bolton skipped a groundball to shortstop John (Blondy) Ryan, who flipped to middle man Critz for the start of a game-ending double play.

The DP, a pitcher's best friend, was especially close to Hubbell, whose knack for keeping the ball down, whether throwing the screwball or any other pitch, was no small factor in his large success.

It figured heavily in the greatest moment of his career. The moment, that is, which always will be remembered as the greatest, though in the harsh light of reality it must be remembered that the All-Star Game still is only an exhibition and, therefore, not as vital as one of those classic Dean-Hubbell duels for team supremacy in the National League.

It's impossible, however, to minimize the theatrics of the 1934 All-Star Game at New York's Polo Grounds, Hubbell's own park, when it's remem-bered that King Carl faced a Hall of Fame batting order with the fences only a chip shot away at either foul line. All starting members are in the Hall of Fame with belated recognition of Lefty Gomez at Cooperstown.

The strategy, of course, is to keep the batters from pulling the ball in a park like the old Polo Grounds. Keeping the ball away, Hubbell got a curve over the plate and Charley Gehringer, Detroit's lefthanded-hitting second baseman, led off with a single to center.

Pitching carefully, again keeping the ball away, Hubbell walked another lefthanded hitter, Heinie Manush, on a full-count pitch. And the National League infielders—Terry, Frisch, Travis Jackson and Traynor—surrounded the mound, nervously.

Hartnett, the tomato-faced catcher of the Cubs, trundled out from behind the plate, too, mask and cap off.

"To hell with pitching carefully, Hub," said Hartnett. "Throw 'em the thing. It always gets me out."

The next hitter was the one and only Babe Ruth, fat and 39, but still dangerous enough to have won the first All-Star Game the previous year with a home run.

Hubbell can remember a bull-voiced guy yelling, "Take the bum out before it's too late."

Against Ruth, Hubbell recalled wasting a fastball and throwing three straight screwballs. The Babe took the called third strike that brought up Lou Gehrig, his partner in mayhem for so many years with the Yankees. Hubbell frankly was looking for a double play, but Gehrig fanned on four pitches.

The crowd was roaring as Gehrig, passing slugger Jimmie Foxx, paused to say a word, which, was:

"Don't wait for him to bring the ball up. He won't."

By now, especially with a righthanded hitter at bat, Hubbell and Hartnett were going for the strikeout. They concentrated so much on Foxx that Gehringer and Manush executed a double steal, but Hubbell said he didn't care. King Carl threw three more screwballs and Double-X went down swinging, too. Twelve pitches and three strikeouts by three of the top hitters in history.

Wait, that's not all. After Frisch homered off Gomez for the National League in the first inning, Hubbell went back to the mound and ran his strikeout string to five by fanning two more top-flight hitters, Al Simmons and Joe Cronin. Bill Dickey then singled to center, bringing up the droll Gomez.

Lefty addressed himself to Hartnett. "You are now looking at a man whose batting average is .104. What the hell am I doing up here?"

Gomez struck out and talked about it ever since, linking himself with Ruth, Gehrig, Foxx, Simmons and Cronin as great hitters who succumbed to King Carl on a day when the National League won more than it lost. The game went down the drain after Hubbell's three-inning scoreless stint, 9-7, but the sensational start by the great pitcher remains one of the most talked about moments in big league baseball's first 100 years.

If Hubbell couldn't top that one for single-day supremacy, he contrived two years later to capture the country's attention again with a spectacular pitching surge that brought another New York pennant.

Although troubled for the first time by the arm soreness and elbow swelling that would lead finally to surgery and a lessening of skill, Hubbell was a big winner in both 1934 and 1935, but both times the Giants faltered down the stretch and lost leads and pennants, one to St. Louis and the other to Chicago.

By mid-July 1936, it appeared that the Giants wouldn't even have the chance to be frontrunners again. Even the great Hubbell was not pitching with the consistency that made him a model.

A funny thing happened on July 17 in Pittsburgh. Funny, as an oddity, not amusing. Joe Moore, Mel Ott, Hank Leiber and Eddie Mayo hit triples in the first inning, tying a major league mark of four three-base blows in one round. When

Hubbell shut out the Pirates that afternoon on three hits, 6-0, his record stood at 11-6.

Nobody knew it then, but both Hub and his teammates were off and running. Two days later, pitching in relief, Hub beat Cincinnati, 4-3.

In another two days, facing Dean and the Cardinals, who were contesting the Cubs for the lead, King Carl topped Ol' Diz in 10 innings, 2-1, on a homer by Dick Bartell.

So it went for the Giants and for Hubbell. The ball club clinched the pennant on September 24, a day after Hub's 16th consecutive victory, 5-4, this one over the Philadelphia Phillies.

Time ran out on the 33-year-old lefthander before he could challenge the major league mark of 19 consecutive conquests, set 24 years earlier by another New York southpaw, Rube Marquard. Fact is, Hub started right in with eight straight victories in 1937, giving him 24 National League victories in a row before the Brooklyn Dodgers, always his nemesis, clobbered him on Memorial Day, 10-3.

Some baseball historians sought to make Hubbell's record a carryover 24, but the professional himself would have no part of it.

"I happened to remember," he said at the time, "that the Yankees beat me in the World Series."

Which they did indeed, 5-2, in the fourth game of the all-New York Series, a result of a two-run homer by Gehrig in the third inning. Hubbell had defeated the Yankees and Red Ruffing in the '36 Series opener, 6-1. And so great was Hub's ability and reputation that Gehrig would regard his game-winning blow in the fourth game as the greatest of the Iron Horse's fabulous career.

"If," Gehrig said, "we hadn't defeated Hubbell in game No. 4, we probably would have had to face him in a seventh game—and that would have been no fun."

After a 22-8 season in '37 when he again led the National League pitchers in won-and-lost percentage, Hubbell split two more World Series decisions against the Yankees. So King Carl had accounted for two of only four Series defeats the Bronx Bombers absorbed in 36 blue-ribbon battles from 1927 through 1941.

Thereafter, as a result of the arm trouble so freely predicted years before, Hubbell was little better than a .500 pitcher for his last six seasons with the Giants, whose decline coincided closely with the loss of their Meal Ticket.

Hubbell was married in 1930 to his high school sweetheart, the former Lucille Herrington of Shawnee, Okla. They had two sons of whom the old lefthander was extremely proud. Carl, Jr., became a career major in the United States Marines after having graduated from Oklahoma State University. Son Jim, who attended Southeastern Oklahoma at Durant and the University of Oklahoma, went into business in McCook, Neb.

The first Mrs. Hubbell died a quarter-century ago and the Giants' farm director married the former Julia Stanfield, an attractive brunette from Casa Grande, Ariz., where the Giants' farm clubs train. Hub died in 1988 at 85.

Hubbell, his gray-green eyes studying raw young talent the way he scrutinized hitters so successfully from the 60-foot, six-inch distance, still commanded in painful retirement the same kind of respect he kept in the majors from the time he threw that first screwball to Hafey in 1928, until he gained victory No. 250, shortly before he quit in 1943.

The Giants were playing Pittsburgh at Forbes field, and in the sixth inning Elbie Fletcher, the Pirates' first baseman, told slugger Mel Ott, Hubbell's long-time roommate: "If we can't win it, I hope Old Shinbones gets the no-hitter."

The next inning, Fletcher socked a homer for Pittsburgh's only hit and run, depriving Hubbell of a dramatic departing gift and proving, as King Carl certainly knew from the game's competitive trials, that sentiment exists only until a guy steps into the batter's box.

CARL OWEN (KING CARL) HUBBELL
Born June 22, 1903, at Carthage, Mo.
Height 6-1 Weight 175
Threw left and batted righthanded.
Named to Hall of Fame, 1947.

YEAR	CLUB	LEAGUE	G.	IP.	W.	L.	Pct.	H.	R.	ER.	SO.	BB.	ERA.
1923	Cushing	Oklahoma St.					(No records available)						
1924	Cushing	Oklahoma St.					(No records available)						
1924	Ardmore	West Assn.	-	12	1	0	1.000	-	-	-	-	-	-
1924	Oklahoma City	Western	2	15	1	1	.500	19	10	-	3	4	-
1925	Oklahoma City (a)	Western	45	284	17	13	.567	273	172	-	102	108	-
1926	Toronto	Int.	31	93	7	7	.500	90	42	39	45	44	3.77
1927	Decatur	I.I.I.	23	185	14	7	.667	174	61	52	76	48	2.53
1927	Fort Worth	Texas	2	3	0	1	.000	7	-	-	0	3	-
1928	Beaumont	Texas	21	185	12	9	.571	177	69	61	116	45	2.97
1928	New York	Nat.	20	124	10	6	.625	117	49	39	37	21	2.83
1929	New York	Nat.	39	268	18	11	.621	273	128	110	106	67	3.69
1930	New York	Nat.	37	242	17	12	.586	263	120	104	117	58	3.87
1931	New York	Nat.	36	248	14	12	.538	211	88	73	155	67	2.65
1932	New York	Nat.	40	284	18	11	.621	260	96	79	137	40	2.50
1933	New York	Nat.	45	309	23	12	.657	256	69	57	156	47	1.66
1934	New York	Nat.	49	313	21	12	.636	286	100	80	118	37	2.30
1935	New York	Nat.	42	303	23	12	.657	314	125	110	150	49	3.27
1936	New York	Nat.	42	304	26	6	.813	265	81	78	123	57	2.31
1937	New York	Nat.	39	262	22	8	.733	261	108	93	159	55	3.19
1938	New York	Nat.	24	179	13	10	.565	171	70	61	104	33	3.07
1939	New York	Nat.	29	154	11	9	.550	150	60	47	62	24	2.75
1940	New York	Nat.	31	214	11	12	.478	220	102	87	86	59	3.66
1941	New York	Nat.	26	164	11	9	.550	169	73	65	75	53	3.57
1942	New York	Nat.	24	157	11	8	.579	158	75	69	61	34	3.96
1943	New York	Nat.	12	66	4	4	.500	87	36	36	31	24	4.91
Major League Totals			535	3591	253	154	.622	3461	1380	1188	1677	725	2.98

a Obtained by Detroit from Oklahoma City in 1925, and after spring trials in 1926 and 1927 was released outright to Beaumont in 1928.

WORLD SERIES RECORD

YEAR	CLUB	LEAGUE	G.	IP.	W.	L.	Pct.	H.	R.	ER.	SO.	BB.	ERA.
1933	New York	Nat.	2	20	2	0	1.000	13	3	0	15	6	0.00
1936	New York	Nat.	2	16	1	1	.500	15	5	4	10	2	2.25
1937	New York	Nat.	2	14 1/3	1	1	.500	12	10	6	7	4	3.77
World Series Totals			6	50 1/3	4	2	.667	40	18	10	32	12	1.79

BARNEY: Walter Johnson's private nickname, caused by his heavy-footed driving, actually referred to his pitching, too. His fastball was faster than most cars of his time.

WALTER JOHNSON

One night many years ago, when Washington first baseman Joe Judge was trying to hurry Walter Johnson through the hotel lobby to catch a diverting movie after a 1-0 loss in St. Louis, the great pitcher's jinx city, a baseball fan intercepted Johnson.

Judge stood by impatiently for 20 minutes as Johnson talked pleasantly to the man. Afterward, Joe complained,

"Do you have to stop and talk to every fan who approaches you?"

"But, Joe," Walter explained, "that fellow was

from Kansas, too, and he said he knew my sister."

"Your sister!" exclaimed Judge. "I didn't know you had a sister."

Johnson smiled: "I don't," he said, "but I had to be nice to the man."

If ever a story summed up the sweet nature of a man, that would have to be it because Walter did have a sister. Two in fact. But he was just too nice even to complain about the amusing exaggeration that grew out of his patience. Except perhaps in his trying managerial years, especially at Cleveland,

Walter Perry Johnson must have been as kind and as even-dispositioned a man as ever pulled on a big league uniform.

And if you'll look at the cold figures and forget the warm person who compiled them, the sandy-haired, ruddy-complexioned Kansas farm boy must have been as great as any pitcher who ever blew a fastball past a hitter.

Even though he pitched for 21 seasons in Washington, described only partly in jest as first in war, first in peace and last in the American League, Johnson scored the league's victories (416), pitched the most shutouts (113), the most complete games (531) and had the most American League strikeouts (3,508).

Because he was a good hitter on a light-hitting team—he batted a remarkable .433 in 1925 when he was nearly 38 years old—Johnson was tied up regularly in pressure-cooker, low-score contests.

Sixty-four times Walter was involved in 1-0 decisions, including the one the day he politely made small talk with the man who knew the sister he didn't have, and 38 times he walked off a winner.

An exercise completely more pleasant and gratifying than hitting against Johnson, who fired incredibly fast from a sweeping, easy-does-it side-armed delivery, the guessing game among teammates and rivals alike as to just how many he might have won if he had served his time with a more robust team. Washington didn't win a pennant until 1924, when he'd toiled for the Senators for 18 seasons—and the Big Train wasn't the caboose then, either.

Fact is, Johnson, at almost 37, led the American Leauge in victories, won-and-lost percentage and earned-run average as his contribution toward the Holy Grail for which this pure-hearted Sir Galahad of the diamond had warred since 1907. Although this was small talk by comparison with his overpowering peak, a nation rejoiced after his 23-7 season and 2.72 ERA, when the American League's Most Valuable Player salvaged a decisive victory in the final game of the 1924 World Series.

One of the A.L.'s distinguished senior citizens, the Nats' Bucky Harris, who was the Boy Wonder manager of Washington's 1924-25 pennant winners, once observed that he felt the only true box office attractions in the league's history had been Babe Ruth, Ty Cobb, Bob Feller, Ted Williams—and Johnson.

The Big Train, nicknamed by Grantland Rice at a time in the country's history when rails expressed the fastest thing in man's imagination, was a gate draw, all right. Who else, after all, ever prompted an owner of an opposing team to help meet the money necessary to keep him in the league?

Meagerly paid early in his career, Johnson was at his positive peak in 1913 when he followed up a 32-victory season with an astonishing 36-7 record, including winning streaks of 10, 11 and 14 games. He pitched 12 shutouts and five one-hit games, hurled 56 consecutive scoreless innings and posted the lowest earned-run average for a 300-inning pitcher, 1.14, until the St. Louis Cardinals' Bob Gibson shaded it 55 years later with 1.12.

So Johnson, who followed up with 28 victories in 1914, giving him a three-season total of 96 triumphs, felt entitled to more than the $12,000 the Senators were paying him.

When the Chicago club of the new Federal League offered $16,000, plus a $10,000 bonus for signing, Johnson's loyalty to Washington wavered.

Over the protest of manager Clark Griffith, the Washington club president, who never would have qualified for the striped-pants' set of the diplomatic service, sent the Kansan a letter in which the man long since forgotten told the man long since remembered that he hadn't been worth what he'd been paid because he'd won "only" 28 games.

Properly furious, Johnson was ready to defect to the Feds. Only by playing on Walter's deep love for his wife, to whom Washington was home, could the cunning Griffith keep the great pitcher in line—and then only by meeting the new circuit's terms.

Griffith breathed a deep sigh, but just until he

realized that, though it would be one thing to sweet-talk the Senators' board of directors into upping the ante to $16,000, there was no way he could pry from them the necessary $10,000 bonus.

Griff's daring gamble seemed desperate when the man he'd helped form the American League—Ban Johnson—flatly refused to contribute league funds. The only hope left was another fellow conspirator in the birth of the American League, Charles Comiskey, who owned the Chicago club.

The Old Roman of Chicago told the Old Fox in Washington to go whistle Dixie until Griffith posed this question:

"How, Commy, would you like to see Walter Johnson pitching for the Chicago Feds on the North Side next season and drawing all those fans away from the White Sox park?"

Griffith got Comiskey's check, cashed it and turned the money over to Johnson, who, as related by Shirley Povich in his informal history of the baseball Senators, promptly paid a $10,000 debt of a brother who just had been swindled by a worthless partner in a new garage business.

To have taken Johnson out of Washington would have been to lose the best part of an opening-day custom which has enriched baseball tradition through the first century of professional play.

Back in 1910, William Howard Taft, 26th president of the United States and a corpulent baseball fan from Cincinnati, was invited by Griffith to throw out the first ball for Washington's opening game with Philadelphia. Appropriately, tall, long-armed Johnson caught the ball and started to take it to the mound, where he intended to throw one pitch and then ask for a new one.

A modest, humble man himself, the corn-fed Kansan had a sense of the historic, but so did the highly literate umpire, Billy Evans, who gave him another ball so that the pitcher could keep the one from the President.

With Taft watching, Johnson promptly shut out the Athletics, 3-0, allowing only one hit, a wind-blown double by Frank (Home Run) Baker. At the bashful Johnson's request, a friend took the ball to the White House for the President's signature.

Taft did more than sign it. "To Walter Johnson," he wrote, "with the hope that he may continue as formidably as in yesterday's game. William H. Taft."

Thirteen times thereafter, Johnson pitched opening-day games for Washington, winning eight more and winding up with autographed baseballs thrown by Woodrow Wilson, Warren G. Harding, Calvin Coolidge and Herbert Hoover.

A sixth, bearing the name of Theodore Roosevelt, who preceded Taft in office, was added to the collection, which Johnson kept carefully in a box specifically designed for them, with a brass plate explaining their significance.

When Johnson was dying of a brain tumor in December 1946, shortly after his 59th birthday, his old boss and good friend, Clark Griffith, would visit him in the hospital and reminisce.

Griff thought Walter's greatest performance had been 22 scoreless innings Johnson hurled against the mighty Philadelphia Athletics on two consecutive days in 1912, but the Big Train held out sentimentally for his final opening-day appearance.

In 1926, at an advanced baseball age, Johnson went 15 innings to beat Philadelphia's Eddie Rommel, 1-0. And if, in spring training of 1927, he hadn't suffered the broken leg which ended his career just before he reached 40, the Big Train undoubtedly would have been on hand for more openers. His right arm was that resilient and remarkable.

Never more so, however, than back in 1908, his second season in the majors, when the gangling 20-year-old kid with the plow-jockey gait shut out the Highlanders, as the Yankees then were known, three times in a four-day series at New York.

Exactly what either manager Joe Cantillon or Johnson was trying to prove that September is fuzzy in research, but it's a fact that Walter shut out the

Highlanders on five hits Friday, 3-0, on three hits Saturday, 6-0, and on two hits in the first game of a Monday doubleheader, 4-0.

The only reason he hadn't pitched Sunday was because of a Sabbath blue law that prohibited baseball in New York at the time. For that kind of extreme durability and precision pitching, Washington then was paying Johnson the princely sum of $2,700.

Salary difficulties once prevented an opening-day assignment for Johnson, who was sidelined until June in 1908 because of mastoid surgery. He also missed his opening turn in '09 because of a heavy cold.

In 1911, after winning 25 games, Walter sought a pay increase from $4,500 to $9,000. The club countered with $6,500 and, two days after the season opened, they compromised at $7,000.

Thereafter, opening-day and Johnson pitching for Washington were happy harbingers of a new season. And, as a result of a gift from his son, Eddie Johnson, the Big Train's collection of presidential signatures now is on display in the baseball Hall of Fame at Cooperstown, N. Y., where the great pitcher was one of the first five named in 1936 and inducted in '39.

Eddie Johnson, second of Walter's five children, shared his father's deep-seated love of the land. A graduate of University of Maryland and, unlike his older brother, Walter, Jr., Eddie never aspired to a baseball career.

He lived on a farm of approximately 200 acres at Comus, Md. His children attended at Bethesda the Walter Johnson High School, which was named for their famous grandfather.

Ever hear of a high school named for an athletic figure?

Walter Johnson was an unusual man, born at Humboldt, Kan., on November 6, 1887, to Frank Edwin and Minnie Johnson, farm folks whose forebears had gone west with the wagon trains from Pennsylvania. Fabulous tales of oil fields lured the poor farmers to Olinda, Calif., in 1901.

They struck no oil, but managed a living by providing horse and mule teams to oilmen who wanted supplies hauled to their fields.

At 14, Walter had the broad shoulders of his father and he was, incongruously, the strong-armed catcher of the Oil Field Juniors. Modestly, he allowed as how he could throw harder than the pitcher, but, alas, the kids couldn't find anyone good enough to catch him.

In 1906, at 16, Johnson turned professional, but he wasn't ready for Tacoma, Wash., in the Northwestern League. He was pitching and digging post holes for the Weiser (Idaho) Telephone Co. in '07 when a traveling liquor salesman badgered Washington manager Joe Cantillon with letters and telegrams about the phenom he'd seen pitching.

When catcher Cliff Blankenship became injured, Cantillon dispatched him to sign an outfielder at Wichita named Clyde Milan and to take a look at that big Swede the traveling salesman was pestering them about.

Blankenship saw Johnson's flame-thrower in a 12-inning game, lost on errors, 1-0. The catcher turned scout flashed a $100 bill as a bonus and offered $350 a month for the rest of the season if Johnson would join Washington.

The 19-year-old kid inquired about traveling expenses to Washington and, before his father would sign an improvised contract on a piece of brown wrapping paper the next day, there was one more question. What about a return train trip if the boy failed?

Walter Johnson never would have returned home, if he hadn't cared to, but, strangely, Washington almost missed the greatest player in the rather drab history of a perennial also-ran.

Not only was a Seattle scout en route to sign Johnson at the very moment Blankenship bundled him on the train for Washington, but manager Fred Clarke and Pittsburgh already had missed a chance because, failing to act on a tip, they had passed up a look-see that previous spring.

For $9, the price of a railroad ticket to Hot Springs, Ark., where they were training, the Pirates had missed a chance to team Johnson with another all-time great, Honus Wagner, on a ball club that won three straight pennants and which, with the Big Train, undoubtedly would have won many more.

What Washington saw was a sight to compare with the Japanese cherry blossoms in spring. Shirley Povich put it so well:

"Here, they quickly realized, was everybody's country cousin, a big, handsome, modest hick. Even the rube in him, that was brought into bolder relief by the high-button shoes and celluloid collar that were high fashion in Idaho, couldn't obscure the rare nobility of his facial features.

"Sandy hair with a reddish tint bristled generously, if somewhat wildly, atop his strong-looking face. He knew little of the pomades that were advertised. The eyes were blue, naturally. The jaw a good one, firm and square cut, if on the shallow side.

"The nose, a straight one that was to be a model for laterday plastic surgeons. If there was a gimmick to the strength of the Johnson countenance—well, it registered the blush more readily than the smile…"

The big kid brought the ball up straight in front of his face, wheeled in a sweeping motion so that the ball was visible on the far side of his body as he pivoted, and then he fired in a sweeping side-armed motion.

"They kept the mound so flat for him at Washington," cracked Waite Hoyt, a more recent Hall of Fame choice, "that pitching in Griffith Stadium was like hurling out of a hole."

Johnson made his big league debut in August 1907, against, of all teams, the pennant-bound Tigers. Sam Crawford homered for Detroit, but Walter led until the eighth inning when Ty Cobb beat out his second bunt, raced to third on another bunt and then scored the leading run.

Walter went out for a pinch-hitter then and the Senators lost the game, 3-2.

But Cobb would remember that game and the amazing first impression of a pitcher who relied almost exclusively on his fastball for years and never did develop more than a fair curve, which he promptly telegraphed.

Cobb took advantage of good nature, he would explain, by crowding the plate so that the well-mannered Johnson would pitch away from him, but Clark Griffith remembered that the Big Train frequently had struck out the greatest hitter.

And Nick Altrock, a fine old pitcher who became Al Schacht's partner in baseline-coaching comedy, loved to recount a bit of Johnson's derring-do in 1909.

"Detroit filled the bases in the ninth inning on two boots and a walk," Altrock would say, "and had three great lefthanded hitters coming up—Ty Cobb, Sam Crawford and Bobby Veach. Barney struck 'em out on nine pitches."

Barney was the nickname used by the Senators to liken Johnson's resemblance to the most famous early racing-car speedster, Barney Oldfield. Not because of the hummer Walter threw, but because he had a heavy foot on the accelerator himself.

He didn't smoke, he didn't drink, he didn't swear and, until later years, he didn't play cards. It must have surprised his teammates when the big, bashful guy finally found romance.

In 1913, as he warmed up one day near the field boxes at Griffith Stadium, a Nevada congressman introduced himself and, to the delight of the pitcher who had admired her from afar, his tall, stately, blonde daughter, Hazel Lee Roberts.

Miss Roberts liked baseball and Walter's second love, hunting.

She soon became his first love and they were married in June 1914. The marriage produced three sons and then two daughters.

Johnson pitched so many low-hit games, including five one-hitters in 1913, that a guy could lose count. But his only no-hitter came the only season in which he had a sore arm, 1920, and he'd arrived at the ballpark in Boston just an hour before game-time. He'd been detained by the illness of his five-year-old son, Walter, Jr.

If young Bucky Harris hadn't kicked a groundball by Harry Hooper, the no-hitter would have been a perfect game.

"Goodness gracious, Bucky, forget it," Johnson said, but Harris didn't.

When Manager Harris was criticized by American League President Ban Johnson for going all the way with Walter in the circus-sawdust, rain-soaked atmosphere of the seventh game of the 1925 World Series, won by Pittsburgh, 9-7, Bucky snapped:

"No man is going to tell me that when I need a pitcher in a pinch, Walter Johnson isn't the man for me. I'll go down the line with him until they carry either of us off the field."

They carried Johnson off in spring training in 1927, a result of a line drive off the right leg by roommate Joe Judge. The broken leg, following a 15-16 year, preceded another subpar season, 5-6.

And when Walter lost 35 pounds in the spring of 1928, a victim of a severe case of influenza, Clark Griffith arranged for him to become manager at Newark.

A year later, Johnson replaced Harris as manager at Washington. His four seasons as skipper of the Senators were not happy ones. He didn't win and he lost the stoical patience he had shown pitching for a poor club.

Aging fellow stars, Judge and Sam Rice, even found him surly. At Cleveland, where he finally wound up managing in 1933, his critics of that time tabbed him as cold, aloof and distant.

One of the reasons those several seasons as a field foreman weren't more successful, or at least more tolerable, could have been the acute loss Johnson felt in 1930 when his 36-year-old wife died, leaving him with their five children ranging from 15 years down to five.

In 1936, he reenacted George Washington's legendary accomplishment of hurling a silver dollar across the Rappahannock River at Fredericksburg,

Va. And in World War II he put on his uniform at Yankee Stadium, at age 54, to pitch in batting practice for another bright superstar, Babe Ruth, in a benefit that sold considerable war bonds to a capacity crowd of 70,000.

By then he was farming his Maryland acres, after earlier having consented to nomination as a Republican for a place on the three-man board of county commissioners. He put in a year as the Senators' play-by-play radio announcer and reluctantly ran for Congress and lost a close race in the Sixth Maryland District in 1940.

Farmer Johnson was happiest in those all-too-few last years on his 552 Maryland acres near Washington. He raised purebred cattle and loved fox hunting.

To be more precise, Walter didn't ride to the hounds. It was more of a chase. He had 36 Walker foxhounds, an English breed, and would be out with them three and four nights a week.

"He really loved dogs," son Eddie recalled. "He'd open the bedroom window and listen to the hounds baying as he lay there, and he could tell you which hound was leading, which was second, and so on."

Lying there before and, perhaps, after the brain tumor that paralyzed him in April 1946, and then took his life in December, Walter Perry Johnson might have replayed, too, a few moments of a serene, wholesome life and of a great career that probably could have been even more fabulous if he'd actually not been afraid of hitting a batter.

Only once did he throw at a hitter. Goaded by teammates, he fired one up and in on Home Run Baker. When the Philadelphia third baseman dropped, just in time, Johnson turned pale, relieved that in giving in momentarily to impulse, he had been spared a painful repentance.

Ray Chapman, who would die one day (1920) when he couldn't avoid one of submarine righthander Carl Mays' deliveries, watched one of Johnson's sizzling fast ones hiss over the plate in 1915.

"Strike two!" called plate umpire Billy Evans.

Chapman, the crouching Cleveland shortstop, suddenly threw down his bat and headed toward the bench.

"That's only strike two!" yelled Evans.

Chapman, turning, retorted, "I know it. You can have the next one. It won't do me any good."

When Ty Cobb was asked once to comment on life's most embarrassing moments, the fearless, peerless Georgia Peach said a lot with a little:

"Facing Walter Johnson on any dark day in Washington."

WALTER PERRY (BARNEY) JOHNSON
Born November 6, 1887, at Humboldt, Kan.
Died December 10, 1993, at Washington, D.C.
Height 6-1 Weight 200
Threw and batted righthanded.
Named to Hall of Fame, 1936.

YEAR	CLUB	LEAGUE	G.	IP.	W.	L.	Pct.	ShO.	H..	R.	ER.	SO.	BB.	ERA.
1907	Washington	Amer.	14	111	5	9	.357	2	100	35	-	70	16	-
1908	Washington	Amer.	36	257	14	14	.500	6	196	75	-	160	52	-
1909	Washington	Amer.	40	297	13	25	.342	4	247	112	-	164	84	-
1910	Washington	Amer.	45	374	25	17	.595	8	262	92	-	313	76	-
1911	Washington	Amer.	40	322	25	13	.658	6	292	119	-	207	70	-
1912	Washington	Amer.	50	368	32	12	.727	7	259	89	-	303	76	-
1913	Washington	Amer.	48	346	36	7	.837	12	232	56	44	243	38	1.14
1914	Washington	Amer.	51	372	28	18	.609	10	287	88	71	225	74	1.72
1915	Washington	Amer.	47	337	27	13	.675	8	258	83	58	203	56	1.55
1916	Washington	Amer.	48	371	25	20	.556	3	290	105	78	228	82	1.89
1917	Washington	Amer.	47	328	23	16	.590	8	259	105	83	188	67	2.28
1918	Washington	Amer.	39	325	23	13	.639	8	241	71	46	162	70	1.27
1919	Washington	Amer.	39	290	20	14	.588	7	235	73	48	147	51	1.49
1920	Washington	Amer.	21	144	8	10	.444	4	135	68	50	78	27	3.13
1921	Washington	Amer.	35	264	17	14	.548	1	265	122	103	143	92	3.51
1922	Washington	Amer.	41	280	15	16	.484	4	283	115	93	105	99	2.99
1923	Washington	Amer.	42	261	17	12	.586	3	263	112	101	130	69	3.48
1924	Washington	Amer.	38	278	23	7	.767	6	233	97	84	158	77	2.72
1925	Washington	Amer.	30	229	20	7	.741	3	211	95	78	108	78	3.07
1926	Washington	Amer.	33	262	15	16	.484	2	259	120	105	125	73	3.61
1927	Washington	Amer.	18	108	5	6	.455	1	113	70	61	48	26	5.08
1928	Newark	Int.	1	0	0	0	.000	0	0	0	0	0	1	0.00
Major League Totals			802	5924	416	279	.599	113	4920	1902	1103	3508	1353	-

WORLD SERIES RECORD

YEAR	CLUB	LEAGUE	G.	IP.	W.	L.	Pct.	H.	R.	ER.	SO.	BB.	ERA.
1924	Washington	Amer.	3	24	1	2	.333	30	10	6	20	11	2.25
1925	Washington	Amer.	3	26	2	1	.667	26	10	6	15	4	2.08
World Series Totals			6	50	3	3	.500	56	20	12	35	15	2.16

250

ALL-AROUND AL: Ability to do it all made Detroit's Al Kaline second only to Mickey Mantle as the best outfielder of his time.

AL KALINE

The New York Yankees, kings of baseball under Casey Stengel, had two men on, two out in the ninth inning, trailing by two runs. A pinstriped, bull-necked Bronx Bomber leaned into a pitch, and in the pressbox the voice of the Yankees, Mel Allen, went into a southern-fried paroxysm of joy.

Shrilly, melliflous Mel screamed, "The Yankees win, 5-to-4…they win, 5-to-4."

And down in the visitors' clubhouse at cavernous Yankee Stadium, Detroit's equipment manager angrily turned off the radio and waited for the conservatively cut kids in gray-and-blue to mope in from the playing field, late and heads abending low.

But, quickly, they appeared, yelling and laughing. That "home run" Allen had called too quickly had suddenly become merely a long, game-ending out, though spectacular. The Tigers' right fielder, Al Kaline, had raced to the auxiliary scoreboard in front of the low field-girdling wall at the Stadium and, bracing him against the scoreboard with his bare hand, he had leaped and backhanded the ball with his glove, clutching it in collision with the barrier.

"Mr. Colleen," as Stengel used to pronounce respectfully but inaccurately the surname properly phoneticized "Kay-line," merely had done it again. He proved that as an all-around athlete he was so good that he wouldn't have had to become the 10th man ever to achieve 3,000 hits to flash Hall of Fame credentials.

Why, he was barely more than a babe out of Baltimore, signed in 1953 for a bonus expected to pin him indefinitely to the Detroit bench, when he became a full-fledged regular at only 19 years old in his second season in the majors. And it was the beginning when his glove outstripped his bat that the moon-faced, bland, seldom-smiling boy showed that there's still room in the man's version of the game for defense.

One day at almost the outset, Kaline outdid...well, even himself against the Chicago White Sox. First, he threw out Freddie Marsh, trying to score from second on a single. Next, he flagged down Minnie Minoso, trying to stretch a single into a double. Finally, he gunned down Chico Carrasquel in an attempt to go from first to third on a single.

Of such accomplishments are legends born, and Kaline was legendary almost too soon in a town that had known such indisputable class as Ty Cobb and Charley Gehringer, forgetting other top talent in between. From the time Al hit .340 in 1955 to become, at 20, the youngest batting champion in history, fanatical Detroit, of which there is none whicher, expected more than even that graceful guy with the most famous No. 6, other than Stan Musial's, could deliver.

Like Musial at St. Louis, Kaline at Detroit suffered just a bit from lack of regular exposure to the Big Apple, but, again, like Stan the Man, Al the Antelope saved his greatest derring-do for New York, obviously inspired by the tradition of that oddly shaped Stadium and the number and importance of the metropolitan press and other men of media.

So even though he wound up with 22 seasons in Detroit, with a street named for him, with his two sons given college scholarships as part of a whopping "day" he insisted be devoted more to the less fortunate, Kaline heard more boos than a team man of his talent and A-1 effort ever should have heard. Eventually, moody at the outset and at times almost curt when he really was more bashful, Al understood Tigertown as it did him.

"Because of my early success at bat, they expected more of me," said Kaline, the first batter ever to achieve 3,000 hits with a career average (.297) below .300, "but they didn't realize that hitting hadn't come that easy for me. The other parts of the game, yes, but not hitting."

H'mm, try to tell that to victims of two home runs in an inning and three in a game and to the St. Louis Cardinals, victimized by his robust .379 average in 1968, the one and only World Series in which he played. With Kaline delivering the key base hit in the critical fifth game when Detroit faced elimination, the Tigers bounced back behind Mickey Lolich's inspirational pitch for a seven-game upset.

To Kaline, the long-awaited Series represented a highlight above and beyond that batting championship 13 years earlier. But it did not supersede hit No. 3,000, seven before he called it quits after the 1974 season, because, nearly 40, ONLY Kaline knew how often he had played hurt to (1) help the club first and (2) aid Al quite incidentally.

It wasn't until he was well along in a career in which he never played a full schedule and only 10 times got into more than 140 games, that Kaline zeroed in to become the first American Leaguer to reach 3,000 hits since Tris Speaker and Eddie Collins got there the same season, 1925.

Oddly, at the end, the 6-2, 184-pound veteran was almost obsessed to become the only Detroit player other than immortal Cobb to reach 3,000. And to get there, just as strangely, the once-magnificent defensive player needed the assistance of the American League's new designated-hitter rule because, frankly, as both he and manager Ralph Houk put it, Kaline no longer was a good outfielder, much less a Kaline, which meant simply great.

He'd played a reasonably shallow right field and played the hitters extremely well, coupling his knowledge and judgment with a quick jump on the ball, speed and the courage to dive and to challenge walls. And he threw hard and accurately.

One manager, his personal favorite, Bob Scheffing, labeled him "better all-around than (Willie) Mays or (Mickey) Mantle" and another, Charley Dressen, for whom Kaline had less personal regard and yet from whom he said he learned the most, termed Al as "overall more valuable than Jackie Robinson or Henry Aaron."

Whether both Scheffing and Dressen were completely candid or merely trying to help build not only Kaline's self-confidence but also to establish public recognition of a relatively unrecognized superstar, is one for the psychiatrist's couch.

Suffice, of the master players mentioned, only Mantle, who played with legs bric-a-brac from boyhood osteomyelitis, knew anywhere the suffering Kaline experienced from childhood in that brown-front row-house neighborhood with three identifying smoke stacks in south Baltimore.

There, at only eight years old, he was diagnosed as having osteo, too—a persistent bone disease that prompted doctors to remove two inches of bone out of his left foot, leaving jagged scars and permanent deformity.

If you saw Kaline, you'll remember now that, though he ran extremely well until late in his career, his left foot curled ever so slightly over and in—even when he was in the batter's box—and after a long afternoon or night, his trace of a limp became more noticeable.

Combine that basic handicap with other injuries and their aftermath—a broken cheekbone, a fractured right hand, a broken right arm and a cracked collarbone suffered, characteristically, when diving for the final out to preserve a 2-1 victory over the Yankees—and you begin to understand (1) the intensity with which Kaline played, (2) his inability to be in there EVERY day and (3) ultimately, the desire to prove he WAS durable and consistent.

Only the durable AND the consistent get 3,000 hits.

Kaline merited the batting-order break by which the Rembrandt of outfielders put down his pallette...er, glove in 1974 and, as a result, played—or, rather, batted—in the most games, 147, since 1961. That year the Tigers almost won a pennant under Scheffing as Kaline hit .324, one of his nine .300-plus seasons.

In 1974, 13 years later, manager Houk, the tough-hewn major of Rangers in World War II, sprayed tobacco in the spring-training dugout at Lakeland, Fla., as he explained that, yes, he expected Kaline to play more often, but not in the outfield.

"Let's face it," said Houk, who always does. "Al has lost something afield and on the bases. But he's still one of the most dangerous clutch hitters I ever saw. He won't drive in runs in clusters, but he'll drive in the big ones, the ones in close, low-score games. And he'll get the big, two-out hits.

"He's a great competitor and he'd go all-out. At his age he's more subject to injury if he played regularly. This fella was, without doubt, an underrated star, and I guess the only reason is that he wasn't a home run hitter."

"Or," said the Major, grinning around that chaw in his cheek, "when he hit 'em, he hit 'em only in the lower deck, not the upper deck."

Seriously, though, Houk insisted, "I want that bat in the lineup more often than Detroit has had it lately..."

Hence, the role as the 10th regular, a seemingly weird one for one of the best-ever outfielders, but one that worked. Kaline got almost as many hits, 194, as he had the two previous seasons combined and, in fact, hit safely more often than in any season since 1954. So it came to pass that No. 6 stepped up there in the fourth inning of the September 24 game at Baltimore's Memorial Stadium where his mother and father were in the stands.

His left knee, injured in a pickup basketball game back in Detroit the previous winter, was heavily taped, but he still hobbled. The right leg, which he'd grab with reflex motion in pain whenever he ran hard, was wrapped to protect a pulled hamstring. But he'd hit .262 in 147 games and homered 13 times and, sure, he could remember that first time up in the majors 22 years earlier.

He'd weighed only 155 pounds then and he was really no physical match for big league pitching, but Fred Hutchinson, the gruff-but-kind man's man who had been a schoolboy phenom himself, had told him to relax and to sit next to the manager. Hutch could explain the whys and hows of things that happened. And then suddenly Al had been sent up to pinch-hit in a game lost and he flied softly to center field.

But now time was running out and, though he would have preferred to save the Big One for Detroit, Manager Houk and general manager Jimmy Campbell had urged him to stay in the lineup because, as Musial once had said when he got to 3,000 with 43 hits in 22 games at the start of one (1958) season, a guy never knew when he might get hit in the can by a cab.

The Baltimore pitcher was lefthander Dave McNally, a cutie who had won 20 games regularly. Before the game prophetically, McNally had told the guys on the Orioles' bench, "He'll get it off me. Hell, he's had 500 others. So why not No. 3,000?"

Mac's first pitch in the fourth was a fastball and Kaline swung with that sweet swing and lined it to the opposite field, just inside the right-field line, and, heck, he said to himself, it's going foul. But he'd hit it hard, and the ball bounded on the grass two feet inside the right-field chalk—fair.

Kaline pulled into second base with a double. "I said a prayer," he said, happily afterward, "a prayer of thanks."

Provocatively, Houk would comment afterward,

"To me, getting 3,000 hits is better than Hank Aaron's 715th home run. You've got to realize that Kaline was competing against every hitter who ever played the game for nearly 100 years. Aaron was competing against the big power hitters, of whom there haven't been really many, and actually against only one—the Babe."

As Houk put it, Kaline had been no Punch-and-Judy hitter, getting more than 20 home runs nine times, topped with 29 in 1962, he'd hit two in the '68 World Series, one in the 1972 championship series and two more in All-Star Games. But his American League regular-season total stood at 399 when the Tigers closed out the '74 season and Kaline's career on October 2, 1974.

The crowd of 4,671 was sparse, but noisy and when Kaline went hitless in two trips and then left the lineup, hitless with 3,007 for his career, the fans booed. They booed because they wouldn't get to see Al round out the HR total with an even 400.

"I was just punching the ball up there," confessed an ailing Kaline. "There was no way I could hit one out of there. I told Ralph (Houk) I couldn't swing and to take me out of the game.

"There was no sense in staying in there. I'm glad it's over. I think I've played as long as I can and I'm going out on a good note, getting 3,000 hits. You can't go out much better."

No, not with the class of the unprepossessing star who became a $100,000 ballplayer and turned from the playing field to the broadcast booth, where he teams with George Kell, former standout third baseman, to go do color analysis on televised Tiger road games. In addition, as for years, he makes goodwill appearances.

Al and his lovely high-school sweetheart, the former Louise Hamilton, live in Bloomfield Hills, one of Detroit's nicest suburbs, and they have two good-looking spectacled sons, Mark who was 17 when Kaline hung up his famous "6," and Mike, then 12. They were old enough to appreciate the old man.

Later, Mike would play high school hockey and baseball and Mark would major in communications at Michigan State, moonlighting as a student on a Lansing-Jackson television station on which Joe Garagiola's younger son, Notre Dame graduate Steve, was sports director.

At the time Kaline was inducted into the Michigan sports Hall of Fame in 1978, the required minimum three-year wait of his retirement and two years before he became eligible for the baseball Hall of Fame, the former ballplayer quipped in prophecy:

"I can see Mark doing TV for a station Mike will own."

The bow to the active cerebrum of his younger son came from a man who, himself, had only a high school education in which studies were second fiddle to an awesome baseball schedule cram-course arranged by Al's father and his uncles. The Kalines were—in a word—baseball batty.

Grandpa Philip caught semi-pro ball. So did two of the boy's uncles and his father, Nicholas, a broommaker. So Albert William Kaline, born of German-Irish extraction in that unpretentious south Baltimore house in December 1934, had two older sisters and a burning ambition. Yeah, a burning ambition to play ball and, as his father found out when he hunkered down to catch him, a burning fastball.

Dad Kaline showed the boy a variety of pitches and Al, at 12, was 10-and-0 with a neighborhood team. About that time the gangling kid with the long arms flung a baseball 173 feet 6 inches at a picnic. The picnicking judges thought—oops!—they'd miscalculated in their contest measurements. So Albert Kaline did it again.

The man who deserves credit for putting Kaline where he could do the most good was Bill Anderson, baseball coach at Baltimore's Southern High School. He put the skinny, 135-pound, power-armed freshman in the outfield.

Kaline came so fast, hitting .333, .418, .469 and .488 in his high school seasons, that scouts flocked around the devout young Methodist like vultures around a cadaver, just waiting for him to graduate.

Because Baltimore had such a good youth baseball program and the senior Kalines were so eager to see Al play for fun and a possible future, he'd often change uniforms in an automobile that whisked him from one game to another. He'd play four a day at times and as many as 100 a summer, stealing bases and enemy base hits when he wasn't banging out his own.

In Kaline's judgment, only the Philadelphia Phillies, St. Louis Cardinals and Detroit Tigers stayed in the bonus running when the day of decision neared, and Al leaned to Detroit because, thanks to the persistent face-guarding of scout Ed Katalinas, the Tigers had shown the most consistent interest.

"And," said Kaline later, "I thought I might get a chance to play oftener with them."

Smart boy. He got a $15,000 bonus, $15,000 salary in 1953, freezing him to the Detroit roster for presumably two years of inactivity, but Manager Hutchinson managed to get him into 30 games for 28 times at bat and a .250 average in '53, including his first big league home run.

Growing up fast, Kaline paid off the mortgage on his parents' home and paid for an operation to save his mother's failing eyesight. He was a tall, lean-muscled, crew-cut kid and Hutch was impressed at once by his outfielding, which meant that the boy, if used, would be no liability defensively.

So when Steve Souchock, the regular right fielder, broke his right wrist in the Cuban winter league and Kaline looked good in spring training, Hutchinson boldly put the 19-year-old kid in right field to open the 1954 season, a heady experience which neither panicked the poised lad nor inflated his $6\frac{7}{8}$" hat size. He hit .276.

Sufficiently entrenched, Kaline mustered up the courage to ask for the hand of Louise, the girl whose lunch he'd help eat at high school.

The blue-eyed queen of the campus was a good

cook as well as a pretty one, and Al came to camp in 1955 at 175 pounds.

En route to the greatest season of his career at only 20, the season he hit .340, the kid just two years out of high school started the All-Star Game, the first 16 in which he played and batted .324.

Others might groan about wishin' they were goin' fishin', but, to Kaline, denied World Series opportunities, the All-Star Game glittered. So did Al, chafing at times over questions about his inability to match 1955 or even '56 when, batting .314, he hit 27 homers for the second straight year and drove in a career high of 128 homers.

More brisk than brusque, retiring around strangers, Al didn't make the best interview for many reporters and others eager to stick a notebook or microphone in front of those blue eyes that could lose patience. But if you didn't ask him silly questions, you didn't get silly answers.

After all, Al Kaline wasn't the kind of guy who wore his aches and pains on the sleeve of that conservative Detroit uniform he wore with such dignity or on those tight lips, either. He didn't tell, for instance, that only two of his toes on the left foot touched the ground because when doctors operated on him as a boy, they left him with sharply swept-back toes.

So only if you noticed that when he ran, he did so with a special technique—on the heel and toes of his right foot and on the side of his left foot—would the go-get-'em outfielder acknowledge discomfort.

"It's like," he put it well, "a toothache in the foot."

But if he knew and trusted you, he'd explain changes he had seen in games. That is, the sophisticated relief pitching, for example, which made hitting more difficult because a batter didn't get four chances to look at the same delivery off a starter who tired and stayed on.

He'd talk, too, about pitchers and players he'd faced or watched.

"I've been very impressed with Frank Robinson

as a player and leader," he said that last spring when he was determined to get No. 3,000 or, if necessary, gut out another season, too.

"I was so glad Roberto Clemente got there because he was the best ballplayer in either league the last three years or so he played.

"I believe Bob Lemon was overall the toughest pitcher I faced, but that entire Cleveland staff of 1954 when they won 111 games—Mike Garcia, Early Wynn and the rest—were great and Bob Feller was even past his peak. The Yankees had such great ones, like Whitey Ford and Vic Raschi, and when Nolan Ryan gets his breaking ball over, you think you're looking at a righthanded Sandy Koufax."

Kaline paused. "The best, though," he said, "was probably Bob Gibson in the World Series."

THE World Series, the one and only in the double decades of Detroit's joy through most of the unproductive years. In 1967 when the Tigers narrowly missed in a close race, Kaline battled Boston's Carl Yastrzemski for the batting title before falling back to .308.

In 1968, however, with Denny McLain strutting to a spectacular 31-game season, Mayo Smith's Tigers came through at a time critical to Detroit's civic safety. With an unpopular war in Vietnam and national unrest reflecting itself in race riots and other disorders, Detroit had a relatively safe and sound hot summer as one and all—black and white, young and old—rallied around the baseball favorites.

However, the No. 1 Tiger, Kaline, was limited to 102 games by injuries. He played some first base as well as the outfield and, to show his team spirit, he'd even hurry out to warm up pitchers between innings. But his batting average was only .287 and his 10 home runs and 53 RBIs were the fewest since...well, would you believe that first full season, 14 years earlier?

Still, though Manager Smith's outfield of Willie Horton, Mickey Stanley and Jim Northrup was doing better than all right, Smith knew he wanted

Kaline in the World Series. The way Mayo saw it, Al deserved it and, additionally, the former Phillies' and Reds' field foreman just knew that the thoroughbred would react to the challenge.

So for the Series, daringly, Smith moved Stanley in from center field to shortstop, not to find Livingstone, but to find a place for Kaline, the right field that was the best of the 16-season veteran's positions.

Sentimentally, nationally as well as in Detroit, Albert William Kaline, long overshadowed by players who were his peers at best, not his betters, delivered dramatically and decisively. His 11 hits for .379 were good for 19 bases and he drove in eight runs and scored six.

Beaming afterward, the glow of victory blended with the glow of the glass that cheers, Mayo Smith told an old friend:

"Damn, I'm happy—happy for everyone from the clubowner on down—but especially for No. 6. He's so smart, a manager's dream as a team player who manages himself and makes no mistakes. He's great in the clutch—I just knew he'd come through—and he's the best player, all-around, I ever had."

Just about the only thing Al Kaline didn't do, as Ralph Houk said that time with both tongue and tobacco in cheek, was to hit 'em in the upper deck, not the lower. But don't tell Mel Allen that when he shrieked, "Yankees win, 5-to-4," that Kaline himself didn't leap into the upper deck at the Stadium for that game-saving catch.

ALBERT WILLIAM (AL) KALINE
Born December 18, 1934, at Baltimore, Md.
Height 6-2 Weight 184
Threw and batted righthanded.
Named to Hall of Fame, 1980.

YEAR	CLUB	LEAGUE	POS.	G.	AB.	R.	H.	2B.	3B.	HR.	RBI.	B.A.	PO.	A.	E.	F.A.
1953	Detroit	Amer.	OF	30	28	9	7	0	0	1	2	.250	11	1	0	1.000
1954	Detroit	Amer.	OF	138	504	42	139	18	3	4	43	.276	283	16	9	.971
1955	Detroit	Amer.	OF	152	588	121	200	24	8	27	102	.340	306	14	7	.979
1956	Detroit	Amer.	OF	153	617	96	194	32	10	27	128	.314	343	18	6	.984
1957	Detroit	Amer.	OF	149	577	83	170	29	4	23	90	.295	319	13	5	.985
1958	Detroit	Amer.	OF	146	543	84	170	34	7	16	85	.313	316	23	2	.994
1959	Detroit	Amer.	OF	136	511	86	167	19	2	27	94	.327	364	4	4	.989
1960	Detroit	Amer.	OF	147	551	77	153	29	4	15	68	.278	367	5	5	.987
1961	Detroit	Amer.	OF-3B	153	586	116	190	41	7	19	82	.324	379	10	4	.990
1962	Detroit	Amer.	OF	100	398	78	121	16	6	29	94	.304	225	8	4	.983
1963	Detroit	Amer.	OF	145	551	89	172	24	3	27	101	.312	257	5	2	.992
1964	Detroit	Amer.	OF	146	525	77	154	31	5	17	68	.293	278	6	3	.990
1965	Detroit	Amer.	OF-3B	125	399	72	112	18	2	18	72	.281	195	3	3	.985
1966	Detroit	Amer.	OF	142	479	85	138	29	1	29	88	.288	279	7	2	.993
1967	Detroit	Amer.	OF	131	458	94	141	28	2	25	78	.308	217	14	4	.983
1968	Detroit	Amer.	OF-1B	102	327	49	94	14	1	10	53	.287	283	14	7	.977
1969	Detroit	Amer.	OF-1B	131	456	74	124	17	0	21	69	.272	257	11	7	.975
1970	Detroit	Amer.	OF-1B	131	467	64	130	24	4	16	71	.278	530	34	6	.989
1971	Detroit	Amer.	OF-1B	133	405	69	119	19	2	15	54	.294	234	7	0	1.000
1972	Detroit	Amer.	OF-1B	106	278	46	87	11	2	10	32	.313	148	9	1	.994
1973	Detroit	Amer.	OF-1B	91	310	40	79	13	0	10	45	.255	347	13	1	.997
1974	Detroit	Amer.	DH	147	558	71	146	28	2	13	64	.262	0	0	0	.000
Major League Totals - 22 years				2834	10116	1622	3007	498	75	399	1583	.297	5938	235	82	.987

CHAMPIONSHIP SERIES RECORD

YEAR	CLUB	LEAGUE	POS.	G.	AB.	R.	H.	2B.	3B.	HR.	SB.	B.A.	PO.	A.	E.	F.A.
1972	Detroit	Amer.	OF	5	19	3	5	0	0	1	1	.263	12	0	1	.923

WORLD SERIES RECORD

Shares records for most at-bats, hits and runs, inning (2), October 9, 1968, third inning.

YEAR	CLUB	LEAGUE	POS.	G.	AB.	R.	H.	2B.	3B.	HR.	RBI.	B.A.	PO.	A.	E.	F.A.
1968	Detroit	Amer.	OF	7	29	6	11	2	0	2	8	.379	18	0	0	1.000

DANDY SANDY: When Sandy Koufax in late 1966 became the first National League pitcher since Dizzy Dean in the mid-'30s to repeat with 25-plus seasons, he smiled.

SANDY KOUFAX

If Robert Louis Stevenson had needed baseball inspiration for "Dr. Jekyll and Mr. Hyde," still one of the most fascinating stories ever to be re-read, re-told and re-captured by the silver screen, he would have found his analogy in the strange case of Sanford Braun and Sandy Koufax, one and the same person.

Of course, Sandy Koufax was only Sanford Braun for the first three years of his life, until his mother divorced his father and married a lawyer named Koufax, a man the boy would think of affec-

tionately as his own parent. The difference in names is mentioned here only because Harry Jekyll and Edward Hyde also were the same man, but, oh so different in temperament and accomplishment, too.

For the first six years he was in the big leagues Koufax' pitching was as undistinguished as a guy named Sanford Braun. He had his moments over that period, including a record-tying 18-strikeout performance in the Los Angeles Coliseum, where the lights were meant for football, not baseball, and he'd lost a tough 1-0 game in the 1959 World Series. But at the ripe old age of 25, Koufax had reason to wonder if he'd indeed gambled with his future and lost when he dropped out of college after one year to go into professional baseball.

He'd received a tidy sum, yes, but nothing spectacular from the Dodgers, then located in his native Brooklyn. Certainly $14,000 and even a share of three World Series, two of which he'd appeared in only as a spectator, couldn't compare with the value of a college education.

Fact is, he was so seldom seen in those early days as a bonus player, frozen to the roster by a rule which denied a ball club the right to option out a free agent given more than $6,000 to sign, that when he asked to be excused from classes at Columbia University for the World Series, a professor asked, "Why?"

A transfer student from the University of Cincinnati where he'd been attracted in part by his basketball skill and the Bearcats' basketball tradition, Sandy hadn't stuck with college after that one year he'd transferred to Columbia. For one thing, there was winter ball, necessary to make up for his lack of summer activity, and another time there was a six-month service call that could be satisfied between playing seasons.

So the family dreams of his following in the footsteps of uncles who were architects proved to be merely castles in the air by 1961. For all intents and purposes, he'd blown it. What 'n hell was a smart, handsome Jewish kid doing taking a salary cut from $19,000 to $18,000—and with little prospects for improvement—when he could be college-trained and just getting his teeth into a profession or business with a future?

No one probably ever will know or appreciate the anxiety or frustration that was Koufax' in those days when he was a lone wolf, amiable enough around the guys, but a bit distant, too. No, of course, he wasn't mean like Stevenson's evil Mr. Hyde, but he was almost as grim when he toed the pitching rubber and he was hot-tempered, angry at

himself, because he couldn't get the ball to do his bidding.

Big and strong, bigger than he looked and stronger than anyone realized unless they felt the hard muscles of a powerful back, Koufax could throw a grape through a battleship, but he wanted to hear the guns roar. He was wild and the harder he'd try to throw, as pitching coach Joe Becker pointed out, the more he'd tense those muscles so that he really wasn't getting either the lively velocity or direction he might have achieved otherwise.

"The expression you hear—'reach back and get something extra'—was never more misapplied than in Sandy's case," Becker would explain later. "He needed a loose wrist, to get snap in the ball at the position of release, not more muscular tension than he already was creating. But it was hard to get that point across."

The low point for Koufax came when after that record strikeout game and excellent World Series performance in 1959, an 8-6 season, he fell back to 8-13 in 1960 and, as mentioned, the Dodgers cut his salary. His record to that moment for six seasons in the majors was only 36 victories and 40 defeats, and he'd finally even sounded like Mr. Hyde in a public jawing session with general manager Buzzie Bavasi in the runway under the Coliseum one night.

"What does a guy have to do to get to pitch around here?" Koufax complained.

"Get somebody out," snapped Bavasi, a pretty good switch-hitting conversationalist.

"But how can you get 'em out when you don't get to pitch?" the kid sassed.

"Get the ball over when you do pitch," bellowed Bavasi. "You've got one pitch—high."

An unintentional eavesdropper—anybody with ears could hear 'em—was Willie Mays, the San Francisco slugger, and Mays, smiling, said to a Los Angeles writer, Mel Durslag, "I wish they'd get mad enough to trade him to us."

That's how much the baseball world loves a pitcher with mustard, the ability to play hard ball with the hitters, as they call it. Besides, Mays had been among the victims that night in '59 when Koufax had fanned 18. But Bavasi wasn't about to give up on Koufax, especially when in trying to swing a big interleague deal for Elston Howard, the Yankees' catcher, he found general manager George Weiss of the perennial champions interested not in Johnny Podres, a slick established southpaw, but in Koufax, the unpolished and unproven pain to a club contending in close races.

The Dodgers had signed Sandy originally for three good reasons. He could throw hard and he was from Brooklyn and he was Jewish. The Dodgers, Giants and Yankees all longed for a nice young Hebrew lad who would spin the turnstiles. But Bavasi reasoned that Weiss' interest in a major deal had to go beyond the boy's attractive background.

So Koufax, though disappointed and discouraged in his career up to then, still was with the Dodgers in 1961, a year he said in his autobiography probably would have been his last if he hadn't turned the corner to success.

Dodger reserves were bussing it to an exhibition game out of Vero Beach, Fla. in '61 and Sandy was seated with the young catcher who would be behind the plate that day. The world might little note nor long remember Norm Sherry, whose distinction up to then had been that he was the brother of Larry Sherry, relief ace of the stretch run and World Series in 1959, but Norm played a part in Koufax' conversion from a marginal liability to a major asset.

"Why not have some fun out there, Sandy?" said Sherry. "Don't try to throw so hard and use more curveballs and change-ups."

It was the mood and the manner, the informality of the B-team game and, ergo, the right thing to say at precisely the right time. Mr. Hyde became Dr. Jekyll. Throwing less hard, but just as fast, if you get the distinction, Sandy found control of the ball and of himself. He pitched beautifully that day and thereafter. He quit gnashing his teeth and the hitters began gritting theirs.

The next six seasons the Los Angeles lefthander was probably as overpowering as any pitcher who ever lived, winning 129 games and losing only 47. He pitched a record four no-hitters, including a perfect game. He tied the 18-strikeout record again, this time in the broad daylight of Chicago's Wrigley Field, and went from there to become the first pitcher to strike out more than 300 batters in each of three seasons. His 382 strikeouts in 1965 became a single-season major league mark.

Named Most Valuable Player in the National League in 1963 and winner of the Cy Young award as the majors' top pitcher in 1963-65-66, Koufax set numerous other records, including five successive seasons leading the National League with lowest earned-run average.

The most astonishing thing in the transformation from Mr. Hyde to Dr. Jekyll is that Koufax suffered first from a circulatory ailment, one which almost cost him the index finger of his left hand in 1962 and definitely cost the Dodgers a pennant lost in a playoff to San Francisco.

Then, after putting together perhaps the finest season ever in 1963, Koufax developed traumatic arthritis of his left elbow, a condition which made pitching a physical misery or, more accurately, the life of a pitcher miserable. When the fear of becoming a permanent cripple finally hit him harder than the discomfort, Koufax dramatically quit at the peak of his career.

He was not quite 31 years old, a professional ball player for 12 seasons, a $125,000-a-year pitcher who could have looked forward to a sizable increase for 1967 at the time he faced reporters, cameras and television and radio microphones in late November 1966. He'd just won 27 games and lost only nine and posted a 1.73 ERA for 323 innings in which he'd fanned 317 and walked only 77.

Intelligent and articulate, shy and quiet, celebrated but withdrawn, Koufax stood there with the poise with which he'd pitched and, not just incidentally, also had faced reporters politely whenever he'd lost, which, naturally, hadn't been often in the sensational six seasons.

"If," said Becker, "Sandy had pitched more as a kid, it would have helped, but he would have been helped even more if he could have been farmed out. Why, even if he had been able to pitch regularly with a weak club in the majors, one that wasn't in the pennant fight every year, he might have been a top star twice as fast."

The process was so slow and discouraging, and the boy didn't have as much patience as the ball club. As a rookie, he got into only 12 games and worked just 42 innings, but his figures then actually were better than they would be as he began to press harder. He was 2-2 with a 3.00 ERA, striking out 30 and walking 28. In August, when the Dodgers were breezing to the pennant, they gambled on him as a starter. He pitched a two-hit shutout at Cincinnati and fanned 14. He shut out Pittsburgh, too, but then relapsed into wildness and ineffectiveness.

By 1958, when the Dodgers flopped to seventh in their first season on the West Coast, Alston was able to work the kid into 40 games and 159 innings. He was 11-11, but he walked 105 men, a fact which reflected itself in his 4.47 ERA.

The Dodgers of '59 were one of the gamest clubs ever, bouncing back not only from seventh the year before, but repeatedly in ball games as well as they moved into the limelight and finally the lead. It was, basically, a comeback by Gil Hodges and Duke Snider and by Wally Moon, obtained from St. Louis, that showed the way, but everyone contributed, including Koufax.

Sandy's 18-strikeout performance came against San Francisco on the last night of August before more than 82,000 in the Coliseum, where the Dodgers advanced to within one game of the league-leading Giants. Koufax had struck out 13 at Philadelphia in his previous start, so he not only broke Dizzy Dean's 26-year-old National League single-game record, but he set a two-game major league mark of 31, which would become 41 for a three-game high his next time out.

Koufax fanned only three Giants the first three innings, but then he got two in the fourth, three in the fifth, three in the sixth, two in the seventh, two in the eighth and, knowing he was closing in on the record, the young southpaw hitched up his belt and struck out the side in the ninth, getting Danny O'Connell to tie Dean's league record and pitching opponent Jack Sanford to match Feller's major league mark.

Manager Alston, who almost had lifted Koufax for a pinch-hitter in the seventh when the Dodgers trailed, 2-1, let Sandy bat for himself to lead off the home ninth with the score tied. Koufax singled. With one out, Moon, using the inside-out swing that permitted him to take advantage of the close left-field fence at the Coliseum, arched a three-run homer over the barrier for a 5-2 Los Angeles victory.

Koufax' well-pitched World Series game came in the fifth contest when the Dodgers had a chance to wrap up the Series before their third successive 92,000 crowd in the Coliseum. Sandy gave up a run in the fourth inning on singles by Nellie Fox and Jim Landis, followed by Sherm Lollar's double-play grounder. And when Jim Rivera turned in a clutch fielding play for the White Sox in right field, Chicago got away with a 1-0 win. L. A. had nine hits off Bob Shaw, Billy Pierce and Dick Donovan. Chicago got only five off Koufax, who walked just one and fanned six in seven innings.

For those of us who thought the World Series had put him over the hump, Sandy's slip from 8-6 in '59 to 8-13 in '60 must have seemed almost as discouraging as it did to the young man who had reason to wonder then if he hadn't made a mistake in baseball as a career. But he wouldn't quit. By then, what else offered a bright future?

Becker would tell him, "Don't rush, Sandy. Damnit, nothing can start until you get damn good and ready to pitch."

Koufax strode too far, tried to throw too hard and couldn't retain an easy, natural rhythm, Becker pointed out, because he was overeager. And then along came catcher Norm Sherry, the right man with the right way to phrase the right thought at the right time.

Everything fell into place at once, and Sandy pitched well in spring training, good enough to start in rotation and win six of his first seven starts in 1961.

"If there was any magic formula," he said, "it was getting to pitch every fourth day, knowing I'd start again even if I had a bad outing. What comes first? Confidence or success? I don't know. That's like the one about the chicken and the egg, but they're closely related. You have to be confident to succeed and yet you need some success to have confidence."

The 18-13 season in '61, with a 3.52 ERA and a league-leading 269 strikeouts in 256 innings, compared with only 96 walks, proved that a star had been born. Yet if either Koufax or the Dodgers had known the physical problems that were to follow, it's doubtful either could have believed that in the next five years, twice sidelined for repairs, this incredible toe-plate talent would win 111 games and lose only 34.

It's necessary first to understand a bit about Koufax' physique. At 6-2 and around 200 pounds, though he'd played no football, he had muscles that would shame a blacksmith. Manager Alston patted him at the waist one time to kid him about a two-inch roll of fat and pulled back his hand in amazement. He'd struck muscle, hard muscle.

The Dodgers' trainer at the time, Wayne Anderson, formerly with the Reds, said he'd never seen such back muscles and Anderson trained big Ted Kluszewski at Cincy and giant Frank Howard with the Dodgers.

"The strangest thing is that, of all people, a pitcher should have these muscles," said Anderson, who labored long before each pitching appearance to help Sandy loosen those powerful muscles. He used a red ointment that would burn the hide off most people to help penetrate and provide pleasing warmth.

Watching Koufax stretch, bend and gyrate on the mound in the early innings of his games made it look as if the spectators were intruding on a calisthenics class or a belly dance. Sandy did everything except hip wiggle like Stan Musial in the batter's box.

So this was a massively muscled man whose circulation also was suspect, as was evidenced by a most unusual disability in mid-season 1962 when he had the Dodgers apparently coasting to a pennant. He was 14-4 when he was forced out by the numbness of his left index finger. Not, however, before he pitched the first of his four no-hit games.

The trouble began, the way Koufax tried to reconstruct it, when as a righthanded batter he decided to switch to the left side to minimize risk of getting hit on his pitching arm. Unable to move as well batting lefthanded, he was jammed by a pitch thrown by Pittsburgh's Earl Francis. The ball hit the bat just above his left hand, breaking an artery on the fleshy part of the hand, the part that sends blood into the index finger.

The finger was numb when he faced the Mets the night of June 30 at Los Angeles. "Wait him out," Casey Stengel told his hitters. "This feller can be kinda wild. Don't go swingin' at no early pitches. Wait him out."

Koufax struck out the first three batters on nine pitches. The veteran Gene Woodling said no one ever had thrown a pitch past him faster than Koufax did. In the second inning, Maury Wills went into the hole for a good stop and threw out Frank Thomas. That was the only tough fielding chance of Sandy's first hitless game.

Walking five and fanning 13, Koufax coasted to a 5-0 victory. Midway in the game, Solly Hemus, coaching third base, increased the tempo of early needling about the no-hitter.

"I've had one a lot later than this," Koufax retorted.

Throwing fastballs two out of three pitches and the rest curves—"his curve collapses at the plate like a folding chair," said catcher John Roseboro—

Sandy made up his mind only that he'd stow the change-up in the late innings.

"I'd have felt sick if someone had got a hit off a letup," he said. "They were going to have to hit the fastball or my curve."

Three starts and three victories after a thrill he compared then with his first big league victory back in '55 and his 18-strikeout game against San Francisco, Koufax was through, for practical reasons, for the season. The loss of the index finger was threatened because he had suffered Reynaud's Phenomenon, a constriction or obstruction of the blood vessels and the same kind of circulatory ailment that struck golf's Ken Venturi.

Circulation into the left index finger was so impaired that if he pressed the finger, it turned white and stayed that color for hours. His thumb and middle finger grew colder. The index finger began to get gangrenous and the skin was falling off.

"There was no pulse at all in it and it was insensitive," explained Koufax. "For the last 10 days when I tried to pitch, it was oversensitive."

Drugs and intravenous injections designed to dissolve blood clots arrested the condition and then cleared it so that after being sidelined from July 17 to 10 days before the end of the season, he tried pitching in St. Louis and was bombed out in the first inning, then went five against Houston finally, he was kayoed by the Giants in the first inning.

"In a way," said Koufax, "it was like spring training all over again. I felt I'd recovered, but I couldn't be sure."

The National League was sure in 1963—and the American, too—when he bounced back with the spectacular 25-5 season for which he would get top billing in the Branch Rickey rating of pitchers. He struck out 306 batters and walked only 58 and finished with a 1.88 ERA.

Early that season, a stiff shoulder caused him to miss three turns, but he tuned up at St. Louis with an 11-1 victory for his second no-hitter, which was achieved before a crowd of nearly 50,000 at Los An-

geles on May 11. And the victims, 8-0, were the hard-hitting Giants.

Aided by a couple of good plays, Koufax had a perfect game until he walked Ed Bailey on a 3-and-1 pitch in the eighth inning. Willie McCovey also walked in the ninth of a game in which the strikeout champion fanned only four and got by with 112 pitches, of which 73 were strikes.

"Because of my finger and shoulder injuries and the caliber of the Giants, this would have to be my biggest thrill," said Koufax afterward. Yes, even more than whiffing 18 Cubs in the sunshine at Wrigley Field.

When the Dodgers upset the Yankees four straight in the 1963 World Series, Koufax was front and center with two impressive victories, including a 15-strikeout performance, a record since broken by Bob Gibson when he fanned 17 against Detroit in 1968. Sandy allowed the Bombers just three runs and 12 hits in two games, striking out 23 and walking only three.

Irving Koufax, stricken with a heart attack, was recovering at his Los Angeles home and, when his wife left his side, he sneaked on the television set against doctor's orders, just in time to see Sandy leap for joy, apparently watching his teammates execute a Series-ending force-out. But the ball was dropped for an error, filling the bases, and Irving quickly turned off the set.

When he saw his son, Mr. Koufax explained, "I thought it was over and it wasn't and I just couldn't watch it. It would have been too much excitement. I thought I felt a flutter in my heart."

"Dad," said Sandy, "the apple doesn't fall too far from the bough. Right then, I felt a flutter, too."

A year later, Koufax felt something else, the first distressing inroads of the traumatic arthritis which would make his last three seasons misery. In his autobiography, Koufax explained what happens to a pitching arm:

"When you begin to stretch the muscles again during training, scar tissue and adhesions, which do not stretch, are torn away. Take a rubber band, stretch some mucilage over it, let the mucilage dry, then stretch the rubber band, The mucilage will crack and break loose. Same thing. The difference is that we are dealing with living tissue. When the scar tissue tears away, a certain amount of bleeding and swelling will take place, and a pitcher may be out of action for 10 days to two weeks."

In 1964, the adhesions didn't tear loose until Koufax was pitching his third regular-season start at St. Louis. He was knocked out and did no more pitching for 12 days. Later, June 4, he would gain his third no-hitter, 3-0, at Philadelphia, walking one and fanning 12.

Richie Allen was the only baserunner when a 3-and-2 fastball was a trifle low in the fourth inning—and Koufax second-guessed himself afterward:

"Doug Camilli called for a curve, but I shook him off. Then, right in the middle of my windup, I realized I had made a mistake, that Allen would be looking for the fast one. But just as you don't stop a golf shot on the backswing, I kept right on going. The ball was low."

In August, diving back into second base on a pickoff play at Milwaukee, Koufax landed hard on his elbow. The arm soreness and throbbing customary after he pitched a game persisted and became more acute. By August 20, after beating the Cardinals with 13 strikeouts and only one walk, he had won 15 of his last 16 starts and his record was 19-5, but the next morning when he awakened he just couldn't believe it.

"I had to drag my arm out of bed like a log," he related. "That's what it looked like—a log. A water-logged log. Where it had been swollen outside the joint before, it was now swollen all the way from the shoulder down to the wrist; inside, outside, everywhere. For an elbow, I had a knee; that's how thick it was.

"The elbow was so swollen that the whole arm was locked in a sort of hooked position. I couldn't straighten it out and I couldn't bend it. I didn't have more than an inch's worth of movement in any direction. By just moving it that tiny distance, I could actually hear the sound of liquid squishing around, as if I had a wet sponge in there."

That's when X-rays by Dr. Robert Kerlan, the Dodgers' surgeon, disclosed evidences of traumatic arthritis, The fluid was aspirated, drawn out with a needle, and the inflammation was treated by injections of cortisone, plus oral medicine. Arthritis can be controlled, but not cured. It's a degenerative condition, which, as Koufax said, "means it gets worse."

The arm did not come around immediately and with the Dodgers far back and only about two weeks to go, the recommendation was complete rest over the winter.

The arm acted up discouragingly again in spring training, 1965. Koufax felt Dr. Kerlan could lay the needle into the elbow joint again and knock the swelling down, but the doctor wasn't that optimistic. He feared Sandy might have to become a once-a-week pitcher. The superstar came up with a super idea. Why not let him skip his customary sideline throwing on the second day between starts? Maybe he could get by from start to start without throwing in between.

It worked—beautifully. The elbow would puff up and hurt, but it would calm down just about the time Koufax pitched and, getting all the ink and attention about his "bum arm," he went out and won 26 games, lost only eight and established that blockbuster record strikeout total, 382 in 336 innings.

Moreover, on September 9 he became the first man ever to pitch four major league no-hitters and, friends, he did it with a flourish with a perfect game, a 1-0 thriller over Chicago southpaw Bob Hendley before a 29,139 crowd that came within a bloop seventh-inning double by Lou Johnson of seeing a double no-hitter.

Curiously, the hit didn't score or set up the run. In the fifth Johnson walked, was sacrificed to second, stole third and continued home on catcher Chris Krug's high throw.

Koufax, striking out 14, was blazing as the game progressed, getting seven strikeouts the last three innings. He was throwing so hard that three times his cap detached itself from his black locks in his follow-through. What was he throwing?

"Everything I had," he said.

"He tried to throw the ball right past us," said Ernie Banks, "and he did."

Koufax saved the pennant and then won the World Series, beating Minnesota in the finale, 2-0, when he worked with only two days' rest and Alston pitched him in preference to better-rested Don Drysdale. Sandy was embarrassed as he talked about his arm.

"You know, Dick Sisler over at Cincinnati keeps saying, 'Yeah, some sore arm! It's sore except between the first and ninth innings,' and I don't blame him, but that's really the truth. The act of pitching seems to pump fluid out of the elbow joint and through the arm, where it would be more easily absorbed. It does feel better when I pitch."

But, of course, it was the pitching that created the condition which became more and more unbearable, despite the pain-killing orange-and-white pills he took, despite the red-hot red salve, despite the ice-cold elbow baths he endured for half an hour after every game he pitched. Yes, despite all medical skill and all the care given it and himself by an athlete who drank or smoked little and took care of himself, there was only one way to ease the condition and avoid possibly more serious consequences.

Koufax must have given it long thought many a night in his fancy bachelor diggings, whether alone with a good book or good music, both of which he enjoyed or with feminine companionship as a most eligible bachelor who could have his pick of the pack.

In 1966, posting a 27-9 record with a career low ERA, 1.73, the Man With the Golden Arm, as they called him on the West Coast, once more picked up a light-hitting ball club on his back and pitched it to a pennant at the wire. Except for a couple of flyballs

dropped in center field for errors and three unearned runs, he probably would have avoided a four-game skunking for the sleepwalking Dodgers at the hands of the bright-eyed and bushy-tailed Orioles in a World Series surprise. Dandy Sandy's ERA for eight World Series games told it all—0.95.

Koufax' decision to quit on top was a surprise, but understandable. To the Dodgers, it was a shock in the standings and at the box office. At one time, management didn't like it when wheelhorses Koufax and Drysdale, tired of being played off against each other at contract time, had declared themselves partners in a double holdout which paid off handsomely. But the Dodgers weren't the same without Sandy and then Don.

The value of a Koufax to a ball club is incalculable, just as it's certain Sandy's grit did more for fellow arthritis sufferers than an older remedy, a raw potato in the hip pocket.

Happily married to an attractive girl, well-heeled with good investments and a reported $100,000-a-year contract for 10 years with the National Broadcasting Company, dandy Sandy Koufax, the Mr. Hyde who became the Dr. Jekyll of the pitching mound, summed up his own value—most unintentionally.

In baseball's centennial season, three years out of uniform, he told how much he missed his teammates and the camaraderie, how even the rigors of baseball travel didn't seem so rugged when you considered the companionship of the gang.

"Above all," he said, getting to the point with close friend Phil Collier, "I miss playing late in the season when there's a pennant at stake."

It was Koufax who clinched the National League championship for the Dodgers on the next-to-last day of the 1965 season. It was Koufax who pitched with only two days rest to beat Minnesota in the seventh and deciding game of the '65 World Series. And it was Koufax who again pitched with two days' rest in 1966 when the Dodgers won another pennant in the final game of the season at Philadelphia.

Sandy Koufax, not Sanford Braun. The polished competitive professional, master of all he surveyed, not the frightened kid who pouted and pressed impatiently. "When you're playing, you think, 'Why did it have to come down to me again?' " he said. "But once you're away from baseball, you see how much you enjoyed the responsibility."

Impeccably and conservatively dressed, except when he wore one of his favorite alpaca sweaters— the dark, handsome Koufax did the most for the color of California orange than anyone since Sunkist—he had a full head of dark hair, heavy eyebrows over narrow, clear, brown eyes and good features. At times, that handsome face brooded and seemed to be a mask which, as writer Bill Libby put it, seemed to conceal so many secrets. But, telling it like it was, Koufax explained he couldn't go on. His left arm was shortening, he found when he tried to shave, and he couldn't reach his face without leaning over.

"I've had a few too many shots and too many pills because of arm trouble," he said. "I didn't want to take the chance of disabling myself. I don't regret for one minute the 12 years I've spent in baseball, but I could regret one season too many.

"I'm young. I want to live a lot of years after this and I don't want to become bitter because I pitched one year too many. I've got a lot of years to live after baseball and I would like to live them with the complete use of my body."

These were strong words, almost frightening, but they apparently did not exaggerate the physical condition of a player who became the youngest elected to baseball's Hall of Fame. Koufax was just 37 years old five seasons after retirement, when he was elected to Cooperstown in 1971.

Even though his career totals were not monumental because he was little more than a benchwarmer for six years and a superstar for six, his 165-87 lifetime record adds up to a sparkling .655 percentage and his career earned-run average is an excellent 2.76. In 2,325 innings, he walked 817 and

struck out 2,396, better than one an inning, accounting for a major league standard of 97 games— out of 397—in which he struck out 10 or more batters. And, naturally, in most of those contests early in his career he wasn't on the firing line long enough to fan 10.

As veteran New York baseball writer Tommy Holmes pointed out, baseball brain Branch Rickey maintained that the won-and-lost percentages and earned-run averages, though helpful barometers to a pitcher's performance were affected by team effort in too many ways. Rickey felt the purest form of measure was (1) the ratio of base hits allowed to the number of innings pitched and (2) the margin by which a pitcher's strikeout total exceeds his bases on balls.

This, Rickey insisted, reduced the problem to man-against-man, pitcher-against-pitcher, with the only outside influence the limited one of a better fielding team making a put-out more now and then behind one pitcher than another hurler might benefit from. Holmes, seeking to apply Rickey's rating to the best seasons in pitching history, adapted a mathematical formula. He awarded a point-plus for each inning pitched in excess of hits allowed and for every strikeout more than walks yielded.

Holmes took the best season for the top pitchers through 1966. The top 12 in order were:

Dizzy Dean, 1934, W-30, L-7, 144 points; Lefty Grove, 1931, 31-4, 153; Dazzy Vance, 1924, 28-6, 256; Juan Marichal, 1966, 25-6, 265; Bob Feller, 1946, 26-15, 289; Grover Alexander, 1915, 31-10, 300; Denny McLain, 1968, 31-6, 312; Bob Gibson, 1968, 22-9, 313; Christy Mathewson, 1908, 37-11, 327; Ed Walsh, 1908, 40-15, 334; Walter Johnson, 1912, 32-12, 336; and SANDY KOUFAX, 1965, 26-8, 431.

Holmes' system admittedly was only for one season and places a great premium on strikeouts.

Sandy Koufax, king of the hill, was born Sanford Braun on December 30, 1935, at Brooklyn. His father, Jack, was a pretty good athlete in his day and was a sizable man from whom Sandy would get his own height and heft. Braun and the boy's mother, Evelyn, were divorced when Sandy was three. The father used to see the son for a few years. Jack Braun had a delightful photo of an eight-year-old boy, knee socks falling down, short pants, long-sleeved shirt, tongue stuck out with determination and swinging a baseball bat that was much too heavy. Sandy, sure.

Bitterness over insufficient support—Braun had remarried—and the love of a man who had married his mother led to Sandy's looking upon attorney Irving Koufax as his own father. So Sanford Braun became Koufax, the first syllable to rhyme with "go," which Sandy did, but usually on the basketball court.

Sandy's older sister, Edith, who became Mrs. Robert Nicholson, reminisced with amusement about the handsome, neatly dressed athlete who became a highly sought-after bachelor until he married Anne Widmark, daughter of actor Richard Widmark. Mrs. Nicholson couldn't resist noting the differences:

"He was a funny kid, a very healthy, dirty-faced kid. You'd go into his room and find clothes piled high. My, how he has changed. He's so neat. I remember one time he came in the house when several of my girlfriends were combing their hair and putting on makeup. So we decided to make him our guinea pig. We combed his hair, put on lipstick, gave him a kerchief and a dress. We all thought he looked awfully pretty.

"As a teenager, he became a very good cook whose specialty was spaghetti. We had an agreement that he'd cook if I'd clean up. He always was eating catsup then. He put it on everything. One day I said, jokingly, 'Why don't you put some catsup on your cereal.' He did. We made him leave the table. Now, he doesn't eat catsup at all."

It must be emphasized that she was very proud of his accomplishments. "As a boy, he was persistent," she said, relating how he would wire the

Koufax house for sound and also came over to her place when she was first married and spent three hours fixing a toy sewing machine. "He proved then, as he did later, that he could see a thing through. I'm awfully proud of that boy. He's pretty special. If your children have to have a hero, they can't have a better one. He does everything well."

At Lafayette High School, Brooklyn, he did well without taking his textbooks home at night to study. He was most interested in basketball, which he could play fiercely, rebounding savagely, winter or summer. Baseball was something to do between times.

The man who spotted him first as a potential ballplayer was Milton Laurie, delivery driver for the old *New York Journal-American.*

"I first saw Sandy with the Tomahawks in the Ice Cream League," said Laurie, a long-time sandlot manager. "He walked nine men in two innings, but still I asked my son, Walter, his high school classmate, to invite him to join our team.

"He refused, saying basketball was his game. When I saw him playing first base at Lafayette and throwing bullets across the infield, I begged again. Finally he joined us, but he worked in camps every summer and didn't pitch much. But, boy, when he did—16 to 18 strikeouts."

About this time, presumably, lawyer Koufax for the first and only time decided to watch his son play an amateur game. Sandy, pitching, was surprised and pleased to spot his father's car at the game. When the boy came home for dinner that night, Mr. Koufax addressed Mrs. Koufax:

"Why don't you give the boy the money to buy himself a pair of new spikes? Do you want him to break his leg or something?"

Sandy smiled as he remembered the look of amazement on his mother's face.

"All this time," he said, "I'd been playing in a pair of old, torn spikes that I'd borrowed from some other kid, and I'd been begging for the money to get a new pair, and Dad had been saying, 'You don't need them. It's only a waste of money. A baseball player you're not going to be.' "

Jimmy Murphy, covering prep sports for the old *Brooklyn Eagle*, tipped off Al Campanis, Dodger scout, to Koufax and eventually the Dodgers got him to Ebbets Field for a workout at which Bavasi and manager Walter Alston saw him. He'd thrown maybe only a dozen games all told, but that strong, lively arm interested them.

However, University of Cincinnati scouts had seen him playing basketball at high school and at the Jewish Community House, and offered an athletic scholarship. The family was proud that he would follow in the footsteps of his uncles, the architects. This was a well-educated family. Mr. Koufax was a lawyer, Sandy's mother was an accountant and his sister, Edith, had gone to Adelphi University on Long Island.

As a freshman at Cincinnati in the 1953-54 basketball season, Sandy averaged 10 points and then, when he found the baseball team would take a southern trip, he went out for the ball club and struck out 51 batters in 32 innings, 34 in two consecutive games.

During vacation that June, the Giants invited him to the Polo Grounds for a tryout, but he was tense and frightened and, as a result, even more wild than usual. The Giants lost interest, but other clubs didn't, particularly the Dodgers.

Time and again, Campanis would call. At one point, Mrs. Koufax told her son, "At least, you'll be able to finish your education with the bonus money. We'll put it away and won't touch it."

Persuasion finally won in December 1954, when Sandy was back in college, talking to his father by phone every Sunday. They decided to take the Dodgers' offer of a $14,000 bonus and $6,000 salary. Mr. Koufax shook Campanis' hand.

As Campanis left the Koufax home, he met a Pittsburgh scout, who said he was authorized by Branch Rickey, then running the Pirates, to top Brooklyn's offer by $5,000.

"I just shook Mr. Campanis' hand for less," said the senior Koufax. "I may be wrong, but the way I live, a deal is a deal and a handshake is a deal."

After the deal was consummated, the Milwaukee Braves came in too late with a $30,000 offer. The Koufaxes weren't envious. They would have their boy at home, but not for too many years, it turned out, because the Dodgers surprised the baseball world after the 1957 season by pulling out of Brooklyn and heading for Los Angeles.

"And I felt guilty in having signed Koufax," said Campanis, general manager on the West Coast.

A few years later, after his parents visited him in Los Angeles and fell in love with the climate, Sandy urged them to leave Brooklyn, too. He bought a new place for himself in 1963 and his parents moved into the one he'd had previously. Mr. Koufax found legal work for the government. Sandy himself had a short-lived TV deal, then turned to coaching.

At the outset, when he went to spring training in 1955 just 19 years old and painfully inexperienced, Sandy was so nervous and tense he couldn't throw for a week at Vero Beach. Then he tried to throw so hard that he got a sore arm and couldn't throw for another week. When he resumed, he was so wild that pitching coach Becker recalled taking him to warm up in isolation behind the barracks so that the kid wouldn't be embarrassed.

When he came out of hiding, the other players went in. "Taking batting practice against him is like playing Russian roulette with five bullets," one Dodger said. "You don't give yourself much of a chance."

SANFORD (SANDY) KOUFAX
Born December 30, 1935, at Brooklyn N.Y.
Height 6-2 Weight 198
Threw left and batted righthanded.
Named to Hall of Fame, 1972.

YEAR	CLUB	LEAGUE	G.	IP.	W.	L.	Pct.	H.	R.	ER.	SO.	BB.	ERA.
1955	Brooklyn	Nat.	12	42	2	2	.500	33	15	14	30	28	3.00
1956	Brooklyn	Nat.	16	59	2	4	.338	66	37	32	30	29	4.88
1957	Brooklyn	Nat.	34	104	5	4	.556	83	49	45	122	51	3.89
1958	Los Angeles	Nat.	40	159	11	11	.500	132	89	79	131	105	4.47
1959	Los Angeles	Nat.	35	153	8	6	.571	136	74	69	173	92	4.06
1960	Los Angeles	Nat.	37	175	8	13	.381	133	83	76	197	100	3.91
1961	Los Angeles	Nat.	42	256	18	13	.581	212	117	100	269	96	3.52
1962	Los Angeles	Nat.	28	184	14	7	.667	134	61	52	216	57	2.54
1963	Los Angeles	Nat.	40	311	25	5	.833	214	68	65	306	58	1.88
1964	Los Angeles	Nat.	29	223	19	5	.792	154	49	43	223	53	1.74
1965	Los Angeles	Nat.	43	336	26	8	.765	216	90	76	382	71	2.04
1966	Los Angeles	Nat.	41	323	27	9	.750	241	74	62	317	77	1.73
Major League Totals			397	2325	165	87	.655	1754	806	713	2396	817	2.76

WORLD SERIES RECORD

YEAR	CLUB	LEAGUE	G.	IP.	W.	L.	Pct.	H.	R.	ER.	SO.	BB.	ERA.
1959	Los Angeles	Nat.	2	9	0	1	.000	5	1	1	7	1	1.00
1963	Los Angeles	Nat.	2	18	2	0	1.000	12	3	3	23	3	1.50
1965	Los Angeles	Nat.	3	24	2	1	.667	13	2	1	29	5	0.38
1966	Los Angeles	Nat.	1	6	0	1	.000	6	4	1	2	2	1.50
World Series Totals			8	57	4	3	.571	36	10	6	61	11	0.95

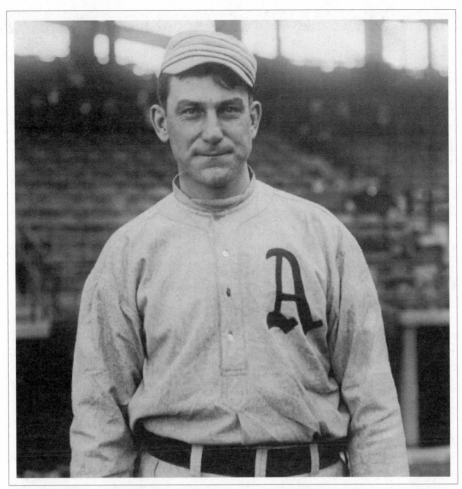

NAPOLEONIC ERA: Best hitter (by far) when the American League came into existence was solid Philadelphia Athletics' second baseman, Napoleon (Larry) Lajoie.

NAPOLEON LAJOIE

Back in the early years of this century when Napoleon Lajoie was as smooth as Napoleon pastry and as sharp as Napoleon brandy, a Detroit pitcher named George Mullin decided he knew how to take the snap out of the Cleveland second baseman's line-drive swing.

Mullin served up a slow ball, which the righthanded-hitting Lajoie pulled savagely. The ball skidded off third baseman George Moriarty's shoulder and into the outfield for a hit.

Mullin was unconvinced. The next time Lajoie batted, the Detroit pitcher again tried a change-up. Again, the Cleveland slugger slammed one down the third-base line. Moriarty, handcuffed, ducked just in time as the ball whizzed past his ear for another hit.

White-faced and red-necked, Moriarty, later a two-fisted American League umpire, walked to the mound and let Mullin have it orally.

"If you give that Frenchman another slow ball," the sharp-tongued Tiger third baseman told his pitcher, "so help me, I'll kill you—unless he gets me first."

Lajoie, properly pronounced LaZhwa, but called La-joyee and best known as Laj-a-way, low-bridged perhaps more infielders than any hitter who ever sizzled a line drive. He batted .339 for 21 seasons and finished with 3,251 hits, 650 of them doubles.

Looking back from the 20th century's last decade, no position has had more glittering stars than second base.

Second basemen enshrined at Cooperstown sound like a Who's Who in baseball: Eddie Collins...Rogers Hornsby... Frank Frisch... Charley Gehringer... Johnny Evers... Billy Herman... Bobby Owen... Red Schoendienst... Tony Lazzer... and, so help me, the least appreciated and remembered—Lajoie!

In this case, the last definitely shall be first because the big Frenchman was the first of the great second basemen to win Hall of Fame honors. He was, in fact, just the sixth player to be named, a year after the annual election began with selection of five superstars in 1936.

Was Lajoie the best ever as a second baseman, all-around? It's difficult to get a thorough appraisal because, fact is, the man was at his peak so many years ago that few observers now were old enough then to be able to evaluate him with the twin advantages of age and experience.

Nap—or Larry, as he was more often called—played big league ball 21 seasons, but he finished in 1916 and, for that matter, wasn't putting his best foot forward either as a batter or fielder a few years before he hung it up at age 41.

Based on what can be deduced, Lajoie was second only to Hornsby among second basemen as a hitter and, for that matter, trailed perhaps only the Rajah and one or two others for clothesline clouting as a righthanded hitter. One, in Larry's own opinion, would be his longtime Philadelphia teammate in the Naughty Nineties, Ed Delahanty.

Only Gehringer, if any second baseman, was as graceful as the 6-1, 200-pound hack driver from Woonsocket, R. I. But, gliding effortlessly, could the thick-legged giant, admittedly not as fast as Frisch or Collins, cover as much ground as those two, say, or Gehringer?

Regardless of the answer, Lajoie was recognized as the peerless second baseman at least until Cocky Collins came along. And there are still some who consider Lajoie, who once batted .422, as No. 1 at the position which produced so many glittering stars.

It's typical of Lajoie's stoicism, it would seem, that he lived 43 years in retirement from baseball and never once let out a protest over a typographical error that for years trimmed 17 precious points off his astonishing average in 1901.

The .422 shrank to .405 for years because an early baseball guide showed only 209 hits, not 229, the accurate figure that was discovered in a laborious recount undertaken by baseball buff John G. Tattersall.

The premier baseball historian, Lee Allen, whose Cooperstown column was a delightful feature of *The Sporting News* before his death in 1969, disclosed that in the fantastic season at the turn of the century, Lajoie was held hitless in only 17 of 131 games.

Hornsby, by contrast, was blanked in 24 of 143 contests in 1924, the year he posted the highest batting average of the 20th century, .424. However, as Allen explained in fairness to all, the foul-strike rule adopted by the National League in 1901 was not accepted by the new American League until two years later. The old rule ignoring the foul ball as a potential penalty was, as a result, at least a marginal advantage for Lajoie over contemporary hitters.

It's not likely, however, that Larry needed much help, even though members of the old St. Louis Browns tried to aid him in 1910 in what amounted to a minor scandal.

By then a three-time American League batting champion, the 35-year-old Lajoie was considerably more popular among his teammates and even rival players than was Ty Cobb, 24, seeking the fourth of nine successive hitting titles.

The Georgia Peach, the fanatical competitor who

finished in front 12 times all told, left a sour taste with his extreme aggressiveness, and they didn't like it when he smugly sat out the last two games of the 1910 season to protect his batting average.

A Chalmers automobile, offered by the long-extinct company of that name, was the individual prize at stake.

The final day, when Cleveland played a double-header at St. Louis, Lajoie came up with eight hits off rookie pitching, but, startlingly, six of them were on safe bunts. The never-speedy Lajoie's bunted hits brought an outcry from Cobb's followers and the investigative eye of Ban Johnson, founder and first president of the American League.

Johnson didn't like what he saw, heard, and smelled. It developed that after Lajoie had creamed a triple, John (Red) Corriden, rookie St. Louis third baseman, had been ordered to play deep by Browns' manager Jack O'Connor, even though Lajoie then beat out bunt after bunt after bunt.

When Lajoie hit a sharp groundball for which the St. Louis official scorer charged shortstop Bobby Wallace with an error at one point, a mysterious note was received by the scorer, offering to buy him a suit of clothes if he changed the error to a hit.

The scorer flatly refused, ultimately costing Lajoie the batting title by seven ten-thousandths of a point, .3848 to .3841. As consolation, Lajoie, like Cobb, received an automobile from the Chalmers company, but Manager O'Connor of the Browns and coach Harry Howell, who also had shown an uncommon interest in the batting race, were fired from their big league jobs.

If these sound as negative highlights of Lajoie's career, it's unfortunate, but, then, maybe that's one of the penalties of having played and lived in a less-than-colorful manner.

The witty quotes by, or exciting anecdotes about, were not part of the Lajoie legend, even though the Frenchman titillated some. For instance, George Trevor of the late, *New York Sun* wrote this purple prose:

"Every pose was a picture, yet there was no striving on Lajoie's part for artistic effects. His gracefulness was innate, a part of this eye-filling D'Artagnan of the diamond. Ruskin referred to architecture as 'frozen music.' Lajoie's batting and fielding might with equal propriety be termed 'living poetry.'"

Less flamboyantly, one Cleveland admirer put it this way:

"Old Nap Lajoie was the only man I ever saw who could chew scrap tobacco in such a way as to give a jaunty refinement to a habit vulgar and untidy in so many others."

He was a handsome fellow, big and dark, with bold features and arresting eyes. He wore his cap cocked on the side of his head, which was covered with thick, dark, wavy hair. And the Frenchman wore the uniform roll collar of his day casually, partly turned up, to make an attractive frame for his face.

With the flourish of an instinctive artist, he habitually drew a line in the dust alongside home plate with the business end of his bat, a prelude to facing the pitcher.

Like Hornsby, who was just breaking in when he was going out, Lajoie stood deep in the batter's box. But bat choked, hands held apart like Cobb, the Frenchman strode into the ball, swung smoothly and hit wickedly.

The bat spoke eloquently in his salad season— .363, .380, .422, .366, .381, .384, .365— for a total of 16 above .300.

Like George Sisler, another all-time great, Lajoie never played in a World Series, coming closest as player-manager at Cleveland in 1908, when Detroit won a four-way race. He didn't get on a pennant-winning ball club until he led Toronto to the International League championship in 1917, the year after he'd finished in the majors.

On the way up, Sandy Lajoie, as they called him as a kid, needed just one season in the minors to reach the majors, but he almost didn't get there at all.

His parents were French Canadians, and Napoleon was the youngest of eight children born to John Lajoie, a day laborer, and the former Celina Guertin. His father died when he was only five years old.

Working as a kid in the cotton mills around Woonsocket, Lajoie began to play ball when he was about 10, enthralled by the magic names put on a baseball scoreboard outside a pool hall in his hometown.

Years later, shortly before his death in 1959, at 83, he would recall King Kelly, Old Hoss Radbourn, John Clarkson, Con Daily, John Montgomery Ward and the other names that fascinated him.

Lajoie was a catcher and played some first base and outfield in semi-pro ball. He was driving a hack for a livery stable in 1895, driving to funerals and delivering wood and coal, when the manager of the Fall River team of the New England League walked into the office.

"Can you tell me where I can find that big French kid named Sandy?" asked Charley Marston.

Lajoie, making $7.50 a week as a hack driver, jumped at the $100-a-month contract Marston drew up on the back of an envelope.

He needed just three months in the New England League, hitting .429, and then was with Philadelphia in the National League, his pay doubled. But it's amusing how Boston missed him and Philadelphia got him.

Frank Selee, managing Boston, was tipped off about him and sent one of his top outfielders, Tommy McCarthy, to take a look. McCarthy was the kind of guy who probably would have laughed at Columbus, scoffed at the Wright brothers and kidded Henry Ford about the horseless carriage.

"That big Frenchman never will hit," said McCarthy. Selee never let the Irishman forget how far he'd missed on that one.

Marston, though, really didn't know what he had, either. When manager Billy Nash of the

Phillies made a scouting trip, interested in Fall River's right fielder, Phil Geier, he offered $1,500 for Geier, spot cash.

"I'll throw in Lajoie, too," said a happy Marston, who next year had Geier back on his hands.

Larry Lajoie, nicknamed by Bollicky Bill Taylor, a Philadelphia pitcher to whom "Larry" was the closest he could come to the Frenchman's last name, joined the Phillies in August 1896.

Ed Delahanty was playing first base because Dan Brouthers had quit the Phillies, but when Lajoie joined the club, the veteran returned to the outfield and the rookie played first. He began his 20-year romance with second base in '98.

The hitter was a hit from the outset, batting .328 in 39 games in 1896, then posting averages in successive seasons of .363, .328, .380 and .346. But he was a victim of a league salary ceiling of $2,400 a player in 1899.

Many players received money under the table, Lajoie recalled years later in an interview with Lee Allen for *The Sporting News*. Larry knew that Delahanty had been receiving $3,000 because he'd seen the checks. Silently, he accepted unhappily the extra $200 a month Col. John I. Rogers, the Phillies' club owner, would give him.

When the American League was founded in 1901, the Athletics organized by Connie Mack offered $24,000 for a four-year contract. Lajoie accepted, but then, as a salary war broke out, suddenly found Colonel Rogers willing to pay $25,000 for two years.

"If, Colonel," the Frenchman said, "you'll pay me the $400 you owe me, we can talk about 1901." Rogers insisted he owed Lajoie nothing. Larry walked out—an American Leaguer.

Lajoie immediately had the greatest season of his career, as the two major leagues hassled in the courts. Opening day, 1902, just after Nap singled off Baltimore's Iron Man Joe McGinnity, a telegram was received by Lajoie, notifying him that his former employers, the Phillies, had obtained an injunction restraining him from playing for the Athletics.

So Mack was forced to bench his greatest star, who sat on the sidelines for a couple of months until it was decided the injunction was good only in Philadelphia. Reluctantly, therefore, but for the good of the new league's cause, Connie sold Lajoie to Cleveland on June 2.

The catch was, however, that when Cleveland appeared in Philadelphia, the great second baseman couldn't play. He stayed out of Pennsylvania, enjoyed himself in nearby Atlantic City and, though limited to 87 games, he hit .366.

In 1905, Lajoie became manager at Cleveland, where they began calling the team the Naps, just as the Brooklyn Dodgers often were called the Robins in the period when Wilbert Robinson managed them.

In the four-plus seasons Lajoie managed them, the Naps were a better than .500 club, but they came close to a pennant only in 1908, when Detroit beat them out on the final day.

Years later, Lajoie would suggest that perhaps he was too lenient with the players. If not too lenient, the Frenchman certainly was most understanding. In 1907, brooding because he'd been moved down in the batting order, first baseman George Stovall argued with his manager, then hit Lajoie over the head with a chair.

With majestic reserve, Napoleon shrugged it off and when asked if he'd keep Stovall with the ball club, he said, "Why not? He's a good player and we need him. That chair episode was just one of those things."

Replaced as manager in the 1909 season, Lajoie was relieved. He figured that, without the worries of managing, he'd hit better, which he did. Twice, as manager, he'd had his first two seasons under .300. In 1910, he zoomed from .324 to .384.

In 1911, he had another big season, batting .365 for another manager, the guy who'd conked him on the head with the chair, Stovall. Considerably more

phlegmatic than the French are supposed to be, Larry gave it his best, uncomplaining and with no thought of asking to be traded.

A year later, celebrating the brilliant ballplayer's 10th season in Cleveland, the Forest City fans arranged a day for Lajoie, presenting him with a giant floral horseshoe, considerably taller than the sizable athlete. Wired in with the roses were 1,009 silver dollars contributed by the fans.

Lajoie treasured the thought as the finest of his baseball career until he helped dedicate the Hall of Fame at Cooperstown, June 12, 1939.

By then, he was seldom seen around baseball. The big Frenchman silently had slipped away.

He'd known one more big season, 1913, when, at 38, he batted .335. He dipped the next year to .258 and was released by the Indians and picked up by his old friend, Connie Mack, who just had broken up his championship club.

Lajoie hit .280 for Mr. Mack in 1915, dropped to .246 in 1916 and knew it was time to say goodbye when he committed five errors in one game.

"Forget it, kid," said old Connie, who seemed as embarrassed as the old superstar himself.

Lajoie did manage to hit .380 in a full season at Toronto in 1917, quite an accomplishment for a man 41 years old, but a year later he hung up his glove, spikes and that specially-made Louisville Slugger on which Bud Hillerich had put an extra knob because of Larry's spread grip.

Lajoie and his wife, the former Myrtle Everturf, a Missouri girl he'd married when playing at Cleveland in 1906, went back home east of the city at Mentor-on-the-Lake, O.

Long popular in Cleveland, Larry was put up as Republican candidate for sheriff of Cuyahoga County, but he lost the election.

Briefly, he was named commissioner of the old Ohio and Pennsylvania League.

For several years, developing an abiding interest in golf, he was a salesman for a rubber company, but, more and more, he found himself spending time in Florida. So in 1925 he retired and moved first to Lake Worth and then to Holly Hill, a suburb of Daytona Beach.

The pipe-puffing old pro shunned reunions. He told Lee Allen he hadn't seen a big league game since the 1920 World Series in which the pitcher he'd faced in his final contest four years earlier was a three-game hero. That would be Stanley Coveleski, a fellow Hall of Famer. Lajoie tripled for his last hit in his final game.

Among his souvenirs in those twilight years when he followed baseball closely, but quietly from a distance, was a throbbing left hand, which had been broken years earlier. And he could remember, too, the day he'd lost his composure with an umpire.

Flagrantly missing one, umpire Frank Dwyer, whom Lajoie called Blinky, allowed Chicago runners to move up on a pitch that glanced away when it was apparent that a White Sox batter, squaring around to bunt, had fouled the ball.

Indignantly, Lajoie hit Blinky squarely in the eye with his chaw of tobacco and drew a five-day suspension from American League president Ban Johnson.

Built like a tiger competing with tabbies and just as graceful as a giant jungle cat, Lajoie seldom showed his fangs except when he addressed the ball.

Russell Ford, who did everything except salt and pepper the ball with foreign substances that were legal, finally found the Frenchman's one weakness one day in 1910.

Three times Ford, then pitching for the New York Highlanders, tried to give Lajoie an intentional pass in the manner of a day in which catchers were not allowed to move from behind the plate until the ball was thrown. Three times Larry reached out with one long arm and lined doubles to right field.

The fourth time Lajoie stepped up to hit with a man on base. An intentional pass was the proper strategy, and Ford achieved the goal which had frustrated him on an afternoon as long as Larry's arm.

The pitcher threw four pitches behind the batter. Not even Napoleon Lajoie, the fabulous Frenchman, had learned how to hit 'em off his backside.

276

NAPOLEON (LARRY) LAJOIE
Born September 5, 1875, at Woonsocket, R.I.
Died February 7, 1959, at Daytona Beach, Fla.
Height 6-1 Weight 195
Threw and batted righthanded.
Named to Hall of Fame, 1937.

YEAR	CLUB	LEAGUE	POS.	G.	AB.	R.	H.	2B.	3B.	HR.	SB.	B.A.	PO.	A.	E.	F.A.
1896	Fall Riber	N. Eng.	OF	80	380	94	163	34	16	16	-	.429	280	30	23	.931
1896	Philadelphia	Nat.	1B	39	174	37	57	11	6	4	6	.328	360	11	3	.992
1897	Philadelphia	Nat.	1B-OF	126	545	107	198	37	25	10	22	.363	1112	43	20	.983
1898	Philadelphia	Nat.	2B	147	610	113	200	40	10	5	33	.328	434	431	48	.947
1899	Philadelphia	Nat.	2B	72	308	70	117	17	11	6	14	.380	222	242	21	.957
1900	Philadelphia (a)	Nat.	2B	102	451	95	156	32	12	7	25	.346	283	345	27	.959
1901	Philadelphia	Amer.	2B	131	543	145	229	48	13	13	27	.422	403	374	30	.963
1902	Phila.-Cleveland	Amer.	2B	87	352	81	129	34	5	7	19	.366	284	278	15	.974
1903	Cleveland	Amer.	1B-2B	126	488	90	173	40	13	7	22	.355	355	426	35	.957
1904	Cleveland	Amer.	2B-SS	140	554	92	211	50	14	5	31	.381	354	400	39	.951
1905	Cleveland	Amer.	2B	65	249	29	82	13	2	2	11	.329	148	177	3	.991
1906	Cleveland	Amer.	2B	152	602	88	214	49	7	0	20	.355	374	455	26	.970
1907	Cleveland	Amer.	2B	137	509	53	152	32	6	2	24	.299	314	461	26	.968
1908	Cleveland	Amer.	2B	157	581	77	168	32	6	2	15	.289	450	538	37	.964
1909	Cleveland	Amer.	2B	128	469	56	152	33	7	1	13	.324	282	373	28	.959
1910	Cleveland	Amer.	2B	159	591	92	227	51	7	4	27	.384	387	419	28	.966
1911	Cleveland	Amer.	1B-2B	90	315	36	115	20	1	2	13	.365	479	109	14	.977
1912	Cleveland	Amer.	1B-2B	117	448	66	165	34	4	0	18	.368	412	261	24	.966
1913	Cleveland	Amer.	2B	137	465	66	156	25	2	1	17	.335	289	363	20	.970
1914	Cleveland	Amer.	1B-2B	121	419	37	108	14	2	1	14	.258	487	233	22	.970
1915	Philadelphia (b)	Amer.	2B	129	490	40	137	24	5	1	10	.280	251	332	23	.962
1916	Philadelphia	Amer.	2B	113	426	33	105	14	4	2	15	.246	254	325	16	.973
1917	Toronto	Int.	1B	151	581	83	221	39	4	5	4	.380	875	263	23	.980
1918	Indianapolis	A.A.	1B	78	291	39	82	12	2	2	10	.282	661	89	10	.987

American League Totals				1989	7501	1081	2523	513	98	50	296	.336	5523	5524	386	.966
National League Totals				486	2088	422	728	137	64	32	100	.349	2411	1072	119	.967
Major League Totals				2475	9589	1503	3251	650	162	82	396	.339	7934	6596	505	.966

a Jumped to Philadelphia A.L., but Philadelphia N.L. club got injunction against his playing for Athletics and he joined Cleveland in June 2, 1902.

b Contract assumed by Philadelphia Athletics, January, 1915.

TURNAROUND TERROR: Baseball's most powerful switch-hitter, Mickey Mantle, persevered through a persistent leg injury to hit more than 50 homers twice, 536 total, plus a record 18 in the World Series.

MICKEY MANTLE

In his highly publicized, provocative book *Ball Four*, for which he was slapped on the wrist by baseball Commissioner Bowie Kuhn, former Yankee pitcher Jim Bouton saw fit to evaluate a famous teammate.

"Mickey Mantle announced his retirement the other day," Bouton told his baseball diary, "and I got to thinking about the mixed feelings I've always had about him. On the one hand, I really liked his sense of humor and his boyishness, the way he'd spend all that time in the clubhouse making up in-

volved games of chance and the pools he got up on golf matches and the Derby and things like that.

"I once invested a dollar when Mantle raffled off a ham. I won, only there was no ham. That was one of the hazards of entering a game of chance, Mickey explained.

"I got back by entering a fishing tournament he organized and winning the weight division with a 10-pounder I'd purchased in a store the day before. Two years later, Mantle was still wondering why I'd only caught that one big fish and why all the other

278

fish that were caught were green and lively while mine was gray and just lay there, staring.

"I also remember the time I won my first major league game. It was a shutout against the Washington Senators in which I walked seven guys and gave up seven hits and had to pitch from a stretch position all game. They were hitting line drives all over the place and Hector (What a Pair of Hands) Lopez bailed me out with about four leaping catches in left field. When the game was over I walked back into the clubhouse and there was a path of white towels from the door to my locker, and all the guys were standing there, and just as I opened the door Mickey was putting the last towel down in place. I'll never forget him for that.

"And I won't forget the time—1962, I guess it was—in Kansas City. I was sitting alone in a restaurant eating, when Mickey and Whitey Ford came in and Mickey invited me to eat with them and picked up the tab and it made me feel good all over and like a big shot besides."

"On the other hand," wrote Bouton, "there were all those times when he'd push little kids aside when they wanted his autograph, and the times when he was snotty to reporters, just about making them crawl and beg for a minute of his time. I've seen him close a bus window on kids trying to get his autograph. And I hated that look of his when he'd get angry at somebody and cut him down with a glare. Bill Gilbert of *Sports Illustrated* once described that look as flickering across his face 'like the nictitating membrane in the eye of a bird.' And I don't like the Mantle that refused to sign baseballs in the clubhouse before games. Everybody else had to sign, but Little Pete (the clubhouse man) forged Mantle's signature. So there are thousands of baseballs around the country that have been signed not by Mickey Mantle, but by Pete Previte."

"Like everybody else on the club, I ached with Mantle when he had one of his numerous and extremely painful injuries," Bouton continued. "I often wondered, though, if he might have healed quicker if he'd been sleeping more and loosening up with the boys at the bar less. I guess we'll never know.

"What we do know, though, is that the face he showed in the clubhouse, as opposed to the one he reserved for the outside world, was often one of great merriment.

"I remember one time he'd been injured and didn't expect to play, and I guess he got himself smashed. The next day he looked hung over out of his mind and was sent up to pinch-hit. He could hardly see. So he staggered up to the plate and hit a tremendous drive to left field for a home run. When he came back into the dugout, everybody shook his hand and leaped all over him, and all the time he was getting a standing ovation from the crowd. He squinted out at the stands and said, 'Those people don't know how tough that really was.'

"Another thing about Mantle. He was a pretty good practical joker. One time he and Ford told (Joe) Pepitone and (Phil) Linz that they'd finally arrived, that they were ready to go out with the big boys. Mantle told them to get dressed up, tie and all—this was in Detroit—and meet them in a place called The Flame. Mickey gave them the address and said to be sure to ask for Mickey Mantle's table.

"Pepitone and Linz were like a couple of kids at Christmas. They couldn't stop talking about what a great time they were going to have with Mickey Mantle and Whitey Ford. They got all fancied up, hopped into a cab and told the driver to take them to The Flame. After about a half-hour, the cab pulled up in front of a place that was in the heart of the slum section, a hole-in-the-wall with a broken plate-glass window in front and a little broken-down sign over the door: THE FLAME. No Mantle. No Ford. No table."

Reaction to these revealing, peek-a-boo passages written inside out from the cloister of the clubhouse was remarkable. Former teammates of Mantle were enraged, acting as if Bouton had come out against motherhood. A player whose marital problems and other peccadilloes have been reported in the press summed up the Yankee rationale when he said, "I don't care what they say about me, but they shouldn't say anything about Mickey."

Mantle, himself, responded with a perfect squelch when asked for comment about the book by Bouton, a 21-game winner in 1963 and a two-game World Series victor in '64 before arm trouble turned him into a part-time pitcher and keyhole commentator. "Jim who?" drawled Mantle.

The fact is, Bouton saw Mantle pretty much as Mickey was—a cutup in the clubhouse among his contemporaries, a withdrawn person among strangers, a man of moods that saw him go out of his way either to give autographs to kids or to ignore them, a superstar with a warm spot for young players and a pretty fast-living performer who certainly had more excuse than most of us, athletes and benchwarmers alike, if he chose to burn the candle a bit at both ends.

With a grandfather, father and two uncles having died shortly before or after the age when they say life really begins, meaning 40, Mantle had good reason not only to be fatalistic, but also to savor every golden drop of enjoyment.

The question is not really whether Mantle should have been a Boy Scout on and off the field, but whether, completely sound, he would have been the best ballplayer, all-around in the first 100 years of professional baseball.

"He's the best one-legged player I ever saw," said Casey Stengel one time in what amounted really to understatement rather than exaggeration. Before he limped out of spring training in 1969, unable to face the torture of a 19th season in the majors, the 37-year-old Mantle had two bad legs, a bum shoulder and a case history right out of Dr. Kildare or Marcus Welby, M.D. But more of the medical details later.

The point is that playing under a physical handicap from the time he contracted osteomyelitis when kicked in the leg in a high school football game, the bullnecked, broad-backed blond with the bric-a-brac legs became the most powerful switch-hitter ever, the author of 536 regular-season home runs and a record-breaking 18 in World Series competition.

The temptation is to wonder, in view of the fast getaway professionally as well as from the plate, just how much longer The Switcher might have played if he hadn't been reduced to a hobbling, hollow shell. There's good reason to believe that he would have liked, if possible, to become a 20-year man, which he would have become before he was 40.

But a former teammate and home run rival, Roger Maris, could have said it best when he first questioned how much longer the thick-set Mantle might have made it. He noted that except for Enos Slaughter, former St. Louis and New York outfielder, the only 20-year players he'd known had been trim and with little weight in the thighs and lower legs.

"I doubt that Mickey would have played longer," said Maris, "but I know he would have played more comfortably and he probably would have set even more records."

The one record Mantle didn't get was the prize that fell to Maris in 1961, the year the No. 3 and 4 men in the middle of the Yankees' batting order put on a head-to-head homer duel in an assault on Babe Ruth's majestic 60-mark set 34 years earlier.

Mantle had come reasonably close in 1956, a savage season in which he joined the select few able to win the Triple Crown of batting. The 24-year-old kid from Commerce, Okla., clobbered the ball for a league-leading .353 average and also led in homers, 52, and RBIs, 130.

Maris' best shot had been 39 homers in 1960, his first season with the Yankees and only his fourth in the majors. When in the first season of expansion to 10 teams and a longer schedule the blond bombers of the Bronx Bombers began to hit homers in tandem, most members of the Yankees and other major league clubs predicted that if either player matched Ruth's magic mark, it would be Mantle. Suddenly, too, as he became the underdog to the interloper, Mickey became a favorite of the crowd.

Funny thing, to that point, Mantle had been a brilliant ballplayer, but he'd never been quite accepted by the fans. Between 1954 and '58, for instance, he'd posted batting averages of .300, .306, .353, .365 and .304, averaging better than 38 homers and 100 RBIs a season. But because he'd had such a buildup, they expected more. Even Stengel expected more from the injury-prone body beautiful who could swish to first base from his lefthanded stance in a breathtaking 3.1 seconds and, even with his gargantuan power, drag bunt for a hit with two strikes.

"He still swings too hard, still strikes out too much and if he'd learn to bunt toward third base, he'd hit for higher average," said Stengel, who obviously saw in this mass of muscle the finest specimen of combined speed and power ever to grace a big league diamond.

Fans at Yankee Stadium were critical because they couldn't quite appreciate the pain with which Mantle played. They couldn't appreciate what they considered his unfriendliness in the outfield and they just couldn't understand that when he pulled up short on a flyball he couldn't reach, refusing to leave his feet, he was doing what was necessary to protect his peanut-brittle knees. From the time he stepped in the indentation of an outfield drain in the 1951 World Series, his rookie year, he had been troubled by one knee and finally by the other.

So they'd booed too often at times, but now in 1961 they cheered. Sympathy sided with Mantle against Maris in the battle of the long ball. Although they seldom socialized together, they shared an apartment near Yankee Stadium and shared mutual respect, too. But Mantle's eyes widened as he saw a rift widen between Rog and the press that pressured him down the stretch. By then, tired, Mickey had fallen behind in the climb to the top.

"I can't take it," Maris complained one day when they were together in the clubhouse.

"You've got to, Rog. That's part of what goes with it," said Mantle, who previously had been difficult for reporters, too. Shy around strangers, he'd warmed slowly and then he had become curt. His way to evade a question was simply not to answer it in silence that could become embarrassing.

Said Maris later, "When Mickey saw my problems, he looked into the mirror and saw himself. He relaxed more with reporters and then received what he should have had all along—the recognition and admiration of just about everyone."

Maris, of course, hit the 61 homers, which earned him fame, fortune and a sour reputation until he put in two pleasant, pennant-winning seasons at St. Louis before becoming a prosperous Anheuser-Busch beer distributor in Gainesville, Fla. Rog, only 51, died of cancer in 1985.

Mantle, hitting a career-topping 54 homers in '61 drove in 128 runs and batted .317 in a season many regarded as the greatest of his career, even better than the Triple Crown season of 1956. In 1956, '57 and again in '62, he would win the American League's Most Valuable Player award, but in '61 the prize went to Maris for a second successive season. Rog, playing eight more games than Mantle, had those seven more homers and 14 more RBIs, a league-leading 142, but his .269 average was 48 points lower.

"With no reflection on Roger, Maris had Mantle hitting behind him, assuring him of getting a good ball to hit more often," a New York writer said, "and Mickey hit more big home runs and drove in more game-deciding runs than any time before or afterward."

Mantle would begrudge Maris nothing, particularly when, as mentioned, the pendulum swung so abruptly to the well-scrubbed, dimple-cheeked slugger who became in his last several seasons a folk hero. Pestered everywhere for his time and autograph, though he no longer had to fight his way off the field as he'd done in the face of an over-friendly mob one time at Yankee Stadium, he became bigger than life, a legend in his time.

The legend first breathed life in Spavinaw, Okla., population 300, on October 20, 1931, just after a fellow Oklahoman named Johnny Leonard Roosevelt (Pepper) Martin had run wild for the St. Louis Cardinals in the World Series. The Cardinals were the favorite team of the boy's father, Elven Mantle, a strapping man they all called "Mutt," but Mutt's favorite player was the catching star of the Philadelphia Athletics, Mickey Cochrane. So the boy was named Mickey Charles Mantle.

When Mickey was four, his family moved to Commerce, population 2,500. Commerce, located in the northeast corner of Oklahoma, is in the tri-state area bordering Kansas and Missouri. Mutt Mantle went down in the lead mines for the Eagle-Picher Co., to raise a family that became five. Mutt was certain of two things: (1) Mickey would become a ballplayer and (2) he'd switch-hit.

Mutt saw to it that over the youngster's protests Mickey learned to bat lefthanded. Mickey's grandfather would throw to him lefthanded so that he could hit righthanded, which he enjoyed, and then his father threw to him righthanded so that he would have to bat from the left side. The kid didn't like it and once he even ventured to bat righthanded in a kid's game, but his father came along to spot him and raised such a storm that the lad fearfully turned back to bat lefthanded.

Mickey Mantle's affection for his father, who died of Hodgkin's disease little more than a year after the boy reached the big leagues, is deep and tender, but amateur psychiatrists have tried to make something out of the superstar's sometimes sulkiness and surliness by trying to correlate it with resentment over having had to do what he didn't want to do as a boy.

What if Mantle hadn't switched? Chances are, based on conversations with him and others, he would have hit for higher average, but probably would have hit fewer home runs, partly because Yankee Stadium was built in a lopsided way to favor lefthanded hitters. The power alley for righthanded

batters, just left of left-center, was a whopping 402 feet from home plate.

Mantle hit more line drives righthanded, but hoisted the ball better lefthanded and, therefore, took advantage of the closer porch in right field. At times he'd hit almost .400 righthanded and as little as .200 lefthanded. But the difference was not so marked early in his career, though the first gimpiness in his right leg seemed to affect his balance more when he batted lefthanded. Still, when Mickey connected, bad wheels or no, no ballpark was big enough to hold the moon shot.

Why, they talked for years about the one he drilled 565 feet, by the measurement of an enterprising tub-thumper, Arthur (Red) Patterson, after Mickey teed off righthanded against Senator' southpaw Chuck Stobbs at Washington's old Griffith Stadium early in the 1953 season. The ball went over the back wall in deep left-center of the towering bleachers and landed in a yard behind a three-story tenement.

"Yeah, that's where the ball landed," an elderly black woman said, hanging out of her window. "The neighbors thought it was a flying saucer."

Three years later, Mantle missed by only about two feet of becoming the first man ever to hit a fair ball out of triple-tiered Yankee Stadium. Hitting lefthanded against Washington righthander Pedro Ramos, Mickey smashed the ball against the gingerbread front of the facade at the top of the right-field stands.

"Fah-sahd, h'mm, I always thought that was pronounced fah-kaid," said Mantle, not the first to guess wrong on that one, but a man sensitive to cracks about his Southwest twang or the double negatives he dropped.

Even before he knew a double negative from a double-dipped ice cream cone, The Mick was murdering 'em with king-sized homers down on the "Alkali," a flat stretch of Oklahoma plain where lead-mine shafts had been sunk and abandoned. Chat piles, heaps of exhausted ore, some higher than houses, made mile-long shadows in the early morning, as Mantle described it in his autobiography, *The Education of a Baseball Player*, and dry summer winds would sift the alkali dust from the tops of the chat piles and sprinkle it over the plains, burning the grass and undergrowth.

Cave-ins and old shafts, closed off by sagging fences any kid could climb through or over, made the area dangerous in the minds of worrisome parents, but Mantle still managed to sock many a ball that skipped over the hard ground like the Oklahoma jack rabbit Mickey became.

They say Mutt Mantle ordered a baseball cap for his son before Mickey was a year old and a complete uniform when he was six. By 10, he was playing in the Pee Wee League, so small at 80 or 90 pounds that they called him "Little Mickey." He was a catcher then, which would have pleased the man whose name was given to the 12-14 age-group in which he next played in the tri-state area. The Gabby Street League was named for a colorful old Joplin catcher who had managed the Cardinals to pennants in 1930 and '31, but by then, though a year under age, Mickey was playing second base and shortstop for the Commerce-Picher team.

Now and then, Mutt Mantle would take his starry-eyed kid the 300-plus miles to St. Louis, where they'd watch the Cardinals play and even stop at the Fairgrounds Hotel, then a residence for ballplayers near old Sportsman's Park. When Mickey was 14 or 15, his father bought him for Christmas a $22 Marty Marion glove. The boy recognized that his Dad had spent more than a third of a week's wages on the model. And then a couple of years later, Mickey blossomed as a member of the fastest teenaged team in the territory, the Baxter Springs (Kan.) Whiz Kids, a Ban Johnson League club managed by a perceptive person named Barney Barnett.

One night in the lighted park at Baxter Springs, young Mantle hammered three homers, the third into a river which marked the outfield boundary in center field, some 500 feet away. Appreciative spectators passed the hat and handed him $54, a whopping sum, but, he sadly learned, he couldn't keep if he wanted to retain his high school football and basketball eligibility.

When Mantle decided to play professional baseball rather than college football, the University of Oklahoma lost a potentially great one. Mantle eventually became close with the former Sooner star, Darrell Royal, who coached the University of Texas. Living in Dallas, his home for many seasons, Mickey also has become almost as devoted to the Dallas Cowboys as he is to golf, a game at which he's extremely long off the tee.

Kicked in the lower leg in football practice one day in high school, Mantle awoke the next morning to feel the ankle hot and clumsy, swollen twice its normal size and a dirty blue. His father didn't go to work that morning, but rushed him to the doctor before breakfast. Hurried X-rays confirmed the doctor's suspicion of osteomyelitis, infectious bacteria in the bone marrow. Hospitalization in Tulsa for penicillin treatments over a two-week period arrested the condition, which led to Mickey's military deferment, a source of concern and even embarrassment in the Korean War when the Army rejected the hulking athlete as physically unfit for service.

"Over the years," wrote Harold Rosenthal, New York writer to whom Mantle painstakingly printed an articulate letter before he ever played big league ball, "Mickey has gained a justified reputation for moodiness and introspection. This black period of youth could have been the well-spring for this…a high school star athlete suddenly given crutches and the idea he might never run again."

What better tonic for a stricken youth than a trip to the World Series to see his favorite team? Mutt Mantle arranged with the superintendent of Blue Goose No. 1 mine for a couple of days off and trundled up Highway 66 bound for St. Louis and the mecca of every baseball-smitten boy, the World Series.

When he came back, Mickey put aside his crutches and told his mother to burn them. The kid was on the way.

A year later, when he wasn't even 16, his Baxter Springs manager, Barnett, tried to interest Tom Greenwade, Yankee scout, in his shortstop-pitcher, but Greenwade, who farmed at Willard, Mo., wasn't impressed. He had his eye on a third baseman.

A year later, after Mickey had worked out with the Yankees' Western Association farm club at Joplin, Mo., the Joplin manager, former New York first baseman Johnny Sturm, passed along a favorable report to the nerve center back east at Parsons, Kan. Still looking at the third baseman, Greenwade did a double-take when he saw Barney Barnett's shortstop, now 20 pounds heavier, a strapping kid with power—and Yankee scouts had been urged to keep an eye out for shortstops.

Greenwade made up his mind that Mantle was his No. 1 project. Mickey's high school baseball coach, Johnny Lingo, persuaded the school superintendent, Albert Stewart, to give Mantle his high school diploma the afternoon of the night he was scheduled to graduate so that he could play under the lights at Baxter Springs with the Yankee scout in attendance.

Greenwade, scheduled to go down to Broken Bow, Okla., to look over a prospect, watched the Friday night game and asked Mutt Mantle, the former semi-pro player, not to sign with anyone before he got back Sunday. The St. Louis Browns had muffed a chance when Mantle was rained out of a workout at Sportsman's Park at a time when the Browns had the good selling point that they were so bad they could offer a short cut to the majors. C. A. (Runt) Marr, veteran Cardinals' scout, was on the trail too. But there had been no offer by the time Greenwade and the Mantles sat in the scout's car after the Sunday game at Baxter Springs was washed out.

Greenwade offered a Class D contract, $140 a month, but the elder Mantle balked. "He can make that much playing Sunday ball around Spavinaw and working in the mines during the week," Mickey's father complained. And how much, the scout wondered, would that come to for the summer? They figured $1,150, so that's what Greenwade offered as a bonus, payable by the Yankees' Independence club in the old K-O-M League.

"Until that club folded, they had that check framed in the office," the scout who signed Mantle would relate later, smiling.

At Independence, Kan., only 75 miles from home, Mantle made his professional debut in 1949 for a manager fresh from the big league playing ranks, Harry Craft, who also would be on the way up. The kid's power impressed Craft in the 89 games in which he hit .313, but he didn't range to his right well enough for a shortstop, Harry reasoned. Craft's recommendation—third base or the outfield.

A year later at Joplin, though he erred 55 times in 137 games, the good-looking, 19-year-old strong-boy hit .383, belted 30 doubles, 12 triples, 26 homers and 136 RBIs. At the World Series that fall, between the Yankees and Philadelphia, the tall, lean Greenwade went around talking about just one thing—Mantle.

This was a period in which the Yankees faced for the first time in more than a quarter-century the prospects of playing without a box office superstar. Joe DiMaggio, the successor to Babe Ruth and Lou Gehrig, was ailing with bad legs, especially a painful heel spur. So the Yankees invited the kid from Class C to train with them in '51 in Phoenix, Ariz. Only they forgot to send him a ticket and, naively, the country boy sat there until they sent for him.

By then, the Yankees already had given him a trip around the league in September 1950. He'd roomed with a former Purdue football player, fresh off the campus, Moose Skowron and, awed by hotel meal prices, they lived on hamburgers, malted milks and French fries at short-order eating places.

By the time he took the train belatedly for Phoenix, Mantle was very much in love. He'd become attracted to a pretty, redheaded majorette for rival Picher High School and they began dating. Her name was Merlyn Louise Johnson.

"Marry Merlyn and have a redheaded, freckle-faced kid," said Mutt Mantle, already ailing. Mickey's first-born, Mickey, Jr., is redhaired and freckled. He was 16 when his father retired from baseball. There are three younger, also husky sons, David, Billy and Danny. So all four boys got to see Pop pop a few even if they weren't as awed—naturally—as so many other men's kids were by the might of Mickey Mantle.

Mantle has said he and Merlyn wished they hadn't named their first-born Mickey, Jr., because the handle made it more burdensome for the boy in kids' games. The instant recognition put the pressure on young Mantle. But when Mickey himself went west, he already was under pressure to live up to unbelievable ballyhoo.

At the tag end of a rookie school that produced infielder Gil McDougald and pitcher Tom Morgan, Stengel said he'd keep the three young "M" men around "a little while longer" in varsity spring training, but daily two things about Mantle became evident. He wasn't a shortstop and, as Stengel said, he switch-hit hard and ran as fast as anybody he ever saw in baseball.

In the first squad game, Stengel moved Mantle to center field and the powerful kid tripled, homered, bunted out, walked and flied out. From then on, everywhere the Yankees went that one spring in which they swapped training camps with the Giants so that part-owner Del Webb could show off his champions in Arizona and California, crouds flocked to see the star on his way out, DiMaggio, and the one on his way up, Mantle. Joe Dee announced in spring training that 1951 would be his last year and it would become evident that it would be The Switcher's first.

Despite the first of a series of distracting draft examinations, Mantle hit hard and the high command made its decision. Mickey would play right field, tutored by Tommy Henrich. At Brooklyn, where the Yankees played the Dodgers in a final, pre-season series, Stengel sauntered out to explain the tricky carom off the slanting right-field fence at Ebbets Field.

"You mean you played here?" the kid exclaimed, innocently.

"You don't think I was born 60 years old, do you?" growled Stengel.

That day, Mickey singled home a run off Preacher Roe and threw out a runner at the plate. That night, the Yankees announced that the contract of Mickey Charles Mantle, 19, had been purchased off the Binghamton roster. Mickey celebrated the next afternoon by getting four straight hits against the Dodgers in his first appearance at Yankee Stadium, including a home run. So the blond Paul Bunyan of the bushes wound up the amazing spring with a .402 average, nine homers and 31 RBIs.

With Mantle in right field, McDougald at third base and Morgan pitching, the Yankees were scheduled to open the American League season the next day at Washington. It rained, so they trained back to New York, where a crowd of 44,000 at Yankee Stadium saw Mickey Mantle play his first big league game in an outfield with Jackie Jensen and the man Mickey was certain to follow into the Hall of Fame, DiMaggio.

Jensen had the big day with a triple and homer off Boston lefthander Bill Wight, off whom Mantle got his first big league hit in the sixth inning, a line single over Vern Stephens' head at third base. Before the season went along too far, the kid would need to be shipped down to Kansas City to get his bearings. They were getting him out high and tight lefthanded and low and away righthanded. The temporary demotion momentarily demoralized him. Mickey is obviously a more emotional man than his later playing-field demeanor would indicate. Early, he was hot-tempered, quick to kick a helmet in disgust and to sulk.

His father brought him up short. Mutt Mantle, who would be dead of cancer by the following May, pep-talked him bluntly on a visit to Kansas City.

"It takes guts to make it, not moaning," said an affectionate father for whom the boy would be his big league alter ego. The alternative, Mutt reminded Mickey, was to grub out a living like the senior Mantle, whose best payday had been $75 a week.

The message took effect on the boy's morale. Mickey began to hit after a slump at KayCee and was recalled by the Yankees, for whom he played 96 games and hit .267 with 13 homers and 65 RBIs. With his father watching, the kid collapsed in the outfield in the second game of the Series with the Giants, the right knee buckling when he turned the leg in the slope of the drain.

"I'm sorry Dad never really saw me make it big," Mantle would reflect later. His father became more seriously ill at the Series and wound up in the hospital bed next to the son. Mickey later would support his mother and his brothers and sisters.

With the specter of heredity hanging over him, Mantle now began a race to stardom, a race with those fleet, beautifully proportioned legs which would suffer the brunt of the injuries that, year by year, one by one, took their toll.

The Yankees' team surgeon, Dr. Sidney Gaynor, first put Mickey under the knife after the '51 Series mishap to remove torn cartilage from the right knee. As late as 1965, Mantle underwent surgery on his right shoulder at a time his once-powerful throwing arm had been reduced to the point he hardly could get the ball back to the infield. Eventually, he wound up at first base, where with his instinct and natural ability he got along well enough for a couple of seasons before calling it a career. As mentioned, he waited until spring training in 1969 and then decided he just couldn't endure it or do the job.

By then, his big league medical case history, in brief, read something like this:

1951, right knee cartilage operation; 1952, the right knee again; 1954, knee cyst removed; 1955, pulled groin muscle; 1956, left knee sprain; 1957, right shoulder injury; 1959, broken finger; 1961, hip abscess; 1962, left knee injury; 1963, broken metatarsal bone in the left foot; 1965, right shoulder surgery, right elbow and left knee injuries.

"Let's see," Dr. Gaynor summarized at the end, "he had two operations on that right knee and finally developed arthritis in it. He had operations on his left knee, right hip and shoulder. He had a broken foot and several broken fingers. He had at least six painfully pulled hamstring muscles and numerous tears in his thighs and groins.

"For more than the last 10 years, he played with elastic bandages wrapped around his right leg from mid-calf to upper thigh, and the last few years he wrapped his left leg the same way for support."

Was Mantle brittle?

"No," insisted Dr. Gaynor. "It was just the demands he made of himself, the stopping, the starting, the turning. It's truly remarkable that Mickey could play 18 years on his legs and it took a remarkable amount of determination for him to do it. He wanted to play every day and he'd minimize his injuries to get to play. He's the kind of guy you'd like to have in your outfit in war."

Indeed, Mantle was a good soldier, which means he learned not to question why, but to do or die. And it's apparent that because of his great ability, managers encouraged him to play when discretion would have been the better part of valor.

Mantle, talking about his managers, looked upon Stengel as a father. He lamented that old teammate Yogi Berra had been let out after one pennant-winning season and expressed regret that he hadn't been more help for Johnny Keane. Far and away his favorite, however, was Ralph Houk, the tobacco-chewing former major who was a third-string catcher when Mickey came up.

Houk, challenging Mantle with responsibility, seemed to draw from Mickey the maturity and leadership the Major envisioned. Houk also saw Mantle in one of his most inspirational moments when he played two games in the '61 World Series with a painful abscess on his hip. When the abscess was removed, there was a hole in the buttock big enough to hide a golf ball, but they packed the wound and Mickey played until midway through the fourth game when, with the Yankees en route to a championship in five, the blood seeped through his bandages and onto his uniform.

"Get on base and I'll get a runner for you," said Houk. Mantle was limited to a single because he couldn't run before he limped off to the showers.

The Switcher really wanted that 1961 championship because he had wept unashamedly in the visitors' clubhouse at Pittsburgh's Forbes Field the year before when Bill Mazeroski's dramatic home run gave the rallying Pirates the title in a peculiar Series in which they were widely outscored, yet managed to get the odd game. Mantle's team qualities showed at their shiniest then because if ever a man personally had done his share, it was the most famous No. 7 this side of a dice table. Mantle, a .257 hitter for 12 World Series with those record 18 homers and 40 RBIs, hit savagely against Pittsburgh with 10 hits in 25 trips, batting .400 and driving in 11 runs. He belted three homers, one of them a line shot over the center-field brick wall, 438 feet away. The ball still might be bouncing around in adjacent Schenley Park.

Before he was 21 years old, Mantle was a World Series star. He followed up a .311 season in 1952 by homering twice and batting .345 in a triumph over borough rival Brooklyn. A year later, though batting only .208 in another Series victory over the Dodgers, Mickey experienced one of his biggest thrills. When manager Charley Dressen made a pitching change, bringing in righthander Russ Meyer to face him with the bases loaded in the third inning of the fifth game, The Switcher switched to the left side and slashed a grand-slam blow into the upper left-center field seats at Ebbets Field. Pretty good for a guy whose left hand had been hit with a line drive in batting practice and frozen with a pain-killing spray so he could play.

The thrills were many for the Mantle of greatness. In June 1955, he hit a tremendous smash off Kansas City lefthander Alex Kellner over the hitters' backdrop in dead center field at Yankee Stadium, just to the right of the 461-foot mark and 30 feet up. Landing in the ninth row, it was modestly calculated at 486 feet.

Coach Bill Dickey, who had been with the Yankees a long time, said in the clubhouse, "I remember one Lou Gehrig hit off Willie Sherdel in the 1928 World Series. It went on a line to the general area of Mantle's hit, but it struck the screen and didn't have the carry Mickey's homer had. I'd say this home run was the longest I've ever seen hit into the center-field bleachers. What makes it all the more remarkable is that the ball he hit was a change-up. Mantle had to supply all the power."

A year later, as related earlier, The Switcher darn near hit one out of the place and then showed that at his peak he was an excellent outfielder when he preserved Don Larsen's perfect game after breaking a scoreless tie with a fourth-inning homer off Sal Maglie.

The run was the only one Larsen needed in his historic 2-0 conquest, but in the fifth Don needed help to maintain his perfect performance. Gil Hodges lined a ball to deep left-center. Mantle raced rapidly to his right and stretched his left arm to its limit to make a backhanded catch, with his back practically to home plate as he squeezed the ball in front of the auxiliary scoreboard.

In 1963, a season of especial misfortune because of a broken left foot which sidelined him for 61 games, Mantle contributed two of his most memorable moments. To break up an 11-inning game against Kansas City, he hit a homer off righthander Bill Fischer with a smash that hit the right-field facade even harder than the one off Ramos several years earlier. This one, they say, was still going up. A scientist suggested that, unimpeded, the ball would have traveled 620 feet.

"How," quipped Houk, "would you like to have that one chopped into singles for the year?"

In August, almost two months to the day after he'd been hurt at Baltimore when he mangled his foot under the wire center-field fence, Mickey went up as a pinch-hitter in the same park before 38,555 fans. Even though Baltimore was clinging to a 10-9 victory behind southpaw George Brunet, the Orioles' fans gave Mantle such a rousing welcome that he said he felt like his hair was standing up at the back of his neck before he stepped into the batter's box.

"I had goose bumps all over my arms, too, and all I was thinking was that if I could hit a groundball or a long fly or something, I'd be happy."

Instead, he homered to left-center, leading the Yankees to victory, and went around the bases smiling to himself, "I'm a lucky stiff. Gee, I'm lucky…"

In the 1964 World Series, one in which the Cardinals ran on his ailing arm and he didn't field with the flair of the Mantle of old, Mickey still managed to make his Series swan song noteworthy. He batted .333 with eight hits, five of them for extra bases and three of them homers. One off Redbird reliever Barney Schultz on the first pitch in the ninth inning of the third game ripped high up into the right-field stands for a 2-1 Yankee victory—and it knocked Babe Ruth out of the Series home run record that had seemed almost as impregnable as the Bambino's single-season 60.

It's too bad, really, that Mantle didn't step out then but he was only 33 and those $100,000 paychecks were mighty good, particularly since some of his early investments hadn't panned out. The innocent Oklahoman had been shorn a few times as a financial lamb.

If he had gone out after the 1964 World Series, when it was painfully apparent that the Yankees were really imposters, he'd have missed breaking Lou Gehrig's club record for games played in the pinstriped uniform of the Yankees. He wouldn't have hit 500 homers, either, but he also wouldn't have struck out a record 1,710 times.

Comfortably over .300 for his career despite the tendency to miss too many pitches, Mantle stayed for four final seasons in which he hit only 82 homers, nothing compared to previous standards, and batted progressively worse—.255....288 ....245 ....237.

At the Ft. Lauderdale press conference at which he announced his retirement on March 1, a date he ordinarily would have begun to get ready for another season, Mantle stood somberly and said:

"I'm not going to play any more baseball. I was really going to try to play, but I didn't think I could. I have had three or four bad years in a row and, as a result, received the greatest disappointment of my career by falling under .300 (to .298) as a lifetime average. I was actually dreading playing another season.

"I just can't play anymore and I know it. I can't hit. I can't go from first to third when I want to. I can't steal second when I want to"—he'd stolen as many as 21 bases in a season—"and I can't score from second on a hit anymore. It really breaks me up to feel I can't do these things and I figure it is best for the team that I stop now . . .

"Even when I was thinking of working out, I knew in my heart that I was only kidding myself. I really hated to think about trying to play again. It has become embarrassing to have young kids throw the ball past me. When I talked to Ralph and told him my feelings, he admitted if he were me, he would prefer to make it quick and sharp. That's the way I wanted it, too. Now it is over, and I am glad."

Doubtless at that emotional moment, Mickey Mantle felt about as wrung out and as old as those scarred knees from which cushioned cartilage long since had been removed.

There was one pleasant postscript at Yankee Stadium and, of course, there was another at Cooperstown, in 1974, the year he became eligible for election to the Hall of Fame. At New York, where they'd honored him with a day four years before and where they'd earlier set up a cancer fund in his father's name, they again honored the handicapped hero who had gone from displeasure to demigod.

On June 8, 1969, with 61,000 on hand to salute him, including teammates of the Yankees' championship past, Mantle participated in ceremonies in which close friend Whitey Ford presented him with his uniform No. 7, retired now like Babe Ruth's 3, Lou Gehrig's 4 and Joe DiMaggio's 5. Mickey and Joe Dee, who really hadn't been as openhearted to him when Mickey was a kid as Mantle became with rookies, exchanged plaques to be hung on the center-field wall at the stadium.

Then, baring his large teeth as he squinted back the tears, the Mantle of greatness spoke in a choked voice and thanked the fans for years of loyalty.

"I would have cried, but I was too nervous about my speech," he said. "Playing 18 years in Yankee Stadium before you folks is the greatest thing that could happen to a player. To have my number retired with Nos. 3, 4 and 5 tops everything I've ever done.

"I've always wondered how a man who was dying could stand here and say he was the luckiest man in the world. Now I know how Lou Gehrig felt."

MICKEY CHARLES MANTLE

Born October 20, 1931, at Spavinaw, Okla.
Height 6-0 Weight 201
Threw right and batted left and righthanded.
Named to Hall of Fame, 1974.

YEAR	CLUB	LEAGUE	POS.	G.	AB.	R.	H.	2B.	3B.	HR.	RBI.	B.A.	PO.	A.	E.	F.A.
1949	Independence	K-O-M	SS	89	323	54	101	15	7	7	63	.313	121	245	47	.886
1950	Joplin	W.A.	SS	137	519	141	199	30	12	26	136	.383	202	340	55	.908
1951	New York	Amer.	OF	96	341	61	91	11	5	13	65	.267	135	4	6	.959
1951	Kansas City	A.A.	OF	40	166	32	60	9	3	11	50	.361	110	4	4	.966
1952	New York	Amer.	OF-3B	142	549	94	171	37	7	23	87	.311	348	16	14	.963
1953	New York	Amer.	OF-SS	127	461	105	136	24	3	21	92	.295	322	10	6	.982
1954	New York	Amer.	OF-1	146	543	129	163	17	12	27	102	.300	334	25	9	.976
1955	New York	Amer.	OF-SS	147	517	121	158	25	11	37	99	.306	376	11	2	.995
1956	New York	Amer.	OF	150	533	132	188	22	5	52	130	.353	370	10	4	.990
1957	New York	Amer.	OF	144	474	121	173	28	6	34	94	.365	324	6	7	.979
1958	New York	Amer.	OF	150	519	127	158	21	1	42	97	.304	331	5	8	.977
1959	New York	Amer.	OF	144	541	104	154	23	4	31	75	.285	366	7	2	.995
1960	New York	Amer.	OF	153	527	119	145	17	6	40	94	.275	326	9	3	.991
1961	New York	Amer.	OF	153	514	132	163	16	6	54	128	.317	351	6	6	.983
1962	New York	Amer.	OF	123	377	96	121	15	1	30	89	.321	214	4	5	.978
1963	New York	Amer.	OF	65	172	40	54	8	0	15	35	.314	99	2	1	.990
1964	New York	Amer.	OF	143	465	92	141	25	2	35	111	.303	217	3	5	.978
1965	New York	Amer.	OF	122	361	44	92	12	1	19	46	.255	165	3	6	.966
1966	New York	Amer.	OF	108	333	40	96	12	1	23	56	.288	172	2	0	1.000
1967	New York	Amer.	1B	144	440	63	108	17	0	22	55	.245	1089	91	8	.993
1968	New York	Amer.	1B	144	435	57	103	14	1	18	54	.237	1195	76	15	.988
Major League Totals				2401	8102	1677	2415	344	72	536	1509	.298	6734	290	107	.985

WORLD SERIES RECORD

YEAR	CLUB	LEAGUE	POS.	G.	AB.	R.	H.	2B.	3B.	HR.	RBI.	B.A.	PO.	A.	E.	F.A.
1951	New York†	Amer.	OF	2	5	1	1	0	0	0	0	.200	4	0	0	1.000
1952	New York	Amer.	OF	7	29	5	10	1	1	2	3	.345	16	0	0	1.000
1953	New York	Amer.	OF	6	24	3	5	0	0	2	7	.208	14	0	0	1.000
1955	New York	Amer.	OF-PH	3	10	1	2	0	0	1	1	.200	4	0	0	1.000
1956	New York	Amer.	OF	7	24	6	6	1	0	3	4	.250	18	1	0	1.000
1957	New York	Amer.	OF-PH	6	19	3	5	0	0	1	2	.263	8	0	1	.889
1958	New York	Amer.	OF	7	24	4	6	0	1	2	3	.250	16	0	0	1.000
1960	New York	Amer.	OF	7	25	8	10	1	0	3	11	.400	15	0	0	1.000
1961	New York	Amer.	OF	2	6	0	1	0	0	0	0	.167	2	0	0	1.000
1962	New York	Amer.	OF	7	25	2	3	1	0	0	0	.120	11	0	0	1.000
1963	New York	Amer.	OF	4	15	1	2	0	0	1	1	.133	6	0	0	1.000
1964	New York	Amer.	OF	7	24	8	8	2	0	3	8	.333	12	0	2	.857
World Series Totals				65	230	42	59	6	2	18	40	.257	126	1	3	.977

† Injured right knee in fifth inning of second game: did not play for rest of Series.

"M" STANDS FOR MUSCLES: For Eddie Mathews, too. The Braves' slugger (left) had 47 homers in 1953 before he was 21. Posing with homer-hitting Roy Campanella of the Dodgers.

EDDIE MATHEWS

At one time in the center-cut prime of Eddie Mathews' 18 seasons in the major leagues, an astute baseball observer described the handsome, olive-skinned, apple-cheeked slugger as "part Slaughter, part Foxx."

Except that Mathews hit lefthanded, the baseball man's appraisal of him was right on. Eddie did hustle with the fury and fire of an Enos Slaughter. He did hit with the tape-measure power of Jimmy Foxx.

In fact, at one point in a career that carried him to Cooperstown in 1978 as the best long-ball-hitting single-season and overall home run producing third baseman until Mike Schmidt, the 6-1, 200-pound performer with the quick temper and quicker swing was belting 'em at a rate that gave him, not Henry Aaron, the ghost of a chance to break Babe Ruth's record.

Uh-huh, either the Babe's 60 or Roger Maris's 61 and the monumental 714, the Mt. Everest that, lo, Aaron climbed, surprisingly when it was Mathews who had homered 299 times in the majors before he was 27 years old. Why, bless his low boiling point, Eddie was just coming into a ballplayer's prime then, and two other National League hitters of note, Stan Musial and Ralph Kiner, put him in Ruth's company. Yeah, the Babe's for frequency and, as that disremembered baseball observer said, Double-X's for distance.

Four of his first eight seasons in the bigs, Mathews banged 40 or more homers, becoming the first third baseman since Heinie Zimmerman in 1912 to lead the league, which he did with 47 at just age 20 in 1953, the Braves' first year in Milwaukee, and again with 46 in 1959. That year, never one to hit for average, Eddie slugged 46 out of the park when batting .306 and accomplishing the fourth of his five 100-plus RBI seasons.

Even a couple of years later, the Texas-born, California-reared athlete still was hitting the long one frequently enough to have exceeded his personal hopes of at least passing the 600 mark. In late April 1963, for instance, I wrote for the *St. Louis Post-Dispatch* a column, accompanied by a chart, that showed Mathews and Mickey Mantle, each 31, virtually tied for career homers. (Mick had 406, four more than Eddie.) At the time, ninth among active players, was a 29-year-old named Aaron who had 305.

Trouble was—for Mathews—the former hot-corner hothead who had cooled off his temper had cooled off as a hitter, too, a result of a severe shoulder injury suffered the year before, 1962. The harmful hurt came when he swung viciously at a pitch thrown by Houston's Dick (Turk) Farrell at claptrap Colt Stadium, the stopgap predecessor to the AstroDome.

From then until Mathews bowed out at 37 with a pinch single in three times up for Detroit in the Tigers' 1968 World Series surge past the St. Louis Cardinals, he had neither the savage strength nor pop in his bat to hit even enough average-sized homers, much less those breathtaking blows of old. Ultimately, too, he became a part-timer when dealt by the Atlanta-based Braves to Houston late in 1966.

So for the last 10 seasons his name appeared in major league boxscores, he hit only 213 more homers, an average of 21.3 compared with the 37.4 rate of those salad seasons. The result: A total of 512 home runs.

Now then, if you consider that Mathews was only the seventh player ever to achieve the 500-home run plateau, this should be construed as neither criticism nor complaint nor apology for the brown-eyed collar lad who had to beat off the gals when he was the most eligible of bachelors as the Braves moved from obscurity in Boston to fanaticism at Milwaukee in 1953.

It's just to show how hard and often the sweet swinger with the quick last-second cut could go for the downs. But even though he was a big man who could run extremely well, throw hard and accurately and field from less–than–fair–to–better–than–good as he developed, Mathews needed five tries in the annual Baseball Writers Association of American poll before he could muster the 75 percent approval necessary for Hall of Fame induction.

The point is that it HAD been a long time, probably too long, for even younger 10-year men on the baseball beat to remember when us older pressbox geezers called him Home Run Mathews, teaming with Aaron to hit even more homers in tandem than Babe Ruth and Lou Gehrig as the most productive 1-2 punch ever.

Summarily shipped to Houston and addressed coldly and incorrectly as "Edward" by the Braves at 35, Edwin Lee Mathews, Jr., made it plain when he came back five years later as manager of his nomadic major league alma mater that he regarded only old teammate Aaron as an Atlanta "untouchable."

By the time Aaron went back to Milwaukee by choice, finishing the illustrious playing career that would produce a staggering 755 home runs, Mathews was packing it in as a manager, too, headed back to Sudsville as West Coast scout for the Brewers.

From early tipping frugality, they called him,

unfairly, "cheap" when he was a rookie walking around with his glove and shoes in a brown paper sack—but they probably never had to hold a benefit for the $60,000-a-year-plus star even though he went through the costs of a couple of divorces.

In February 1977, Eddie Mathews, a son of poverty, married a long-time young friend, attractive Elizabeth Busch Burke, daughter of August A. Busch Jr., board chairman of Anheuser-Busch and president of the baseball Cardinals. Ed's two sons and a daughter by his first marriage were in the wedding party at Pasedena, Calif. Subsequently, Ed wed a third time.

If Liz Busch wasn't exactly society, it's only because the Busches preferred to do their own thing their own way, but the former Junior Leaguer and equestrienne from St. Louis did represent a crock pot-to-gold-gabboon come-up in the life of a lad once struggling. Mathews and his loving parents found it as tough to get through the Depression as he later did in turning play from a liability into an asset.

Eddie was the grandson of a genial giant named Bird Mathews, a man who seems by legend almost as big as Texas, to which Bird migrated from Georgia just after the turn of the century. Even bigger than that strapping grandson would become, Bird Mathews was a batting powerhouse for the Bonham Blue Stockings, an independent ball club that cut down even the top professional teams in central Texas.

The folk hero spawned a son, ultimately Eddie's father, who had the old man's love for the game, if not ability. A Western Union operator, Ed Mathews, Sr., was delighted to be assigned to dit-dot-dash press copy for writers in spring training of John McGraw's 1918 New York Giants. And when the Scotch-Irishman married an Iowa girl of German background a few years later, he would fill her head and their only child's with baseball yarns, just as Pap-Paw Mathews did whenever young Eddie was around. Grandfather Bird had known

Ross Youngs, Rogers Hornsby and other Texas ball players of prominence.

Eddie was born at Texarkana in October 1931, but when he was of kindergarten age, Ed, Sr., moved the family to scenic Santa Barbara, Calif. Times were tough, and now and then Bird and Grandma Mathews would help out, but from the time Eddie could toddle, his father had given him a dimestore bat. The righthanded lad picked it up and assumed a lefthanded stance. Just like that.

Like Bob Feller's father and probably others, Ed Mathews, Sr., went above and beyond the point of parental interest in helping his son develop, even insisting on a steady and increased regimen of push-ups, an exercise Ted Williams also used to help develop his Popeye arms. Powerful Eddie at 13 posted in his room at home photographs of two players—Williams and Ruth.

Eddie's high school coach, Clarence Schutte, a one-time star fullback at Minnesota, broke the kid of a bad habit—Eddie flipped the ball like a girl—and then the coach saw the burgeoning boy develop into such a football prospect that, if it had happened now with the pro gridiron so attractive, baseball might have lost a great one.

When Santa Barbara played St. Anthony's of Long Beach in 1948 at the Los Angeles Coliseum for the mythical state prep championship, triple-threat Mathews put on a brilliant show. He literally knocked out his No. 1 rival, Johnny Olszewski, later of California's Rose Bowl fame and the Chicago Cardinals. And to scouts from Southern Cal, Cal, UCLA, Stanford and other West Coast schools came Wally Butts, the squatty pass master of the University of Georgia.

But Eddie had taken a battering—one that didn't help his knees, particularly in those later years in baseball—and he frankly wasn't sufficiently interested in education. If he could have majored in watching western films, a favorite hobby when he was a beer-sipping ballplayer, just maybe he'd have opted for college first.

Instead, he wanted baseball and baseball wanted him, enough that one club offered $40,000 at a time of a rigid $6,000 maximum or a bonus-clause penalty that froze a kid to a big league roster for two years. Branch Rickey at Brooklyn offered $10,000 for the boy and $30,000 for his family, which could have used it. But Ed, Sr., reportedly nixed it.

If Rickey arched his bushy brows, he wasn't alone. More than one ball club suspected foul play in the form of under-the-table payment when Johnny Moore, former outfielder scouting for the Braves, slipped Eddie away from his high school graduation dance a minute after midnight, the first possible second the kid could be signed. The price, $6,000, meant the youngster could be optioned out.

The Mathews' explanation, father and son, was that they had studied big league rosters and regarded the Braves' Bob Elliott as the oldest third baseman and, further, neither father nor son wanted Eddie riding a big league bench when he could be out somewhere learning how to play. Besides, the Braves had promised that if the junior Mathews made it to the majors, they'd make it worth the family's while.

So less than 18 in 1949, Eddie Mathews found himself two days later in the visiting clubhouse at Chicago's Wrigley Field, where Boston manager Billy Southworth wanted a look-see before the highly touted prospect was shipped out. Smart aleck Charley (Red) Barrett, a master of variable velocities pitching batting prospect, didn't give the kid a chance—or a fastball. Eddie felt more foolish then than he did later carrying that brown paper bag with glove and spikes.

At High Point-Thomasville in the North Carolina State League, the homesick kid hit .363 with 17 homers in 63 games, and Dixie Walker, former batting champion then managing the Braves' Atlanta farm club in the Double-A Southern Association, persuaded general manager John Quinn to let him have the young fella in 1950.

Under Walker, Mathews blossomed with 32 homers in 106 RBIs, batting .286, and Dixie and coach Whit Wyatt worked to get him off his heels and onto his toes in the field. The defensive redo was completed by Billy Jurges, former slick Cubs' and Giants' shortstop, when Eddie was a Braves' rookie in '52. Jurges got him to bend his back, not only his knees, when addressing a groundball. The rest was work—hard work.

Although Braves' manager Tommy Holmes considered benching the kid against lefthanded pitching, Mathews hung in there stubbornly against the breaking ball that prompts many a batter to flinch backside. Ed's blind spot then, actually, was a high and tight fastball and he struck out frequently, but he felt helpless only against Philadelphia's herky-jerky Curt Simmons and the Cardinals's gangling Wilmer (Vinegar Bend) Mizell.

From the time, however, that he hit his first big league homer, a gargantuan wallop off Phillies' southpaw Ken Heintzelman over the high, distant fence in right-center at Shibe Park, Mathews struck some of the mightiest blows ever seen anywhere.

Charlie Grimm, one of his best boosters, raved about one to the center-field scoreboard at the back of Wrigley Field's bleachers. Eddie hit one so far over the pavilion roof into St. Louis's Grand Avenue that the wincing Cardinals thought the Babe was back. Eddie, himself, felt the most powerful was a shot that landed the third row from the top of Crosley Field's towering bleachers at Cincinnati and was still going up when it landed.

To cap that freshman season in which he batted only .248, 23 points under what he'd hit in what amounted really to an all-or-nothing-at-all career at the plate, Mathews left his farewell at Boston on the next-to-last day of the 1952 season, the Braves' last in New England.

Actually, the site was Brooklyn's Ebbets Field, where the brown-eyed slugger became the first rookie ever to hit three homers in a game. He got the range against Joe Black once and Ben Wade twice, finishing with 25 homers to break the National League neophyte mark for four-base blows set by Ralph Kiner six years earlier at Pittsburgh.

As the saying goes, they hadn't seen anything from the brown-eyed Baptist. The Braves moved—lock, stock and tepee—to new County Stadium at Milwaukee, where the good brewers went bananas over big league ball. And young Mathews responded with a .302 season of 135 RBIs and a league-leading 47 home runs.

"And," said positive Donald Davidson, the dwarf who, like Mathews, was the only man to accompany the ball club from Boston to Milwaukee to Atlanta, "if we'd still been playing at Braves Field, where the 'jury box' in right field was closer in right-center, Eddie would have hit 17 more."

Although stormy days were ahead, Mathews was the Man of the Year as the young seventh-place Braves of Boston surged home second to Brooklyn in their first season at Milwaukee.

Honored with a special "night," he got five television sets, 15 expensive wrist watches, a $400 outboard motor, personal jewelry and enough other pirate's booty to make Captain Kidd cry with envy in his garlic soup.

But the shy, pestered 22-year-old, nerves frayed from fighting off autograph seekers and well-wishers who ripped his shirt, ruined a $100 suit with leaky pens and tried to get into his downtown hotel room and even his bed, finally exploded. Booed when he made two errors in a game lost, he refused to come out between a doubleheader's contests to receive an award as the National League's All-Star third baseman. Not even Manager Grimm or coach Bucky Walters could persuade him to avoid the slight that would be misunderstood.

Stubbornly, Mathews refused beginning for what a time became a love-hate relationship with the public and press, reflecting that hot streak which manifested itself in things foolish and furious. They ranged from a slightly tipsy cops-and-robbers' chase in which, booked, he threatened to break a photographer's arm, to fights on and off the field.

The diamond doozy was one they still talk about, one that would make misty-eyed the old guard that acted as if the men went off to fight in World War II and never came back. Aggressive Frank Robinson, sliding as hard as Mathews himself would, rode high into the protesting, angry Milwaukee third baseman in 1960.

One word led to another and before you could say Jack Robinson or Frank, the powerful Mathews had decked the Cincinnati outfielder. Yep, just like that.

Marriage to the former Virjean Lauby, a Marshfield (Wis.) maiden who must have been the only girl in the baseball-batty state who didn't recognize or know him, helped settle down the Braves' powerful No. 41 and also slow the pursuit of the ladies of all sizes, shapes and ages who pursued him.

Although he would remain moody on the field, affable one day and as silent as he had been as a shy kid the next, Mathews matured further in on-and-off-the-field actions after the death in August 1954 of the father he had worshipped. His dear mother, who worked for years and would be with him when he married years later into beer baron Busch's big and colorful family, can remember as well as Eddie about Ed, Sr's., dedication. The tall, frail man would pitch batting practice to his robust son and have the boy's mother shag those drives that became long and l-o-n-g-e-r.

In 1951, the father went down with tuberculosis. He fought a losing three-year battle for which his slugging son paid heavy medical bills almost as heavy as his heart. Pop never had seen Eddie play a big league ball game.

By the time the Braves acquired Red Schoendienst, long-time St. Louis star, in a deal with the New York Giants prior to the 1957 season, manager Fred Haney had the last piece in the pennant jigsaw. The calm professional redhead at second base had a saluatary effect on the third baseman, as young Mathews would remember. With Aaron and the peach of a pitching pair, Warren Spahn and Lew Burdette, they were the key men of the first club other than Bill Veeck's hoopla, circus-atmosphere Cleveland Indians of 1948 to draw more than 2,000,000 rabid rooters. Every day—or night—was Sunday at County Stadium.

Although hitting more homers on the road than at home, Mathews was the model of consistency from his debut at Boston. At Milwaukee, in succession he hit 47 homers... 40... 41... 37... 32... 31... 46... 39... 32...

In 1957, that first pennant season, the output was 32 homers with 94 RBIs and a .292 average. But in the World Series against the Yankees, Mathews was as bush—at first—as New York writers called those exuberant beer-and-bratwurst patrons at the National League ballpark.

Although the Yankees pitched cautiously to him, walking him now and then, Eddie was hitless as the Yanks won two of the first three games. But his second blow of the fourth contest was a big one. The Yankees had tied on Elston Howard's ninth-inning blast off Spahn and had gone ahead in the 10th. A Series rout seemed at hand.

But Nippy Jones, pinch-batting, proved to plate umpire Augie Donatelli that a low-skipping pitch from wild man Tommy Byrne had shoe black on the ball, proving Jones had been nicked by the delivery. Nippy was awarded his base. Felix Mantilla ran for him and when righthander Bob Grim replaced southpaw Byrne, shortstop Johnny Logan plugged the gap in left-center with a game-tying double.

Here, the mighty Mathews—Home Run Mathews—struck with a long home run for a 7-5 Milwaukee victory, evening the Series.

A game later in the sixth inning of a duel between Burdette and Whitey Ford, Eddie showed his speed, deceptive for a big man. Timed at 3.5 seconds getting down to first base, though he regarded himself as a slow starter who really burned the gas once he shifted into high, Mathews let out on a two-down high hopper to Jerry Coleman at second base.

Rather than try a difficult charge for an in-between, do-or-die grab, Coleman waited for the big bounce. In a bang-bang play, big No. 41 surprisingly beat it out. That infield hit, prolonging the inning, won the game because Aaron and Joe Adcock followed with hits to score Mathews. Eddie's run was the only one Burdette needed—or got—in a 1-0 masterpiece.

Mathews batted only .227 in the 1957 Series, but he proved a big-play man throughout such as in the seventh and final game at Yankee Stadium when the Yanks filled the bases with two out in the ninth inning. They trailed Burdette and the Braves, 5-0, but that lead seemed trimmed to two runs when Moose Skowron hit a scorcher over third base for an apparent bases-clearing double.

However, Mathews had not put in those hours and days for sheer exercise. He converted himself from a mediocre third baseman to a good one. Eddie lunged quickly to his right, backhanded the ball beautifully and stepped on the bag for a sudden—and sensational—Series-ending stop.

"That Series was my greatest thrill and that play ranked right up there with breaking the 500-homer barrier," Mathews would recall, "because I'd had a hard time shaking what was really a bum rap about my fielding. I'd made better plays—in fact, Casey Stengel raved about one on a slow-hit ball earlier in the Series—but that big one in the spotlight stamped me the way I wanted to be remembered."

Indeed, he's remembered as an all-around player—I once saw the slugger score from first base on a single to beat St. Louis in extra innings—and as a team player. A little tense at times, subject to hot and cold streaks at bat, but a team man first.

Said Schoendienst when Mathews was elected to the Hall of Fame, "He deserved it, richly, and I know Spahn, Burdette and Aaron feel the same because we've all talked about it at reunions."

Mathews wanted the honor and recognition, too, and sounded off briefly when he got only 118 votes his first time eligible, far from election. But then he bided him time, probably aware that some of the young writers didn't know about that shoulder injury in 1962, the one that short-circuited his power. He no longer had that quick, late swing, one by which he seemed almost to jerk the ball out of a catcher's glove and pull it for distance.

So Edwin Lee Mathews, Jr., broke neither Babe Ruth's single-season nor even career home run records, as the most optimistic suggested when he broke in hitting the long ball more often and farther than any young player.

But it was a full, satisfying career, one that made Mathews the All-Star 10 times in seven seasons and four years, 1955-57-59-60, earned him a place on *The Sporting News'* annual end-of-the-season major league All-Star team.

Eddie probably put it best when his number came up late in the 1974 seasons after two years managing the Braves, the former Boston ball club of which he was the Last Man Out. He'd been a special hero at Atlanta, where he'd whaled the whey out of things as a kid at Ponce de Leon Park on the way up. But by the time the Braves moved from Milwaukee to the southern metropolis in 1966, he was damaged goods.

The dark, curly hair had receded and a mustache adorned the upper lip of history's top homer-hitting third baseman, but, though he might look mod, he lamented the unwillingness, as he put it, of current kids to give the game their all for purposes of practice and improvement, the find that had put him in the Hall of Fame.

But, philosophically, interviewed when the axe fell on him as field foreman at Atlanta, Eddie Mathews phrased it well, solemnly and sincerely:

"I've had my day in the sun," he said.

Definitely, many a day and many a night, too.

EDWIN LEE (EDDIE) MATHEWS JR.
Born October 13, 1931, at Texarkana, Tex.
Height 6-1 Weight 195
Threw right and batted lefthanded.
Named to Hall of Fame, 1978.

YEAR	CLUB	LEAGUE	POS.	G.	AB.	R.	H.	2B.	3B.	HR.	RBI.	B.A.	PO.	A.	E.	F.A.
1949	H. Point-Th'ville	N.C. St.	3B	63	240	62	87	20	3	17	56	.363	71	126	21	.904
1950	Atlanta	South.	3B	146	552	103	158	24	9	32	106	.286	159	218	24	.940
1951	Atlanta	South.	3B	37	128	23	37	5	4	6	29	.289	31	62	7	.930
1951	Milwaukee	A.A.	3B	12	9	2	3	0	0	1	5	.333	1	0	0	1.000
1952	Boston	Nat.	3B	145	528	80	128	23	5	25	58	.242	160	259	19	.957
1953	Milwaukee	Nat.	3B	157	579	110	175	31	8	47	135	.302	154	311	30	.939
1954	Milwaukee	Nat.	3B-OF	138	476	96	138	21	4	40	103	.290	133	254	15	.963
1955	Milwaukee	Nat.	3B	141	499	108	144	23	5	41	101	.289	140	280	21	.952
1956	Milwaukee	Nat.	3B	151	552	103	150	21	2	37	95	.272	133	287	25	.944
1957	Milwaukee	Nat.	3B	148	572	109	167	28	9	32	94	.292	131	299	16	.964
1958	Milwaukee	Nat.	3B	149	546	97	137	18	1	31	77	.251	116	351	22	.955
1959	Milwaukee	Nat.	3B	148	594	118	182	16	8	46	114	.306	144	305	18	.961
1960	Milwaukee	Nat.	3B	153	548	108	152	19	7	39	124	.277	141	280	22	.950
1961	Milwaukee	Nat.	3B	152	572	103	175	23	6	32	91	.306	168	281	18	.961
1962	Milwaukee	Nat.	3B-1B	152	536	106	142	25	6	29	90	.265	208	285	16	.969
1963	Milwaukee	Nat.	3B-OF	158	547	82	144	27	4	23	84	.263	176	277	19	.960
1964	Milwaukee	Nat.	3B-1B	141	502	83	117	19	1	23	74	.233	184	252	17	.962
1965	Milwaukee	Nat.	3B	156	546	77	137	23	0	32	95	.251	113	301	19	.956
1966	Atlanta (a)	Nat.	3B	134	452	72	113	21	4	16	53	.250	114	237	20	.946
1967	Houston (b)	Nat.	1B-3B	101	328	39	78	13	2	10	38	.238	594	73	11	.984
1967	Detroit	Amer.	3B-1B	36	108	14	25	3	0	6	19	.231	120	40	4	.976
1968	Detroit	Amer.	1B-3B	31	52	4	11	0	0	3	8	.212	37	13	1	.980
National League Totals - 16 Years				2324	8377	1491	2279	351	72	503	1426	.272	2809	4332	308	.959
American League Totals - 2 Years				67	160	18	36	3	0	9	27	.225	157	53	5	.977
Major League Totals - 17 Years				2391	8537	1509	2315	354	72	512	1453	.271	2966	4385	313	.959

a Traded with Pitcher Arnold Umbach (transferred from Richmond to Oklahoma City) and player to be named later to Houston Astros for Outfielder Dave Nicholson (transferred from Oklahoma City to Richmond) and Pitcher Bob Bruce, December 31, 1966. Infielder Sandy Alomar sent to Astros to complete deal, February 25, 1967.

b Traded to Detroit Tigers for cash and player to be named, July 22, 1967. Pitcher Fred Gladding sent to Astros, November 22, 1967 to complete deal.

WORLD SERIES RECORD

YEAR	CLUB	LEAGUE	POS.	G.	AB.	R.	H.	2B.	3B.	HR.	RBI.	B.A.	PO.	A.	E.	F.A.
1957	Milwaukee	Nat.	3B	7	22	4	5	3	0	1	4	.227	9	19	1	.966
1958	Milwaukee	Nat.	3B	7	25	3	4	2	0	0	3	.160	5	13	1	.947
1968	Detroit	Amer.	PH-3	2	3	0	1	0	0	0	0	.333	0	1	1	.500
World Series Totals—3 Years				16	50	7	10	5	0	1	7	.200	14	33	3	.880

HIGH-BUTTON SHOES: Christy Mathewson wore big shoes and a small glove. Big Six was one of the first five men elected for the National Baseball Hall of Fame in 1936.

CHRISTY MATHEWSON

Ring Lardner, a reformed baseball writer famous for his short stories, was a man of biting sarcasm, as reflected more than once in the all-too-brief lifetime of a wry, deadpanned literary figure.

There was, for instance, the time in the South a pompous caricature of a deep-dyed-in-Dixie aristocrat gushed forth the pedigree of his illustrious ancestry. Lardner, bored and annoyed by the lily-white blueblood, routed the Confederate snob with this casual interruption:

"I was born in Niles, Mich., of colored parents."

Lardner's sharp-edged humor was as considerable as his courage. Well-oiled with regret and remorse because his common sense had told him that not all was well in the infamous 1919 World Series, the Chicago baseball writer rolled through the private railroad cars of the notorious Black Sox, singing a parody to a popular tune of the period:

"I'm forever blowing ball games . . ."

This was the same man who had written with almost maudlin tenderness a poem three years earlier to the towering knight of the toeplate, Christy Mathewson:

> *My eyes are very misty*
> *As I pen these lines to Christy*
> *Oh, my heart is full of heaviness today.*
> *May the flowers ne'er wither, Matty,*
> *On your grave at Cincinnati*
> *Which you've chosen for your final*
> > *fadeaway.*

Mathewson wasn't dead or even dying when Lardner penned that poem, though Cincinnati did seem a graveyard of big league ballplayers at the time the 36-year-old pride of the New York Giants, arm weary after a fabulous 15-plus seasons as a model in pitching perfection and manhood, moved over to the Reds to become player-manager.

But the gentle, wistful, poetic strains seemed to capture the sweet tragedy that was Mathewson's career and life. He wound up his career by winning a complete-game farce that September from his Chicago rival of many competitive classics, Mordecai (Three-Finger) Brown. The score was 10-8, more runs than Matty would allow in a month.

His lungs damaged by poison gas in World War I, Christopher Mathewson came back to find himself eased out as manager at Cincinnati and with a cough that drove him into the sanatorium at Saranac Lake, N. Y., in a fight against tuberculosis. When he couldn't resist in 1923 the temptation to return to baseball as president of the Boston Braves—strong men don't believe they'll ever die— he wrote his death sentence.

The end came for Matty when he was just 45 in October 1925. The World Series, in which he once had been the brightest of stars, pitching three straight shutouts 20 years earlier, was just starting in Pittsburgh when the word reached Forbes Field. Mathewson's No. 1 adversary for pitching acclaim, Washington's veteran Walter Johnson, turned pale and silent. A year later, Johnson would toe the rubber at the Polo Grounds in an all-star benefit that

raised funds for a memorial tribute to Matty at Bucknell University and for the American Legion tubercular station at Saranac Lake.

Mathewson looked like a Greek god, or better still, a blue-eyed Viking with a blond cowlick. He was tall at 6-1½, taller for his day, of course, and slightly knock-kneed. At 195 pounds, he looked like the football star he had been at Bucknell, where he was an honor student, a great drop-kicker and all-around good fellow. His campus romance with Jane Stoughton, whom he'd married a few years later after he established himself with the Giants, was as delightful as their 22 years together.

Jane Mathewson learned to live with tragedy because she had the kind of fortitude that her son Christy Mathewson, Jr., a pilot, displayed after he lost his bride and a leg in a plane crash in 1933. Young Matty persevered to walk on an artificial limb and eight years later, when World War II came, he talked and battled his way back into the Air Corps and trained flyers.

Mrs. Mathewson lived 42 long years after her husband, maintaining a close relationship with Mrs. John McGraw, widow of the manager whose affection for his meal ticket of the mound far transcended gratitude even though Muggsy would fine Matty now and then for playing golf in the baseball season.

Annually, the two widows would make the pilgrimage to Cooperstown, N. Y., where their spouses had long since been enshrined in the Hall of Fame.

Mrs. Mathewson's affection for Ken Smith, director of the baseball museum, was deep and abiding. But when she died in 1967, the octogenarian left her meticulous collection of Mathewson memorabilia neither to Cooperstown nor to Bucknell. It went to the hometown school in Factoryville, Pa., where Christy Mathewson began the trip that made him a national idol.

Keystone Academy, as the current junior college then was known, was founded by Christy's great-grandmother. Factoryville, 16 miles from Scranton, was named for a cotton factory that failed. Christy, born in 1880, was the oldest of five children and he had a wonderful boyhood because his mother had some money and his father was a gentleman farmer.

"Husk," as they called the large, muscular lad, began pitching when he was 11 years old against boys several years older. By the time he attended the academy, the teenager was offered a dollar a game to pitch for a nearby town. He walked both ways, a distance of 12 miles.

When he was just 16, he was sitting in the grandstand at Scranton watching a professional team play when a ballplayer, recognizing him, came over and appealed to him to pitch in place of a regular who hadn't shown up. Matty put down his sack of peanuts, warmed up—and struck out 15 men.

Even at the time he attended Bucknell, he pitched semi-pro ball summers for $200 a month, room and board. In college, aside from falling for the pretty Jane, whom he married, the Frank Merriwell from Factoryville played football, baseball and basketball. He was class president, a member of the Glee Club and of two literary societies. Years later, when he was approached by a newspaper syndicate to do a baseball column, he reportedly turned down a ghost writer.

"Nobody ever has done my work for me so far," Mathewson is supposed to have said. "I'll manage."

Where does the truth end and fiction begin in researching or recapping the career of an early-day superstar, especially one who, like Mathewson, was treated with awe by many pressbox pioneers?

They wrote, for example, that Matty didn't drink, smoke, etc. Fact is, though he didn't play Sunday baseball out of respect to his mother, a deeply religious woman, he knew the difference between Scotch and rye. He appreciated the aroma of a good cigar, puffed a pipe and also smoked cigarettes. He knew how to fill a straight at poker, too, though he probably played more hearts, bridge and a game that captivated him almost as much as golf—checkers.

"He was a good man, a very good man," Mrs. Mathewson tried to set it straight one time, putting it so very well, "but he was not a goody-goody."

There's a story that Mathewson got his nickname, Big Six, because Sam Crane, a former ballplayer who wrote sports in New York, likened him to a prominent horse-drawn fire engine of an earlier period. But a gentle writer named Frank Graham, an accurate reporter, expressed considerable doubt. Graham thought perhaps the nickname was derived simply from an exchange something like this:

First Player: "How big do you think that big kid is?"

Second Player: "Six feet."

First Player: "He's the biggest six you ever saw—a big six."

Whether likened excitingly to a fire engine or less imaginatively to his size, Big Six lent himself to incredible yarns, which he tried to debunk whenever possible. With Mathewson honesty was the only policy, as Hal Chase found out when Matty, managing the Reds, suspected the great first baseman of contriving to drop a ball game here and there.

Mathewson's reputation for veracity was so well-established by 1908 that in the confusing and recriminating aftermath of the unforgettable moment when young Fred Merkle failed to touch second base, Matty calmed many Giant players, officials and fans who thought they'd been robbed.

"I don't believe Merkle touched second base," said Mathewson, breaking the New York party line when asked for an affidavit in the course of an investigation that led to an official league ruling. The league upheld umpire Hank O'Day's decision, which created a tie game, eventually a pennant tie and, ultimately, the greatest disappointment of Matty's career.

But that's getting ahead of the tale about the fairy tales that must be accepted or rejected if Mathewson is to come forth as just a helluva man, not something too good to be true.

At Taunton, Mass., where he began his professional career in the New England League in 1899 for $90 a month when the club could afford to pay him, Matty found something more valuable than the few bucks the club didn't have.

He did not, however, he insisted scrupulously, invent the pitch referred to most accurately by Branch Rickey as "the reverse curve." But he saw it thrown by a Taunton pitcher who, like most since, didn't know what to do with the freak delivery or how to handle it.

This became Mathewson's famed fadeaway, the pitch they called the "butterfly" when another outstanding pitcher for the Giants, Carl Hubbell, became a big winner 30 years later. It's the delivery known as the screwball, a pitch thrown with a counterclockwise twist of a righthander's wrist so that the ball breaks just the opposite of the curveball, though not as sharply. It goes down and in to the right-handed hitter, down and away from the lefthanded batter.

Mathewson, who had a good fastball and pretty good curve, relied more and more on the fadeaway as he lost the hop on his high hard one but, always, the fadeaway was a psychological threat. If a hitter guessed with Matty, he was guessing with a master of control and cunning. John McGraw, hard to please, called all battery signs from the bench, unwilling to trust either his catcher or pitcher. But not when Mathewson pitched.

"I warned him one time about not throwing a fastball to Jimmy Slagle of the Cubs," McGraw reminisced later. "Slagle beat him with a home run. Matty never forgot after that."

McGraw, playing third base briefly at St. Louis after a rousing career at Baltimore and before he took over the Giants, was the first big league batter Mathewson faced in 1900, McGraw liked to tell people.

Muggsy liked to give the impression, too, that he had taken Mathewson off first base, but the fact is that one Horace Fogel, for whom Christy pitched in 1901, merely played Matty at first temporarily because his seventh-place ball club was hurting for

personnel. And Mathewson, batting cross-handed then, could hit.

Mathewson, first baseman, hardly could have approached the superstar status of Mathewson, pitcher, but think how a bit of National League history might have been rewritten if Matty had gone to Philadelphia rather than New York.

When Matty was pitching for Norfolk, Va., in 1900—his record was 20 and 2—the manager, one phenom John Smith, called him aside one day in late July and said he'd received offers from both the Phillies and Giants.

"Which team would you rather be with?" he asked.

Christy would have liked Philadelphia, which was closer to home, but he carefully studied the pitching rosters and decided that the Giants needed more help and that, therefore, the opportunity with the New York club should be better.

At the age of 19, Christy Mathewson nervously joined the Giants. The manager, George Davis, wanted to see quickly what he had coming for the club's $2,000 investment. The rookie pitched in morning batting practice.

"Throw everything you've got," directed Davis from the batter's box.

The manager nodded approvingly at the fastball, frowned at an old roundhouse curve he promptly drove to deep center field and wondered if the kid didn't have an overhanded curve? A drop, they called it in those days.

He did. Davis swung and missed. "Pretty good," said the manager. "Anything else?"

Mathewson, still nervous, walked in toward the batter's box. "I've got a sort of freak ball, sir," he said. "I've been practicing up on it."

Matty returned to the mound and twisted his wrist to the left, throwing the ball down and in on Davis, who swung and missed.

"Throw that one again, kid," he yelled. Matty delivered and Davis, lunging, missed again. Eyes bulging, he walked out to the pitcher.

"What the hell do you call that one?" he asked.

Matty didn't know what to call it. "It's awfully hard to control," he said, "but I'm getting better at it."

Davis called out some lefthanded hitters to try to hit the odd delivery. They had their troubles, too.

"It's the darndest thing," said Davis, who then pinned on the pitch a name that is more appropriate than anything used since. "It sort of fades out of sight, a fadeaway curve."

But Mathewson and the fadeaway weren't ready immediately because Christy pitched in only six games the last two months of the season, absorbed three losses and was returned to Norfolk.

Although Ring Lardner sympathized with Matty because he ended his career at Cincinnati, the great pitcher almost began and ended down by the O-hi-o. He was drafted by the Reds from Norfolk for $100 and then was promptly traded back to the Giants for Amos Rusie, a one-time pitching standout who had been sidelined with an ailing arm for two years.

Was Zinzinnati done in? In one of the strongest indictments possible against syndicate ownership in sports, it's enough to report that John T. Brush, the Reds' owner who generously sent Mathewson to New York, was en route there himself to become boss of the Giants. What better place to hide the bright prospect who would know only one losing season in the next 14?

Matty, like June, was ready to bust out all over. A 20-game winner in 1901, his first full season in the majors, he slumped to 14-17 in 1902, McGraw's first season as manager, but then he began an incredible string.

In 1903, he not only posted a spectacular 30-13 record, but he also scored eight straight victories over the pennant-winning Pittsburgh Pirates, a team that included Honus Wagner, Fred Clarke, Tommy Leach and other standouts.

In 1904, Mathewson improved to 33 victories and the Giants won the pennant, but there was no World Series. A year later, when he was 31-9, the Giants finished first again, and Matty turned in his unforgettable three-shutout performance in the five-game 1905 World Series, one in which the Philadelphia Athletics were blanked four times, the Giants once.

The Giants trotted onto Philadelphia's Columbia Park for the first game of the '05 Series dressed in new black uniforms, a bit of psychology by McGraw. The A's must have recognized pallbearers when they saw them.

Mathewson blanked them in the opener on four hits, 4-0. After Chief Bender shut out New York in the second game, rain delayed the third contest a day, excuse enough for McGraw to come back with Matty. Christy pitched another four-hitter, 9-0. And after Iron-Man Joe McGinnity outdueled Eddie Plank, 1-0, a Saturday crowd of 25,000 elbowed into the first Polo Grounds to see Mathewson brought back with only one day's rest.

He bested Bender, later a staunch golfing rival when both could shoot in the 70s. The score was 2-0 and Matty scattered six hits, giving him a 27-inning total of only 14, a total unmatched until St. Louis' Bob Gibson turned back Boston three times 62 years later. Mathewson walked just one batter and struck out 18.

Big Six' control was even more remarkable than those three Series shutouts, his 94 victories over a three-year stretch, his modern N. L. record of 37 in one season and, yes, even his career total of 373 triumphs, the league high that was matched in 1929 by Grover Cleveland Alexander.

Mathewson in 1913 pitched 68 consecutive innings without giving up a base on balls. His ratio of strikeouts over walks could be astonishing. For instance, in 1908, his 37-victory season, when he fanned 259 and passed only 42 in 391 innings. In '13, he walked just 21 in 306 innings.

"A woman could have caught Matty," said a great receiver, Roger Bresnahan.

Where most pitchers used about 125 deliveries a game, Mathewson always planned on throwing only 75 to 80 times, even though he got his share of strikeouts. Except in a jam, though, he really didn't try to strike out a hitter. He outdid himself one game when he needed just 67 pitches to walk off the winner.

A loyal roommate, Laughing Larry Doyle, a great second baseman who also contracted tuberculosis and was confined at Saranac Lake, always contended that Mathewson would loaf when he had a large lead, unconcerned about his reputation or records.

"He was great only when he had to be, at his best in a pinch," said Doyle. A book by and about Matty in 1912 was aptly titled *Pitching In a Pinch.*

Was Mathewson the greatest pitcher who ever lived?

McGraw, understandably prejudiced, thought so. Connie Mack, whose devotion to the American League would almost match McGraw's fanatic attachment to the National League, made an even more telling case one time when he was quoted as saying:

"Mathewson was the greatest pitcher who ever lived. He had knowledge, judgment, perfect control and form. It was wonderful to watch him pitch—when he wasn't pitching against you."

Mr. Mack, the baseball patriarch, had more than a few great ones of his own, including Rube Waddell, Chief Bender, Eddie Plank, Jack Coombs and Lefty Grove, and he knew more than a little about Cy Young, Walter Johnson and, presumably, Old Pete Alexander.

Old Connie, if quoted accurately, was not misled, apparently, by either Mathewson's final World Series record—five defeats in 10 decisions. Or by the fact that his own Athletics took two out of three from Big Six in 1911 and split a pair of games with him in 1913. Philadelphia won both Series.

Actually, with any luck, Mathewson might have been unbeaten in World Series competition because he had a sparkling 1.15 earned-run average for 101⅔ innings of blue-ribbon competition. He

yielded 76 hits and 22 runs, only 13 of which were earned, striking out 48 and walking a mere 10.

The triumphs and tragedy of Mathewson, as indicated at the outset, were bittersweet. He was a serene man, shy almost to the point of aloofness with fans and strangers, though it's obvious, too, as Grantland Rice wrote: "Christy Mathewson brought something to baseball no one else had ever given to the game—not even Babe Ruth or Ty Cobb. He handed the game a certain touch of class, an indefinable lift in culture, brains, personality…"

Superlative, but mortal. Powerful but, alas, not indestructible. Unusual, but not perfect. Either Matty or his literary ghost, if by then he had consented to use one, couldn't understand in print one day in the 1911 Series how Rube Marquard could have given Philadelphia's Frank (Home Run) Baker the pitch by which the Athletics' third baseman had hit a game-winning homer.

The next day Matty had the A's down in the ninth, 1-0, and two strikes on Baker when Home Run hit a homer that tied the score and won his nickname. After the Athletics went on to win the game in the 10th, 3-2, it was Marquard's turn to retort in print.

In 1912, the Giants played butterfingered baseball behind their bread-and-butter man, giving up six unearned runs in three Series games with the Red Sox so that the best he managed was an 11-inning tie, 6-6. Still, Matty and his mates might have pulled it out in the final game of the Series.

The old money man of the mound was leading in the last of the 10th, 2-1, when Fred Snodgrass muffed a fly in center field and then, after Chief Meyers, the catcher, and Fred Merkle, the first baseman, had bluffed each other out of an inning-ending catch on a pop foul hit by Tris Speaker, the Gray Eagle spanked a game-tying single. Larry Gardner's long outfield fly then drove in the decisive run.

Merkle was, of course, the unfortunate reason a playoff was necessary to decide the pennant in

1908, Mathewson's greatest season. The rookie first baseman, following custom, had failed to complete the 90-foot run from first base to second on an apparent game-winning single by Al Bridwell. One way or another, with second baseman Johnny Evers of the Cubs alertly screaming for the ball, Chicago got a forceout after the crowd had surged onto the field.

So that certain 2-1 New York victory became an official 1-1 tie, necessitating a replay to decide the pennant when the Giants and Cubs wound up the season exactly even.

"I'm not fit to pitch today," Mathewson told his wife the morning of the replay. "I'm dog-tired."

If, though, center fielder Cy Seymour hadn't decided suddenly that he knew more about baseball than the master craftsman, Matty might have made it in the bitter climax to the sweetest season of his career.

A Mathewson nemesis, Joe Tinker, the light-hitting Chicago shortstop, came up in the third inning with two on, and, coolly, Matty motioned Seymour deeper. The center fielder drifted out, but, certain he knew more about hitters than the old master, he moved in again when Christy turned his back. So Tinker's long fly to center, a ball which could have been caught, went for a triple that led to a four-run inning and a 4-2 pennant payoff for the Cubs over 37-game winner Matty, a loser in the biggest game of his career.

In the mood again of Ring Lardner, the soft-hearted cynic:

My eyes are very misty
As I pen these lines to Christy
Oh, my heart is full of heaviness today.

CHRISTOPHER (BIG SIX) MATHEWSON
Born August 12, 1880, at Factoryville, Pa.
Died October 7, 1925, at Saranac Lake, N.Y.
Height 6-1 1/2 Weight 195
Threw and batted righthanded.
Named to Hall of Fame, 1936.

YEAR	CLUB	LEAGUE	G.	IP.	W.	L.	Pct.	ShO.	H.	R.	ER.	SO.	BB.	ERA.
1899	Taunton	N. Eng.	17	-	5	2	.714	-	-	-	-	-	-	-
1900	Norfolk	Va.	22	187	20	2	.909	4	119	59	-	128	27	-
1900	New York (a)	Nat.	6	34	0	3	.000	0	34	32	-	15	20	-
1901	New York	Nat.	40	336	20	17	.541	5	281	131	-	215	92	-
1902	New York	Nat.	34	276	14	17	.452	8	241	114	-	162	74	-
1903	New York	Nat.	45	367	30	13	.698	3	321	136	-	267	100	-
1904	New York	Nat.	48	368	33	12	.733	4	306	120	-	212	78	-
1905	New York	Nat.	43	339	31	9	.775	9	252	85	-	206	64	-
1906	New York	Nat.	38	267	22	12	.647	7	262	100	-	128	77	-
1907	New York	Nat.	41	315	24	12	.667	9	250	88	-	178	53	-
1908	New York	Nat.	56	391	37	11	.771	12	281	85	-	259	42	-
1909	New York	Nat.	37	274	25	6	.806	8	192	57	-	149	36	-
1910	New York	Nat.	38	319	27	9	.750	2	291	98	-	190	57	-
1911	New York	Nat.	45	307	26	13	.667	5	303	102	-	141	38	-
1912	New York	Nat.	43	310	23	12	.657	0	311	107	73	134	34	2.12
1913	New York	Nat.	40	306	25	11	.694	5	291	93	70	93	21	2.06
1914	New York	Nat.	41	312	24	13	.648	5	314	133	104	80	23	3.00
1915	New York	Nat.	27	186	8	14	.364	1	199	97	74	57	20	3.58
1916	N.Y. (b)-Cinn.	Nat.	13	74	4	4	.500	1	74	35	25	19	8	3.04
Major League Totals			635	4781	373	188	.665	83	4203	1613	-	2505	837	-

a Joined Giants midseason, 1900. Turned back to Norfolk at end of campaign, but drafted by Cincinnati and traded to Giants for pitcher Amos Rusie.
b Traded with outfielder Edd Roush and infielder Bill McKechnie to Cincinnati for infielder Charles Herzog and outfielder Wade Killefer, July 20, 1916.

WORLD SERIES RECORD

YEAR	CLUB	LEAGUE	G.	IP.	W.	L.	Pct.	ShO.	H.	R.	ER.	SO.	BB.	ERA.
1905	New York	Nat.	3	27	3	0	1.000	3	14	0	0	18	1	0.00
1911	New York	Nat.	3	27	1	2	.333	0	25	8	6	13	2	2.00
1912	New York	Nat.	3	28 2/3	0	2	.000	0	23	11	5	10	5	1.57
1913	New York	Nat.	2	19	1	1	.500	1	14	3	2	7	2	0.95
World Series Totals			11	101 2/3	5	5	.500	4	76	22	13	48	10	1.15

SAY HEY: Which was just about all grinning Willie Mays would say when he came up to the Giants in 1951 and exploded at bat, on the bases and especially afield as New York won a storybook pennant and Wonderful Willie launched a fairy-tale career.

WILLIE MAYS

One wintry night in early 1954 when a cold wind shimmied like a belly dancer up the Potomac into Washington, two of the nation's law-enforcing finest came up on a suspicious-looking pair at the airport. For good reason, the FBI men were as jumpy as Willie Mays scaling an outfield wall for a baseball blast.

That day on Capitol Hill, where the solons were accustomed to taking oral and literary potshots, wild-eyed Puerto Rican patriots literally had taken pot shots as members of the House assembled. The manhunt was on.

There, at the airport, a natural spot to look for the farthest if not necessarily quickest getaway, were two men of a different color, darker-complexioned, and entirely furtive or, at least, strange or unorthodox to the two G-men.

One suspect, middle-aged, shivered in a suit coat, newspapers plastered for warmth against his chest. The other, younger, wore an overcoat obviously too large and one that might have belonged to someone else, including the older guy, whose nervousness was obvious in contrast to the kid's calm.

One government agent asked for identification and the older black man, really café au lait in color, heavy on the cream, pointed to his young companion and said, huffily, "This is Willie Mays."

The FBI man snorted, "Yeah, and I'm Sherlock Holmes."

Now, under the circumstances, Frank Forbes, a former Negro National League player, part-time New York state boxing judge, promoter and baseball talent scout, might have been wise to let the G-man's wisecrack take second, unmolested.

Instead, because he was so high strung, Forbes responded sarcastically to "Sherlock Holmes" by growling, "Yeah"—meaning the other FBI fella—"and who's this? Dr. Watson?"

Well, years later as Willie Mays breezed into the baseball Hall of Fame despite 23 blind or bigoted baseball writers out of 432, Forbes could remember with a chuckle the quarter-century earlier episode, explaining:

"I guess I'm lucky I didn't talk Willie and me into the hoosegow, but, hell, I was more afraid of Leo Durocher than I was of those two guys."

You see, the New York Giants, who hadn't heard that they soon would be playing at Candlestick Park by San Francisco's Bay rather than at the Polo Grounds near the Harlem River, were waiting most impatiently in spring training at Phoenix, Ariz., for the return of the prodigal, the precocious Say-Hey Kid who had spent nearly two full seasons in the Army after having helped make possible the Little Miracle of Coogan's Bluff in 1951. You know, the sensational surge climaxed by Bobby Thomson's dramatic playoff home run that done in—oops, did in, Eliza—the interborough rivals, the Brooklyn-based Dodgers.

No one better than Durocher, the dapper field foreman of the Stonehams, knew the value and importance of the return of 23-year-old center field wunderkind Mays, though Horace's nephew and unofficial general manager, Chub Feeney, later National League president, was the official timekeeper.

Each morning, cheerfully at practice, Feeney would sing out, "Only three (or two) days before Willie comes marchin' home!"

But the Giants knew that in his age of innocence, Willie might stray—even if no one played street stickball games in mid-winter, heck, many a curvaceous, long-legged wolf in sheep's or more likely mink's clothing might want to distract that good-looking hunk of young manhood. So they dispatched Forbes to Fort Lee in Virginia to bring back the "pennant."

Frank acted as if they'd asked him to guard Fort Knox, partly because Forbes knew a superstar even before it barely had time to glitter and, sure enough, the generals at camp wanted to shake the hand of the good-natured, gifted soldier of whom they were fond. Uh-huh, and there'd been a brief dalliance of a more intimate nature and, to Forbes's dismay and disgust, they'd missed connections to the Washington airport.

Irresponsibly, Willie had forgot his overcoat, but Forbes, again recognizing that he'd never seen the day, even when younger, when he could carry Mays' glove, bat or baseball shoes, appreciated the greater value of the athlete. So he literally gave the kid the coat off his back and they'd gone into town, killing time at a movie before the flight to Phoenix, and then Uncle Sam had stepped in to make the anxious babysitter's job more difficult. Yep, the FBI men physically put the two men on the airship to Arizona and watched to make certain they didn't get off.

Forbes was tempted to stick out his tongue at them on takeoff—imagine a governmental gum-shoe not recognizing Willie Mays!—but Frank needn't have considered the disrespectful gesture. Willie stuck out his tongue figuratively for friend, foe and the Durocher's guys, in turn, did the same to the National League in 1954.

Willie was indeed back, leading the NL in hitting with an average, belting 41 homers, driving in 110 runs, and leading the pennant. That was the year, with Jim (Dusty) Rhodes drinking the right stuff and Durocher making the right moves, especially in beckoning for Dusty to do his stuff as well as to drink it, New York won the World Series in four straight, the Giants knocked off a Cleveland ball club that had compiled a record American League victories, 111.

If, in retrospect, there's really only a surprise or two in Mays' career, other than the plays he pulled, especially afield and at bat, it's only that he was given just two National League Most Valuable Player awards, 1954 and '56, and that he played on really only four pennant-winning ball clubs—the Giants of '51, '54 and '62 and the Mets of '73.

One thing more, other than the question of whether Willie Howard Mays, Jr., was the greatest player ever and absolutely no doubt that he played a year or two too long, is the relative standing of the man as a home-run hitter.

On the record alone, playing 21-and-a-fraction seasons, Mays totalled 670 career home runs, third only to Henry Aaron and Babe Ruth. Twice, 1955 and 1965, he achieved the rare 50-homer plateau (51 and 52), but his last two seasons he hit only 14 total. Even so, there's good reason to believe that if it hadn't been for nearly two years in service, he would have been the first to climb the towering target of the Babe's apparently unsurmountable 714.

Not that Aaron necessarily wouldn't have prevailed with his 755. Fact is, if Mays had pushed farther if not longer, each of the early black standouts of the post-Jackie Robinson breakthrough might have hit more out of parks.

Incidentally, there's no doubt, at least in this judgment, that Mays had more difficult home run targets than Aaron, especially when Henry moved from Milwaukee to the higher altitude of Atlanta, where the Braves even pulled in the left-field fence for him. New York's Polo Grounds did have chummy fences at the foul-lines, but was cavernous in left-center, right-center and straightaway. And Candlestick Park's chilly, ill wind was punishing to righthanded pull-hitters so that Willie had to learn

to go the other way with the ball. Too many hitters can't do that.

Conditions improved over the years in SanFran, including dimensions of the park and added construction that diminished the wind some, but Candlestick was not conducive to righthanded power-hitting or, when the grass grew long in that damp climate, to hitting in general.

Significantly, Mays' first major league hit was a home run off none other than the masterful Warren Spahn in 1951, the year the Giants brought up the dusky southern-born Paul Bunyan batting a staggering .477 average at Minneapolis. Willie, who'd hit so powerfully in the Association was so helpless at the outset in the National League that he pleaded with Durocher to send him back.

But The Lion already had seen evidences of what would be the A-1 talents Mays possessed—speed, strength of arm and incredible ballhawking skill. The ability to hit and to hit for power would come—and they did.

When Mays reported, wide-eyed, eager to please, ready to smile at the slightest kind word and yet frown fearfully over what he envisioned shortcomings, his arrival prompted a lineup change that turned the Giants from pretenders to contenders. They'd come strong in 1950, a result largely of Sal Maglie's emergency as a pitcher of renown and Jim Hearn's toeplate contributions to Larry Jansen's. In fact, the third-place Giants of '50 went to the post as pennant favorites in '51.

But the Jints, as the field announcer at the Polo Grounds used to call them, lost 11 of their first 13 games. The rival Dodgers, meanwhile, managed by Charley Dressen, were off briskly to what seemed a runaway.

Mays' arrival did make a difference because Durocher, who had brayed and roared about "my kind of ball club" after an ironic twist that took him from hated rival across the bridge in Brooklyn to Coogan's Bluff, promptly shook up his lineup. Mays went into center field, Thomson moved into third base, Whitey Lockman shifted to first and Monte Irvin also went from first back to the outfield, where his throwing arm and Mays' created baserunning traffic jams.

It was Irvin, by the way, who hung onto Mays the nickname most popular among the players—"Buck." Willie, in his high-pitched voice that said "Say Hey" a lot less often or not so frequently as the newspapers would indicate, used with no malice the feminine form—"Orlanda"—in referring to his long-time teammate, fellow slugger Orlando Cepeda.

Cepeda, who came along as the Giants moved lock, stock and batting cage to San Francisco, was Frisco's first hero, not Willie the Wonder. Somehow, before and after the Giants began playing at Seals Stadium before Candlestick went up in too big a hurry and in the wrong location, the Bay area expected more from the brilliant outfielder who by then had followed up grandly that 121-game rookie season of .274 with 20 homers and 68 RBIs.

In 1955, he had dipped some in average from .345 to .319, but his home runs swelled to 51 and he drove in 127 runs. Moreover, that year Willie became the first big leaguer ever to hit 50-plus homers and steal more than 20 bases (24) in a season. The next year, though falling farther to .296, he became the first National Leaguer and only fifth leaguer with 30 homers and 30 thefts in the same season (36 and 40). And a year later, 1957, the last for the Giants at the address of John McGraw and glamor associates, Mays did it again when batting .333. Not only did he hit 35 homers and steal 38 bases, but he also tripled 20 times.

At San Francisco, Willie's figures were good, but not great in the early years. Home runs, for instance, were 29, 34 and then (at Candlestick) 29 again and his RBIs a solidly steady 96, 104 and 103. Averages, too, at .347, .313 and .319.

Maybe they resented that this was a darker Joe DiMaggio or, perish the thought, even better than Joe Dee. Maybe they didn't want to compare him

as a hitter with their old Pacific Coast League idol, Lefty O'Doul. Maybe the New York press and ball club had been too lavish in praise. Maybe, therefore, they expected him to wear blue leotards and that red "S" for Superman instead of the black-and-orange-trimmed white home or road gray uniforms of the Giants.

So they took Baby Bull Cepeda to their hearts more than they did Willie, but, to the everlasting credit of the often-pouting, occasionally sulking star who was considerably more sensitive than many realized, Willie made him home among them. As a man of a different color, he ran into housing problems at first, but, eventually, he got what he wanted. Willie had the good sense to recognize that, if you could slacken the wind and take a bit of the bite out of it, SanFran was paradise. And San Francisco began to appreciate Mays, who had outstripped Stan Musial as the National League's best and—again!—was either the best ever, as Durocher and other champions maintained, or certainly rated in the first division of all-time, all-around talent.

Why, take 1962, for example, when, led by Alvin Dark, the Giants gave San Francisco its first and only pennant. As usual, Willie was climbing the wire outfield fence within the fence or charging in for shoetop catches—somehow, he didn't seem to have to leave his feet often—and he was throwing with strength, accuracy and an intuitiveness summed up best one time by another Giants' manager, Bill Rigney.

At spring training, Rig was instructing his infielders. "When a ball goes out to or near Mays, go to the nearest base. Don't ask me to explain it, but just do what I tell you because sometimes you'll get the damndest, most unexpected surprises if you're as on your toes as he is. Somehow, he knows which runner has rounded a base too far, which has become over-confident or if failing to concentrate, and—bang!—he'll slap the ball in behind or ahead of the man, so, again, be there!"

Like the last day of the '62 season. After hitting

.304, pounding 49 homers and driving in 141 runs, Mays led the Giants in a charge that caught the slumping Dodgers. And Buck teed off on Houston's Turk Farrell for a pennant-tying home run.

In a three-game playoff with the Dodgers, L.A. looked to be in command with a 4-2 lead in the final inning of the final game, thanks to Maury Wills' excellence the year he broke Ty Cobb's record with 104 stolen bases. But Ed Roebuck, the Dodgers' relief ace, had gone to the rubber once too often. Arm weariness robbed him of his control, and the sinkerball expert issued two walks that filled the bases with one out, Mays coming up.

Now, for a guy who sparkled in All-Star play with his record 23 hits in 24 games and a .307 average, Mays was no super-hitter in playoffs, Championship Series or World Series. But against Roebuck when a sharp groundball could have been an inning-ending double play or any other kind of out would have meant that Cepeda's subsequent fly would have ended it, Willie measured his man and hit a tremendous shot. It was a line drive back through the box. The ball tore off Roebuck's glove for a run-scoring single, the catalyst to a four-run inning and a 6-4 victory that meant the pennant.

Willie, characteristically basket-catching at his belt the Dodgers' final out in the home half of the ninth, was so jubilant that he turned, wheeled and flung the ball into the center-field bleachers of depressed Dodger Stadium. Won, a pennant. Lost, a potentially valuable souvenir.

Willie Howard Mays, Jr., tossing away any ball, much less a memento, had come a long way from the kid born in Fairfield, Ala., in 1931, son of a steel-mill hand who never earned more than $2,000 a year. If though, Kit Kat Mays, as they called the cat-like father of the superstar, had been white or even Willie's paternal grandfather, Walter, the family might have had three generations reach the big leagues.

When Willie was only 14 months old, the story goes, Kit Kat would roll a ball across the carpet of the living room, to the utter delight of the infant, who cried when the father wearily ended the game. Later, father and son would have catches. By the time Willie was six years old, he'd fungo skyward flyballs to himself and run them down. Nice work if you can get it—or do it.

Reared by an aunt to whom he was devoted, Willie attended Fairfield Industrial High School and, to no amazement of anyone fascinated by his athletic ability or that rock-hard body with the bulging biceps and slightly bowed legs, he was outstanding in football and basketball as well as baseball. Once, he threw five touchdowns in a game and did something he rarely did on a ball field—kicked a ball—and out of sight.

Willie loved football so much that he shinnied up a tree once to watch a game and fell out of the tree, breaking a leg. Years later in the Army he would fracture the ankle of his other leg, but for years, man, he was s-w-i-f-t.

For Kit Kat Mays, however, baseball was THE one sport for his son, and young Willie was swinging against semi-pros when he was only 14 years old. One day his father took him to see Lorenzo (Piper) Davis, manager of the Birmingham Black Barons, a Negro National League team. Piper liked what he saw.

Years later, tracing Willie's career for its first of two decades in the bigs, author Arno Hano said Davis could remember that the 17-year-old broke into the Barons' lineup and, though Willie did well at once, Piper opened his stance a trifle so that he would aim at the pitcher, not peek toward him.

For the young man barnstorming with the Birmingham black league ball club, it was a round of baseball, pool-shooting, rummy, pinball, western movies, television, Nat King Cole, Johnny Nash and soft drinks. One day the $300-a-month kid got so engrossed in a pool hall that he blew the Barons' bus, grabbed a car and overtook the bus, screaming to manager Davis:

"What you gonna do? You gonna leave me? I'm a pro ballplayer, hear? You can't leave me."

No matter how modest they seem, the good ones ALWAYS know they're good. The Giants, scouting another player, didn't need to see much of Mays to know that he was Rembrandt and the other guys house painters. Although Branch Rickey, as the pioneer who deserved everlasting credit for cracking the insidious color line with Robinson, was loathe to give any black league player or club a bonus, Stoneham's Giants peeled off $5,000 for Mays and $10,000 heart balm for his ex-employers.

So at 19, playing in the Inter-State League at Trenton, N.J., not far from where he'd make his mark in the Big Apple, Willie went to work in the white man's world he would dominate. For 81 games in 1950, before the aforementioned Bunyanesque .477 at Minneapolis in the Triple-A American Association in '51, Mays hit a .353 that was promising—almost as promising as his fielding.

To anyone who ever saw him, as well as, hopefully, those who read this, Willie was a 7-come-11 natural as a ballplayer, one who defied some of the basic do's-and-don'ts of the diamond. For instance, running the bases, you're not supposed to look back over your shoulder because just about everybody slows down to look, as Satchel Paige would say, to see if anything was gaining on him. And, besides, what 'n heck you got a third-base coach for? Yet the managers Willie respected most—probably Durocher, Alvin Dark and Herman Franks, an investment counselor to him, too—all recognized that this man was unique. His judgments were, too, and uncanny.

Why, when he was 40 years old and time had robbed him of much of his speed if not the old elan and eclat, Willie homered to tie a game against the Mets in the eighth inning. Then he won it, pure and simple, in the 10th, 2-1.

Mays walked, took second on a sacrifice and when Alan Galagher grounded to third, Mays stopped in front of Tim Foli, rookie third baseman who would prove to be a short-fused ballplayer. Then Willie bolted away again, and Foli, swiping at him, missed the tag and was too late to get Gallagher at first. So Mays scored the winning run on a flyball by Tito Fuentes.

Said Mays afterward of Foli, "I think he got confused when I stopped…" Understated.

The Mets' manager, Gil Hodges, put it so well. Said Hodges, "It was simply a case of experience versus youth, and experience won. What is there to say about Mays that hasn't been said 100 times before? He's simply the best."

For all of his zest, his practical jokes, whether as perpetrator or foil, Willie had his troubles. Twice, he ran afoul marital shoals, once after having adopted an infant son, Michael, who couldn't have been treated more tenderly than if he were the superstar's own. He wasn't mature enough to handle the disappointment of a disappointing marriage then, and his moods carried over at times to his relations with others.

At times he could play himself into sheer exhaustion, dropping dizzily on the diamond, and, withdrawing more, he could sleep the clock around, retreating to his hotel room on the road to sleep long and watch TV there, even eating his meals in the room to avoid autograph seekers and others who sought to fawn over him or to use him.

When he'd quit playing and was on the road to hustle one product or cause or another, the Atlanta Journal's sports editor, Furman Bisher, wrote for *The Sporting News* a column which he told a "friendly flack" on the phone in New York that he wasn't interested in seeing Mays. For eight years, Bisher said, Willie had apporached Atlanta's city limits "as if they were off the field," observing:

"I tried to talk to him in the dugout, the clubhouse, by the batting cage. I called him at his hotel and invited him to breakfast, to lunch. 'Pick a meal,' I said, 'just any old meal.' Willie didn't want to see me. Gee, I like you. You're a nice guy. An old friend. For you, I'd be happy. But after eight years shut out and turned down by Willie Mays, I have one message for him, 'Go to hell.' "

A mite strong, no doubt, but, as the "friendly flack" told Bisher, "I didn't realize this was going on. I've been getting the same reaction from a lotta guys."

Mays could be difficult at times and probably for good reason, such as his early trouble at San Francisco, where he'd hit one up the shaft and a pressbox cynic would crow, "Another $80,000 popup."

Actually, Willie's pay doubled that amount even before either inflation or the free-agent fiasco turned baseball's poor peons into instant millionaires, but, ultimately, with age taking its toll of Mays' talent and Stoneham's shrinking financial base bringing criticism from other Giants' stockholders, Stoneham sorrowfully dealt the 41-year-old athlete. Horace sent Willie to the New York Mets in May 1972 for cash and one Charley Williams, a pitcher. Criminy, some 18 years earlier when Anheuser-Busch had bought the St. Louis Cardinals, Stoneham laughed when Gussie Busch wondered if friend Horace would take $1,000,000 for his center fielder.

For a wonderful sportswoman, Mrs. Charles Shipman Payson, nee Joan Whitney of the horse-racing family, to obtain her long-time idol, was a dream come true. Mrs. Payson arranged for financial security down the road for Willie, consigned by then to occasional outfield and/or first-base play. Distressingly, the sensational center fielder looked almost amateurish on wobbly legs at Oakland in the 1973 World Series, his swansong. Time had done to Willie Mays what none other could do. Why, time was pumping figurative fastballs past him.

After they hung up uniform No. 24, the famed double dozen of the diamond, Willie seemed to have trouble adjusting to even an informal time-table as part-time coach and instructor for the Mets. After Mrs. Payson's death, it just seemed as if the front office was content to let Mays collect his de-

ferred-payment check and come and go as he played. At one time he'd seemed almost childishly to run through his money. Fact is, he was suspended by one commissioner, Bowie Kuhn, for working for a gambling casino, then reinstated by another, Peter Veberroth.

Although Mays over the years said many things that represented baseball etiquette, including San Francisco protocol that DiMaggio had been his idol and rated as the most outstanding, he changed his tune—refreshingly—when it was announced in January 1973, that Willie had become one of the rare ones to win Hall of Fame election his first time eligible.

At first he dodged a particular question, then smiling and voice hitting the high-C-over-C of a male Yma Sumac, he consented to answer a persistent question. "I," he said, emphasizing the first-person promoun, "was the best I ever saw."

Well said, just as his observation that, though he'd been a hitter for pretty good average and even greater power and, of course, an alert, unorthodox and effective baserunner, he'd always felt his fielding was the top of his game. Right on.

Afield, Mays was so good that the celebrated catch he made off Vic Wertz in dead center field of the distant Polo Grounds in the 1954 World Series was almost routine—for Willie, that is. Why, running back to the plate, breaking instinctively and rapidly, he'd even had time to pound his mitt like a catcher under a pop foul before glowing the long drive. More astonishing, I always thought, was his whirling, off-balance throw on the button to second base. Otherwise, a runner on second could have scored after the good, not-great-for Mays catch.

A greater catch, I'm sure, was one I saw one night at Forbes Field, the brickwalled big park that was Pittsburgh's home field until Three Rivers Stadium. Roberto Clemente lashed one to deepest left-center near where the Pirates stored their batting cage. Mays took off at full speed, angled back and caught up with the ball only by flinging his glove backhanded and outstretched, just before he reached the barrier that would have catapulted him right through the wall into Schenley Park beyond.

The one, meaning catch-and-throw, that Willie always singled out—even though he was quoted as saying cleverly, "I catch 'em and you rate 'em"—was in the heat of a Giant-Dodger series at New York.

With the Brooks' Billy Cox on third, Carl Furillo lined one to right-center, an apparent double or triple. Dutifully, Cox, a professional, tagged up. Mays, racing to his left, flung out his glove, miraculously caught the ball and then, pivoting full tilt like a discus thrower revved up, he cut loose blindly an on-the-fly throw that nipped a startled Cox at the plate.

Huffed chesty Cholly Dressen of the Dodgers, characteristically hitching his pants, "H'ummph, I'd like to see him do THAT again!"

So that's Willie Howard Mays, Jr., about whom escort Frank Forbes was so miffed with the law back there a quarter-century earlier when the FBI, though familiar with its own Ten Most Wanted List, didn't recognize the young man already en route to the Hall of Fame as well as to Phoenix.

In that spring of 1954, if you'll forgive dating the piece a bit an anonymous writer, who got to Arizona shortly after Willie and Forbes did, sent back this description:

"Willie Mays is 10 feet, nine inches tall. He can jump 15 feet straight up…He's a step faster than any line drive ever hit…Willie hits balls that even Willie couldn't catch…Willie can do more for a team's morale than Marilyn Monroe, Zsa Zsa Gabor and Rita Hayworth, put together."

WILLIE HOWARD (SAY HEY) MAYS JR.
Born May 6, 1931, at Westfield, Ala.
Height 5-11 Weight 187
Threw and batted righthanded.
Named to Hall of Fame, 1979.

YEAR	CLUB	LEAGUE	POS.	G.	AB.	R.	H.	2B.	3B.	HR.	RBI.	B.A.	PO.	A.	E.	F.A.
1950	Trenton	Int. St.	OF	81	306	50	108	20	8	4	55	.353	216	17	5	.979
1951	Minneapolis	A.A.	OF	35	149	38	71	18	3	8	30	.477	94	5	1	.990
1951	New York	Nat.	OF	121	464	59	127	22	5	20	68	.274	353	12	9	.976
1952	New York (a)	Nat.	OF	34	127	17	30	2	4	4	23	.236	109	6	1	.991
1953	New York	Nat.							(In Military Service)							
1954	New York	Nat.	OF	151	565	119	195	33	13	41	110	.345	448	13	7	.985
1955	New York	Nat.	OF	152	580	123	185	18	13	51	127	.319	407	23	8	.982
1956	New York	Nat.	OF	152	578	101	171	27	8	36	84	.296	415	14	9	.979
1957	New York	Nat.	OF	152	585	112	195	26	20	35	97	.333	422	14	9	.980
1958	San Francisco	Nat.	OF	152	600	121	208	33	11	29	96	.347	429	17	9	.980
1959	San Francisco	Nat.	OF	151	575	125	180	43	5	34	104	.313	353	6	6	.984
1960	San Francisco	Nat.	OF	153	595	107	190	29	12	29	103	.319	392	12	8	.981
1961	San Francisco	Nat.	OF	154	572	129	176	32	3	40	123	.308	385	7	8	.980
1962	San Francisco	Nat.	OF	162	621	130	189	36	5	49	141	.304	429	6	4	.991
1963	San Francisco	Nat.	OF-SS	157	596	115	187	32	7	38	103	.314	397	7	8	.981
1964	San Francisco	Nat.	OF-1-2-3-S	157	578	121	171	21	9	47	111	.296	376	12	6	.985
1965	San Fransisco	Nat.	OF	157	558	118	177	21	3	52	112	.317	337	13	6	.983
1966	San Francisco	Nat.	OF	152	552	99	159	29	4	37	103	.288	370	8	7	.982
1967	San Francisco	Nat.	OF	141	486	83	128	22	2	22	70	.263	277	3	7	.976
1968	San Francisco	Nat.	OF-1B	148	498	84	144	20	5	23	79	.289	310	7	7	.978
1969	San Francisco	Nat.	OF-1B	117	403	64	114	17	3	13	58	.283	205	4	5	.976
1970	San Francisco	Nat.	OF-1B	139	478	94	139	15	2	28	83	.291	303	9	7	.978
1971	San Francisco	Nat.	OF-1B	136	417	82	113	24	5	18	61	.271	576	29	17	.973
1972	S.F (b)-N.Y.	Nat.	OF-1B	88	244	35	61	11	1	8	22	.250	213	5	4	.982
1973	New York	Nat.	OF-1B	66	209	24	44	10	0	6	25	.211	246	6	4	.984
Major League Totals				2992	10881	2062	3283	523	140	660	1903	.302	7752	233	156	.981

a Entered military service May 29.
b Traded to New York Mets for cash and Pitcher Charlie Williams, May 11, 1972.

CHAMPIONSHIP SERIES RECORD

YEAR	CLUB	LEAGUE	POS.	G.	AB.	R.	H.	2B.	3B.	HR.	RBI.	B.A.	PO.	A.	E.	F.A.
1971	San Francisco	Nat.	OF	4	15	2	4	2	0	1	3	.267	5	0	0	1.000
1973	New York	Nat.	PH-OF	1	3	1	1	0	0	0	1	.333	1	0	0	1.000
Championship Series Totals—2 Years				5	18	3	5	2	0	1	4	.278	6	0	0	1.000

WORLD SERIES RECORD

YEAR	CLUB	LEAGUE	POS.	G.	AB.	R.	H.	2B.	3B.	HR.	RBI.	B.A.	PO.	A.	E.	F.A.
1951	New York	Nat.	OF	6	22	1	4	0	0	0	1	.182	16	1	0	1.000
1954	New York	Nat.	OF	4	14	4	4	1	0	0	3	.286	10	0	0	1.000
1962	San Francisco	Nat.	OF	7	28	3	7	2	0	0	1	.250	19	0	0	1.000
1973	New York	Nat.	O-PH-PR	3	7	1	2	0	0	0	1	.286	1	0	1	.500
World Series Totals—4 Years				20	71	9	17	3	0	0	6	.239	46	1	1	.979

100 GRAND HANDYMAN: Stan Musial, one of baseball's most successful hitters with seven batting championships and three MVP awards, was the first big leaguer to play 1,000 games each in the infield and outfield.

STAN MUSIAL

Stanley Frank Musial was baseball's Horatio Alger, the poor Polish immigrant's son who struck it rich by playing a boy's game better than most men.

A living legend, a homer-hitting grandfather at nearly 43, Musial set more than 50 major and National League records for batting and durability in the course of 22 years. He played more games for one team than any player in the first century of professional baseball. And he finished first in career total bases (6,135) and extra-base hits (1,377) temporarily and second only to Ty Cobb in hits (3,630).

At his peak with the St. Louis Cardinals, for whom he later became a championship-winning general manager and then senior vice president, Musial was a swift baserunner, talented outfielder and good first baseman. As baseball's highest-paid handyman ($100,000) ever to smooth a troubled manager's furrowed forehead, he was the first player to put in 1,000 games each in the infield and outfield.

Although he'll be remembered long statistically, millionaire Musial will be remembered most by many for personal qualities that made him rate exceptionally high as a popular celebrity. He didn't have quite the booming bat, or the naturally blithe spirit of Babe Ruth, but he was a lighthearted, serious-playing performer who knew how to balance business with pleasure and, in effect, to whistle while he worked.

"The greatest thrill," he said, repeatedly, making the trite seem palatable as well as true, "is just putting on the big league uniform every day, especially for the opener of a new season."

The Man, nicknamed by respectful Brooklyn fans, played with youthful fervor to the point he almost won an eighth batting championship when he hit .330 only six weeks shy of his 42nd birthday. A trim athlete and good family man, Musial made news on the field, seldom off it. Yet he reached the public everywhere with his talent, team consciousness and even temperament.

Polite, patient and proud, he was at one and the same time the ballplayer's ballplayer, a manager's man and a fan's favorite. And if that sounds as if he was too good to be true, a Sir Galahad in baseball britches, you'll have to forgive the personal prejudice of one who watched Musial closely for 13 years on the road and seldom saw him do the wrong thing—and never say it.

As he said in his autobiography, shortly after he finished his playing career in 1963, Musial was no mental heavyweight, but he was no dummy, either, no automaton. He had his own opinions and impressions, but he kept them to himself or rarely expressed them to persons he could trust.

A superstar without a first-person complex, he was dedicated to doing things the team way, refusing to fly by himself when he couldn't sleep on trains because he didn't want to leave the ball club. He shared gifts and samples with his teammates, making certain that the rawest rookie was favored as often as road roommate Red Schoendienst. He shared batting and playing tips, too, particularly if asked, but not his opinions, especially about his managers.

Musial has received many tributes in baseball, much more meaningful than this one. For instance, he was honored at every city in which he played on the final swing of his career. In addition, he had been honored previously in New York and later at Los Angeles. He wound up with more decorations than a Mexican general and he even found himself cast in bronze for an 18-foot statue outside St. Louis' new Busch Memorial Stadium, where even the pigeons were respectful.

But, in this judgment, the finest tribute paid Stan the Man was by the nine managers for whom he played in a career that saw him spoiled with four pennant-winning seasons his first four full years in the majors, then suffer through the frustration of trying 18 more times to match in maturity the youthful joy of competing for baseball's big apple in October.

Musial, incidentally, had to be one of the finest hitters down the stretch. In most cases there has to be too much by-guess and by-golly, a result of insufficient statistical evidence, but the late baseball bloodhound, Lee Allen, a historian with a heart and a sense of humor, dug deep in research for Musial's book to provide a most revealing dossier on the consistency and class of the Cardinals' apple-cheeked athlete with the ample nose and lopsided grin.

Although playing more than 150 games a season 11 times and moving from outfield to first base and back again, Musial hit his highest down the wearisome stretch Allen proved. Stan batted .438 in brief regular-season October competition and next best was September—.344.

By "fantastic coincidence," as Allen put it, Musial collected exactly as many hits on the road as he did at home, 1,815, as he hopscotched from position to position as well as from town to town. He played 299 games in center field, 699 in right, 907 in left and, counting games in which he played both infield and outfield, he was at first base more than 1,000 times.

"I'd rather play the outfield because I think I hit

better there, and I actually prefer right field to any position," he would say without bitterness or complaint. Allen's figures showed he batted .336 as an outfielder, .324 as a first baseman and .263 as a pinch-hitter.

Although he was playing his ninth big league season in 1951 before he participated in more night games than day contests in a season, Musial finished playing only 242 times fewer times under the lights. I remember back in 1948 when, as Allen's figures refresh the memory, Musial hit .399 at night and I suggested he was better off under the lights.

Stan dissented. "I don't care what the figures show," he said, stoutly, "I like to play day games and I know I'm a better hitter in the day time."

His career bore him out. He hit .340 for 1,634 day games, .320 for 1,392 night games. And even though he batted better in every park except two, his favorite park was Chicago's Wrigley Field, where he hit .308.

"I think," he said, smiling, "I liked Wrigley Field best because they were all day games."

Club by club, except for Houston, which saw him only his last two seasons and then before it had the air-conditioned Astrodome to benefit a 40-year-old gaffer, National League teams had good reason to be glad to bid The Man good-bye in his final grand tour in '63. Home and away, he missed by just one point against Milwaukee, successor to Boston, of hitting .300 or better against every club except the Astros, then called the Colts.

On the road, Musial was at his best in savage showdowns at Brooklyn, .356, followed by Boston, .347; New York, .343; Pittsburgh, .339; Los Angeles, .337; Philadelphia, .318; Cincinnati, .314; Chicago, .308; San Francisco, .306; and Milwaukee, .288.

At home, he batted .336, just 10 points higher than on the road for his career. The Man batted .360 against Boston, which was replaced in 1953 by Milwaukee. His other averages at old Sportsman's Park, St. Louis, were .359, Philadelphia; .355, New

York; .341, Pittsburgh; .331, Brooklyn; .326, Chicago; .323, Cincinnati; .311, Milwaukee; and against the two Coast franchises, which were in business his last six seasons, he hit .311 against Los Angeles and .305 against San Francisco.

The capital "C" for consistency that made Musial stand out in a game of inconsistency was reflected, too, particularly until the end, in his batting figures for each of his nine managers. You see, thorough friend Allen even includes Stan Hack, who filled in for a week.

For former teammate Marty Marion, his manager in 1951, Musial batted .355; for Eddie Dyer, 1946-50, .348; for Billy Southworth, 1941-44, .344; for Eddie Stanky, 1952-55, .332; for Fred Hutchinson, 1956-58, .331; for Harry Walker, 1955, .323; for Stan Hack, 1958, .321; for Johnny Keane, 1961-63, .293; and for Solly Hemus, 1959-61, .273.

Virtually to a man—and this is getting back to the greatest tribute The Man ever received—each manager when he departed went out of his way to salute Stan for having made the departing field foreman's job easier. For playing when he was hurt, for moving from position to position, for not asking for special favors and for never complaining or second-guessing, Musial won full appreciation from managers who didn't have his stature either with the press, public or—for that matter—front office.

Curiously, respecting the problems of managing, Musial wisely—if you'll accept the editorial adverb—declined to become a manager. Not because he feared the pressure or even because he recognized that eventually the almost constant cheers he'd known as a player would turn to the hisses of disapproval that managers hear.

"Everybody thinks I'd be too easy as a manager," said Musial with Alfred Hitchcock timing when we were working on his book. "The truth is, I'm afraid I'd be too tough, that I'd demand too much from the players as other gifted players have done as managers, and I just don't need that grief. I like people too much to go through that when I don't have to."

Only one manager, Hemus, the former self-made shortstop Stan had helped by suggesting a thin-handled bat so he could pull the ball better, ever found Musial a problem or, in turn, disappointed him.

Taking over in 1959, Solly was a party to the ill-conceived plan, in which Musial and the field and front office command concurred. They agreed that The Man should take it easier in the spring of '59. He'd run down in '58, the year he reached the 3,000-hit goal, and the conclusion, as he reached 38, was that he needed to conserve himself by running less and playing fewer exhibition games.

The decision was wrong, 100 percent. Musial, who had relied only on off-season diet and constant playing to keep in shape, needed more work as an older player, not less. He never did reach playing peak in 1959 and when he failed to hit .300 for the first time in 18 years, dipping to .255, the logical conclusion was that he'd had it.

Not to Musial, though, because he reasoned that if his reflexes really had gone back that far, pitchers would have been throwing the fastball past him. He couldn't quit with the gnawing question of doubtful physical preparation eating at him. So in mid-August general manager Bing Devine called him in, to ask his plans so that Stan wouldn't run into the question daily throughout the league in September.

Musial said he wanted to return, to which Devine readily agreed. Stan was surprised when he was put in mothballs for the last few weeks as the club looked at young players, but he shrugged and determined to be in the best possible condition, which he was in 1960. In the off-season he worked at St. Louis University with physical education director Walter Eberhardt, whose efforts in Musial's behalf prompted Devine to hire him to work every spring since then at the Cardinals' camp.

Musial, working hard, hit well in spring training, 1960, and for a few days, too, but then tailed off with a slumping ball club. By mid-May, though driving in runners and moving up men at a higher percentage than all other regulars, the .260-hitting veteran was benched.

At Chicago, Hemus told him before the first game of a Sunday doubleheader, "Be ready to play the second game, Stan." In the opener, however, the Cardinals won their first road contest in 13 tries, and Hemus stuck with the same righthanded-hitting lineup even though a sidearming righthander, Don Cardwell, was pitching for the Cubs.

"You were just kidding about playing me, Solly," said Musial in mild rebuke, which Hemus acknowledged some time later. That afternoon, Cardwell pitched the first no-hitter thrown at the Cardinals since Hod Eller of Cincinnati in 1919.

Musial, who had spoiled no-hitters in '59 for Chicago's Glen Hobbie and San Francisco's Jack Sanford, played in only four of the next 12 games and hit safely in three of them before an embarrassing moment at Philadelphia, one which Musial didn't mention, but the St. Louis newspapers did.

With the score tied in the ninth inning, another lefthanded hitter, Carl Sawatski, squatted on deck to pinch-bat until Daryl Spencer tripled with one out. Then, figuring an intentional walk, Hemus pulled back Sawatski and sent up Musial to take the purposeful pass. Then Sawatski reappeared to pinch-bat and did indeed hit a run-scoring sacrifice fly.

Hemus was convinced Musial was through. For a fact, Stan didn't field as well either at first base or in left field as he had for so many salad seasons and he no longer ran, as Fred Hutchinson put it, like a wounded turkey. But his bat still seemed important, and didn't the wishes of a superstar who'd never complained mean anything?

"I've got 25 players and I've got to treat them all alike," said Hemus, who had come right out of the players' ranks to manage.

When the Cardinals turned a late May deal with Pittsburgh, Musial apparently went to the bench for good. Devine gave up southpaw pitcher Wilmer (Vinegar Bend) Mizell, the later North Carolina

Congressman who would help Pittsburgh to win a long-awaited pennant in 1960. The Redbirds received, in return, a rookie second baseman, Julian Javier, who would contribute to three St. Louis pennants in the decade just beginning.

At the same time, Hemus put young Curt Flood in center field, where he became a master after Johnny Keane made the appointment permanent. Bill White, a slick first baseman trying to play center field on a ball club loaded with first basemen, moved back to his normal position. At Grant's Farm, August A. Busch, Jr.'s, estate, the Redbird president and his top hands, Executive Vice President Dick Meyer and General Manager Devine, tried to break it gently to Musial that Hemus preferred to go with a different, younger lineup.

Musial was hurt because, he would say later, he saw no bright young star on the horizon, but he told top management, "Whatever you want is all right with me, though I think I can still help the ball club."

Most superstars I've known, past or present, would have had their say, but Musial bided his time, devoting himself to in-season conditioning he'd learned from pinch-hitter deluxe, reserve first baseman George (The Judge) Crowe. Stan worked as he watched Hemus go through a medley relay of left fielders—Leon Wagner, Ellis Burton, John Glenn (no, not the astronaut), Walt Moryn and Bob Nieman.

Near the trading deadline, Danny Murtaugh, managing the Pirates, was in town. "What's the matter with the Polack?" he asked. The old friendly rival shook his head as he added, "I'd sure like to have him, but Stan never would leave the Cardinals."

Oh, wouldn't he? Back in 1956, when Frank Lane was trading everything that wasn't nailed down, Musial's sharp business partner, the late Julius (Biggie) Garagnani, had insisted without verification to an Anheuser-Busch official that Musial wouldn't report if traded to Philadelphia for pitcher Robin Roberts, as rumored.

Now, however, in 1960, when I mentioned to Musial that Murtaugh thought Stan could make the difference for Pittsburgh in the pennant race, The Man said, softly, "I never thought I'd ever say this, but, yes, I would play elsewhere. I've worked too hard this year to prove a point, not to have a chance to play it out. And I would like to get into one more World Series."

Joe L. Brown, Pittsburgh's general manager, explained off-the-record shortly thereafter why Musial would remain, as Stan eventually was happy to be, "a Cardinal forever."

"As much as we'd like to have Stan," said Brown, "I couldn't do this to Bing Devine, an honorable man. Sure, if Musial were released, we would grab him. As Murtaugh said, we can't give up one of our better young players for him. And to offer too little would be taking advantage of the public sentiment, which is sure to be strongly behind Musial, not the ball club. Devine would be on the spot where I don't care to put him."

Musial had his own ethics. Pride and ethics. He wouldn't ask for his release. After he'd been on the bench nearly a month, Nieman was hurt, and, looking around and seeing he'd exhausted all left field candidates, Hemus turned finally to Musial. The date was June 24 at Philadelphia. By the time of the All-Star Game three weeks later, Musial was hitting .300, a result of a torrid 20 for 41, and the Cardinals had come from nowhere.

Hemus was grateful. "Musial," he said, "has delivered the last two or three weeks the most big hits I've seen any player get in years."

Named sentimentally to the National League's All-Star team—he hit .317 with a record six homers for 24 All-Star appearances and 63 times at bat—The Man was as blazing as the heat in Kansas City. There, he pinch-singled off Detroit's Frank Lary. Two days later at New York, appearing in Yankee Stadium for the first time since the 1943 World Series, he creamed one of Gerry Staley's sinkers into the third deck in right field for a pinch-homer.

The standing ovation Musial received brought tears to more than one eye, including Mayo Smith, former Philadelphia and Cincinnati manager and later skipper at Detroit. When you touch the professionals, you've struck pay dirt. Larry Goetz, then recently retired as an umpire, was another who reported he choked up.

"I kept seeing him as a kid 20 years earlier," Goetz said. "I remember the first time I worked the plate behind him and Van Mungo, who really could fire the ball, was pitching for Brooklyn. Twice, even though Musial stood back from the plate, Mungo knocked him down with pitches. Stan got up and hit the third one into left-center for a triple and, as I brushed off home plate, I couldn't resist yelling to Mungo, 'Hey, Van, you sure scared hell out of that kid, didn't you?'"

The 1960 Cardinals certainly scared hell out of Pittsburgh. Musial, though tailing off to .275 after the race was settled, hit productively and used three of his 17 home runs to beat the Pirates three times in August. Even friends in Western Pennsylvania who'd always wished him well over the years were a bit grim, unable to see the humor in a hometown hero—the old buck—trying to keep the young Bucs from Pittsburgh's first pennant in 33 years.

Why didn't Musial, personally vindicated, hang it up after the bittersweet season of '60? Because, heck, he grinned, now baseball was fun again and now management wanted him back in '61.

Stan's hunch that the Cardinals would win the pennant—he was almost as optimistic annually as Ernie Banks at Chicago—was all wet even though the grand old man boosted his average to .288 and drove in 70 runs, starting just about two-thirds of the Cardinals' games. He proved again his theory that a performer can concentrate better when he isn't feeling up to par.

Troubled by a pulled leg muscle and cold which kept him from sleeping, he developed a miserable abscessed tooth one evening. Trainer Bob Bauman was afraid Stan would roll off his rubbing table because of the pain, but he played against the Giants, anyway, and hit two home runs, one a grand slam. His RBI total that night was seven. Then he rushed out of the ballpark to keep a midnight date with his dentist.

The day the disappointing sixth-place season ended in Philly, Musial was called aside by Johnny Keane, the wiry little coach who had replaced Hemus as manager in early June. Stan actually hadn't hit as high for Keane as for Hemus, but Keane surprised him.

"Stan," Keane said, "I want you back, not to play less, but to play more. I've watched you and I'm convinced that you could have played more. What do you think?"

Musial welcomed the challenge.

"Good," Keane said. "Get yourself in the best possible shape. If next year is going to be your last one, make it one to be remembered. You can do it."

Musial, looking forward to expansion and a return to New York and the Polo Grounds, where he'd always hit well, trimmed down at one point to 175 pounds, his rookie weight, 12 fewer than he'd played at recent times. Too weak and drawn, he leveled off at 180 and said he felt the benefit of the weight loss most in his sliding, which hadn't been as aggressive as in his earlier years.

From the time he went 3-for-3 opening night at St. Louis in the first major league game played by the Mets, who weren't amazin' then, Musial had a remarkable season for a man closing in on 42. In early May, he played his first doubleheader in nearly four years—under unusual circumstances.

Over the years, Musial had developed a knack with a runner on third base of lifting a run-scoring flyball to left field, not necessarily deep, but deep enough to bring home the run. By not pulling the ball, he reduced his chances of jerking his head and popping up. So when he popped up unusually with one out and the bases loaded in the ninth inning of a May doubleheader at Cincinnati as the Cardinals lost by one run, he sat brooding at his locker. Keane walked by.

"Buck up, Stan," said the manager, slapping him

on the back. "you're playing the second game and you'll get four hits."

Musial played, but didn't get four hits, only three. The third one off Moe Drabowsky in the ninth inning was a homer which broke up a scoreless game and gave St. Louis a 3-0 victory.

Although the Cardinals once again ran out of the pennant race, Musial actually played enough to qualify for the batting title, appearing in 135 games and collecting 143 hits, including 19 homers and driving in 82 runs. He hit .330, enough to win some batting titles, but the Dodgers' Tommy Davis had a great year, hitting .346.

On the final weekend Musial and his mates knocked Los Angeles out of a pennant and into a disastrous three-game playoff with San Francisco, but not before it looked as if Stan might have done in his old friend, Horace Stoneharn, president of the Giants.

For years, Stan and Red Schoendienst had a late-season ritual of dropping in for a farewell drink with sportsman Stoneham. As they parted before the clubs' final game the next afternoon, Stoneham said, smiling, "I'd ask you to take it easy on us tomorrow, Stan, except that the last time I did that was in your restaurant the night before (1954) you had those five home runs against us."

Musial laughed. "That's right, Horace," he said, "don't ask."

The next afternoon, The Man went 5-for-5 for the final time in his career and when the Cardinals beat the Giants, San Francisco trailed Los Angeles by three games with only four to play. The Dodgers never got the one more victory they needed.

The 1962 season was unforgettable for Musial even though, as a team man, he smarted under a second-division finish. Snapping a 1-for-25 slump, he singled off the Dodgers' Ron Perranoski to a rousing reception earlier at Los Angeles, to break the National League record for career hits held by the lovable, legendary character from his home area, Pittsburgh's Honus Wagner.

Stan's wife, Lil, had fallen asleep in the late-night broadcast from the West Coast and had missed the big moment on radio. The next evening at the St. Louis airport when she waited for the club's plane coming in from L. A., Mrs. Musial quipped, "I guess I'm too old for the game. It's for young people like Stan."

Musial's family, which he'd had to see on a hit-and-run basis through most of his long career, shared big moments with him in '62. At New York, where friends Toots Shor, Horace McMahon, Arthur Godfrey, Ed Mosler, Fred Corcoran and others whipped up a night for him at the Polo Grounds, Stan's family, including his mother, were with him as he accepted a plaque from Casey Stengel and turned over funds to "Lou Gehrig's college," as he put it, for a scholarship at Columbia University.

Musial, though he'd become wealthy playing baseball after passing up the college education his immigrant father wanted him to take, insisted over the years that if he'd had it to do over again, he'd complete his education first.

"I think," he said, in the closest admission of an inferiority complex a well-adjusted person ever made, "that it takes a man who hasn't had one to know what he's missed, especially when he's exposed to so many college men."

So Musial, who had missed his own high school graduation, was delighted and proud to be able in '62 to attend his son Dick's commencement at Notre Dame, where the first college man in the Musial family had lettered on the track team. Three daughters, Geraldine, Janet and Jean, also attended college.

The same summer Dick Musial graduated from college, to become a reserve officer in the Army and then affiliated with his father in Musial's "Stan the Man" sports products, the old boy received a considerable honor. Monmouth (Ill.) College made Stan an honorary Doctor of Humanities.

Doc Musial glowed over participation of his

family in his big moments that season though they put him down with the delightful nonchalance by which a prophet is without honor in his own kitchen. Stan Musial, his batting stance copied by every kid in town and by many around the country, was a hero everywhere except in his own household.

Fact is, as far back as Dick's diaper days in 1941 when Stan and Lil were teenage parents, the kids had a way of deflating the old man. For instance, when Stan hit three home runs in one game for Springfield, Mo., in the Class C Western Association, an exasperated Lil Musial missed all of them because they coincided with innings in which young Master Musial needed a change of diapers.

Thirteen years later, when The Man homered three times in the first game of a doubleheader against the Giants at St. Louis, he was happily munching on a ham and cheese sandwich when he was called to the phone. It was Lil. She hadn't been able to get to the game because No. 2 daughter had come up with a sore throat.

That one, May 2, 1954, was a red-letter day in the career of a man who had as many moments as just about anyone who ever pulled on baseball flannels. In the first game he homered twice off southpaw Johnny Antonelli and once off righthander Jim Hearn.

The lights were on because of overcast when Stan ripped the third one with two on, breaking a 6-6 tie and winning the game. The crowd roared then, but booed when the second game began and he drew a first-inning walk.

Next time up, Musial hit a ball about 410 feet to the base of the right-center field fence, where Willie Mays made the catch. The wind that day blew toward left field, favoring righthanded hitters. If it had blown to right or even if there had been no wind, Stan the Man probably would have made a remarkable record even more astonishing by having two three-homer games on the same day.

In the fifth inning, facing relief ace Hoyt Wilhelm, he hit a slow curve over the towering

right-field pavilion. The record fifth homer in one day came in the seventh inning of the rain-delayed second game and Musial was the proudest that it had been stroked off Wilhelm's wicked knuckleball. No. 5 went farther than the fourth.

By the time Musial batted in the ninth, most of the crowd was still there even though the time was near 8 o'clock. The Giants were in front, 9-7, when Stan led off the ninth. Overeager against Larry Jansen, The Man bit on a fastball that was too far up and in. He hit the ball high, but only to the first baseman. The crowd groaned, then cheered—and rushed for the exits.

When Stan walked into his living room later, beaming, scooping up five-year-old Janet and playfully mussing the blond hair of 13-year-old son Dick, the boy said, gravely:

"Gee, Dad, they sure must have been throwing you fat pitches today."

Lil and Stan had trouble prying Janet away from her horse in 1962 so that the 12-year-old equestrienne would accompany her parents to New York and then to Washington for the All-Star Game.

The heat in Manhattan was sweltering and Mrs. Musial and her daughter saw the sights with friends, passing up a Friday night game and Saturday afternoon doubleheader with the Mets at the Polo Grounds. Pinch-hitting Musial hit an eighth-inning home run to win the second game Saturday, 3-2. Lil Musial would not be dissuaded from passing up Sunday's single game.

"I've got to be out there today," she said as the family came out of Mass that morning. "I've got a hunch."

Musial made it four successive homers, tying a record, by getting three that afternoon, the first two off righthander Jay Hook and the third one off young lefthander Bill Hunter. The last one had The Man smiling—for two reasons—as he trotted around the bases.

"For one thing," he said, "I remembered the look on Hunter's face. He threw me a fastball high and inside—too far inside—but I didn't believe in letting an inside pitch get away at the Polo Grounds with that close fence. I liked to bet on getting a ball to the fence before it curved foul. I tomahawked that one against the right-field roof."

Circling the bases, Stan thought of Lil's having missed those two other three-home-run performances because she had been, first of all, a dutiful mother and he smiled. As he stepped on home plate, he could see Lil and Janet in their first-row box behind the visitors' dugout, standing and clapping.

Afterward, asked for her reaction, Janet told a St. Louis reporter she had been surprised.

Surprised?

"I was afraid," she said, deflatingly, "that Daddy would strike out."

Old Daddy proved he was a pretty big man at least in other people's eyes when the Musials took the train that night to Washington and the 1962 All-Star Game. There, six years earlier, representing J. G. Taylor Spink, long-time editor and publisher of *The Sporting News*, Bob Feller had presented Musial with an award he prized.

It was *The Sporting News'* first Player of the Decade award, and in a vote of players, managers, umpires and writers, Musial had won out over stars, young and old, players like Feller himself, Joe DiMaggio, Ted Williams, Willie Mays, Jackie Robinson, Warren Spahn and Robin Roberts.

For one who wasn't the most articulate, Musial had a way with words at times. Expressing appreciation at a showcase luncheon held at Washington's Touchdown Club, he'd said, "I can't throw like Feller, field like DiMaggio or hit like Williams."

In the National League's 7-3 victory over the American at old Griffith Stadium, Williams hit a tremendous home run off Spahn in the sixth inning. By the time statisticians thumbed through their record books, Musial was batting in the visitors' seventh against Tom Brewer, Boston righthander.

Over the pressbox intercom, Bob Addie of the *Washington Post* announced, "Attention, press, Wil-

liams' home run was his fourth in All-Star competition and tied Stan Musial…"

Musial swung and lined the ball into the left-center field seats.

"Sorry," said Addie, to laughter, "Mr. Musial has just untied the record."

Now, six years later at the new D. C. Stadium, which would be renamed for Robert F. Kennedy, Musial was informed through an aide that President John F. Kennedy wanted to see him at his box seat. Musial had campaigned for JFK, but had met him only once before a couple of years earlier.

Stan had been standing in front of the Schroeder Hotel in Milwaukee, waiting for the team bus that would take the Cardinals to County Stadium. A man came up to him and said:

"You're Stan Musial, aren't you? My name is Jack Kennedy. I'm glad to meet you."

Of course, Musial recognized the photogenic senator from Massachusetts, then campaigning in the Wisconsin primary for the Democratic presidential nomination.

"They tell me," the senator said, pleasantly, "you're too old to play ball and I'm too young to be president, but maybe we'll fool them."

Musial reminded Kennedy of that amusing remark as they conversed in the ballpark, and JFK chuckled when Stan added, "I guess, Mr. President, we fooled them, all right."

In the sixth inning of the All-Star Game, the next-to-last in which he would play and the last the martyred president would see, Musial was summoned to pinch-hit by Fred Hutchinson, his old St. Louis boss and a good man for whom, like JFK, time was prematurely running out. Hutch died of cancer two years later.

When Musial stepped up to face Camilo Pascual, Minnesota Twins' righthander with a good old-fashioned over-hand curve, the game was scoreless. President Kennedy leaned over to an aide and said, "I hope the old man gets a hit."

Musial lined a two-strike curve into right field for

a single and trotted off to a warm reception, replaced by Maury Wills, whose baserunning and daring led directly to a 3-1 National League victory.

Musial's good friend, Sen. Stuart Symington, a reformed sportswriter, had arranged a capital tour for the family the next day, and Stan glowed as Janet's eyes bugged when they were taken into the president's office for a pleasant visit and were escorted through the First Family's living quarters.

Musial would reflect again later, appointed special consultant on physical fitness by President Lyndon B. Johnson, if only his father, Lukasz Musial, could have seen his boy then…

This was, you see, a story too incredible and too hokey even for Hollywood. Who would believe, anyway, a Grade-B plot about a poor deadarmed kid with a wife and baby to feed becoming a big league batting star overnight?

As they say in the fairy tales, "Once upon a time…"

Stan Musial was born in Donora, Pa., November 21, 1920, the fifth of six children. He had four sisters, all older, and a younger brother Ed, called "Honey," who looked a good bit like him and played minor league ball until nearly five years of military service curtailed his chances.

Stan's mother, Mary Lancos, a hearty woman with a hearty laugh, was born in New York City, to Czechoslovakian immigrants who moved to Donora, 28 miles south of Pittsburgh in western Pennsylvania's industrial Monongahela Valley. At eight, Mary went out to work housecleaning. As a teenage girl, she used to row her father across the Monongahela River in a skiff early each day and row him back again in the evening. He worked in a coal mine four miles beyond the river. He walked there to spend 12 hours underground, for which he was paid 90 cents a day.

To survive in the rugged climate of the steep, smoke-choked valley whose belching stacks meant business and a livelihood required rugged inhabitants. Most were immigrants from Russia and Germany and Poland. Language difficulties compelled them to clan together in their churches and social clubs.

In 1910, when she was 14, Mary Lancos went to work in Donora's wire mill. There, sorting nails, she saw a shy, little Pole named Lukasz Musial. He worked in the shipping department, handling 100-pound bundles of wire, wrestling them into freight cars. Born on a farm in Warsaw, he had little education and knew no English, but Mary knew enough Polish to understand him when they met at a dance. They were married before Mary was 18. Lukasz brought home $11 every two weeks and they paid $4 a month rent.

Stan was christened Stanislaus, changed to Stanley in school. His father called him Stashu, and the boy's earliest recollection of a toy is of a ball. And whenever he needed a ball, his mother would sew one together out of a little bit of this and a little bit of that.

As a toddler, Stashu created an economic calamity when he developed a taste for the canned milk used to sweeten coffee. To avoid a paddling, he'd hold his breath, but his Grandmother Lancos put a stop to that. Wham! She thumped a ground-rule double off his bottomside a couple of times and Stan grew up with a respect for authority and an appreciation of discipline.

Although he would drool over the "hunky" dishes his mother turned out when she could afford the ingredients, he learned to marvel at her method in making a little go a long way. Fresh milk and meat were too expensive. Every two weeks, she would buy a 50-pound sack of potatoes and a 100-pound sack of flour, 25 pounds of sugar and 15 pounds of coffee. She baked bread in an outside oven, 10 loaves at a time. The kids picked blackberries and elderberries for jelly and, incongruously, dug into their own private coal-mine on a hill behind the house.

From the time he was only eight years old, Musial dreamed of becoming a big leaguer. He lived next door to a Joe Barboa, a pleasant man of Spanish-Belgian descent. Barboa had played minor league ball as a pitcher and outfielder. His hard, hot work as a short-shifter in the zinc mill gave him more free time. He managed the plant team and he'd play catch in the daytime with those two lefthanded Musial boys. At night, sitting overlooking the lights twinkling below on the Monongahela, he'd fill their heads with dreams of the major leagues.

Although people tell Musial he was "frail and skinny" in his early teens, Stan scoffs. He was wiry and strong, he insists, underscoring physical fitness, because of his father's insistence on the gymnastics and acrobatics of the Old World turnverein idea.

Baseball equipment was scarce, but Stan played whenever and wherever he could. His first clipping is of a game when he was 14 and envisioning himself first as Lefty Grove and then Carl Hubbell. He pitched for the Heslep All-Stars, as they called themselves, against Cement City, so-called because they were sons of foremen and supervisors who lived in sturdy concrete houses rather than cheaper frames. The kids from the wrong side of the track won, 24-2. Musial had four hits, three of them doubles, struck out 14 and walked two in a game that took FIVE HOURS.

As a batboy for Barboa's team, the 5-4, 140-pound Musial kid, just 15, was shooed into the game as pitcher one day by his neighbor when the Donora's starting pitcher was knocked out at Monessen. Facing men, the boy fanned 13 in six innings.

He was in, but, curiously, Barboa was out as manager, dismissed by grumbling members of the Donora Zinc Works A.A. because he'd used a player who was not a dues-paying member. The dues? Two bits!

The Zincs played most of their games at Americo Park down close to the river, near the plant. Railroad tracks ran just beyond the first-base line and inter-city trolley tracks fringed left field,

making it considerably shorter than right. That inviting topography taught Musial at an early age what so many lefthanded hitters find most difficult—how to hit to left field.

The first time Barboa's successor used Musial as a pinch-hitter, Stan was so excited that he swallowed his gum and struck out. Barboa returned as manager—and Stan celebrated by breaking his friend's ankle with a line shot when Joe was coaching first base.

Playing with the men, Musial naturally was even more outstanding when he competed in junior American Legion and high school ball against boys his own age. His high school coach and close friend, the late Ki Duda, became Dr. Michael Duda, president of California (Pa.) State College. Stan starred in basketball for Coach James K. (Jimmy) Russell, who turned out championship football teams and outstanding athletes.

Musial's father thrilled over the prospect of a basketball scholarship for his son at the University of Pittsburgh and balked stubbornly when Stan tried out with the Cardinals at their nearby Monessen farm club and wanted to turn pro for only $65 a month. He was only a high school junior at the time, 1937.

The Monessen manager, Ollie Vanek, recommended that Musial be signed, but business manager Oliver French found the senior Musial adamant, unwilling to give parental consent. Finally, Stan cried and his mother said sternly to her husband:

"Lukasz, why did you come to America?"

"Why?" asked the puzzled little man in his broken English. "Because it's a free country."

"All right," she said. "And in America a boy is free NOT to go to college, too."

Stan, from his own standpoint, had wrestled with the college-versus-baseball problem until he'd talked to the high school librarian, Helen Kloz. Miss Kloz knew that the bashful, backward boy wasn't really a good student, though conscientious, and she recognized his sincerity.

"Stan," she said softly, "I've never known a boy who wanted something more than you do. College is a wise course for a man to follow, but you've got to want it enough—almost as much as you want baseball. If you're going to try baseball, the younger you start, the better. You can't afford to lose your head, but you can afford to follow your heart."

Twenty-five years later one night at Philadelphia when they met with the wind whipping in from right field at Connie Mack Stadium, Miss Kloz said, "I believe this is the last time I'll see you play ball, Stan. Won't you hit a home run for me?"

By then, The Man's home runs were few and far between, but he belted a pitch that rode through the wind and over the fence. He laughed for joy as he circled the bases.

Musial always was confident that he could hit. His favorites no longer were pitchers, but hitters—Paul Waner, Mel Ott and Babe Ruth. He'd saved his money in 1935 to go into Pittsburgh to see the Babe, but he'd been a soft touch and lent it to a friend. So he'd missed the dramatic day Ruth hit those three from memory at Forbes Field. It wasn't until after his father actually had agreed that he could play for the Cardinals in 1938 that he got to see his first big league game.

Stan accompanied Johnny Bunardzya, young Donora sports editor, and watched as New York southpaw Cliff Melton beat the Pirates, 5-3. After a few innings, Stan turned to Bunardzya and said, "John, I think I can hit big league pitching."

Armed with letters from Cleveland and the New York Yankees, who had invited him to tryouts, Musial worked out with Pittsburgh three or four times early in 1938, convinced the Cardinals had forgotten him. The Pirates' manager, Pie Traynor, finally talked contract.

"I'd like to, Mr. Traynor," said Stan, a Pirate fan, "but I signed this agreement with the Cardinals late last summer. I don't know, though. I guess they've forgotten me."

Traynor shook his head. "I doubt that, son," he said. "You'll be hearing from them one of these days. If they do release you, let us know. Good luck, boy."

Musial was signed as a pitcher, but he's convinced that he never would have made it with the toeplate because of inadequate control. The first two seasons, reporting late from high school to Williamson, W. Va., in the Mountain States League in 1938 and '39, Stan hit better than he pitched.

By the time he went to spring training for the first time in 1940, his third season and yet first full year in pro ball, he was married at the ripe old age of 19 and his wife was expecting their first child.

Lillian Labash, a cute little blonde, was a daughter of the corner grocer in Donora. At 14, watching a ballgame with her father, a former ballplayer, she had been advised, "Keep your eye on that Polish kid."

She did. Lil likes to tease and say that when Stan was playing high school basketball, she fell in love with his legs. She insists, in turn, that Stan didn't fall in love with her, but rather with the lunch meat and milk he wolfed down at her father's store whenever he'd come calling on her.

They double-dated first after a basketball game when he was a junior. A few months after the high school graduation at which Lil stood in for him, they were married on the young ballplayer's 19th birthday.

When Stan was pitching and filling in for Dick Kerr's club in the outfield at Daytona Beach, Fla., in 1940, Dick and his wife Corinne—called "Pep"—took them in so that their baby wouldn't have to be born in a bandbox hotel. As a pitching hero of the infamous Black Sox World Series in 1919, Dick Kerr had reason to be sour on baseball because he'd been blacklisted a couple of years later for refusing to accept a pittance raise from pinch-penny Charley Comiskey of the White Sox.

Little Dickie never lost his good spirits, however. In later years, to Musial's embarrassment, the story came out that for the Kerrs' retirement in Houston, Stan and Lil had presented a house in gratitude to a couple which died just months apart in 1963, Musial's last season as a player. The Musials' son— Richard Stanley Musial—was named after Dick Kerr.

At Daytona Beach, Stan posted an 18-5 record and hit .311, but in late August at Orlando, playing center field, he dived for a ball. Time and again, the trained gymnast would make tumbling, diving, somersaulting catches, but this time he landed heavily and painfully on his left shoulder. A lump formed.

The next spring, assigned to Columbus, O., of the American Association, then Double-A, Musial reported to manager Burt Shotton for training at Hollywood, Fla. He couldn't throw, but he could hit. By then, Stan already had told Bernard Kahn, Daytona Beach sports editor, that he thought his future might be with a bat instead of on the mound.

Shotton sent the lame-armed lefthander to the larger minor league camp at Albany, Ga., with the notation that he could hit. Veteran scout Joe Mathes saw Musial hit and called him to the attention of Branch Rickey, who was impressed, too. The manager of the Columbus (Ga.) club, Clay Hopper, insisted Musial pitch part of a disastrous exhibition against the big league Cardinals, stopping through as they barnstormed back to St. Louis. But no club in Class A or Class B wanted even a deadarmed outfielder when it came time to reassign players late in training.

A Class C manager spoke up. "I'll take him, Mr. Rickey," said Ollie Vanek, the man who'd first recommended that Musial be signed. Vanek, in 1941, was player-manager at Springfield, Mo.

Vanek smoothed out Musial's outfielding at Springfield. The hitting just naturally took care of itself. With Rickey in the stands one night against St. Joseph, Musial ripped a triple, homer and single. After 87 games in which he'd clobbered 26 homers and 94 RBIs, hitting .379, he was switched to Rochester, N. Y., in the International League, a top minor league.

The slender kid bugged the eyes of Tony Kaufmann, managing Rochester. The Red Wings were playing bitter rival Newark, the flagship of the Yankees' minor league system. Hank Majeski, Newark's third baseman, had a habit of charging fast whenever he anticipated a bunt, making it difficult to sacrifice a runner along.

When Musial came up in the 11th inning, Kaufmann, coaching third base, called him aside, "I'm giving you the bunt sign, kid, but if Majeski charges, try to push the ball past him."

Musial squared around, faked the bunt, then doubled past the third baseman. In the 13th, the score still tied, Musial again faked the bunt. Majeski, thinking the rookie wouldn't or couldn't do the same thing twice, charged—and Stan lined the ball past his ear for a game-winning double.

Rickey had to see the wunderkind again. Musial knew B. R. was there at Newark the night he went 4-for-4. When Rochester was eliminated from the playoffs, Musial who had batted .326 in 54 games, was called up by the crippled Cardinals, gallantly battling leading Brooklyn in September.

Musial reported timidly in St. Louis, and captain Terry Moore, the center fielder, couldn't believe it when Stan said they'd met before and told him where. Moore called to Johnny Mize, the slugging first baseman, "Hey, John, Musial is the kid lefthander we hit those long homers off at Albany this spring."

The Cardinals' outfield was thinned by injuries, so manager Billy Southworth told the 6-0, 175-pound lefthanded hitter that he'd start him in the second game of a weekday doubleheader with the Boston Braves, managed by a gent named Casey Stengel. The Cardinals trailed Brooklyn by only two games.

Against the first knuckleball he ever saw, Musial popped up facing veteran righthander Jim Tobin his first time up. The next trip, two on and two out, Stan rattled one to right-center for the first of his record 725 National League doubles. He also singled in that game as the Cardinals and 20-year-old lefthander Howard Pollet won on a ninth-inning homer by the veteran Estel Crabtree, 3-2.

The next day Musial got one hit against Boston, the third afternoon he went 3-for-3 against Chicago, leading up to a Sunday doubleheader which would end St. Louis' home schedule.

In the first game, playing left field, Musial made two good catches and threw out a runner at the plate. At bat, he doubled off the right-field screen in the first inning. Next time up, he singled to center and stole second. On his third trip, he doubled off the screen again. The fourth time, with the score tied in the ninth, 5-5, he hit a one-out single for his fourth straight hit and moved to second on an infield out.

After Cubs' manager Jimmy Wilson ordered Frank (Creepy) Crespi passed intentionally, Coaker Triplett swinging hard, squibbed a little grounder in front of the plate, toward third base. The Cubs' catcher, Clyde McCullough, pounced out, fielded the ball and fired to Babe Dahlgren at first base. Umpire Lee Ballanfant spread his palms—"safe."

Dahlgren whirled to argue with Ballanfant. McCullough stood watching, hands on hips. Rounding third base, Musial saw his chance and, without breaking stride, he raced home and slid across, ahead of Dahlgren's hurried return throw to McCullough, who was scrambling back to cover homeplate. The Donora Greyhound, as J. Roy Stockton called him, had scored the winning run from second base on a hit that traveled about 15 feet.

In the second game, Musial played right field in a 7-0 victory. He dived to his right for one low line drive and charged for another, turning a double somersault. He bunted safely toward third base and singled to center for a memorable six-hit day of all-around delight, but not for Chicago.

"NOBODY, but nobody, can be that good," exploded Jimmy Wilson.

No, but until he became long in the tooth, Musial did far more than swing a bat. If, in fact, his throwing arm, which picked up strength in the middle years of his career, had been as strong as it was before he was hurt, Stan would have been a perfect ballplayer.

At Pittsburgh, with his friends and relatives watching, Musial hit his first big league homer off Rip Sewell, then finished with .426 for 12 games as the Cardinals couldn't quite catch the Dodgers. He'd started that Cinderella season of '41 as a deadarmed lefthanded pitcher from Class D and he'd finished it in the majors with a contract that would pay him $4,250 his first full year up.

Musial, now a sensation, didn't hit in spring training, but Casey Stengel tut-tutted. "Don't worry," he told the writers in Florida, "you fellers are going to be writin' about this feller for 10 . . . 15 . . . 20 years."

As the shyness left, Musial became happy-go-lucky, one of a group that practiced musical murder in the clubhouse before Cardinal games. Their legacy was Pepper Martin's Missouri Mudcats of the Gashouse Gang and colorful trainer Harrison J. (Doc) Weaver's mandolin and phonograph. Musial, who liked polkas, could beat out time with aluminum coat hangers or play a mean slide-whistle.

These were the St. Louis Swifties, as New York cartoonist Willard Mullin referred to them, lean and hungry and incredibly quick. The speed, defense and opportunism of the 1942 Cardinals, of whom pitcher Harry Gumbert and center fielder Terry Moore were the only players 30 or over, made them an exceptional team with exceptional pitching. The depth, which included Mort Cooper, Johnny Beazley, Max Lanier, Ernie White, Howard Pollet, Murry Dickson, Howard Krist and Gumbert, might have been as impressive as any club ever had.

They spotted the Dodgers a 10-game lead in August, then reeled off 43 victories in their last 52 games to nip the Brooks by two games even though the Dodgers won their last eight starts. Musial's first grand-slam homer beat Sewell and Pittsburgh in a key final-week victory.

Although platooned early in the season, Musial

batted .315 with 72 RBIs and 10 homers. He hadn't yet summoned the power that would mark his post-war production. The 1942 Cardinals, following their spectacular 106-48 season, upset the New York Yankees in the World Series, winning in just five games against a ball club that hadn't lost a Series since 1926 (to St Louis) and, in fact, had lost precious few games.

Musial's contributions were limited in the Series, though he did hit safely twice in one inning of a six-run rally in the fourth game. Defensively, Stan teamed with the master center fielder, Moore, and ever-reliable right fielder, Enos Slaughter, to save the third game with circus catches. White's shutout, 2-0, the first suffered by the Yanks since Jess Haines blanked them in the '26 Series, was preserved particularly when Moore dived over Musial, who had slipped in left-center to deprive Joe DiMaggio of a run-scoring triple with a diving backhanded catch.

When the Cardinals rolled out of Penn Station, headed back for St. Louis and their victory celebration, Marty Marion, their great shortstop, remembers that Musial actually cried. Stan was heading home to Donora assured of more money for one week ($6,192.53) than he'd earned all season.

With long-time friend Frank Pizzica trying to help him negotiate, Musial effected a modest compromise to $6,250 in 1943 when he held out and sought $10,000 at a time owner Sam Breadon offered only $5,500. Stan won his first batting championship and first Most Valuable Player award in '43, another pennant-winning season, and in addition to hitting .357, he also led the league in hits, doubles and triples.

So Breadon put him under a three-year contract, scaled at $10,000, $12,500 and $13,500, and Musial missed another batting championship only because he was hurt in an outfield collision and tailed off at bat. His 146 games in '44 would be the fewest the durable Donora dandy would play from his rookie season until he suffered a fractured shoulder in 1957, when he was almost 37 years old.

A .347 hitter in '44, Stan batted .304 and hit a home run as the Cardinals defeated their St. Louis rivals, the Browns in a wartime streetcar World Series. Then he was drafted into the Navy and, happily for Uncle Sam, became a ship repairman who never tried to repair a ship. Playing service ball in the States and in the Pacific, he altered his batting stance and hitting philosophy somewhat to accommodate his fellow G.I.s.

Musial went down on the handle and edged a bit closer to the plate, to pull the ball more. When he came back from service in 1946, he gravely shook hands with a false thumb, howling with joy that he constantly fooled teammates with the amateur magic at which he did a better job than when he tried to tell jokes. Trouble is, Stan always has laughed at his own punchlines.

The Musial who stepped into the batter's box that first post-war season crouched more than anyone had seen before, to handle outside pitches and to get the ball down more often. He hunched his back, coiled up like a spring, looking over his right shoulder "like a guy peeking around the corner to see if the cops are coming," as someone once said. He stood deep in the batter's box, feet close together his right foot pointed at the pitcher, his knees bent and his bat held perpendicular to the ground.

At times he would overstride. At times, too, he would get carried away with a home run swing, but, generally, he strode no more than 12 inches and went into the ball with an ability to hit to all fields.

"The secret of hitting," Musial wrote in his autobiography, "is to relax, concentrate—and don't hit a fly ball to center field."

Noting that Ted Williams was the only high-average, one field hitter he'd ever seen, Musial said he cocked his right knee like the trigger of a gun and he shot for either foul line, to avoid the deep part of the ballpark. He explained, too, how he could concentrate and relax at the same time.

"It's necessary to have mental tenacity at the

plate, but to avoid physical tension," he said. "Ever watch a tomcat stalk his prey? The tail swishes slowly until just before he's ready to spring. I think the movement keeps him from becoming too tense. Just before he pounces, the tail stops.

"I moved my tail, too, in what I guess was a pretty humorous wiggle that, frankly, I wasn't aware of. It was part of an instinctive effort to relax at the plate. I'd take a deep breath, shrug my shoulders to loosen the back muscles, wiggle my fanny to unlock the hips and flex my fingers to make certain my hands and wrists weren't tight in overeagerness. All these things gave me absolute freedom of movement, but I did them automatically. My entire thinking was on just two things: The pitcher and the ball in his hand."

In 1946, the year Brooklyn fans nicknamed him The Man, Stan turned down a $75,000 bonus in cash and $125,000 contract for five years from Jorge Pasquel, the marauding Mexican baseball buff. At only $13,500, he stayed in St. Louis to put together a season that won him his second MVP award and the Cardinals a pennant.

Asked in mid-June to move to first base—"his annual move," as Mike Haley of the *Globe-Democrat* later quipped—Musial led the league in six offensive departments in a .365 season featured by 228 hits, of which 50 were doubles, 20 triples and 16 home runs. He batted in 103 runs.

In the famous head-to-head encounter with Williams in the World Series, Musial did not distinguish himself, either, but he did better than his rival. Stan batted .222 to Ted's .200 and included five extra-base hits among his six blows, driving in four runs. Williams had five singles and one RBI.

Terry Moore has enjoyed re-showing a well-worn film of the Cardinals' seven-game upset over the Boston Red Sox just to show again Musial's speed in racing to third with a triple at Fenway Park. Another teammate, Harry Walker, a frequent manager, has repeatedly told his players that one of the main reasons Musial broke Cobb's career record

for total bases and Ruth's mark for extra-base blows was that he left home plate in full-stride.

"Most hitters want to wait until they're close to first base before deciding, ah, I can get two or three," said Walker. "That's too late. Musial was going all-out for the extra base when he left the batter's box."

Musial wound up the kind of agreeable guy to whom, honestly, a clubowner actually paid more than he'd agreed, but Stan hadn't met Gussie Busch by the time he practically hand-wrestled Sam Breadon in a 1947 holdout to get up to $31,000 just after the Cardinals had drawn 1,000,000 paid admissions for the first time.

A balky appendix took its toll in '47 when The Man was flattened once for five days and only a practical knowledge of athletic medicine by Dr. Robert F. Hyland kept Musial from losing more time and probably the Cardinals more games. Dr. Hyland, referred to as the "surgeon-general of baseball" by Judge Landis, offered to freeze the appendix and remove it after the season.

Musial, hitting only .188 in late May, struggled uphill to bat .312 and then underwent surgery for removal of both the appendix and infected tonsils. He came out in '48, healthier and stronger, and—at 27—put together the greatest season of his career.

The first time the Cardinals went into Brooklyn's Ebbets Field, his happiest hitting grounds, Musial ripped 11 hits in 15 trips, including four doubles, a triple and a homer. And the way he hit all season seemed almost an extension of that hot streak.

Batting .376 and winning MVP again, Musial missed by just one rained-out home run of leading in an unprecedented sweep of offensive departments. He had the most runs (135), the most hits (230), the most doubles (46), the most triples (18) and the most RBIs (131). Down at the end of the bat, yet still able to keep his strikeouts to 25 or fewer, he hit 39 home runs, one under the league lead shared by Ralph Kiner and Johnny Mize.

The Musial of 1948 actually had a piece of several great hitters' best seasons. He had the first .700 slugging percentage in the National League since Hack Wilson in 1930. His 103 extra-base hits were just four shy of Chuck Klein's league record set in 1930 and his 429 total bases were only 21 behind the league high established by Rogers Hornsby in 1922.

Four times that season, tying a record set by Cobb, Musial collected five hits in a game. Once, he did it in a game in which he got all five hits with two strikes. The last time . . .

Well, there's a little preamble to the afternoon at Boston when Musial forced the Braves to delay by one day the celebration of their first pennant in 34 years. Over his career, Stan prided himself on his fielding, particularly when he didn't hit. Playing center field at Brooklyn, where for once he was stopped at the plate, Musial made two diving catches and once charged into the exit gate in left-center for a gloved grab that saved a 3-2 victory.

"Stash, if you could only hit . . ." Terry Moore ribbed him.

Musial had jammed his left wrist diving, and the next afternoon The Man halted the game in the ninth inning to suggest that with the winning run in scoring position, manager Eddie Dyer put in Erv Dusak, who could grip the ball to throw and had a stronger arm. The move was made, but the thoughtful strategy failed. Pete Reiser singled in the decisive score.

Hit on the right hand by Carl Erskine that game, Musial went into Boston with both wrists taped. For once, the wind blew out toward the Charles River behind the right-field fence.

"A great day for the hitters, Banj," I suggested. It was ridiculous to call a great hitter "Banjo," but Musial never minded.

"Yeah," he said, a bit bitterly, "but I can't hit like this."

In disgust, he ripped off the restrictive tape and that afternoon, facing Warren Spahn and replacements, Musial needed just five swings to get his record-tying five hits. For the record, he batted .314

over a career against Spahn, the slick southpaw, and hit 14 home runs, but most of them came early when Warren tried to challenge him with the fastball, he insisted.

Musial's father died that winter, a result of the poison smog which gripped Donora in October and drove the elder Musials to St. Louis. Later, Stan's mother insisted on returning home to the Donora house he'd built for her and, to his despair, would mow the lawn and shovel snow even though he had neighbors spying on her for him. Stan had deep affection for his father, but it was his big, strong and handsome mother he seemed to resemble.

At the '59 All-Star Game in Pittsburgh, Mrs. Musial waved frantically for Stan to come over to her box in practice. "Look," she said, triumphantly holding up an autographed scorecard, "I just got this from my favorite player—Ted Williams."

Musial, trying to hit home runs like Williams, came a cropper the first half of the '49 season, but good ol' Ebbets Field and a three-hit All-Star Game there including a home run, started him to roll. He finished strong with a .338 average, 36 homers and 123 RBIs, but he missed another batting title almost as closely as the Cardinals did the flag in a third straight second-place finish.

In 1950, hitting over .400, Musial slipped in loose dirt rounding first base at Pittsburgh and when he tried to get up, he couldn't, his left knee hurt. "Thank God for the restaurant," he said to himself.

Despite the elastic, steel-ribbed brace he needed the rest of that season and on and off thereafter, Musial began a string of three consecutive batting championships—.346, .355 and .336.

At the All-Star Game in Detroit in '51, Preacher Roe, witty Brooklyn veteran, listened as Ed Lopat, chesty Yankee southpaw, said he knew how to pitch to Musial. The next afternoon Stan hit Lopat's first pitch into the upper right-field stands and Roe crowed, "I see . . . I see. . . Hell, I knew how to pitch him that way."

Roe once walked Musial on four pitches at

Brooklyn, pitching too carefully, and then picked Stan off first. The next day when Eddie Dyer was holding his clubhouse meeting, the Preacher stuck his head in the door and gloated with a grin, "I found Musial's weakness."

As Musial stepped up to bat in the 12th inning of the 1955 All-Star Game at Milwaukee, he found friend Yogi Berra of the Yankees, grumbling behind the plate.

"What's the matter, Yogi?" Stan inquired.

"It's these extra innings," said the catcher. "Really tough on a guy catching every day."

Bull-voiced, beet-red Bill Summers, the plate umpire, chimed in, "How about me? It's getting just as tough back here."

"Yeah, I'm tired, too," said Musial. Bam! He lined Frank Sullivan's first pitch high into the right-field bleachers for a game-winning home run.

"He owed me that...he owed me that," shrilled the National League's manager, Leo Durocher, who had been victimized by Musial for years at Brooklyn and New York.

By 1956, his batting average having dwindled to .310, though his power production was still good, Musial made two errors in one game at first base against Brooklyn in St. Louis and went hitless. He was booed, lustily, for the first time.

"It was," he said realistically afterward, "a long time coming." The next day a group of fans took out full-page ads in the St. Louis newspapers to apologize to him.

Musial accepted a $5,000 salary cut to $75,000 at Frank Lane's request, cut out smoking and bounced back in 1957 with a spectacular year for a man nearly 37, hitting .351 to gain his seventh batting title. The Redbirds rebounded, too, and almost won a pennant that went to Milwaukee. Young Henry Aaron barely shaded old man Musial for the MVP award even though Stan suffered a hairline fracture in his right shoulder in late August ending his consecutive-game record at 895. The mark was later topped by Chicago's Billy Williams.

Although written off for the season, Musial insisted on returning to the lineup and, just punching the ball, because he couldn't swing properly, he collected 16 hits in 31 times at bat. And when he'd agreed with new general manager Bing Devine to a contract for $91,000 for 1958, big boss Gussie Busch had Devine call Stan back.

"Mr. Busch," said Devine, smiling, "wants you to have $100,000."

Musial's burning goal for some time, other than another pennant, had been 3,000 hits. "I want to get them in a hurry," he said at the outset of the '58 season. "Who knows? I might get hit in the can with a cab."

The Man needed only 22 games to get 43 hits. He achieved No. 3,000 on May 13 at Chicago. St. Louis' Union Station was crowded that night with well-wishers, young and old, even though the Cardinals' delayed train didn't arrive until nearly midnight.

"Now I know how Lindbergh felt," Musial said when escorted through the cheering crowd to a speaker's platform.

"What did he hit?" someone yelled.

Musial giggled. "No school tomorrow, kids," he said, impulsively, bringing down the house.

A night later, before a standing-room crowd which had hoped to see No. 3,000, The Man made No. 3,001 a first-inning homer. The old boy had a bit of ham in him, all right, a touch of the theatrics.

When the Cardinals rallied spectacularly in September 1963, just after Musial had announced his retirement by saying he'd hoped to go out with a winner, 19 victories in 20 games brought a showdown series with the Dodgers. Just before it, both Musial and wife Lil had awakened early one morning, sharing an uneasiness. Mrs. Musial put on the coffee pot because neither of them could sleep. The phone rang. It was son Dick calling from Fort Riley, Kan.

Their daughter-in-law Sharon had given birth to their first grandchild just a couple of minutes after the senior Musials had awakened. The first time up that night, Stan hit the first pitch thrown by the Cubs' Glenn Hobbie for a home run.

"That one," said Musial grinning, "is for Jeffrey Stanton Musial." And how many boys can ever say that their grandpas celebrated their arrival by hitting a home run in the big leagues?

The Dodgers closed out the Cardinals in a magnificent three-game sweep, an extremely well-played series. The excitement when Musial tagged southpaw Johnny Podres for a game-tying homer, 1-1, in the seventh inning of the opener still can be remembered even though St. Louis since celebrated three pennants, the homer was the 475th and last of Musial's career.

Stan the Man, hitting .325 against the pennant-winning Dodgers that season, didn't have enough help in that show-down in St. Louis. So he closed out his career in the spotlight the final day of the '63 season.

Emotion was high. The pressure was on Musial from the minute he got up until he stepped onto the field for pre-game ceremonies. A capacity crowd and a television audience peeked over his shoulder then the way reporters and camera crews had from early morning. Cincinnati, with a chance to finish third and the fear of winding up fifth, was pitching flame-firing Jim Maloney, a 23-game winner.

The first time up, Musial struck out and the crowd groaned, but in the fourth inning he singled for the first hit off Maloney. Then in the sixth, with Curt Flood on second, the count ran to 2-and-1, and the sharp-eyed man of nearly 43 years picked up the spin of a quick-breaking curveball, low and inside. For the last time the wrists flashed—and Musial pulled the ball into the hole for a run-scoring hit.

It was, Johnny Keane decided, a great way to go, and the manager lifted the old superstar, who sat around and waited until the Cardinals won, 3-2, the same score by which they'd won the day he broke in with two hits 22 years before.

Then everybody went over to Musial's place for a helluva blow-out. A big retirement dinner in October drew most of the great players and other personalities in the game. The Man fascinated an old friend even more with a remark the following year when the Cardinals acquired Lou Brock from Chicago in mid-June and then went on to win their first pennant in 18 years, with Brock playing sensationally.

"The Cardinals couldn't have won with me in left field," said Musial, matter of factly saying what many other great ones never would admit to themselves, much less to others.

If the storybook script had held up just a bit longer, the Cardinals would have won that game the year before against the Dodgers when Musial homered off Podres and when he singled late for the first hit off Sandy Koufax the next night. Stan the Man could have gone out with a championship as a player just as he did as a general manager four years later.

The joy of playing kept Musial going even more than his concern for his weight and his waistline. As far back as 1941, leaving Daytona Beach for spring training of the fateful season in which he went magically from nowhere to somebody, The Man put his feelings in perspective for sports editor Benny Kahn.

"Naturally," he said, "I want to play with Columbus, but the Cardinals will probably farm me out to Asheville or some other B team. I won't want to play any more D ball, but, if I have to, I want to play it right here in Daytona Beach. I'd play in an E league if they told me to. I like baseball too much to ever give it up."

This is a man of whom former Commissioner Ford Frick said, the day Musial retired, "Here stands baseball's perfect warrior...here stands baseball's perfect knight."

This is a man—better make that, as they did first in Flatbush, The Man—who summed up the charm of baseball's first century as well as his own credo when he said at his induction into the Hall of Fame at Cooperstown in 1969:

"I say baseball was a great game, is a great game and will be a great game. I'm extremely grateful for what it has given me—in recognition and records, thrills and satisfaction, money and memories. I hope I've given nearly as much as I've gotten from it."

STANLEY FRANK (THE MAN) MUSIAL
Born November 21, 1920, at Donora, Pa.
Height 6-0 Weight 180
Threw and batted lefthanded.
Named to Hall of Fame, 1969.

YEAR	CLUB	LEAGUE	POS.	G.	AB.	R.	H.	2B.	3B.	HR.	RBI.	B.A.	PO.	A.	E.	F.A.
1938	Williamson	Mt. St.	P	26	62	5	16	3	0	1	6	.258	7	22	6	.829
1939	Williamson	Mt. St.	PH-P	23	71	10	25	3	3	1	9	.352	5	19	3	.889
1940	Daytona Beach	Fla. St.	O-P	113	405	55	126	17	10	1	70	.311	183	69	11	.958
1941	Springfield	W.A.	OF	87	348	100	132	27	10	26	94	.379	185	7	3	.985
1941	Rochester	Int.	OF	54	221	43	72	10	4	3	21	.326	102	5	1	.991
1941	St. Louis	Nat.	OF	12	47	8	20	4	0	1	7	.426	20	1	0	1.000
1942	St. Louis	Nat.	OF	140	467	87	147	32	10	10	72	.315	296	6	5	.984
1943	St. Louis	Nat.	OF	157	617	108	220	48	20	13	81	.357	376	15	7	.982
1944	St. Louis	Nat.	OF	146	568	112	197	51	14	12	94	.347	353	16	5	.987
1945	St. Louis	Nat.								(In Military Service)						
1946	St. Louis	Nat.	1-OF	156	624	124	228	50	20	16	103	.365	1166	69	15	.988
1947	St. Louis	Nat.	1B	149	587	113	183	30	13	19	95	.312	1360	77	8	.994
1948	St. Louis	Nat.	O-1B	155	611	135	230	46	18	39	131	.376	354	11	7	.981
1949	St. Louis	Nat.	O-1B	157	612	128	207	41	13	36	123	.338	337	11	3	.991
1950	St. Louis	Nat.	OF-1B	146	555	105	192	41	7	28	109	.346	760	39	8	.990
1951	St. Louis	Nat.	O-1B	152	578	124	205	30	12	32	108	.355	816	45	10	.989
1952	St. Louis	Nat.	O-1-P	154	578	105	194	42	6	21	91	.336	502	18	5	.990
1953	St. Louis	Nat.	OF	157	593	127	200	53	9	30	113	.337	294	9	5	.984
1954	St. Louis	Nat.	O-1B	153	591	120	195	41	9	35	126	.330	307	15	5	.985
1955	St. Louis	Nat.	1-OF	154	562	97	179	30	5	33	108	.319	1000	94	9	.992
1956	St. Louis	Nat.	1B-OF	156	594	87	184	33	6	27	109	.310	954	95	8	.992
1957	St. Louis	Nat.	1B	134	502	82	176	38	3	29	102	.351	1167	99	10	.992
1958	St. Louis	Nat.	1B	135	472	64	159	35	2	17	62	.337	1019	100	13	.989
1959	St. Louis	Nat.	1B-OF	115	341	37	87	13	2	14	44	.255	624	63	7	.990
1960	St. Louis	Nat.	OF-1B	116	331	49	91	17	1	17	63	.275	300	19	3	.991
1961	St. Louis	Nat.	OF	123	372	46	107	22	4	15	70	.288	149	9	1	.994
1962	St. Louis	Nat.	OF	135	433	57	143	18	1	19	82	.330	164	6	4	.977
1963	St. Louis	Nat.	OF	124	337	34	86	10	2	12	58	.255	121	1	4	.968
Major League Totals				3026	10972	1949	3630	725	177	475	1951	.331	12439	818	142	.989

WORLD SERIES RECORD

YEAR	CLUB	LEAGUE	POS.	G.	AB.	R.	H.	2B.	3B.	HR.	RBI.	B.A.	PO.	A.	E.	F.A.
1942	St. Louis	Nat.	OF	5	18	2	4	1	0	0	2	.222	13	0	0	1.000
1943	St. Louis	Nat.	OF	5	18	2	5	0	0	0	0	.278	7	2	0	1.000
1944	St. Louis	Nat.	OF	6	23	2	7	2	0	1	2	.304	11	0	1	.917
1946	St. Louis	Nat.	1B	7	27	3	6	4	1	0	4	.222	60	2	0	1.000
World Series Totals				23	86	9	22	7	1	1	8	.256	91	4	1	.990

PITCHING RECORD

YEAR	CLUB	LEAGUE	G.	IP.	W.	L.	Pct.	H.	R.	ER.	SO.	BB.	ERA.
1938	Williamson	Mt. State	20	110	6	6	.500	114	75	57	66	80	4.66
1939	Williamson	Mt. State	13	92	9	2	.818	71	53	44	86	85	4.30
1940	Daytona Beach	Fla. State	28	223	18	5	.783	179	108	65	176	145	2.62
1952	St. Louis	Nat.	1	0	0	0	.000	0	0	0	0	0	0.00
Major League Totals			1	0	0	0	.000	0	0	0	0	0	0.00

A LEG UP: Mel Ott, a major leaguer at only 17, became a 500-homer hitter hoisting his right leg in the batter's box.

MEL OTT

John McGraw was master of all he surveyed when the Polo Grounds was the palace of big league ballparks. He could tongue-lash a smart aleck to ribbons, but the often tyrannical 30-year manager of the New York Giants could recognize sincerity, too, even when it sounded down right ridiculous.

Back there in the spring of 1926, McGraw just had asked a short, stocky, thick-thighed catcher if he'd ever played the outfield.

"Only when I was a kid, Mr. McGraw," came the polite reply from Melvin Thomas Ott as the fa-mous manager sought to suppress a smile. After all, the youth in front of him just had turned 17.

Over the years, the Giants would tease Ott in the clubhouse because they knew their man. They'd call him Bright Eyes and Little Spring Time. The press, recognizing the tender age at which he'd appeared and the early point at which he'd established himself as a star, would refer to him at Master Melvin.

But, more and more as the lad from Louisiana became a senior citizen in baseball knickerbockers, he became Ottie, a name that would be used with affection even in Brooklyn, where the only good Giant was as dead as the one in Jack and the Beanstalk.

Another extremely likeable guy named Stan Musial came along and systematically ripped away most of Mel Ott's records, some of which the littlest Giant, as he was known, had wrested from the National League's legendary hero, Honus Wagner. But even when Ott's name was disappearing from the record book, he was winning new recognition just as surely as he'd won ball games for the Giants for two decades with a big bat, good glove, strong arm and know-how.

Ott's savvy was more than just native intelligence. He'd benefited from perhaps the finest cram course to which a big league ballplayer ever was subjected.

When he rode the Giants' bench for the greater part of his first two years in the majors—imagine signing a big league contract at 16!—he sat next to the portly McGraw in one corner of the dugout.

Sure, the kid would have liked to slide down to the other end, where other benchwarmers crowded, to avoid the wrath of the Old Man. But McGraw insisted that the curly-haired kid with the big brown eyes listen to what amounted to a frequently sulphuric, yet educational commentary on the games that would unfold before them.

Why, now and then the Old Man would forget himself and direct his four-letter scorn to the young man next to him. Ott would protest softly in a syrupy southern drawl, "But, Mr. McGraw, I'm not even playing."

"I know, Ott," the Old Man would catch himself, "but I just don't want you to make the same stupid mistakes as those dumb such-and-such, so-and-sos out there now."

Ott didn't. He wasn't fast but he ran the bases wisely and well. He knew how to hit the cutoff man from the outfield. With a strong arm and an ability to play the carom off the short right-field wall like a billiard champion, he hung up runners frequently enough to make them proceed with unnatural cau-tion. Yet he rarely was trapped in throwing to the wrong base.

Even though he was one of the leading home run hitters in history, the National League's champion until Willie Mays and Henry Aaron, etc., Ott could bunt when he had to and, if necessary, go to the opposite field. Basically, though, he was an extreme pull-hitter as he compiled a .304 lifetime average, 511 homers and 1,860 runs batted in.

Fact is, except for the novelty of his extreme youth as a big leaguer and the steady, high-level performance of play that brought him Hall of Fame election in 1951, Ott was most unusual for his distinctive batting stance.

The lefthanded hitter, taking dead aim on the right-field fence, only 257 feet away at the foul line in the Polo Grounds, planted his feet far apart. He raised his right leg to knee height while the pitcher was preparing to deliver the ball. Then Ott planted the right foot on the ground again, just before impact with the pitch. The stride was no more than a couple of inches.

Wait, that's not a good enough word picture if you never saw the former New York Nationals' famed No. 4 swing. Try this: Ottie squared away to a pitch as if he were going to beat a rug. Crowding the plate with feet spread, he reared up his front leg, not unlike the family canine finding a favorite hydrant. At the same time he pulled back the bat, stepped lightly forward as the right foot descended, and then swung.

The swing was a good level stroke, one which caught McGraw's eye in an early workout at the Polo Grounds. Mel was signed in September 1925, for $400. He stayed there a quarter-century, including nearly seven undistinguished seasons as a manager and the last two-plus as assistant to his old friend and former teammate, Carl Hubbell, in the Giants' farm system.

It was Ott who inspired Leo Durocher's classic quote, "Nice guys finish last." Although Durocher doesn't embarrass easily, The Lip didn't mean for that one to see the light of day because, like everyone else, he had high regard for Mel as a man and a player.

Embarrassingly then, it was Durocher who came across the Brooklyn Bridge at the All-Star break in 1948 to succeed Ottie as manager when Horace Stoneham, a longtime admirer, decided he'd gone about as far as he could go with an old idol.

Stoneham trod slowly and softly because as he'd said earlier in the managerial reign which produced just two first-division finishes, "If I fired Mel, my mother and sister wouldn't speak to me."

The affection of the fans for Ott had been captured in a night given for him in 1940. He would remember that as his biggest baseball thrill even though, a hitting hero of two World Series, he contributed just one single in five times at bat of a game lost to Brooklyn, 8-4.

By then, the Dodgers, who for years had been ground under the heel of the Giants, suddenly had gained the upper hand in the battle of the baseball boroughs. But a grand old man at only 31, Ottie was grateful first that Stoneham had picked a night when the Dodgers were at the Polo Grounds so that no one could accuse anyone of trying to build up a crowd with a phony promotion. Giant-Dodger battles in New York were classical, hotter, if possible, than the same two franchises' feud since they've located in California.

So the added incentive of a tribute to the littlest Giant, plus a pitching hookup between Hubbell and former teammate Freddie Fitzsimmons, packed 53,997 persons in the Polo Grounds.

Ott was given a 208-piece set of flat silver, a coffee and tea set imported from England, a silver water pitcher, a complete set of golf clubs and bag from his fellow players, a couple of plaques and even a gold membership card in the Baseball Writers' Association of America.

Except for a brilliant running catch, with a leaping back-handed grab deep in the Giants' bullpen in extreme right-center of the spacious horseshoe-shaped stadium, Ottie did little that night. But he remembered cheers and the good fellowship—even from the leather-lunged Flatbush faithful.

When he got back to the Greenwich Village apartment he rented summers for himself, his wife and two daughters, a special delivery letter awaited him. It was from former silent screen star Marguerite Clark, widow of Harry Williams, a wealthy Louisiana lumberman who had been prominent in the saga of Master Melvin Ott.

"Do you mind if I add a little something to the gifts which all Giant fans are proud and happy to contribute?" Mrs. Williams wrote in advance of sending a matching salad set. "If Harry were alive, he would want me to, I know. It would have made him very happy."

Harry Williams already had made Mel Ott very happy when the kid was quite sad. Born March 2, 1909, in Gretna, deep in Louisiana's bayou country, Mel played high school football, basketball and baseball, but his heart was in baseball, the sport in which his father and an uncle had been pretty good semi-pro hands.

At 16, little 5-9 Ottie and his high school batterymate, Lester Ruprich, crossed the Mississippi to New Orleans to ask the owner of the Southern Association's New Orleans Pelicans for a job.

Alex Heinemann liked what he saw in pitcher Ruprich, who was three years older than Ott, but he told the runty catcher, "You're too small, son, and too young, anyway."

Mel blubbered a bit, he would recall with a smile in later years, and Heinemann suggested that if the kid really wanted to play desperately enough, the New Orleans club owner could fix him up with a semi-pro team "in the country where they play three or four times a week." The town about 90 miles from New Orleans, was Patterson, La.

"Just tell Harry Williams I sent you," said Heinemann. Ott would remember Williams with deep affection. The rich sportsman gave him a ball-playing job for $150 a month and expenses. "That really meant all expenses, including haircuts, movies and sodas," Mel recalled. "Whenever I—or any player—hit a home run, the fans at Patterson would pass the hat so that I found myself making more than my salary in extras."

Six weeks later, hitting hard, young Ott received a Southern Association contract from Heinemann at New Orleans, offering $300 a month. Eager to accept, the kid thought it was only fair to show the contract to Williams.

"That's nice," the man said, almost casually, "but forget about it."

Ott thought to himself, "Here I've got a chance to go to New Orleans and he wants to keep me in Patterson for the rest of his life," but Mel's loyalty kept him in rural Louisiana even when Williams and his wife went to Europe.

Late in August, Ott received a penny postcard sent by Williams from New York on his return from abroad. "Report to John McGraw at the Polo Grounds for a tryout on September 1," the card read.

No one could fool the world-wise 16-year-old from the bayous. Master Melvin Ott recognized a joke when he saw one. So he was still catching for the Patterson Braves when Williams returned.

"What are you doing here when you're supposed to be in New York?" asked the ballplayer's benefactor.

Williams gave him a train ticket to New York, by way of New Orleans, but first, Mel stopped at home at Gretna, where his mother was upset that her young son, still wet behind the ears, would venture alone to the Big City. Ottie's father convinced Mrs. Ott not to worry.

Mama had a point, all right. When Mel reached New York, carrying a straw suitcase, he became so confused by the vast subway system that he saw Coney Island before he did the Polo Grounds. But he made it, finally, and reported to McGraw's office, where a timid knock brought a gruff command to enter.

Whether McGraw was disappointed in his first look at the sturdy little fellow recommended by his good friend, Harry Williams, it's difficult to determine. But he became impressed one morning when he stepped out into the ballpark early and saw a newcomer hitting the ball hard in morning batting practice.

"Who's that?" McGraw asked.

"The kid, Ott," he was told, and, reflecting the Old Man's baseball sagacity, McGraw not only put the 16-year-old boy under contract to the Giants, but he made a bold decision.

He would keep the kid with the big club. "I don't want anyone tinkering with that natural swing," McGraw growled. He even turned down his former outfielder, Casey Stengel, who managed Toledo in the American Association the next couple of years and who said he'd be delighted to work with young Ott.

Master Melvin sat at the Old Man's knee, became McGraw's last favorite and, the way Mrs. McGraw remembered, the great manager's personal pet, next to his money man of the mound when both McGraw and Christy Mathewson were young.

Ott played nearly seven years for McGraw or, to be more accurate, he was a regular the last five seasons of McGraw's long reign. Ott's greatest regret was that, coming up just after the Old Man had won his last four pennants in a row, the Giants couldn't give McGraw one more.

"We fought hard and came close," said Ott, remembering close calls in 1927, 1928 and 1930, "but we just couldn't make it for him."

McGraw came to an early conclusion that for one so thick-thighed, Ott would become painfully slow and risk considerable leg trouble if he continued to catch. So the schooling of Ottie as an outfielder began, including lessons from a track coach on how to get away from his teeth-jarring, flatfooted running technique.

For all of McGraw's perspicacity, those heavy thigh muscles popped one charley horse after another over the years. They led, in fact, to Ott's virtual retirement after the wartime season of 1945 when he was 38 years old, still able to hit 21 homers and drive in 79 runs. He batted just 68 times in 1946, getting his 511th and last homer among only five hits, and went to the plate just four fruitless trips as a pinch-hitter in 1947.

That year, the Giants hit a National League record total of home runs, 221, WITHOUT one from the first man in league history to break the 500-homer barrier. And when the slow-moving, power-packed Giants could finish no higher than fourth, the handwriting was on the green outfield wall of the Polo Grounds for Ott as a manager.

As a veteran player, Ottie tried ways and means to keep his legs in shape. At first, he nursed them with massage and vitamin injections. Finally, he tried a cure popular in his grandfather's day—an olive oil rubdown.

As carefully nursed by McGraw, Mel struck out his first time at bat in 1926 when he was only 17, but though batting only 60 times, he hit phenomenally. He ran off five straight pinch-hits before he failed twice-in succession.

A friendly New York writer, Fred Lieb, long-time contributor to *The Sporting News*, had dinner with the lad, who was distressed.

"I held the bat the same way and swung just the same as when I made the hits," said the teenager who was batting over .400. He finished the season in which he appeared in only 35 games by hitting .383, which would be the highest average of his career.

Ottie's first big league home run came against the Chicago Cubs at New York in the 1927 season, one in which he got into 82 contests and batted .282. That first homer, his only one that season, came on a drive on which Hack Wilson slipped in the mud so that the ball skipped past him for an inside-the-park, four-base hit.

Offhand, Ott could remember only one other homer that didn't leave the playing field, and it had amusing aspects.

In 1931, the only year one Frank Watt pitched

in the majors, Ottie teed off on the Philadelphia hurler just as regularly as he did on his favorite cousin, Larry French, a talented southpaw for Pittsburgh, Chicago and Brooklyn.

Off Watt, it seemed, the littlest Giant homered in every game he faced him until the last one of the final series between the New York and Philadelphia clubs. As Ott stepped up for his last turn at bat, Watt said, sarcastically, "Here's your last chance to keep your record, Mel."

Ott hit a line shot to deep right-center in the cavernous Polo Grounds and as the ball ricocheted around down to the bullpen and No. 4 circled the bases, Watt cussed him every inch of the way.

Watt really shouldn't have felt too bad because Ott led or tied for the league home-run leadership six times, with a career high of 42 in 1929, a year in which he drove in 151 runs while batting .328. His highest batting average was .349 a year later, but he batted over .300 11 times.

In the spring of 1930, Ott came up to McGraw in spring training one morning and said, "I found a man in my room this morning, Mr. McGraw."

The Old Man was taken aback until, smiling, the warm young star added triumphantly, "I'm 21 today!"

By then, Ott was quite a man, having established himself defensively as an outfielder who was versatile enough to move around in a pinch. Why, back in 1928 when Andy Cohen became incapacitated, Mel's fooling around at second base in practice paid off.

Later, when Bill Terry took over as manager, the brilliant right fielder would shift to third base and play capably because the Giants needed him there more than they did in right field.

One year when Ottie had been particularly valuable and hadn't received the recognition Terry deemed appropriate to his deeds, the big first baseman said to the little Giant, "Why don't you do something colorful so they'll notice you, like come out wearing a red bandana—or get drunk?"

Ottie drank, all right, but the little guy with the

passive southern accent and an active taste for crayfish bisque, New Orleans style, was too well-disciplined to do anything reckless. Not until he became a playing manager of a second-division ball club did he lose his equanimity with umpires—and then you'd have to charge part of it to the effects of a nervous stomach which put him to bed for two weeks.

Ott was a movie addict, a crossword puzzle devotee and partial to gin rummy, bouillabaisse and oysters Rockefeller. He didn't mind betting a few bucks on the horses now and then. He played golf very well, shooting in the mid-70s, and he played the way he threw, righthanded. He chopped wood the way he batted—lefthanded.

Ott married a New Orleans girl, Mildred Wattigny, and they had two daughters. Having invested wisely, Mel was in no pinch or hurry when the Giants let him go after the 1950 World Series, ending what had seemed to be an endless love affair. Typically, Ottie would make no complaint.

He sought, momentarily, to take the same path back to the big leagues as a manager that Casey Stengel and Charley Dressen had trod, putting in the 1951 and '52 seasons as skipper of the Oakland Oaks, then in the Pacific Coast League. However, the results were undistinguished. So maybe, though it's this writer's feeling that no manager is better than his material, Master Melvin was just too fundamentally nice to be a successful field foreman. On him, a scowl seemed foreign.

At any rate, living in suburban New Orleans at Metairie, gainfully connected in a contracting business, Ott found himself happily in demand as a baseball broadcaster, first with radio's traveling "Game of the Day" program and then for three seasons on the Detroit Tigers' network.

On November 14, 1958, a foggy night, Ottie and his Mildred had dinner near Bay St. Louis, Miss. They pulled out onto the highway in their station wagon and found themselves in a head-on collision with another car. The driver of the lighter vehicle, a father of seven who apparently had lost the center line of the highway with limited visibility, was killed outright.

The Otts were critically injured, especially Mel. He underwent surgery in Gulfport for four hours to repair two broken legs, but his internal injuries were grievous and he was moved to the famed Touro Infirmary in New Orleans, where an artificial kidney machine was used to reduce pressure on the bladder. A son-in-law, Dr. Philip Loria, was included in the battery of medical men who fought desperately, but futilely, to save Mel Ott's life. Uremia, kidney damage and multiple fractures claimed him a week later, on November 21. He was only 49 years old.

The little man who was as solid as Louisiana cypress, left indelible impressions, as witness his election to the Hall of Fame only four years after he quit playing.

He'd starred for the Giants in the 1933 World Series they won from Washington. In the first inning of the first game after a fumble by Buddy Myer at second base brought up New York's doughty little cleanup man against southpaw Walter Stewart, Ott creamed a 400-foot home run.

That blow served to stand up for a 4-2 victory for friend Carl Hubbell, who was aided further by a run-scoring single by Ott. In his first World Series game at the ripe old age of 24, all the eight-year veteran did was post 4-for-4.

Ottie won the last game of the '33 Series, which was the fifth, just as he did the first, but more dramatically. In the 10th inning of a game at Griffith Stadium, with the score tied, Ott lifted a long drive to center, where Fred Schulte went back and leaped.

The ball deflected off Schulte's glove and into temporary bleachers, disappearing among the customers. Umpire Cy Pfirman first ruled the ball a ground-rule double, but on the heated protest of the Giants that the ball hadn't touched the ground, the umpire reversed himself and awarded the home run which, to pressbox observers with a better view, was entirely justified. Ott's blow gave the Giants a 4-3 victory and the world championship.

A .389 hitter in that Series, Ottie had his eighth straight 100-RBI season in 1936, batting .328, getting 33 homers and driving in 135 runs, to help the Giants to the first of two straight Series against the Yankees, Mel batted .304 in the six games and included a home run off Lefty Gomez.

Gomez again was tagged by Ott for a homer in the '37 Series, which went to the Yankees in five games. Ott, playing third base in that one, hit only .200.

As a home run slugger, Ottie was indeed favored by the beckoning right-field barrier at the Polo Grounds, where he hit 323 of his 511 homers. The last one came there on opening day, 1946, as Mel teed off his first time up against Philadelphia lefthander Oscar Judd.

Actually, earlier in his career, Ott needed no home-field advantage. In his biggest home run season, 1929, 22 of the 42 came on the road. Through 1939, at a time he had 369 home runs, only 51 percent had been stroked at New York. It is a well-publicized fact, of course, that once the Phillies moved in 1938 from the Baker Bowl bandbox to Shibe Park, as Connie Mack Stadium then was called, the National League's long-time home run king did not homer again in Philadelphia.

When Ott died, John C. Tattersall, baseball historian and statistician, listed for *The Sporting News* a breakdown of Ott's home runs, showing that he'd hit one every 18.5 official times at bat, that he'd accounted for 48 percent of his RBIs with home runs and that he'd hit two homers in a game 48 times.

In 1930, the year he was married, Ott hit three in a game for the only time, belting two off Boston southpaw Tom Zachary and one off righthander Ben Cantwell at the Polo Grounds. In the same game, he doubled and narrowly missed a fourth homer on a drive to deep right.

Ott's pleasant personality made him a special person. His sportsmanship, too, as Stan Musial brought out at ceremonies at Cooperstown in July, 1969, when Stan the Man joined Ottie and superstars of the past in baseball's Hall of Fame.

"When I was moving in on his records for extra-base hits, total bases and others, he'd not only wish me well, but he'd actually encourage me to spur me on," said Musial, "and I was impressed then by Ottie's sense of honor, his sportsmanship. When my records fall, I hope I'm as gracious as Ottie was."

Although the littlest Giant was facetiously referred to as the first white child born at the Polo Grounds, it only seemed that way. Still, he was a mighty young man when he came along, as close friend and roommate Fred Lindstrom discovered one time when they were talking to a writer seeking to learn big league stars' boyhood idols.

Lindstrom's had been Tris Speaker and George Sisler, said the blond third baseman from Chicago. And Ott's boyhood favorite?

"Lindy was my hero," said Mel.

"What!" roared Lindstrom, leaping out of his chair.

"What are you trying to do, you little pipsqueak, make an old man out of me?"

"No," said Ott, "I'm serious. How old were you when you played in the 1924 World Series?"

"Eighteen," said Lindstrom.

"All right," said Ottie. "I was 15 and in high school in Gretna. Maybe you don't know it, but you were the hero of every high school kid in the country that fall."

Mel Ott winked at the reporter. "Little did I think," he said, "that I'd grow up to room with the great Lindstrom."

"Nuts," said Lindstrom, looking at his watch. "It's time we were getting to the ballpark. Come on, SONNY BOY."

MELVIN THOMAS OTT
Born March 2, 1909, at Gretna, La.
Died November 21, 1958, at New Orleans, La.
Height 5-9 Weight 170
Threw right and batted lefthanded.
Named to Hall of Fame, 1951.

YEAR	CLUB	LEAGUE	POS	G.	AB.	R.	H.	2B.	3B.	HR.	RBI.	B.A.	PO.	A.	E.	F.A.
1926	New York	Nat.	OF	35	60	7	23	2	0	0	4	.383	18	3	2	.913
1927	New York	Nat.	OF	82	163	23	46	7	3	1	19	.282	52	2	1	.982
1928	New York	Nat.	OF	124	435	69	140	26	4	18	77	.322	214	14	7	.970
1929	New York	Nat.	OF	150	545	138	179	37	2	42	151	.328	335	26	10	.973
1930	New York	Nat.	OF	148	521	122	182	34	5	25	119	.349	320	23	11	.969
1931	New York	Nat.	OF	138	497	104	145	23	8	29	115	.292	332	20	7	.981
1932	New York	Nat.	OF	154	566	119	180	30	8	38	123	.318	347	11	6	.984
1933	New York	Nat.	OF	152	580	98	164	36	1	23	103	.283	283	12	5	.983
1934	New York	Nat.	OF	153	582	119	190	29	10	35	135	.326	286	12	8	.974
1935	New York	Nat.	OF-3B	152	593	113	191	33	6	31	114	.322	304	42	6	.983
1936	New York	Nat.	OF	150	534	120	175	28	6	33	135	.328	250	20	4	.985
1937	New York	Nat.	OF-3B	151	545	99	160	28	2	31	95	.294	198	126	10	.970
1938	New York	Nat.	OF-3B	150	527	116	164	23	6	36	116	.311	163	241	15	.964
1939	New York	Nat.	OF-3B	125	396	85	122	23	2	27	80	.308	190	45	11	.955
1940	New York	Nat.	OF-3B	151	536	89	155	27	3	19	79	.289	240	92	12	.965
1941	New York	Nat.	OF	148	525	89	150	29	0	27	90	.286	256	19	9	.968
1942	New York	Nat.	OF	152	549	118	162	21	0	30	93	.295	269	15	3	.990
1943	New York	Nat.	OF-3B	125	380	65	89	12	2	18	47	.234	219	12	6	.975
1944	New York	Nat.	OF	120	399	91	115	16	4	26	82	.288	200	19	7	.969
1945	New York	Nat.	OF	135	451	73	139	23	0	21	79	.308	217	11	4	.982
1946	New York	Nat.	OF	31	68	2	5	1	0	1	4	.074	23	2	0	1.000
1947	New York	Nat.	PH	4	4	0	0	0	0	0	0	.000	0	0	0	.000
Major League Totals				2730	9456	1859	2876	488	72	511	1860	.304	4716	767	144	.974

WORLD SERIES RECORD

YEAR	CLUB	LEAGUE	POS	G.	AB.	R.	H.	2B.	3B.	HR.	RBI.	B.A.	PO.	A.	E.	F.A.
1933	New York	Nat.	OF	5	18	3	7	0	0	2	4	.389	10	0	0	1.000
1936	New York	Nat.	OF	6	23	4	7	2	0	1	3	.304	12	0	1	.923
1937	New York	Nat.	3B	5	20	1	4	0	0	1	3	.200	5	9	1	.933
World Series Totals				16	61	8	18	2	0	4	10	.295	27	9	2	.947

LEGGY LEGEND: Leroy (Satchel) Paige was a fantasy as a pitching great even before in athletic old age he pitched in the majors.

SATCHEL PAIGE

As the Yankees did what came naturally for them in their record run of five straight world championships through 1953—that is, rally to win when they didn't do it going away—little Phil Rizzuto scampered from first to third with the potential tying run and, chest stuck out triumphantly, the Scooter pranced up and down the baseline toward home plate as the lowly St. Louis Browns made a pitching change.

Out of the distant bullpen at Yankee Stadium ambled in Stephin Fetchit gait the game's most cer-

tainly colorful colored legend and character. He shuffled with brown bullet head, face expressionless behind a large lower lip. Tall, skinny, stork-legged and big-footed, it was the one and only Leroy (Satchel) Paige, the Methusaleh of the mound.

Ol' Satch, already closer then to 50 than his corner-cutting pitches to the black border of the plate, was a first-class exception on a second-class ball club, a prince of pitchers playing with the paupers of talent scraped, borrowed and—maybe—even stolen by his good friend, Bill Veeck. Veeck had brought

Paige at long last into the bigs at Cleveland in the pennant-winning season of 1948.

Except when baby-faced Ned Garver started a game for the bumbling Browns or old man Paige shuffled out of the bullpen, the Brownies were as inept as some of the semi-eye pros Paige had faced in pursuit of coffee and cakes, then silk shirts and Cadillacs in the period when Jim Crow kept the black men out of organized professional baseball and often—even the shade of major league grandstands as cash customers, too.

By the time Ol' Satch ambled up the foul line at Yankee Stadium, Korean War vintage, the gangling geezer most thought was old enough to have been the drummer boy at Shiloh, was a $25,000-a-season full-fledged big leaguer full of funny philosophy and pragmatic psychology as well as cunning, control and just enough of the old mustard on his famed fastball. Er, "trouble ball," as he called it.

Passing the keyed up, chesty Rizzuto pawing the dirt in his eagerness to score, Paige threw a casual comment at the sawed off litttle star shortstop of the big bad Bronx Bombers:

"Calm down, Sonny, you ain't goin' nowhere."

No how. No runs, no hits and only one error, the grievous one that prevailed in baseball in bigotry since Cap Anson, the first pioneer superstar, huffed off the field with his Chicago White Stockings at Newark, N.J., in April 1887. To Anson's discredit, he refused to face George Stovey, a light-skinned Canadian Negro who had won 35 games in the Eastern League.

By the most ironic—no, make that the most caustic—of coincidences, the first black professional player had been born in Cooperstown, N.Y., which would become baseball's Mecca as home of the national Hall of Fame. He was John W. (Bud) Fowler, who played for pay in 1872 with a white team at New Castle, Pa.

In 1884, brothers Welday and Moses Fleetwood Walker reached the big leagues briefly with Toledo when the Ohio metropolis and the American Asso-

ciation were in the majors. Fleetwood Walker, then 27 years old and a native of Mt. Pleasant, O., attended both Oberlin College and the University of Michigan.

When organized ball slammed the door shut in 1890, the door Anson had begun to close earlier, Walker and others would watch in frustration the extreme right-wing reaction to the Reconstruction era. Athlete, intellectual, businessman and journalist, Fleetwood died in 1924 without having seen fulfillment of his personal dream, i.e., mass migration of the American Negro to Liberia.

So for some 60 years, a couple of generations, the official recognition and records, the acclaim and affluence were denied to only God knows how many men would have been major leaguers of achievement before Branch Rickey in 1947 brought in at Brooklyn a college-trained former Army lieutenant and all-around athlete—Jackie Robinson.

Through superior knowledge or sheer envy, though reconizing that Jackie deserves a bow for standing up to the spotlight and pressure, many black baseball ancients don't regard Robinson as the best their race had to offer it, had someone had the guts to say "Open sesame" to the men of a different color.

Undoubtedly, the honor roll would include the likes of Josh Gibson, Cool Papa Bell, Buck Leonard, Oscar Charleston, Judy Johnson, Monte Irvin, John Henry (Pop) Lloyd and Martin Dihigo, all of whom joined Robinson, Paige and Roy Campanella in the Hall of Fame before Ernie Banks led the parade of more modern black standouts. Yes, and such others as Smoky Joe Williams, described by some as faster and better than Paige, and by later inductees Andrew (Rube) Foster, pitcher-manager-league founder, Ray Dandridge and—.

Room doesn't permit here a detailed rundown of these and other candidates, but recommended reading, if you would prefer the plight of the player of wrong pigmentation through that period of blacklisting blacks, would include John Holway's assortment, among them *Voices from the Great Black Base-ball Leagues* (Dodd, Mead and Co.) and Robert Peterson's *Only the Ball Was White*, published by Prentice-Hall, Inc.

To pick up the saga of the symbol of the black-balled black who rode to the rescue was a white knight in shining armor—Satchel Paige—Peterson has summed up the bus-league blacks who scrounged barnstorming for a buck, baloney and flea-bug housing.

"They were," he wrote, "saints and sinners, college professors and illiterates, serious men and clowns, teetotalers and Saturday night drunks. Negro baseball was at once heroic and tawdry, a gladsome thing and a blot on America's conscience."

Overall, handicapped by exaggeration that is as natural as most tales retold too often and by the lack of substantative statistics, black league teams won a good two out of every three post-season exhibition games Holway learned in tireless research. But the competition of black league baseball was, as Peterson determined from interviews when he toured the country to interview Negro League veterans, probably no better than Class Double-A or Triple-A, at best.

But when a Paige at age 59 could start for the Kansas City Athletics in 1965 and pitch three scoreless innings against the Boston Red Sox, allowing only one hit by the obviously classy Carl Yastrzemski, it's obvious that the great gaffer of dark hue might have been younger what garrulous, self-confident Dizzy Dean proclaimed him after a 13-inning, 1-0 post-Series loss to Paige:

"You're the greatest, podnuh, the greatest and the fastest. It's a damned shame you ain't white."

"Mr. Diz," as Ol' Satch would call him thereafter with mutual respect and regard, wasn't just a-woofin' because back there in the mid-30s, whether pitching for the champion Pittsburgh Crawfords of the Negro National League or doing a solo in '35 to lead Bismarck, N.D. to the first National Semi-pro Baseball Congress at Wichita, Kans., the pencil-thin Paige was in his pinpoint prime.

If, as suggested, Ol' Satch as young was so impressive that he would wind up pitching an estimated 2,500 games and win 200 of them—shucks, some estimates have it higher because Paige did pitch so often—it's hard to disbelieve anything about the gadfly who finally stood still long enough to tell it all, even with tongue in cheek, to Dave Lipman.

Lipman, working for the *Star* in Kansas City (Satch's home) before the collaborator became managing editor of the *St. Louis Post-Dispatch*, teamed in 1962 with the legend for Doubleday's aptly entitled Paige autobiography, *Maybe I'll Pitch Forever*. Heck, seven years later, nailing down enough time to qualify for the baseball pension plan, thanks to the thoughtfulness of Bill Bartholomay and the Atlanta Braves, Paige "coached" for a season-plus and even pitched a scoreless exhibition inning on Easter Sunday.

Thanks to Lipman's reportorial nose for news, it can be said that, no matter the fun and games Ol' Satch and others have had over age-guessing, the erect geezer with the heavy hornrimmed glasses that gave him a professorial mien was 63 years old. Lipman learned through research that Leroy Paige, then spelled "Page," was born in Mobile, Ala. in 1903.

Parenthetically, let it be known that, though he preferred his first name spelled with a capital "R" in the middle and pronounced "Lee-roy" and that he thought of his nickname with double "l" at the end, he signed his name when running for the Missouri state legislature from Kansas City in the late '60s just the way the country has come to know him—Leroy (Satchel) Paige.

So be it. Satchel, once called "Satchelfoot" even though he stoutly denies that it's the size and shape of his long narrow foot, stuck high in the face of a hitter from the end of a windmill windup, that led to his nickname. Satch said he got the distinctive label penned on him by boyhood pals when he was a small-fry baggage-smasher at the Mobile railroad station, tying together luggage on a pole-and-rope gadget so that he could carry more bags and also not have one or any bark his toothpick shins.

Yeah, they called him "Satchmo" at times, too, with what would be good reason if you knew that the blithe spirit, gamboling down the highway of life, liked to sit in at times with friend Louie (Satchmo) Armstrong and pick a tune on a Spanish guitar.

The elusive legend who collected victories and expensive pieces of china, flashy clothes and block-long cars could get lost almost as much as he'd good-time Charley with his cash. If he didn't go hunting or fishing—and "hunting" when he was a young buck meant moonshine and roses, dancing all night— he'd bed down somewhere and sleep all day.

Even though closer to 75 than to three-score-and-10, he made personal-service appearances as a Hall of Famer for A. Rae Smith the wealthy Tulsa oil man and baseball buff, Ol' Satch treated the clock with the disdain he had before becoming the twice-married father of seven. For Paige, time stood still until his death in 1982 at 76. He was something special ever since he quit bouncing rocks off annoying skulls with accuracy that helped put him in a reform school to develop an ability to pitch endlessly and tirelessly with a remarkably resilient right arm.

Doctors who raved about his youthful demeanor were positively ecstatic about that long, supple pitching weapon that knew just mysterious—and apparently career-crippling—spell of soreness in a career that began professionally at Chattanooga in 1926. Trouble is, everybody who ever saw a slender hard-throwing black pitcher thinks the guy was Paige. Heck, he not only didn't get into the second battle at Bull Run. He missed the first, too.

As full of blarney as the wittiest, most unctuous politician this side of "The Last Hurrah," Paige would insist that when he lived among Sioux Indians out there in North Dakota, when he took

French leave from the Negro National League for better pay and to pitch Bismarck to that first national semi-pro title, he was given "secret snake oil" for his pitching arm.

Trainer Bob Bauman, smiling, would explain:

"That 'secret snake oil' was really only chloroform liniment with cologne, but I'll say this: Satch has positively the smoothest, most pliable arm I've ever massaged in more than 50 years. It's velvet."

That velvet arm—by the pitcher's own admission—probably would have taken him nowhere from the poverty of the cardboard castle of the stacked house on Mobile's South Franklin street—stacked because four ramshackle rooms ran back in a row.

He would wind up with fame and a squandered fortune, a poor boyhood and an extravagent manhood, because of deadly accuracy throwing at bottles, birds and batters. Barnstorming and boasting, he followed the sun daily from coast to coast summers and in the Caribbean winters, following a trail of amusement and amazement. It all developed because Lee-roy could throw rocks with God-given marksmanship and because he was a tattered, skinny little nigger kid who couldn't resist sticking a desiring little nose against a toystore window and then helping himself to a few toy rings. He got caught.

The Paige boy, seventh of 11 children born to a gardener and a church-going mother from whom he developed his longevity, had plunked one too many white heads with rocks in self-defense. He'd played hooky once too often from school and frustrated an infuriated truant officer. So despite Lula Paige's tears, they committed the lightfingered, dark-skinned lad in July 1918 to an industrial school for Negro children at Mount Meigs, Ala.

In his autobiography—*Maybe I'll Pitch Forever*—Ol' Satch looked upon that trauma at 12 as the turning point in his life because on the Mount they taught him many things, including refinement of baseball-throwing he had begun a couple of years earlier. By the time he was about 15, he'd reached his height of manhood, 6-foot 3½-inches, fully 40 pounds fewer than the barely 180 he carried throughout most of his career. The long-legged kid, who pursed that shovel lip when he pitched, learned to kick that big foot so that, as he put it, it looked like he "blackened out the sky" and he learned, too, how to swing around that velvet right arm so that the smoke he threw was difficult to pick up.

Above all, from a coach whose name he disremembers, Leroy Paige learned in reform school to watch a batter like a bullfighter watches a bull.

"I never look at a batter anywhere except at the knees, just like a bullfighter," Paige told collaborator Lipman. "The bullfighter can tell what a bull is going to do by watching his knees. I learned the same. When a batter swings and I see his knees move, I can tell just what his weaknesses are. Then I put the ball where he know he can't hit it…"

Oh, along the way, he did learn to throw a dinky curve and, working straight over the top, he learned to come three-quarter, sidearmed and even drop down to submarine delivery, breaking speeds with a classic change-up. Also, his celebrated "hesitation" pitch, one in which he'd stride with that narrow sized 12 foot before arching the ball—alley oop!—for a strike.

Natch—from Satch—just like the direction of his human radar, the well-placed velocity of his Long Tom, the "trouble pitch" as he called his easy-does-it delivery from the time he moseyed over to Mobile's Eureka Gardens in 1924, where he expected to see older brother Wilson working out with the semi-pro Tigers, a black team. Wilson wasn't there, but the manager was working out a kid pitcher by cuffing his stuff from yon to yonder.

The thin wafer recently released from reform school asked for a chance—no, not begged, not Satchel, never—and when the manager swung and missed 10 straight times, the boss man asked:

"Do you throw that fast consistently?"

The truant who would develop his own colorful vocabulary shook his head. "No, sir," he said, "I do it all the time."

When the manager gave him a crinkly piece of green paper with George Washington's photo, that dollar bill turned the boy Paige into a man, an amateur into a professional, fun into business. Why, shoot, this was better 'n goin' to the mound from first base at aged 10 for the first time in relief and striking out 16 and pitching no-hit ball. Over the years, unofficially, he pitched something like 250 shutouts and 45 no-hitters, not counting those exhibitions in which—to work more often and bring in the buckerinoes more rapidly—he'd work just the first three innings, guaranteeing to strike out all nine men.

Before he became a one-man traveling baseball circus, Satchel Paige had to prove himself, which is what the 18-year-old kid did, when picking up soda bottles and helping clean up the Mobile Bears' park, he was persuaded for a bet to throw against the white Southern Association ball club. Swish… swoosh…swash. The Bears fanned, Satch picked up the buck bet and then, he said later, heard for the first time from one of the Mobile players the line that woud gnaw at his innards even more than that fried liver on which he lived for too long in the Islands because he couldn't communicate in Spanish:

"If you were only white…"

It's silver dollars to sugar doughnuts that he'd have been in a World Series long before 1948 when he mopped up briefly for Cleveland and in an All-Star Game before Casey Stengel—one old man admiring another—picked him in 1952 and in the Hall of Fame before 1971 when a special committee on blacks was established, primarily to bring to Cooperstown for enshrinement the embodiment of the spurned stars of the darker hue. Natch, Satch.

The l-o-n-g road to the scenic little upstate New York village that sired Abner Doubleday and Bud Fowler began for Leroy Paige in 1926 with the Chattanooga Black Lookouts of the Negro Southern League, where he got all of $50 a month, some of which dutifully was sent home to Mom in Mobile. He pitched a two-hitter to beat New Orleans' professional blacks, 1-0.

At Chattanooga, he was so good that he'd call in his outfield and—at times—find the merry men of the meadow lying on the green or talking to spectators, backs to the plate. With the Birmingham Black Barons, who brought his contract in 1928 and gave him a whopping $275 a month, the struck-it-rich kid tooled around in a racy roadster and displayed—in reverse—his incredible control.

At St. Louis, where years later he would astonish batterymate Clint Courtney by warming up for the Browns with only a gum wrapper as "home plate," Paige faced the Negro National League champion Stars, a ball club that, though perhaps not the equal later of the Homestead Grays or Pittsburgh Crawfords or even the Kansas City Monarchs when Satch was the king of KayCee, had outstanding talent. Included was a future Hall of Famer, center fielder James (Cool Papa) Bell, and a couple of others who undoubtedly deserved similar recognition, slugging Mules Suttles and hard-hitting, sharp-fielding shortstop Willie (Devil) Wells.

Over the years, typical of athletes white or black or, as civil rights' champion Bill Veeck would say, "purple with pink polka dots," there were salary jealousies. Like Babe Ruth, better paid by far than his colleagues in the coffee-and-cake circuit of the colored leagues, which barnstormed weekdays and nights so they could afford to play league games weekends in big league parks or their own, Paige prospered by comparison with his comrades. In later years, in fact, when he had become more a national curiosity than a one-club contributor, he got up to $35,000 or more a year. By contrast, next highest paid, power-hitting Josh Gibson, earned up to maybe $10,000 a year and the rest, no matter how talented, tagged along.

One, the slender, swift, switch-hitting center fielder for St. Louis and other clubs, Cool Papa Bell, would comment wryly on how difficult it was to get

more than a few hundred bucks so the slick-fielding, leg-hitting, batting-title and basestealing contender also followed the bouncing ball south of the border many winters. Bell never begrudged Paige a payday.

In return, though Ol' Satch considered Gibson the greatest hitter he ever faced and the Detroit Tigers' silk-smooth second baseman, Charley Gehringer, as the most troublesome white batsman, Bell rated No. 1 all-around with Paige.

"Fast," Ol' Satch would drawl. "That Cool was so fast that when he'd turn out a hotel room doorway switch at night, he'd be in bed before the light went out."

With his audience laughing and only a flicker of a smile creasing the corner of his lips, Paige would tell another one that the Chicago Cubs' great Gabby Hartnett loved to repeat. Said Satch by way of Gabby:

"One time I was facin' Cool and jammed him with a pitch that sent a ball back through the box so slow that I misjudged it. Know what? That ball went right through my legs, and Cool was so fast that as he slid into second base for a double, the ball hit him and he was out for interference."

Apochryphal, white lies or just damned fibs, they made good listening and, as one occasionally got into print, good reading, too. As the years passed, Ol' Satch loved to sit and hold court with younger players, as for example the time he told baby-faced Garver about his most trying moment. Now, Garver was young then—later mayor of Ney, O.—but winner of 20 only 52 the bumbling Brownies won, a .305 hitter and...

So, intently, Ned from Ney listened as Paige painted the picture: Bases loaded, Monarchs leading by a run, none out when with a 3-and-2 count on the hitter, the Kansas City manager beckoned for Ol' Satch. The ancient one, hurrying an impromptu warmup, pocketed the practice ball, strolled to the mound and, here, he'd pause for effect.

Well?

"Well," he'd say deadpanned, "I'd slipped the

warmup ball into my glove so that, winding up, I fired the practice ball to third and the game ball to first, picking off two men, and my motion was so good that the batter swung and, of course, missed. Side out. Game over!"

Which is the way everything seemed to be for Ol' Satch back in 1934, his prime when he'd won four of six post-season masterpiece games from Series hero Dizzy Dean. Down in Mexico that winter, the stomach miseries that first had hit him in Venezuela worsened and sweat popped out all over him more than he did when he'd loosen up over the years for pitching by taking a scalding-hot shower before a game and another afterward. Suddenly, the hurtin' hurler couldn't even lift his arm and a Mexico City specialist told him gravely:

"Satchel, I'm afraid you'll never pitch again."

No longer would the incomparable Paige, it seemed, do what he'd done to the St. Louis Stars back there in 1928 when, exhibiting unbelievable control as they greedily crowded home plate, young Satch had hit the first three men painfully on the thumb. The third one took after the retreating pitcher in rage, slung the bat at Paige near second base and missed. So Satch picked up the wood and chased the guy right out of the center-field exit gate at Stars' Park.

No longer, if that arm didn't come around, would Paige field a bunt or bounder back to the box and, staring straight at his catcher, retire the batter with an across-the-body, under-the-left-arm peg or flip to the first baseman.

And if he didn't make it back, how would mutual admirers Marty Marion, Bob Bauman and the rest of the long-gone St. Louis Browns remember vividly the venerable one's all-around exhibition to win three bets from Scrap-Iron Clint Courtney, his deep-dyed-in-Dixie battermate who learned the hard way to appreciate Ol' Satch's competitive smarts?

First—for money, of course, not marbles or chalk—Paige put on catcher's gear and gunned down Courtney at second base in a simulated attempted steal. Next, standing at shortstop as a coach fungoed a groundball, the old man ranged far to his right, backhanded the ball and fired across the diamond to retire Scraps at first base. Finally, with Courtney tagged up at third, Paige stood out in left field at Sportsman's Park, went back for a long fungoed fly and then unfurled a strong, accurate throw that cut down Courtney at the plate.

Yes, too much of the lore of the legend would have been missed if the arm had stayed dead. But J.L. Wilkinson and Sam Baird, co-owners of the Kansas City Monarchs, gambled that the box office magic would work even if the thin man played first base on their second unit. And, lo, a couple of years later the pain disappeared, the fastball reappeared and, young and frisky and happy again, the cock of the walk of KayCee's 18th and Vine Streets met and married a snippy drugstore clerk named Lahoma Brown. Leroy's every-loving Lahoma gave him contentment and a large family.

Finally, thanks to Veeck and to his friend, the Harlem Globetrotters' Abe Saperstein, 42-year-old Satchel Paige got his chance in 1948 with Cleveland, contending for its first pennant since Tris Speaker's world champions of 1920.

Lou Boudreau, the inspirational playing-manager shortstop of the Indians, was skeptical at a tryout at Cleveland Stadium on Paige's 42nd birthday—July 7, 1948. He wondered if the geezer could throw like he used to?

"Not half as fast as it used to be, but as fast as anybody pitchin' now," sniffed the dusky dean of the toeplate, "and I can still pitch it where I want to."

After catching Paige in a private warm-up and then hitting against him—or trying to—batting-champion Boudreau agreed that the old man would do. Indeed. He won six out of seven decisions, including three shutouts, one of which was a three-hit masterpiece in his starting debut at home before a Cleveland crowd of more than 78,000.

After he'd slumped somewhat in 1949, distressed

by stomach ailment that required extensive dentistry and store teeth, Cleveland cut him adrift and he went back to barnstorming, doing better than ever even though black baseball was fast becoming as extinct as the dodo. Then, old friend Veeck resurfaced in St. Louis and sent out an S.O.S. for Satch.

With the Brownies, a bad ball club, Paige was good and funny, as for instance when bigoted, hardnosed manager Rogers Hornsby wanted him to run regularly with the young pitchers, and the short-end, game-saving specialist said with a sigh:

"Mr. Hornsby, are you trainin' Ol' Satch to pitch relief or for the U.S. Army?"

Paige didn't care much for Rog, who couldn't see the wisdom—and justice—in Veeck's observation that he was interested only in a player's opinion, not whether he was white or chocolate or strawberry. Ol' Satch hadn't grown his mustache or put on those thick-shelled cheaters as yet and hadn't shown his own lower-ranged racial intolerance.

Later, he would seem more moody—even sullen with the press that had helped his image—in part with repeating his credo:

"Avoid fried meats which angry up the blood…

"If your stomach disputes you, lie down and pacify it with cool thoughts…

"Keep the juices flowing by jangling around gently as you move…

"Go very lightly on the vices, such as carrying on in society—the social ramble ain't restful…

"Avoid running at all times…

"And don't look back. Something might be gaining on you."

That last one has become part and parcel of Paige's legend and more: It's in the national idiom now and forever, part of the country's philosophy. Uncle Sam—to Ol' Satch, the government is plain "Sam"—might have included even a petulant Leroy (Satchel) Paige as a national treasure.

Take the time when pitching for the Browns in relief at Washington, the tall man hired for short-order work found himself hooked up for 10 in-

nings and a brilliant game that went into the 17th before the Brownies poked a nose in front. Grumbling agitatedly in the box next to the visitors' dugout at old Griffith Stadium, traveling secretary Bill Durney Slattery warned that the railroad just couldn't hold any longer the train back to St. Louis and—.

"Will nine pitches do it, boss?" Ol' Satch said, quickening his pace to the mound.

Ten pitches later, the game over, the Browns showered hurriedly and rushed in triumph to the depot, just in time to catch the train. Manager Marty Marion, the man Paige had said "played shortstop the way Duke Ellington plays the piano," wondered why the ancient hero of the hour wasn't smiling.

"Because," said living legend Satchel Paige who might have been the best ever to throw a baseball 60 feet six inches at the black borders of a 17-inch target, "because I promised the man (Slattery) only nine pitches— and that empire had to go and miss one."

LEROY ROBERT (SATCHEL) PAIGE
Born July 7, 1905, at Mobile, Ala.
Died June 8, 1982, at Kansas City, Mo.
Height 6-4 Weight 190
Threw and batted righthanded.
Named to Hall of Fame, 1971.

YEAR	CLUB	LEAGUE	G.	IP.	W.	L.	Pct.	H.	R.	ER.	SO.	BB.	ERA.
1948	Cleveland	American	21	73	6	1	.857	61	21	20	45	25	2.47
1949	Cleveland	American	31	83	4	7	.364	70	29	28	54	33	3.04
1950							(Out of Organized Ball)						
1951	St. Louis	American	23	62	3	4	.429	67	39	33	48	29	4.79
1952	St. Louis	American	46	138	12	10	.545	116	51	47	91	57	3.07
1953	St. Louis	American	57	117	3	9	.250	114	51	46	51	39	3.54
1954-55							(Out of Organized Ball)						
1956	Miami	International	37	111	11	4	.733	101	29	23	79	28	1.86
1957	Miami	International	40	119	10	8	.556	98	35	32	76	11	2.42
1958	Miami	International	28	110	10	10	.500	94	44	36	40	15	2.95
1959-60							(Out of Organized Ball)						
1961	Portland	Pacific Coast	5	25	0	0	.000	28	12	8	19	5	2.88
1962-63-64							(Out of Organized Ball)						
1965	Kansas City	American	1	3	0	0	.000	1	0	0	1	0	0.00
1966	Peninsula	Carolina	1	2	0	0	.000	5	2	2	0	0	9.00
Major League Totals—6 years			179	476	28	31	.475	429	191	174	290	183	3.29

WORLD SERIES RECORD

YEAR	CLUB	LEAGUE	G.	IP.	W.	L.	Pct.	H.	R.	ER.	SO.	BB.	ERA.
1948	Cleveland	American	1	2/3	0	0	.000	0	0	0	0	0	0.00

AN OLD SMOOTHIE: Herbert Jeffries Pennock, the squire of Pennsylvania's Kennett Square, was a cunning corner-cutting southpaw for most of his 22 years in the majors.

HERB PENNOCK

Of all the high-type players who lent class to professional baseball in its first century, foremost was Herbert Jeffries Pennock, Hall of Fame pitcher for the New York Yankees and the man who laid the groundwork for a flanneled phenomenon, a National League pennant for Philadelphia.

Pennock looked more like a headmaster of the kind of fashionable suburban prep school he attended than a baseball player. He seemed tall at six feet because he was slender, almost frail in appearance. He had a long, thin face and a fascinating nose that looked as if it belonged on an ancient Greek statue or on a Roman senator in the reign of the Caesars.

Pennock portrayed a country gentleman, which he was even when he was one of the best pitchers over much of his 22-year big league career and certainly the craftiest. Even though he lacked control as a kid, he soon shattered the myth that lefthanders are wild.

By his conduct on and off the field, well-contained and reserved, he looked as if he might be commuting to Wall Street rather than Yankee Stadium. Most of his salad seasons with the Yankees, he managed to make the trip regularly to his birthplace and home, a farm near Kennett Square, in the extreme southeast corner of Pennsylvania, about 40 miles from Philly.

Pennock, a farmer at heart, raised flowers and gardened. He raised silver foxes, rode to the hounds and lived in a style and manner that made him fit comfortably the nickname he wore so well—the Squire of Kennett Square.

Just short of 54 and, in fact, 25 years to the day he was traded to New York in a deal that clinched the Yankee dynasty, Pennock died of a cerebral hemorrhage, January 30, 1948, as he prepared to step into a National League meeting at New York's Commodore Hotel. As general manager for five years of the Phillies, the moribund franchise of the majors, he wisely had spent sportsman Bob Carpenter's money.

Carpenter, prophetically, lamented, "I'm sorry Herb didn't live to see the fruits of his labors. They are inevitable."

The Phillies' Whiz Kids won a pennant in 1950, the club's first in 35 years and its last in a World Series until 1983. More than one baseball man has expressed the opinion that if Pennock had lived longer, Philadelphia's pennant enjoyment would not have been so short-lived.

Pennock's own preference for the life of the country gentleman, though it didn't prolong his own, rubbed off on his family. Daughter Jane married Eddie Collin, Jr., son of Herb's former teammate and close friend, the great second baseman of the Philadelphia Athletics and the man who steered Herb into a front office career after his playing career. Eddie, Jr., worked for his father-in-law at Philadelphia, rather than with his own father at Boston, but junior Collins, a former ballplayer, quit the pressure pace of professional baseball—he had become farm director of the Phillies—to follow the path of the suburban pedant, teaching and raising

his family in the area that enchanted Herb Pennock.

Considering Pennock's physique—he never weighed more than 165 pounds—and his fondness for his home and hearth, it's hard to believe that he pitched in the big leagues until he was 40 years old. Why, when he was just 31, disenchanted by the slump of the Yankees to seventh place and a series of close, low-score defeats, he talked seriously of quitting.

He owned $45,000 worth of silver foxes, he said back there in 1925, and he had 33 acres in Kennett Square devoted to them. Furthermore, he told New York writer Tom Meany, he had additional interest in a fox ranch in the Miramirchi region of New Brunswick.

"With pelts worth from $700 upward, I think it would be worth incorporating a $250,000 fox-breeding business and I know where I can get the backing," Pennock declared. "I'm a certified member of the American Fox Institute and I have won blue ribbons exhibiting some of my animals."

The reporter didn't want to spoil a good story but how, he wondered, could a pitcher who had won 40 games and lost only 15 the two previous seasons consider quitting?

"I'm over 30 and the way things are going, I'll feel even older by the end of the season," said Pennock. "Our club isn't what it was and I must be slipping, too. So, maybe, I should try to get into a line where I might do better."

Pennock was only a 16-17 pitcher in '25, the season of Babe Ruth's big belly ache, but his steadiness and 2.96 earned-run average, extremely good for a brisk-batting era, weren't lost on the Yankees' beetle-browed front office boss, Ed Barrow. The general manager raised his salary for 1926 and Pennock, happily, changed his mind.

By then, Herb was getting more than $20,000 a year—how much more I can't say—but it had been a hard pull. From 1912, when he turned professional, quite unexpectedly, until 1919, when he was a World War I veteran who posted a 16-8 record for the Boston Red Sox, his top salary was $3,000, and it took a $500 end-of-the-season bonus from theatrical man Harry Frazee, the Red Sox owner, for Herb to get to three grand.

Back to 1926, which is really a roundabout way of getting to the beginning, the reluctant ruralist from Pennsylvania put together his most robust season, posting a 23-11 record. In addition, he beat the Cardinals twice in St. Louis' first World Series, which was won by the Redbirds on the heroics of ancient Grover Cleveland Alexander.

When the Series shifted to old Sportsman's Park for the third game, the courtly Pennock politely went out of his way to take his teammates to a field box occupied by a little St. Louis optometrist, Albert Aloe.

"Gentlemen," he said to Babe Ruth and his buddies, "I'd like you to meet the greatest prep school catcher of all time."

Aloe, until his death in 1965, would glow whenever he retold that one, explaining that Pennock and he had indeed been good friends and that he'd attended daughter Jane's wedding.

"But I couldn't be the greatest prep school catcher," said Aloe, "because I think I dropped 10 third strikes the first game Herb ever pitched."

Aloe went East to Cedar Croft, a fashionable prep school in suburban Philadelphia. There, he met the Pennocks, George and Herb, members of a Scotch-Irish family of Pennsylvania Quakers. Their grandparents addressed each other as "thee" and "thou." Herb was born at Kennett Square on February 10, 1894.

Grandfather Pennock invented road-building machinery. Herb's father sold it and then retired to the family farm outside Kennett Square, where he lived as if to the manor born.

Earmarked for the University of Pennsylvania, Herb attended the Friend's School of West Town, Pa., but then, because he liked baseball, switched to Cedar Croft. Herb played first base and older brother George pitched until one day George quit the squad, leaving the lads without a pitcher. That's

where short Albert Aloe entered tall Herb Pennock's life in one of the strangest Mutt-and-Jeff combinations this side of the old-fashioned comic strip.

Playing catch with tall Herb, short Al made a startling discovery and walked over to the team's coach. "Don't worry about our pitcher, coach," said Aloe. "We've got one. Everything Herb throws breaks. He can't throw a straight ball."

The Cedar Croft coach watched and agreed. Pennock, 16 years old, pitched his first game and struck out 19. "And," said Aloe, "I set a record for the most passed balls, but he won for us—again and again—and Connie Mack began to notice."

Mack arranged for him to pitch what euphemistically was—and still is—known as "summer ball," a semi-pro brand in which not enough money changes hands to bring a charge of professionalism, yet enough is available to enable a guy to get by. Herb, pitching at Atlantic City, opened more eyes, including those of batterymate Earle Mack, Connie's son, when he pitched a no-hit game against the St. Louis Stars, a team of topflight black professionals.

The first big league ballplayer Herb ever faced, Cincinnati's Bob Bescher, belted a 3-and-2 pitch off him for a home run in a summer exhibition game at Atlantic City when blue laws prevented major league Sunday play in Philadelphia.

Pennock, transferring that fall to Wenonah Military Academy, to brush up on his preparatory work for Penn, was invited to work out with the Athletics in May 1912. This was, you must understand, a championship-dynasty club Mr. Mack had, much less a teenager's favorite team. Herb leaped at the chance, figuring it would be fun until he went to college and—.

He never got to college and, in fact, barely left the big leagues for more than two decades. The second day at Shibe Park, he was sitting in the corner of the dugout, watching Jack Coombs get whomped by the Chicago White Sox, when he heard Connie call:

"Boy, warm up."

Pennock looked around, but he was the only boy and there was no place to hide. In a semi-daze the 18-year-old prep school kid went down to the bullpen. Minutes later, the skinny southpaw was on the major league mound and the megaphone-toting field announcer informed the pressbox and small crowd:

"Bennock now pitching for Philadelphia."

The sports pages reported the next day that a kid named "Bennock" had done very well. Indeed he had, yielding only one hit, two walks and one run in a four-inning stretch.

Seldom seen his first two seasons with the smooth A's of the championship period, Pennock worked 50 innings the rest of the '12 season and only 33 in '13, but he was watching and studying. From Chief Bender, the cunning Cherokee, he picked up the screwball, a pitch he did not use extensively, but one which helped over the years.

After he was 11-4 in 1914 as a 20-year-old without minor league experience—he had a good 2.78 ERA and even worked three scoreless innings in the World Series—it's unthinkable that Mack let him get away in a breakup of championship veterans who had been swept in four straight by the Boston Braves in the famed 1914 Series upset.

One version is that the mild, studious Pennock angered the manager by flouting instructions in a pitching situation in 1915. Angrily, Connie is supposed to have asked waivers on the kid. That one probably makes more sense than the alternate suggestion that, in Mr. Mack's judgment, Herb just didn't have it.

Come to think of it, that wouldn't have been too hard to decide, either, because Pennock never was an overpowering pitcher. He rarely threw his fastball, which, ultimately, through the element of surprise, would come in faster than it seemed. Essentially, he was—or, rather, became—a master of the breaking ball, a consummate curveball specialist with the most remarkable control.

In 55⅓ World Series innings—10 games over a period from 1914 through 1932—Pennock walked just eight men. That pinpoint control and a 1.95 earned-run average are two reasons he finished with a spotless Series record, 5-0.

Pennock threw with such style and grace, overhanded or side-armed, that the fluid, easy-does-it delivery heightened his deception. Detroit's Gerald Walker summed it up one time late in Pennock's career.

"You go up there against the old man feeling real good," said Gee Walker. "You know he won't hit you and, hell, even if he did, it wouldn't hurt. You get four pretty good licks and then when the day is over, you're oh-for-four and you wonder how he did it. But you're still horsecollared."

One day at New York, when Pennock was warming up with battermate Benny Bengough, a spectator seated nearby yelled to the catcher:

"How does he get anybody out with that stuff? He looks so easy to hit."

The pink-pated, cherubic Bengough grinned. "That," he yelled back, "is what the hitters think. Why don't you grab a bat and find out?"

The spectator was smarter than Detroit's stocky powerful Bob (Fat) Fothergill, who crowed to a fellow righthanded batter, hitting master Harry Heilmann of Detroit, that there hadn't been a lefthander born who could get him out. Fothergill drooled watching the artistic Pennock warm up. Then, as Gee Walker said, he went a comfortable oh-for-four.

"I can't understand it," Fothergill grumbled to Heilmann afterward. "What the hell happened?"

"You didn't face a lefthander," said Heilmann. "You faced Herb Pennock."

Before the 1927 World Series, a New York writer who had been covering the National League warned the Yankees that the Pirates were death on southpaws.

Pennock, despite his previous Series excellence, didn't take the firing line until the third game of the

Series at New York. He held Pittsburgh hitless until one out in the eighth and then breezed home with a three-hit, 8-1 victory.

The Yankees' Bob Meusel beckoned to the New York writer in the clubhouse. "I thought," growled Meusel, sarcastically, "that you said no lefthanded pitcher could beat Pittsburgh."

The writer recovered neatly. "No National League lefthander," he said, smiling. "Naturally, I excluded Pennock."

The assumption, generally, is that Pennock favored that Series gem as the rarest in his collection, which included 240 regular-season victories as well as five in Series competition. He was beaten 162 times.

Herb's personal choice, however, was a 15-inning game he won against Lefty Grove and the Philadelphia Athletics in 1925, the year the Yankees fared so poorly that Pennock nearly quit.

The game with fellow Hall of Famer Grove was a Fourth of July classic before a crowd of close to 55,000 at Yankee Stadium. It was the first game of the traditional holiday doubleheader and even though the contest went 15 innings, it lasted only two hours and 50 minutes.

One reason is that in the marathon contest the corner-cutting Pennock did not walk a batter. He struck out five, yielded just four hits, two of them to Jimmie Dykes, and faced only 18 batters in the first six innings and 21 the last seven.

The Yankees won in the 15th, 1-0, when Bobby Veach singled, Meusel sacrificed and Steve O'Neill delivered New York's 14th and final hit, a single to center.

Pennock, falling behind only three hitters on the ball-and-strike count, went to 3-and-2 on just one hitter, Al Simmons.

"But then he always did scare me a little," Herb recalled with a smile.

Pennock, calling on his long playing and front office experience, always regarded Joe Jackson and Babe Ruth as the best natural hitters he ever saw and Ty Cobb as the greatest.

Nothing exceptional as a hitter, though he did belt four big league homers in his 22 seasons, Pennock liked to tell about the time at Fenway Park, pitching for the Red Sox just after Ruth had gone over to the Yankees, he stopped the Babe and then beat the Yanks with an inside-the-park homer himself.

Actually, as a close student of both hitting and pitching—after all, hitters were his business— Pennock was consulted often by Yankee hitters when they were in a slump, including the one and only Ruth.

Even though he and the Babe traveled different routes, to and from the big leagues, including to and from the ballparks daily, the gentlemanly blue-ribbon man of the mound was a favorite with Ruth. The Babe was dying of cancer himself in '48 when Pennock suddenly expired.

"He was a honey," the Babe croaked hoarsely.

Honey—bees, anyway—played a part in a bizarre episode in the otherwise orthodox career of pitcher Pennock. When the Squire of Kennett Square was struggling with a lame arm in 1928, a season the Yankees were riddled with injuries and still won, he became desperate enough to listen when a friend suggested a drastic remedy. The arm could be restored, Herb was told, if he would submit to a stinging of bees.

What happened?

"They brought out the bees—one at a time— placed them on my left arm and let them sting me," Pennock related years later in the presence of the friend, Ed Holly. "Then they brushed off the bees and removed the stingers with a pair of pliers."

And?

"Nothing," said Pennock, glancing at Holly, "all I got out of it was an arm that was both lame and sore for a time."

Holly coughed uncomfortably. "It was a mistake to use domestic bees," murmured the friend. "We should have used wild ones."

Pennock, if he couldn't be cured by a quack idea

or practical joke, was able to use a straight face to help a teammate one time. Despite his reputation for remedying batting slumps, Herb couldn't detect a thing wrong when center fielder Earle Coombs asked the pitcher to study him at the plate.

Perplexed, yet certain that, psychologically, any answer would be better than none at all, Pennock told Coombs, "You're just overstriding a bit, Earle." The Kentucky Colonel bounced out of his slump with two hits that day.

Pennock, years later when he had become a successful executive, described overstriding as the curse of good hitting.

"There's nothing," he said, "that can more quickly break up the hair-trigger coordination of eye and muscle, so necessary to effective hitting, than to drop the body below the level of the pitch, which happens in the swing of the hitter who overstrides."

Excepting Babe Ruth, Pennock ticked off the names of the most consistent hitters—Cobb, Paul Waner, Joe DiMaggio, Stan Musial and Ted Williams—and noted that all of them took a short stride. He made special mention of Joe Sewell, chunky little former Cleveland and New York Yankee shortstop and third baseman.

"Like DiMaggio, Sewell practically put his front foot down in the same spot," Pennock said, "and striking out only a few times a season, he not only was hard to fool, but he was a consistent hitter, too."

Although an agreeable man, Pennock had his positive opinions. He took issue with his old boss, Ed Barrow, when the Yankees long-time general manager tabbed the 1938 Bronx Bombers as superior to the 1927 Murderers' Row.

"You'd have to find a place for DiMaggio in any lineup and, of course, for Bill Dickey, a great catcher, but otherwise I'd take the 1927 team, the greatest ever assembled," Pennock said, flatly.

The '27 team, you know, won 110 games in a 154-game schedule and swept through Pittsburgh in the World Series. Lou Gehrig, Tony Lazzeri, Mark Koenig and Joe Dugan were in the infield, Ruth, Coombs and Meusel in the outfield. The

catching was shared by Bengough, John Grabowski and Pat Collins. The foremost pitchers were Pennock, Waite Hoyt, Urban Shocker and Wilcy Moore.

"We had an excellent outfield, great infield, good pitching and adequate catching," the well-respected analyst summed up the '27 powerhouse.

One of Pennock's most provocative opinions probably was his assessment of shortstops he'd seen from Honus Wagner to Phil Rizzuto, Marty Marion, Pee Wee Reese and Lou Boudreau, all of whom were at their approximate peaks at the time he died.

The best defensively, Pennock said shortly before his death, was Leo Durocher, a Yankee teammate for a couple of seasons when The Lip was a brash kid.

"Leo played on his nerve," said Herb. "He wasn't born great; he made himself great by keying himself to any emergency. In the pinch, he was superb and never made a bad throw. With two out in the ninth, the ball hit to short and the tying run coming home, a pitcher could walk off the field without looking behind him. Leo wouldn't let him down."

The late publisher of *The Sporting News*, J.G. Taylor Spink, persuaded Pennock one time to list Ten Commandments for pitchers. The old master demurred, but Spink persisted and this is the way Pennock laid it down for young pitchers:

"1. Develop your faculty of observation.

"2. Conserve your energy.

"3. Make contact with players, especially catchers and infielders, and listen to what they have to say.

"4. Work everlastingly for control.

"5. When you are on the field always have a baseball in your hand and don't slouch around. Run for a ball.

"6. Keep studying the hitters for their weak and strong points. Keep talking with your catchers.

"7. Watch your physical condition and your mode of living.

"8. Always pitch to the catcher and not to the hitter. Keep your eye on that catcher and make him your target before letting the ball go.

"9. Find your easiest way to pitch, your most confortable delivery—and stick to it.

"10. Work for what is called a rag arm. A loose arm can pitch overhanded, side-arm, three-quarter, underhanded—any old way—to suit the situation at hand."

Pennock added, "I might give you an eleventh commandment and, that is, don't beef at the umpire. Keep pitching with confidence and control of yourself as well as of the ball. Don't get it into your head the umpire is your worst enemy. Fury is as hard on you physically as emotionally.

"I had to be concerned with conservation of energy because I appreciated my handicap, lack of weight and strength. By throwing with a nice, easy motion, changing speeds and hitting the corners, I was able to develop control and, as a result, use fewer pitches."

Connie Mack said over the years that his dismissal of Pennock on waivers in June 1915, represented the worst deal he ever made. Until Early Wynn came along, the man on whom Connie gave up belied his frail physique to share with Cy Young and Sam Jones the record for most seasons pitched in the majors, 22. Wynn made the mark 23.

Pennock was farmed out in both 1915 and '16 before he returned to the majors to stay in 1917. He was married after the 1915 season to Esther Freck, his school sweetheart. The Frecks owned an inn at historic Kennett Square for generations.

Herb and Esther did not raise a family until after his return from World War I. A highlight for Pennock, serving aboard a Navy destroyer, was a command performance on July 4, 1918, when he pitched in England and beat an Army team, 2-1. A 40,000 crown in Chelsea's soccer football stadium included King George V and Queen Mary.

The student prince of pitching, a man of poise, principle and breeding, should have been at home with the purple because Herb was baseball royalty. Son Joe Ted, who captained the Kennett Square

High School team, wanted to follow his father into baseball before World War II intervened, but, wisely the young one didn't try to become another Pennock as a pitcher. He went to the University of Delaware.

Herb's career turned dramatically as he and Mrs. Pennock arrived back from a trip to Japan in January 1923. Dockside, he learned that he had been shipped figuratively to the Yankees by the Red Sox for outfielder Camp Skinner, infielder Norm McMillan, pitcher George Murray and a commodity close to a bankrupt ball club's heart—cash.

To that point, counting development as a kid who came up too soon and the problem of pitching for a bad ball club. Pennock had been in parts or all of 10 previous seasons with a big league record of 76-72.

From then on, given better support at New York, Pennock was all quality, beginning with a 19-6 season in 1923, helping the Yankees to their third straight pennant and, significantly, their first world championship. The Yanks had lost eight straight Series games to their rivals and former Polo Grounds landlords, the New York Giants, until the blue-chip pitcher beat them the first of two times that October.

That year, 1923, was the first for Yankee Stadium and it marked an 11-year honeymoon for the student prince of pitching. As late as 1932, when he was 38 years old, Pennock pitched effectively twice in relief for Joe McCarthy in the World Series. The Yankees ripped the Chicago Cubs four straight.

"At my age, I think maybe I got as much satisfaction out of saving a game this time as I did starting and winning them when I was at my prime," said Pennock.

Released by the Yankees in January 1934, after a 7-4 season, Herb was honored for meritorious service at the New York baseball writers' dinner and then signed with the Red Sox as a relief pitcher. He recorded a record of 2-0 in '34.

Eddie Collins, general manager, then named him as a minor league manager, business manager, coach and scout for the Bosox. He was farm director of the Red Sox when Carpenter, taking over the Phillies, called in December 1943, with a generous offer to become vice president and general manager of the Philadelphia Nationals. This meant homecoming for the Squire of Kennett Square.

The lifelong American leaguer spent $1,250,000 of Carpenter's fortune to build up the futile National League Phillies. Included were two young pitchers, Robin Roberts and Curt Simmons, who would justify once again the judgment and wisdom of the student prince of pitching, Hall of Famer Herbert Jeffries Pennock.

HERBERT JEFFRIES PENNOCK
Born February 10, 1894, at Kennett Square, Pa.
Died January 30, 1948, at New York City, N.Y.
Height 6-0 Weight 165
Threw lefthanded and batted left and righthanded.
Named to Hall of Fame, 1948.

YEAR	CLUB	LEAGUE	G.	IP.	W.	L.	Pct.	H.	R.	ER.	SO.	BB.	ERA.
1912	Philadelphia	American	17	50	1	2	.333	48	31	-	38	30	-
1913	Philadelphia	American	14	33	2	1	.667	30	24	19	17	22	5.13
1914	Philadelphia	American	28	152	11	4	.733	136	56	47	90	65	2.78
1915	Providence	International	13	90	6	4	.600	72	28	-	57	38	-
1915	Phil. (a)-Boston	American	16	58	3	6	.333	69	50	41	31	39	6.36
1916	Boston	American	9	27	0	2	.000	23	11	9	12	8	3.00
1916	Buffalo	International	15	113	7	6	.538	99	-	21	76	36	1.67
1917	Boston	American	24	101	5	5	.500	90	49	37	35	23	3.30
1918	Boston	American					(In Military Service)						
1919	Boston	American	32	219	16	8	.667	223	78	66	70	48	2.71
1920	Boston	American	37	242	16	13	.552	244	108	99	68	61	3.68
1921	Boston	American	32	223	12	14	.462	268	121	100	91	59	4.04
1922	Boston (b)	American	32	202	10	17	.370	230	108	97	59	74	4.32
1923	New York	American	35	224	19	6	.760	235	86	83	93	68	3.33
1924	New York	American	40	286	21	9	.700	302	104	90	101	64	2.83
1925	New York	American	47	277	16	17	.485	267	117	91	88	71	2.96
1926	New York	American	40	266	23	11	.676	294	133	107	78	43	3.62
1927	New York	American	34	210	19	8	.704	225	89	70	51	48	3.00
1928	New York	American	28	211	17	6	.739	215	71	60	53	40	2.56
1929	New York	American	27	158	9	11	.450	205	101	86	49	28	4.90
1930	New York	American	25	156	11	7	.611	194	95	75	46	20	4.33
1931	New York	American	25	189	11	6	.647	247	96	90	65	30	4.29
1932	New York	American	22	147	9	5	.643	191	94	75	54	38	4.59
1933	New York (c)	American	23	65	7	4	.636	96	46	40	22	21	5.54
1934	Boston	American	30	62	2	0	1.000	68	31	21	16	16	3.05
Major League Totals			617	3558	240	162	.597	3900	1699	1403	1227	916	3.60

a Claimed on waivers by Boston Red Sox, June, 1915.
b Traded to New York Yankees for outfielder Camp Skinner, Infielder Norman McMillan, pitcher George Murray and cash, January 30, 1923.
c Released by New York Yankees and signed by Boston Red Sox, January 1934.

WORLD SERIES RECORD

YEAR	CLUB	LEAGUE	G.	IP.	W.	L.	Pct.	H.	R.	ER.	SO.	BB.	ERA.
1914	Philadelphia	American	1	3	0	0	.000	2	0	0	3	2	0.00
1923	New York	American	3	171/3	2	0	1.000	19	7	7	8	1	3.63
1926	New York	American	3	22	2	0	1.000	13	3	3	8	4	1.23
1927	New York	American	1	9	1	0	1.000	3	1	1	1	0	1.00
1932	New York	American	2	4	0	0	.000	2	1	1	4	1	2.25
World Series Totals			10	551/3	5	0	1.000	39	12	12	24	8	1.95

WHIZ KID: Robin Roberts came out of Michigan State to spark the Phillies to a long-awaited pennant and stayed long enough to make the Hall of Fame.

ROBIN ROBERTS

When Robin Evan Roberts was attending that little red school house, which it literally was, on the outskirts of Springfield, Ill., just before World War II, a prominent bistro boss about town brought out a tall, quiet, knock-kneed man, weathered with early age and late hours.

Now, for the pink-cheeked, teenaged kid sitting there with ears on point because the tall visitor was described as a former big league star, his idol was the one and only Lou Gehrig. Lou's pictures were plastered all over the boy's room in the modest family

home until his mother complained. Then he told her, "Please, Mom, and don't worry. Some day I'll build a house for you the way Lou did for his mom."

Yes, Gehrig, even blockier and bigger than young Mr. Roberts, a big boy, was his idol, but the tall weathered man, Grover Cleveland Alexander, gave it to him as straight as Alex took his whiskey.

"Boys," Old Pete said softly, "I had my day and made big money for the times, but I wasted the years and the money. Don't let it happen to you."

By coincidence, Robin Roberts' father, a Welsh immigrant with a give-away accent who had come to Springfield to work in the coal mines, had fallen hard for baseball and for Alexander in 1926, the year Old Pete pitched the St. Louis Cardinals to their first pennant and world championship.

By even greater coincidence, the pink-cheeked boy whose antennae ears had got on Alex' wavelength that pre-war afternoon in the little old red school house, went on to achieve stardom with the same Philadelphia Nationals for which Alexander had done his best pitching a quarter-century previously. In face, though controversially, when baseball franchise's fans were asked in the centennial professional season of 1969 to pick an All-Star team, Roberts, the six-season-in-a-row 20-game winner, was picked as the Phillies' No. 1 all-time pitcher ahead of Alexander, who only won 22, 27, 31, 33 and 30 for five seasons at Baker Bowl. Slyly Alex was dealt to Chicago so he could become the Cubs' cannon fodder if he failed to return from World War I.

If Roberts wasn't Alexander's equal—and how many ever were?—he was amongst 'em, as Dizzy Dean would say. The durable righthander who pitched the Phillies in 1950 to the first pennant since Alex' 31-10 season in 1915 took the old alcoholic's advice to heart, quite profitably on and off the field.

Not only through clean living and perseverance did he achieve a lifetime 286-245 record, one that undoubtedly would have been better if through overwork he hadn't suffered in mid-career an arm injury that took away the p-f-f-t off his fastball, but he also saved and invested well his baseball earnings.

As a result, in 1977, a year after his election to the baseball Hall of Fame, Mr. Roberts was able to give up the hurly-burly of go-go "civilization" for the relaxed life of a suncoast squire. He gave up commuting from Philadelphia to a New York brokerage business. He dispensed with his interest in a minor league hockey team and his part-time radio color commentating. The father of four grown sons just picked up his dear wife and possessions and moved to Tampa, where he became baseball coach at the University of South Florida.

Only a man desperately in need of money and a job would drop down to USF—no reflection intended on the burgeoning college by the bay—but university baseball coaches just don't make THAT kind of money, not even if they agreed not to bring along their golf sticks, which Robby certainly didn't intend to do in what amounted to a graceful, gentle, warm-weather semi-retirement.

Because the toeplated Boy Scout who labored usually in the second division with Philadelphia, winning far more of the percentage of his games than his team did, lingered through mediocrity in the majors until he was 40, the feeling existed that he was hardheaded as well as a hard competitor. They thought he was record-conscious, pursuing that elusive 300-victory plateau above and beyond the normal or even logical.

But as late as 1947, when he tried a comeback for manager Frank Lucchesi and the Phillies' farm club at Reading, Pa., he was both an inspiration and a joy. He'd lug bats not even the professional rookies wanted to carry. He'd pitch batting practice until the perspiration cascaded off his forehead and skied down the slope of his nose. And, oh, how he tried to pitch.

He sought again the fastball best described by St. Louis's long-time second baseman and later 12-season manager, Red Schoendienst. Red said:

"Robby's fastball seems to get up to the plate, an inviting appetizer, and then suddenly skids across the strike zone as if on a cake of ice."

Roberts threw with a deceptive, easy-does-it motion, using a curveball that wasn't much, but relying essentially on his equivalent of the high hard one. Only it was low, a bristling pitch down around the knees and thrown to spots with control that impressed both Cy Perkins and Benny Bengough when they were a couple of wise old catchers as coaches for the Phillies from the late '40s.

A $25,000 bonus baby from Michigan State University, aided by alma mater coach John Kobs and even more so by the University of Michigan's Ray Fisher in a New England summer college league, Roberts was a .500 pitcher from the time he finished his first FULL season in the majors, 1949. And after that 15-and-15, he reeled off six straight seasons of 20 or more:

20-11… 21-15… 28-7… 23-16… 23-15… 23-14…

By the end of the 1955 season when he was just 29, you'd have bet that here would be one of the best ever and a shoo-in for 300. Why, he was 179-120 and still growing so strong that—.

Or was he?

Without ever a murmur of criticism for having worked 300 or more innings each of six straight years, topped by 346 in 1953, Roberts disclosed that near the end of the '55 season, something sinister had happened.

As old-fashioned as high-button shoes in his ability to finish what he started, yet throwing the greased-lightning ball that made even eighth-spot humpty-dumpty hitters threats to belt a home run, Robby had had to be a bear down guy all the way. Oh, he'd had the ability to reach back for something extra, to use the language of the dugout, when he needed a strikeout with a man on third base and none or one out. They'd call it "hitching up the belt," though what Roberts did was to hitch up the back of his right leg uniform at the knee and then pour on the coals.

But, disdainfully declining to throw up and in so as to intimidate hitters, he'd simply overpower 'em at his peak, keeping 'em from pulling the ball. They'd hit four shots to pretty deep center field at spacious Connie Mack Stadium and feel pretty good about it, too, until they realized—oops!—they'd gone for the collar. And as Schoendienst would say, you'd have a big day off the great righthander—"single, double and homer until you

came up in a jam and then he'd skid that cake of ice past you for Strike Three."

Roberts, who grew up listening to Red and other glamorous Cardinal teammates because Springfield, the state capital of Illinois, is just 99 miles north of St. Louis, could remember with pleased amusement one night when he'd faced three standout lefthanded hitters in succession—Schoendienst, Stan Musial and Enos Slaughter.

"They were great, excellent, but that night with the bases loaded and none out, I struck out the three of them in a row on just 10 pitches," he recalled proudly.

Kinda like the tense pennant-deciding moment the last day of the 1950 season at Brooklyn's Ebbet Field when the floundering Phillies looked as if they were going to back into a playoff for which they'd have little momentum. Even after Richie Ashburn came up with the throw of his life, playing a bit shallow in center field and grabbing Duke Snider's hot line single and pegging out Cal Abrams at the plate, the Phillies still were in even more hot water than Milt Stock, the Dodgers' third-base coach who had waved Abrams in to be tagged out a good 15 feet with none down.

One run, any kind, would win the game in the last of the ninth and end the race in a tie. The Dodgers had runners on second and third, too, Jackie Robinson up. A tough man in a pinch, of course, and Robby and manager Eddie Sawyer, the tough-looking, soft-hearted Phi Beta Kappa, decided to fill the bases with an intentional pass.

Next up was Carl Furillo. Year-in, year-out in Brooklyn's pennant bids, the Brooks' right fielder was their best September hitter. But Roberts tugged at that right pants' leg at the knee and threw the smoke, and Skoonj Furillo popped up the elevator shaft to Andy Seminick, Roberts' batterymate. One to go. Gil Hodges. The blacksmith first baseman didn't hit to right field very often, but, heck, no one was pulling Mr. Roberts now. Gil hit an inning-ending can of corn to right. Side out.

In the 10th inning, you'll recall, Dick Sisler then hammered a three-run opposite field homer off Don Newcombe for a 4-1 victory that gave Philadelphia its first pennant in 35 years and made Dodger scout George Sisler, seated in the stands, the man with the oddest feeling in the park. The great star who never got into a World Series in 15 seasons himself didn't know whether to laugh or to cry because son Dick had done in George's friend and employer, Branch Rickey.

But now to get ahead to the moment of crisis in 1955, the Phillies were in what amounted to a five-club race and the opposition was Brooklyn once more and, well, let Roberts himself tell the tale of work and woe that turned a superstar into something considerably less:

"I'd pitched nine innings and won on a Friday night. The next afternoon I warmed up to go in and get Don Newcombe, a heckuva hitter as well as pitcher, and on Sunday I warmed up again. Then, Tuesday night, I went nine again. The next day I barely could straighten the right arm."

The embers were still there, but not the flame. For the sixth straight season, Roberts did win more than 20 games, but, as a likely telltale that the fuzzy tail was gone from his fastball, he yielded a record 41 home runs. And in 1956, he fell to 19-18. Then he descended rapidly, winning more than he lost in just five of his last 12 seasons.

In 1974, famed Pulitzer-Prize winning author, James A. Michener, a Philadelphia fan particularly devoted to Roberts, took talented pen in hand for the *New York Times* and wrote huffily that the Yankees' Whitey Ford had been favored over Robby in Hall of Fame elections among baseball writers because Ford had played in the "Big Apple."

Wrote the author of *Tales of the South Pacific*, further immortalized in words and music by Richard Rodgers and Oscar Hammerstein II:

"Ford had a lifetime record of only 236 victories and Roberts had 286. The important fact was that Ford had been the subject of hilarious stories during his entire career. He owned a race horse he drove at state fairs. He was photographed drinking beer with his cronies. He was good copy and a delightful human being, and he had played for the Yankees in 11 World Series, often winning the big game.

"Roberts, on the other hand, had played for the Phillies, which of itself brings his intelligence into question. He was a big, capable, quiet man from Springfield, Ill., around whom stories did not accumulate. A graduate of Michigan State University, he conducted himself like the gentleman he was, pitched his heart out when the team was giving him no runs and compiled a dazzling record."

But he was not colorful. His teammate, Richie Ashburn, wrote of him:

"Despite the fact that Robby was a pitcher, he has some good qualities. He is a good family man, he goes to church regularly. He's honest. He pays his bills. And he's a Republican."

Funny fella, that little Ashburn, the slick bunt-and-run center-field star of a team that had too few who were A-1 in Roberts's era, as Michener would complain, but, the truth is, too, in defense of at least younger 10-year baseball writers eligible to vote for the Hall of Fame, the Roberts they knew wasn't a Cadillac or even Chevrolet compared with the Ford.

Whitey, after all, did log 139 fewer defeats in 16 big league seasons to the Springfield Rifle's total in 19 years. More important, the rifle was more often a popgun the last 10 seasons during which Mr. Roberts won only 107 games and lost 125. THAT was the Roberts to many younger BBWAA members knew. So it took an extra election or two for Robby to make the Hall of Fame, just as it did for Early Wynn, another big winner who was also a large loser.

Why did Roberts hang on so long? He endured seasons of 10-20... 17-14... 15-17... 12-16 and then 1-10 at Philadelphia before making what amounted to at least a modest comeback in the American League at Baltimore, where he was 10-9 in 1962... then 14-13... and 13-7. In 1965, dividing time with the Orioles (5-7) and with Houston (5-2) back in the National League, he was 10-9, but between the Astros and the Chicago Cubs he reached the end of the line at 40 in 1966, a season his combined won-and-lost record was 5-and-8.

For part of the answer of the pitcher's perseverance, you've probably got to dig into the background of Robin Evan Roberts and his family—by the way, around Springfield they still call him "Evan"—just as the way his proud Welsh father, Tom, planned to dig coal when he came to this country.

Tom had come up from the back-breaking labor and pocket-pinching strikes of a coal mine in Lancshire, England, where he'd met the woman who as his wife would bear him four girls and four boys. No, they didn't name that one boy for Robin Hood, the legendary stick-it-to-the-rich-and-help-the-poor pixy of Nottingham Forest, or not even for Robin Goodfellow, the mythical English house sprite. The name as the senior Roberts used it was just a handy substitute for Robert.

As a boy, Robin relegated everything to playing games on the farm on the outskirts of Springfield, and, though happy to be working above ground rather than below it and with an immigrant's attachment to baseball, Tom Roberts didn't like it a dam site when the kid deliberately broke a hoe to avoid working the modest place.

Pop, outraged, took a fly swatter and belted a ground-rule double across his husky seven-year-old son's well-padded bottom. The elder Mr. Roberts explained the fly swatter:

"You don't hurt your hand and you don't mark the kid."

The consideration was duly noted, but not sufficiently impressive enough to keep the all-around athlete from constantly going around with a ball, as his dear mother, Sarah, would remember, when he'd sweet-talk her out of his chores with a promise he did indeed keep with his professional bonus:

"Naw, Mom, I'm no farm hand, I'm a ball-player. You just wait until I get into the major leagues. Then, like Lou Gehrig did for his mother, I'll build you a house."

Even Robin's father, with the understatement characteristic of the Welsh, came to respect the determination that—remember?—would keep Robby toeing a rubber even at Reading, Pa., when it was merely a matter of principle, certainly not principal.

When Rob was a boy and couldn't get one of his three brothers to play catch with him, he'd prop an old mattress against the garage door and fire away for hours at a hole in the middle, all the while listening to a play-by-play of the Cardinals or, more often because they played only day games at Wrigley Field, the Chicago Cubs.

En route to fame and fortune, Roberts pitched and played third base at Springfield and Lanphier high schools. He also was a fair enough end on the football team and a pretty shot-putter, to, but at Michigan State, where he enrolled at 18 in 1944, he was good enough in basketball to win an athletic scholarship in that sport. So he was a bit tardy when he reported to baseball to John Kobs, whose Spartans had been hitting in indoor cages all winter.

Kobs told the kid, politely, that he'd already picked his travel roster, but the strapping lad insisted. Kobs had to tell him that, whether batting righthanded or switch-hitting, he didn't impress enough, but Roberts persisted with a wait-and-watch-me-pitch plea to the coach. Kobs did and liked the way the boy threw hard and, above all, threw strikes.

So it was in the Green and White of Michigan State that Roberts took his collegiate shove off the pitching slab, but he got his biggest break from the man who coached the Maize and Blue of bitter rival Michigan. Ray Fisher, who had pitched in the majors with the Yankees and Cincinnati, liked the raw talent—even if Roberts was so raw that he threw eagerly before getting the catcher's signs and fell down awkwardly when fielding bunts.

So Fisher took him in 1946 to Montpelier, Vermont in the old Northern League, a college kids' summer league on the straw-hat circuit, and put on the finishing touches so well that by the end of the second summer there, the St. Louis Browns had offered Roberts $225 a month to play Class B ball and the Phillies offered $10,000 to sign. He hesitated. The Phillies went to $15,000. The bewildered boy was tongue-tied. So they went to $25,000, and he reached for a pen at Chicago.

When he worked out with the Phillies at Wrigley Field, Cy Perkins, the old catching smoothie who had worked with Lefty Grove and helped take the rough edges off the guy who took his own job with the Philadelphia A's, Mickey Cochrane, buttonholed Babe Alexander, then the Phillies' traveling secretary.

"Don't let the kid out of the park unsigned," Perkins pleaded.

Over the years, Perkins and Fisher would exercise technical influence over the pink-cheeked 4-H boy who reduced pitching to simplicity. Once, after that arm weariness or injury in 1955 took its toll late in the season against the Dodgers, Robby dropped off at Ann Arbor and asked the former rival college coach to have a look.

"You've changed your delivery, haven't you?" said Fisher gently to the superstar. "You're throwing sidearmed rather than three-quarter overhand."

Smiled Roberts, "That's what I wanted to know, Coach, thanks. At Philadelphia, I'm Robin Roberts and they won't tell me anything."

Earlier, though, when he was not quite so certain, Perkins would reassure him, such as the day the gallant competitor warmed up feeling like a million bucks and then, most unlike Roberts, was belted out in the first inning.

Perkins followed him into the clubhouse with consoling encouragement. "Don't worry, kid," Cy said, "I warmed up Grove the day I thought Lefty had the best stuff I ever saw and he faced eight Yankees and didn't get one out."

Roberts remembered that when he was inducted at Cooperstown. "Imagine," he said, "here I was a kid just 24, barely in my third big league season and Cy told me something than that was really startling. 'Kid,' he said, 'I've watched and worked with some great ones—Grove, Johnson, Alexander and Pennock—and you belong right up there with them.'"

By that time, Robby had gone back to Michigan State to get a degree in physical education and, wearying of watching movies on the road, he'd asked sister Nora if she knew any girls he might date, and Nora introduced him to a young grade school teacher just out of the University of Wisconsin. A year later pretty brunette Mary Ann Kalnes married the ballplayer and they moved, to of all addresses, a suburban Philadelphia home in Meadowbrook on Robin Hood Road.

The $60,000 pitcher with the smooth-as-silk delivery was particularly close to fellow bonus teammate and neighbor, Curt Simmons, who went to Roberts' defense when it was suggested that Robby not only was hanging on too long, but that he also stubbornly refused to change.

"He can't change-up as easily as I did," said Simmons, whose herky-jerky delivery made the once flame-throwing Egypt (Pa.) southpaw a master of variable velocities.

Roberts, emphasizing that he enjoyed the challenge even down there at Reading, where he hoped futilely once more to prove to the Phillies or any others that he was a major league pitcher, looked back philosophically on having prolonged his career to the point where—.

"To where," he said, "I not only never could second-guess myself that I'd quit too soon, but that I'd played myself out of the little boy's urge. The sheer joy of playing the game was so persuasive."

Robin Roberts would bristle only when it was suggested he was too bullheaded to change and that he hadn't prepared himself for the decline the way his chief rival, 363-game winner Warren Spahn, had over the years.

"First thing," the old Springfield Rifle would explain in handsome middle age with only a touch of thickness in the jowls, "I did break speeds on my fastball more than people thought and, actually, I improved my curve, too, or I couldn't have come back the way I did at Baltimore. But I just no longer had that little extra zap. And I didn't have the arsenal of different pitches Spahnie had before he lost his best fastball. I guess I wasn't as smart…"

H'mm, no player should—or could—buy that self-assessment if he knew the role Robin Evan Roberts had played in improvement of the ballplayers' brilliant pension and their strong players' association or, if you will, union.

No militant or radical, if that's a fair description, Roberts actually had angered J. Norman Lewis, the attorney who first represented the players after the pension plan had been originated by Mr. Shortstop, Marty Marion, and trainer Harrison J. (Doc) Weaver of the Cardinals in July 1946. Farsighted clubowners had helped. After all, old Pete Alexander's grateful boss, St. Louis' Sam Breadon, was slipping the National League $100 a month to pass along as if it were a league pension to the reeling, down-and-out boozer who one day would inspire Roberts.

Robby's interest grew just before he lost his one and only World Series game, 2-1, on a 10th-inning home run by Joe DiMaggio in 1950. That day the commissioner at the time, A.B. (Happy) Chandler, visited the Phillies' clubhouse and told them the importance of continuing to vote World Series radio and television money into the pension plan to keep it solvent.

By then, as Roberts remembered, Pittsburgh's Ralph Kiner and the Yankees' Allie Reynolds, as the major league's top player representatives, had hired Lewis, who ultimately was ousted in favor of Judge Robert C. Cannon, Milwaukee municipal jurist. Cannon's father, a lawyer, represented the ousted eight players in the Black Sox scandal of 1919.

One day, taking a stroll in New York when still pitching, Roberts dropped into the commissioner's office to ask questions about the pension plans. He found answers vague or non-existent, not indicating dishonesty, but carelessness or at least lack of adequate concern. He looked through the pension files made available to him and left, disturbed.

Roberts called for stronger reaction and supervision by his fellow player representatives. In turn, he was asked to follow up in pursuit of a full-time representative. Judge Cannon was reluctant to give up the bench or to leave Milwaukee.

So Robby called a University of Pennsylvania man, George Taylor, whom he knew had settled numerous labor disputes, and told Dr. Taylor what he wanted—"a strong man of established character and one whom we could count on to represent the best interests of the game as well as the players…"

Dr. Taylor recommended a man duly forwarded by Roberts to his fellow players. You've heard—certainly baseball has—of Marvin Miller, dynamic economist and former assistant to the United Steelworkers, a man whose forceful leadership improved the lot of players immediately, past, present and future.

And at pension age as he passed the half-century mark when he headed from the wintry blasts of Pennsylvania to the relative warmth of Florida, Robin Evan Roberts could reflect that he had come a long way from listening to a broken-down old pitcher in that little red school house outside Springfield, Ill.. A long way to trying to teach his own tricks of the trade he practiced so well to those eager young University of South Florida baseball players at Tampa and then to accept appointment to the baseball Hall of Fame at Cooperstown.

ROBIN EVAN ROBERTS
Born September 30, 1926, at Springfield, Ill.
Height 6-1 Weight 201
Threw right and batted right and lefthanded.
Named to Hall of Fame, 1976.

YEAR	CLUB	LEAGUE	G.	IP.	W.	L.	Pct.	H.	R.	ER.	SO.	BB.	ERA.
1948	Wilmington	Int. State	11	96	9	1	.900	55	25	22	121	27	2.06
1948	Philadelphia	National	20	147	7	9	.438	148	63	52	84	61	3.18
1949	Philadelphia	National	43	227	15	15	.500	229	101	93	95	75	3.69
1950	Philadelphia	National	40	304	20	11	.645	282	112	102	146	77	3.02
1951	Philadelphia	National	44	315	21	15	.583	284	115	106	127	64	3.03
1952	Philadelphia	National	39	330	28	7	.800	292	104	95	148	45	2.59
1953	Philadelphia	National	44	347	23	16	.590	324	119	106	198	61	2.75
1954	Philadelphia	National	45	337	23	15	.605	289	116	111	185	56	2.96
1955	Philadelphia	National	41	305	23	14	.622	292	137	111	160	53	3.28
1956	Philadelphia	National	43	297	19	18	.514	328	155	147	157	40	4.45
1957	Philadelphia	National	39	250	10	22	.313	246	122	113	128	43	4.07
1958	Philadelphia	National	35	270	17	14	.548	270	112	97	130	51	3.23
1959	Philadelphia	National	35	257	15	17	.469	267	137	122	137	35	4.27
1960	Philadelphia	National	35	237	12	16	.429	256	113	106	122	34	4.03
1961	Philadelphia (a-b)	National	26	117	1	10	.091	154	85	76	54	23	5.85
1962	Baltimore	American	27	191	10	9	.526	176	63	59	102	41	2.78
1963	Baltimore	American	35	251	14	13	.519	230	100	93	124	40	3.33
1964	Baltimore	American	31	204	13	7	.650	203	69	66	109	52	2.91
1965	Baltimore (c)	American	20	115	5	7	.417	110	51	43	63	20	3.37
1965	Houston	National	10	76	5	2	.714	61	22	16	34	10	1.89
1966	Houston (d)-Chicago	National	24	112	5	8	.385	141	66	60	54	21	4.82
1967	Reading	Eastern	11	80	5	3	.625	75	25	22	65	7	2.48
American League Totals—4 Years			113	761	42	36	.538	719	283	261	398	153	3.09
National League Totals—16 Years			563	3928	244	209	.539	3863	1679	1513	1959	749	3.45
Major League Totals—19 Years			676	4689	286	245	.539	4582	1962	1774	2357	902	3.40

a Sold to New York Yankees, October 16, 1961.
b Released April 30, 1962; signed with Baltimore Orioles, May 21, 1962.
c Released July 31, 1965; signed by Houston Astros, August 6, 1965.
d Released; signed by Chicago Cubs, July 13, 1966.

WORLD SERIES RECORD

YEAR	CLUB	LEAGUE	G.	IP.	W.	L.	Pct.	H.	R.	ER.	SO.	BB.	ERA.
1950	Philadelphia	National	2	11	0	1	.000	11	2	2	5	3	1.64

BIRDS OF A FEATHER: Brooks Robinson (left) teamed with Frank Robinson to give the Baltimore Orioles powerful, middle-of-the-lineup offensive production.

BROOKS ROBINSON

When Baltimore, the crabcake-and-race course capital of the country, said hail and farewell to its all-time baseball favorite, the Robinson who simply had rolled on like a babbling brook or Brooks for 23 years, first baseman Lee May stole the show. Almost as neatly, in fact, as the famed No. 5 in the orange-and-black trim of the Orioles had swiped base hits from May and the 1970 World Series from the Cincinnati Reds.

Some 51,798, then the largest crowd for a regular-season game in the Maryland metropolis spoiled by Brooksie's ability, the Orioles' success and the competitive lure of the two-dollar window at one of the area's thoroughbred-racing emporiums, stood up and cheered as one. Baltimore celebrated B. Robinson's retirement.

"Thanks Brooks Day," they called it, and it was as cheerful as the soft-spoken, articulate, kindly athlete who had come out of Little Rock, Ark., to become a big man in good ol' "Bal'mer," as the natives pronounce that Chesapeake Bay center.

Typically, Brooksie, a sissy name affectionately

used by virtually all for a man's man, wanted no gifts, so life-saving equipment he'd wanted for Johns Hopkins Hospital Children's Center was donated in his name. Still, there were the inevitable presents, including sense and nonsense, such as when Doug DeCinces, Robinson's young successor, simply reached down into the infield at Memorial Stadium, plucked out the third base Brooks had protected so marvelously so long and simply handed it to the legend.

But it remained for May, the foe who had become a friend, to put the figurative frosting on the farewell cake. In the elaborate pre-game ceremonies the first baseman presented the hot hand at the hot corner with a well-traveled vacuum cleaner.

Referring to Robinson's wife, Connie, the former airline stewardess beauty Brooks captured with a rare display of courage overcoming shyness, a smiling May told the slow-moving old-timer with the fast-receding hairline:

"I hope Connie makes you put it to good use in your retirement. You'll see that this vacuum cleaner has a lot in common with you, Brooks. It has a lot of miles on it."

Time—seven years—had healed Mays' wounds from those moments in the '70 Series when Robinson, not only hitting a ton, fielded so brilliantly before the stunned Reds and an awed national television audience as if he were Pie Traynor, Buck Weaver, Jimmy Collins, Billy Cox, Willie Kamm, Ossie Bluege and the Boyer brothers, Clete and Ken all in one inspired body.

Sure, they called him "Vacuum Cleaner" from one disgusted dugout to the other and "Hoover" when they didn't mean Herbert, either, and "Robby the Robber" sprang off the typewriters of many baseball writers trying to come within spittin' distance journalistically of the Pulitzer Prize play they'd seen by the Baltimore third baseman, a .429 hitter and—hands down—the Series hero.

Now, if it hadn't been for Brooksie, that blindly good-and-lucky honky as May understandably might have called him, the Cincinnati first baseman well might have emerged from the World Series with the laurel wreath, too.

Take the first game, which, oddly enough, Robinson began by misplaying his first chance for an error. The muscular May drilled a sure-fire double down the third-base line, but in one lightning motion Brooks whirled to his right, snared the ball backhanded across the foul line and threw off-balance to snip the tape just ahead of May at first base.

Next game, Lee blistered another shot down the foul stripe, but Robinson speared it on one knee and turned the hot shot into a double play. Rubbing it in on the Reds in what became a five-game rout of the National League powerhouse, Robby the Robber stole another base hit from Cincinnati in the third game with an incredible diving catch. And when Cincy's slugging Johnny Bench grumbled that the only way to get one by Robinson was "to hit it over his head," Brooksie leaped high on thick ankles to send Bench to the bench with an AB instead of basking in the middle of the infield with a 2B.

Said Pete Rose, the hit-hungry hustler bound for a record 4,256, "The guy can field a ball with a pair of pliers."

The Cincinnati manager, Sparky Anderson, said it with three little words:

"Robinson beat us."

As pleased almost as the punch Brooksie had provided—two doubles and two homers among nine hits for six runs driven in and five scored—the bantam field boss of the Birds, Earl Weaver, smiled benignly on gushing members of the media who crowded around the Baltimore manager when they couldn't get to Robinson himself.

"Welcome, gentlemen, to the American League," said Weaver in oblique reference to the obvious. Ink-stained pressbox wretches and fur-draped, bejeweled World Series spectators from the high-rent district just had seen a sample of what the Orioles themselves and their shirt-sleeved faithful were accustomed.

Why, heck, even Harold (Pie) Traynor, the gentlemanly Hall of Fame third base standout and a career .320 hitter, said he'd never seen anyone play his old bag the way B. Robinson did in the '70 Series or again in '71 when Brooksie rose to the occasion at bat, hitting .318, and also well for anyone else, routinely for Robinson. That Series, however, belonged to the late Roberto Clemente, a fitting memorial.

For 18 full seasons and parts of five others Brooks, who flowed past his 40th birthday, was an in-and-out hitter and, overall, though powerful enough, really not a good one. His career average was .267 and just twice did he exceed .300, once when winning the Most Valuable Player award, 1964.

But in the spotlight of important play, Brooksie was a clutch hitter. No Frank Robinson, to mention the unrelated outfielder with whom he formed a mutual admiration society from the time F. Robby came over from Cincinnati in 1966 to help B. Robby and associates achieve their first pennant.

The 6-1, 190-pound third baseman immediately homered to help a four-game upset of the Los Angeles Dodgers, but he batted just .214 in that Series and had a dismal 1-for-19 (.053) in the five-game humiliation that wound up four World Series with .263, a result of 14 RBIs in 20 games. His All-Star play for 18 games was a successful .289, too, but he was at his best batting in the showdown of the League Championship Series, that not fully appreciated playoff, regularly scheduled now since 1969, which determines whether a guy heads for home with a few extra bucks in his pocket or lingers for a chance at the blue-ribbon and blue-chips of the World Series.

Not until he was 37 years old, limited to one playoff hit, a home run, in 12 times at bat and an .083 average against Oakland, did the ruggedly game Robinson really have unproductive post-season production for the American League pennant. He hit .500 in 1969, .583 in '70 and .364 in '71.

Although he was .250 in 1973, closer to his norm, the fact is that, though by severe self-analysis essentially a swinger, often a sucker for that high fastball up out of the strike zone, Brooksie was a center-stage star in the televised championship and World Series of 1970-71.

In those spotlighted 18 games, aside from fielding sensationally, Robinson batted a torrid .410, including five doubles and three homers among 27 hits, driving in 15 runs. It's no wonder that to Joe Blow from Breese, Ill., or J. Lee Donuts, the tycoon from Wall Street, B. Robby was BOTH a great hitter AND a great fielder.

Although laterally quick, like another latter-day slewfoot, Ken Reitz, Brooksie couldn't run and he lost base hits that way, just as he did other points on his average by swinging at bad balls and taking an unnecessary time at bat when he could have taken a base on balls.

Even though a free swinger who hit 268 home runs, six times topping 20 a season, and knocking in 100 runs twice and more than 80 eight times, Robinson played it the company way at bat as he did when he'd drag old No. 5 out there no matter how hurt.

As Manager Weaver said by way of one compliment when Robinson's appreciation day followed his voluntary retiring in August 1977, a decision made so that the Orioles could use a valuable spot on the roster for a physically returned player who could help in a valiant division drive:

"I never had to ask Brooksie to take on 2-and-0."

When most hitters chomp at the bit, eager to be turned loose with the count as favorable as at 3-and-1, team man Robinson recognized that he was a double-play threat as well as a good hitter in a jam. So he'd often take one from the pitcher for the good of the cause—the Orioles', not necessarily his.

As for playing hurt, well, from 1960 when returned from brief exile at Vancouver of the Pacific Coast League, the name of B. Robinson never was omitted from the lineup for more than 18 games

(1964 and '75) until Old Father Time began to make it tough in 1976. Even then, in what might have been an awkward situation for the Orioles, Robinson did not want to retire and persisted, as mentioned, until August of '77. His last full season and two fragmentary ones saw Brooksie bat under .200 for 245 games, a plate collapse that might have cost him .270 as an overall bat mark.

Even so, the clean-living Methodist son of a Little Rock fire captain showed his guts in more ways than one as he played more big league seasons with one club than any player ever and more games (2,896) than all except Ty Cobb, Henry Aaron, Stan Musial and Carl Yastrzmski.

Brooksie, sent down to Vancouver on his birthday (May 18) when he was 22, showed his exile that the Orioles merely had uncovered a polished gem tougher than an uncut diamond.

Chasing a foul ball at Vancouver's Capilano Stadium, the kid ran into a dugout guard rail, impaling his right forearm on a steel hook. While Robinson shouted in pain, the arm had to be cut away from the hook. The question was two-fold: Had nerves and tendons been cleanly cut or managled and, ergo, was the uncertain minor league second baseman's potentially brilliant career as a big league third baseman kaput?

Here, B. Robby showed the mark of a champion. Told after 22 stitches that he might never bend the right elbow again, the Razorback to whom a drink meant little or nothing quipped, "Well, in that case I'll stay half-sober the rest of my life."

But within weeks, because the arm had been slashed cleanly, Robinson had battled his way back to Baltimore to stay, though throwing awkwardly.

At Detroit one day, charging a ball fouled into the stands at Tiger Stadium, Robinson crashed face first into a concrete ledge and lay unconscious, his lower unhinged jaw agape. When he came to and the trainer called for an ambulance, the third baseman opened his pale blue eyes and wove to his feet, exclaiming:

"What's the matter? Never see anyone shook up before? Give me a glove and let's play ball."

True grit even before they began working on a fractured jaw and loosened teeth. As a boy, he'd broken his arm and collarbone in second grade and refused to cry. He didn't weep, beef or show the white feather, either, when he was beaned with pitches seven times.

Criminy, most guys would bellow bloody murder at the pitcher or become hopelessly gun shy. B. Robinson merely stood his ground at bat as well as afield, and he would talk Weaver out of benching him when he wasn't doing well, which was part of the time.

"Because," the manager explained, "I found that when I DID rest Brooksie, his bat really became inactive. Besides, you KNEW his glove would save more than his bat failed to produce."

Indeed, thanks to constant practice—super-scout Jim Russo noted that the premier third baseman took 50 or more grounders even before hot weather games—and thanks also to his ability and to that national exposure, Robinson did more for defensive recognition than even the Rawlings Gold Glove he won eight times as the No. 1 third baseman.

Just when he hung up that quivering leather which had thrilled so many and displeased so few, I informally polled sportswriters and scouts, local and national, in the pressbox at St. Louis' Busch Memorial Stadium. Essentially, mind you, the writers at least were National Leaguers, but they had seen B. Robby in person or on TV. I wondered how each man figured Robinson's Hall of Fame chances, meaning whether soon or late or at all?

The result was a startling disparity, ranging from the suggestion he'd make it with the top superstars his first time eligible for consideration by the Baseball Writers' Association of America, meaning five seasons after retirement, to never because he hadn't hit enough at an offensive position.

My own feeling was that reality probably lay somewhere in between, that Robinson wouldn't make it with the minimum wait, but that he'd be tapped for induction by the BBWAA before the 20-year time limit after which, following another five seasons in the Cooperstown waiting room, a highly placed also-ran becomes eligible for consideration by the Hall of Fame's Committee on Veterans. Proving I'm full of beeswax, B. Robby made Cooperstown in his first try, 1983, a tremendous tribute to defense in short smothered by offensive heroes.

Even when his last breathtaking stop was as fresh in the memory as Baltimore's affection for the good neighbor who'd lost heavily in outside investments while giving his time to the needy. I felt in 1977 that he'd follow Frank Robinson into the Hall of Fame. It was good-natured, easy-going, do-your-job-and-forget-your-worries Brooks who had stated publicly no interest in managing, but had forecast that F. Robby could make the first black skipper, which he did.

Even down there in Little Rock, where he'd been born in 1937, he'd been a bright boy, much interested in reading, especially of history. He also read, understood and appreciated even tedious novelist William Faulkner. And his father, who'd played a sharp second base in softball, saw to it that Brooks Calbert Robinson, Jr., began to field groundballs as soon as the boy wouldn't trip over his diapers.

At 14, the lad had a paper route that included a prominent Little Rock citizen, great Yankees' catcher Bill Dickey. Brooksie tried so hard to impress Dickey with the strength of his throwing arm that he fired the *Arkansas Gazette*—or was it the *Democrat*?—onto the roof of Dickey's house. Error: Robinson!

In those days the kid dreamed of a big league career and he even wrote in an English theme that his ambition was to play for the St. Louis Cardinals or Detroit Tigers, but by the time he starred for a junior American Legion post, he'd also made All-Arkansas in high school basketball and run the 880 in track.

As Eberts Post won the Arkansas state legion title, 16 big league scouts liked young Mr. Robinson's bat and glove, but he didn't have either a powerful throwing arm or running speed. With the University of Arkansas and other colleges interested, Brooksie was caught on the ticklish horns of dilemma between baseball and education. A smart parent let the boy make his own decision, noting only that many were called by the majors, but so-o-o few were chosen.

On his own, therefore, with $4,000, the bonus limit that could be given a free agent without freezing him to a major league roster, handicapping both the boy and the team, B. Robinson opted for baseball and the Baltimore Orioles, only recently (1953) the sorriest club in the majors as the old St. Louis Browns.

In 1955 at York, Pa., in the Piedmont League, Brooks hit .331, convincing Orioles' organization men that as a pretty fair second baseman, he'd make a better—and then some!—third baseman. And Paul Richards, rebuilding the Browns (oops, Orioles) with youth and money, even called up the kid to Baltimore late in the season.

Brooksie actually started against Washington's Chuck Stobbs and doubled and singled, but in 20 more times at bat, he got no more hits, struck out 10 times and was optioned out.

At that time Robinson had no power and it was suggested he try switch-hitting. The boy protested that he couldn't hit—or throw—lefthanded. But, observers noted that he ate, wrote, played golf and table tennis, bowled and shaved lefthanded. Why couldn't he turn-around?

A couple of years before Buck Weaver's silence in the Black Sox scandal had cost him his career, another brilliant third baseman, Weaver of the world champion 1917 Chicago American's, had improved his hitting dramatically by switching? Why not Robinson?

Nope, not stubborn, but just ineffectual, so he was a banjo-batting righthander, though already a great fielder, called to breakfast by Manager Richards at Detroit early in the 1959 season. Brooksie thought tall Paul wanted to wish him a happy birthday, instead, the taciturn Texan said the kid was going out.

"Show me something," said King Richards, "and I'll bring you back at the All-Star break."

Shocked because he thought he'd beaten out Billy Klaus and Jim Finigan for the Baltimore third-base job, Robinson took demotion like a champion, as Vancouver manager Charley Metro learned after the lad's long plane ride.

"You'd have thought he had promoted, not de-moted," said Metro. "He grabbed a bat and within 20 minutes was friends with everybody."

Out of the severe arm gash mentioned earlier came a new batting stroke and, suddenly, the little hitter from Little Rock was hitting big. Recalled by Baltimore, where fans already remembered his glove, he was given a rousing hand even though his first batting effort was a pop fly up the elevator shaft.

So began a love affair almost as tender as the one between Brooksie and the United Airlines stewardess he met on a chartered flight one night from Boston. Pretty Constance Butcher listened, amused, as the fumbling fellow cautioned, "Watch out for those other guys. They're all married. I'm the only single man aboard."

Connie had heard, much less seen, better lines than the one the lanky bashful ballplayer, good-looking and so serious, was giving her. In October 1960, they were married and had a couple of handsome boys, one of whom came home sniveling near the end of the player's career to say, "The other kids say we're going to lose our house."

Always the optimist, Brooks assured his young-ster it wasn't so, but, indeed, it was. A sporting goods venture with partners who seemed to have no more time for the business than for the goodwill ambassador who did good deeds for people when he wasn't doing them for the Orioles.

Although an unpaid bank loan was reduced, a circuit judge ordered Robinson's handsome home in Lutherville, Md., auctioned off for a mortgage foreclosure suit brought by a York (Pa.) bank. When you've lost close to $250,000…well, as wife Connie said it with feeling:

"Now we all know why he hasn't been able to play ball the past two years. I told him he worked 22 years playing ball, saving money and he has to start all over again. Poor Brooks!"

No, not when you're as sunny-dispositioned, as light on your feet, laterally if not straight ahead, figuratively if not literally, as the fair-skinned Ernie Banks of the American League. He was, in truth, the fair-haired boy of a community that knew Babe Ruth, Lefty Grove, John McGraw, Wee Willie Keeler, Uncle Wilbert Robinson, Jack Dunn and sports editor Bob Maisel's father and a local favorite, Fritz Maisel.

Immediately, phone calls poured in with offers of financial help for the athlete who was close to the end of earning, much less commanding, a contract well in excess of $100,000. And as dear Connie predicted, Brooksie was too proud to take a penny.

Almost as proud, in a different way, of course, as when he ran off with the American League's Most Valuable Player award in 1964, 18 first-place votes to runner-up Mickey Mantle's two and 269 points to The Mick's 171. That year, Brooksie hit .317 and led the American League in runs batted in, 118, while clubbing 28 homers.

Even then, there was a shadow because Balti-more, leading the race most of the season, lost out in September when Yogi Berra's New York Yankees obtained Pedro Ramos on waivers from Cleveland. Ramos wasn't eligible for the World Series, but there was nothing illegal about his final-month con-tributions out of the bullpen.

Still, when the end came for Brooks Calbert Robinson, Jr., to take off No. 5 after the 1977 sea-son, turning to the television booth as a commenta-tor for Oriole road games sent back home and for a non-affiliated job in which the man's popularity and personality figured to play a part, Brooksie had friends. When the baseball commissioner's office gave him its second award several years ago for off-the-field contributions to baseball, the selection was laughable. Not that Robinson was chosen, but that either he or Banks or both hadn't been picked the first time around rather than Willie Mays.

Robinson had had his moments, all right, including a raft of fielding and durability records for a major league third baseman and for having tied the major league mark for consecutive games hitting grandslam homers, 1962, and for belting two opening game homers in 1973. Yeah, and on the other hand, fast-moving old slowpoke had grounded into the most double plays one season and gone another year without so much as stealing a base.

Nine times *The Sporting News* had named him to its American League All-Star team and had picked him as AL Player of the Year in '64. Sixteen straight times he'd been tapped by the national sports weekly as its No. 1 defensive third baseman in his league. Yet not even was that quite enough.

As super-scout Russo of the Orioles put it, "I get accused of niggardliness in declining to use the word 'great,' which I believe is overworked by sportswriters, press agents and politicians. So in rating players numerically as we do in scouting—2 to 8, meaning 'poor' to 'outstanding'—I usually stop at 7, which is considered 'very good.'

"But Brooksie WAS great afield, so good that long before he won the Hickok belt as Professional Athlete of the Year (1970), he'd figured most unusually to kill off a unique deal. In 1958, Paul Richards and the man who then owned the Kansas City Athletics, Arnold Johnson, were set to swap rosters, 25 players for 25 players, but, suddenly, Richards remembered young Mr. Robinson and said, nixing the deal, 'There is a young player we'd like to keep…'"

Johnson, the Canteen Corp. of American tycoons who milked the A's of their profits before Charley Finley arrived in town on his mule, recog-

nized that Paul was a poker player with talent. The kid HAD to have something. So the roster-swapping was abandoned.

Good thing for Baltimore. The transplanted Browns might have gone as long there without winning as they had in St. Louis. After all, taking just one look at Brooks Robinson, wearing the fastest glove in the West or East, ex-umpire Ed Hurley summed him up best.

Said Hurley, amazed, "That kid looks as if he just came down from a HIGHER league!"

BROOKS CALBERT ROBINSON JR.
Born May 18, 1937, at Little Rock, Ark.
Height 6-1 Weight 190
Threw and batted righthanded.
Named to Hall of Fame, 1983.

YEAR	CLUB	LEAGUE	POS.	G.	AB.	R.	H.	2B.	3B.	HR.	RBI.	B.A.	PO.	A.	E.	F.A.
1955	York	Pied.	2B-3B	95	354	72	117	17	3	11	67	.331	184	226	14	.967
1955	Baltimore	Amer.	3B	6	22	0	2	0	0	0	1	.091	2	8	2	.833
1956	San Antonio	Texas	3B-2B	154	577	72	157	28	6	9	74	.272	213	396	26	.959
1956	Baltimore	Amer.	3B-2B	15	44	5	10	4	0	1	1	.227	9	25	2	.944
1957	San Antonio	Texas	3B-SS	33	124	10	33	5	1	1	9	.266	34	59	4	.959
1957	Baltimore	Amer.	3B	50	117	13	28	6	1	2	14	.239	34	66	3	.971
1958	Baltimore	Amer.	3B-2B	145	463	31	110	16	3	3	32	.238	157	283	22	.952
1959	Vancouver	P.C.	3B	42	163	20	54	9	2	6	30	.331	54	93	8	.948
1959	Baltimore	Amer.	3B-2B	88	313	29	89	15	2	4	24	.284	92	187	13	.955
1960	Baltimore	Amer.	3B-2B	152	595	74	175	27	9	14	88	.294	174	330	12	.977
1961	Baltimore	Amer.	3B-2B-SS	163	668	89	192	38	7	7	61	.287	155	334	14	.972
1962	Baltimore	Amer.	3B-SS-2B	162	634	77	192	29	9	23	86	.303	165	340	11	.979
1963	Baltimore	Amer.	3B-SS	161	589	67	148	26	4	11	67	.251	153	331	12	.976
1964	Baltimore	Amer.	3B	163	612	82	194	35	3	28	118	.317	153	327	14	.972
1965	Baltimore	Amer.	3B	144	559	81	166	25	2	18	80	.297	144	296	15	.967
1966	Baltimore	Amer.	3B	157	620	91	167	35	2	23	100	.269	174	313	12	.976
1967	Baltimore	Amer.	3B	158	610	88	164	25	5	22	77	.269	174	405	11	.980
1968	Baltimore	Amer.	3B	162	608	65	154	36	6	17	75	.253	168	353	16	.970
1969	Baltimore	Amer.	3B	156	598	73	140	21	3	23	84	.234	163	370	13	.976
1970	Baltimore	Amer.	3B	158	608	84	168	31	4	18	94	.276	157	321	17	.966
1971	Baltimore	Amer.	3B	156	589	67	160	21	1	20	92	.272	131	354	16	.968
1972	Baltimore	Amer.	3B	153	556	48	139	23	2	8	64	.250	129	333	11	.977
1973	Baltimore	Amer.	3B	155	549	53	141	17	2	9	72	.257	129	354	15	.970
1974	Baltimore	Amer.	3B	153	553	46	159	27	0	7	59	.288	115	410	18	.967
1975	Baltimore	Amer.	3B	144	482	50	97	15	1	6	53	.201	95	326	9	.979
1976	Baltimore	Amer.	3B	71	218	16	46	8	2	3	11	.211	59	126	6	.969
1977	Baltimore	Amer.	3B	24	47	3	7	2	0	1	4	.149	6	28	0	1.000
Major League Totals - 23 Years				2896	10654	1232	2848	482	68	268	1357	.267	2712	6220	264	.971

CHAMPIONSHIP SERIES RECORD

YEAR	CLUB	LEAGUE	POS.	G.	AB.	R.	H.	2B.	3B.	HR.	RBI.	B.A.	PO.	A.	E.	F.A.
1969	Baltimore	Amer.	3B	3	14	1	7	1	0	0	0	.500	6	10	0	1.000
1970	Baltimore	Amer.	3B	3	12	3	7	2	0	0	1	.583	3	5	0	1.000
1971	Baltimore	Amer.	3B	3	11	2	4	1	0	1	3	.364	4	7	0	1.000
1973	Baltimore	Amer.	3B	5	20	1	5	2	0	0	2	.250	2	14	1	.941
1974	Baltimore	Amer.	3B	4	12	1	1	0	0	1	1	.083	4	13	0	1.000
Championship Series Totals—5 Years				18	69	8	24	6	0	2	7	.348	19	49	1	.986

WORLD SERIES RECORD

Shares record by hitting home run in first series at-bat, October 5, 1966, first inning.

YEAR	CLUB	LEAGUE	POS.	G.	AB.	R.	H.	2B.	3B.	HR.	RBI.	B.A.	PO.	A.	E.	F.A.
1966	Baltimore	Amer.	3B	4	14	2	3	0	0	1	1	.214	4	6	0	1.000
1969	Baltimore	Amer.	3B	5	19	0	1	0	0	0	2	.053	1	16	0	1.000
1970	Baltimore	Amer.	3B	5	21	5	9	2	0	2	6	.429	9	14	1	.958
1971	Baltimore	Amer.	3B	7	22	2	7	0	0	0	5	.318	6	17	2	.920
World Series Totals—4 Years				21	76	9	20	2	0	3	14	.263	20	53	3	.960

FEARLESS FELLA: Plate-crowding Frank Robinson, defying pitchers to hit him, was a rare Most Valuable Player in both major leagues.

FRANK ROBINSON

The situation was s-o-o typical of Frank Robinson, the broad-backed, bulging-biceped slugger with the high tailgate and long legs that were incredibly skinny. A heavyweight from the waist up, a welterweight from the belt down, he was all man and—now—he'd become the first black manager in 100-year-old big league history.

It was opening day, 1976, at Cleveland's mammoth lakefront stadium, where a crowd of 56,715, lured more by the curiosity of the Indian field foreman's color than Cleveland's unlikely pennant prospects, attended to watch and wait.

F. Robby, as the headline writers long since had labeled the only player ever to be tabbed Most Valuable in EACH major league, was closing in on 41 years old and nothing in his immediate background of diminishing return indicated he really had the power and pizzazz to achieve 600 home runs and 3,000 hits, both within reach if—.

If, that is, as the majors' first playing pilot since

Kansas City's Hank Bauer (briefly) nearly 15 years earlier, Robinson didn't reach into the reserve of a great clutch player's past to shoulder the burden and shed the years. The Texan who grew up in California and starred in Ohio and Maryland had never been much for records or for popularity contests. Winning had been his thing.

So now, signed to play AND manage, the shrill-voiced, tilt-nosed 20-year man listed himself as Cleveland's Designated Hitter, a convenient device for a guy who felt that in this day and age a manager's place was on the bench rather than on the field. And in the first inning on April 8, 1976, the well-traveled accomplished No. 20 stepped into the batter's box as the Indians' second-spot hitter.

The crowd applauded enthusiastically. After all, the old dogs among them could remember when the great Napoleon Lajoie and graceful Tris Speaker were superstars who had led the Tribe as playing pilots. And who could forget 1948 when Lou Boudreau pushed not only all the right buttons in Cleveland's first pennant since Spoke's '20 team. Whiz-kid Lou also had a fabulous season climaxed with two homers and two singles in the one-game playoff with the Boston Red Sox.

Robinson faced the New York Yankees' Doc Medich, bat cocked and—bang!—swung, the ball arced over the fence in left-center for a home run that almost brought down the house. The dramatic blow signaled a 5-3 Cleveland victory.

Said the happy, grinning manager afterward, "I couldn't and wouldn't have wanted for anything better, but the biggest thing was that we won."

A typical retort from a team man who, as even admiring Baltimore super-scout Jim Russo said, once had "a tainted" reputation. Cleveland's general manager, Phil Seghi, the man who'd hired F. Robby as field foreman, was ecstatic.

"I never dreamed Frank would break in the way he did, but knowing him as I do after all these years, I'm not surprised by anything about that man's ability to rise to an occasion," said Seghi, who had been in Cincinnati's front office when Robinson did unto National League pitchers what he would do to the American's.

Summing up, Seghi shook his head in amazement: "My wife and I had dinner with Frank and his wife afterward and he acted as if it were just all in another day's work. Frank Robinson's doing the unusual is only usual for him."

Well-said, Phil, and so. So true.

If only the rangy righthanded Robinson who teed off on Medich on Day One as manager had been a few years younger, chances are that he would have fulfilled his ambition to manage five years at Cleveland. That was his goal.

Unfortunately, Robby was really only a shell of the superstar who had won the National League's MVP in 1961 at Cincinnati and then, traded unwisely and unwell, had duplicated at Baltimore in 1966 with one of the most inspirational examples of "I'll-show-those-guys" ever.

It's unlikely that the dark-skinned Robinson who teamed with the lighter one, Brooks, the brilliant third baseman, ever had a more effusive follower as well as loyal friend than the Orioles' special assistant to the GM, super-scout Russo. Russo, who had worked for Bill DeWitt with the old St. Louis Browns, remembered the Cincinnati club president's oral boo-boo after the super-sleuth had helped Orioles' general manager, Harry Dalton, another DeWitt disciple, put together the deal for Robinson.

Cincinnati needed pitching and Robinson was not in best favor with the front office and probably even Fred Hutchinson's field command. So, in December 1965, F. Robby was dealt to the Orioles in a then rare inter-league transaction for starting pitcher Milt Pappas, reliever Jack Baldschun and outfielder Dick Simpson.

DeWitt, justifying the deal, described Robinson as "an old 30." That did it.

An enraged Robinson, always extremely aggressive and intent in his play, was a dynamo, won the

Triple Crown to lead Baltimore to its first pennant and then signaled a four-game upset over Los Angeles with a first-game homer. In the regular season, aside from running hard, sliding savagely and fielding extremely well, he gritted his teeth to force a sore arm to make a strong, accurate throw in the pinch, Robinson hit .316 and also led the AL in homers with 49 and runs batted in with 122. He was the league's pacesetter in runs scored, too, with exactly the same number he'd knocked in.

That Robinson, hailed by Russo as "the most intense" player and "one of the best competitors" in the super-scout's more than 30 years in the game, would have done wonders managing Cleveland by leading through example.

Said Russo, "He'd come to Baltimore with that tainted reputation, but he'd matured to become the Orioles' team leader for six seasons and four World Series.

"If a player made a mistake—a mental mistake, not a physical one—Hank (Bauer) or Earl (Weaver) didn't have to get on him. Robby—'The Judge,' they called him—would do it. He could be quite critical and yet the players idolized him. Our center fielder, Paul Blair, thought he could walk on water."

Russo's smile faded. "You've seen clutch hitters. I've seen clutch hitters, but I never—repeat, never—have seen a guy who could come through as often with that big eighth or ninth-inning single or home run that tied or won a game."

Yeah, the Robinson who turned around the Orioles was something, all right, as good and dedicated as the same player who, dissatisfied with a subpar World Series at Cincinnati after winning the MVP award, responded in 1962 with an even better season—.342, 208 hits good for a .624 slugging percentage (208 hits, 51 doubles, two triples and 39 homers), and 136 RBIs and 134 scored.

Inspired, which he was more often than not after he got over a pistol-packing papa reputation in Cincinnati, Robinson was a one-man gang, a terror. Uh-huh, even if in zeal he slid so hard one time into Eddie Mathews, then Milwaukee's no-nonsense

third baseman, that when Robby got up to exchange words with an angry Mathews, Eddie decked him. To Frank, that was all part of the job—of the game—so no hard feelings. Just a couple of lumps on his fighting phiz.

But at Cleveland, despite that first-game homer, the platoon sergeant couldn't lead his troops into action. That hurt. Robinson got into only 49 games in 1975, hitting just .237 with nine homers and 24 RBIs. He vowed that '76, the centennial of big league baseball, would be his last as a player. He played rarely, getting into only 15 games and batting just .224 with three homers among 10 hits good for 15 runs.

So only 57 hits short of 3,000 and merely 14 homers short of 600, tempting proximity that would have prompted many a player—especially one with managerial clout—to make himself obnoxious in a bid for batting milestones, F. Robinson put down his quivering bat and hung up his glove. His career batting average, which had been .300 even in the National League, was .294 for nearly 21 seasons.

Really, therefore, for most of his two-plus seasons as the trail-blazing black pioneer manager in the majors, Robinson did not have his most important weapon, his own blazing bat. Considering that Cleveland hadn't done well for years, his 79-80 record for fourth place in 1975 wasn't bad, and his 81-78 figure for fourth again in '76 marked the most victories for the Tribe since 1968.

At the time of his dismissal in a draggy 1977 season, one in which the Indians bit the dust with a sorry 71-90 mark under Robinson and Jeff Torborg, Frank graciously wished well his former coach, a catcher he had encountered in an ill-fated 1972 season at Los Angeles, probably the most dismal in F. Robby's glamorous career. Third time around back at Baltimore, Robinson won manager-of-the-year acclaim with a 1989 near-miss with a ball club that had finished last.

Of friend Frank's first failure to achieve that five-year managerial plan, Russo had this observation:

"I'm afraid not enough of Frank's players had his

dedication to the game or, at least, couldn't sustain it. Early, I thought I saw in the Indians the earmark of the man himself, but then, as I told him later, I saw a difference. I thought they'd quit on him and, I'm sorry to say, that the very blacks who I thought would rally around him the most seemed unable to put-out well enough or long enough for him."

Strong language, but honestly given by a white man sorrying for the black man he admired. Frank Robinson himself, though he'd prepped for that precedent-shattering berth by putting in six winter seasons managing in the Caribbean, didn't take it so hard. No one understands the hard way more than a black who has lived it.

Take, for instance, "Pencils," as he was called in Oakland because of those bird legs. Born in Beaumont, Tex., youngest of 11 children in a broken home, he never knew his father well, but he was pleased later to be able to buy a home for a mother he referred to "as most deserving," quietly observing that a woman who could raise a football-sized family deserved a medal and a place to display it.

The Robinsons grew up in Oakland, Calif., and attended McClymonds High School, almost legendary for athletes it turned out, including Curt Flood and Vada Pinson, who followed Robinson into the Cincinnati outfield. Frank had a tall, stringy schoolmate named Bill Russell. By coincidence, Russell not only would become equally great in his sport—basketball—but also would break the color barrier as a coach.

Robinson, 6-foot-1 and stoop-shouldered, was not yet filled out to the muscular upper-torsoed 194 that stopped pitches unflinchingly like a human pin-cushion. Before he was 18, in 1953 he signed with Cincinnati's astute talent hunter, scout Bobby Mattick. Why the Reds?

"Only because they gave me the best offer," said Robinson, to whom in 1953 a few thousand dollars seemed almost as sizable as the $180,000 he'd get from Cleveland as player-manager.

At Ogden, Utah, in the Pioneer League, playing

first base and third as well as the outfield, Frank immediately began to justify the front office expenditure okayed by Gabe Paul, the former Rochester bat boy who had succeeded his friend and mentor, Warren Giles, as Reds' GM when Giles became National League president.

Within a year, though, the Reds' investment was jeopardized and Robinson's future imperiled by the most serious of the mishaps this hardy athlete would endure over the years in which he felt both pain and growing pains.

At Columbia, S.C., in the South Atlantic League, Robinson hit almost as well in 1954 as he had out West in '53, but, suddenly, his arm began to feel when he threw, as he put it, as if "someone had stuck me with a needle."

In winter ball, the pain was so intense that the man with the high-pain threshold was forced to quit. In 1955 spring training, the arm went dead. So did Robinson's batting average and his second season at Columbia, where he played in only 80 games and batted just .263. He was angrier than when he'd reported in Carolina and learned that the color of his skin was more significant than it had been in California.

About the arm, doctors would give different evaluations. A bone spur, one would say. Calcium deposit, said another. Another almost boiled over the high-blooded 20-year-old kid's quick temper by saying there was nothing wrong, period.

At spring training with Cincinnati at Tampa, Fla., in 1956, Robinson found in Birdie Tebbetts a psychology major who practiced what he had learned at Providence College. The Reds' manager brushed off the rookie's throwing difficulties and, purposely within earshot of F. Robby at the batting cage, the former catcher would suggest that here would soon be one of the great hitters.

Robinson responded so well that, even though his throwing was only poor to fair at first, Tebbetts stuck him in the Cincinnati lineup and Robinson responded in 1956 with a spectacular freshman season. He crowded the plate and couldn't be driven back even though he was pinked or plunked 20 times, a record for a first-year man. And he tied a more meaningful rookie mark, belting 38 home runs, tying a high set by Wally Berger with the old Boston Braves in 1931. With the high-scoring Reds, who powered their way home a surprising third, the newcomer in left field hit .290 with 83 RBIs. And as muscle men such as Ted Kluszewski, Wally Post, Gus Bell, Ed Bailey and Robinson teed off, rookie F. Robby led in runs scored, 122.

A good, instinctive runner, Jackie Robinson's (sur) namesake also had the knack of begging, borrowing—or stealing—his way around the bases to score.

Still, he was just a boy, and boys will be boys, black or white or purple with pink polka dots. And to the annoyance of such a veteran as Don Newcombe, for instance, he'd lay prone on the outfield grass, spreading the oral manure with the groundskeepers when he was out of the lineup.

First, he was skulled in 1958 by Washington's Camilo Pascual in spring training, 1958, and, gun-shy for the first time, he needed the All-Star interlude to dig in as of before, but he fell from .322 to .269. But by 1959 he'd proved to himself—and all others—that he could take a blow without flinching, driving in 125 runs with 36 homers and hitting .311. He even stole 18 bases, a pretty good total for that era.

"I wish we'd run more because it helps a ball club win," said Robinson prophetically. "If the other club knows you're not going to steal, they don't have to throw as many fastballs with men on, but can use the curve and change-up more."

Nine times a .300 hitter, F. Robby early disturbed author teammate Jim Brosnan as too nonchalant, but Fred Hutchinson, who had succeeded Tebbetts as manager, noted Frank was "a big guy with a lumbering gait that makes it look as if he's not hustling."

The crisis came in February 1961 when, climax-

ing problem-child attitude, a chip-on-the-shoulder racist temporarily, Robinson got into it with the law when, beered up, he was hauled into a district police station with a polished Italian Beretta automatic handgun he'd brandished after a bar argument.

"A foolish thing, foolish," F. Robby repeated after drawing a fine and court costs, totaling $301.30. The indiscretion hurt his image with the Reds' management and fans.

The center cut of Robinson's Cincinnati career came in DeWitt's first two years of operating the Reds after acquiring them from the estate of Powell Crosley. Brosnan, the pitcher turned part-time writer, saluted Robinson's new leadership in the .323 pennant-winning season of 1961, one in which Frank homered 37 times and drove in 124 runs. And then, as mentioned earlier after he'd hit only a tepid .200 and permitted a flyball to fall in against the Yankees in the '61 World Series, Robinson outdid himself in '62.

Injured and sick, he leveled off considerably the next year, dropping to .259, but by the time DeWitt dealt him to Baltimore after the 1965 season, he'd just come off a season of 33 homers and 113 RBIs, a year in which he'd batted .296. He'd forgotten racial differences that once had led him to slug the Phillies' Robin Roberts in an argument. And he'd seemed to weather what DeWitt considered personal indiscretions.

Still, as Branch Rickey's former office boy and disciple at St. Louis, DeWitt prided himself that he knew just when to get rid of a player, meaning as B.R. always did, a year too soon rather than a year too late. Besides, Robby's reported $60,000 salary was large for Cincinnati and its cozy Crosley Field, especially back there in the mid-1960s.

So the deed was done, the three-for-one deal that was supposed to give the Reds important pitching help and an outfielder who was a sweet-swinging sleeper as a hitter. But Simpson didn't cut it, Pappas wasn't the golden Greek of Baltimore as a starter and Baldschun wasn't a Wilcy Moore or

Firbo Marberry or Hugh Casey or Joe Page as a re-liever or any of the then more recent big-name knights of the bullpen.

Meanwhile, Frank Robinson had come a long way from the boyhood when, mother Ruth Shaw remembered, his father had bought him a bat, ball and glove at only three. "Pencils" had been so sen-sitive about those toothpick legs that he wore a couple of extra pair of socks, McClymonds coach George Powles remembered, and began the custom of wearing pants long and cutaway stirrups high so that the white sanitary stockings showed more. Too much, in fact.

In high school, twice bloodied, he'd quit foot-ball, but, though barely just an average student, he'd shown Powles the instinct that indicated he had the athletic smarts. Shy, a loner except when on the playing field, he had such powerful wrists, Powles recalled, that he could check a swing better in the middle of a cut than any hitter the sagacious coach ever saw, majors or minors.

Frank came a long way before he was jolted by that trade from Cincinnati, which he regarded as home. Big George Crowe, bespectacled black who was father-confessor to many young Afro-Ameri-cans, could see that the anger which burned within Robinson had now been directed toward the play-ing-field situation rather than racial discrimination.

"He was spoiled," said Crowe, "but, remember, he was very young and such a poor boy that, heck, the $6,000 major league minimum salary, doubled within a year, made him seem rich. So you get the glamour, the big car and, if you're like Frank was then years ago, a gun, too. But he really matured."

Right on, George, and with the Orioles he was a crusader, the exact time of day of that December deal—4:20 P.M.—etched deeply in his memory.

Opening day, 1966, exactly 10 years since he'd broken in with the Reds, F. Robby stood up there for the first time in the American League, slightly crouched, bat held high and the arms vir-tually in the strike zone as if the gutty guy were saying, "Okay, big boy, here I am. Let's see you drive me back."

Sure enough, first time up at Boston opening day, he was hit with a pitch and trotted down to first base. He'd passed the AL's test.

Later in the game, Frank Robinson hit his first American League home run, and Baltimore won. Next day, first time up, F. Robinson homered again and then B. Robinson homered, too, and the Ori-oles were off and swinging to 12 victories in their first 13 games.

In early May back there at Baltimore's Municipal Stadium, Luis Tiant, the canny Cuban who later would make a grand comeback with Boston, was squirting tobacco juice figuratively in hitters' eyes for Cleveland. El Tiante had pitched three straight shutouts and retired the first batters when F. Robinson languidly strolled up to the plate, head down, like the weary old athlete DeWitt had sug-gested he might be.

Pow! Robby came alive on a low inside fastball. The ball went out deep to left field. Over the fence. Over the head of the awed spectators. Over the back wall and, finally, it landed in a parking lot, where slide-rule engineers went to work. The ball, they said, had traveled 451 feet on the fly and stopped 540 feet from home plate.

It was the first ball ever hit out of Memorial Sta-dium. Today, there is a flagpole on the spot where Robby's rocket left the bleacher area. On the flag-pole is a banner. It has one simple word—"Here."

Legs bandaged to protect a charley horse, the motivated man played and slid hard, breaking up double plays and taking an extra base. And at bat he homered and homered and pitcher Jack Fisher smiled and smiled, explaining:

"Before the season, I bet Pappas five cigars that Robinson would hit 25 homers, five more he hits 30, five on 35 and—."

Bless Winston Churchill's king-sized stogies, Fisher could have been cigar-enough rich to open his own tobacco shop. Robby rapped 49, and Warren Giles, National League president, grumbled at his headquarters in Cincinnati:

"I don't like to see the National League trade a superstar—any superstar—to the American League. We need to keep our own box office."

Younger Baltimore players had heard that Robinson was a clubhouse lawyer, a player difficult to know and like, but Hank Bauer, the hard-nosed former Marine then managing the Orioles, said:

"Anybody who can adopt a child can't be all bad. I talked to Willie Mays about Frank, and Willie said we've got one helluva ballplayer. All I know is that Robinson averaged 32 homers and 100 RBIs a year for 10 seasons at Cincinnati. I'll take that."

Bauer got more, of course, and Dick Sisler, who had coached at Cincinnati and then filled in "for a dying Hutchinson as manager," set the record clear on at least one point:

"Robinson was a leader, a cheerleader, in the game more than anyone on the club, even including men on the bench. He'd tell guys about different pitchers—everything. Only thing I can figure is that the front office wasn't aware of how many ways he helped the club."

Baltimore knew—from the start—and through pennant seasons of 1966, '69, '70 and '71.

By then, sure and certain, the unofficial "judge" of kangaroo courts by which Orioles fined each other and just about anyone else who invaded the Baltimore clubhouse, Frank Robinson was as loose as ashes except when the game was on. No longer was he the shy kid who attended Xavier University briefly when he wasn't spending more time in a movie house than the chewed-out gum stuck under the seats.

Finally, with Baltimore's blessings and thanks, Frank Robinson was dealt back to the National League, to the constantly contending Dodgers at Los Angeles in his native California. He went out there in 1972, then going on 37, and, hurt and perhaps pressing, he hit only .259 with just 19 homers and 59 RBIs in 103 games. He didn't like manager

Walter Alston too much, either, though Alston managed the Dodgers successfully for nearly a quarter century.

F. Robby had become almost too articulate. He knew how to hit and he'd teach it. He knew the game and he'd help umpire it, especially Emmett Ashford, whom he would have undressed as well as addressed if teammates hadn't pulled him off the first black umpire. Frank had his own ideas about managing—his own ambitions—and he didn't mind voicing them.

At times it seemed as if, proving his impartiality as well as understanding of players, the guy was speaking too much about that burning desire, the one that, fulfilled, helped Larry Doby, the American League's first black ballplayer, move in near mid-season, 1978, as skipper of the Chicago White Sox. For years folks had been suggesting Doby would be the first black manager or maybe Maury Wills, but it was Frank Robinson who broke the barrier and proved certainly no worse if not better. Ergo, taking his dismissal with poise, F. Robby made it easier for Doby and other men of a different color who would follow by becoming leaders, too, especially after his success and Tito Gaston's at Toronto in '92.

Managing aside, I feel as if there was too much a tendency to think of the aging Robinson as almost a freak because of that managerial breakthrough. Actually, at nearly 38, hitting .266, he still belted 30 homers and drove in 97 runs after the Dodgers dealt him down the highway toward Disneyland. The trade a year later to Cleveland was as obvious as the broken-bridge, tilted tip of his nose. Frank Robinson was sought on the shores of Lake Erie for his date with dugout destiny.

First, yes, he would break in dramatically as manager with that opening game homer in 1975 and he'd squabble with the Perry brothers, Gaylord and Jim, a couple of Carolinians who probably didn't cotton too much to having a "colored" call the shots. But the great Gaylord insisted it was only a ploy to get one buck more from management for

pitching than F. Robby was getting for more managing than hitting.

Now, if it had been only a few years earlier,
Gaylord wouldn't have gotten away with that approach, and I'm not talking about his having to
eat—or Robinson—a knuckle sandwich. It's just
that in the decade of the 1960s, despite the presence
of Willie Mays, Henry Aaron, Roberto Clemente,
Mickey Mantle, Harmon Killebrew, Sandy Koufax,
Brooks Robinson, Pete Rose, Willie McCovey and
Carl Yastrzemski, the player who got the MOST
votes for the annual Most Valuable Player award
was the only man ever MVP in each league.

Yep, Frank Robinson.

FRANK ROBINSON
Born August 31, 1935, at Beaumont, Tex.
Height 6-1 Weight 194
Threw and batted righthanded.
Named to Hall of Fame, 1982.

YEAR	CLUB	LEAGUE	POS.	G.	AB.	R.	H.	2B.	3B.	HR.	RBI.	B.A.	PO.	A.	E.	F.A.
1953	Ogden	Pion.	O-3B-1B	72	270	70	94	20	6	17	83	.348	105	28	18	.881
1954	Tulsa	Tex.	2B-3B	8	30	4	8	0	0	0	1	.267	17	15	1	.970
1954	Columbia	Sally	OF-3-2B	132	491	112	165	32	9	25	110	.336	258	63	18	.947
1955	Columbia	Sally	OF-1B	80	243	50	64	15	7	12	52	.263	203	3	4	.981
1956	Cincinnati	Nat.	OF	152	572	122	166	27	6	38	83	.290	323	5	8	.976
1957	Cincinnati	Nat.	OF-1B	150	611	97	197	29	5	29	75	.322	487	36	6	.989
1958	Cincinnati	Nat.	OF-3B	148	554	90	149	25	6	31	83	.269	314	24	6	.983
1959	Cincinnati	Nat.	1B-OF	146	540	106	168	31	4	36	125	.311	1049	78	18	.984
1960	Cincinnati	Nat.	1-OF-3	139	464	86	138	33	6	31	83	.297	775	62	10	.988
1961	Cincinnati	Nat.	OF-3B	153	545	117	176	32	7	37	124	.323	284	15	3	.990
1962	Cincinnati	Nat.	OF	162	609	134	208	51	2	39	136	.342	315	10	2	.994
1963	Cincinnati	Nat.	OF-1B	140	482	79	125	19	3	21	91	.259	238	13	4	.984
1964	Cincinnati	Nat.	OF	156	568	103	174	38	6	29	96	.306	279	7	4	.986
1965	Cincinnati (a)	Nat.	OF	156	582	109	172	33	5	33	113	.296	282	5	3	.990
1966	Baltimore	Amer.	OF-1B	155	576	122	182	34	2	49	122	.316	282	6	5	.983
1967	Baltimore	Amer.	OF-1B	129	479	83	149	23	7	30	94	.311	207	8	2	.991
1968	Baltimore	Amer.	OF-1B	130	421	69	113	27	1	15	52	.268	193	5	7	.996
1969	Baltimore	Amer.	OF-1B	148	539	111	166	19	5	32	100	.308	367	19	5	.987
1970	Baltimore	Amer.	OF-1B	132	471	88	144	24	1	25	78	.306	262	11	4	.986
1971	Baltimore (b)	Amer.	OF-1B	133	455	82	128	16	2	28	99	.281	449	20	11	.977
1972	Los Angeles (c)	Nat.	OF	103	342	41	86	6	1	19	59	.251	168	6	6	.967
1973	California	Amer.	OF	147	534	85	142	29	0	30	97	.266	38	3	1	.976
1974	Calif. (d)-Cleve.	Amer.	1B-OF	144	477	81	117	27	3	22	68	.245	23	0	1	.958
1975	Cleveland (e)	Amer.	DH-PH	49	118	19	28	5	0	9	24	.237	0	0	0	.000
1976	Cleveland	Amer.	1B-OF	36	67	5	15	0	0	3	10	.224	11	0	0	1.000
National League Totals - 11 Years				1605	5869	1084	1759	324	51	343	1068	.300	4514	261	70	.986
American League Totals - 10 Years				1203	4137	745	1184	204	21	243	744	.286	1832	72	36	.981
Major League Totals - 21 Years				2808	10006	1829	2943	528	72	586	1812	.294	6346	333	106	.984

a Traded to Baltimore Orioles for Outfielder Dick Simpson and Pitchers Milt Pappas and Jack Baldschun, December 9, 1965.
b Traded with Pitcher Pete Richert to Los Angeles Dodgers for Pitchers Doyle Alexander and Bob O'Brien, Catcher Sergio Robles and First Baseman-Outfielder Royle Stillman, December 2, 1971.
c Traded with Infielders Billy Grabarkewitz and Bob Valentine and Pitchers Bill Singer and Mike Strahler to California Angels for Third Baseman Ken McMullen and Pitcher Andy Messersmith, November 28, 1972.
d Released on waivers to Cleveland Indians, September 12, 1974; Indians sent Outfielder Rusty Torres and Catcher Ken Suarez to Angels, December 4, 1974, as part of deal.
e Player-manager.

CHAMPIONSHIP SERIES RECORD

Shares major league records for most at-bats, inning (2), October 3, 1970, fourth inning; hitting home run in first series at-bat, October 4, 1969, fourth inning.

YEAR	CLUB	LEAGUE	POS.	G.	AB.	R.	H.	2B.	3B.	HR.	RBI.	B.A.	PO.	A.	E.	F.A.
1969	Baltimore	Amer.	OF	3	12	1	4	2	0	1	2	.333	2	0	1	.677
1970	Baltimore	Amer.	OF	3	10	3	2	0	0	1	2	.200	2	0	0	1.000
1971	Baltimore	Amer.	OF	3	12	2	1	1	0	0	1	.083	7	0	0	1.000
Championship Series Totals—3 Years				9	34	6	7	3	0	2	5	.206	11	0	1	.917

WORLD SERIES RECORD

YEAR	CLUB	LEAGUE	POS.	G.	AB.	R.	H.	2B.	3B.	HR.	RBI.	B.A.	PO.	A.	E.	F.A.
1961	Cincinnati	Nat.	OF	5	15	3	3	2	0	1	4	.200	5	0	0	1.000
1966	Baltimore	Amer.	OF	4	14	4	4	0	1	2	3	.286	6	0	0	1.000
1969	Baltimore	Amer.	OF	5	16	2	3	0	0	1	1	.188	13	0	0	1.000
1970	Baltimore	Amer.	OF	5	22	5	6	0	0	2	4	.273	7	0	0	1.000
1971	Baltimore	Amer.	OF	7	25	5	7	0	0	2	2	.280	12	0	0	1.000
World Series Totals—5 Years				26	92	19	23	2	1	8	14	.250	43	0	0	1.000

TRAILBLAZER: A versatile all-around athlete, Jackie Robinson stiffarmed tradition by becoming the first black big league player in this century.

JACKIE ROBINSON

In the Twentieth Century, big league baseball saw the game go from day to night, from coast to coast and then border to border in growth and expansion. By far, in this judgment, the most significant change of this century was the one by which a blue-black athlete named Jack Roosevelt Robinson opened the 1947 season at first base for the old Brooklyn Dodgers.

At the end of baseball's first 100 years, a time when the biggest stars were blacks, including Willie Mays, Henry Aaron, Roberto Clemente, Frank Robinson, Ernie Banks and Bob Gibson, among others, it was hard to realize the impact of the break with tradition by which Robinson became first a minor league infielder at Montreal in 1946 and then, as mentioned, broke into the bigs with Brooklyn in '47.

"Bigs"—that's a colorful colloquialism brought into baseball by the blacks, along with "ribbies" for RBIs and at least one incestuous vulgarism that turned on corpulent former National League President Warren Giles as completely as if he'd been told he'd have to go on a starvation diet. Giles made the horrendous hyphenation automatic grounds for ejection from a ball game.

As far back as 1872, only three years after the Cincinnati Red Stockings began touring as professionals, a Negro infielder named Bud Fowler, appropriately from the home of baseball's Hall of Fame, Cooperstown, N. Y., played with an otherwise all-white team at New Castle, Pa. And in 1884, a well-educated black man, Moses Fleetwood Walker, caught 41 games for Toledo at a time the Ohio Metropolis and the American Association both were in the major leagues.

Four years later, as a result in part of the backlash of the Civil War's ill-fated Reconstruction Era, the Negro disappeared from the bigs for almost a half-century. It reflects absolutely no credit on Adrian (Cap) Anson that the baseball pioneer, the game's first 3,000-hit player, was prominent in the prejudice by which an unwritten law, a mislabeled gentlemen's agreement, deprived men of one color of equal opportunity in the national pastime.

Negro league baseball, to which former college star and World War II lieutenant Jackie Robinson turned in 1945, was largely guess and by golly, an irregular tour by bus along the tanbark trail. To make ends meet and to paper the pockets of the bosses, the dusky traveling salesman of the diamond played as many mid-week exhibitions barnstorming the nation's byways as they did league games weekends in the metropolises they supposedly represented.

Except for legendary Satchel Paige and homerhitting catcher Josh Gibson, they played for peanuts. So Robinson was receptive when he was approached by scout Clyde Sukeforth and told that Branch Rickey wanted to see him. Robinson was certain Rickey, then president of the Dodgers, was following through with his announced intentions to form the Brooklyn Brown Dodgers in what would be the United States League, an all-black circuit.

This was, of course, a smoke screen, a red herring by which Rickey had sought to cast aside suspicion as he assigned sharp-eyed scouts to look over the best of the black talent available. Although his Christian conscience certainly glowed over the thought of doing a good deed at a time New York's feisty little mayor, Fiorello LaGuardia, was agitating for anti-discrimination in all areas, Rickey was motivated most by the opportunity to explore virgin territory.

As father of the farm system, the incredibly successful self-development program by which a major league club raises its own talent like home-grown tomatoes, Rickey had enabled rag-tag St. Louis to compete with and then surpass wealthier New York and Chicago franchises in the National League. He'd done so well that by the time he was eased out of an $80,000-a-year job by Sam Breadon after the 1942 season, the Cardinals just had won the pennant and world championship with one of the finest young teams in baseball history.

Rickey, taking over at Brooklyn, where freespending Larry MacPhail quickly had put together a winner, winced at trying to compete against St. Louis over any period of time with a veteran team and limited supply from the farms. He had two ideas, one of which he bounced off the bank-operated Brooklyn ball club's board of directors and the other merely off the president of the Brooklyn Trust Company, George McLaughlin.

At a time the rest of baseball was retrenching, Rickey told the board, he proposed to sign 15 and 16-year-olds, gambling that an end of World War II within two or three years would give the Dodgers an edge. On McLaughlin, a former New York police commissioner and civic leader with a deep knowledge of social affairs, Rickey sprang his trial balloon. "We're going to beat the bushes and we'll take whatever comes out," said Rickey, "and that might include a Negro player or two."

McLaughlin had no objections and so B. R., who liked nothing better than a chance to play chess with human pawns, began to make the plans that more than two years afterward in late August 1945, just a couple of weeks after the war ended, would have Robinson seated across his desk in the Dodgers' office on Brooklyn's Montague Street.

In what would amount to a historic baseball confrontation, the 26-year-old Robinson found himself facing a bespectacled, bushy-browed man of 63, chewing a cigar and able to run the vocal scale with pipes that would have been at home on a pulpit or on the Chautauqua circuit.

The young man Rickey studied with eyes alternately squinting and bulging from beneath those bushy brows was almost six feet, dark skinned, close to 200 pounds. His shoulders were wide, his legs strong and heavy—almost too heavy— and he walked pigeon-toed with the springy step of the track man he had been.

He had what Rickey sized up immediately as a sensitive, intelligent face with strong features, a high forehead, wide and somewhat brooding eyes, a full mouth and determined chin. He smiled easily, but laughed infrequently. And he spoke rapidly with a high-pitched voice and with diction completely free of the thick-toned dialect usually associated with the uneducated Negro.

What Rickey didn't know about Robinson's background and ability wasn't worth knowing. The old man had had the younger one cased completely. He knew that Jackie had been born in Cairo, Ga., January 31, 1919. A year later, his father had deserted his mother, who, left with five children, took her brood overland to Pasadena, Calif., where she worked as a domestic servant to raise and feed them.

It wasn't easy. In fact, years later when he was a high-salaried star and a father expected to serve a good example for his children at the table, Robinson related that wife Rachel had to remind and coax him to eat green vegetables. You see, he'd grown up, practically, on day-old bread dunked in sugar and milk. The habit didn't help his sweet-tooth tendency toward diabetes.

As the youngest child, Jackie was taken care of by his sister, Willie Mae, two years older, so that Mrs. Robinson could work for the family's support. When Willie Mae went to school, Jackie tagged along and played in the schoolyard until his sister got out of class.

School authorities, who didn't want the responsibility for a three-year-old on their hands, complained to Mrs. Robinson, but they couldn't resist the logic of the woman's reply. If she had to stay home to mind the baby in the family, she couldn't work and the family would have to go on relief, and wouldn't it be cheaper for the city to let her little man play in the sandbox?

When he was old enough to leave the sandbox and go to school on his own, Jackie reached a point where he proudly told his mother she could save food by not fixing a lunch for him. He was the best athlete in his class and the other kids brought him sandwiches and even dimes for the movies so they could play on his team.

"So you might say that I turned professional at an early age and that I had to win from the start if I wanted to eat as well as the rest of my friends," Robinson reminisced when he announced his retirement as a player in January 1957.

Years later, when interviewed for this series about baseball, Jackie talked tenderly about his mother, who died in 1968:

"Yes, I did what I could for her, but it was nothing," he said. "She was a great lady. With no education, to do what she did for us kids was fantastic."

A deeply religious woman and extremely well-adjusted, Mrs. Robinson wrote her Georgia relatives when she was living on Pasadena's Pepper Street and earning just eight dollars a week, "I'm living on the outskirts of heaven."

Pepper Street was a combination of Mexicans, Japanese and Negroes, Robinson recalled, and kids there raided orchards for plums, oranges and grapes, and they threw clods of dirt at passing automobiles, taking off in all directions when the police approached. Then a man named Carl Anderson came along and organized sports teams and the trouble disappeared. This made an impression on Robinson and led to his adult interest in sports as a curb for juvenile delinquency.

Jackie's oldest brother, Mack, became a celebrity of the neighborhood, a track star who finished a close second to Jesse Owens in the 200 meters at the 1936 Olympic Games in Berlin.

Jack (Be Quick) Robinson was fast, not as fast as Mack, but how he could twist, turn and change pace. He went first to Pasadena Junior College and then to UCLA, combining a part scholarship with campus jobs, lettering in four sports at both schools. When he was named to *Sports Illustrated*'s Silver Anniversary All-America in 1965, he was labeled UCLA's only four-sport letterman—baseball, basketball, track and football.

In track, Jack broke the Pacific Coast Conference's broad-jump record. In basketball, he was high scorer in the league. In football one year, he averaged 12 yards a carry to become the leading ground gainer in the country. The only other baseball player who might have been his all-around equal would have been another great second baseman, Frank Frisch, a generation earlier.

Robinson wasn't a scholar. His mother wanted him to become a doctor or a lawyer, but he wanted physical education, to be an athlete and to coach. To teach, Jack would have had to go back to the campus at Westwood to pass that elusive French.

Over the protests of his mother and of the man he most admired, the Rev. Karl Downs, the Methodist minister for whom he taught Sunday School, Robinson left college as soon as his athletic eligibility ended in his senior year. He thought he could help better to make ends meet at home, he said. First, he worked as an assistant director with the National Youth Administration, a pet project of Mrs. Franklin D. Roosevelt. Then, in 1941, he played professional football for the Los Angeles Bulldogs.

En route back by ship from the season-ending game in Hawaii, Jackie Robinson was playing cards

in the ship's lounge when he saw a seaman painting the portholes black. That's how he and the other passengers found out that the Japanese had attacked the American fleet at Pearl Harbor.

A few months later, he did basic training in the Army and was transferred to a cavalry troop at Fort Riley, Kan. He got into Officer Candidate's School and was commissioned a lieutenant in cavalry. Chipped bones from an old ankle injury kept him from overseas duty and he was discharged a first lieutenant in November of 1944.

Returning to civilian life, hopeful of following friend Carl Anderson in the social service field with youngsters, Robby coached basketball at Samuel Houston, a black college in Austin, Tex., and then joined the Kansas City Monarchs in 1945 as a shortstop at $400 a month. A fellow soldier, Bob Alexander, who pitched for the Monarchs, had urged him to write Tom Baird, a white man who ran the itchy-footed Kansas City club in partnership with J. L. Wilkinson.

Although the Negro leagues were drawing well, despite a shortage of manpower, there was considerable informality that bugged the college-trained, Army-disciplined Robinson. Paige, for instance, would pitch only two or three innings, travel by private car instead of by bus with the team and would work for various all-star teams the rest of the week.

One day at Baltimore, the Monarchs played a lopsided game. In one inning they scored five runs. Only two showed on the scoreboard. The Kansas City club looked for the official scorer to straighten it out, but he had disappeared. He got bored with the game and went home early, reminisced a rueful Robinson, not at all certain the .345 he supposedly hit for the Monarchs was at all official.

Back in April, when the Red Sox were seeking favorable Sunday baseball legislation in Massachusetts, Robinson, Sam Jethroe and another black who would not make the majors had been flown into Boston for a one-day tryout with the Bosox. Elfish, elderly Hugh Duffy, who had hit .438 for

Boston back in 1894, conducted the workout, and gave a noncommittal all's-well afterward, but nothing had come of it. Still, even if only to get to New York and into another Negro league of more substance, Robinson was glad to sit across from Branch Rickey at Brooklyn on August 28, 1945.

They'd hardly shaken hands when Rickey asked unexpectedly, "Do you have a girl, Jackie?"

Robinson stammered slowly, "I don't know."

"What do you mean, you don't know?" Rickey retorted.

The truth is, Jackie didn't know whether pretty Rachel Isum, the UCLA coed he'd met, really would wait. Although she had been his constant companion on campus, she'd almost broken their engagement when he told her he was going to barnstorm with the Monarchs. An Army-necessitated absence was one thing, but traipsing around with a traveling ball club, eating bad food, sleeping in poor hotels and sleeping irregularly was something else again.

Over the years, Branch Rickey played Dan Cupid often. For one thing, he'd had a long, happy married life himself. For another, he felt that all ballplayers were better off married. This would be especially true of a black to whom he would offer the opportunity and challenge of the lonely life as a trailblazer.

"Of course you have a girl," said Mr. Rickey, "and you ought to marry her as quick as you can."

Then the Mahatma startled the young black man by telling him that he wanted to bring him into organized professional baseball at Montreal, then in the Triple-A International League, and maybe even with the Dodgers themselves.

For three hours, former lawyer Rickey grilled Robinson as if the old man were a prosecuting attorney. He knew that this was no Uncle Tom, but a black who had spoken out against discrimination and prejudice from his boyhood.

"Talk back," as the whites put it. He was a man of a different color who had endured a service court-martial—and won—because of a hassle. He disobeyed a surly bus driver who was ignorant as well as biased. Jim Crow was outlawed on an Army post. Robinson didn't have to sit in the back of Uncle Sam's bus.

No, Rickey had not tapped Amos 'n Andy or a Stepin Fetchit caricature or even old Satch Paige or young Roy Campanella, both of them more pliable than Robinson. He had chosen a black who would fight or at least bristle at even a hint of racial prejudice. B.R.'s job was to convince the proud athlete not to fight.

In this pivotal moment in baseball history, the old boy was never better. He portrayed an insulting waiter in a restaurant, a haughty room clerk in a Southern hotel, a sarcastic railroad conductor. Then the dialogue went like this:

"Suppose they throw at your head?"

"Mr. Rickey, they've been throwing at my head for a long time."

"Suppose I'm an opposing player in the heat of an important ball game. Suppose I collide with you at second base. When I get up, I yell, 'You dirty black bastard.' What do you do then?"

Rickey's executive assistant, former newspaperman Arthur Mann, an observing witness, saw Robinson blink, lick his lips and swallow.

"Mr. Rickey," Jackie said, puzzled, "do you want a ballplayer who's afraid to fight back?"

Almost savagely, Rickey responded, "I want a ballplayer with guts enough not to fight back. You've got to do this job with base hits and stolen bases and by fielding groundballs, Jackie. Nothing else!"

Rickey stormed from behind his desk, removed his jacket, Mann wrote later, and said:

"Now, I'm playing against you in the World Series. I'm a hotheaded player. I want to win that game, so I go into you spikes first. But you don't give ground. You stand there and you jab the ball into my ribs and the umpire yells, 'Out!' I flare—all I see is your face, that black face, right on top of me—so I haul off and I punch you right in the cheek."

An oversized white fist swung through the air and barely missed Robinson's sweating face. The dark eyes blinked but the head didn't move.

"What do you do?" Rickey roared.

The heavy lips trembled for an instant and then opened. "Mr. Rickey," Jackie Robinson whispered, "I've got two cheeks—is that it?"

Branch Rickey nodded and blinked away the mist from his own eyes, Arthur Mann said. That scene assured success in B. R.'s bold venture, the noble experiment, because Robinson was some ballplayer as he proved in a 10-year major league career which landed him in the Hall of Fame the first time he was eligible, 1962.

Robinson married the girl and accepted the scorn and skepticism, the segregation and the threats which followed first the announcement that he would play for Montreal in 1946 and then the delayed word that he would move up to Brooklyn in '47. Not even an umpire has to live as lonely or as neutral a life as that one black man did in a white man's game.

Jackie didn't drink or smoke, but, my, how he could move around a ball field. He didn't have a shortstop's arm, scouts Clyde Sukeforth and George Sisler agreed, but he'd be brilliant on the right side of the infield. And when he made a particularly outstanding stop in spring training in Florida with the Montreal club, Rickey exclaimed, "Did you ever see a human being make that kind of play?"

"Mr. Rickey," said Mississippi-born Clay Hopper, the man for whom Robinson would play at Montreal, "do you think he IS human?"

Rickey was getting it from all sides. The minor leagues' president, Judge W. G. Bramham, a southerner, called B. R. a "carpetbagger" and said, "Father Divine will have to look to his laurels, for we can expect Rickey Temple to be in the course of construction in Harlem soon."

Down in Florida, where Robinson was cruelly treated that first spring with Montreal, Hopper wondered how the publicized rookie would hit topflight pitching. Former Cincinnati star Paul Derringer, working for Indianapolis, said he'd help an old friend find out.

"Tell you what I'm going to do, Clay," said Derringer. "I'm going to knock him down a couple of times and see what makes him tick."

The first time Robinson dropped to avoid a high and tight pitch, he got up and singled. The next time Derringer decked him, Jackie leaped up and lined a curve into left-center for three bases.

"He'll do, Clay," Derringer yelled from the mound to the Montreal bench.

Opening at Jersey City, after games were canceled in Florida towns which would not stand for a Negro competing with whites and after Jackie and bride Rachel were compelled to leave the training base at Sanford, the bell rang—and Robinson came out fighting with his bat, glove and talented legs.

First time up, Jackie grounded out and, over-eager, he made an error, but he put on a helluva show. He homered with two on, got three more hits, stole two bases, scored four runs and twice rattled opposing pitchers into balks, enabling Montreal to breeze to a 14-1 victory.

Robinson went on to lead the International League in hitting with a .349 average. At a late-season meeting, Rickey questioned whether Robinson was ready for the major leagues. Dixie's Clay Hopper, who earlier had wondered whether the black was human, proved that baseball is color blind, after all.

"Don't worry about the boy," Hopper told the glowing Mahatma, "he'll make it. He's a great athlete and competitor—and a gentleman."

Although, shamefully, much of official baseball didn't like it at the time and a good bit of America, either, Robinson became officially a big leaguer, breaking the color barrier, in spring training of 1947. Two days after the furor caused by the season-long suspension of manager Leo Durocher by

Commissioner A. B. (Happy) Chandler, who found The Lip guilty of associating with questionable characters, the Dodgers quietly announced that they had purchased the contract of Jack R. Robinson.

Robinson, who had received a $3,500 bonus and $600-a-month contract at Montreal, was en route to the recognition that would bring him up to $42,500 for his top contract, plus the share of six World Series and other baseball-connected earnings. He made his reputation as a second baseman and the last four years he played third base and the outfield, too—in fact, one season he played five positions—but he broke into the bigs as a first baseman.

With Eddie Stanky, the Dodgers had a winning ballplayer at second base, but they had been inadequate at first base in 1946 when they lost the pennant to St. Louis in the first playoff series in major league history. Robinson broke in against the Boston Braves and cunning righthander Johnny Sain.

"I not only went hitless against Sain," Robinson would recall later, amused, "but, all I saw was curveballs—curves of different sizes, shapes and speeds—and I wondered whether maybe I'd soon be back in Montreal."

Jackie didn't remember his first major league hit. It came in his second game off Boston southpaw Glenn Elliott. It was a safe bunt. The first homer came the next day at New York's Polo Grounds off Giant lefthander Dave Koslo.

Rickey had warned Robinson that he would have to wear "an armor of humility" and the aggressive, outspoken instincts of the fierce defender of civil rights, muzzled by the Mahatma, were tested sorely in the Dodgers' first series with the Philadelphia Phillies. Ben Chapman and his players ripped Robinson with racial slurs to the point where he almost dropped his bat and took off for the Philadelphia dugout, but he remembered the turn-the-other-cheek admonishment. Stanky helped, too.

The Philadelphia-born second baseman, a long-time resident of Mobile, Ala., shouted at the Phillies' field foreman, "Chapman, why don't you get on somebody who can fight back?"

Robinson credited Stanky, the man he would replace a year later at second base, and the Dodgers' captain and classy shortstop, Kentucky-born Pee Wee Reese, for supporting him in a time when he faced what could have been a one-man fight. The truth is, some of the Brooklyn players were resentful enough that a petition was in the process of circulation when veteran righthander Kirby Higbe, though himself a Southerner, found his conscience bothering him.

The colorful Higbe, a hard drinker who became an evangelist and author of an interesting, asbestos-lined biography, *The High Hard One*, told his troubles to traveling secretary Harold Parrott in Panama that spring.

"Ol' Hig just won't do it," drawled Higbe. "The Ol' Man (Rickey) has been fair to Ol' Hig. So Ol' Hig ain't goin' to join any petition to keep anybody off the club. That's all."

Rickey, tipped off, was able to head off potential trouble, though the Peepul's Cherce, popular Dixie Walker, asked to be traded and then, reconsidering finally, stayed to help the Dodgers to the 1947 pennant before he finally was dealt to Pittsburgh. The Walker brothers, Dixie of the Dodgers and Harry of the St. Louis Cardinals, were informal ringleaders in what really wasn't an organized attempt to keep Robinson out of the game or to boycott baseball.

To one who was traveling with the Cardinals when the story broke in New York early that 1947 season that the Redbirds would have gone on strike if National League President Ford Frick hadn't issued a play-or-else ultimatum, the whole thing was magnified. Frick's action was crisp and correct, more positive and authoritative than he would be at times later as commissioner, but it wasn't really necessary. Some of the gum-beating by ex-GIs, notably from the South, had alarmed Sam Breadon, owner of the Cardinals, who was panicky when his world champions lost 11 of their first 13 games and was looking for unreasonable reasons for the slow start.

Fact is, as Robinson pointed out more than

once, Louisiana-born, Texas-educated Eddie Dyer, manager of the Cardinals, went out of his way to wish Jackie well the minute Dyer saw him. Enos Slaughter, a slashing, hustling player, spiked Robinson one game at first base and Stanky insisted it had been intentional. Slaughter insisted it hadn't. Funny thing, twice the previous season the extremely aggressive Slaughter put Stanky out of the lineup with savage rolling blocks. Once, Eddie even went to the hospital, but Stanky never complained.

St. Louis-Brooklyn games throughout the decade of the '40s were usually decisive and frequently were a throwback to the Gashouse Gang days and even to the brawling Baltimore Orioles of the gaslight 1890s. But Robinson was not thrown at by the Cardinals nearly so much as other players were. Even though some players would insist that umpires went out of their way to protect the first black player of the century, it wasn't a matter of fear of authority or of reprisal nor even of Dyer's courtesy that kept the Cards from trying to strongarm Robinson.

"Hell, pal" drawled Dyer, himself a former football star who was impressed by Jackie's gridiron credentials, "you can't intimidate this man any more than you could a player like Frank Frisch. He's like Frisch, in fact. The madder you get him the harder he's going to try—and the better."

As a footnote to personalities involved—and to prove a point about man's progress—it must be emphasized that some of the unhappiest players at the time the color barrier was broken became admirably color blind. Bobby Bragan even managed in the Brooklyn organization and handled big league ball clubs before becoming president of the Texas League. Dixie Walker also managed and coached, and Harry Walker's rapport with black players featured his career as a baseball teacher. When he was at Pittsburgh, where he almost won a pennant, other players might have sworn at him, but Roberto Clemente swore by him.

So Jackie Robinson's arrival erased inbred prejudice. In a noteworthy speech before the season,

Rickey urged Negro leaders and fans, particularly in the New York area, not to lionize the player, not to ruin his chances. Rickey could remember how another minority group had unintentionally damaged its pride and joy. Andy Cohen, taking over at second base for the New York Giants in 1928, not only had the disadvantage of trying to fill the ample shoes of brilliant predecessors, Frisch and Rogers Hornsby. When he got off to a good start, Jews wined and dined him out of the league.

In Robinson's case, Rickey couldn't prevent happy Negroes from packing the parks around the National League and from cheering everything Jackie did, to bring about a temporary backlash from white spectators who knew you didn't applaud a pop fly, but gradually Jackie won over the crowd with his exciting play. Rickey encouraged the "spirit of adventure," evaluated open-throttle antics, and the great athlete thrived on the unexpected and the spectacular.

Although Robinson's stolen-base totals were not high by standards that were reached after Maury Wills' record shattering 104 in 1962 brought about a grand revival of a lost art, Jackie did lead the league with 29 steals in 1947 and again with 37 in '49. As he pointed out, with the power-packed Brooklyn lineup in the cozy hitter's paradise of Ebbets Field, percentage wasn't sound in running wild. But Jackie's jockeying on practically every pitch, the tireless way he drove himself and also practically drove opposing pitchers to distraction, titillated crowds and set up runs and Brooklyn victories.

Off the field, it was no fun. Why, in St. Louis and Philadelphia, at first, he couldn't even stay in the same hotel with his teammates. He was forced to live in second-rate Negro hotels without air conditioning. Cincinnati was rough also.

Over the years as Robinson established himself, he quit turning the other cheek. He established himself as a hairshirt to the country's conscience and even as "a professional agitator," as Bob Feller called him. Curiously, the white man accepted the black so completely—in sports, at least—that the whites forgot the insults, inconveniences and injustices baseball's first Negro big leaguer of this century had been forced to endure. A sensitive man, he seethed inwardly in his lonely room, forced to keep his temper in check and his tongue silent, in those perilous days when he was the flanneled guinea pig in Rickey's noble experiment.

The fight to restrain himself rather than fight the foe—umpire Larry Goetz later had to keep him from tangling under the stands with Philadelphia pitcher Russ Meyer—had its rewards. Jackie glowed, for instance, he recalled later, about a clutch game down the stretch in 1947 at St. Louis. When he hurtled courageously into the visitors' dugout, risking his neck to catch a pop foul, husky teammate Ralph Branca stood up, braced himself and caught Jackie in mid-air. "NYU tackles UCLA," we quipped in the pressbox, aware both men had been college football players, but Robinson, grateful to Branca, was grateful also for something else—the rousing applause his play and his teammate's pluckiness had produced in a town where seating segregation in the ballpark had ceased to exist only a couple of years earlier.

Robinson, selected as Rookie of the Year by *The Sporting News*, missed only three games in 1947, played well at the strange position, first base, and hit 12 homers and drove in 48 runs. He batted .297 with his stiff-wristed, sweeping swing and pitchers jammed him better at the outset than they would be able to do later. Some pitchers beefed bitterly that if they had been able to throw tight on Robinson more often without causing practically a federal case, they'd have been able to get him out more often.

"He likes the ball out over the plate," they'd say, but, come to think of it, who the hell doesn't, especially if he's a righthanded hitter striding into the ball?

By Branch Rickey's estimate, Robinson cost the Dodgers a chance to repeat as pennant winners in 1948 because he ballooned from 190 pounds to 230 when he succumbed to the banquet circuit. No doubt, as Rickey said, Robinson's slow start until he reduced his weight contributed to Brooklyn's failure to beat out Boston, which was winning its first National League pennant in 34 years. Playing second base with Stanky a member of the rival Braves, Jackie dropped a point in hitting from his freshman season, though he boosted his RBIs to 85.

Another reason the Dodgers didn't win in '48 was that Rickey, who loved to tinker, had encouraged Leo Durocher to use various lineup combinations. At one time they had three catchers in the lineup—Bruce Edwards at third base, Gil Hodges at first base and a Negro newcomer named Roy Campanella behind the plate.

In seventh place on July 3, shortly before the All-Star break switch in which Durocher went across the bridge to replace Mel Ott as manager of the Giants and Burt Shotton returned to Brooklyn, the Dodgers actually wrested the lead around Labor Day before falling back when beaten head-to-head by the Braves.

Robinson, stung by Rickey's criticism, responded in 1949 with the greatest season of his career. The Dodgers nipped St. Louis for the pennant by one game and they wouldn't have come close if Robinson hadn't proved, as Clay Hopper and Eddie Dyer among others had said, that he was a great competitor. The only hotter Brooklyn hitter in those torrid September finishes in that period was the right fielder, Carl Furillo.

Robinson led the National League in hitting in '49 with a .342 average, beating out both Slaughter and Stan Musial of St. Louis in a close three-way race. He had 203 hits, including 38 doubles, 12 triples, 16 homers and 124 RBIs. He won the National League's Most Valuable Player award.

By now, Jackie no longer was turning the other cheek. Back in 1948, he had been ejected by an umpire for the first time at Pittsburgh when Walter (Butch) Henline ran him. In the heated finish of '49, he was chased by Bill Stewart in a critical situation and might have cost the Dodgers a ball game when he clutched his throat in a choke-up gesture to the veteran arbiter. An instant later, with Eddie Miksis playing second base, Joe Garagiola singled off Miksis' glove for a hit that gave the Cardinals and Max Lanier a 1-0 victory over the Dodgers and Don Newcombe, the third member of the Negro trio that brought Brooklyn a series of pennants.

Garagiola, now a national radio and television celebrity, cost himself probably his own career in an effort to avoid ruining Robinson's in a game the following June 1950, the year St. Louis fell back in the baseball version of the feudin' Hatfields and McCoys. Garagiola, hitting .350 at the time, tried to keep from stepping on Jackie's leg when Robinson was covering first base. Joe broke stride, tripped over the Brooklyn second baseman's leg and fractured his shoulder. Garagiola never was quite the same and ended his career four years later to take a highly successful fling with his lively larynx and sparkling wit.

Robinson's greatest single heroics almost saved the 1951 pennant for Brooklyn in a race that Jackie, like just about everyone else, thought the Dodgers had wrapped up when they opened up a 13-game lead by mid-August. But the Giants went on a 16-game winning streak and kept coming to the point where they actually had the pennant won the last day of the season if the Dodgers lost at Philadelphia.

Down 6-1, Brooklyn rallied to tie, but in the 12th inning with the bases loaded, two out, Eddie Waitkus of the Phillies hit an apparent game-winning, pennant-deciding line shot to the second baseman's right. Robinson, whose fielding hasn't been described adequately here, made a running dive at the ball and make a backhanded grab, just inches off the ground, but the momentum of his big, strong body drove his right elbow into his stomach when he was falling. The pain was excruciating and he landed face down, unconscious.

Jackie's wife, Rachel, watching the game, began to cry. She thought he was dead. Robinson awakened to the syrupy assurances of Pee Wee Reese. The

captain's psychology kept him in the game, Robinson would say later, and Jackie hit a two-run homer in the 14th to win the game and set up the playoff that was won by the Giants on Bobby Thomson's dramatic ninth-inning home run off Branca.

By then, the natural interborough battle between Brooklyn and Manhattan had reached heated proportions and Robinson, who had fussed or feuded with the best, took on Durocher.

"After being on the receiving end in such a lopsided way early, I got a boot out of it," Robinson told Jack Orr for a *Sport* magazine profile after he retired. "Durocher was the best jockey I ever went up against. He was good and knew how to get the most out of it. In all the years, he never race-baited me, but we had some hot times. Carl Erskine once said he couldn't think of what he was doing when we were playing the Giants. The yelling between Durocher and me was too much.

"Jockeying wakes a club up. Often I would go to the ball park, say for a day game after a night game, and I'd just feel that the club was dead and needed shaking up. I found I could do it by beginning to ride the other bench. Any kind of crazy thing would do. Once I accused Durocher of wearing his wife's (Laraine Day's) perfume and I got a lot of mileage out of that."

Robinson, playing for his favorite manager, Charley Dressen, hit and played hard to help win pennants in 1952 and '53, even moving to third base and to the outfield as Cholly saw fit. Against the Yankees in '53, he had his best World Series, batting .320.

By the time the Dodgers won their first world championship in 1955, Walter Alston's second season as manager, Robinson's successive seasons of robust .300-or-better hitting had dissolved at six. Hitting .256 and playing third base, Jack contributed little to the Series win with a .182 average. The 36-year old pro did steal home against Whitey Ford in a first-game decision disputed by Yogi Berra, but the Yankees won that game.

A year later, picking up 19 points in average, two more homers and seven more RBIs than in 1955, Jackie still wasn't Robinson at his peak, but he played as many as five positions that year and gave the Dodgers a lift as they grabbed a pennant that seemed certain to go to Milwaukee.

Robinson's swansong of a compact 10-season career that can't be capsuled in his .311 lifetime average came in the sixth game of the 1956 World Series won by the Yankees. Reliever Clem Labine and Yankee ace Bob Turley dueled scorelessly into the 10th at Ebbets Field. With Jim Gilliam on second base, two out, Casey Stengel elected to pass dangerous Duke Snider intentionally, Robinson who had left five men on base, then lined a shot to left for a hit that gave the Dodgers a 1-0 victory.

Two months later, the Dodgers announced they had traded Robinson to the rival Giants for pitcher Dick Littlefield and $35,000. A month later, Robinson announced in an exclusive series for *Look* magazine that he had quit baseball, precipitating a bitter exchange between Jackie and the Dodgers' general manager, Buzzy Bavasi, who insisted Robinson had let down the daily press by withholding the retirement announcement. Jack's rejoinder was that he'd lived up to terms of a contract with the magazine and that Bavasi wasn't his brother's keeper.

Through vice president Charles S. (Chub) Feeney, the Giants offered most generous contract terms for 1957. With their attendance down to little more than 600,000, looking west to San Francisco if the gate didn't pick up, the Giants were prepared to pay heavily for the box office attraction. But, as Robinson said for this article looking back 13 years later, "My legs were gone and I knew it. It would have been unfair to Horace Stoneham and the Giants to take their money."

Besides, Chock-Full O'Nuts, a restaurant chain in New York, had offered him an attractive $30,000-a-year job as vice president in charge of personnel relations. Eighty percent of the company's employees were Negroes.

Giving up baseball meant a chance to be home more often with Rachel and his children at their fashionable home in Stamford, Conn. The family included son Jack, Jr., daughter Sharon Mitchell, and son David, who went to Stanford with the thought of studying journalism. Young Jack, a Vietnam war veteran, then had a publicized drug problem, but the young man and his famous father faced up to it manfully. Together they went out and spoke against the danger of narcotics until death silenced them. Young Jack's loss in an automobile accident hastened his loving dad's departure in 1972.

Robinson, to whom civil rights and social problems always have struck a nerve, left Chock-Full O'Nuts in 1964 to branch out into banking, radio and television and to become more active in politics. A strong supporter of Nelson Rockefeller, the governor of New York, Robinson refused to support the national Republican ticket in both '64 and '68 because he considered Barry Goldwater a warmonger and Richard Nixon not sufficiently sympathetic to the Negro's cause.

His curly hair prematurely white, Robinson at last trimmed back to his best playing weight, 190. He finished his career too heavy at 234 and then went up from there on the scales until diabetes and a mild heart attack in 1968 forced him to slow down and also to diet. He tried to get out more on the golf course, where he played with an eight-handicap, but a seafood franchising company and other projects had a way of taking up the time of a tense man whose hypertension should come as no surprise.

Robinson, certain that pressbox bigots would at least delay his election to baseball's Hall of Fame, made it the first time he was eligible, 1962, but he stayed away from most ceremonies in apparent protest against the black man's inability to win managerial or front office recognition. Jackie was certainly aware that he was too outspoken and controversial to be a pioneer himself in any other area of baseball progress.

"Maybe I wasn't the ideal man for the role Mr.

Rickey had in mind," Robinson has said. "But after I stored all that stuff they gave me my first couple of years, it was enough. I had to be able to squawk when I thought I had a squawk coming. I found I could play better by letting off steam."

Rachel Robinson can bear witness to his sleepless nights, to the inability to eat and to other areas of pressure and frustration, which, a doctor told both husband and wife, threatened the trailblazer that first critical season, 1947. My, that seems so long ago because of the Afro-American's full acceptance and strength in baseball now. The peppery pioneer, blinded by diabetes, was only 53 when he died of a heart attack in 1972.

Some will choose to remember Jackie Robinson as one writer did—"the hotheaded popoff, the poor loser, the acid-tongued agitator, the quick-tempered, blazing-eyed man with the big No. 42 on his back."

But I like to remember him as beloved Bojangles Bill Robinson, the master hoofer, did when the unrelated young man of the same surname burst upon the big league scene to make life more bearable for Negro boys taking their first swing at a battered ball in the back alleys of the ghettoes.

"You know what he is?" said Bojangles Bill of Jack Roosevelt Robinson. "He's Ty Cobb in Technicolor."

JACK ROOSEVELT ROBINSON
Born January 31, 1919, at Cairo, Ga.
Died October 24, 1972, at Stamford, Conn.
Height 5-11½ Weight 225
Threw and batted righthanded.
Named to Hall of Fame, 1962.

YEAR	CLUB	LEAGUE	POS.	G.	AB.	R.	H.	2B.	3B.	HR.	RBI.	B.A.	PO.	A.	E.	F.A.
1946	Montreal	Int.	2B	124	444	113	155	25	8	3	66	.349	261	385	10	.985
1947	Brooklyn	Nat.	1B	151	590	125	175	31	5	12	48	.297	1323	92	16	.989
1948	Brooklyn	Nat.	INF	147	574	108	170	38	8	12	85	.296	514	342	15	.983
1949	Brooklyn	Nat.	2B	156	593	122	203	38	12	16	124	.342	395	421	16	.981
1950	Brooklyn	Nat.	2B	144	518	99	170	39	4	14	81	.328	359	390	11	.986
1951	Brooklyn	Nat.	2B	153	548	106	185	33	7	19	88	.338	390	435	7	.992
1952	Brooklyn	Nat.	2B	149	510	104	157	17	3	19	75	.308	353	400	20	.974
1953	Brooklyn	Nat.	INF-OF	136	484	109	159	34	7	12	95	.329	238	126	6	.984
1954	Brooklyn	Nat.	INF-OF	124	386	62	120	22	4	15	59	.311	166	109	7	.975
1955	Brooklyn	Nat.	INF-OF	105	317	51	81	6	2	8	36	.256	100	183	10	.966
1956	Brooklyn (a)	Nat.	INF-OF	117	357	61	98	15	2	10	43	.275	169	230	9	.978
Major League Totals				1382	4877	947	1518	273	54	137	734	.311	4007	2728	117	.983

a Traded to New York Giants for pitcher Dick Littlefield and reported $35,000, December 13, 1945; Robinson announced retirement from game, January 5, 1957, canceling trade.

WORLD SERIES RECORD

YEAR	CLUB	LEAGUE	POS.	G.	AB.	R.	H.	2B.	3B.	HR.	RBI.	B.A.	PO.	A.	E.	F.A.
1947	Brooklyn	Nat.	1B	7	27	3	7	2	0	0	3	.259	49	6	0	1.000
1949	Brooklyn	Nat.	2B	5	16	2	3	1	0	0	2	.188	12	9	1	.955
1952	Brooklyn	Nat.	2B	7	23	4	4	0	0	1	2	.174	10	20	0	1.000
1953	Brooklyn	Nat.	OF	6	25	3	8	2	0	0	2	.320	8	0	0	1.000
1955	Brooklyn	Nat.	3B	6	22	5	4	1	1	0	1	.182	4	18	2	.917
1956	Brooklyn	Nat.	3B	7	24	5	6	1	0	1	2	.250	5	12	0	1.000
World Series Totals				38	137	22	32	7	1	2	12	.234	88	65	3	.981

THE MOSTEST MAN: One and only, unconquerable Babe Ruth, pitch-captain-and-bat-first guy who could have made the Hall of Fame as a pitcher had he not switched to the most productive bat ever.

BABE RUTH

A half-century after Babe Ruth was laid to rest at Mt. Pleasant, N. Y., relieved of the spreading throat cancer that turned his booming baritone voice into a harsh whisper, it's still hard to believe that he was such a fantastic performer and personality. It's hard to realize also that baseball failed to utilize its best goodwill ambassador after his retirement.

Sure, the Babe was crude, vulgar and an animal with an animal's instincts, but he had a warm image with people, a child-like charm reflecting the mentality of the bad boy who really never grew up. A

generation of protective sportswriters put aside their pads and pencils at times when the pure animal took over Babe. So, too, did more than one policeman who came upon the good-natured slob when he'd exceeded even his apparently limitless appetite for drink and life in general and, out of character, had become abusive.

All could be—and was—overlooked because Ruth was a wonder man, a magnetic figure whether wearing the pinstriped uniform of the Yankees with the No. 3 on the back or tooling about town in a big roadster, wearing the familiar brown cap, camel's hair coat, big cigar and a bigger grin.

He was the No. 1 box office attraction in baseball history, the greatest home run hitter, one of the best pitchers, an exceptionally fine fielder and baserunner and a hero to a world of kids. With children, the former poor kid who'd spent time in a Catholic institution in Baltimore for incorrigibles, had the fine, soft touch.

Although barely literate and certainly not learned, the Bambino had excellent penmanship. And it was something to get a growled good word from him and his flourishing "Babe Ruth" as an autograph.

He did do thoughtful things, like visiting sick kids in hospitals. He did hit home runs on request, by happy coincidence, even though he really didn't call his shot in the 1932 World Series at Chicago's Wrigley Field.

But mainly, he maintained a rapport with the fans in the stands, especially the young ones, with admirable patience even when grimy hands pawed his snow-white jackets, and ink stains made the cloth look as if it had measles.

Until free agency began in 1976, much more than inflation, moderns didn't come close to the equivalent of the $80,000 he was paid during the depths of the depression. Counting the heavy increase in taxation and the even greater decrease in the value of the dollar, a five-star player would have to pull down around 10 times that amount to equal the Babe's spending power. And brother, Ruth's spending power was as remarkable as his power at the plate.

This went on until a good business manager, Christy Walsh, and a conscientious second wife, the former Claire Hodgson, contained him.

Though Roger Maris hit 61 home runs in 1961, playing eight more games than Ruth in an expanded schedule and Henry Aaron totaled 755, no one has ever matched the Babe as a home run hitter. Maris made no pretense of having replaced the

Babe. For one thing, though he'd spent his first four seasons in the majors as a pitcher, Ruth still walloped an amazing 714 home runs. For 41 more homers, Aaron batted nearly 4,000 times more.

Putting it another way, few men in baseball history ever approached 50 home runs in one season, but the Babe did it four times. And when he clobbered 60 in 1927, he hit nearly 13 percent of the entire homer total that season in the American League. At the recent overall output, a player of today would have to come close to 150 homers a season to achieve the Ruth ratio of '27.

"He's got to be the greatest power hitter, the greatest player," said Stan Musial, who, with Aaron, surpassed the Bambino's career total for extra-base hits.

"Look at it this way," said Stan the Man. "He was good enough to pitch and bat fourth, like the star of a high school team. And even though he struck out more than 1,300 times, he still had a career average of .342."

Asked once if the Babe felt he could have hit .400 by bunting more and going for the hit more often on the ball pitched away form him, Ruth snorted disdainfully.

"Four hundred, hell, kid," he said, "I could have hit .500."

When he batted .393 in 1923, Ruth collected 205 hits and drew 170 bases on balls in 152 games. To hit in front of the Bambino in the Yankee lineup was nice, but batting just behind him was even nicer. The Big Monkey, as the opposition called him, was on base more than the canvas that covered the square sawdust hassocks.

To try to recapture Ruth with cold statistics would be like trying to keep up with him on a night out. The Babe's appetite for wine and women was enough to give a lesser man an inferiority complex.

A pretty good trencherman, Paul Derringer, sat in awe one morning at breakfast on a train as he watched Ruth down a pint of bourbon and ginger ale with a porterhouse steak, four fried eggs, fried potatoes and a pot of coffee.

Derringer was impressed to learn that this was only standard fare for the creature who ballooned to 265 pounds in some off seasons, 35 pounds heavier than his playing weight, which, by any current standard, was too much.

The Babe was partial to the pickled eels put up by the mother of fellow slugger Lou Gehrig. Ma Gehrig would bring a quart of the pickled eels whenever the Yankees played a doubleheader in New York, and Ruth would send out between games for a quart of chocolate ice cream and mix the concoction, which he considered delicious.

When you consider that little George Herman Ruth was allowed to run undisciplined as a child— his saloon-keeper father could not cope—it's no wonder he had weird dietary ideas as an oversized man with oversized desires.

His loyal teammate and good friend, acerbic Waite Hoyt, always insisted that if you sawed the Babe in two, half the concessions of Yankee Stadium would flow out.

Even though it's apparent the press was covering up when the Bambino collapsed in the spring of 1925 with the world's most famous "bellyache," the 30-year-old Ruth could have had enough hot dogs, soda and beer to have led to a gastric revolt. The same season, he was fined $5,000 by manager Miller Huggins for repeated violations of training rules and curfew.

The big Babe thought he'd put little Miller in his place, but the fine stuck. Rebounding after a winter of taking care of himself instead of larding it up, Ruth then had one of his greatest seasons in 1926. He hit three home runs in a World Series game in St. Louis.

He did it again in '28 when he batted .625 in a four-game rout of the Cardinals. In '27, he cracked those 60 homers and had 164 RBIs, just six shy of his high set in 1921.

So it's no wonder his salary soared like one of his towering home runs, one of which was measured at nearly 600 feet one spring at Tampa, Fla. By the time Babe got up to $80,000, the economy had collapsed with the stock market on Black Tuesday in October 1929.

When Ruth held out in spring training at St. Petersburg, Fla., a New York writer suggested as a friendly thought that the holdout might not look good to the Bambino's legion of admirers, with breadlines forming and people selling apples on the street corner.

Why, the writer pointed out, even the president of the United States, Herbert Hoover, was paid only $75,000 a year.

"Yeah" scoffed the Babe, "but I had a better year than he did."

Enamored with Alfred E. Smith, the New York governor who ran unsuccessfully against Hoover in 1928, Ruth tried to avoid meeting Hoover, a genuine baseball fan. In fact, the Babe never got around to voting until he registered and cast a ballot for Franklin D. Roosevelt's fourth term in 1944.

The Babe brought a chuckle from stone-faced Calvin Coolidge, Hoover's predecessor in the White House, when Silent Cal made one of his infrequent appearances at Griffith Stadium on a humid day.

Politely, correctly, each of the Yankees met and shook hands with the president. When Ruth's turn came, he stuck out a friendly mitt, grinned and said, "Geez, it's hot, ain't it, Prez?"

More than one young writer was rewarded by Ruth's informality and the willingness to give of himself. This trait prompted him to play exhibition games in the rain and, in fact, to play first base in a downpour in Tokyo with a bright Japanese parasol over his shoulder. The Japanese loved it, just as they did "Beibu Rusu" on his triumphant tour in 1934.

The prosperous, progressive people of the little island were so smitten by the big Bambino that on Pacific Atolls in World War II they thought they could taunt American troops into reacting when they chanted, "To hell with Babe Ruth."

This was the compliment supreme from an enemy that still worships the memory of the friendly big man (6-2) with the cabbage head, wide nose, thick lips, big mouth, bulging belly, spindly legs, small feet and pigeon-toed walk. He ran in short, mincing steps, waved cheerfully and even kept his temper when the ordinarily polite Nipponese took the "Do Not Disturb" sign off his hotel room and awakened him early for his autograph.

In front of huge Koshien Stadium in Osaka, a bronze plaque commemorates Ruth's visit. Japan's annual baseball day, held to promote the game among the small fry, is called Babe Ruth Day. Some years back, a leading Japanese weekly listed the most famous personalities in Japan during a 40-year period. All the names were Japanese except one—the Babe.

Just before his last Yankee season, the aging giant was late for an exhibition game at Nashville, but he patiently stood outside the ballpark, ignoring the exhortations of his teammates, to answer questions put to him by a Tennessee tenderfoot reporter.

That's how many of us learned that the Babe's favorite actor and actress were the softhearted tough guy, George Bancroft, and petite, sweet Janet Gaynor, star with Charles Farrell of a famed film of that era, *Seventh Heaven.*

Later a guy would learn that, like Clark Griffith, Ruth most enjoyed the radio serial, "The Lone Ranger." And his favorite song was "Deep Purple." From the young reporter, a reader found that the Babe preferred hunting birds on the wing even more than birdies on the links, and he was a fine golfer with a natural lefthanded swing almost as smooth as the baseball stroke he adopted from Shoeless Joe Jackson.

The young reporter who never forgot him and wrote feelingly of the Babe's patience when Ruth died in August 1948, was a southern-fried redhead named Will Grimsley, a legendary globe-girdling sportswriter for the Associated Press out of New York.

Ruth wouldn't have remembered, naturally. If he remembered faces, he had a helluva time with names. So he greeted the young with a breezy "Hiya, Kid," and the bald and middle-aged with "Hiya, Doc."

One spring late in his career, when the Yankees stopped off in Baltimore for an exhibition game, a longtime Baltimore friend wondered what the Orioles' greatest alumnus, the Babe, thought about their newest major league prospect, Don Heffner.

"Who?" asked the Babe, puzzled.

Heffner had been playing second base for nearly a month in front of Ruth, but the famous right fielder didn't know Don's name.

George Herman Ruth came out of Baltimore as an uncontrolled kid who had been filching nickels, sipping beer and chewing tobacco from the time he was seven years old. In and out of reform school, he had done better in St. Mary's Industrial School, an institution at which he made the most strides under the firm but kindly hand of Brother Matthias, a man he deeply respected.

It was Brother Matthias who saw baseball talent in the big coveralled kid playing lefthanded with a righthanded catcher's glove.

At Brother Matthias' request, Jack Dunn, owner of Baltimore's International League club, took a look at the 10-year-old Ruth in 1914 and was impressed. The gawky kid rode a bicycle in training camp and stuffed snuff under his lip, a can at a time, when he pitched for the Orioles.

He was some "Babe," all right, as they tagged him with the nickname that became famous. However, he was referred to more often by his Yankee teammates as Jidge and as the Big Monkey by opposing players with whom he traded insults.

Before the 1914 season was out, Ruth had been sold to the Red Sox and owned two major league victories as a powerful lefthanded pitcher. His mound credintials are wrapped up in a 94-46 career record and 2.28 ERA, three World Series victories and an even more dazzling 0.87 earned-run average for Series competition. Until Whitey Ford broke it in 1961, the Bambino also held for 43 years the record for most consecutive scoreless innings by a Series pitcher, 29.

The Babe was such a fine all-around athlete, despite his torso, that at the age of 38 in 1933, he toed the rubber at Yankee Stadium for a percentage of the gate receipts. It was the last game of the season and would have drawn virtually no one, but he attracted 25,000 and pitched splendidly.

Although he had pitched just one American League game previously in 12 years, Ruth shut out the Red Sox for five innings. When it was suggested he bow out with his arm stiffening, he insisted on going all the way. Hitting a home run, he held on for a 6-5 victory.

He was so exhausted afterward that he couldn't get out of uniform for an hour. Even so, some 5,000 fans waited outside Yankee Stadium and when he appeared, they paid him a rare tribute. Instead of cheering, they applauded him like a virtuoso, which he was.

Babe stood there for a long moment, basking in one of the last ovations he would receive as a ballplayer. He finally acknowledged it by tipping his cap. With his right hand, that is, because he couldn't raise the left.

This must have been the way it was back in 1919 when the Red Sox, with whom he was playing, stopped off in Baltimore for a spring exhibition game so that George's hometown friends and the good brothers at St. Mary's could see him in action. Then just making the transformation from the toeplate to the batter's box, he belted six straight home runs against the Orioles, four one day as an outfielder, the other two pitching the next afternoon.

What would have been baseball history if bushy-browed Ed Barrow hadn't changed Ruth from a great pitcher to a great hitter? What if theater producer Harry Frazee, the Red Sox owner suffering from financial shorts, hadn't sold Ruth to New York in January 1920, for $125,000 and a $350,000 mortgage on Fenway Park?

Would the Red Sox have remained a power, in-stead of winning only two pennants in nearly a half-century? Would the Yankees have gotten off the launching pad in 1921 to their incredible 40-year dominance of baseball? Would their ownership have had reason to put up in '23 the House That Ruth Build—after Ruth had raised the home run record from 29 to 54 and then to 59?

Could one man mean that much to a franchise? To a city? To a game? If the man was Babe Ruth, yes.

After the Black Sox scandal of 1919 broke across the land in the 1920 pennant stretch, all of baseball could be thankful that the country was buzzin, cousin, over the homer-hitting of the Babe, whose 54 that season must have seemed as far-fetched as a moon shot would have been just a few decades ago.

Ruth raised sights, salaries and, unbelievably in view of his personal habits, baseball standards, too. There was only one thing almost as exciting as the Babe hitting a homer. It was a Ruth strikeout, a thing of beauty and, if you were rooting against the Yankees, a joy forever.

The mighty Casey of mythical Mudville never went down with more graceful menace than the Sultan of Swat turned suddenly into a corkscrew by a third strike that slipped past the fury of his flailing bat.

Ah, he was something, all right, even to the pathetic end of his career in 1935 with the Boston Braves. There came a May day at Pittsburgh when the Babe, hitting an embarrassing .180, limped into a National League city he'd terrorized in the 1927 World Series.

Before the game, a Pittsburgh reporter, smiling, told manager Pie Traynor of the Pirates not to worry, that he'd kept the old boy out doing the town until 5 A.M. Ruth merely unleashed three homers that day, his last Herculean feat. Shucks, even at 40, the Babe could both burn the candle and drink the midnight oil like a college kid on Easter recess.

Years before, Al Schacht, the Clown Prince of Baseball, had baited a trap for the Babe at Washington by turning him over to Goose Goslin, also a pretty good man at touching all the bases after dark. They ate, drank and made merry until mid-morning, when the Babe, without benefit of sleep, hurried to Walter Reed Hospital to autograph baseballs and visit the sick.

Gratefully, Goslin dived into the sack for a few hours of shut-eye before the 3 P.M. game.

That afternoon, the bleary-eyed Babe belted two homers and a double. Goslin went hitless in five trips, committed two errors and Schacht was in the Senators' doghouse for a month.

Ruth, whose memory for baseball details was as good as his faculty for names was faulty, once lost a bet that he had homered off Schact in the majors, not the minors. Paying off, the Babe said:

"Well, I guess I hold another record that I didn't know about."

"What's that?" inquired the baseball comedian turned restaurateur.

"It looks," cracked Ruth, "as if I'm the only big league ballplayer who didn't ever hit a home run off Al Schacht!"

When Ruth showed up at Pittsburgh's Forbes Field in May 1935, long in the tooth and short of sleep, Traynor gratefully shrugged him off as the Pirates went over the hitters. "Don't worry about Ruth," said Traynor.

"I wouldn't say that," cautioned an old Ruthian teammate and playmate, Waite Hoyt, who was then earning his keep as a pitcher with the Pirates.

That day, which really should have been his last day in the majors, the Babe reached back into the intuitive talent of an instinctive athlete to clout a trio of home runs—long, longer and for years, the longest at Forbes Field, the first blast atop the towering right-field stands.

Hoyt could grin then as he did later when relating many moments of joy with the Babe, on and off the field. He could recall with a straight face the touching moment when Waite had been traded by the Yankees to Philadelphia and he'd bade farewell to the Babe.

"Good luck, kid," said Ruth, choked up at losing a fellow blithe spirit. "Take care of yourself…WALTER!"

Could a man who couldn't manage himself manage others? The Yankees thought not when they passed over Ruth at a time playing pilots were the popular—and economic—thing to do. The Babe blew a chance when he didn't answer a call from Detroit's Frank Navin, who had permission to talk to him after the '33 season when the Bambino was on the West Coast.

Navin turned to Philadelphia, instead, and landed a pennant-winning player-manager, Mickey Cochrane.

Unwisely, Ruth turned down a chance to manage the Yankees' top farm club at Newark in 1935. A coaching job offered by Larry MacPhail at Brooklyn in 1938 didn't last after Leo Durocher, who had sassed the Babe with the Yankees 10 years earlier, took over as manager of the Dodgers.

But why didn't someone or anyone, much less ALL of baseball, see in the immensely popular Bambino the kind of goodwill guy he became for the Ford Company and the American Legion baseball program the last summer of his life? Then he was a dying man with a croaking voice and clothes that hung on him as loosely as a burlesque comedian's pants.

A good friend and former Fordham second baseman, Francis Cardinal Spellman, brought the Babe back into the church before the end came, mercifully, at 53. Six thousand persons crowded into St. Patrick's Cathedral and many thousands mourned outside.

Prominent pallbearers, active and honorary, included several of Ruth's former teammates, who carried the casket into the fierce heat of the August afternoon at the cemetery in Mt. Pleasant, N. Y.

"Lord," whispered Jumpin' Joe Dugan, the old third baseman, "I'd give my right arm for an ice-cold beer."

Waite Hoyte, turning, nodded and murmured, "So would the Babe."

GEORGE HERMAN (BABE) RUTH
Born February 6, 1895, at Baltimore, Md.
Died August 16, 1948, at New York, N. Y.
Height 6-2 Weight 215
Threw and batted lefthanded.
Named to Hall of Fame, 1936.

YEAR	CLUB	LEAGUE	POS.	G.	AB.	R.	H.	2B.	3B.	HR.	RBI.	B.A.	PO.	A.	E.	F.A.
1914	Balt.-Prov.	Int.	P-OF	46	121	22	28	2	10	1	---	.231	20	87	4	.964
1914	Boston	Amer.	P	5	10	1	2	1	0	0	0	.200	0	8	0	1.000
1915	Boston	Amer.	P-OF	42	92	16	29	10	1	4	20	.315	17	63	2	.976
1916	Boston	Amer.	P-OF	67	136	18	37	5	3	3	16	.272	24	83	3	.973
1917	Boston	Amer.	P-OF	52	123	14	40	6	3	2	10	.325	19	101	2	.984
1918	Boston	Amer.	OF-P-1	95	317	50	95	26	11	11	64	.300	270	72	18	.950
1919	Boston (a)	Amer.	OF-P	130	432	103	139	34	12	29	112	.322	270	53	4	.988
1920	New York	Amer.	OF-1-P	142	458	158	172	36	9	54	137	.376	259	21	19	.936
1921	New York	Amer.	OF-1-P	152	540	177	204	44	16	59	170	.378	348	17	13	.966
1922	New York	Amer.	OF	110	406	94	128	24	8	35	96	.315	226	14	9	.964
1923	New York	Amer.	OF-1B	152	522	151	205	45	13	41	130	.393	378	20	11	.973
1924	New York	Amer.	OF	153	529	143	200	39	7	46	121	.378	340	18	14	.962
1925	New York	Amer.	OF	98	359	61	104	12	2	25	66	.290	207	15	6	.974
1926	New York	Amer.	OF	152	495	139	184	30	5	47	155	.372	308	11	7	.979
1927	New York	Amer.	OF	151	540	158	192	29	8	60	164	.356	328	14	13	.963
1928	New York	Amer.	OF	154	536	163	173	29	8	54	142	.323	304	9	8	.975
1929	New York	Amer.	OF	135	499	121	172	26	6	46	154	.345	240	5	4	.984
1930	New York	Amer.	OF-P	145	518	150	186	28	9	49	153	.359	266	10	10	.965
1931	New York	Amer.	OF-1B	145	534	149	199	31	3	46	163	.373	237	5	7	.972
1932	New York	Amer.	OF-1B	133	457	120	156	13	5	41	137	.341	212	10	9	.961
1933	New York	Amer.	OF-P	137	459	97	138	21	3	34	103	.301	215	9	7	.970
1934	New York (b)	Amer.	OF	125	365	78	105	17	4	22	84	.288	197	3	8	.962
1935	Boston	Nat.	OF	28	72	13	13	0	0	6	12	.181	39	1	2	.952
National League Totals - 16 Years				2475	8327	2161	2860	506	136	708	2197	.343	4665	561	174	.968
American League Totals - 2 Years				28	72	13	13	0	0	6	12	.181	39	1	2	.952
Major League Totals - 17 Years				2503	8399	2174	2873	506	136	714	2209	.342	4704	562	176	.968

a Sold to New York Yankees for $125,000, January 3, 1920.
b Released to Boston Braves, February 26, 1935.

WORLD SERIES RECORD

YEAR	CLUB	LEAGUE	POS.	G.	AB.	R.	H.	2B.	3B.	HR.	RBI.	B.A.	PO.	A.	E.	F.A.
1915	Boston	Amer.	PH	1	1	0	0	0	0	0	0	.000	0	0	0	.000
1916	Boston	Amer.	P	1	5	0	0	0	0	0	1	.000	2	4	0	1.000
1918	Boston	Amer.	P-OF	3	5	0	1	0	1	0	2	.200	1	5	0	1.000
1921	New York	Amer.	OF	6	16	3	5	0	0	1	4	.313	9	0	0	1.000
1922	New York	Amer.	OF	5	17	1	2	1	0	0	1	.118	9	0	0	1.000
1923	New York	Amer.	O-1B	6	19	8	7	1	1	3	3	.368	17	0	1	.944
1926	New York	Amer.	OF	7	20	6	6	0	0	4	5	.300	8	2	0	1.000
1927	New York	Amer.	OF	4	15	4	6	0	0	2	7	.400	10	0	0	1.000
1928	New York	Amer.	OF	4	16	9	10	3	0	3	4	.625	9	1	0	1.000
1932	New York	Amer.	OF	4	15	6	5	0	0	2	6	.333	8	0	1	.889
World Series Totals				41	129	37	42	5	2	15	33	.326	73	12	2	.977

GEORGE HERMAN (BABE) RUTH

PITCHING RECORD

YEAR	CLUB	LEAGUE	G.	IP.	W.	L.	Pct.	H.	R.	ER.	SO.	BB.	ERA.
1914	Balt.-Prov.	Int.	35	245	22	9	.710	219	88	---	139	101	---
1914	Boston	Amer.	4	23	2	1	.667	21	12	10	3	7	3.91
1915	Boston	Amer.	32	218	18	8	.692	166	80	59	112	85	2.44
1916	Boston	Amer.	44	324	23	12	.657	230	83	63	170	118	1.75
1917	Boston	Amer.	41	326	24	13	.649	244	93	73	128	108	2.02
1918	Boston	Amer.	20	166	13	7	.650	125	51	41	40	49	2.22
1919	Boston	Amer.	17	133	9	5	.643	148	59	44	30	58	2.97
1920	New York	Amer.	1	4	1	0	1.000	3	4	2	0	2	4.50
1921	New York	Amer.	2	9	2	0	1.000	14	10	9	2	9	9.00
1930	New York	Amer.	1	9	1	0	1.000	11	3	3	3	2	3.00
1933	New York	Amer.	1	9	1	0	1.000	12	5	5	0	3	5.00
Major League Totals			163	1221	94	46	.671	974	400	309	488	441	2.28

WORLD SERIES RECORD

YEAR	CLUB	LEAGUE	G.	IP.	W.	L.	Pct.	H.	R.	ER.	SO.	BB.	ERA.
1916	Boston	Amer.	1	14	1	0	1.000	6	1	1	4	3	0.64
1918	Boston	Amer.	2	17	2	0	1.000	13	2	2	4	7	1.06
World Series Totals			3	31	3	0	1.000	19	3	3	8	10	0.87

BY ANY OTHER NAME: Whether as Aloysius Szymanski or Al Simmons or as Bucketfoot Al, Sim was one of the greatest hitters ever and defensively versatile, too.

AL SIMMONS

One spring, Thomas Alva Edison, the only Ft. Myers winter resident more distinguished than Connie Mack, was invited by baseball's patriarch to an exhibition ball game in the pleasant Florida Gulf Coast community.

As an inventor, Edison, whose incandescent light alone made every man's life brighter, didn't have much time for baseball. When he was introduced to the Athletics' Al Simmons, he asked, politely:

"Ah, what is your position, Mr. Simmons?"

"I'm an outfielder, Mr. Edison," said Simmons, slightly taken aback.

"Is that so?" said the aging inventor. "I thought you were a batter."

Al beamed. The old boy might not know a shortstop from a short circuit, but he'd heard about the great Sim, a swaggering, confident slugger, and that was good enough for Bucketfoot Al and made it even. Sim had heard about Edison, too.

Although as a player he was never as noisy as

when he became a coach, a mighty good third-base traffic cop, Simmons had extreme self-assurance from the time he was a 19-year-old professional rookie training with Milwaukee at Caruthersville, Mo., in 1922.

Addressing himself to teammate Oscar Melillo, a little second baseman, Simmons boasted, "We're in, Osk. We're the two greatest prospects in the history of baseball. We should be in the majors right now."

The next day, Milwaukee, then a Class Double-A American Association ball club, shipped both Simmons and Melillo to Class D. And Osk said to Al, sarcastically, "So we're the greatest rookies, huh?"

Simmons heading for Aberdeen, S.D., as his little pal went to Winnipeg, Man., patted Melillo on the back and smiled patronizingly.

"Don't worry, Osk," he said. "They just made a little mistake. We'll be right back."

Before the season was over, Simmons was right. Milwaukee recalled both players. Melillo became a slick-fielding second baseman who lasted 12 seasons in the American League. Simmons became one of baseball's greatest hitters and pulled on a player's uniform in the majors for 20 years.

They called him Bucketfoot Al at first because of an unorthodox batting stance, but the description was as annoying to Simmons as the burly outfielder was to opposing pitchers for 16 seasons. Those last few years an impostor played in place of Aloysius Harry Szymanski.

Simmons, who took his baseball surname from a hardware company billboard, put the screws to enemy pitchers with a career batting average of .334, which tells only part of the story.

Fifteen times he batted over .300, the first 11 seasons consecutively, and over one seven-season stretch, 1925 through 1931, he averaged better than .370, hitting this way: .384, .343, .392, .351, .365, .381, .390.

Despite the aforementioned consistency and prowess, Simmons won just two batting champion-

ships, 1930-31, reflecting the competition he faced in a hitting era. More than a quarter-century after he finished as a big leaguer by batting .500 with three hits in six times up for the Philadelphia Athletics in 1944, it's apparent that the Duke of Milwaukee never quite got the acclaim he deserved.

The Baseball Writers' Association of America did select him for *The Sporting News'* All-Star major league team six times over an eight-year period, 1927-34, but Simmons doesn't get now the general overall recognition he would seem to merit. Was it because of questionable personal popularity?

Five years after Al played his last big league ball game, he was coaching for his old boss, Connie Mack, when the 1949 Philadelphia Athletics made a motion at getting into the pennant race. A reporter wondered which player Connie figured as his key man, expecting the old man to name one of his current players.

"I wish," said Mr. Mack thoughtfully, "I had nine players named Al Simmons."

Whether Szymanski or Simmons, the Duke of Milwaukee made a considerable impression on his fellow professionals, as was evident in 1953 when he was elected, at 50, to baseball's Hall of Fame.

Joe Cronin, himself a Hall of Famer and a long-time playing rival, brought up a side of Simmons that many, not only Thomas Edison, hadn't considered.

"He was great all-around, running, fielding and throwing, as well as hitting and as a competitor," said Cronin at the time of Sim's death in 1956. "There never was a greater left fielder in going to the line and holding a double to a single. He'd even dare you to make the wide turn at first on a ball hit to his right."

Ralph (Cy) Perkins, a defensive catching star and shrewd observer of Philadelphia's pennant-winning peak, 1929-31, summed up Simmons at the time of his Hall of Fame induction this way:

"He had that swagger of confidence, of defiance, when he came up as a kid. He was as sensational as a rookie as he was as a star. I've always classed him next to Ty Cobb as the greatest player I ever saw. He could hit to all fields. He and Rogers Hornsby, in my opinion, were the best righthanded hitters.

"I don't think I ever saw Al make a mistake. He never threw to the wrong base when he played left field for Mr. Mack, and he never made a mistake when he was third-base coach for the Athletics. He had remarkable baseball sense. He was what I would call the 'perfect player.'"

High praise, indeed, and even when he began to spend more time with the sauce in his last professional baseball job, as a coach for Cleveland in 1950, Simmons took pride in proper techniques and methods.

I came across Sim and actor Bill Frawley, a baseball buff, in the long, narrow bar of the Hollywood Plaza Hotel in the spring of 1950. The Indians had come to the West Coast from Tucson for a series of games with the St. Louis Browns, Chicago Cubs, Pittsburgh Pirates and Pacific Coast League clubs based there.

Simmons and Frawley had started out to break bread together, but they had had a liquid dinner and now sounded as if they would break each other's skull. Shouting at each other in the dark, semi-deserted bar, they would take turns scurrying the length of the mahogany. The reason for the argument? Trying to reach agreement on the right way for an outfielder to break back on a flyball.

Simmons, a restless, lonely man after his marriage broke up, remained single because of religious convictions, but he let down his guard one time, talking to sports columnist Ed McAuley in Cleveland shortly before he quit as a coach in '51.

Explaining to McAuley his affection for Connie Mack, Al said, "Mr. Mack seemed to look on me as his son. He never stopped feeling sorry for me about the breakup of my marriage. He told me, 'Al, you and Mrs. Simmons ought to patch things up. I stayed single for 18 years after the first Mrs. Mack died, and all the time I didn't know the meaning of the word happiness.'"

Overweight and unable to stay on a diet or on the wagon, either, when he lost out at Cleveland, Simmons did get back briefly into baseball's fringe area in 1954. Rabbit Maranville died and at the urging of a mutual friend, Herb (Curly) Perry, New York American's sports editor Max Kase put Sim in charge of Hearst's juvenile baseball program.

At one time, Simmons would have made that job a joy for himself as well as for the kids who had the benefit of his baseball knowledge and experience, but he had become his own worst enemy. The last time I saw him was in the spring of 1956 when he staggered out of a taxicab one midnight at the Milwaukee Athletic Club, arms loaded with bottled companionship.

Barely a month later, loaded within and without, Sim staggered out of another cab at the same Milwaukee A. C., his summer home, and collapsed. Increasingly heavy-legged, he had been hospitalized earlier in the spring for phlebitis, an inflammation of the lower leg, but he had no history of coronary trouble.

Survivors included his ex-wife, the former Doris Lynn Reader of Racine, Wis., a resident of Miami; a son, John Allen Simmons, then a student at the University of Georgia, and two brothers and three sisters, all of whom lived in the Duke of Milwaukee's hometown. Six days past his 53rd birthday, he was buried in St. Adalbert's Cemetery.

Aloysius Harry Szymanski, born in happier days to Polish immigrants, grew up on Milwaukee's South Side, a poor kid, but a good athlete who went for a time to Stevens Point Teachers College as a football player. He had only one ambition—to be a baseball player.

He took a shine to Roger Bresnahan, then managing at Toledo, and the kid who would become the Duke of Milwaukee wrote to the famed old Duke of Tralee for a tryout. His letter went unanswered.

If Bresnahan had managed to see Simmons, chances are the former catching star of the New York Giants would have been impressed enough to take a hard look. Chances are, too, the way Bresnahan made available his top talent to old boss John J. McGraw, that Simmons would have wound up under McGraw rather than Mack.

"I couldn't have liked McGraw as much as I did Mr. Mack," Simmons would suggest, smiling, "but as much as I liked Shibe Park, oh, how I'd have enjoyed a career at the Polo Grounds with those short fences."

Simmons, playing with a laundry team on Milwaukee's South Side, was given a couple of bucks' railroad fare to play semi-pro ball at Juneau, Wis., in the old Lake Shore league. A man named Eddie Bodus, managing at Juneau, remembered Al's first game.

"He sat down on the bench next to my 10-year-old nephew," recalled a smiling Bodus years later, "and looked at the horrible hunk of leather he had for a glove and then at the pretty good glove I'd given my nephew. Next thing you know, he'd made a deal with the kid for his glove—a swap and 50 cents in cash. Trouble is, the nephew never did get the half a buck."

Simmons walked off the bench as a pinch-hitter in the seventh inning that day and hit an inside-the-park homer for a 1-0 victory over Eddie Stumpf's Milwaukee Red Sox. So the word got to the Brewers, the Milwaukee (American Association) club, and the business manager, Lou Nahin, called him into the Brewers' office.

Al walked in, wearing a bow tie and a checkered cap, just as the Brewers' big boss, Otto Borchert, wearing swallow tails, stalked into the outer office of his suite. He took one look at the husky lad and glared.

When Nahin minutes later gleefully told Borchert that he had signed Simmons for 1922— "he'll bring you a fortune some day," the business manager prophesied—the club owner was unimpressed.

"Not," he said, "until he throws away that ugly cap."

Simmons was a hot hitter in spring training in '22, as mentioned in Al's optimistic dialog with Oscar Melillo, but, over the protests of manager Harry Clark and the Milwaukee press, Borchert farmed him out to Aberdeen.

A .365 hitter there, Simmons was optioned to Shreveport in 1923. One day Nahin received a wire in which the Texas League club's manager messaged:

"Simmons won't do. Will give him his unconditional release."

Nahin, aware Al was hitting over .300 and fielding well, shot back a telegram to Shreveport:

"Don't release Simmons. Return him to Milwaukee immediately."

Shortly, Shreveport reported:

"Simmons doing little better. Will buy him for $1,500."

Now, both Nahin and Borchert were furious. Borchert wired, "If Simmons is worth $1,500 to you, he's worth $15,000 to me. Send him back."

The Brewers' boss later told Sam Levy, longtime baseball writer for the *Milwaukee Journal,* "Can you imagine that guy in Shreveport trying to outsmart me? He'd pay me $1,500 for a player he wanted to release the week before."

After Sim added a .398 mark in 24 games at Milwaukee to .360 at Shreveport, Connie Mack bought him for about $70,000 in cash and players. Fortunately for Al, if he ever needed any help, Mack paid even more for a much-publicized player, Paul Strand, who had hit fabulously with Salt Lake City in the Pacific Coast League. Playing in 194 games, Strand batted .394—and had 325 hits.

So the spotlight was entirely on Strand in spring training. Poor Paul couldn't lug along the rarefied atmosphere, where pitchers found it extremely difficult to break off a curve and where flyballs floated out of sight.

Strand was a bust, batting only .228 in 47 games, before he was shipped back to a healthier climate. By then, quietly, Simmons had gotten off to a good start and was on his way to a .308 rookie season.

What they saw when Simmons stepped up to the plate was a 6-0, 200-pound athlete with grey eyes, brown hair, dark brows and a light complexion that never seemed to tan. The more intense a hitting situation or the angrier Simmons became, the whiter his face.

He wore his uniform sleeves extremely long, well below his elbows, affecting the style of his favorite player, Ty Cobb, with whom he was delighted to become teammates in 1927 and '28, the old Georgia Peach's last two seasons in baseball. Al pumped him with questions, and Ty enjoyed having as a pupil a man who already had established himself as one of the best hitters in baseball.

An awkward outfielder at first, Simmons, as indicated, became far better defensively than many now remember. At bat, where he made his reputation, he was a righthanded hitter who had an extremely comfortable stance. He stood deep in the batter's box, feet close together and took a long stride with his left foot.

Because he strode toward third base, however, rather than toward the pitcher, it was suggested that he was "stepping in the bucket," an expression used in the old days when a hitter with a cowardly posterior looked as if he'd put his front foot in the old-fashioned water bucket that decorated every bench or dugout.

Simmons didn't like the Bucketfoot Al nickname because of the connotation that it questioned his courage. The way he hit, he need never have worried, because if there was anyone for whom to feel sorry, it was the pitchers he belabored. In truth, though, Simmons really didn't bail out. His hips and weight were going into the pitch even if the front foot wasn't.

Only a hitter taking a long stride can go to the opposite field when beginning from deep in the batter's box, and only a hitter using a long bat—Simmons generally swung a big brown betsy—and putting his body into the pitch, if not that front leg, could hit with as much power to the opposite field as Al did. Charley Gehringer said Sim hit harder to the second-base side than lefthanders Ruth or Gehrig.

Early efforts to alter his unorthodox batting stance failed and Connie Mack told everyone to mind his own damn business and to let that big Polish kid do what came naturally to him.

Man, that Simmons had a sophomore season in the majors. In 1925, playing 153 games, he collected 253 hits, scored 122 runs, belted 43 doubles, 12 triples, 24 homers and drove in 129 runs. He hit .384, one of several seasons he did NOT win batting championships with an average that was outstanding.

By the June trading deadline in '25, the A's, rebuilding from a decade of disaster, actually were leading the American League. They wouldn't win a pennant for another four seasons, but they were beginning to make noises like this one:

Playing Cleveland and trailing in the eighth inning, 15-4, the Athletics had only one on and one out when they began an assault that prompted Tris Speaker, the player-manager of the Indians, to use four pitchers.

Simmons, sixth up, singled and by the time Al came up again with two down, two on, Philadelphia had scored 10 times. George Uhle, Cleveland's ace, was on the mound when Sim stepped into the batter's box.

Just a few days earlier, he had become the first player to put a ball on the newly build left-field roof of Shibe Park. Now, he found the roof again with his second hit of the inning, a three-run blast, that gave the A's a remarkable 13-run round and a hard-to-believe 17-15 victory.

For a moment there in '27, proving that he was good enough to play center field, Simmons found himself as the middle man between two aging big-name stars, finishing up with Mr. Mack. How about an outfield of Cobb, Simmons and Speaker, friends? In name, anyway.

By 1929, when the Athletics began an impressive run of three straight pennants with one of the best ball clubs ever assembled, Simmons was 26 years old and at his peak.

"Them pitchers," he would growl, "are trying to take meat and potatoes off my plate."

He resented knockdown pitches and feuded with Fred (Firpo) Marberry, giant Washington reliever. When Marberry couldn't think of what to throw Simmons—and that was most of the time—he would decide to deck the big cleanup man in the Athletics' awesome lineup. When Lefty Grove was pitching, there were four future Hall of Famers in the batting order. Mickey Cochrane, Simmons and Jimmie Foxx, hitting 3-4-5 were superstars.

"I don't know what Sim is complaining about," said Foxx one time. "I get knocked down more than he does. Not because of what I've done, but because of what he's done. He rips 'em for a double, triple or homer. Up I come and down I go."

In 1929, though sitting out 11 games, Simmons knocked in 157 runs, batting .365 and belting 34 homers. He was named the American League's Most Valuable Player.

In Philadelphia's five-game World Series win over the Cubs that fall, Simmons figured prominently as he did in all spotlighted situations. It's no wonder he was at his best against the A's arch-rivals, the Yankees. The man was a competitor at his best in blue-ribbon events, as witness a .462 average for the first three All-Star games and a .329 mark for four World Series, the last of which when he was little more than a shell of his old savage self as a part-time performer with the 1939 Cincinnati Reds.

A decade earlier, though, Simmons and Company caved in the Cubs just before the stock market collapsed in 1929 to throw the country into the depths of the infamous depression.

Simmons touched off probably the most remarkable inning in World Series history when he led off the home seventh of the fourth game. The A's were leading the Series, two games to one, but just barely because the Cubs and Charley Root were in front, 8-0.

Sim slugged one of Root's pitches atop the roof at Philly and the roof caved in on the Cubs. The A's

batted around. Aided by Hack Wilson's monumental misjudgment of Mule Haas' line drive, which became a three-run homer inside the park, the score was narrowed to 8-7 by the time Simmons batted again.

With Cochrane on first base, Simmons faced righthander Fred (Sheriff) Blake, the third Chicago pitcher. Al singled Mickey into scoring position, and Foxx delivered a game-tying safety. Pat Malone replaced Blake, plunked Bing Miller with a pitch and then yielded a decisive double to Jimmie Dykes, making it an historic 10-run round and an unforgettable Philadelphia victory, 10-8.

The next day, with President Herbert Hoover in the stands, Malone shut out the A's until the ninth inning when Haas hit a two-run homer to tie the score. With two down, Simmons doubled for his sixth hit and third extra-base blow, bringing his Series batting average to .300. After Foxx was intentionally passed, Miller doubled Sim home with the run that gave the Mackmen a 3-2 triumph and the world championship.

The A's repeated in 1930. If there was any question about the race, Simmons settled it early when Washington came to town for a Memorial Day doubleheader, leading the league. This was, as he understandably said, Sim's greatest day in baseball.

They were playing a morning-afternoon double dip, two games for the price of two. Grove, who liked to face the foe when they hardly had their eyes open, was hit hard and the Senators held a 6-3 lead into the ninth inning.

Two were on, two were out when Simmons faced the submarining serves of righthander Ad Liska. Hitless in four trips, Sim recalled later that some of the fickle fans had booed him. The white left Al's face and he walloped a game-tying, three-run homer.

In the 11th inning, he doubled. No score. In the 13th he singled. No score. In the 15th he got his fourth straight hit, a double, and when Foxx dribbled a grounder down the third-base line, beating it out for an infield hit, Simmons rounded third and was trapped. He scrambled back to the bag safely, but as he dived he felt something snap in his right knee.

Standing on the bag, waiting for Eric McNair to come through, which he did with a single for a 7-6 Philadelphia victory, Simmons said he could feel the knee swelling. He hobbled home on McNair's hit and limped into the clubhouse.

The A's team physician, a devoted baseball fan, came in and examined the knee. "It's a broken blood vessel," he said. "You'll be all right, but not right now."

A worried Connie Mack wondered whether the doctor would take Simmons to the hospital immediately?

"Not until after the second game," said the sportsminded medical man. "I came to see a doubleheader. Al can't play, but he could pinch-hit if you need him. Hit one so you can walk, Al."

Simmons sat on the bench, but not for long. By the fourth inning, with the Athletics trailing, 7-4, Philadelphia filled the bases. Mack beckoned his limping slugger. "This," he said, "is what Dr. Carnett must have been talking about, Al, you know what he said. Walk around the bases if you can."

Simmons pounded a grandslam homer to put the Athletics ahead and Washington on the way out of the race. Philadelphia won the game, 14-7, and the pennant. And Old Fox Clark Griffith, stung by Simmons' clutch hitting, kept tabs the rest of the season.

Afterward, the Senators' boss told Mack that he figured that 14 of Sim's 36 homers that season had come in the eighth and ninth innings and had tied or won ball games for the A's.

In the World Series that fall, as Philadelphia beat St. Louis in six games, Simmons hit two more home runs. Burleigh Grimes, the stubble-bearded old competitor on the mound for the Cardinals, groused after the first one.

"Where the hell's this guy's weakness—right over the plate?" beefed Burleigh. "I had him two strikes and nothing and tried to waste a pitch out-

side. He reached across and hit it over the right-field fence."

A .381 hitter and batting champion with 36 homers and 165 RBIs in 138 games, Simmons held out, stubbornly, to the point that he did not train with the A's in 1931 and in fact, did not sign with the Shibes and Macks until minutes before the opener at Philadelphia.

When the game began and the familiar, long-sleeved, burly figure trotted out to left field, the A's fans gave him probably the most thunderous ovation he ever received.

"Showboat," growled one New York correspondent to another, Tom Meany, whose smile widened as his fellow writer grumbled. "Why the hell did he have to wait until the last minute to sign? Who does he think he is? The U.S. Marines going to the rescue?

Not a bad imitation. Sim hit the first professional pitch he'd seen that spring for a home run, proving that he not only appreciated the three-season contract for $33,333.33 each that he'd whittled out of management, but that he'd taken to heart what Mack had told him.

"The challenge for a batting champion, Al, is to repeat," said Connie, who knew he was touching Simmons' pride then added:

"That's what Ty Cobb used to do."

Simmons repeated, all right, hitting .390 and driving in 128 runs in the same number of games. He had 22 homers and collected two more in the Series, giving him a total of six homers and 11 extra-base blows in 23 World Series hits for the A's. In the '31 Series alone, Sim had nine hits and drove in eight runs, but the A's lost their world championship to the Cardinals. With the Reds, he added one double in the '39 series.

The Philadelphia dynasty became a victim of the Depression. Attendance that had lagged with the surfeited victory habit was even lower in 1932 as the Yankees wrested the pennant from the A's. Simmons, dipping to .322, still whacked 35 homers and knocked in 151 runs in 154 games, but at the end of that season he was dealt with third baseman Dykes and center fielder Mule Haas to the White Sox for $150,000.

The Comiskeys, better able to handle Simmons' sizable salary, welcomed Al by moving home plate closer to the fences in their pitchers' park. Al did all right there, hitting .331 and getting 14 homers as he drove in 119 runs in 1933. But he lost some spark, too.

After he had come out early one morning, asking extra men to pitch to him, another Chicago regular came forth and asked, "How come you're out here trying to show us up?"

Now if he really had been like his idol, Cobb, Simmons would have chewed out the other guy and told him to tell the rest of the Chisox to go take a flying leap into Lake Michigan. But Sim apparently had accepted the Sox' second-division syndrome. He laid off the extra practice, he lamented later in self-confession.

Practice or no, Simmons still could hit, as he proved with a .344 season, 18 homers and 104 RBIs in 1934, but after he dipped below .300 for the first time with a .267 season in '35, the White Sox decided to unload him.

His old Philadelphia teammate, Dykes, then managing the White Sox, called to say he had two cash offers for Simmons and that he'd take the one Sim requested. Quick now, which would it be? Detroit or New York?

Another of Al's teammates just had won two straight pennants at Detroit, a hitter's park and especially better for a righthanded batter than Yankee Stadium. The Yankees just had bought a young phenom named Joe DiMaggio, so—.

"I'll take Detroit," Simmons said, explaining later that the decision was the worst he'd ever made.

Although he was past his prime, as he frankly put it, he batted .327 and drove in 112 runs in 143 games, but he hit only 13 homers. The Tigers didn't win the pennant and so there was a tendency among the fans, Simmons felt, to blame the new man, especially one for whom the club had paid $75,000.

"If I'd gone with the Yankees, I'd have been on four pennant winners," Simmons would say, acting as if it were a foregone conclusion that he would have remained in New York's pinstripes. The old dog never lost that swagger.

"If any player ever has the choice I had," said Sim, "I'd advise this: Don't select a club that has won pennants and will have the attitude they won without you and don't need your help. Take the club that has been down and has a chance to climb."

From Detroit in '36, Simmons bounced to Washington in '37, to the Boston Braves and Cincinnati in '39, then back into the American League and Philadelphia in '40. He sat out the '42 season as a coach, returned to the playing roster with the Boston Red Sox in '43 and then got into just four games as a player-coach at Philadelphia again in '44. From then through 1949 Sim coached for the A's. He was a Cleveland coach in 1950.

His last couple of years as a player, Aloysius developed—too late—an obsession for 3,000 hits, a goal that came to his attention in 1942 when Paul Waner climbed the Mt. Everest of hitting. Simmons struggled hard, but not soon enough. He was 73 hits short at the finish.

So, when he met another Polish immigrant's son one time in the late '40s when the A's were leaving Philadelphia just as the National Leaguers were coming in, Sim gave him quite a pep talk about the importance of playing regularly and of making every time at bat count.

"From a hitter as great as Al Simmons, I learned a lesson and got inspiration that helped me get where he wanted so very much to go himself and then wanted me to reach in his place," said Stan Musial, ultimately the author of 3,630 major league hits.

ALOYSIUS HARRY (BUCKETFOOT) SIMMONS
Born May 22, 1903, at Milwaukee, Wis.
Died May 26, 1956, at Milwaukee, Wis.
Height 6-0 Weight 210
Threw and batted righthanded.
Named to Hall of Fame, 1953.

YEAR	CLUB	LEAGUE	POS.	G.	AB.	R.	H.	2B.	3B.	HR.	RBI.	B.A.	PO.	A.	E.	F.A.
1922	Milwaukee	A. A.	OF	19	50	9	11	2	1	1	7	.220	16	3	1	.950
1922	Aberdeen	Dakota	OF	99	395	91	144	26	16	10	---	.365	209	19	0	1.000
1923	Shreveport	Tex.	OF	144	525	96	189	36	10	12	99	.360	335	31	13	.966
1923	Milwaukee	A. A.	OF	24	98	20	39	2	3	0	16	.398	58	2	1	.984
1924	Philadelphia	Amer.	OF	152	594	69	183	31	9	8	102	.308	390	17	10	.976
1925	Philadelphia	Amer.	OF	153	658	122	253	43	12	24	129	.384	447	8	16	.966
1926	Philadelphia	Amer.	OF	147	581	90	199	53	10	19	109	.343	333	11	9	.975
1927	Philadelphia	Amer.	OF	106	406	86	159	36	11	15	108	.392	247	10	4	.985
1928	Philadelphia	Amer.	OF	119	464	78	163	33	9	15	107	.351	231	10	3	.988
1929	Philadelphia	Amer.	OF	143	581	114	212	41	9	34	157	.365	349	19	4	.989
1930	Philadelphia	Amer.	OF	138	554	152	211	41	16	36	165	.381	275	10	3	.990
1931	Philadelphia	Amer.	OF	128	513	105	200	37	13	22	128	.390	287	10	4	.987
1932	Philadelphia (a)	Amer.	OF	154	670	144	216	28	9	35	151	.322	290	9	6	.980
1933	Chicago	Amer.	OF	146	605	85	200	29	10	14	119	.331	372	15	4	.990
1934	Chicago	Amer.	OF	138	558	102	192	36	7	18	104	.344	286	14	4	.987
1935	Chicago (b)	Amer.	OF	128	525	68	140	22	7	16	79	.267	349	5	7	.981
1936	Detroit	Amer.	OF	143	568	96	186	38	6	13	112	.327	364	8	5	.987
1937	Washington (c)	Amer.	OF	103	419	60	117	21	10	8	84	.279	240	7	4	.984
1938	Washington (d)	Amer.	OF	125	470	79	142	23	6	21	95	.302	232	4	4	.983
1939	Bos.(e)-Cin.(f)	Nat.	OF	102	351	39	96	17	5	7	44	.274	172	8	4	.978
1940	Philadelphia	Amer.	OF	37	81	7	25	4	0	1	19	.309	51	1	2	.968
1941	Philadelphia	Amer.	OF	9	24	1	3	1	0	0	1	.125	16	0	0	1.000
1942	Philadelphia(g)	Amer.						(served as coach)								
1943	Boston(h)	Amer.	OF	40	133	9	27	5	0	1	12	.203	66	3	1	.986
1944	Philadelphia	Amer.	OF	4	6	1	3	0	0	0	2	.500	3	0	0	1.000
American League Totals				2113	8410	1468	2831	522	144	300	1783	.337	4828	161	90	.982
National League Totals				102	351	39	96	17	5	7	44	.274	172	8	4	.978
Major League Totals				2215	8761	1507	2927	539	149	307	1827	.334	5000	169	94	.982

a Sold with third baseman Jimmie Dykes and outfielder George Haas for $150,000 to Chicago White Sox, September, 28, 1932.
b Sold to Detroit Tigers for $75,000, December 10, 1935.
c Purchased by Washington Senators for $15,000, April 4, 1937.
d Sold to Boston Braves, December 20, 1938.
e Sold to Cincinnati Reds, August 31, 1939.
f Released by Cincinnati Reds after season closed and signed by Philadelphia Athletics as free agent, December 11, 1939.
g Released following 1942 season and signed by Boston Red Sox as active player, February 2, 1943.
h Released by Boston Red Sox, October 15, 1943, and signed as player-coach by Philadelphia Athletics, December, 1943.

WORLD SERIES RECORD

YEAR	CLUB	LEAGUE	POS.	G.	AB.	R.	H.	2B.	3B.	HR.	RBI.	B.A.	PO.	A.	E.	F.A.
1929	Philadelphia	Amer.	OF	5	20	6	6	1	0	2	5	.300	4	0	0	1.000
1930	Philadelphia	Amer.	OF	6	22	4	8	2	0	2	4	.364	12	1	0	1.000
1931	Philadelphia	Amer.	OF	7	27	4	9	2	0	2	8	.333	19	0	0	1.000
1939	Cincinnati	Nat.	OF	1	4	1	1	1	0	0	0	.250	3	0	0	1.000
World Series Totals				19	73	15	24	6	0	6	17	.329	38	1	0	1.000

GORGEOUS GEORGE: Before a gimmick wrestler sullied the sobriquet, that's what they called George Sisler often regarded as the perfect player. He hit .420 in 1922.

GEORGE SISLER

They called George Harold Sisler, a picture-book performer, poetry in motion and, as the supreme accolade, the perfect player. Certainly he was a perfectionist, an athlete to whom good wasn't good enough.

Sisler's standards for Sisler were so high that he considered his career to have ended, in effect, with eye trouble in 1923, even though three times thereafter he collected more than 200 hits a season and batted .326, .327 and .345.

"I didn't consider that real good hitting," said the man who in 1922 batted .420, a record American League high—and still didn't consider that his best season.

Sisler's best came two years earlier when he played every inning of 154 games for the old St. Louis Browns. Month by month, in 1920, he batted this way:

.333 in April, .360 in May, .407 in June, .325 in July, .442 in August and .448 in September.

In only 23 games was he hitless all season. Just twice did he fail to get a base hit for two successive games. He finished with 257 hits, the major league record, and collected 49 doubles, 18 triples and 19 homers, a total second only to Babe Ruth. He scored 137 runs, drove in 122 more and stole 42 bases.

Afield, he used his great speed and quickness to start 13 first-to-short-to-first double plays. And he finished with a flourish a season in which the Browns could finish only fourth, despite his .407 average and all-around derring-do.

The last day of the season against the White Sox, Sisler got three hits, scored two runs and stole three bases, including home. And he also pitched the final inning, striking out two men, even though he hadn't hurled competitively for four seasons.

THAT, you see, friend, WAS a season, but again it didn't afford Sisler the greatest thrill or the most treasured moment of a career frustrated by too many seasons in the second division, total absence of World Series joy and the misfortune of the serious sinus infection that almost cost him his sight and did cost him additional batting records.

Over the years, whenever he could be persuaded to reminisce, the modest and retiring Sisler would always remember first the moment as a rookie when he pitched against—and beat—his boyhood idol, Walter Johnson.

Sisler's dual contract signings with St. Louis and Pittsburgh helped destroy the troika that then ran baseball as the National Commission. Sisler was only two months off the Michigan U. campus in 1915 when a St. Louis sports editor, Billy Murphy, beat the drums for a Sunday hookup of the stylish 22-year-old southpaw and Washington's 28-year-old fireball righthander, Johnson. The Big Train, in his ninth major league season, already had won more than 200 games.

The Browns' manager, Branch Rickey, the man who had coached Sisler in college and preceded him to St. Louis, recognized a compelling matchup when his sense of showmanship smelled one. On Saturday, he told his tenderfoot of just a few big league games that he would face the master the next day.

"I couldn't sleep all night," Sisler recalled. "I got up early, ate breakfast and was the first man at the ballpark. I had mixed emotions over the obvious opportunity, the magnitude of the challenge and my natural regard for Johnson, whom I had learned to admire as a man as well as a pitcher.

"During the pre-game warmup, I even watched him and had to resist imitating him. Then I walked to the mound, extremely nervous, but after I threw a strike to the first batter, my concern suddenly vanished."

Sisler struck out the Senators' leadoff man, Dan Moeller, but singles by Eddie Foster and Clyde Milan put runners on first and third, from where Foster scored on an outfield fly by Howie Shanks.

It wasn't, certainly, a promising start when you consider the caliber of the pitching opponent. But then Johnson, like Sisler, labored in the vineyard of team mediocrity most of his valiant years.

So, after Tilly Walker singled in the second inning for St. Louis, Baby Doll Jacobson—uh-huh, that's what they called 'em in those days, ma'am—bunted in front of the plate. Washington's catcher Alva Williams, threw wild to first, Walker scoring and Jacobson reaching third.

When Del Howard singled, Sisler led, 2-1, and the young guy they later would call Gorgeous George and The Sizzler, made that lead stand up, inning after inning. He scattered six hits, walked two, struck out three and slipped away with a triumph over his idol.

"I looked over as soon as the game ended to see if Johnson was in the dugout," Sisler recalled. "I had the impulse to say something—maybe even tell him I was sorry—but he was gone."

Sisler, was mannerly, genteel, different from most of the players, especially in a period when the college-trained athlete was less frequent, but he was no lace-ruffled sissy. They called him Sis in the dugout, but that was merely an abbreviation of his last name.

Rickey, who always regarded Sisler as the greatest player he'd ever seen, partly through the honest prejudice of appreciating the athlete's virtues of a man, could tell how George made it painfully plain that his politeness was no sign of weakness.

At a time when he was still a kid freshly converted to first base, he couldn't reach a high throw and by the time he retrieved the ball, the runner was on second base. The Browns' pitcher, Bob Groom, was losing and the mishap did nothing to dampen the fuse of a short temper.

"Listen you … college boy," he said to Sisler in the dugout, "you run harder for those … balls. Where the hell do you think you are, at a … tea party?"

No one ever had talked like that to Sisler before—and no one would ever do so again. His face turned white, Rickey recalled, and he stared in disbelief at Groom for an instant, then walked over and decked the startled pitcher with a left hook. Once he even slapped umpire George Hildebrand with his glove and drew a brief suspension.

George was indeed a different breed of cat. He was pleasant but aloof, a modest, sober man who appeared to smile much more than he did because he squinted and bared his teeth in concentration during his playing days. In later years he wore a grimace of pain from arthritis when he had to struggle into ballparks to continue scouting for Pittsburgh.

For a time in the big leagues, Sisler incongruously called Manager Rickey "Coach," using the collegiate appellation that seemed rah-rah to many who wouldn't understand the respect and affection it implied. Even though George was past 70 when Branch died, Sisler still addressed his old mentor as Mr. Rickey.

They were inducted together into the Missouri Sports Hall of Fame in November 1965, along with the late J. G. Taylor Spink, long-time publisher of *The Sporting News*. Rickey, though close to 85, insisted on not only leaving a St. Louis hospital for the occasion, but also on watching in cold weather a Missouri-Oklahoma football game which preceded the induction dinner at Columbia.

What followed was distressing because, with the grand eloquence that made him a spellbinder, B. R. collapsed in the midst of reciting a Biblical parable in which he distinguished the difference between physical, mental and spiritual courage.

He never regained consciousness and died a few weeks later.

There was no better way, with an audience in the palm of his hand, that Mr. Rickey, if he'd had his choice, could have wanted to go.

But Sisler was so moved that, politely and yet firmly, he tightened his already rigid policy against attending banquets or other public functions.

Like Babe Ruth, George Sisler undoubtedly could have made his mark as a pitcher except that just as Ed Barrow saw that Ruth's bat was too valuable to keep him on the bench between pitching starts, Rickey recognized that every fourth day would be a waste of Sisler's talents.

George was built well but trim, 5-10½ and 170 pounds at his peak, so quick, nimble and graceful—"truly poetry in motion, the perfect player," said Frank Frisch. And he proved it for Rickey by moving from the pitching mound to the outfield and finally to first base.

In fact, in an emergency at the outset, he even played an inning or two, here and there, at second base and third base, no mean achievement for a lefthanded athlete.

"But then I'd been a shortstop as a kid back home in Ohio," said Sisler, who died a day short of his 80th birthday. Until then he was chauffeured regularly from his suburban St. Louis home to scout big league games at Busch Memorial Stadium for the Pirates.

Filling in at second base in the big leagues, had southpaw Sisler ever been required to pivot on a double play?

"No," was the thoughtful answer and a chuckle, "but, somehow, I think I would have managed."

Although modesty is a Sisler characteristic, so is self-confidence. "Hitters," he said, "have to believe in themselves. They can't be afraid of the ball, the pitcher or the situation. Rogers Hornsby was always so certain of his own ability to dominate that he actually felt sorry for the pitcher."

Hornsby and Sisler came up to the big leagues the same year, 1915, and together the handsome roughneck from deep in the heart of Texas and the well-mannered Michigan grad gave St. Louis probably the greatest competitive perfection at the plate any big league city ever has enjoyed.

Neither the Browns, with whom Sisler finally settled at first base to become defensively great, nor the Cardinals, for whom Hornsby became a good second baseman, went far through most of the 11 seasons George and Rog were rivals in the same town. So the spotlight focused on the righthanded-hitting Hornsby and the lefthanded-hitting of Sisler.

If the heavier, huskier Hornsby was the harder hitter, Sisler was no "tickie" hitter, which a later generation of Pirates would say when they tried to tease the hitting coach for whom they had great admiration and respect.

George could leg out an infield hit or a safe bunt, but using a heavy 42-ounce hickory bat with a choked grip, he could pull with power as well as punch, push and slash.

He's proud of the fact, despite his ability to lay the ball down and hotfoot for first base, that he didn't bunt once to prolong his 41-game hitting streak in 1922.

That one, the record until Joe DiMaggio's famed 56-game string in 1941, was snapped in a crucial late-season game when Sisler's right shoulder was so badly hurt that he had to lift his right gloved hand with the bare one on throws that were above the waist.

"I told the other infielders to keep the throws low in that big series with the Yankees," Sisler said later, "but I couldn't tell New York's pitchers to do the same. I should not have been in there, but we so desperately wanted to win the pennant."

And Lee Fohl, the manager, recognized the obvious: A Sisler with one arm was better than anyone else available with two, even though he was held to

a hit each of the first two games and then blanked in the decisive third one when the Browns blew a ninth-inning lead, losing the late-September series—and the 1922 pennant—by one game.

Failure to play on better clubs undoubtedly cost Sisler money and acclaim at a time when, as Eddie Collins put it, George was caught between the fiery flamboyance of Ty Cobb and the boisterous brilliance of Babe Ruth. How could a quiet, clean-living superstar expect to win headlines?

Yet, if you tend to grieve for Sisler, 15 years a big leaguer without experiencing the rich thrill of playing in a World Series, just consider how drab the existence of the old Browns would have been without St. Louis's greatest American League star.

Long after the Browns' wartime pennant in the streetcar Series of 1944 becomes misty in the memory and faceless and nameless, baseball folklore will record the deeds of a chap called Sisler with a team known as the Browns.

The Sizzler warmed many a cold winter for followers of a team whose inferiority complex was almost as obvious as the Cardinals' until the National League neighbors won their first of 12 pennants under Hornsby in 1926. By then The Rajah and Gorgeous George had slumped at bat, though they both would rebound elsewhere, if never again quite so savagely. Here, year by year, is the way they went at it in a rivalry that drew distinct lines of difference like the one between the Republican elephant and the Democratic donkey:

	HORNSBY	SISLER
1916	.313	.305
1917	.327	.353
1918	.281	.341
1919	.318	.352
1920	.370	.407
1921	.397	.371
1922	.401	.420
1923	.384	(Did Not Play)
1924	.424	.305
1925	.403	.345
1926	.317	.289

Before the 1927 season, St. Louis—and baseball—was shocked by the trade in which Hornsby went to the New York Giants for Frank Frisch and pitcher Jimmy Ring. At the end of the '27 season, Sisler was gone, too.

After returning from an illness-imposed exile in 1923, a year poisonous sinusitis affected his optic nerves and gave him double vision for a time, Sisler reluctantly became player-manager. As he said later, he should have known better. He'd seen things become so discouraging with the Browns that one time in 1918, after they'd blown a five-run lead in the ninth inning and lost at Washington, their manager of the moment, Fielder Jones, walked out the clubhouse door—and never came back.

A $25,000 contract, the best of his career, induced Sisler to manager at a time when he frankly felt he wasn't ready. Even though, however, he wasn't stern enough as some observers felt, the fourth and third-place finishes the next two seasons were better than par for the Browns' course. After a sag to seventh in 1926, however, Sisler suggested he be returned to the ranks. And as a buck private he batted .327 in 149 games, collected 201 hits and drove in 97 runs. Surprisingly, an ownership that once had turned down $200,000 for his contract, sold the 34-year-old first baseman to Washington for $25,000.

Sisler did considerable mountain-climbing and heavy hunting that winter, hoping to bring back the spring into his legs, but he wondered later whether he might have overdone it. He was slowed painfully with the Senators and, in late May, he was sold to the National League, claimed by of all people—his old rival, Hornsby, then player-manager of the Braves.

"I always liked Rog," George said. "We respected each other's ability and I liked the fact that you always knew where you stood with him."

Sisler stood high with Hornsby. Together, playing for a bad ball club, they put on quite a show. George batted .340 and Rog, three years younger, led the league with .387.

Hornsby was traded to Chicago, but Sisler stayed on at Boston to hit .326 in 1929. Even though at 36 he was able to get 205 hits, that was one of the seasons he didn't particularly relish.

"Our manager," he recalled, "was the club owner, Judge Emil Fuchs, a nice man, but entirely out of place on the bench. Johnny Evers, coaching third base for us, would be looking in for a sign, and the Judge would be telling jokes."

The Braves finished a happy eighth, dead last, before Judge Fuchs brought in a good baseball man, Bill McKechnie. Sisler, slowed even more afield and on the bases, batted .309 in 116 games in 1930 and then caught on with a winner at Rochester after he was released by the Braves.

At 39, Sisler batted .287 on part-time duty as player-manager at Shreveport-Tyler in the Texas League in 1932 and then got out of professional baseball.

"I regretted the 10 years I was away," he looked back when he returned as a scout and special hitting instructor with Brooklyn, just after Branch Rickey went to the Dodgers as president and general manager in 1943.

In the interval, Sisler hadn't been idle. Earlier, as a player, he had been associated with a St. Louis printing company that bore his name. For a time later, he was interested in a sporting goods house, which also carried the magic Sisler label, and he operated two depression-period night softball parks when there was no air conditioning to keep people inside on hot nights and no major league competition under the lights.

For several years, too, he served as commissioner of the National Baseball Congress for Ray Dumont, supervising the annual national semi-pro tournament played then and now in Wichita, Kan.

Sisler followed Rickey from Brooklyn to Pittsburgh and stayed behind after B. R. left the Pirates, though eventually the Sislers returned to St. Louis. Mrs. Sisler, the former Kathleen Holznagel of Detroit, met George on the campus at Ann Arbor.

They had a daughter in St. Louis, Mrs. William Drochleman, one of the three Sisler boys lived there and another worked in the city where their father made his fame. The boys have done more than all right in baseball, too.

George, Jr., a Colgate graduate bothered by weak eyes, played professionally one year in the Browns' organization as a pitcher-infielder before beginning a front office career in the Cardinals' chain. He eventually became general manager at Rochester and, ultimately, president of the International League and operated the Yankees farm club at Columbus, O.

Dick, bigger and stronger than his father, yet not nearly so well-coordinated, played first base and the outfield for the Cardinals and Phillies from 1946 through 1953. Dick, later manager at Cincinnati and then a coach with the Redbirds, gave his father one of the greatest moments of mixed emotions a parent ever could have.

In 1950, with the pennant at stake on the final day, George's No. 2 son hit a 10th-inning home run for Philadelphia at Brooklyn, where his father, seated in the stands, was on the Dodgers' payroll.

The third son, Dave, a basketball star at Princeton, pitched for Boston, Detroit, Washington and Cincinnati from 1956 through 1962 and became a prominent stock broker in St. Louis.

The senior Sisler, a reserved man, was proud of his boys in a quiet way. "They made it on their own," he said. "I really never was able to play with the older ones, so the most we did was just talk, and I tried to answer questions rather than offer advice."

Maybe that's the way George learned it back home in Nimisila, O., which is close to Manchester, in turn close to Akron. His grandfather Sisler had farmed the area and then gone into the grocery business. George's father, Cassius Sisler, and his mother, the former Mary Whipple, were graduates of Hiram College. Like George and his Kathleen, they were college sweethearts.

George was born into an athletic family on March 24, 1893. His father, supervising a coal mine, and two older brothers were good athletes. George moved to Akron to live with an older brother at 14 so he could go to high school. An uncle was mayor of the rubber capital.

With a choice of scholarships at the University of Pennsylvania and Western Reserve, young Sisler, then a magnificent all-around athlete at 140 pounds, insisted on paying his own way at Michigan so that he could be with his high school batterymate, Russ Baer, who wanted to study law at Michigan. Baer became a banker in Akron.

At 17, before going off to Ann Arbor, Sisler signed a piece of paper that almost turned baseball inside out. He signed with Akron of the Ohio-Pennsylvania League, a farm team of Columbus' American Association club. He received no money and played no game professionally and the University of Michigan later waived the transgression.

The kid impressed Branch Rickey so much that Rickey even remembered that Sisler was wearing a blue sweater the first time the former big league catcher and graduate lawyer saw George when Rickey was coaching baseball at Michigan.

"I knew at once," he would say, "that this was a once-in-a generation athlete, a remarkable young man who instinctively knew how to handle a bat—and he could run as fast as any ballplayer I had ever seen."

Rickey implored Fielding H. (Hurry-Up) Yost, Michigan's famed football coach, not to use the slender youth, fearing he would be hurt. And then B. R. shrewdly let it be known around the American League that if any ball club really was interested in Sisler, it might do well to speak to his coach first. Rickey became a scout for the Browns in 1912 and manager a year later.

By the time George graduated in 1915 with a degree in mechanical engineering, the Browns had his name on a contract. So did the Pittsburgh Pirates, who had purchased that earlier contract from Columbus.

A hassle followed, a tug of war in which the three-man National Commission, then running baseball, finally voted two out of three in favor of St. Louis. National League President John K. Tener favored Pittsburgh.

American League President Ban Johnson favored St. Louis. Cincinnati club president Garry Herrmann cast a decisive vote for the Browns, perhaps taking into strong consideration the fact that Sisler had been a minor who had signed without parental consent.

The Pirates' owner, Barney Dreyfuss, refused to speak to Herrmann, and the tottering troika collapsed in the wake of the 1919 Black Sox scandal, with selection of Judge K. M. Landis as commissioner.

Sisler went directly from college commencement to the big leagues. He made his debut with the Browns on June 28, 1915, at Chicago, pitching three scoreless innings in relief and getting a hit in two trips off a 24-game winner with the awesome nickname of Death Valley Jim Scott.

As mentioned, the 2-1 victory two months later over the man he worshipped as a person and player, Walter Johnson, made Sisler believe he really belonged. A year later, he faced Johnson again and blanked the Big Train, 1-0.

Although he had only a 5-7 won-lost record for the pitching he did over the two-year period—and he appeared in only 27 innings on the mound in 1916—George had an earned-run average, 2.32, which spoke better for his effectiveness. Thereafter, he would appear as a pitcher in only four season-ending games.

Meanwhile, he had begun to win games and a reputation with his scientific bat, gifted glove and daring legs.

In 1918, batting .341, he led the league with 45 stolen bases and committed only 13 errors. In 191, he hit .352 and, ranging wide off the gab, turned in 120 assists.

Then began an incredible three-year stretch which in many ways was more outstanding than the five-season period, 1921 through '25, in which Hornsby averaged nearly .400. Sisler, 1920 through '22, was close to .400, too, with those individual averages of .407, .371 and .420. Moreover, he collected 719 hits and stole more than 125 bases. He was voted the American League's Most Valuable Player in 1922.

He was doing the darnedest things defensively, too. Like the day he fielded a groundball and flipped it softly toward first base, only to find, by Judas Priest, that the pitcher wasn't covering the bag. Before you could say George Harold Sisler, The Sizzler had leaped forward, Mr. Rickey said, and caught his own throw on the bag for a putout.

Dubious? Then you never saw Gorgeous George. One day the Browns were playing Washington in St. Louis and a situation arose in which the hallmarks of the perfect player—intuition, speed, precision and sheer artistry—permitted Sisler to do this:

With Washington's Joe Judge breaking from third base, Roger Peckinpaugh bunted down the first-base line. Sisler, sensing the play, had bolted with the pitch. Scooping up the ball only about 15 feet from the plate, inches in fair territory, George tagged Peckinpaugh and in one continuous motion he threw to Hank Severeid, who tagged out the sliding Judge.

Asked about the long-talked-about double play on a groundball squeeze bunt, Sisler smiled. "I'll never forget it, either," he said.

George Sisler was at his best when he was speaking his piece about hitting, a subject on which he obviously was an authority and one articulate enough to get his points across.

"Hitters can't guess, they've got to think," he would tell the batters he helped, always insisting it was their own aptitude that permitted them to improve.

"They've got to look for the ball, not for a particular pitch. They can afford to be selective, meaning they should only swing at strikes, but they can't be defensive up there. They've got to have a balanced stance, level swing and keep their front shoulder into the ball so they're going into the ball, whether they're pulling the pitch or hitting the ball to the opposite field."

Inducted together as true giants of baseball at the first ceremony at Cooperstown in July 1939—Christy Mathewson, Willie Keeler and John McGraw already were dead—were Ty Cobb, Babe Ruth, Honus Wagner, Walter Johnson, Cy Young, Larry Lajoie, Eddie Collins, Grover Cleveland Alexander, Tris Speaker, Connie Mack and Sisler.

Thirty years later, when the grand old game reached 100, only Sisler was alive and he still wasn't drinking, a fact which startled W. C. Fields years ago in Boston when the bulbous comic expressed a desire to meet his favorite player.

Fields, playing in *Poppy*, the show in which he used his unforgettable line, "Never give a sucker an even break," had been watching Sisler at Fenway Park. The ballplayer obliged by visiting the comic backstage at the Majestic Theater.

Although this was prohibition, Fields' dressing room was stacked with more cases of whiskey than would be found in a high class speakeasy.

"You fascinate me, George," said Fields in his famous nasal tenor. "I've seen you many times and have admired your artistry very much. Help yourself to the snake-bite cure."

"No, thanks," replied Sisler, politely, "I don't drink."

A look of keen disappointment came over the classic Fieldian features and, helping himself to a beaker of rye, W. C. said, philosophically, "Oh, well, not even the perfect ballplayer can have everything."

GEORGE HAROLD (GORGEOUS GEORGE) SISLER
Born March 24, 1893, at Manchester, O.
Died March 26, 1973, at St. Louis, Mo.
Height 5-10 1/2 Weight 170
Threw and batted lefthanded.
Named to Hall of Fame, 1939.

YEAR	CLUB	LEAGUE	POS.	G.	AB.	R.	H.	2B.	3B.	HR.	RBI.	B.A.	PO.	A.	E.	F.A.
1915	St. Louis	Amer.	P-1-O	81	274	28	78	10	2	3	29	.285	413	38	7	.985
1916	St. Louis	Amer.	1-P-O	151	580	83	177	21	11	4	74	.305	1493	86	24	.985
1917	St. Louis	Amer.	O-1B	135	539	60	190	30	9	2	55	.353	1384	101	22	.985.
1918	St. Louis	Amer.	1B	114	452	69	154	21	9	2	45	.341	1244	97	13	.990
1919	St. Louis	Amer.	1B	132	511	96	180	31	15	10	83	.352	1249	120	13	.991
1920	St. Louis	Amer.	1B	154	631	137	257	49	18	19	122	.407	1477	140	16	.990
1921	St. Louis	Amer.	1B	138	582	125	216	38	18	11	104	.371	1267	108	10	.993
1922	St. Louis	Amer.	1B	142	586	134	246	42	18	8	105	.420	1293	125	17	.988
1923	St. Louis	Amer.					(Out with eye trouble)									
1924	St. Louis	Amer.	1B	151	636	94	194	27	10	9	74	.305	1326	112	23	.984
1925	St. Louis	Amer.	1B	150	649	100	224	21	15	12	105	.345	1343	131	26	.983
1926	St. Louis	Amer.	1B	150	613	78	178	21	12	7	71	.289	1467	87	21	.987
1927	St. Louis(a)	Amer.	1B	149	614	87	201	32	8	5	97	.327	1374	131	24	.984
1928	Washington(b)	Amer.	1B	20	49	1	12	1	0	0	2	.245	45	0	0	1.000
1928	Boston	Nat.	1B	118	491	71	167	26	4	4	68	.340	1188	86	15	.988
1929	Boston	Nat.	1B	154	629	67	205	40	9	1	79	.326	1398	111	28	.982
1930	Boston	Nat.	1B	116	431	54	133	15	7	3	67	.309	915	81	13	.987
1931	Rochester	Int.	1B	159	613	86	186	37	5	3	81	.303	1401	125	20	.987
1932	Shrev.-Tyler	Tex.	1B	70	258	28	74	15	2	1	23	.287	637	33	15	.978
American League Totals				1667	6716	1092	2307	344	145	92	966	.344	15375	1276	216	.987
National League Totals				388	1551	192	505	81	20	8	214	.326	3501	278	56	.985
Major League Totals				2055	8267	1284	2812	425	165	100	1180	.340	18876	1554	272	.987

a Sold to Washington for $25,000, December 14, 1927.
b Purchased by Boston N. L. for $7,500, May 27, 1928.

PITCHING RECORD

YEAR	CLUB	LEAGUE	G.	IP.	W.	L.	Pct.	H.	R.	ER.	SO.	BB.	ERA.
1915	St. Louis	Amer.	15	70	4	4	.500	62	26	22	41	38	2.83
1916	St. Louis	Amer.	3	27	1	3	.250	18	4	3	12	6	1.00
1920	St. Louis	Amer.	1	1	0	0	.000	0	0	0	2	0	0.00
1925	St. Louis	Amer.	1	2	0	0	.000	1	0	0	1	1	0.00
1926	St. Louis	Amer.	1	2	0	0	.000	0	0	0	3	2	0.00
1928	Boston	Nat.	1	1	0	0	.000	0	0	0	0	1	0.00
Major League Totals			22	103	5	7	.417	81	30	25	59	48	2.13

SUPER SOUTHPAW: *Warren Spahn, winningest lefthander ever, shows the high-kicking craftsmanship by which he fooled batters and also picked off many opposing baserunners.*

WARREN SPAHN

Affluent as well as affable and extremely able, Warren Spahn, a frugal man and yet not nearly as stingy with his money as with enemy hits, missed a chance to include among his many baseball records the granddaddy of all contracts, one that would have made even Babe Ruth's Depression-era document look like a bunt.

Back in 1952, the Boston Braves nosedived to seventh place amid the groans of only 281,278 patrons. Spahn, four times a 20-game winner, had dropped to a 14-19 record in his sixth full major league season and had been asked to take a pay cut. Spahn, who never balked on the mound, balked now at the salary terms offered by Lou Perini, the contractor who had bought out the two other members of the Three Little Steam Shovels, Guido Rugo and Joe Maney.

Spahn wouldn't hold still for a $5,000 cut from $25,000. He insisted on the same salary because, to tell the truth, his 2.98 earned-run average with that young, inexperienced ball club behind him in '52 had been lower than in three of his big seasons.

"How about 10 cents a head?" said Perini, proposing a contract based on attendance. Spahn declined with thanks. He'd seen that Braves' gate decline steadily every year following their pennant season of 1948.

So the crafty king of lefthanders, the shrewd Spahnie, got his $25,000, but he blew a contract for $182,639.70. Before the first ball was thrown in 1953, the Braves had been moved to Milwaukee, the land of milk and honey, and the attendance increased nearly seven-fold from one season to the next.

Spahn can tell that story now, a crazy, crooked smile on his lips, because that bonanza was about all he missed in a 20-year career in which he won more games than any southpaw—past, present or probably future—and built his holdings into a 2,800-acre spread southwest of Hartshorne, Okla.

Warren Spahn's Diamond Star cattle ranch is a far cry from the chilblains of Buffalo, N.Y., where he grew up as the son of a baseball-batty wallpaper salesman, but the improbabilities geographically are even less than the chances Casey Stengel would have given for his future in a spring training game in 1942 in Florida.

Spahn, not quite 21, had been a big winner at the Braves' Class B farm club at Evansville, Ind., and had been invited to train with the big league club, then managed by the jug-eared, sandy-haired, mobile-featured man who himself had a date with baseball destiny. Stengel might have seemed like a clown managing seventh-place misfits at Brooklyn and Boston, but there wasn't anything funny about those New York teams he turned out in championship sequence at Yankee Stadium.

For all his quips and quotes, Ol' Case was a member of the old school, a disciple of John McGraw, and he expected his men to be able to play the game rough and tough. So his exasperation soared in a spring exhibition game against Brooklyn when he flashed the sign for a brushback pitch and his pitcher failed to comply.

The Dodgers had been swiping the Braves' battery signs and with Pee Wee Reese at bat and a runner on second, Stengel reasoned that nothing would shake up Dodger confidence more in their ability to crack the Braves' code than to send the batter back on his heels with a high, hard one when the teammate on base was wig-wagging that a curve was coming.

Three times Stengel gave the brushback motion from the bench, but three times young Spahn merely threw a fastball inside to Reese, and Casey came storming out of the dugout to the mound and took the ball out of the pitcher's hand.

"Young man," the manager growled, "you've got no guts."

Spahn not only remembered, but so did Stengel, a man with an elephantine memory.

"Casey lifted me because I hadn't decked Reese," the famous pitcher would relate, smiling, "and then he stopped me in the dugout and told me to pick up my railroad ticket to Hartford."

Stengel, grinning, would add in his raspy voice, "Yes, I said 'no guts' to a kid who wound up a war hero and one of the best pitchers anybody ever saw. You can't say I don't miss 'em when I miss 'em."

Indeed, Ol' Case missed that one almost as much as National League hitters did when they tried to zero in on the serve of the left-kicking, smooth-throwing, stylish southpaw whose 363 victories left him fifth on the all-time list of major league pitchers even though he spent three years in service in World War II.

It's not that Spahn was ready for the big leagues by 1943, not even after having followed that 19-6 and 1.83 ERA season at Evansville with a 17-12 record and 1.96 efficiency rate in Class A at Hartford. But there's no doubt that he would have been able to post his first big league victory a couple of years before mid-season, 1946, when he was 25.

The way Spahn walked right out of the Army early in the 1946 season, did sideline training with the Braves and then broke in with four consecutive victories would indicate that only military duty kept him from achieving probably a National League record for victories and maybe even 400 games.

When Warren won 23 and lost only seven as a 42-year-old wonder in 1963, he felt confident that he could pass the 373 at which Christy Mathewson and Grover Cleveland Alexander were tied and even join Cy Young and Walter Johnson in the exclusive membership of 400-plus.

The strong, supple left arm, singularly free of trouble over the years, never did give out, but the trim, well-built legs, which had taken a tremendous toll, finally betrayed him. Three times, astonishingly, Spahn had experienced and bounced back from surgery on his knees. Finally the old wheels gave out and, as further proof of the problem the pitcher had experienced and endured, he was nearly crippled until he underwent further surgery on both knees in 1970 when he was managing Tulsa, the Cardinals' Triple-A farm club located only a couple of hours from his expensive diggings.

A wheelchair for life was the medical alternative to the double surgery performed after the '70 season—"I'd reached the limit of my tolerance for pain," Spahn said—and a poignant sight at the annual Florida governor's baseball dinner, this one in St. Petersburg, was the man who wasn't yet 49 years old.

His weight was down from 195 to 167, his face gaunt, accentuating the generous nose for which he had been chided over the years. His head was almost bald except for a warlock which had made him in the passing years look like a Mohawk chief. The Last of the Mohicans barely could hobble out of a wheelchair with crutches to accept an especial award to a thunderous ovation, but before the Oilers broke camp and headed north, Spahnie had filled out somewhat and he was gimping along with his canes, showing the same kind of guts that Casey Stengel didn't think he had those many years before.

Among the big winners in baseball history, Spahn's position is unique. Not only did he record

more victories than southpaws of the unquestioned quality of Eddie Plank, Lefty Grove, Carl Hubbell, Herb Pennock and, later, Steve Carlton—must we go on?—but he pitched his entire career in the era of the lively ball. Only Johnson and Alexander of the previous 300-plus winners were still on the active list when Warren Spahn was born in 1921. Johnson, who pitched until 1927, and Alexander, a big leaguer until '30, endured the juiced-up ball, which came in when the spitter and other foreign substances were outlawed in 1920. But the bulk of their careers, like those of their illustrious predecessors, came in an era when a pitcher could afford to coast or to pace himself.

Spahn might not have faced as many good hitters—and this is not to say he didn't—but the free swingers and the hypoed horsehide did create a combination which made every man a home run threat and, therefore, permitted the pitcher no luxury with the lightweights in the enemy lineup. When catcher Hobie Landrith of the San Francisco Giants beat him, 3-2, with a two-run, ninth-inning homer late in his career, Spahn felt the sting more than if he had been tagged by an old nemesis, Stan Musial.

Spahn and Musial—they even looked somewhat alike until Warren began to thin out on top—put on quite a show over the years they battled against each other when, fact is, the Cardinals were the lefthander's favorite cousins. He beat them nearly 70 times.

The lefthanded-hitting Musial hit .314 for his career against southpaw Spahn and belted 14 home runs in their confrontations which ended in 1963, The Man's last year, when Stan knocked Warren off the mound and out with a hot line smash. As usual, Spahn won the game.

"Sure, I hit him pretty good," said Musial, "but most of those long balls came early in both our careers when he could really throw hard and I had quicker reflexes and he'd try to buzz one by me. Over the years, I learned I had to give in, to go to the opposite field against him, to wait on the ball a split-second longer, or I wouldn't have had a chance.

"With Spahn's control, I wouldn't try to get out in front of the ball. So I wouldn't be off-stride against changing speeds, I'd hit quite a bit from left field to right-center against him. Facing Warren was the greatest challenge I knew because this man was a pitching scientist, an artist with imagination."

Spahn not only was a master of control and cunning, but also of the most difficult thing to achieve in baseball by batter and pitcher alike—consistency. His 13 seasons with 20 victories were the most ever by a lefthander. In fact, only Cy Young, winning 511 games had more 20-game seasons—16. No pitcher ever bettered Spahn's string of consecutive seasons with 100 or more strikeouts—17.

At one time, wonderful Spahn was a blow 'em down pitcher whose rising fastball alone was a considerable weapon. His curveball was just pretty good and he had a pretty good change. In 1948, when the Braves broke a 34-year drought by winning a pennant, Spahn started the second game of the World Series against Cleveland at Braves Field and was lifted in the fourth inning, trailing Bob Lemon by the 4-1 score that became final that day.

Twice thereafter in the Series, won by the Indians in six games, Spahn relieved at Cleveland's mammoth lake-front stadium and, with the adrenaline flowing because of crowds of more than 86,000, the young lefthander put on a strong-armed show.

In the fifth game, replacing Nelson Potter in the fourth inning, Spahn fired five and two-thirds innings of scoreless ball, allowing just one hit, walking one and fanning seven. The 11-5 Boston victory deservedly was his.

In the sixth and deciding contest won by Cleveland, 4-3, Warren worked two innings and yielded a precious run, but, more important for the point that is being pursued here, he fanned four in the two frames. In the company of Bob Feller, Johnny

Said, Lemon and the other good men of the mound who worked in that Series, Spahn seemed the most overpowering pitcher.

Actually, in that long-awaited season of joy for the Boston Nationals, the chant of "Spahn and Sain and a day of rain" was not quite accurate. For one thing, it was the tall tobacco-chewing righthander, Sain, a 24-game winner, who deserved top billing. And with a 15-12 record, even though typically he came on the second half of the season, Spahn didn't deserve that much better notices than other members of the Boston staff.

Over the years, of course, he would outdistance them all, including Sain, who became an outstanding pitching coach and, therefore, a man who could evaluate his former teammate as well as any, if not better.

"Spahn was able to change over from being a power pitcher," said Sain. "Go through the records and find out how many pitchers were able to do that. Not many.

"He was completely thorough. He hit well enough to stay in a close game late. He fielded extremely well. He ran the bases well and his move to first base was superb. I can remember that he picked off Jackie Robinson twice in one vital game during a Labor Day doubleheader at Boston in '48 when Robinson was the best basestealer in the league.

"Spahn became great because of these things and because he's one of the smartest men ever to play the game," Sain went on. "He came up with a screwball to help when his fastball began to fade and then he added the slider. And consider this when you marvel at the ability of a man able to pitch no-hit games and even jerk up big strikeout performances when he's 40 years old.

"A young fellow can blow it past the hitters and fan maybe a dozen in a game. No older pitcher should strike out that many. The older fellow will be doing fine if he strikes out three or four, but in the spots he picks. He'll know from his experience which is the important situation and he'll be able to muscle up the necessary power to do it once or twice in a game. That's where Spahn is so great. Still, he managed to fan 15 in one of his no-hitters at an age when most pitchers long have had it."

Pitching student Sain made this further observation about pitching student Spahn:

"He had to change all the time because he's been around so long the batters had to get to know him. Did you ever notice how a good hitter will look so bad striking out the first time up? The second time, maybe he'll get a piece of the ball. And if he's still up against the same pitcher the third or fourth time, he could make a lot of trouble. Spahn, learning all the time, has been good at changing and fooling the good hitters right in the middle of a game."

Traveling with the Cardinals for the *St. Louis Post-Dispatch* through the heart of Spahn's career—hell, he outlasted me on the road—I used to like to listen to Chief Hooknose, as some of the players would call him disrespectfully. Talking to Spahn as a St. Louis reporter after he beat the beloved Redbirds made it practically a continual conversation.

When he heard I was getting off the caravan to become sports editor in 1958, the year the National League went coast to coast and became an aerial circus, he reminisced and then said:

"I'll tell you the secret of consistent pitching: you have to be able to throw strikes, but you try not to whenever possible."

Ever since his father, Edward Spahn, stormed over any display of wildness as a kid athlete, Warren Spahn has had an acute sensitivity to the importance of control. "The plate is 17 inches wide," he explained, "but I've always figured the middle 12 inches belong to the hitter. I want the couple inches of the plate, inside and out, but only if I need them."

To illustrate his point about the ability to throw strikes, but the desire not to, Spahn went back to two central figures in Cleveland's 1948 success. Handsome lefthander Gene Bearden and righthander Bob Lemon were 20-game winners that season. Lemon went on to put together six more

20-win seasons, but Bearden soon was out of the league.

"Lemon's good sinker was generally below the knees, not above," said Spahn. "The difference between Lemon and Bearden, say, is that whenever batters did lay off Lem's pitch, he still could come in there with another good pitch. When batters began laying off Gene's knuckler, finding out it was breaking into the dirt, he couldn't throw anything above the knees that was effective."

The "pitching scientist, an artist with imagination," as Musial called him, Spahn was six feet tall and trim until near the end and, as he pointed out, his legs had no excess weight, either. For years, Warren and his fun-loving pitching partner, Lew Burdette, would stay in shape, they'd say, by teasing the kids at Brooklyn's Ebbets Field and then running to the safety of the outfield.

"If you ever got hit with an overripe banana or tomato, you'd find you had amazing speed," Spahnie said, smiling.

Off the mound, Spahn liked to horse around, almost as loosey-goosey as Burdette, but on the mound he was a picture of perfection. Head cocked to one side, he'd take the battery sign on the rubber, then go into a slow rock-back with a high, fluid kick of his right leg, his bent knee almost hiding his glove. Then out of the front of the uniform, so that it would be more difficult for the batter to pick up the pitch, he'd deliver the ball overhanded in a flurry of arms and legs.

The thinking man's pitcher learned first to mix the size and speeds of curves. Next, he picked up a sinker. As far back as 1950, he began to develop on the sidelines a screwball, a pitch which would break down and away from a righthanded batter, but he waited until he faltered in 1955, dropping below 20 victories for only the second time in seven seasons, to introduce the new delivery to unhappy National League hitters.

Even after he became the most prominent pitcher of this period, Spahn was not too bashful to seek advice, just as back there at Boston in 1942 he learned from Willard Donovan, a little-remembered lefthander, the magical move that glued enemy runners to first base as if they were playing girls' softball. They swore that at times he threw to the plate when he was looking at first base, but it only seemed that way. His keen concentration permitted him to coordinate a head fake with good body balance and a right foot that looked as if it would go to the plate and yet would be put down in a line directly enough toward first base to win approval from the umpires.

In 1958, even though he was posting 21 victories with almost the same pleasant monotony he put on uniform No. 21 at Milwaukee, Warren went to Whitlow Wyatt, the Braves' pitching coach. Spahn wanted help with a slider, the pitch that had enabled Wyatt to bloom late in his career.

"The slider," Spahn told me, "has done more to help the pitcher than anything. It not only makes the batter aware that he's got to look for a pitch difficult to detect, but it gives a righthanded pitcher, for instance, a pitch he can use in tight on a pull-hitting lefthanded batter. And any time you've got the pitches to work in and out on a batter as well as up and down, you're a lot better off, and" he grinned, "the batter isn't."

When the Ponce de Leon of pitching came along back in April 1921, his father, Edward P. Spahn, couldn't decide whether he wanted his son to become a big league baseball player or president of the United States. So he named him after the president then, Warren G. Harding, and set out to teach him baseball.

Pop Spahn, with eventually four daughters and another son, managed to find a lot of time away from selling wallpaper in Buffalo to play catch with his son. Mr. Spahn had a big, old-fashioned catching glove and insisted that the boy hit the target. If he didn't, the father scolded the young southpaw, who looked back later with pleasure on Pop's persistence and perspicacity.

"He taught me how to follow through with my shoulder and body, how to throw without any strain, how to get the most out of my pitch and out of my weight even when I was a skinny kid," a grateful Spahn recalled. "He taught me how to roll a curveball, how to let it go off my fingers at the last moment. He taught me to pass my right knee with my left elbow.

"I thought it was a lot of drudgery. It was lots more fun just to pick up the ball and throw, but Dad wouldn't let me play catch unless I did it correctly."

As the boy became older, Ed Spahn would take him out to watch the Buffalo Bisons of the International League. Bill Kelly, the first baseman, was his favorite because Warren thought then that he wanted to be a first baseman. By the time he was nine years old, his father encouraged him to join the Lake City Athletic Club, which had a midget team in a league sponsored by the *Buffalo Evening News.*

"I'll never forget that first uniform," the major league star would say years later. "I petted it like a puppy and I'd go to the club two hours before game time, just to put it on and wear it around."

Three years later, Warren joined the Casenovia Post Junior American Legion team, still as a first baseman, and also served as batboy for the team on which his father played.

"Every Sunday, Dad would take us all to church. Then we'd hurry home, grab a bite to eat, pack our baseball clothes and go. Those were happy years. By the time I was 15, I was playing for three teams six days a week—the Legion team, my high school and in the Buffalo Municipal League."

One year father and son were on the same club. Ed played third base, Warren was the 110-pound first baseman, and the old man gunned the ball across the diamond until the boy's hand hurt.

"When I made a mistake, I heard about it." Spahn said. "My dad's philosophy was, 'It's okay to make a mistake once, but never twice.' He didn't only dish it out, though, because if I thought he'd done something wrong in a game and mentioned it, he thanked me."

Spahn's father must have been quite a man.

"You have only so much time on this earth, son," he would say. "Be an economist. Don't waste it. Use it for something constructive. You wouldn't throw gravel into the valves of an engine, would you? Well, then, don't throw any gravel into the greatest engine in the world, your body.

"That goes for your mind, too. Don't litter it with a lot of garbage and then have to spend half your time cleaning it up."

The senior Spahn's advice was also sound when it came to the boy's relations with other people. "Don't pop off too much," the father told the son. "The guy who is noisy, always blowing off, is the fellow who has an inferiority complex. Be yourself, be polite, respect other people's feelings and treat them with deference."

Warren Spahn learned his lessons well. When he couldn't beat out the high school first baseman, he switched to pitching and the years of his father's harping on control and a smooth throwing motion, plus his own tireless effort, paid off. Father and son glowed in 1940 when scout Bill Myers, a former umpire, offered him a small bonus to play with Bradford in the Class D Pony League.

The story is that Myers was scouting for the Red Sox and was so miffed when they wouldn't sign Spahn at a modest figure that he transferred over to the Braves and took the kid with him. If that one is true, the Sox lost one who proved almost too good to be true.

At Bradford, working for a grizzled old ex-big league catcher and coach, Jack Onslow, later manager of the Chicago White Sox, the 19-year-old Spahn twice pulled tendons in his left arm. He was 5-4 with a 2.73 ERA, but then pitching at Evansville for another old catcher, Bob Coleman, later boss of the Braves, he began to roll with that 19-6 mark in '41 and 193 strikeouts in 212 innings.

As mentioned, Casey Stengel questioned his courage in spring training, 1942, before he was assigned to Hartford, but late in the season he was called up by the Braves and worked in four games,

16 innings, during which he yielded 10 earned runs, striking out seven and walking 11. The control wouldn't ripen until after the war.

Spahn couldn't very well forget his major league debut. Stengel brought him out of the bullpen in the eighth inning at New York's Polo Grounds, with the Braves trailing, and Babe Barna greeted him with a three-run triple—but Boston won the game.

"On a forfeit," Spahn said, smiling. "There were thousands of kids in the place that day free. They got in for bringing a few items of scrap iron or aluminum for the war effort. But when I got the side out finally in the eighth, the kids swarmed all over the field and wouldn't clear it even under threat of forfeit to the visiting club. So the umpires finally awarded the game to the Braves."

This was not, of course, the first of Spahnie's 363 victories. Before he could win that one, a lot of water would flow under the bridge, including the famed Remagen bridge where he nearly lost his life in World War II.

Years later, Spahn won—and then lost—a judgment for $10,000 against a publisher who brought out a juvenile book about him, a book which the pitcher figured fabricated too much, blowing up out of proportion, for instance, his role in World War II.

No matter how he might try to play down his contribution, the young hawknosed hurler from Buffalo did win a battlefield commission in 1945 at a time officers were being picked off at a fast pace. Spahnie later got a Purple Heart for a shrapnel wound in the foot and he won a citation for bravery, but his near-miss came in a tragedy at Remagen.

At Remagen, the bridge the Americans grabbed and held before the Germans could blow it up, thereby permitting Allied men and armor to penetrate more quickly across the Rhine, Spahn was being shown around in late afternoon to see what his engineers could do about completing repairs. The Nazis had bombed the three-span bridge, over which the U. S. planned to move trucks with weapons for the front.

Spahn was walking toward the bridge when suddenly there was "a terrible, deafening roar as the bridge collapsed," he would recall with feeling, "throwing many of the men and much of the equipment into the deep gorge and water below. We just ran for our lives, but then we did finally manage to rescue some of the men. Many had been crushed by the falling debris and others had drowned.

"All I know is that I was a mighty lucky guy to get out of that alive."

Discharged from the Army on his birthday in 1946—April 23—Spahn had a double-date in mind. He wanted to get back to baseball in a hurry, but he also kept waiting in Oklahoma a young lady he'd met early in his career. His fiancee, Lorene Southard, had her heart set on a June wedding, but John Quinn, general manager of the Braves, talked fast and Lorene, who would prove to be a strong partner in a happy marriage, relented.

So Spahnie joined the Braves on the road and manager Billy Southworth gave him a couple of tune-up relief assignments before starting him at Pittsburgh on a hot Sunday afternoon, July 14, 1946. He opposed a veteran lefthander, Fritz Ostermueller, who was caught by a man who would win a reputation as a manager—Al Lopez.

Spahn won that game, 8-5, but needed relief, something he seldom required over the years. The contest is mentioned only because it was, after all, No. 1 of the eventual 363 wins. And Spahn reeled off five straight victories before he finally persuaded Southworth that marriage would wait no longer. Warren and Lorene were married in August and he lost four in a row, but he finished strong again with an 8-5 record that proved a cornerstone for the great career that would follow.

His first full year in the majors, 1947, Warren Spahn led the league in innings pitched (290) and, winning 21 games and losing only 10, also paced N.L. pitchers with a 2.23 earned-run average. That's how quickly, when given the chance, the former Army lieutenant was able to find the groove.

The pennant season of '48 was not a great one for Spahn, but he improved down the stretch, buoyed by the birth of his son, Greg, and he turned back the Dodgers twice in critical late-season series after Brooklyn, rallying from seventh-place on the Fourth of July, actually nosed ahead of the Braves just before Labor Day. Warren won both games by the same score, 2-1, the second one in 14 innings. Over the years, the Dodgers would be as bad for Spahn as Greg was good, but the two things were in close juxtaposition that momentous year.

Until late in his career, when they were on the West Coast and he'd altered his pitching again, the Dodgers as a ball club could cream Spahn the way Willie Mays did as a hitter. The Brooklyn bandbox, Ebbets Field, and a lineup of powerful righthanded hitters formed a combination too formidable for even the finest pitcher of his generation. Head to head, by the way, Spahn was 8-3 against Philadelphia's brilliant righthander, Robin Roberts.

Despite the Dodgers' ability to beat Spahn twice as many times as he beat them, they paid him the ultimate compliment when Branch Rickey introduced at their Vero Beach (Fla.) training camp a new machine, which had a long steel arm which threw strikes monotonously, with an overhanded, mechanical motion.

"The Warren Spahn," the Brooks called it.

Spahn's stature was established in three consecutive 20-game seasons at Boston even before he blew the big contract with Perini because of financial conservatism. The pitcher had just entered into a business deal in Boston for the construction of a diner on Commonwealth Avenue, hard by Braves Field, when Perini broke the half-century logjam of major league franchises. Braves' fans were resentful, but not to the extent that they boycotted the beanery of their boy, Spahnie.

Spahnie—and if it's silly to use that kind of diminutive for a grown man, don't blame me, podnuh—actually had a good season for himself after that 1952 season because he'd lost six games by one run. Included were two successive contests in which he struck out a total of 29, 18 of them in a 15-inning game lost to the Cubs, 3-1.

So Spahn was due for a good break and he got one at Milwaukee, where the incredible enthusiasm of the beer-and-bratwurst metropolis and, in fact, all of Wisconsin's dairyland, made every day or night a holiday at County Stadium. Of all the heroes except for possibly Henry Aaron, who began his career there, the favorite of the fans was Spahn.

By then 21 years old and a veteran of seven seasons in the majors, Warren said he found himself caught up in the extreme fanaticism of the crowd, which drove the young team into close pennant contention. The old pro still looks back on his opening day victory in the first game at Milwaukee, 3-2 over the Cardinals in 10 innings in 1953, as one of the highlights of his career. Rookie Billy Bruton's disputed homer, the only one the young center fielder hit that year, won the game before an hysterical packed house.

A good opening day pitcher, though traditionally not a good April pitcher, Spahn managed one of his 63 shutouts in an opener, an 8-0 cakewalk at Pittsburgh in 1959.

The first year in Milwaukee, 1953, was Spahn's best season—23-7 with a league-leading 2.10 ERA—and it followed, astonishingly, the first of the series of knee injuries which eventually caved him in to the point he'd have been extremely knock-kneed in retirement, doctors told him if he could stand at all.

Down in spring training at Bradenton, Fla., Spahn stepped in a hole and tore cartilage in his right knee. "Funny thing, but I learned to follow through more on my delivery because my knee was weak, and it helped me have that best season," he recalled.

In the off-season, the right knee was operated on and in 1954 Spahn was batting against Cincinnati when Art Fowler brushed him back with a pitch. "I twisted away from it, but my spikes caught and the left knee went," Spahn said, "I needed an operation on it."

Not, however, until he'd done what came naturally to him. That is, win 20 games, to be exact, 21. Three years later, Dr. Donald O'Donohue, the Oklahoma orthopedic surgeon who has done so well by him, "went in and flushed out about 20 bone chips" in the left knee.

Despite these experiences, Spahn said he wasn't prepared for the ordeal of pain and discomfort that began early in November 1969. Dr. O'Donohue had recommended the operations earlier, to avoid the possibility the former pitcher might never be able to walk again because of locked knees. Spahn hadn't wanted to jeopardize his start as a manager. So he delayed until he no longer could bear the burden.

When he underwent the knife this time, Dr. O'Donohue, who does surgery for the University of Oklahoma football teams, found he needed to go into each knee twice—to cut a wedge of bone from the nearly locked joint and then to shorten the tendons and complete surgical repair. The painful convalescence followed.

"I really got down over Christmas and became more susceptible to pain," said Spahn, "and I really got to feeling sorry for myself. There were times when I thought I'd never walk again."

Yes, but a man who could pitch with bad wheels could do most anything, except, it seemed for a time, get into another World Series. In '56 when the Braves blew it in a season-ending series at St. Louis, as Brooklyn eased past Pittsburgh to the pennant, Spahn pitched his heart out in a 12-inning classic the next-to-last game of the season. With his own defense questionable and the Cardinals' Bobby Del Greco playing an inspired center field, the master of the mound lost to Herman Wehmeier, 2-1.

As he walked off the hill to the dugout, trying unsuccessfully to fight back the tears, Associated Press photographer Jack Hogan caught the poignant picture—and almost got Spahnie's glove in the face as the angry and embarrassed pitcher threw it at the cameraman.

A year later, with the pitching twosome of Spahn

and Burdette bolstered by the acquisition of the veteran Red Schoendienst to play second base and the full flowering of young Henry Aaron as a batting star in the outfield, the Braves finally brought to Milwaukee the pennant with which the beer-and-bratwurst metropolis had flirted.

In the World Series, Spahn lost the opener to the Yankees' Whitey Ford at New York, 3-1. He won the fourth one in 10 innings, 7-5, when Eddie Mathews homered, but it was Burdette's Series. Lanky Lew beat the Yankees three times, twice on shutouts, to give Milwaukee the world championship.

A year later, the reliable Spahn was the usual comfortable 22-game winner as the Braves repeated in the National League race and gave Milwaukee high hopes for another fall out of the mighty Yankees. He beat 'em in the opener in 10 innings on a hit by Bruton, 4-3, and then came back at New York in the fourth game for a two-hit masterpiece against Ford, 3-0.

The Yankees were down, three games to one, a deficit no team had been able to overcome in the World Series other than Pittsburgh against Washington in 1925. But the Yankees won the fifth game as Bob Turley blanked Burdette, 7-0. Then Spahn, working with two-days' rest, drove in a run for the third straight game himself, but got little batting support and lost the sixth contest in 10 innings, 4-3. Actually, Gil McDougald's homer put New York ahead and reliever Don McMahon then yielded the extra run which proved decisive. And Turley then bested Burdette in the windup, 6-2.

So that was it for Warren Spahn as a World Series performer. The Braves lost a pennant playoff in '59 to the Dodgers, and the old pro just kept on winning. Even though the Milwaukee attendance began to go into reverse, he had built himself up to an $80,000-a-year salary, which made life pleasant for him, Lorene and Greg. Lorene's stew was a favorite dish before he pitched, and Spahn's wife and son were at the ballpark regularly. Sadly, Mrs.

Spahn died. Greg, a well-mannered, husky kid who went to the University of Oklahoma, was an athlete good enough to please and excite the old man. He particularly liked football, but he had the great pleasure of watching his dad reach pitching heights at a time most of his young friends' fathers were lucky if they could cut the grass without breathing hard.

At 39, Spahn pitched his first no-hitter against Philadelphia on September 16, 1960, before only 6,117, the second-smallest crowd to that point in Milwaukee, where the baseball honeymoon had ended. The triumph, his 20th of the season, came by a 4-0 score in a game in which he walked two and struck out 15.

"Why, I actually threw some fastballs down the middle and got away with them. Can you imagine! At my age, my fastball was my best pitch tonight."

Only 34 of the 105 pitches he threw in the 15-strikeout performance were called balls.

A year later, April 28, just past his 40th birthday, Spahn pitched his second no-hitter, beating the San Francisco Giants at County Stadium, 1-0, before 8,518. Only Cy Young, at 41, had been older when he pitched a hitless game.

"I was lucky this time," said Spahn afterward. "Let's face it. I walked a man to start an inning—a cardinal sin with a one-run lead—and not once, but twice. And I made a really bad pitch to Mays, a pitch Willie ordinarily would hit the daylights out of, and he bounced one right back to me. You have to be lucky to have those things happen."

Maybe, but as batterymate Charley Lau said, "When Spahn talks about mistakes, he means the ball didn't always go quite where he wanted it. Spahn would call those mistakes, but nobody else would."

Furthermore, only the fancy-fielding pitcher's barehanded grab and backhanded flip to Joe Adcock on an almost perfect bunt by Matty Alou in the ninth inning saved the no-hitter of which Mays said:

"He deserved it, no matter what he says. He wasn't fast, but he was all pitcher and he had amazing control. He kept the hitters off balance with his changing speeds and he never put the ball where you could get much bat on it."

Two days later in the same park and against the same club, but not against the same pitcher, Mays hit four home runs in one game.

It honestly seemed almost too easy then and when, after an 18-14 season in '62, Spahn came back at the age of 42 and put together a 23-7 season in '63—and with a 2.60 ERA, too—it seemed almost unbelievable. It's too bad, in a way, with 350 victories and only 216 defeats that he didn't hang it up the night he was honored at County Stadium in late September. A crowd of 33,676 came out and, at Spahnie's suggestion, they poured their contributions into a scholarship fund in his name. The amount was $30,000 even before the returns were in.

Hall of Famers he would join as soon as he became eligible were on hand, including two other great lefthanders, Grove and Hubbell. It was an emotional night and, therefore, a tough one on which to pitch, and Spahn didn't. Not very well, anyway, giving up four runs on five hits as the Braves went down to their eighth straight defeat, 11-3.

Among the gifts was a scroll from the Dodgers, whom he had defeated four times that year in their drive to the world championship. The inscription read, "You have our vote for the Hall of Fame—if you retire now."

Ah, but who quits when he's making it look so easy? Sure, the paychecks were good, but now it was pride, dedication and determination—uh-huh, some "ego," too, as grumbling Bobby Bragan put it—that was driving Spahn toward 373 and then hopefully on to 400. He never got to either goal, of course, and he stepped on the toes of men for whom he played. Like Bragan, for instance.

Spahn insisted that he still could win, that he'd merely lost his pitching rhythm, that his right heel was striking the ground first, that he'd be all right if he kept starting, that he'd always been a slow starter. Fading stars can be a problem for a ball club and the

new Braves' management, already looking for a chance to duck to Atlanta, sold the high-salaried gaffer in the fall of 1964 to the Mets. He'd won only six, lost 13 and had a 5.28 ERA.

The Mets, still trying to out-glamorize the Yankees, had grabbed Yogi Berra after he was cut loose following a pennant-winning season in what would seem to be a king-sized gaffe by the Yankees. With Spahn, 44 and Berra, 40, the Mets could have the oldest battery this side of Medicare. "The ugliest if not the oldest," quipped Spahn.

But the joke was on Spahnie. Yogi retired wisely to the first-base coaching lines after a few swings and a couple of games behind the plate. Spahn, pitching coach, insisted on keeping himself in the starting rotation when he might have helped more in relief. Finally Stengel, the first big league manager with whom he now had come full circle, suggested that he'd be better off elsewhere.

"I'm afraid he's lost it," Casey said, "because the pitchers are hitting him."

Released by the Mets, Spahn might have gone on in the American League, but he was pursuing a National League record—remember?—so he caught on with the San Francisco Giants on July 22. That didn't work, either. He'd aged and lost it overnight. His combined 7-16 record and 4.00 ERA for the final 198 innings of his major league career meant only that he had sacrificed a couple of things that were precious to him—his career .600 won-and-lost percentage and his career ERA under 3.00.

Still feeling the urge, the last to know and a bit bitter as some of the great ones are at the end, Warren Edward Spahn even went down to Mexico City in 1966, pitching a few innings, and later, with Tulsa (Pacific Coast), he pitched in three games, all of which meant only that his eligibility for the Hall of Fame would be delayed to 1973, because a player must be retired completely—from the majors and/or minors—for five seasons.

"I didn't quit, baseball retired me," said Spahn, crossly, but baseball hadn't forgotten him any more than it could forget his skill and durability as the Ponce de Leon of pitchers. A merry man, Spahnie never was the kind who could stay unhappy long, anyway, and he proved as manager at Tulsa that he could handle young pitchers and others in a fashion that would win him a trip back to the majors as a coach or skipper—if he wanted to leave his spread in Oklahoma.

"I'm only a windshield rancher, the kind of cowboy whose horse grazes on gasoline," he said, propped temporarily on his canes, displaying once more the crazy, crooked grin and courage that combined with control of himself as well of the ball to help make Warren Edward Spahn the winningest lefthander ever.

WARREN EDWARD SPAHN
Born April 23, 1921, at Buffalo, N. Y.
Height 6-0 Weight 183
Threw and batted lefthanded.
Named to Hall of Fame, 1973.

YEAR	CLUB	LEAGUE	G.	IP.	W.	L.	Pct.	H.	R.	ER.	SO.	BB.	ERA.
1940	Bradford	Pony	12	66	5	4	.556	53	27	20	62	24	2.73
1941	Evansville	I. I. I.	28	212	19	6	.760	154	62	43	193	90	1.83
1942	Hartford	Eastern	33	248	17	12	.586	148	65	54	141	130	1.96
1942	Boston	Nat.	4	16	0	0	.000	25	15	10	7	11	5.63
1943-44-45	Boston	Nat.					(In military service)						
1946	Boston	Nat.	24	126	8	5	.615	107	46	41	67	36	2.93
1947	Boston	Nat.	40	290	21	10	.677	245	87	75	123	84	2.33
1948	Boston	Nat.	36	257	15	12	.556	237	115	106	114	77	3.71
1949	Boston	Nat.	38	302	21	14	.600	283	125	103	151	86	3.07
1950	Boston	Nat.	41	293	21	17	.553	248	123	103	191	111	3.16
1951	Boston	Nat.	39	311	22	14	.611	278	111	103	164	109	2.98
1952	Boston	Nat.	40	290	14	19	.424	263	109	96	183	73	2.98
1953	Milwaukee	Nat.	35	266	23	7	.767	211	75	62	148	70	2.10
1954	Milwaukee	Nat.	39	283	21	12	.636	262	107	99	136	86	3.15
1955	Milwaukee	Nat.	39	246	17	14	.548	249	99	89	110	65	3.26
1956	Milwaukee	Nat.	39	281	20	11	.645	249	92	87	128	52	2.79
1957	Milwaukee	Nat.	39	271	21	11	.656	241	94	81	111	78	2.69
1958	Milwaukee	Nat.	38	290	22	11	.667	257	106	99	150	76	3.07
1959	Milwaukee	Nat.	40	292	21	15	.583	282	106	96	143	70	2.96
1960	Milwaukee	Nat.	40	268	21	10	.677	254	114	104	154	74	3.49
1961	Milwaukee	Nat.	38	263	21	13	.618	236	96	88	115	64	3.01
1962	Milwaukee	Nat.	34	269	18	14	.563	248	97	91	118	55	3.04
1963	Milwaukee	Nat.	33	260	23	7	.767	241	85	75	102	49	2.60
1964	Milwaukee(a)	Nat.	38	174	6	13	.316	204	110	102	78	52	5.28
1965	New York(b)-San Fran.	Nat.	36	198	7	16	.304	210	104	88	90	56	4.00
1966	Mexico City Tigers	Mex.	3	10	1	1	.500	14	7	5	7	1	4.50
1967	Tulsa	P. C.	3	7	0	1	.000	8	6	5	5	5	6.43
Major League Totals			750	5246	363	245	.597	4830	2016	1798	2583	1434	3.08

a Sold to New York Mets, November 23, 1964.
b Released by New York Mets, July 19, 1965, and signed by San Francisco Giants, July 22, 1965.

WORLD SERIES RECORD

YEAR	CLUB	LEAGUE	G.	IP.	W.	L.	Pct.	H.	R.	ER.	SO.	BB.	ERA.
1948	Boston	Nat.	3	12	1	1	.500	10	4	12	3	3	3.00
1957	Milwaukee	Nat.	2	15 1/3	1	1	.500	18	8	2	2	2	4.70
1958	Milwaukee	Nat.	3	28 2/3	2	1	.667	19	7	18	8	8	1.88
World Series Totals			8	56	4	3	.571	47	19	32	13	13	2.89

"SPOKE": The past-tense became one of the nicknames for Tris Speaker. The Gray Eagle and center-field defensive master—and a career .344 hitter.

TRIS SPEAKER

To say that Tris Speaker revolutionized outfield play wouldn't be quite right because the suggestion would be that the famed Gray Eagle of Boston and Cleveland set a pattern. The fact is, he didn't. He broke the mold.

Neither before nor since has an outfielder played so shallowly as Speaker did in the course of nearly 22 big league seasons during which he distinguished himself as one of the finest all-around players in baseball history.

Among 10-year men, his lifetime batting aver-age, .344, was surpassed in the 20th century only by Ty Cobb, Rogers Hornsby, Shoeless Joe Jackson and Lefty O'Doul. Tris hit the most doubles in major league history, 793, and stole 433 bases.

For years there has been a general disposition to mention as an entry in outfield of Babe Ruth, Speaker and Cobb as the all-time best. Their careers generally paralleled one another's in the American League. Curiously, Speaker, easy to meet, liked Cobb, who was difficult to know, but didn't care much for the gregarious Ruth.

As the first 100 years of professional baseball passed, there was a tendency among some to ease Speaker out of that mythical all-time outfield in favor of Joe DiMaggio or Willie Mays.

Spoke, as they called him, had considerable career advantages over the great DiMaggio if you'll accept what Branch Rickey would call quantitative quality, and over wonderful Willie, too.

Speaker played nine more seasons than Joe, scored 491 more runs, made 1,301 more hits. He had 404 more doubles, 93 more triples and 403 more stolen bases. DiMaggio owned a sizable home run advantage, 361 to 115, but Joe didn't hit against the dead ball that was used more than half of Tris' career. Ditto Mays, 42 points lower in average, but with 660 homers.

Gordon Cobbledick, the Cleveland chronicler, suggested in a biographical sum-up of Speaker and DiMaggio that fielding statistics are notoriously fallible as indicators of a player's true defensive worth. But no one ever would have to apologize, in fact or fancy, for Speaker's wizardry afield. And even counting the added outfield depth necessary because of the livelier ball, it's remarkable that Spoke would have been credited with three times as many assists as DiMaggio and nearly that large an edge over Mays.

Four times in a big league career that had started in 1907 at Boston and finished in 1928 at Philadelphia, Speaker threw out 30 or more men a season, twice getting 35, the American League record. As late as 1923, when he had been forced by a juiced-up ball to give a bit of real estate to Ruth and the other heavy hitters, the 35-year-old lefthanded-throwing Speaker assisted in 26 put-outs.

As a center fielder, Speaker played so close in for most of the hitters over most of his years that he was a fifth infielder, sure and swift—and cunning.

Twice in one month, April 1918, he executed unassisted double plays at second, collaring low line drives on the run and then outracing retreating baserunners to the bag. At least once—and play this one over slowly in your mind, friend—he figured as the pivot man in a routine double play.

Try that one out on your credulity: Second baseman to center fielder to first baseman.

Time and again, Speaker would sneak in from short-center to take a pickoff throw from the catcher and retire a runner at second.

He also devised and employed for many years a unique defense against an attempted sacrifice bunt with runners on first and second base.

Standard practice in such a situation, of course, is for the first baseman to charge to the plate, for the pitcher to break in and toward the third baseline and for the third baseman to go part way in, yet be prepared to retreat to take a throw, groping for the bag, if the ball is handled by either the first baseman or pitcher.

The shortstop is needed to cover second base, the second baseman to move over and cover first. But because the alert Speaker played so shallowly, Spoke insisted on covering second base when the bunt was put down, freeing the shortstop to cover third so that a charging threesome of the third baseman, pitcher and first baseman could make it more difficult for the enemy hitter to move the runner along.

Speaker, a ruddy-faced, prematurely-gray player, was nearly six feet tall and 193 pounds, built like the football player he had been as a restless Texas schoolboy, but even at the end of his baseball career, he still would startle an infrequent viewer with the defensive position he took, so close that he could charge in for low line drives and short, looping liners. He possessed, however, the ability to scurry back for the long ones.

The Gray Eagle credited baseball's winningest pitcher, the fabled Cy Young, for having helped him develop the ability to go back on a ball so capably. In Tris' early days at Boston, Cy was a pitching veteran skilled at wielding a fungo bat, which he did mercilessly in practice.

Speaker never became an old fogey, living in the past. On the contrary, he could wax enthusiastic over younger players to the end, which came unexpectedly at 70 when he suffered a second heart attack on a fishing trip back home in Texas. But for all his affection for baseball and his fairness to younger playing generations, he just could not understand outfielders who played with their backs virtually scraping paint off the walls.

"I know it's easier, basically, to come in on a ball than go back," he said the last time we met, six months before his death when he visited St. Louis to welcome Stan Musial to the exclusive 3,000-Hit Club, of which Spoke then was vice president to Cobb.

"But so many more balls are hit in front of an outfielder, even now, that it's a matter of percentage to be able to play in close enough to cut off those low ones or cheap ones in front of him. I still see more games lost by singles that drop just over the infield than triples over the outfielder's head. I learned early that I could save more games by cutting off some of those singles than I would lose by having an occasional extra-base hit go over my head."

To try to single out this defensive virtuoso's finest fielding performance would be difficult, but fans long in the tooth in Cleveland would vote for a catch that they believe won the 1920 pennant for the Indians.

The Tribe was engaged in a down-to-the-wire fight with the defending champion White Sox, whose hose hadn't quite been found out as soiled. The Yankees, on the threshold of their long dominance, also were threatening.

The Indians needed a lift because their spirits understandably had dropped after the tragic death of their shortstop, Ray Chapman, who had been struck with a pitched ball a short time before. The inspiration came in the defensive genius of a field foreman serving his first full season as manager.

In the deciding game of a series of three with the Black Sox at Dunn Field, which Cleveland's old League Park then was called, Chicago had the sacks loaded with two out when Joe Jackson hit a savage line drive to deep right-center.

Speaker, turning quickly, streaked for the exit gate, timed a tremendous leap and made the catch as, with both feet off the ground, he crashed into the concrete wall. He fell and lay unconscious for several minutes, but they had to pry the ball out of his hands.

The thrill of winning as a player-manager in a season in which be batted .388, belting 50 doubles, 11 triples and eight homers among 214 hits, driving in 107 runs, would have been justifiably the greatest in a great player's career. After all, Spoke also followed by hitting .320 as the Indians beat Brooklyn in the World Series.

His top thrill, however, he said, came eight years earlier in his first World Series, a climax to the 1912 season in which he had won the American League's Most Valuable Player award at Boston, batting .383.

When the Series with the New York Giants got down to its deciding game at Boston, the mighty Christy Mathewson seemed to have the championship wrapped up when the Giants took a 2-1 lead in the 10th inning.

Then, in the home 10th, pinch-hitter Clyde Engle hit a ball that was muffed by Fred Snodgrass, the New York center fielder, who for years was portrayed as the goat of the Series. Speaker would have none of it, however, partly because as an outfield authority himself, he regarded the low liner on which Snodgrass erred as not simply chance.

"The ball was sinking, and Fred's knee hit his elbow as he reached for the ball," Spoke would explain.

Besides, he'd point out, the Giants had more than one chance to get out of the inning. After Harry Hooper flied out, Mathewson walked Steve Yerkes, bringing up Speaker, a lefthanded hitter who always felt he could hit the remarkable righthander.

This time, however, Spoke lifted a high foul between home plate and first base. He felt that the ball, drifting toward first base, would have been an easy out for Fred Merkle, playing there. Hopefully, Tris was just about to call for the Giants' catcher,

Chief Meyers, with the wishful thought that the man in the pads couldn't catch it.

"But before I could open my mouth, I heard Matty calling 'Meyers, Meyers,'" Speaker would relate, grinning as he relived that moment of joyful relief.

Meyers couldn't catch up with the ball that was blowing away from him. Belatedly, Merkle, who had been called off the play, made a stab for it and missed. The blunder, Speaker insisted, was not Bonehead Merkle's as many liked to suggest, bringing up Merkle's misfortune when he failed to touch second base as a rookie four years earlier. The blame was Mathewson's.

Overjoyed and confident, the 24-year-old Speaker needled the 32-your-old pitcher. "You just blew the championship," he yelled at Matty.

Speaker made good his boast. Reprieved, he singled to right, scoring Engle with the tying run. And after Duffy Lewis drew another walk, loading the bases, Larry Gardner hit a sacrifice fly that gave the Red Sox a 3-2 victory and the world championship.

No superstar of baseball probably ever had more trouble convincing people he could play than the kid from Hubbard, Tex.

Born into a large family and losing his father at 10, Tris was close to his mother, who had trouble keeping up with the high-spirited lad who was riding equally high-spirited horses without a saddle or bridle before he was knee high to a stirrup.

As a kid, Speaker broke his right arm in falls bronco-busting wild horses and finally learned to throw lefthanded, which, as already mentioned, he did extremely well. In high school, he played football, but, at 17, he forgot football when he enrolled at Fort Worth Polytechnic Institute.

Following his sophomore season at Polytech, 1906, Tris was pitching for a store team in Corsicana when Doak Roberts, owner of the Cleburne club of the North Texas League, stopped off to scout an outfielder on the same semi-pro club. Roberts saw Speaker pitch, win and hit two home

runs. He forgot the outfielder and asked the lad from Hubbard how he'd like to play pro baseball.

Would a bird like to fly? Roberts gave Speaker a dollar for train fare to Waco, where he was directed to report to the Cleburne manager, one Benny Shelton. Tris pocketed the buck, hopped a freight and reported as directed.

Knowing the deep-voiced, smiling Speaker in later life as a kind, personable man, it's hard to believe that he broke into baseball using his fists and tongue better than he did his pitching arm, but so he did.

A fresh kid, he awakened Manager Shelton at 6:30 in the morning and was told angrily to wait in the hotel lobby until 9:30, after which he was taken to the ballpark, where he warmed up for half an hour, pitched in batting practice, shagged flies and then was told, surprisingly, that he was going to pitch.

"Warm up," Shelton ordered.

"Warm up? Hell, I'm hot now," countered the kid who then held a 2-1 lead into the ninth inning when Shelton, playing first base, held the ball in protest of an adverse call at the bag as the tying and winning runs scored.

The next morning, when club owner Roberts arrived in Waco, he found the second baseman, Mickey Coyle, waiting for him at the railroad platform, complaining about the rookie pitcher.

"He's cussed out Shelton and challenged everybody on the ball club to fight, including me," whined Coyle.

Roberts found Speaker at breakfast. "What's the idea of insulting Shelton?" he asked.

"Who insulted him?" snapped young Spoke. "All I said was he was a butterbrained bum standing around holding the ball, and that monkey-faced second baseman stuck his nose into it, and I told him I could lick him, which I can."

"Son," Roberts said softly, "come upstairs with me. We've got business to talk."

The result was a $50-a-month contract to play for Cleburne, the only condition being that Tris apologize to Shelton. He did. The manager accepted, more or less graciously, as author Cobbledick put it, and the next day he started Speaker on the mound again.

Twenty-two runs later, he led the kid away, bloody, but unbowed. Unbowed, indeed, because when right fielder Dude Ransom was hit in the face with a pitch that broke his cheekbone and Shelton wondered what he'd do, the 18-year-old Speaker spoke up.

"Put me in right field," Tris said. "I'm the best right fielder in the league."

Shelton glared at the brash kid, but put him in the outfield—to stay.

A year later, when Roberts transferred his Cleburne franchise to Houston and the Texas League, Speaker hit .314. The St. Louis Browns' manager, Jim McAleer, had been impressed by the cowboy in exhibition games and had asked Roberts to wire him when he thought the young player was ready.

At mid-season two wires went unanswered, after which Roberts tried again, messaging McAleer:

"SPEAKER READY. YOU CAN HAVE HIM FOR $1,500. I OWN 200 ACRES GOOD TEXAS BLACK LAND. WILL DEED TO YOU IF SPEAKER DOES NOT MAKE GOOD."

Still no answer. So the next day, George Huff, a Red Sox scout, paid just $800 for one of the greatest players ever.

Wait, that's not all.

Although the Red Sox called him up to the American League in September, in time to bat .158 with three hits in 19 times at bat, they didn't regard him highly enough to send him a contract for 1908 by the required February date. So he went to Marlin, Tex., where the Giants trained, and offered his services to John McGraw, not once, but twice.

Rebuffed, Tris paid his own way to the Red Sox training camp at Little Rock, Ark., where Boston reluctantly signed him. The Sox, however, did not take him north. They left him behind in lieu of cash. Ignored by the fans at exhibition games, they

weren't able to pay their rent. They wondered if the owner of the Little Rock club, Mickey Finn, would accept a ballplayer instead?

"What player?" he asked.

The Sox could let him have that promising young outfielder, Speaker, if Finn would give them first right to reacquire the kid for $500.

The Little Rock man agreed to quite a bargain—for him and the Bosox. Spoke batted a blazing .350 at Little Rock, bringing offers from the Giants, Pirates and Senators, but Finn, who had profited from the kid's play, felt a moral obligation to Boston.

The lucky Red Sox? Yes, and no. In his first full season, 1909, Speaker batted .309 for them, beginning a string of seven successful seasons with Boston, including world championships in 1912 and '15. But then Boston blew him in a deal almost as incredibly bad for the Red Sox as their loss of Babe Ruth to the Yankees four years later.

With the baseball salary war at an end, a result of dissolution of the Federal League, the Red Sox owner, Joe Lannin, was determined to retrench. He sent his master center fielder a contract for exactly half the $18,000 he'd received the two previous seasons. Stubbornly, Speaker, who had expected a raise, said he wouldn't play for a penny less than $15,000.

Caught in the middle, manager Bill Carrigan arranged finally for Tris to train with the Red Sox at Hot Springs, Ark., and travel north with them, playing in exhibitions for a fixed fee, hopeful one side or the other would capitulate or, at least, that when a compromise came, the superstar would be ready.

Speaker was ready, all right, as he proved at the end of a brilliant spring when he hit a game-winning home run at Brooklyn's Ebbets Field off southpaw Rube Marquard, two days before the start of a season for which he was still unsigned.

Lannin was waiting for him in the runway. "Great stuff, Spoke," he beamed, putting an arm around Speaker's shoulder. "You win. We'll sign when we get to Boston tomorrow."

Hours later, relieved, Speaker was packing in his

hotel room for the trip to Boston when he received a phone call from the lobby. Bob McRoy, the Cleveland general manager, wanted to talk to him.

Puzzled, Speaker invited McRoy up to the room, where they talked generalities before the visitor asked, "How would you like to play for Cleveland, Tris?"

Tris wouldn't. "You've not only got a bad ball club," he said, "but you've got a bad baseball town."

McRoy hesitated. "I wish," he said, "you didn't feel that way. We've made a deal for you."

Speaker protested, stubbornly insisting he wouldn't report, remembering unhappily that when he'd wanted to go into baseball, he had to coax his mother to win parental permission because Jennie Speaker had refused flatly to allow her boy to be bought or sold "like a longhorn steer."

The deal by which the great Speaker had been shipped to Cleveland for pitcher Sam Jones, infielder Fred Thomas and $50,000 already had been announced, Tris learned with a sinking feeling. Then he insisted he'd go to Cleveland only if he received $10,000 of the purchase money.

Reluctantly, and only when Speaker threatened to go home to Hubbard, did Fannin at Boston agree to the $10,000 slice for the veteran who was always a good businessman. Spoke worked his way up to more than $50,000 a year at Cleveland.

For Cleveland fans, needing a hero to replace Napoleon Lajoie, who had faded away, Speaker was a joyful acquisition, and Spoke didn't disappoint his new friends. In 1916, he won his only American League batting championship, breaking Cobb's stranglehold on the title with a rousing .386.

The fact is, only 1919, the year he replaced Lee Fohl as manager in mid-season, did he slip below .300 in 11 seasons with the Indians. And when he brought Cleveland the long-awaited pennant and championship in 1920, a year he'd batted .388 and knocked in 107 runs, he elbowed his way through the crowd at Dunn field to a boxseat where Jennie Speaker was seated, crying happily.

"This was what I meant, Mom," Spoke said as he embraced her. "This was why I had to play ball."

As a manager, Tris Speaker couldn't match that memorable 1920 season, capped by the Series in which Elmer Smith hit a grandslam homer and Bill Wambsganss executed an unassisted triple play. He platooned expertly at a time when platooning was greeted derisively. He called up Walter (Duster) Mails, a cocky pitcher who won seven straight down the stretch, and he achieved the maximum out of one Ray (Rube) Caldwell with a most unusual contract.

The document insisted that the slim righthander, a well-traveled bottle jockey, was to get drunk after every game he pitched and not show up at the ballpark for one day.

"If I signed this, Tris, you'd fire your stenographer," the pitcher said. "She left out the word 'not' in front of 'get drunk.'"

Speaker assured the pitcher he meant what the contract said. Caldwell, with the joy of breaking training apparently spoiled by the requirement to drink for one day, rather than avoid it completely, contributed 20 victories to the Indians' championship season.

As late as 1925, the year Tris married the former Frances Cudahy of Buffalo, the 37-year-old Speaker hit .389 in 117 games. A year later, with his team rebounding from the second division to finish second, Spoke played 150 games and batted .304.

However, he was let out as manager in December 1926, a victim of the Hubert (Dutch) Leonard charge, as detailed in the Cobb story in this book, that two of the American League's three brightest stars of the era, the Georgia Peach and the Gray Eagle, had contrived to fix a late-season game several years earlier.

When the first commissioner, Judge K.M. Landis, investigated and gave the back of his hand to Leonard for making the charges and American League founder Ban Johnson for believing them, Johnson was forced to resign by his associates.

Cobb and Speaker, exonerated, signed with Philadelphia and Washington, respectively.

Spoke batted .327 for the Senators in 141 games as a center fielder-first baseman in 1927, a pretty handsome figure for a ruggedly handsome guy.

Speaker held his bat low, moving it up and down like the lazy twitching of a cat's tail, before he cocked it, not more than hip high, and he strode into the ball, untroubled by any pitcher except the same Chicago southpaw, Doc White, who earlier had bothered Cobb.

When Clark Griffith found it inconvenient to pay Spoke's robust salary, Tris joined Ty at Philadelphia for Connie Mack in 1928. Speaker, at 40, wasn't much help, dipping to .267 in 64 games.

Speaker managed and played part-time at Newark in the International League in 1929 and '30. He hit well, but quit to become a baseball broadcaster in Chicago.

In 1933, Speaker and an old friend, Lee Keyser, the man who had put up lights two years earlier at Des Moines, and an old admirer of Tris, Joe E. Brown, the comedian, took over operation of the Kansas City Blues. The depression venture was not successful, and Speaker returned to Cleveland briefly as a broadcaster.

There, too, he became associated in the wholesale liquor business and prospered representing a Detroit steel firm.

A star who never lost his love for baseball or his interest in it, Speaker leaped at a chance and a challenge in 1947. Bill Veeck, then the new owner of the Indians, bought the contract of the American League's first Negro player, Larry Doby, and then asked the master center fielder to convert the second baseman into an outfielder.

Obviously, both Speaker and Doby did their job well because Larry was in center field a year later when the Indians won their first pennant and world championship since the Gray Eagle and those other birds in 1920.

In retirement, though he had a healthy glow and never spared himself, making the banquet circuit as an able lower-case speaker who didn't live in the past, Spoke had hard luck. He fell from a roof making repairs and suffered a fractured skull. He narrowly escaped death with a perforated intestine and was hospitalized with a heart attack in 1954.

As friend Gordon Cobbledick put it, however, when the Gray Eagle still could walk in the garden and smell the roses, "The world has done all right by Tris Speaker. He knew what he wanted and he got it with a minimum of frustration and disappointment along the way…

"…His talents brought him fame and a comfortable fortune. He was well-paid in his baseball lifetime (he saw to that!) and he didn't gamble away his money like Hornsby or drink it up like Alex. He didn't die in the prime of life like Matty and Gehrig. He never, as Cobb did, soured on the game that made him and that he helped so greatly to make."

Fact is, when St. Louis' brilliant center fielder, Curt Flood, misplayed a decisive flyball behind Bob Gibson in the seventh game of the 1968 World Series with Detroit, I could just hear the strong-voiced Speaker sympathize with Flood and say, "Don't let it get you down, kid. I'll never forget the first major league flyball I lost in the sun—in the 1915 World Series."

Spoke gave up a run with the one he misjudged in the Series, one of only three he ever misjudged in the majors, but he stepped up to the plate in the next inning and tripled off the Phillies' great righthander, Grover Cleveland Alexander. The Red Sox won the game and the Series.

As Joe Williams once wrote, "There is no manlier man than Tris Speaker."

The Hall of Famer who twirled rope with Will Rogers and lunched at the White House with President Dwight D. Eisenhower came to the end, appropriately, back home in Texas when he and Mrs. Speaker were visiting in Hubbard in December 1958.

Spoke and a friend just had come in from fishing at nearby Lake Whitney and were hooking their boat and trailer to their car when the 70-year-old Gray Eagle collapsed. Fishermen lifted him into the back seat of the car.

He opened his eyes and whispered his last words.

"My name," he said, "is Tris Speaker."

A name to remember.

TRISTRAM (SPOKE and GRAY EAGLE) SPEAKER
Born April 4, 1888, at Hubbard City, Tex.
Died December 8, 1958, at Lake Whitney, Tex.
Height 5-11 1/2 Weight 193
Threw and batted lefthanded.
Named to Hall of Fame, 1937.

YEAR	CLUB	LEAGUE	POS.	G.	AB.	R.	H.	2B.	3B.	HR.	RBI.	B.A.	PO.	A.	E.	F.A.
1906	Cleburne	No. Tex.	OF	84	287	35	77	-	-	-	-	.268	100	43	3	.979
1907	Houston	Texas	OF	118	468	70	147	-	-	-	-	.314	189	29	12	.948
1907	Boston	Amer.	OF	7	19	0	3	0	0	0	0	.158	4	2	0	1.000
1908	Little Rock	South.	OF	127	471	81	165	19	10	3	-	.350	330	37	13	.966
1908	Boston	Amer.	OF	31	118	12	26	2	3	0	10	.220	37	8	0	1.000
1909	Boston	Amer.	OF	143	544	73	168	26	13	7	79	.309	319	35	10	.973
1910	Boston	Amer.	OF	141	538	92	183	20	14	7	62	.340	337	20	16	.957
1911	Boston	Amer.	OF	141	510	88	167	34	13	8	80	.327	297	26	15	.956
1912	Boston	Amer.	OF	153	580	136	222	53	13	9	98	.383	372	35	18	.958
1913	Boston	Amer.	OF	141	520	94	190	35	22	3	81	.365	374	30	24	.944
1914	Boston	Amer.	OF	158	571	100	193	46	18	4	86	.338	425	30	15	.968
1915	Boston (a)	Amer.	OF	150	547	108	176	25	12	0	63	.322	378	21	10	.976
1916	Cleveland	Amer.	OF	151	546	102	211	41	8	2	83	.386	359	25	10	.975
1917	Cleveland	Amer.	OF	142	523	90	184	42	11	2	65	.352	365	23	8	.980
1918	Cleveland	Amer.	OF	127	471	73	150	33	11	0	61	.318	352	15	10	.973
1919	Cleveland	Amer.	OF	134	494	83	146	38	12	2	69	.296	375	25	7	.983
1920	Cleveland	Amer.	OF	150	552	137	214	50	11	8	107	.388	363	24	9	.977
1921	Cleveland	Amer.	OF	132	506	107	183	52	14	3	74	.362	345	15	6	.984
1922	Cleveland	Amer.	OF	131	426	85	161	48	8	11	71	.378	285	13	5	.983
1923	Cleveland	Amer.	OF	150	574	133	218	59	11	17	130	.380	369	26	13	.968
1924	Cleveland	Amer.	OF	135	486	94	167	36	9	8	65	.344	323	20	13	.963
1925	Cleveland	Amer.	OF	117	429	79	167	35	5	12	87	.389	311	16	11	.967
1926	Cleveland (b)	Amer.	OF	150	540	96	164	52	8	7	86	.304	394	20	8	.981
1927	Washington (c) (d)	Amer.	OF-1B	141	523	71	171	43	6	2	73	.327	356	24	12	.969
1928	Philadelphia	Amer.	OF	64	191	28	51	23	2	3	29	.267	111	8	3	.975
1929	Newark	Int.	OF	48	138	36	49	11	1	5	20	.355	57	2	0	1.000
1930	Newark	Int.	OF	11	31	3	13	1	1	0	3	.419	10	1	1	.917
Major League Totals				2789	10208	1881	3515	793	224	115	1559	.344	6851	461	223	.970

a Traded to Cleveland for pitcher Sam Jones, infielder Fred Thomas and $50,000, April 12, 1916.
b Resigned as manager of Cleveland, December 2, 1926.
c Unconditionally released by Washington and signed with Philadelphia, February 5, 1928.
d Played 17 games at first base (G—17, PO—145, A—12, E—2).

WORLD SERIES RECORD

YEAR	CLUB	LEAGUE	POS.	G.	AB.	R.	H.	2B.	3B.	HR.	RBI.	B.A.	PO.	A.	E.	F.A.
1912	Boston	Amer.	OF	8	30	4	9	1	2	0	2	.300	21	2	2	.920
1915	Boston	Amer.	OF	5	17	2	5	0	1	0	0	.294	10	0	0	1.000
1920	Cleveland	Amer.	OF	7	25	6	8	2	1	0	1	.320	18	0	0	1.000
World Series Totals				20	72	12	22	3	4	0	3	.306	49	2	2	.962

A FAVORITE PHOTO OF A FAVORITE FELLA: Mine of Casey Stengel, almost statuesque as he began his remarkable reign of five straight world championships with the Yankees in 1949.

CASEY STENGEL

Before his amazin' Mets played their first-ever ball game in April 1962, a bunch of stiffs greeted by 41-year-old Stan Musial's perfect 3-for-3 manager Casey Stengel obliged one of "my writers," as he always put it possessively, only in this instance it was one of his broadcasters, Lindsey Nelson, prominent play-by-play broadcaster for the newly established New York National League franchise.

Characteristically, Stengel rocked on his heels, hands in the hip pockets of a uniform that by design included the colors of the four different New York clubs for which he had played or managed since Teddy Roosevelt. For Nelson's radio audience, Casey delivered in a loud, croaking, rapid-fire sing-song a lineup that would be historic and historically inept.

"We'll have Ashburn in center field, leading off," said Stengel who, yes, could use a surname when he saw fit, "and Mantilla, shortstop, and Neal, second base, and Thomas, left field, and…er, er…"

For a fleeting instant, the elephant-memoried, colorful codger had forgotten his fifth-spot player, the right fielder, but he plunged on:

"Hodges, first base, and Zimmer, third base, and Landrith, catcher, and Craig, pitcher."

Sparring for time, at which orally he was James J. Corbett, Gene Tunney and Muhammad Ali wrapped into one, Stengel sought in the recesses of his celebrated cerebrum the name of the elusive right fielder.

"We're ready as the bell rings," said Casey, his craggy features lighting up like an electric bulb over the head of a previously befuddled figure in an old comic strip, and, raising his rasping voice another decibel, he added triumphantly:

"And that's his name—Bell, Gus Bell, and he'll play right field and bat fifth and…"

Before he reached 85 some 13 years later, probably at a time St. Peter decided he needed a cutup to explain the cutoff play to him, Charles Dillon Stengel entrenched himself in the public eye as a baseball personality perhaps second only to Babe Ruth—IF to the Babe—for charisma on and off the field. A pretty good ballplayer with Brooklyn, Pittsburgh, Philadelphia, New York (Giants) and Boston in the National League, he had been a good-natured manager with lousy ball clubs and with one outstanding team, the Yankees, who won 10 pennants and a record five consecutive world championships for him, 1949 through '53.

When he'd reached 71, a wealthy man through oil-field good fortune, a wise wife and good long-time income, even when they would pay him NOT to manage, Stengel was at an age and stage when old friends, such as this one, wished he'd stay put. That is, around his orange groves at Glendale, Calif., and the suburban Los Angeles bank there for which he served as vice president under brother-in-law Jack Lawson.

Why, after having needed so many years to prove that he was good and smart as well as good and funny, would the old man risk that glittering record compiled at Yankee Stadium to come back as a manager, especially for misfits such as the Mets figured to be?

"Because," said Stengel, "records aren't sacred, baseball is too much fun and, besides, I'm flattered they asked and I owe it to them, especially to the man with the long pencil (general manager George Weiss, his long-time Yankee associate who also had been put out to pasture.)"

So a man whose career won-and-lost record had been .555, even though he'd managed nine seasons in the second division before putting in a glittering dozen at the Yankee Stadium, returned to finish 10th in a 10-team league three times. He was bound for the coal hole again when he broke a hip after a long, wet night on the town in 1965 with former Giants' teammate Frank Frisch.

Although Stengel won only 175 games and lost 461 at the Polo Grounds and then out there at the Mets' new home, Shea Stadium in Flushing Meadow, he is positively the only man who could have made the losing louts livable, likable and even lovable.

"They're amazin'," Stengel would tell a press that put down every UNDERSTANDABLE word when the ink-stained wretches of the Fourth Estate face-guarded the double-talking Old Professor or The Doctor, as they referred to him more often. So in this book and in a game that has known a Connie Mack, a John McGraw, a Joe McCarthy, a Walter Alston, a Billy Southworth, an Al Lopez and others who won more often and lost less frequently, Casey from KayCee will stand for—and represent—ALL managers.

None probably would object, either, because he could outtalk and outdrink them all and outwit most, and managers good and bad would echo his exasperated lament to his players:

"Can't nobody play this here game?"

In addition to Stengelese, long since accepted as a synonym for non sequiturs, Ol' Case had pet expressions, such as "You could look it up," which few ever had to because the old man's memory was so good; "He done splendid," which said more for the erstwhile dental student's encomiums than his grammar, and "excaute," which was the grand geezer's favorite verb for what it takes to get the job done between the foul lines.

Wherever he went, increasingly with the passing years when he was an honorary vice president and a scout for the Mets, Stengel attracted crowds the way Jack Daniels and Johnny Walker attract alcoholics. And Ol' Case, it must be explained with awe and envy, had a capacity for alcohol almost as unbelievable as for baseball and conversation, making him a tireless triple threat as well as the greatest of company for old friends and new associates.

Stengel was the life of any party or bull session, yet late to bed and early to rise as if he might miss the next golden moment of the 85 years a God bemused and amused, if not confused, graciously granted him and those fortunate enough to have rubbed—or bent—elbows with Stengel.

Although his fractured syntax created a language of his own and made Irwin Corey sound like an English professor, Casey could make a point simply— "now see here, Doctor," he'd say with jut jaw—and as directly as the straightest line to the nearest barroom or ballpark.

With Ol' Case, two was company and three was not only a crowd, but a command performance, a necessity to go into his act. Big-hearted, generous, a check-grabber, Stengel had more ham in him than any packing house. With both young and old, he was the best goodwill ambassador baseball ever had, bar none.

In his own way, pantomiming, grimacing, winking with features both rough and rubbery, the jug-eared, gesticulating gentleman with the chalk-white complexion and slicked-down hair that ranged from natural white to orange, depending on his rinse or dye of the day, was an actor, like his Kansas City high school classmate, William Powell, the suave star of the movies' *This Man* series.

Powell might have had more polish than his fellow lefthander, but the dashing, debonair film figure never drew a bigger, more attentive or appreciative audience than Ol' Case whenever the baseball man stopped to autograph or to hold court for press or public. His gravel voice ranged dramatically from a stage whisper to a roar that could have shattered the walls of those four New York ballparks in which he'd performed—Ebbets Field, the Polo Grounds, Yankee Stadium and Shea Stadium.

In a word or few, Stengel was as colorful as the purple-and-yellow-shirted uniforms he wore at Kankakee, Ill., in 1910, the year the world lost a gabby potential lefthanded dentist and gained a noisy, fun-loving ballplayer who—and you could look it up!—was pretty good anytime and great in the spotlight. In three World Series he batted .393.

At home in Kansas City, where he starred on Central High School teams, they called him Charley or, in reference to his ancestry, "Dutch." It was only when he went away to play ball that be became "Casey," a fast phoneticization of the initials of the home town about which he talked so much—K.C.

By 1912, the year before Charley Ebbets opened that magnificent rotunda in Flatbush as a showcase to a sport he considered still in its infancy, Charley Stengel came up late in the season from Montgomery, Ala., of the Southern League. The only player he knew was the National League's premier left fielder, a fellow Missourian, Zack Wheat.

Before his first ball game at old Washington Park, Stengel was down on the clubhouse floor, shooting craps and winning the pot before an annoyed manager wondered what 'n hell a brash kid was doing there?

So all Casey did his first game in the National League was to go 4-for-4.

It really wasn't that easy, of course, and, playing parts of all of 14 seasons, the lefthanded-hitting Stengel batted .284, hitting over .300 four times. They thought at times he had a screw loose because he'd practice sliding on the outfield grass and, after he'd been dealt to Pittsburgh in 1918, he came back to get the bird at Brooklyn—and to give it back.

Finding a wounded sparrow, Stengel put it under his cap and, booed as he came to the plate, he removed the cap in a sweeping bow that permitted the fine-feathered friend to fly away in a surprising gesture that delighted the crowd, a life-long occupation for Case the clown.

Charley thought life was a bowl of cherries and a few or more bottles of beer—"John McGraw used to say, 'Don't drink the water'"—until he found Pittsburgh penurious. He horsed around so much that he made Barney Dreyfus miserable enough to deal him to Philadelphia, where he played just well enough to win the prize in July 1921. He was dealt to the Giants for $75,000 worth of baseball flesh.

Beaming, Stengel would recall, "I got to New York so fast that Mr. McGraw couldn't change his mind."

The pennant contender brought out the best in the veteran outfielder, concerned only about covering the deep center field of the horseshoe-shaped Polo Grounds when used against righthanded pitching. Frisch, the fresh young second baseman, told him:

"Don't worry, Pop. Play back. I'll be out to handle the short ones (flies)."

A lifelong friendship that carried through years of managerial rivalries when they'd tilt the flowing bowl and trip the light fantastic followed that meeting of the minds between Dutch and the Dutchman.

Stengel, who had hit .364 for Brooklyn in the 1916 World Series, didn't get into the '21 Series with the Giants, but, after batting .368 in 84 games in '22, he got into two October contests of the sweep over the Yankees and singled twice in five trips. A year later the .400 hitter was even hotter (.417) and more productive in a losing cause.

The House That Babe Built, as Fred Lieb called the Stadium, had opened across the Harlem River and in the first World Series game there in 1923, Stengel hit a ninth-inning homer off reliever Joe Bush that won for the Giants. So, in the third game, did his seventh-inning belt into the right-field stands decide a duel between the Giants' Art Nehf and the Yankees' Sad Sam Jones.

In that one, also played at the Stadium, the oversized pixy thumbed noses at the Yankees' executive box as he rounded third base. He drew a reprimand from the commissioner, Judge K.M. Landis, who liked a joke, but not in a ball game.

But it was the dramatic inside-the-park shot to deep left center, winning opener, that drew the most attention, skillfully off the pen of Damon Runyon before the sportswriter became a short story king. Wrote Runyon, in part:

"This is the way old Casey Stengel ran yesterday afternoon running his home run home.

"This is the way old Casey Stengel ran running his home run home in a Giant victory by a score of 5 to 4 in the first game of the World Series of 1923.

"This is the way old Casey Stengel ran, running his home run home, when two were out in the ninth inning and the score was tied and the ball was still bounding inside the Yankee yard.

"This is the way…

"His mouth wide open.

"His warped old legs bending beneath him at every stride.

"His arms flying back and forth like those of a man swimming with a crawl stroke.

"His flanks heaving, his breath whistling, his head far back…"

Out in California, the father of a tall, willowy brunette, Edna Lawson, wondered if her 34-year-old "intended" would last long enough for the wedding, which was performed in the summer of 1924 at Belleville, Ill., where Edna's brother, Jack, was an Army Air Corps captain in lighter-than-air at Scott field, as the government installation then was known.

By then, Casey had been dealt to Boston and early in 1925 he was sent down to Worcester (Mass.) of the Eastern League to serve as player, manager and president of the Braves' farm club.

Did well enough, too, hitting .320, that Toledo of the American Association offered him the player-manager's job at more money in 1926.

Here, Stengel showed the amusing ingenuity that would make him money before and after Randy Moore, a subsequent Boston outfielder, talked Casey and several other visionaries into sinking a few thousand bucks into an oil field Randy's father-in-law was sinking in Texas. They struck gold—black gold.

In '26, player Stengel requested in writing of Manager Stengel his release and Manager Stengel forwarded it in writing to President Stengel of the Worcester club with a similar request for himself. President Stengel not only graciously consented, to the dismay of the Braves and even to Judge Landis, but added a note of commendation to "both."

At Toledo, he done splendid, as Stengel himself would say, though one day he was so intent in conversation that, carrying a fungo stick, he jabbered away at an amused Mudhen player, unaware until he reached the dugout that he'd forgot to put his flannel baseball pants over his long john underwear. Then, he rapped the giggling Toledo player, Jocko Conlan, across the shins with the fungo bat.

Finally, old teammate Max Carey, managing alma mater Brooklyn, called and Casey coached for two seasons, then was asked to replace Carey as keeper of the Daffiness Dodgers. He declined, loyally, until Carey told him not to be silly. If Casey didn't take the job, someone else would.

So in probably his greatest triumph until his championship reign with the Yankees, Stengel's second-division Dodgers came across Brooklyn Bridge with a horde of Flatbush faithful to knock the Giants out of the 1934 pennant, the year New York's Bill Terry facetiously had inquired beforehand, "Is Brooklyn still in the National League?"

Afterward, Stengel and Terry, emerging from their clubhouse, virtually bumped into each other on the stairs leading away from the Polo Grounds.

Terry, the big first baseman, glowered at the smaller (5-10, 175-pound) older man and said:

"If your club had played all year the way it did the last two days, you wouldn't have finished sixth."

"Yas," growled Stengel in retort, "and if yours had played all year the way it did the last two days, you wouldn't have finished second."

Over a Budweiser or bourbon or brandy or whatever you had to offer, Stengel would tell that one, explaining that Terry had taken a step toward him and Ol' Case had said:

"I'm sure you can take me, Bill, but I'll take a piece of you with me."

Funny thing, years afterward, when reminded of that conversation, Casey embarrassingly would change the subject as if no longer willing to humiliate an old teammate. He'd relate, instead, that he and Terry had met on an elevator at the winter meetings after the '34 season, that Bill had spoken to him and that they'd wound up—of course—having a drink together.

Stengel, you see, had compassion even though with an appreciation of skills learned from McGraw, plus his own wit, he could be tart-tongued and could hold up a player or players for ridicule, which meant that even some of his champion Yankees didn't care too much for him. Certainly that would be true of a Boston outfielder, a pretty good hitter, whose dainty defensive play and base-running prompted Stengel to imitate the fellow's milquetoast slide and, grinning a devilish grin, ask:

"Have you met my pansy center fielder?"

Stengel never was so cruel, however, as Boston columnist Dave Egan—"The Colonel"—who waited until Casey's sixth and final season with Bob Quinn's moribund ball club: Then, when Casey was almost killed by a cabdriver on a dark, rainy night at Kenmore Square, Egan wrote that the driver who sidelined Stengel deserved an award as "Boston's man of the year."

Casey wound up with a leg so badly broken that as his personal favorite, Billy Martin, described it, the barrel-chested Stengel's baseball-stockinged leg "looked like a sock with a ball stuffed into it." Did, too.

In 1944, returning to the Chicago Cubs from Milwaukee, where he was surrogate operator and manager for Marine Bill Veeck out in the South Pacific, Charley Grimm disgusted Veeck by saying he'd turned over the Brewers to that Stengel—Veeck regarded him as a "clown" then, but Ol' Case justified Cholly's confidence and, incidentally, became eventually a fast friend of Veeck, the war-wounded promoter who brought the midget to the big leagues.

To listen to Stengel and Veeck or another attuned to Casey's conversational quirks talk hour on end without seldom, if ever, using a proper noun was both mystifying and exhilarating. Ol'Case could go to great lengths at times to avoid use of names such as when one spring at St. Petersburg, Fla., he identified the Cardinals' first baseman as "the bicycle rider."

The bicycle rider? Steve Bilko? How come, Case?

Ah, yes, Eddie Stanky, then managing the Redbirds and a pretty fair hand at hanging nicknames on people, called Bilko "Humphrey" after Humphrey Pennyworth, the big, good-natured, muscle-bound blond who drove a small outhouse-type shanty on bicycle wheels in a Sunday sideline comic strip by Ham Fisher, creator of "Joe Palooka." Casey couldn't remember Humphrey, but he liked Stanky's description of Bilko's resemblance to the "bicycle rider."

You could look it up, but in 1945, KayCee Stengel went back to his hometown, a Yankee farm club, and managed dead last an American Association ball club so sad that it drew only 38,000. Yeah, TOTAL for 77 home games.

But three successful seasons at Oakland, managing the Pacific Coast League Oaks for Brick Laws, brought the blockbuster offer. Imagine, as more than one baseball man and writer put it, a comedian

like Casey Stengel taking over the mighty Yankees, the dignified champions of all they surveyed? But George Weiss, succeeding as general manager when Dan Topping and Del Webb bought out Larry MacPhail after a roisterous, fist-swinging championship celebration in 1947, advised his employers that looks WERE deceiving.

So Stengel, who had hammed it up with the Dodgers and Giants in the National League, returned to the Big Apple in the American League—and it proved to be a wedding made in heaven or, at least almost as good as Ol'Case's 51 years with dear Edna.

Edna, a chic woman with a head for business, outlived Stengel by a year, after which her estate willed $40,000 to the national baseball Hall of Fame at Cooperstown, N.Y., as part of a special exhibit there in the colorful character's honor. A five-year wait for Hall of Fame induction was waived so that Ol' Case could be inducted by the Veterans' Committee into the Hall of Fame in 1966 when, as he put it, "Most people my age are dead."

At the end, meaning the last few years of their lives together, Edna's "think box," as Casey quaintly referred to his helpmate's brain, was fuzzy with senility, but if you'd like a close-up look at Mrs. Stengel as well as the best of the many books written about the man himself, I'd recommend Joe Durso's *Casey*, published in 1967 by Prentice-Hall, Inc.

Although often separated by the continent, the Stengels, a childless couple who doted on nephews and nieces, were as close as one second to another. Edna was Casey's buffer until she became ill and then, as Durso wrote, Stengel babied "and waited on her with the gallantry of a bridegroom."

Edna had been a professional accountant and actress when they met, and she revived her skills later by managing apartment-house properties and serving as chairman of the company that operated their bank's headquarters building. But in a serious moment in which for an instant she'd taken the conversational spotlight from him, Casey could interrupt to say:

"Tell 'em about the time you played with Hoot Gibson."

Once in a while they'd have a typical familial quarrel or disagreement, Durso noted, and Casey could give Edna the silent treatment, such as the time she forgot her exit visa from Mexico City, forcing the Yankees to cool their heels in a plane.

Not until they deplaned at Tampa did gabby Casey break the icy silence by saying he'd look after her baggage. Ten minutes later, Casey returned, climbed aboard a chartered bus, sat alongside the statuesque woman who'd known—and resembled—royalty.

"Yeah," said Stengel, overplaying his efforts to make up for the frosty treatment, "they're all right. They've got all three of 'em packed in."

Edna, after hours of suffering in silence, had her shot at Casey and made the most of it. Tersely, evenly, unemotionally, yet triumphantly, the regal spouse of the king of managers zinged Ol' Case. She said, coldly:

"I had four."

With his players, he was boss even though the Mets would titter late in the going the old man would fall asleep at times on the bench out of age or the hangovers he never showed or perhaps the sheer boredom of defeat. But, basically, he was the master of platooning and hunch playing.

For example, though rugged Hank Bauer had waded ashore with the Marines in critical and bloody Pacific battles and though Bauer would defy the walls to make catches, Stengel noted that Hank flinched from the righthanded curveball. Bailed out, they call it. So he'd not use the hustling ex-Leatherneck against cretain righthanders.

From the tie his Yankees knocked off Joe McCarthy's Red Sox two straight to win the pennant the final weekend of the 1949 season until his friend and former player, Al Lopez, unseated him with a record 111 victories at Cleveland in 1954, Charles Dillon (Casey) Stengel set that record unlikely to be matched: Five world championships in succession.

The personnel changed, but always the man with the long pencil—Weiss—was ready to help with a late-season acquisition, and Stengel wasn't averse to moving a Gil McDougald from one infield position to another or to putting "my assistant manager," Yogi Berra, in the outfield so that the bat and glove of Elston Howard could be utilized behind the plate. And Ol' Case always saw to it that, used too infrequently and certainly not too much, that money pitcher Whitey Ford was ready for the big game. Uh-huh, after Chief Allie Reynolds no longer was available to start to finish a blue-ribbon ball game.

When a player started up to the plate and Stengel wanted a pinch-hitter, he'd holler, "Hold the gun." When a groundball was needed to score a Yankee run, he'd yell, "Butcher boy!"

If he said something was "Ned in the Third Reader," you knew that any dumpkopf ought to be able to understand it. And if he said someone, including the umpires, "had given me the Vaseline pot," you know he intended no compliment to anyone or anything except perhaps the efficacy of the petroleum jelly on the posterior.

As Steve Jacobson noted once in *Newsday*, Stengel used the word "commence" unusually. For example: "Then they commence hitting the ball over a building…"

The Old Professor nickname went w-a-y back to Boston when the Braves were bums with lower-case "b's." The Doctor was a cognomen hung on Ol' Case himself because he'd use it himself, to wit, especially when steamed up by a question or comment:

"Now wait a minute, Doctor. Let me ask you something." Then, as many a New York writer would acknowledge with a grin, it would be Stengel who would proceed to tell the OTHER guy something.

Although not a religious man, he was not really a profane one. An exception was when he first took the Yankees into Ebbets Field at the time Mickey Mantle was a kid playing right field and Stengel walked out to the sloping right-field base of the

Brooklyn fence to show The Mick how to handle rebounds.

Said Mantle innocently, "Did you ever play here, Casey?"

"Crissakes," Stengel snapped, "do you think I was born 60 years old?"

Although he regarded Joe DiMaggio as the greatest player he managed, aware that DiMag had come off the disabled list to rip the Red Sox apart for him in a memorable series at Fenway Park, he often wondered whether body beautiful Mantle, if he'd had two sound knees, might not have been the best.

In the big bashful Oklahoma blond, a swift switch-hitter with extraordinary power, Stengel sought to blend the past with the present. Although Mantle could hit a ball a country mile, he also struck out too often. So, though some modern baseball men might disagree with the strategy, Casey had Mickey learn to drag-bunt, which the multitalented Mantle could do so well that he'd even beat out a crucial hit by bunting with two strikes on him.

There are s-o-o many stories to tell about the old man who finally bowed to cancer in September 1975, at which time the chances are that his excellent liver, the finest filter this side of Smithsonian Institute, probably quivered and lived another three days. It's too bad Ol' Case didn't will the liver to medical science and that brilliant brain, too.

Berlitz hardly would have been able to use his quaint English to teach foreigners. Sen. Estes Kefauver, the late coonskin-capped Ivy League senator from Tennessee, did a double-take at Casey's double-talk when Stengel was invited to testify before a Senate committee considering baseball's exemption from antitrust laws.

Casey "clarified" the situation this way:

"As to why baseball wants this bill, I hafta say I would not know, but I hafta say the reason why they want it passed is to keep baseball going as the highest-paid bill that has gone into baseball. I am in the baseball business and it has been run cleaner than was ever put out in 100 years at the present time."

Huh?

Ol' Case was often as complex as his commentary, which could be concise and clear-cut if he chose, prompting the *New York Times*' H.A. Dorfman to mark the first anniversary of Stengel's death this way:

"During the last year, the man has been referred to in print as a joker and a clowning loser, a Socrates and an original, a public clown, but not a private one…Other sources have provided labels such as master psychologist, Merlin, gadfly, gargoyle, a combination of Donald Duck and Charles de Gaulle.

"Gov. Hugh Carey offered his own composite Casey: 'The mind of a genius, the heart of Santa Claus and St. Francis, the face of a clown.'"

Yeah, and ALL original even though topped at times by a copy-cat. Like the time, feigning a fainting spell at an umpire's decision, he flopped to the ground, eyes closed, then opened one watery blue glimmer just long enough to learn that another delightful screwball, umpire John (Beans) Reardon, had lay down on the field right next to him.

S-o-o?

"So I get up and walk away," Casey Stengel would say, pouring another drink. "Hell, I know when I've run into a guy nuttier than I am."

CHARLES DILLON (CASEY) STENGEL
(The Old Professor)
Born July 30, 1889, at Kansas City, Mo.
Died September 29, 1975, at Glendale, Calif.
Height 5-10 Weight 175
Threw and batted lefthanded.
Named to Hall of Fame, 1966.

YEAR	CLUB	LEAGUE	POS.	G.	AB.	R.	H.	2B.	3B.	HR.	RBI.	B.A.	PO.	A.	E.	F.A.
1910	Kankakee	No. Assn.					(League disbanded in July)									
1910	Maysville	Bl. Grass	OF	69	233	27	52	10	5	2	-	.223	143	11	2	.987
1911	Aurora	Wis.-Ill.	OF	121	420	76	148	23	6	4	-	.352	229	27	8	.970
1912	Montgomery	South.	OF	136	479	85	139	-	-	-	-	.290	295	16	11	.966
1912	Brooklyn	Nat.	OF	17	57	9	18	1	0	1	12	.316	36	1	4	.902
1913	Brooklyn	Nat.	OF	124	438	60	119	16	8	7	44	.272	270	16	12	.960
1914	Brooklyn	Nat.	OF	126	412	55	130	13	10	4	56	.316	173	15	7	.964
1915	Brooklyn	Nat.	OF	132	459	52	109	20	12	3	43	.237	220	13	10	.959
1916	Brooklyn	Nat.	OF	127	462	66	129	27	8	8	53	.279	206	14	8	.965
1917	Brooklyn (a)	Nat.	OF	150	549	69	141	23	12	6	69	.257	256	30	9	.969
1918	Pittsburgh	Nat.	OF	39	122	18	30	4	1	1	13	.246	64	7	2	.973
1919	Pittsburgh (b)	Nat.	OF	89	321	38	94	10	10	4	40	.293	195	7	9	.957
1920	Philadelphia	Nat.	OF	129	445	53	130	25	6	9	50	.292	212	16	11	.954
1921	Phila (c)-N.Y.	Nat.	OF	42	81	11	23	4	1	0	6	.284	33	5	2	.950
1922	New York	Nat.	OF	84	250	48	92	8	10	7	48	.368	179	7	6	.969
1923	New York (d)	Nat.	OF	75	218	39	74	11	5	5	43	.339	115	4	2	.983
1924	Boston	Nat.	OF	131	461	57	129	20	6	5	39	.280	211	12	5	.978
1925	Boston	Nat.	OF	12	13	0	1	0	0	0	2	.077	1	0	0	1.000
1925	Worcester	East.	OF	100	334	73	107	27	2	10	-	.320	175	6	6	.968
1926	Toledo	A.A.	OF	88	201	40	66	14	2	0	27	.328	78	4	1	.988
1927	Toledo	A.A.	OF	18	17	3	3	0	0	1	3	.176	4	0	0	1.000
1928	Toledo	A.A.	OF	26	32	5	14	5	0	0	12	.438	16	0	0	1.000
1929	Toledo	A.A.	OF	20	31	2	7	1	1	0	9	.226	7	0	0	1.000
1931	Toledo	A.A.	OF	2	8	1	3	2	0	0	0	.375	3	1	0	1.000
Major League Totals - 14 Years				1277	4288	575	1219	182	89	60	518	.284	2171	147	87	.964

a Traded with Second Baseman George Cutshaw to Pittsburgh for Infielder Chuck Ward and Pitchers Burleigh Grimes and Al Mamaux, January 9, 1918.
b Traded to Philadelphia Phillies for Outfielder George Whitted, August, 1919; refused to report to Phillies for remainder of season in salary dispute.
c Traded to New York Giants for players valued at $75,000 July, 1921.
d Traded with Shortstop Dave Bancroft and Outfielder William Cunningham to Boston Braves for Outfielder Billy Southworth and Pitcher Joe Oeschger, November, 1923.

WORLD SERIES RECORD

YEAR	CLUB	LEAGUE	POS.	G.	AB.	R.	H.	2B.	3B.	HR.	RBI.	B.A.	PO.	A.	E.	F.A.
1916	Brooklyn	Nat.	OF	4	11	2	4	0	0	0	0	.364	3	1	1	.800
1922	New York	Nat.	OF	2	5	0	2	0	0	0	0	.400	4	0	0	1.000
1923	New York	Nat.	OF	6	12	3	5	0	0	2	4	.417	11	0	0	1.000
World Series Totals—3 Years				12	28	5	11	0	0	2	4	.393	18	1	1	.950

RECORD AS MAJOR LEAGUE MANAGER

YEAR	CLUB	LEAGUE	Position	W.	L.
1934	Brooklyn	Nat.	Sixth	71	81
1935	Brooklyn	Nat.	Fifth	70	83
1936	Brooklyn	Nat.	Seventh	67	87
1938	Boston	Nat.	Fifth	77	75
1939	Boston	Nat.	Seventh	63	88
1940	Boston	Nat.	Seventh	65	87
1941	Boston	Nat.	Seventh	62	92
1942	Boston	Nat.	Seventh	59	89
1943	Boston	Nat.	Sixth	68	85
1949	New York	Amer.	First	97	57
1950	New York	Amer.	First	98	56
1951	New York	Amer.	First	98	56
1952	New York	Amer.	First	95	59
1953	New York	Amer.	First	99	52
1954	New York	Amer.	Second	103	51
1955	New York	Amer.	First	96	58
1956	New York	Amer.	First	97	57
1957	New York	Amer.	First	98	56
1958	New York	Amer.	First	92	62
1959	New York	Amer.	Third	79	75
1960	New York	Amer.	First	97	57
1962	New York	Nat.	Tenth	40	120
1963	New York	Nat.	Tenth	51	111
1964	New York	Nat.	Tenth	53	109
1965	New York	Nat.	Tenth	31	64

Major League Totals—25 Years   1926   1867

WORLD SERIES RECORD

YEAR	CLUB	LEAGUE	W.	L.
1949	New York	Amer.	4	1
1950	New York	Amer.	4	0
1951	New York	Amer.	4	2
1952	New York	Amer.	4	3
1953	New York	Amer.	4	2
1955	New York	Amer.	3	4
1956	New York	Amer.	4	3
1957	New York	Amer.	3	4
1958	New York	Amer.	4	3
1960	New York	Amer.	3	4

A BOW TO THE CZAR: Even independent-thinking Bill Terry, first-base star and manager of champion Giant ball clubs, bent boxside to converse with Commissioner Judge K.M. Landis.

BILL TERRY

For 30 years, John McGraw managed the New York Giants with an authority that helped him win pennants and, in addition to considerable respect and some admiration, even more awe and plain vanilla fear. You either did it Mr. McGraw's way, cousin, or you were long gone. And how do you think you're going to like the laundry service or chow mein in Kankakee?

It wasn't a reign of terror, but it was a Napoleonic era of baseball in which the round little dictator met his Waterloo in an eight-season pennant drought and his Wellington in the person of his first baseman, William H. Terry.

Terry proved he could be as independent as the Old Man, which was one of the more polite descriptions used for McGraw behind the manager's back. Terry preferred later to gloss over their differences. After all, a wealthy Jacksonville (Fla.) automobile dealer, healthy and usually happy to 90, Bill saw only the sunny side of a career in which his own bluntness and aloofness kept him from enjoying a full measure of popularity, especially with the press.

But failure to give complete recognition to Terry's relationship with McGraw would be to miss a large measure of the stern, firm character of the poor boy who lifted himself from a broken home to become an extremely successful ballplayer, manager, businessman, husband and father. Quite a tribute to the moral fiber of the finest all-around first baseman in National League history and the last man in the league to hit .400.

Terry was as impressive a person as he was a performer, and that certainly included facially and physically as well as in demeanor and accomplishments.

At professional baseball's centennial-year Hall of Fame induction at Cooperstown, N.Y., where he was a faithful visitor since his own election in 1954, Bill had a bit of gray in the dark hair that was one of the most attractive features of a handsome, brooding man. Over the years, he gimped a bit with a cane, making him a bit more hunched, but then he'd always been slightly stooped.

Nearly 6-2, weighing more than 200 pounds, Terry was big and strong and graceful with powerful legs. He stood in the batter's box with his feet together, shoulders slightly hunched, chest concave and his arms held close to his body. A lefthanded batter, he hit line drives savagely to left-center and straightaway, a circumstance which hurt him in his home park, horseshoe-shaped Polo Grounds. There, outfielders could bunch him in the middle and range far back for some of his longest shots, but he still had a robust .341 average for 14 seasons.

"When I joined the Giants, I was a pull-hitter," Terry recalled, "but McGraw wanted me to learn to hit to the opposite field. Later on, he wondered why I didn't pull the ball."

Such exasperations would rankle a logical man like Terry, but not enough to keep him from doing what by then had come natural for him. In 1930, beginning a three-year stretch in which he didn't miss a game, Bill became *The Sporting News'* choice as the National League's Most Valuable Player with a .401 average.

Since 1900, only eight major leaguers have hit .400 or better. Two of them—Rogers Hornsby and Ty Cobb—did it three times each. George Sisler made it twice. The others were Nap Lajoie, Joe Jackson, Harry Heilmann, Ted Williams and Terry. The only other National Leaguer was Hornsby.

"Heavens," said Terry in recollection, "I certainly didn't expect to see nearly 40 years go by without a .400 hitter in the league. I thought someone would do it in a couple of years or so."

Hitters had their heyday in 1929-30 when there was as great an imbalance favoring batters as there was the other way in 1968, the Year of the Pitcher. Lefty O'Doul got 254 hits at Philadelphia in 1929 for a National League record, and Terry tied the mark in '30.

Actually, big Bill came up to the final game with a chance to break the year-old mark and, if he had a good day, maybe even match George Sisler's 10-year-old major league standard (257). However, he went hitless, to the disappointment of a 15,000 crowd which had come out to the Polo Grounds just to see Terry's assault on the single-season hit record.

A year later, he was a hit away from a second successive batting title when his .349 lost out to St. Louis' Chick Hafey by a fraction of a point.

In 1932, the year Terry became manager of the Giants, author Sidney Skolsky took a hard look at him and reported that the bronzed, blue-eyed giant of the Giants had a mole on his left leg, eight hairs on his chest, chewed tobacco on the field, smoked a huge cigar off the field and liked a beer or two.

His baritone voice, which he raised on behalf of the church choir in Memphis, was so good, the writer said, that Terry turned down $1,000 a week to play the Palace in New York.

Although he batted and threw lefthanded, he signed his checks righthanded. "He never reads a book, hates the movies, is a poor bridge player, scowls when he loses at poker and is a very strict parent," wrote Skolsky. "He disciplines his kids like a German oberlieutenant."

Indications are that Terry didn't like such invasions of his privacy, and over the years he became a tough interview, refusing to talk to reporters at the hotel when he was on the road, declining to give his unlisted telephone number to baseball writers traveling with the team and, though grudgingly making himself available after a game, he tried to keep the press away from his players.

Terry's aloofness on the one hand—"my business when I'm away from the ballpark is my own," he would insist—and the over-solicitous protectiveness of his players were bound to lead to strained relations with baseball writers. But there was no excuse for the primitive delay by which the gifted ballplayer was voted into the Hall of Fame 18 years after he'd hung up his glove.

Typical of the continuing misunderstanding that seemed to exist between Terry and at least his own generation of the press was the mileage given his first quote when he was notified that he had been elected to the Hall of Fame. "I have nothing to say," he said icily.

But in the sylvan beauty of Cooperstown, surrounded the following summer by superstars against whom he'd played and by the plaques of others whose artistry he appreciated, Terry thawed. And, as mentioned, he became a faithful figure at Hall of Fame functions. Verily, a spirited adviser to less conscientious members.

Chances are, William Harold Terry always was more sentimental than he would let on, but he had his guard up from the time he grew up in a broken home. He became a school dropout at 13, a husband at 18.

He was born in Atlanta, reportedly on October 30, 1898, though baseball greybeards think it was even earlier and that Bill just didn't want to be regarded as more than 23 when he came back to professional baseball a second time.

Bill's parents separated. At 13, he went to work to support himself and at 15 he was doing a man's work, unloading freight cars, throwing sacks of flour into trucks at the railroad yards in Atlanta. The ex-

periences made him grim, almost bitter. They also made him hungry.

Practicing baseball daily after work helped ease the literal hunger, but it created a drive to get ahead, a motivation that baseball at first wasn't able to provide fast enough to satisfy him.

A hard-firing, wild lefthander pitching for a semi-pro team, he impressed a scout for the St. Louis Browns and was invited to go to spring training in 1914 at St. Petersburg, Fla.

The frugal young man who would be called cheap by some in later years even bought a trunk, though he didn't have the clothes to fill it. But while awaiting orders to report, he was released.

That same spring—and he would be only 15 then if his birthdate is correct—Terry tried out with Atlanta of the Southern League, signed a contract and was optioned to Thomasville of the Georgia State League. Pitching there and at Newman in the Georgia-Florida League in '15, young Bill was restless, eager for more bread than he'd seen.

Sold to Shreveport in the Texas League, he had a 6-2 record in 1916 and was married that fall to the former Virginia Snead. After a 14-11 season in 1917 at Shreveport, where he doubled in the outfield and batted .231, the 19-plus family man decided to forget baseball.

"I'd played baseball only because I could make more money doing that than I could anything else," Terry has said with the detached frankness that has been an asset and a liability.

Traveling around the Southern League, he'd spotted something in Memphis. The burgeoning Standard Oil Company was attracted to the sober-faced athlete whose responsibilities had made him old and wise for his years. He went to work for Standard and also played for the company's fine semi-pro team.

The owner of the Memphis Chicks of the Southern League, Tom Watkins, watched the lefthander hit better than he pitched, but Watkins knew he couldn't afford those line drives, not with

Terry's stubborn business sense. So when the world champion New York Giants came to town for a spring exhibition in 1922, Watkins arranged a meeting between Terry and McGraw.

They exchanged small-talk in a suite at the new Peabody Hotel before McGraw asked, "How would you like to come to New York with me?"

"What for?"

"To play with the Giants, maybe."

"For how much?" Terry asked.

McGraw burned. "Do you understand," the master of all he surveyed asked, "what I'm offering you? I'm offering you a chance to play with the Giants—if you're good enough."

The 23-year-old family man understood.

"Excuse me," he said tartly, "if I don't fall all over myself, but the Giants don't mean a thing to me unless you can make it worth my while. I'm doing all right here. I have a nice home and I'm in no hurry to leave it or the job. If I can make much more money going to New York, I'll go. You can't get me excited by talking to me about the New York Giants."

McGraw said he would think it over. Three weeks later, he sent Terry a telegram, offering him $5,000 a season, plus a guarantee that if he were sent to the minor leagues, the Giants still would own him. The offer was a good one for its day.

When McGraw sent Terry to Toledo, he sent instructions to the farm club manager to work him at first base, not as a pitcher. "He may be clumsy, but he's going to be a helluva hitter," said McGraw, prophetically.

Terry, resentful, didn't like the new position and he had particular difficulty making the first-to-short-to-first double play, but he was strong-armed and also strong-willed and more important, strongly willing. He practiced until he mastered the position's demands.

The practice was painful, though, especially for the coach off whose head Terry once ricocheted a throw.

By the time Bill hit .336 and then .377 in two years at Toledo, he was ready for the Giants, playing briefly with them at the end of the 1923 season and then alternating with George Kelly in '24.

Actually, Long George, a versatile, rangy righthanded-hitting athlete who could play second base, too, went to the outfield and not the bench when Terry played first base against righthanders. The rookie, no kid at nearly 26 or so, batted just .239 in 77 regular-season games, but he was such a batting terror in the World Series against Washington that Bucky Harris, the Senators' manager, paid him the supreme compliment.

In five of the six games in which the platoon first baseman had appeared, he had delivered six hits in 14 trips, including a triple and home run. So Harris, after starting righthander Curly Ogden in the seventh game at Washington, switched two batters later to southpaw George Mogridge.

Harris' strategy was to compel Terry to bat against lefthanded pitching or to persuade McGraw to get him out of there. Bill batted twice unsuccessfully against Mogridge and was lifted for a pinch-hitter, after which Washington went to righthanded pitching.

Firpo Marberry and Walter Johnson worked the last seven innings. Johnson, against whom Terry was to hit .572, won the first Series game of his illustrious career—and the championship—in the 12th. Harris had flim-flammed McGraw.

None could have believed it that the first full season for Terry, the greatest first baseman he ever had, would mark the 10th and final pennant for McGraw. Some would even suggest that, pitchers excepted, Terry was the best player McGraw ever had.

If so, that would be a tremendous tribute, for Muggsy's best men included Frank Frisch, Mel Ott, Rogers Hornsby and Ross Youngs, to name a few.

Certainly the infield of Terry, Frisch, Travis Jackson and Fred Lindstrom was one of the greatest—and maybe the best ever.

Terry really came into his own in 1927 when he

hit .326 with 20 homers, drove in 121 runs and began a 10-season stretch of .300-or-better hitting that would continue until he limped painfully through a final pennant-winning season in 1936 with a swollen knee. He hit a career high of 28 homers in 1932, getting three in one April game and six in four games, but he withstood temptation to swing for the fences.

The 1932 season, the year in which he became manager in early June, he batted .350 and drove in more than 100 runs for the sixth successive season, proving that the assumption of authority never did bother a man born to leadership.

As a player, Terry was a hard-playing, reluctant follower because he couldn't quite stomach some of McGraw's dictatorial decisions with the servility of others who weren't as well employed in the off-season as the Memphis oil man.

Why, the lovely home for which he had spent just in excess of $30,000 had soared in value to more than $100,000. To Bill, baseball still was only a means to an end, and he had enough spirit of independence to resent McGraw's worst traits.

There was, for instance, the time Bill and Irish Meusel went to a show in Chicago. It ran a little late and, aware of the club's 11:30 curfew, the two ballplayers sprinted to the hotel and strode through the lobby, where McGraw was seated talking to friends, the time was 11:32.

The next morning there was a note in the players' hotel box, telling them they had been fined $50 each. Terry took out after McGraw and, as he put it, "sassed the old man pretty good" for sticking by a technicality when the spirit of the curfew was really to punish players who were making a night of it.

That afternoon, though Terry always hit well against veteran righthander Grover Cleveland Alexander, the first baseman wasn't in the Giants' lineup. Disdainfully, Terry went to the corner of the visitors' dugout, took off his shoes and tried to sleep, ignoring the game as well as the manager.

The Giants trailed in the ninth, 2-1, and had a man on base when players nudged Terry that McGraw wanted him to go up and pinch-hit. Slowly, defiantly, Bill walked up the dugout and sat down to put his shoes on, right in front of McGraw. Then he went up and belted a game-winning homer.

That evening Terry stepped into a hotel elevator with McGraw and the Giants' secretary, Jim Tierney.

"Give the boy back his money," McGraw ordered the secretary and then, turning to Terry, he said, "Come up to my suite. I've got some beer."

Good beer in Prohibition was a treat. Terry accepted two cases, took them to his room, called Jackson, Lindstrom and a few others to share his good fortune.

"We charged two dollar's worth of ice to McGraw and had a great party," Terry said, his sober face breaking into a smile.

Overweight, ill and apparently old before his time, McGraw began to lose some of the mental sharpness for which his players had admired him even when they couldn't stand his guts.

One day in a game in which Terry couldn't handle a grounder off the bat of Brooklyn's Johnny Frederick, McGraw left in pitcher Larry Benton to the point that Terry called time and appealed to Jackson, the shortstop and captain, to make a pitching change himself.

After the game, lost because Benton lingered too long, McGraw reverted to his favorite clubhouse device of castigating a player. Instead, however, of picking on his captain as his whipping boy, a technique that had forced Frank Frisch into silent revolt, the manager singled out Terry because of his misplay.

Terry took the tirade temporarily, then leaped to his feet and said, "You've been blaming other people for the mistakes you've made for 30 years."

Terry turned and went into the shower, taking his good old sweet time, aware McGraw was waiting for him. When he came out and the manager started to speak, Bill shouted, "Aw, nuts."

McGraw bridled. "No one," he said, "can say, 'Aw, nuts,' to me."

McGraw stormed off and for two years, Terry recalled, neither the manager nor the first baseman spoke to the other.

"I like to think that in the stubborn, uncomfortable period, I tried even harder," recalled Terry, who played every game and extremely well.

Then on June 3, 1932, the 59-year-old McGraw broke the silence. He called the 33-year-old Terry into his office off the clubhouse at the Polo Grounds and told him to prop a chair against the door so they wouldn't be interrupted.

"I thought he was going to tell me I'd been traded," Terry said.

Instead, McGraw became confidential. "Bill," he said, "you don't have to answer now. Wait a while if you like, but would you like to manage the Giants?"

Bill never blinked. "Mr. McGraw," he said, "there's no need for me to wait. I'll take it now."

So an era ended, the Napoleonic era of John J. McGraw, of whom his successor would say repeatedly, "I disagreed with him often, especially in the later years, but he was the greatest baseball man I ever knew, and he showed me his bigness when he didn't let our differences cost him his sense of fairness."

There's reason to believe, of course, that if Frisch hadn't jumped the Giants several seasons earlier, leading to his trade to St. Louis, the Fordham Flash would have succeeded McGraw. The Giants reportedly sought to reacquire Frisch after the 1931 season, but he was then the National League's Most Valuable Player.

No one could have done any better than Terry and few could have done as well after the first baseman took over a floundering ball club. He wouldn't be a McGraw, but he would exercise some of the Old Man's prerogatives, serving as general manager without portfolio.

McGraw, moving upstairs, offered to help.

"We became friends the last couple of years and I'm glad, because he died so soon (1934)," said Terry, "but I didn't ask any advice and he didn't offer any. He came into my office just once, to congratulate me after we won the 1933 pennant."

Terry stayed considerate of his players. He'd see that they had cold beer aboard a hot train on getaway day after a long western trip and he'd even play bartender for them, but he was the boss and properly distant most of the time. He no longer roomed with his good friend, Jackson, though they stayed close enough and he arranged for the shortstop to manage the Jersey City farm club when Jax slowed up.

Lindstrom, shifted unhappily from third base to the outfield by McGraw, apparently thought he should have had the managerial job rather than Terry. Bill traded Lindy that fall to Pittsburgh.

Terry's first move, however, was to fire a trainer the players considered a stool pigeon under McGraw and to bring back a morale-and-massage man they liked, Willie Schaeffer, a former prize fighter who was extremely popular with the players.

The most important trade was one which brought small, agile Gus Mancuso to take over the catching that had been handled by bulky Bob O'Farrell and heftier Shanty Hogan. Terry, shrewdly, wanted a catcher who could get the low strikes without having to stoop.

Umpires' calls are—or were—influenced by the ease with which a catcher handles the ball, and Mancuso could take the downbreaking deliveries of Carl Hubbell, Hal Schumacher, Fred Fitzsimmons and Bud Parmelee and ease them up into the strike zone.

"The best manager I ever played for," said Mancuso of Terry. "He really fought for his players."

Said King Carl Hubbell, the Hall of Fame lefthander who hit his stride in 1933 with his first of five straight 20-game seasons:

"Bill managed like he played. It was business to him, not fun, and he was successful."

Successful indeed. Although hurt when his right hand was hit with a pitch on Memorial Day, Terry batted .322 in 1933 and saw his team, shaken out of its beds in California by an earthquake in spring training, rise to meet all emergencies, though not necessarily quite so dramatically as when a light-hitting former Holy Cross shortstop sent a wire after brief hospitalization:

"We can't lose now. Am en route. J.C. (Blondy) Ryan."

Terry looked back, with good reason, on that 1933 pennant-winning season and five-game World Series conquest of Washington as the greatest thrill of his career. Bill pulled rabbits out of the hat regularly in the Series in which he doubled and homered among six hits.

In the sixth inning of the second game in which the Giants trailed, 1-0, Terry summoned Lefty O'Doul to pinch-hit for his regular center fielder, and O'Doul's two-run hit opened the gates to a six-run inning and a 6-1 victory.

In the same inning, slow-moving Mancuso squeezed home a run with a safe bunt. In the fourth game, an ailing-kneed Jackson, playing only because regular third baseman Johnny Vergez was stricken with appendicitis, beat out a bunt and scored the winning run on a single by Ryan.

In this game, Terry gambled when Washington filled the bases with one out in its half of the 11th. The Senators' manager, Joe Cronin, sent up a lefthanded pinch-hitter, rookie Cliff Bolton. At this point, veteran reserve infielder Charlie Dressen hopped off the Giants' bench to tell Terry that Bolton was slow and could be doubled. Bill ordered his infield back, conceding the tying run if the Giants couldn't get two on a groundball, but Ryan turned Bolton's ball into a game-ending DP.

Terry would use pinch-hitters extremely early for a regular if he thought he saw a chance to break open a game, but he was basically even more conservative—or fundamental—than McGraw in his emphasis on defense and pitching.

Late, long-time director of the Hall of Fame, Ken Smith, then traveling with the Giants as a writer, remembered a reaction that typified Terry's approach

to a game lost, 2-1, when Smitty said in commiseration, "Just another hit there, Bill, and—"

"They shouldn't have scored two runs," insisted Terry stoutly.

Another former baseball writer, the late Tom Meany, suggested that Bill became Terrible Terry in the minds of much of the press after having used the bunt in a manner of writers considered frightfully conservative.

In a game at Pittsburgh, the first three Giants hit safely in the first inning for a run, putting New York players on first and second, none out, bringing up slugger Mel Ott. Surprisingly, Ott was ordered to bunt. He dutifully moved the runners along, after which an intentional pass filled the bases, and a double play ended the Giants' only scoring of the game.

Writers questioned the strategy that had given a reprieve to a pitcher they thought the Giants had on the ropes. When one of them went into Terry's office the next day, the manager gave him a cold smile.

"I see," he said, "you don't like the way I run the ball club. Maybe we should switch jobs."

The writer grinned. "That's all right with me, Bill," he said, "as long as we switch salaries, too."

That should have ended it, but it didn't, Meany pointed out. Terry plainly let the reporter know that he resented his criticism and hinted that no baseball writer had the competence to second-guess him.

Except when he was ferreting out hamlets and places off the highways and byways to take his Giants and their traveling companions, the Cleveland Indians, on lengthy and profitable barnstorming stops in the spring, Terry presumably didn't worry about the fans, either.

But the buzzing borough of Brooklyn really let him have it after a remark innocently made in the winter of 1934 when he was holding a press conference in New York. The Dodgers had been quiet, he acknowledged in answer to a question, and asked with a quip:

"Is Brooklyn still in the National League?"

The last two days of the season, the Giants seemed to have the pennant won. But a faltering finish was climaxed by defeats at the hands of the sixth-place Dodgers, who seemed to bring half the borough across the Brooklyn Bridge to jeer the Giants and gloat.

After the flag had slipped away, a grumbling Terry bumped into the Dodgers' manager, Casey Stengel, who was leaving the Polo Grounds. The husky Terry glowered down at Stengel.

"If," he snapped, "your club had played all season the way it did the last two days, you wouldn't have finished sixth."

"No," cracked Casey, glaring up at the big man, "and if your fellas had played all season the way they did the last two days, they wouldn't have finished second."

Terry, a .354 hitter in the disappointment of '34, batted .341 in '35, but again the Giants faltered and not only were passed once more by St. Louis' Gashouse Gang, but by Chicago, which went past both clubs with a remarkable 21 consecutive victories in September.

A new shortstop, Dick Bartell, had helped in 1935 and Terry traded again in '36, this time for a second baseman, Burgess Whitehead of St. Louis, to succeed his aged sidekick, Hughie Critz. The Giants looked like a contender again, but this time they started poorly, handicapped by the knee miseries of the manager who was nearly 38—at least.

Bill's knees were in such bad shape that when he decided to put himself into the lineup in mid-July, umpire Ernie Quigley urged him, "Don't play, Bill." A spectator, Ford Frick, the former sportswriter who had become National League president, went onto the field and tried to talk Terry out of it.

"One twist and you might be crippled for life," he told Terry.

I tried to find out from Bill whether he really had hurt either or both knees, but he shrugged. "So far back I hardly can remember," he said, "and I aggravated the worse one in spring training that year."

So just after, on a doctor's advice, he had announced that he had retired as a player. When the Giants were 10½ games out, Terry changed his mind. He ignored Quigley's advice and Frick's plea and went into the lineup at Pittsburgh.

He tripled home the winning run and the Giants responded with a 15-game winning streak. They went on from there to a pennant, with the painwracked skipper hitting .310 in his last hurrah as a player.

Terry really earned the $37,000 he said he made that season—a handsome sum for those Depression times—and he closed out his playing career, batting .240 against the Yankees in the World Series won by the New York rivals, but he still drove in five runs in the six games.

As a bench manager, Bill Terry won another pennant in 1937, then signed a five-year contract for a reported $40,000 a season. The Giants dipped into the second division and after Terry finally stepped down as manager in favor of Mel Ott in 1941, he stayed only a season as farm director before heading home for Memphis.

Terry, the poor boy who vowed he'd never be poor again, left baseball a rich man, partly because he'd worked hard off the field, too, and invested well. For years, they called him Memphis Bill because he'd had a cotton plantation and real estate in the mid-South, but then richer opportunities beckoned in an automobile agency in Jacksonville, Fla. The Terry family had three agencies in Dixie. The senior Terrys had four children and 11 grandchildren, seven of them boys.

When Bill was fussing and fighting for more money, as tough a man at contract time as he was at home plate, he knew there would come a time when he would be happily married to dear Virginia, who died before he did in 1989 at a ripe 90.

Far from the maddening crowd for a half-century, he consented for a time to serve as president of the South Atlantic League with headquarters in Jacksonville, but the businessman-ballplayer who set the model for the modern athlete could afford the luxury of independence.

He turned down an offer from Walter O'Malley years ago to manage the Dodgers for $65,000 a season when, quick calculations told him, he'd need just about twice that much to compensate him for losses elsewhere.

Some years earlier, Warren Giles, still running the Cincinnati ball club before becoming president of the National League, had offered $25,000. Terry didn't mean to be impolite or ungracious, but his reply came out this way:

"Warren, I can make that much a month in my automobile business."

"Then," said Giles brightly, "why don't you take the job just for the fun of it?"

That would be the day, apparently, Bill Terry doing anything professionally just for the fun of it. The guy lost his amateur standing when he was just 15 years old and began the backbreaking job of unloading freight cars in Atlanta.

WILLIAM HAROLD TERRY
Born October 30, 1898, at Atlanta, Ga.
Died January 9, 1989, at Jacksonville, Fla.
Height 6-1 1/2 Weight 200
Threw and batted lefthanded.
Named to Hall of Fame, 1954.

YEAR	CLUB	LEAGUE	POS.	G.	AB.	R.	H.	2B.	3B.	HR.	RBI.	B.A.	PO.	A.	E.	F.A.
1915	Newnan	Ga.-Ala.	P	8	-	-	-	-	-	-	-	-	2	11	0	1.000
1916	Shreveport	Tex.	P	19	29	3	7	3	1	0	-	.241	2	14	3	.842
1917	Shreveport	Tex.	P-OF	95	208	15	48	9	1	4	-	.231	51	61	9	.926
1918-19-20-21								(Played semi-pro ball)								
1922	Toledo	A.A.	1B	88	235	41	79	11	4	14	61	.336	417	54	10	.979
1923	Toledo	A.A.	1B	109	427	73	161	22	11	15	82	.377	957	57	7	.993
1923	New York	Nat.	1B	3	7	1	1	0	0	0	0	.143	22	1	0	1.000
1924	New York	Nat.	1B	77	163	26	39	7	2	5	24	.239	325	14	4	.988
1925	New York	Nat.	1B	133	489	75	156	31	6	11	70	.319	1270	77	14	.990
1926	New York	Nat.	1B-OF	98	225	26	65	12	5	5	43	.289	391	31	9	.979
1927	New York	Nat.	1B	150	580	101	189	32	13	20	121	.326	1621	105	12	.993
1928	New York	Nat.	1B	149	568	100	185	36	11	17	101	.326	1584	78	12	.993
1929	New York	Nat.	1B	150	607	103	226	39	5	14	117	.372	1575	111	11	.994
1930	New York	Nat.	1B	154	633	139	254	39	15	23	129	.401	1538	128	17	.990
1931	New York	Nat.	1B	153	611	121	213	43	20	9	112	.349	1411	105	16	.990
1932	New York	Nat.	1B	154	643	124	225	42	11	28	117	.350	1493	137	14	.991
1933	New York	Nat.	1B	123	475	68	153	20	5	6	58	.322	1246	76	11	.992
1934	New York	Nat.	1B	153	602	109	213	30	6	8	83	.354	1592	105	10	.994
1935	New York	Nat.	1B	145	596	91	203	32	8	6	64	.341	1379	99	6	.996
1936	New York	Nat.	1B	79	229	36	71	10	5	2	39	.310	525	41	2	.996
Major League Totals				1721	6428	1120	2193	373	112	154	1078	.341	15972	1108	138	.992

PITCHING RECORD

YEAR	CLUB	LEAGUE	G.	IP.	W.	L.	Pct.	H.	R.	ER.	SO.	BB.	ERA.
1915	Newnan	Ga.-Ala.	8	-	7	1	.875	-	-	-	-	-	-
1916	Shreveport	Texas	19	84	6	2	.750	50	-	10	39	34	1.07
1917	Shreveport	Texas	40	246	14	11	.560	222	108	82	81	116	3.00
1922	Toledo	Amer. Assn.	26	127	9	9	.500	147	75	60	35	59	4.26

WORLD SERIES RECORD

YEAR	CLUB	LEAGUE	POS.	G.	AB.	R.	H.	2B.	3B.	HR.	RBI.	B.A.	PO.	A.	E.	F.A.
1924	New York	Nat.	1B	5	14	3	6	0	1	1	1	.429	43	2	0	1.000
1933	New York	Nat.	1B	5	22	3	6	1	0	1	1	.273	50	1	0	1.000
1936	New York	Nat.	1B	6	25	1	6	0	0	0	5	.240	45	8	0	1.000
World Series Totals				16	61	7	18	1	1	2	7	.295	138	11	0	1.000

HOT STUFF AT THE HOT CORNER: Pie Traynor was a fixture in Pittsburgh the last 52 of his 72 years as perhaps the greatest glove at third base, a .320 hitter, manager, broadcaster and story-teller.

PIE TRAYNOR

Unflinchingly, the greatest of all third basemen, Harold (Pie) Traynor—okay, Brooks Robinson and Mike Schmidt fans, let's hear it—faced and felt the cold steel and hot slides of enemy baserunners. But he shivered with fear one time when he was driving with Charles J. (Chilly) Doyle and the Pittsburgh sportswriter told him, "Turn right at the next corner, Pie."

Traynor, who didn't mind getting shaken up out there at the hot corner, was considerably shaken up at Doyle's command for two good reasons: (1) It

was absent-minded Chilly who was behind the wheel, and (2) Traynor never drove a car in his life.

When professional baseball turned 100 years, Traynor turned 70, still active enough to be able to don a uniform and conduct summer tryout camps for the Pirates at Forbes Field. One of the reasons he reached three-score-and-ten in such splendid physical condition was his life-long habit of walking where others would ride. So his death at 73 in 1972 was a shock. Still, he had a rich quality life.

"I never learned to drive because I was afraid I'd

find an excuse not to walk, which I've found so enjoyable, so relaxing and healthful," said the handsome, silver-haired Traynor in cultured tones that were misleading.

Neither by heredity nor environment, instinct nor inclination, was Traynor cultured, but he had been known as gentlemanly and articulate. His precise diction, an altered New England accent, served him well for more than 20 years as a Pittsburgh sportscaster on radio.

From the time he tramped through the snows of suburban Boston as a boy in Framingham and Somerville, through the years when he sat down at the bridge table only when the weather wasn't fit for hunting, Pie had been a physical culture man with one flaw—he smoked. He was as active as the miners and mill hands who were among his warmest admirers in the 14-plus seasons he gave Pittsburgh positively the finest combination third-base glove and bat in baseball history.

Except for the original Jimmie Collins, a stocky little man who played in the big leagues from 1895 to 1908, there was no other third baseman who had a call when it came to selecting all-time teams. And Collins didn't have the hitting or fielding figures— or size—to compare with Traynor's. Only Schmidt did 50-plus years later.

Traynor was broad-shouldered and rawboned, lithe and supple. He was six feet tall, long-legged and long-armed. He played at 175 pounds and he weighed almost exactly the same at 70 as he did when he took himself off Pittsburgh's playing list, reluctantly, at 37.

Opening day, 1969, living very much in the present, though proudly glorying in the past, Pie stepped out of his apartment in downtown Pittsburgh and surveyed the crowded bus headed for Forbes Field. Mentally, he made note of the bus number and struck out on foot, an uphill three-mile climb to the Schenley district in which Forbes Field is located.

"I didn't push myself," he said, "but I got there before the bus."

As a walking man and part mountain goat, Traynor was incredible. At his playing peak, he confided, he once became lost when hunting in the Wisconsin woods and tramped from five in the morning until nine at night before he found civilization, estimating he'd hoofed about 50 miles.

In his playing years, he'd think nothing of walking from Manhattan's old Alamac Hotel at 71st Street to the Polo Grounds at 157th. Once, he and Jewel Ens, a Pirate coach, walked back to the Alamac all the way from Brooklyn's Ebbets Field.

As recently as the time when both he and this century were in their mid-50s, Pie awakened to find New York bathed in pleasant Indian summer sunshine the early October morning of a Dodger-Yankee World Series. The Pittsburgh broadcaster ate breakfast at his 34th Street hotel and began a leisurely walk up Eighth Avenue toward Yankee Stadium, located at 161st Street.

"En route," he recalled, smiling, "friends in cabs would spot me and stop, but I thanked them. I know the folks in Harlem must have thought I was nuts. The trip took about three and a half hours. Sure, I was tired when I got there, but I was loosened up and relaxed."

The therapy of putting one foot in front of the other—"with motion, there's no emotion," someone once said—was apparent in the longest walk Traynor ever took. Not the longest mileage, but certainly the grimmest and most painful.

In 1938, Pie took a ball club that had only one 15-game winner, relief pitcher Mace Brown, and led the National League so comfortably down the stretch that in September, club officials even ordered a new rooftop press section built for the World Series. Then the Pirates staggered and the Chicago Cubs came on. The seven-game lead dwindled.

At Wrigley Field in late September, ailing-armed Dizzy Dean outfoxed the Pirates with slow stuff, 2-1, cutting Pittsburgh's lead to one-half game. The next day, the Pirates twice blew two-run leads in a game that went into the home 10th tied, 5-5, with darkness casting a gray shadow over the Cubs' park.

By then, Traynor no longer was a player-manager, able to inspire his young Buccos with his bat and his glove, but the Cubs' field foreman was their tomato-faced catcher, Gabby Hartnett. It was apparent that the umpires would call the game if relief ace Brown could retire Hartnett.

With two strikes, however, Mace hung a curve and Gabby belted it over the ivy-covered left-field fence for a famed homer in the gloaming that put the Cubs into first place to stay.

Traynor walked from Wrigley Field to the Pirates' downtown hotel, accompanied by friend Ens and a young Pittsburgh sportswriter, Les Biederman. Not a word was spoken.

"If either of you had said anything, I'd have popped you one," said Traynor, quite understandably out of character.

It was out of character for Pie to be thrown out of a ball game, and there's only one recorded incident of ejection, a bit of unusual news that prompted reporters to question umpire Pete McLaughlin. Why?

"Traynor said, 'I'm sick and tired of such decisions,'" the umpire explained.

Well?

"Since he wasn't feeling well, I excused him for the day," said McLaughlin, sounding like a junior-grade Bill Klem. "I hated to put him out—such a fine young man, too—but he did throw the ball to the ground, and we're instructed to put out any player who makes a gesture indicating disrespect for any umpire."

Pie was a pleasant, personable man and some thought he was too good-natured or easy-going to be a successful manager, but it's a fact, anyway, that in his five-plus seasons he got the Pirates closer to a pennant in '38—and quite surprisingly—than they were at any time in the long drought between victory drinks. That is, between 1927, when he was the star third baseman, and 1960, when he was a Pittsburgh-area scout who did a daily stint on radio.

Traynor returned to Pittsburgh in 1944 to go on the air for one year and he stayed for 22, displaying the kind of consistency and durability that had featured his play. Pie's air work was a blessing, financially, because he'd lost in the stock market crash of 1929 and, astonishingly, considering his baseball skill and his double duty as player and manager, the most money he ever made was $14,000 a season.

This, mind you, even though he had a lifetime batting average of .320 after batting over .300 in each of 10 seasons. He hit as high as .366 in 1930 and also batted .356, .337 and .342 the three seasons immediately preceding, but he regarded 1923 as his top season.

At 23, the four-season professional hit .338 and collected 208 hits, driving in more than 100 runs for the first of seven times. He had 19 doubles, tied for the league lead with 19 triples and hit 12 home runs. He also scored 108 runs.

"I was the first Pittsburgh player ever to bat .300, score 100 runs, drive in 100 and get 200 hits in the same season," said Traynor, aware that his predecessors included legendary Honus Wagner, the Pirate player with whom he was most closely associated.

Pie had considerable affection for old Honus, who coached for him and with whom he was associated in an ill-fated sporting goods business. But he seemed to reserve his greatest respect for blunt, outspoken Rogers Hornsby.

"Hornsby not only was the greatest righthanded hitter I ever saw," said Traynor, "but he was a good teacher. When I appealed to him for help early in my career, noting that I was hitting long outs with not quite enough power to reach the left-field fence often in a big ballpark, he recommended a heavier bat. 'You'll go to right field more often,' he said and he was right.

"I switched to a 42-ounce bat, one of the heaviest in the game, and, as Hornsby predicted, I didn't get around on the ball as quickly. So I began to hit line drives to right field and right-center."

I can recall Pie hitting the ball as tight to the

right-field line—and as deep—as any righthanded hitter I ever saw.

Traynor was understandably a bit sensitive that he didn't receive more recognition for his hitting, which certainly spoke for itself. But, truthfully, Pie's defensive play was so brilliant that it tended to overshadow his hitting, though the Pittsburgh third baseman's all-around excellence was not lost on John McGraw, the long-time Giants' manager who was Mr. National League for 30 years.

"If," McGraw said in 1929, "I were to pick the greatest team player in baseball today, I would have to pick Pie Traynor."

Sure-handed, quick-fielding and strong-armed, Pie once started four around-the-horn double plays in a game against McGraw's Giants. With Glenn Wright, Pittsburgh's shortstop for five seasons in the mid-'20s, he represented probably the finest left side of an infield ever to choke off opposition hits.

At Pie's peak, there was an old telegraphic play-by-play parody that went like this:

"Smith (or Jones or Hornsby or Hafey) doubled down the left-field line, but Traynor threw him out."

Playing virtually even with the bag, Pie could make every play. On balls hit to his left he ranged into the hole, quickly and gracefully. On bunts, he was so alert and adept that batters rarely laid the ball down in his direction.

On pop flies, he ranged from home plate to the field boxes to short left field. And he was positively devastating on the toughest play of them all, the hot ground smash over the bag.

"I've seen him make that play barehanded," said Charlie Grimm, a former teammate and opponent who had a ham-sized hand himself. "Pie had the quickest hands, the quickest arm of any third baseman. And from any angle he threw strikes. Playing first base with him was a pleasure—if you didn't stop too long to admire the plays he made."

They even talk about the kind it's hard to believe. That is, Traynor lunging backhanded to his right, gloving a smash and, losing balance, flipping the ball

to his bare hand and firing a side-armed strike to first base before taking a header into the dirt.

To the premier third baseman, the hardest-hitting pull-hitter he ever faced was the Cardinals' bespectacled Chick Hafey.

"He'd pull the pitch at the last split-second," Pie recalled, "and the ball would be on you in a flash, dipping fiercely or sailing. He was a helluva all-around player who ought to be in the Hall of Fame." (Hafey made it in 1971.)

No player of Traynor's generation, or for that matter, no person inside baseball or out could make more valid evaluations than the 70-year-old master of the hot corner. Not necessarily on the basis of native good judgment, but on the basis of experience—and exposure.

Even though in baseball's 100th year and his 50th in the professional phase of the game, he was doing only filmed television commercials and helping run Pirate tryout camps, Traynor was on top of the game he'd first played for coffee and cakes in 1920.

Down at Bradenton, Fla., in spring training, the old guy was out there in uniform, not getting underfoot, but offering encouragement to 5-4 Freddie Patek when the little man was thrust into the regular shortstop's job because of Gene Alley's persistent arm trouble. Traynor knows, incidentally, what it means to have a career ended by an arm injury.

Sliding home in 1934, the year he took over as manager of the Pirates in June, Pie tried to elude catcher Jim Wilson of the Phillies. Missing the plate as Wilson missed the tag, he thrust his right arm out to touch the rubber just as the whirling catcher came down on the outstretched arm with both knees.

"I felt something snap and was certain I had a broken arm," Traynor recalled. "I didn't, but I couldn't throw well anymore."

He played 57 games in 1935, none in '36 and went to bat just 12 times in 1937.

"With more minor leagues then and more players, you had more seasoned men ready for the majors," he said, "and that's why, with expansion further diluting talent, it's possible now for good players to play longer."

Traynor was explaining, not complaining, because he never permitted himself to become marshmallow sticky in sentiment for the "good old days." Until the end of his life he went to the park regularly and didn't believe that the game and the guys who play it have gone down the drain.

"The best third baseman I've ever seen is Ken Boyer," said Traynor. In fairness, the evaluation was made before Brooks Robinson's sensational 1970 World Series and before Schmidt's fielding was almost as good as his bat. Pie, of course, didn't see Traynor.

"For 10 years before Boyer hurt his back, he was out of this world," said the Hall of Fame third baseman enthusiastically. "He made all the plays, hit for power and drove in big runs. Brooks Robinson is another good one. And the most underrated star I've ever see, white or black, is Henry Aaron."

To Traynor the best pitcher he ever saw was Washington's Big Train, Walter Johnson, and he's extremely proud of having homered off Johnson his first time up in the 1925 World Series, a conquest that provided the greatest thrill of his career.

Traynor rated other great pitchers he'd seen this way:

Lefty Grove: "The hardest-throwing lefthander."

Sandy Koufax: "The best lefthanded curveballer."

Carl Hubbell: "When McGraw retired and Hub was permitted to throw his fastball more often to go with the curve and his excellent screwball, his pitching matched his competitive instinct."

Bob Feller: "Great."

Christy Mathewson: "I never knew Matty and couldn't pass judgment on him."

Grover Cleveland Alexander: "With Dazzy Vance, he had the most stuff and could thread a needle, throwing at three different speeds, deceptively, out of his uniform."

Traynor went along with the general ranking of Mickey Cochrane and Bill Dickey as the top catchers, "but I never saw anyone steal off Hartnett, including Max Carey," Pie said, pausing also to salute Roy Campanella and Ernie Lombardi.

"You couldn't steal off big Lom, either, and even though he couldn't run, how he could hit! He won a couple of batting championships even though they'd throw him out from short left field. And how often do you see a man from a fourth-place club win the Most Valuable Player award as Lombardi did in 1938? Like Hafey, he belongs in the Hall of Fame." (Lom made it, too.)

Traynor singled out George Sisler, Bill Terry and Lou Gehrig among first basemen and mentioned Eddie Collins, Nap Lajoie, Frank Frisch, Charlie Gehringer and Billy Herman among second basemen. He dwelled on Hornsby.

"We used to stop and watch Rog in batting practice," he recalled, "and he could go down to first base as fast as any righthanded hitter I ever saw. Not only was he the greatest righthanded hitter, but he was also a very good infielder and the finest double-play man on the pivot until Bill Mazeroski came along. Until he got fat in the legs, Hornsby covered ground well."

Shortstop? Traynor smiled.

"Who else? Wagner," he said. "If Honus had benefited from the livelier ball the rest of us enjoyed, there's no telling what he would have hit. He had power, speed, those remarkably big hands and tremendous shoulders. It's enough that men like John McGraw, Connie Mack and Clark Griffith thought he was the best."

Traynor rattled off the outfield names of Ty Cobb, Babe Ruth, Tris Speaker, Joe DiMaggio, Ted Williams and Stan Musial, then paused and mentioned Paul Waner and Mel Ott, too.

"All-around, I believe Speaker, Cobb and DiMaggio were the best," he said. "What DiMag did to his old boss, Joe McCarthy, when he came off the injured list in 1949 at Boston was one of the most amazing series a ballplayer ever had.

"Musial, if he hadn't hurt his throwing arm,

would have been a perfect player. I never saw anyone better at turning first base at full speed in an almost square turn without losing a stride."

These were, please understand, rapid-fire, off-the-top-of-the-head comments by peerless Pie, who over the years was ready, willing and quite able to speak warmly to Pittsburgh-area groups. Unless, that is, like his delightful absentminded friend, the late saintly Chilly Doyle, they asked him to turn the corner.

"I've been picked up more than once to make a talk and then have had to walk home because the guy who drove me got too much into the spirit of a festive occasion," he said, chuckling.

Harold Joseph Traynor had a long love affair with baseball even though when he was six years old and pestering older boys to let him play, they played a dirty trick on the son of an Irish printer in suburban Boston. They put him behind the plate without a mask and the first pitch hit him in the mouth and knocked out two teeth.

There are two versions of how the boy got his nickname. One is that his father hung it on him one day when Harold come home covered with dirt. "You look like pied type," James Traynor supposedly remarked, referring to a jumbled, ink-stained mess.

The other version is that an older boy, a neighborhood idol, began to call him "Pie Face" when the Traynor lad would show up at the grocery store looking for his favorite dish. Traynor long since had outgrown his sweet tooth, but the nickname, hung on him when he was only eight years old, stuck like a hot grounder gloved by the master himself.

As one of eight children, Pie went to work at the age of 12, walking three miles into Boston to serve as a messenger and office boy. By the time World War I broke out, turned down in an effort to enlist, he was put to work checking freight cars with munitions, riding a horse 12 hours a day for six months. Maybe that's why he always preferred to walk, not ride.

In 1918, Pie got down off his horse and, at the invitation of a Braves' scout who'd seen him play on the Somerville sandlots, he reported to Braves field. Someone forgot to tell George Stallings, however, and the Braves' manager angrily chased off one of the finest players the club ever missed.

By 1920, wiser and less timid, though still shy, Pie was scouted by both the Philadelphia Athletics and his favorite team, the Red Sox. The Sox still were his favorites even though they'd traded to Cleveland his personal favorite, Speaker. And that's a clue, in part, as to why Pie thought Tris was even better than Ty Cobb.

When one Les Bangs, manager of the Portsmouth club of the Virginia League, wired an offer to the tall, young Somerville shortstop, Traynor took the telegram to Ed Barrow, boss of the Bosox for whom he'd worked out. Should he sign?

"Go ahead," Barrow told him. "We've got a working agreement with Portsmouth. If you look good down there, we'll buy you."

The Red Sox tried to buy him, after he'd hit .270 in 104 games, but Pittsburgh wanted him even more. On the strength of a glowing report from scout Tom McNamara, frequently tightfisted Barney Dreyfuss, owner of the Pirates, bought the kid's contract for $10,000, a pretty tidy sum 70-plus years ago.

Pittsburgh, which had gone through several shortstops since Wagner's retirement three years earlier, gave the 21-year-old Traynor a 17-game look late in the 1920 season. Pie made 12 errors, batted .212, and the Pirates swung an off-season deal by which they obtained baseball's perennial pixy, Rabbit Maranville, Boston's shortstop.

Optioned out to Birmingham, Traynor had a big year, batting .336 and stealing 47 bases. When the Southern Association season ended, the Pirates recalled the infielder as they fought to retain a slender September lead over the Giants. Manager George Gibson played him one game at third base—and it was costly.

Costly not only because young Traynor threw low, allowing Chicago to score the winning run, but, as Max Carey pointed out, even more costly because manager George Gibson hesitated to use the rookie again. He played outfielder Clyde Barnhart at third base.

"Pie could play rings around Barnhart and he didn't get into any of our critical games with the Giants," Carey told writer Lee Greene many years ago.

Traynor began the 1922 season at shortstop, with Maranville at second base. But when Bill McKechnie replaced Gibson as manager in mid-season, Barnhart returned to the outfield, Maranville moved back to shortstop and Traynor began his long spectacular stand as the cool man at the hot corner.

"The hardest thing in going from shortstop to third base was learning to play that much closer to the hitter," Pie explained. "It was very important to know your hitters and station yourself correctly. A shortstop can always gamble a little because he can see the ball better and gets a better jump.

"Actually, though, I had to learn to play third base twice. When I was young and had good legs, I could play in closer and take more chances. But as I grew older and found my reflexes slowing, I found I was second-guessing myself.

"That's when I started over again, playing back and relying more on my positioning."

It's ironic that Traynor suffered his career-shortening injury as a baserunner. Teammates always thought he'd get it defensively. For all his skill, the clever basestealing Carey said, Pie never did manage to avoid barreling baserunners, and he was cut now and then.

But he cut into only two pint-sized shares of the World Series, batting a handsome .346 in the seven-game 1925 classic when, down three games to one, the Pirates rallied and finally beat Walter Johnson in the sawdust circus atmosphere of a rainy showdown, 9-7. Pie had two triples and a homer that time, but he had just one double to show for only

three hits and batted only .200 when the Yankees routed the Pirates in four straight two years later.

As a handsome bachelor, Traynor was one of the boys with the Pittsburgh cutups of the early '20s, though he couldn't qualify for the famed quartet of Maranville, Grimm, Possum Whitted and Cotton Tierney.

"He wanted in," said Grimm, grinning, "but he couldn't sing."

Winters, he was a lone timber wolf, trekking off to Wisconsin to hunt deer and to fish by cutting a hole through the ice of a Wisconsin lake, dropping a baited line into the water.

"There's nothing like the tug of a big northern pike," Traynor said.

Except maybe romance. In 1931, Pie married Eva Helmer, chief operator of the Havlin, a Cincinnati hotel where the ball club stayed. They had no children.

Traynor lost 20 pounds after the agonizing 1938 season and then lost his job at the end of the next season to Frank Frisch, an old foe for whom he had little regard. Pie moved to Cincinnati, his wife's hometown, but then Pittsburgh radio station KQV called him back to become sports director, and he began the double-duty decades as a sportscaster and Pirate scout.

As the only third baseman elected to baseball's Hall of Fame—Jimmy Collins and Home Run Baker were chosen by the Veterans' Committee—Pie Traynor was in a class by himself. Take the word of his long-time radio associate, Jack Henry, a reformed Pittsburgh sportswriter.

Even in blizzard weather, the walking man of the Golden Triangle never wore a hat. Henry wondered why.

"Why, you know, I had my hat stolen at the overcoat exchange," said Traynor. Translated, it meant he'd lost it in a restaurant.

But that had been several years before, hadn't it?

It had, but there'd been another unpleasant experience. Pie, who no longer could look pie in the face, explained with the sad-eyed deadpanned expression that made it difficult to tell when he was telling a tall tale.

"I've never felt the same about a hat since I went to a rack to retrieve one at a restaurant and a gentleman thought I was stealing his umbrella," Traynor told Henry.

But…

"But then the very next day, my wife gave me three umbrellas to take into town for repairs," he said, "and I bumped into the same restaurant patron. He stared at me in disbelief and then muttered, admiringly, 'Man, you sure had a good day today.'"

Indeed. A good day, a good career and a good life, but, say, friend, don't you have the feeling we've been had the way the famous pedestrian was when Chilly Doyle told him to turn right at the next corner?

HAROLD JOSEPH (PIE) TRAYNOR
Born November 11, 1899, at Framingham, Mass.
Died March 16, 1972, at Pittsburgh, Pa.
Height 6-0 1/2   Weight 175
Threw and batted righthanded.
Named to Hall of Fame, 1948.

YEAR	CLUB	LEAGUE	POS.	G.	AB.	R.	H.	2B.	3B.	HR.	RBI.	B.A.	PO.	A.	E.	F.A.
1920	Portsmouth	Va.	SS	104	392	50	106	18	4	8	57	.270	215	334	31	.947
1920	Pittsburgh	Nat.	SS	17	52	6	11	3	1	0	2	.212	35	39	12	.860
1921	Birmingham	South.	SS	131	527	101	177	22	13	5	53	.336	330	382	64	.918
1921	Pittsburgh	Nat.	SS-3B	7	19	0	5	0	0	0	2	.263	4	9	1	.939
1922	Pittsburgh	Nat.	SS-3B	142	571	89	161	17	12	4	81	.282	186	278	31	.937
1923	Pittsburgh	Nat.	3B	153	616	108	208	19	19	12	101	.338	191	310	26	.951
1924	Pittsburgh	Nat.	3B	142	545	86	160	26	13	5	82	.294	179	268	15	.968
1925	Pittsburgh	Nat.	SS-3B	150	591	114	189	39	14	6	106	.320	226	303	24	.957
1926	Pittsburgh	Nat.	3B	152	574	83	182	25	17	3	92	.317	182	279	23	.952
1927	Pittsburgh	Nat.	3B	149	573	93	196	32	9	5	106	.342	212	265	19	.962
1928	Pittsburgh	Nat.	3B	144	569	91	192	38	12	3	124	.337	175	296	27	.946
1929	Pittsburgh	Nat.	3B	130	540	94	192	27	12	4	108	.356	148	238	20	.951
1930	Pittsburgh	Nat.	3B	130	497	90	182	22	11	9	119	.366	130	268	25	.941
1931	Pittsburgh	Nat.	3B	155	615	81	183	37	15	2	103	.298	172	284	37	.925
1932	Pittsburgh	Nat.	3B	135	513	74	169	27	10	2	68	.329	173	222	27	.936
1933	Pittsburgh	Nat.	3B	154	624	85	190	27	6	1	82	.304	176	300	27	9.46
1934	Pittsburgh	Nat.	3B	119	444	62	137	22	10	1	61	.309	116	176	14	.954
1935	Pittsburgh	Nat.	1B-3B	57	204	24	57	10	3	1	36	.279	59	84	18	.888
1936	Pittsburgh	Nat.							(Did not play)							
1937	Pittsburgh	Nat.	3B	5	12	3	2	0	0	0	0	.167	2	8	0	1.000
Major League Totals				1941	7559	1183	2416	371	164	58	1273	.320	2366	3627	346	.945

WORLD SERIES RECORD

YEAR	CLUB	LEAGUE	POS.	G.	AB.	R.	H.	2B.	3B.	HR.	RBI.	B.A.	PO.	A.	E.	F.A.
1925	Pittsburgh	Nat.	3B	7	26	2	9	0	2	1	4	.346	6	18	0	1.000
1927	Pittsburgh	Nat.	3B	4	15	1	3	1	0	0	0	.200	5	9	1	.933
World Series Totals				11	41	3	12	1	2	1	4	.293	11	27	1	.974

THE NATURAL: Jut-jawed, built as if he had been sculpted, John (Honus) Wagner became a ham-handed wonder at shortstop.

HONUS WAGNER

When Ty Cobb reached first base the first time at Pittsburgh's brand new Forbes Field in the 1909 World Series, the fiery Detroit star cupped his hands and shouted to the Pirates' shortstop, "Hey, Krauthead, I'm coming down on the next pitch."

The Pittsburgh shortstop, at 35, was already a legend but John Peter (Honus) Wagner, though a gentleman, had learned years earlier how to meet and handle a challenge.

"I'll be waiting," Wagner answered Ty the Terrible. In this first and actually only confrontation between players regarded by many as the best each major league ever has developed, Cobb came off a painful second best.

When Ty slid into second, spikes high, Wagner was there not only holding his ground to make the putout, but applying the tag so forcefully, trying to stuff the ball down tyrannical Ty's throat, that Cobb wound up with a lacerated lip.

Uh-huh, and a bashful .231 batting average and just two stolen bases in a seven-game Series won by the Pirates, who were aided immeasurably by

Wagner. Honus hit .333 and stole six bases, a record which lasted until Lou Brock stole seven in the 1967 and '68 Series for the St. Louis Cardinals.

By then, most of Wagner's other records had been wiped away, a few by the New York Giants' late Mel Ott and St. Louis' Stan Musial, who, like Honus, came from the coal-blackened soil of western Pennsylvania, neither the Man Stan nor Henry the Hammer broke Wagner's mark of eight National League batting championships and 17 consecutive seasons hitting .300 or higher.

Separating fact from fancy about Wagner, who played his last big league baseball in 1917, is like trying to determine the veracious from the fallacious in the yarns the old man used to tell in those happy later years when he was a Pittsburgh landmark as a coach.

He retired at 75 and slipped away at 81 in December 1955, the same year in which he'd watched tearfully as an 18-foot statue of himself was erected in Schenley Park, a long, loud foul from home plate at Forbes Field.

Tobacco-gnawing, white-haired, craggy-faced and stooped, his famed bowed legs even more parenthetically shaped with the years, the once-shy and always modest Wagner would hold court in the clubhouse or dugout for young ballplayers or reporters.

The ballplayers liked him because, though they knew he was great, he never made uncomplimentary comparisons and the writers liked him because, well, how's this for a starter:

"I'll never forget the time I was playing shortstop and a dog ran onto the field and scooped up the ball as a runner on second broke for third," old Honus would say, massive jaws kneading the tobacco patiently as he delayed the punch line for an ear-twitching audience.

"I wasn't the smartest fella in the world, but I thought fast that time," he would add outrageously. "I picked up the dog, ball and all, and threw him over to the third baseman, who slapped him onto the runner, without hurting the dog or dropping the ball, and the other guy was out."

A Pittsburgh rookie once had the temerity to suggest, "I don't think I can believe your stories, Mr. Wagner."

Old Honus nodded. "That may be so, sonny," replied Wagner, "but I never told you anything that you can't repeat to your mother."

To be sure, Wagner was one of the purest heroes in the first century of professional baseball, if you're not stuffy enough to criticize a kindly, homely man of humble beginnings for icing up a case of beer and sitting around, shoes off, to relax on the porch or in the parlor of his suburban Pittsburgh home.

Except to outdo just about anyone who ever lived with baseball versatility—he's the No. 1 all-time shortstop who proved he could play any position on a ball club—Wagner was moderate, conservative and completely conscious of what he regarded his responsibilities to the youth of more than a half-century ago.

He once exasperated Cobb, who had become one of his greatest admirers, by turning down a whopping offer of $1,000 a week for a short tour on vaudeville. "I'm no actor, Ty," he insisted, "but thanks."

Another time, when sportswriter John Gruber was solicited to break down Wagner's resistance to tobacco endorsements, cigar-puffing Honus held the line firmly, but gently. A cigarette company had offered Gruber $10 if he could get the great National League star's permission to use his picture on cigarette baseball cards, much like the bubblegum cards of a later generation.

Gruber, touched and impressed by Wagner's reply, kept both the letter and check the ballplayer sent. In a treasure of simplicity, Wagner wrote:

"Dear John: I don't want my picture in cigarettes but I don't want you to lose the $10, so I am sending you a check for that sum." The seldom seen card became a collector's item.

If you're inclined to sneer at the tobacco company as stingy or to underrate Wagner's generosity, please remember that a sawbuck was a considerable sum through the years Honus was the underpaid king of at least his league.

At home in Carnegie, Pa., which was then known

as Mansfield, he was one of nine children born to a Bavarian immigrant, a coal miner, and at the age of 12 he'd followed his father into the earth to load coal at 70 cents a ton, a ton a day, for $3.50 a week.

Even though he was trying to follow another brother into barbering, he leaped at the chance to play baseball professionally in 1895 for $35 a week—even though he had only $3 left the first week after he'd had to pay for his own glove, shoes and baseball uniform.

By the time he ripped Atlantic League pitching at Paterson, N. J., a year later, the Dutchman was a hero. A raft of babies born in '96 and '97 were named John Peter. A cigar manufacturer came out with a Honus Wagner perfecto. A brewer named a brand of beer for the pitcher-outfielder-infielder.

The point is, that when Wagner came to the National League midway in 1897 with the Louisville franchise, which happily was transferred to his home Pittsburgh area in 1900, the majors offered no financial bonanza to a ballplayer.

In fact, a salary limit of $2,400 a man in the National League helped not only to create the American League in 1900, but, more significantly, set the stage for contract-jumping which permitted the American League to achieve parity so quickly that the Boston Red Sox beat Pittsburgh in the first modern World Series in 1903.

Wagner was wooed by Clark Griffith, manager of the New York Highlanders, as the Yankees were called then, when Ban Johnson and the American League began their frontal attack on the crusty, tightfisted National League. Without asking Pittsburgh owner Barney Dreyfuss for a penny, the former coal miner turned down the most money he'd ever seen at one time in his life. Griffith had laid before him 20 $1,000 bills.

Honus, who had just won his first batting title with a .381 average in a stirring battle to the final day against Philadelphia's Elmer Flick, became a national attraction, but the highest contract he ever signed was for $10,000, the salary he received in 1909 and thereafter.

So he was a man of more principle than principal. If he'd asked, Wagner probably could have commanded more money before he hung it up in 1917 at 43 with a lifetime .329 average. But each year after he'd reached $10,000 when he threatened to quit after the 1908 season, he and Barney Dreyfuss would talk contract and the Pittsburgh club owner would ask him what he wanted, and he'd say, "Same as last year."

Dreyfuss then would lay before him a blank contract, but Honus merely would affix his signature and the club owner would fill in the amount, which was, indeed, the "same as last year."

Wagner did not hold out for money after hitting .354 in 1908, slashing the beanbag ball the pitchers then threw for 201 hits, of which 39 were doubles, 19 triples and 10 home runs. Only occasionally did the old man who prided himself on 252 career triples wonder aloud just how many home runs he might have hit against the livelier ball that made its first appearance in 1920.

The reason Honus almost quit in 1909 at nearly 35—just before he wiped out a mediocre World Series performance six years earlier—was that his powerful bowed legs bothered him increasingly, a throwback to those cold, damp, unhealthy days digging coal.

The arthritis, which is what they didn't call rheumatism, in those days, bothered the basestealing and batting champion until he called it quits when he'd had his fourth straight season under .300. He batted .265 in 1917 after—and few will remember this—he even managed the Pirates a few days.

A great admirer of Fred Clarke, the rugged left fielder and field foreman for whom he played most of his career, Wagner had no taste for succeeding a friend, much less managing at all, but he humored Dreyfuss and reportedly recommended Hugo Bezdek, the Penn State football coach, and agreed to give Bezdek a hand.

One day at New York's Polo Grounds, with a young Pittsburgh pitcher faltering in the ninth inning, Bezdek looked out to Wagner at shortstop.

The old pro shook his head, a sign to stay with the kid. Bezdek did until, with the bases loaded, none out and the score tied, he walked out to the mound, motioning Wagner to join him.

"What do we do now?" the manager asked dryly.

Honus grinned, sheepishly, "I'd say," he observed, "that YOU'VE got a helluva problem on your hands."

All managers found Wagner a delight to handle because he was a star without temperament, a durable, uncomplaining player who was actually too good-natured until the rowdy Baltimore Orioles—and Clarke—taught him a lesson in his rookie season.

Honus rapped what should have been a triple, but when he made the turn at first base, the Baltimore first baseman, Jack Doyle, gave him the hip. At second, the shortstop Hughie Jennings, forced him wide. At third base, none other than John McGraw blocked him off the bag, then knocked the wind out of him by tagging him hard in the stomach.

Clarke cussed out the 23-year-old newcomer and threatened to send him back to the minors if he didn't fight back. There are two versions of what happened.

In one, beating out a slow roller to McGraw, Wagner ran right over Doyle at first base, so that McGraw's throw sailed over the bag and into the right-field corner, permitting Honus to reach third. In the other—and I like this one better—Honus was quoted years later as recalling:

"I hit another to deep center for extra bases. I dumped Doyle on his behind at first, left Jennings in the dirt at second and trampled all over McGraw's feet coming into third. Clarke was so tickled to see McGraw fuming and cussing that he came over to the coach's box and said, 'Nice day, ain't it, Muggsy?' "

The Louisville regulars, who had run Wagner out of the batter's box only until the slow-to-arouse Honus realized from Clarke that he didn't have to take their guff, could have told McGraw and associates what would happen if the guy got his Dutch up.

McGraw, who died in 1934, always insisted that Wagner was the greatest all-around ballplayer he'd ever seen. Ed Barrow, the man who turned Babe Ruth from pitcher to outfielder and brought Joe DiMaggio to the Yankees, also rated Honus as No. 1.

Barrow, who was 85 years old when he died in 1953, saw much of baseball's first 100 years and could say with authority, "Ruth was the best hitter and the most powerful and Cobb the greatest driving force, but Wagner was the best player overall. He wouldn't have done poorly at any position."

Barrow, like McGraw, might have been a bit prejudiced in Wagner's behalf and not only because Honus was such a completely likeable human being. McGraw, to tease the American League, might have favored Wagner over Cobb and Ruth for purposes of league pride. Barrow might have been a bit blinded by the fact that he'd scouted and signed Honus himself.

The name, of course, was John Peter Wagner, though for the heck of it, he signed his first contract with Steubenville, O., as "William Wagner" because he thought it sounded better. Actually, around home, they used the Germanic pronunciation of Johannes, which, abbreviated, became Hans or, as delightfuly simple and as unaffected as the man himself, just plain Honus.

Just plain Honus was a free agent when Barrow came calling or, rather, walking in the winter of 1895. From directions given him at a railroad station, Barrow struggled up the tracks a couple of miles at Mansfield, Pa., to find a few young fellows chucking hunks of coal at railroad cars. The way Wagner told it, they thought Barrow was a railroad cop and they hightailed from the scene, but Barrow's version was different.

Barrow, who then operated the Paterson ball club, remembered that one young man was clumsy-looking and awkward, yet so obviously strong, and he threw the coal farther and more accurately than the rest. That one, he knew, was the Wagner he'd come to see, though, actually, Honus' older brother, Al, who championed him at a time when few others could see a diamond in the rough on the anthracite diamonds, reached the big leagues too, but just briefly.

Honus' father was a baseball buff and the big-hearted ballplayer got him out of the mines and into the ballpark as a ticket taker so that the old Bavarian could watch his Hans dazzle two generations and write his name permanently into baseball lore, as well as in the record books.

Wagner was a walking caricature, a strapping 5-11 and close to 200 pounds, a bear of a man with a big chest, broad shoulders and legs so bowed that, someone once wrote, they took off at the ankles in a curving sweep to meet in surprise at his waistline. He was, Lefty Gomez once quipped, the only man Gomez ever saw who could tie his shoestrings without bending.

Honus had extremely long arms and huge hands which scooped up infield dirt when he got those powerful lunch hooks on a ball. The hands were so powerful that, once to rattle a young St. Louis fireball righthander who had completely puzzled the Pirates, Wagner took two called strikes, then reached out barehanded, grabbed the next fastball and threw it back to the mound with a deflating comment:

"Change-up, huh?"

The umpire called Wagner out, but the young pitcher, unnerved, immediately walked the next five batters, and the Pirates won the game.

Afield, Honus could glide to his right and rifle out a runner from deep short. His speed, they say, was deceptive and unbelievable for a man of his size and build. He led the National League six times in stolen bases and, in the 1909 Series, the one in which he outdueled his younger rival widely in the advertised confrontation with Cobb, he once stole second, third and home.

Deep in the batter's box, with a stance that made him look as if he were sitting on a bar stool, the righthanded-hitting Wagner would peer sharply over his large hooked nose and then lunge into a pitch with a short, chopping swing.

He hit to all fields and against the best of them, averaging .324, for instance, against the outstanding pitcher of his era, Christy Mathewson.

After he quit playing, just a year following his belated marriage to a Pittsburgh girl, Bessie Smith, who bore him two daughters, Wagner continued playing barnstorming basketball and even baseball for a time. He'd always figured, probably correctly, that one reason he lasted until he was 43 years old was because he'd never had to fight each spring to get himself back into condition.

For a time, he served as basketball and baseball coach at Carnegie Tech. He couldn't stand the inactivity as sergeant-at-arms in the Pennsylvania State Legislature and then, when the bottom dropped out in the depression, he and another Pittsburgh star, Pie Traynor, dropped a bundle in a sporting goods store.

That's when William Benswanger, son-in-law of the late Dreyfuss, brought the Pittsburgh favorite back into uniform. Wagner was nearly 60 when he became a Pirate coach in 1933, but he worked industriously, never interfering with a manager. Until he was past 70, he would retrieve balls on the field. Finally, as feared, a smash hit him in the back one day, forcing the old warrior to retreat wisely to the dugout.

There, or on the banquet circuit, which he followed assiduously in the Pittsburgh area, to the amazement of those who had remembered him as quiet and reticent, John Peter (Honus) Wagner would lend his warmth and his wit.

He'd tell about his fabulous former roommate, roistering Rube Waddell, who insisted on sleeping with water running in the bathtub. Waddell, who lived near a turbulent stream north of Butler, Pa., maintained that the splashing of water on a nearby dam soothed him.

When Wagner was asked if he had continued to room with Waddell, he would quip, "Not by a dam site."

Honus insisted he'd lost a home run one time because he'd hit a ball over the fence just as a steam engine passed, contending with a straight face that the huffing and puffing of the engine coughed the ball back into the playing field.

But, glibly, the grand gaffer would point out that those things had a habit of evening up. Which would remind him that he'd hit a drive up against a left-field screen one time and that, leaping, the left fielder had snagged his uniform shirt on the wire so that he dangled there, helplessly, as Wagner circled the bases for a home run.

He'd spin stories by the hour. Even Bing Crosby, a stockholder in the Pirates, was mesmerized by the legend when it was alive. At a banquet, where Wagner had a habit of asking a question rather than answering one when he was getting weary, Der Bingle heard Honus wind up one night by asking:

"How is it possible for a player to hit a game-winning four-run homer and not have a man touch home plate?"

A bothered Crosby cornered him later. "How, Honus?" inquired the crooner.

Wagner chuckled and smiled. "I'm afraid, Bing," he said, "that a man with four boys never could figure that one. The reason no man touched home plate was because it was a girls' team."

Corn, sure and schmaltz, yes, but Wagner was entirely in character, though on the field he had been quickwitted enough to devise plays that won games. Like the one, for example, with a runner on third, of having the third baseman inch forward, as if expecting a squeeze bunt, to draw the baserunner's attention so that the shortstop, Wagner, could rush over and take a pickoff peg from the catcher.

"The only trouble was that the first time we tried it, I didn't get over to third in time, and Fred Clarke, playing left field, threatened to kill us," Wagner said.

The first time Clarke ordered Honus to "lay one down," Wagner hit away, blasting a home run rather than bunting, and he had a hard time convincing the manager that he'd never heard the expression.

"I thought 'lay one down' meant to 'lay it on,' " said the earnest young athlete, talking his way out of a $50 fine.

The next time Wagner came up in a bunting situation, Clarke called him over.

"Lay one down, Dutch," the manager ordered, adding with a twinkle, "like the last time."

Wagner advised youngsters to practice and to avoid concentrating on any one position until they were 18 years old, so that they not only might better develop versatile skills, but also get a better idea of the position for which they were best suited.

"I was an outfielder who pitched, horribly, and became a shortstop because the Pirates needed one, but I'd always tried to move around," he would explain, "and maybe that's why I was ready."

Wagner had another bit of advice about not bothering the umpires, a policy he preached as well as practiced. But, still, he could enjoy telling one on the umpires in a way that made him a joy to listen to, even for those who weren't fortunate enough to watch him play.

There was the day, for instance, when a rookie named Walter Rehg went up to pinch-hit, unannounced, and plate umpire Bill Klem demanded:

"Who are you batting for?"

"For myself, you fool," replied the brash rookie, almost tossed out of a big league game before he ever got into one.

About the same time, the Pirates had another rookie who was sent up to hit, and Klem asked his name.

"Booe," the player answered.

"What did you say?" the umpire asked heatedly.

"Booe," was the meek reply.

To keep Everett Booe from getting chased, manager Fred Clarke had to hurry out with a scorecard. But no one ever needed a scorecard or program to identify the refugee from Gutzom Borglum's sculpting chisel, baseball's greatest shortstop and perhaps its premier player—Wagner.

JOHN PETER (HONUS) WAGNER
Born February 24, 1874, at Carnegie, Pa.
Died December 6, 1955, at Carnegie, Pa.
Height 5-11 Weight 200
Threw and batted righthanded.
Named to Hall of Fame, 1936.

YEAR	CLUB	LEAGUE	POS.	G.	AB.	R.	H.	2B.	3B.	HR.	RBI.	B.A.	PO.	A.	E.	F.A.
1895	Stuebenville	Int. St.	SS	44	-	-	-	-	-	-	-	.402	-	-	-	-
1895	Mansfield	Ohio St.							No record available								
1895	Adrian	Mich. St.	S-O	20	-	-	-	-	-	-	-	.365	-	-	-	-
1895	Warren	Iron--Oil	SS	65	-	-	-	-	-	-	-	.369	-	-	-	-
1896	Paterson	Atl.	1-3-OF	109	416	106	145	-	-	-	-	.349	802	79	41	.956
1897	Paterson	Atlantic	3B	74	301	61	114	-	-	-	-	.379	104	107	24	.898
1897	Louisville	Nat.	OF	61	241	38	83	17	4	2	-	.344	105	17	11	.917
1898	Louisville	Nat.	1B-3B	148	591	80	180	31	4	10	-	.305	827	165	32	.969
1899	Louisville (a)	Nat.	3B-OF	144	549	102	197	47	13	7	-	.359	197	185	30	.927
1900	Pittsburgh	Nat.	OF	134	528	107	201	45	22	4	-	.381	177	13	6	.969
1901	Pittsburgh	Nat.	1F-OF	141	556	100	196	39	10	6	-	.353	299	279	47	.925
1902	Pittsburgh	Nat.	1F-OF	137	538	105	177	33	16	3	-	.329	526	171	34	.953
1903	Pittsburgh	Nat.	SS	129	512	97	182	30	19	5	-	.355	303	397	50	.933
1904	Pittsburgh	Nat.	SS	132	490	97	171	44	14	4	-	.349	274	367	49	.929
1905	Pittsburgh	Nat.	SS	147	548	114	199	22	14	6	-	.363	353	517	60	.935
1906	Pittsburgh	Nat.	SS	140	516	103	175	38	9	2	-	.339	334	473	51	.941
1907	Pittsburgh	Nat.	SS	142	515	98	180	38	14	6	91	.350	314	428	49	.938
1908	Pittsburgh	Nat.	SS	151	568	100	201	39	19	10	106	.354	354	469	50	.943
1909	Pittsburgh	Nat.	SS	137	495	92	168	39	10	5	102	.339	344	430	49	.940
1910	Pittsburgh	Nat.	SS	150	556	90	178	34	8	4	84	.320	337	413	52	.935
1911	Pittsburgh	Nat.	SS-1B	130	473	87	158	23	16	9	108	.334	471	321	46	.945
1912	Pittsburgh	Nat.	SS	145	558	91	181	35	20	7	94	.324	341	462	32	.962
1913	Pittsburgh	Nat.	SS	114	413	51	124	18	4	3	55	.300	289	323	24	.962
1914	Pittsburgh	Nat.	3B-SS	150	552	60	139	15	9	1	46	.252	339	457	43	.949
1915	Pittsburgh	Nat.	SS	156	566	68	155	32	17	6	78	.274	298	395	38	.948
1916	Pittsburgh	Nat.	1B-SS	123	432	45	124	15	9	1	38	.287	409	272	33	.954
1917	Pittsburgh	Nat.	1-3-SS	74	230	15	61	7	1	0	22	.265	476	74	13	.977
Major League Totals				2785	10427	1740	3430	651	252	101	-	.329	7367	6628	799	.946

a Transferred with 14 other players to Pittsburgh when Louisville dropped out of National League.

WORLD SERIES RECORD

YEAR	CLUB	LEAGUE	POS.	G.	AB.	R.	H.	2B.	3B.	HR.	RBI.	B.A.	PO.	A.	E.	F.A.
1903	Pittsburgh	Nat.	SS	8	27	2	6	1	0	0	3	.222	13	27	6	.870
1909	Pittsburgh	Nat.	SS	7	24	4	8	2	1	0	7	.333	13	23	2	.947
World Series Totals				15	51	6	14	3	1	0	10	.275	26	50	8	.905

POUND FOR POUND: Like boxing's Sugar Ray Robinson, Paul Waner might have been the best hitter for size. Little "Big Poison"—a half-inch shorter than younger brother Lloyd—he was only 5-8½" but he flicked foul-lines left to right for 20 seasons at .333.

PAUL WANER

As a former nursemaid to bottle jockeys of baseball, Charles E. (Gabby) Street, manager of the Cardinals, knew a hangover when he saw—and smelled—one.

On a hot early summer day in the early 1930s, walking toward him at St. Louis' Sportsman's Park, hunched over, eyes squinting painfully in the glaring sunshine, the fumes quivering about his head, was a persistent pain in the Redbirds' reputation—Pittsburgh's Paul Waner.

"Had a rough night, Paul?" asked Street, pleas-

antly, as they passed on the field shortly before game time.

"Rough night?" Waner winced. "What a host that Meine is!"

By happy coincidence for those to whom whiskey was mother's milk, Heinie Meine, a Pittsburgh pitcher, operated a saloon in a St. Louis South County community called Luxembourg, where the gemuetlichkeit was as good as Waner's batting stroke.

Waner, who had spent the night sitting up with

a sick jug, wondered who was pitching for the Cardinals that depression summer afternoon.

"Dean," said Street.

"Oh, no, not Diz," complained Waner. "Tell 'im to take it easy on old Paul, will you, Sarge?"

Gabby Street, the former World War I sergeant, patted the Pittsburgh player patronizingly on the back and said, "Sure, Paul, sure."

To himself, heading for the home team's dugout, Street chuckled. "This," he said, "is one day the little so-and-so won't bother us."

Years later, good ol' Gabby would pause over his punch line, puffing on a pipe. "All Waner did that day," he would say, "was to hit four doubles, tying the record."

Drunk or sober, therefore, Big Poison, as they called him, could hit the finest pitcher of his day, Dizzy Dean. And, pound for pound, Waner might have been the best hitter who ever lived.

Only 5-8½ tall, never weighing more than 153 pounds, the older of the Waner brothers averaged .333 for 19-plus seasons in the major leagues. Eight times he collected 200 hits in a season, matching Wee Willie Keeler's National League record.

And as one of only 10 players who have collected 3,000 or more hits in major league history Paul earned Hall of Fame election in 1952, just seven years after he quit.

Before he died of pulmonary emphysema in 1965 at the age of 62, the wizened Waner had established himself as a capable batting coach who scorned the usual instructions: Keep a level swing and follow through with the wrists.

"Forget the wrists and don't worry about keeping the bat level," Waner would say, emphasizing:

"Turn your head so that you are watching the pitcher with both eyes. Swing down on the ball and turn that bellybutton away from the pitcher when you pivot."

A better-than-average golfer, Waner would add, "You swing down on a golf ball and if you do it in baseball, you're bound to hit the ball more often and harder."

A sharp-featured, thin-lipped little man, tanned the color of an acorn and as lean as an Indian pony from his native Oklahoma, Paul seemed constructed entirely of bone and gristle.

A lefthanded hitter, he'd stand well back of the plate, his feet almost together, but the right foot about three inches in front of the left, toes parallel to the line of the batter's box, about five inches inside the chalkmarks. He raised his right leg slightly as he stepped into the pitch, nothing like the exaggerated leg lift of Mel Ott.

Tomahawking the ball, Waner was a clothesline hitter, hitting sharply to all fields and so straight that his wife could have hung out a week's wash on one of his liners. And, like his younger brother, Lloyd, Pittsburgh's center fielder at the time he played right field, Paul was extremely fast and could leg out infield hits, too.

With Lloyd leading off and Paul batting third, they played together with the Pirates for 14 years through 1940, when both were traded.

The only reason they didn't first-and-third the foe to death, as they'd say in the dugout, was that often Lloyd would hotfoot it all the way home from first when Paul plugged the gaps or flicked the foul-lines at Forbes Field with one of his sharp shots.

Their nicknames, menacing and colorful, were misapplied because, in Brooklyn patois, a respectful fan's attempt to refer to them as "little person" and "big person," though they were the same height, came out sounding like Little Poison and Big Poison.

When, however, Paul Waner's parents gave him the middle name of Glee, back there in 1903 at Harrah, Okla., they acted with a prescience given to few mortals, for fun really was Paul's middle name.

He wasn't a roisterer on the scale of Babe Ruth, nor was he a rowdy, but he liked late hours, liquor and convivial company. And if there are better stories about booze and base hits than about this Merry Mite of baseball, twitching ears that have collected Waner lore for years, I haven't heard them.

Maybe they're not all true, friend, but, personally, I checked out enough with P. G. Waner in his later years to know that there's more truth than fiction to even the tallest tales about this mightiest mite of the majors.

Okay, so maybe there's an exaggeration along the way in the delightful saga of this free-style elbow-bender of incredible capacity, but Pie Traynor, the Hall of Fame third baseman with whom—and for whom—he played, insists this one is true:

Taking over as manager at Pittsburgh, Traynor expressed the thought that maybe his .370-hitting right fielder would bat .400 if he gave up the raw stuff in favor of a little beer.

"For you, Pie, I'd do anything," said Waner, always a good team man.

The first time around the league that year, P. G. was batting a tepid .240. When the Pirates pulled into New York and checked into their hotel one evening, Waner took a walk and Traynor tagged along.

They passed a bar, and Pie suggested that they stop in. The bartender inquired, "What'll you have, gents?"

Traynor said he'd have a beer.

"Me, too," said Waner.

"He will like hell. Give him a shot of whiskey," said Traynor, who swore that the Waner of old then began to rip National League pitching.

Even as late as 1942, when he was 39 years old, the wonderful Waner could astonish no less than Casey Stengel, a man whose own liver was one of the finest filters this side of the tobacco belt.

Stengel then was managing the moribund Boston Braves, who had picked up Big Poison after he had been released unconditionally by the Brooklyn Dodgers. World War II had begun and Stengel would come back from Florida with new respect for Waner's durability.

Paul would get up at dawn to go fishing with his young teenage son, Stengel said. He'd come in, eat breakfast, practice baseball until past noon, have a bite of lunch, then go out for a round of golf. After

dinner, he'd be up to both burn and drink the midnight oil, then repeat the process early the next morning.

One day at DeLand—or was it Sanford?—they sat on the bench, the great old hitter and the great old guy who would be remembered as a great manager. Waner inquired about a sign on the outfield fence.

"You mean," said Stengel, "you can't see it?"

"No," was the reply, "and the ball isn't as big as it used to be, either."

Ol' Case chewed on that one a bit and asked, "Well, how big does the ball look?"

"Oh," said Waner, "about as big as a ball."

Stengel did a double-take. "Now wait a minute," he said. "The ball looks about as big as a ball. How big did it used to look?"

"About as big as a grapefruit," said Waner, explaining that he'd never liked glasses on the field for astigmatism because, though the specs brought the ball in sharper focus, they also made it seem smaller.

"I liked the big blur," he said, "because I just aimed for the middle of it."

Waner's personal life was not lost on the public, as a bull-voiced spectator proved one day at Brooklyn's Ebbets Field when Paul was playing right field for the Braves.

A ground rule did not cover a king-sized knothole in the right-field bullpen bench. So when Dixie Walker skipped one just inside the foul line and into the knothole, the ball was in play, and the alert Waner knew it.

With Walker circling the bases, Paul dropped to his knees, thrust his hand into the opening in the bench and came out clutching a handful of peanut shells. He reached blindly into the grab-bag a second time with the same result.

The third time he tried, with Walker completing an inside-the-park home run, the leather-lunged fan bellowed, "Whatcha looking for, Waner—a bottle of beer?"

The little man had class, as he proved at Boston

when he struggled to achieve 3,000 hits, a goal reached previously by only six players, and just two in the National League, Cap Anson and Honus Wagner.

Some baseball graybeards like to grumble that they did not know there was such commotion over 3,000 hits, insinuating that they could have played longer, rested less often or, indicting themselves, tried harder.

Fact is, however, that there has been especial attention paid to the 3,000-hit milestone at least since Napoleon Lajoie reached it in 1914.

From the time both Tris Speaker and Eddie Collins achieved their 3,000th hit in the same year, 1925, until Stan Musial reached the plateau 33 years later, there was only one man who got there. And it looked as if Waner might be running out of time in 1942.

It hurt in an early season game at Pittsburgh when, with a runner on first, Paul grounded one to deep short, where it appeared unlikely he ever could be thrown out. So when the runner beat a desperate attempted force-out throw to second, Waner and the Boston writers thought the wizened wonder was entitled to a hit, which would have been his fifth that day.

A Pittsburgh writer called it a late fielder's choice. Annoyed, Waner told the sympathetic Boston press that night, "From now on, I want every hit to be clear-cut."

It came to pass, therefore, that when the hits were coming hard—and who knows when even the biggest or strongest man will fall over on his keister?—Paul hit one to shortstop against Cincinnati at Braves Field.

Eddie Joost, young Redleg shortstop, couldn't make the play properly, and an infield hit, a scratch single, albeit legitimate, seemed the logical call.

Before the official scorer could hold up the index finger that would signal No. 3,000, Waner stood at first base, vigorously shaking his head and motioning with both hands, quite plainly, that he wanted to throw the minnow back.

Reluctantly, the scorer stuck up his hand, fingers forming a circle to indicate a boot. And Waner, apologizing to Joost, explained:

"I'm sorry to see you get the error, kid, but I wanted it to be one I could be proud of."

The delay merely heightened the suspense and, furthermore, gave Waner the chance to deliver the big one against his old Pittsburgh club, which conceivably could have been his idea all along, though he really wasn't the vindictive type.

On June 15 at Braves Field, facing righthander Rip Sewell, Paul Glee Waner smashed a hot single up the middle. When he did, a most unusual thing happened:

Umpire Tom Dunn called for the ball and presented it to Waner at first base. Frank Frisch, managing the Pirates, charged out of one dugout, and Stengel, the boss of the Braves, ambled out of the other. Sewell walked down off the mound toward first base, extending his hand, too. And there, interrupting the game, they posed for a picture that looked like an old-fashioned family tintype.

Afterward, Waner collared a Boston writer, chairman of the BBWAA chapter, and said he'd like to throw a party for the players, for the Braves' front office and for the press. Would the writers handle it?

"Sure, P.G.," he was told.

"Do you think $1,000 will be enough?" said Waner, blinking the writer's eyes, because a grand then was like 10 grand now.

This was the little man who, if Pittsburgh arithmetic is correct, never received more than $18,500, though he won three batting championships over there—1927, 1934 and 1936 and hit well over .300 for 12 straight seasons.

He hit .380 in 1927, his second year in the majors, and was voted the National League's Most Valuable Player.

Getting back to the party Waner wanted to throw, the truth is, that even though the Braves then were suffering the financial shorts, the club's president, Honest Bob Quinn, wouldn't let Paul pick up the tab. He'd grabbed enough checks in his time.

Waner's pride rebelled only at the suggestion that he had a Grapes-of-Wrath background as an Okie. He and Lloyd walked barefoot only by choice, not because of necessity, he would insist, explaining that his father was a prosperous farmer, that he and Lloyd each had his own horse and gun and that they both attended East Central State Teachers College at Ada, Okla.

Playing college and independent ball, alternating from outfield to first base and to pitching, Paul reportedly had won 19 straight games as a southpaw pitcher, breaking up 17 with home runs, when a traveling San Francisco Seals' scout gave an Ada druggist a contract to sign him.

"If he makes good," scout Nick Williams is supposed to have said to the druggist, "we'll guarantee you $2,500."

In spring training, Paul suffered a sore arm, the story goes, and Justin Fitzgerald, veteran San Francisco outfielder, assisting manager Jack Miller, apparently recognized that the Seals had a potentially good hitter foolishly wearing a pitching toeplate.

Regardless of how much that might embroider the truth, the fact is that the 20-year-old Waner was spectacular in the Pacific Coast League, where he batted .369 in 1923 and then followed with seasons of .356 and .401.

In the expanded Coast League schedule (174 games), Waner lashed out 280 hits in '25, including 75 doubles. In the National League, only he and Stan Musial ever collected 50 or more doubles three times, and Paul had 62 in 1932.

Sold to the world champion Pirates after the '25 season, Waner hit .336 as a rookie and then blossomed forth in brother Lloyd's rookie season, 1927, with his greatest year. In that .380 season, he had 40 doubles, 17 triples, nine homers, 131 RBIs and 237 hits.

With Lloyd contributing 223 hits, the Waners totaled 460 between them in '27, the only pennant-winning team on which either little man played.

The mighty Yankees did not awe the Waners or,

for that matter, overpower the Pirates in the World Series, but they did sweep four games behind brilliant pitching.

But the Yanks did not keep Lloyd from getting six hits including a double and a triple, for a .400 average. And they could not prevent Paul from collecting five blows, one a double. He hit .333 and drove in three runs.

The elder Waner brother batted robustly to win his batting championships, hitting .380 in 1927, .362 in 1934 and .373 in '36, and he did briskly some years when he didn't win, too. For instance 1928, when he batted .370 to Rogers Hornsby's .387, and .368 in 1930, the year Bill Terry hit .401.

Paul was a good outfielder, especially adept at playing the right-field carom at Forbes Field. He ran well, threw well, hit well and, well, nearly drank the well dry.

Twice married and with one son, Paul struggled through the three seasons of World War II before drawing his release from the Yankees after one game in 1945.

He finished as player-manager at Miami in the Florida International League in 1946, hitting .325, and then called Sarasota home. Over the years, he owned a golf driving range and a batting cage, then bounced around from team to team as special hitting instructor.

Paul Glee Waner undoubtedly would have lived longer and more comfortably if he had been willing to give up his heavy cigarette habit and to forego those occasional extra-inning battles with John Barleycorn, who has a way of coming on stronger the older and weaker the foe.

But, in all seriousness, would the pleasant little man have hit even better if he'd spent more time in the arms of Morpheus than out bending the elbow with Bacchus?

You'll find a debate over that one, though no one is endorsing spirits as preferable to spirit. It's just that the darndest things happened to Waner.

Like the night he overdid it and entered the Pirates' hotel in Chicago, just as his teammates were leaving at noon for a 3 o'clock game at Wrigley Field.

So that manager George Gibson would not see Waner, Fred Lindstrom and a couple of other players spun Paul right out the revolving door and into a taxi cab.

When the cab stopped for a red light at a greasy-spoon restaurant, an onion-reeking hamburger joint near Wrigley Field, Waner jumped out, explaining:

"Gotta get a couple of hamburgers. I haven't had breakfast."

In the clubhouse and on the field before the game, the Pirates screened Waner from Gibson. The hot sun began to sober him up, but not soon enough.

In the first inning, he misjudged a flyball so badly, charging in for a ball hit to his normal position, that when center fielder Lindstrom retrieved the ball at the right-field line and threw to second base, know who caught the ball?

None other than the out-of-place right fielder. Gibson figured probably that even a fine player like Paul can lose one in the sun now and then. But Waner was hitless and helpless all day as the Pirates batted in the ninth, trailing by a run.

Teammates were on second and third, with Waner at bat, when one Bucco stage-whispered on the bench that maybe it would be a good idea to tell Gibson so that he could send up a pinch-hitter.

"No," exclaimed Lindstrom incredulously. "Not after we've connived and contrived all day to fool the man! Hell, he'll fine us all. We've gone this far. Let's go all the way."

So the Corsair conspirators sat on their hands, fingers crossed, and watched as the bleary-eyed Waner, suffering with the granddaddy of bustheads, stepped up against fast-firing Guy Bush, who delivered a tight fastball that jammed the batter's fists.

Waner, handcuffed because he didn't have the fast bellybutton going for him that day, managed to poke the pitch for a blooper just over third base. A

seagull, the players call it, a dying swan, a bashful-looking bird, but as good as a Waner line drive in the boxscore.

The tying run scored, the leading run scored and when the Pirates got the Cubs out in the last of the ninth, Pittsburgh had a happy, laughing—and winning—visitors' clubhouse.

Gibson walked over, put his arm around the grinning hero and addressed the rest of his ball club:

"Maybe the rest of you guys would be great hitters like Waner—if you ate onions."

PAUL GLEE (BIG POISON) WANER
Born April 16, 1903, at Harrah, Okla.
Died August 29, 1965, at Sarasota, Fla.
Height 5-8 1/2 Weight 153
Threw and batted lefthanded.
Named to Hall of Fame, 1952.

YEAR	CLUB	LEAGUE	POS.	G.	AB.	R.	H.	2B.	3B.	HR.	RBI.	B.A.	PO.	A.	E.	F.A.
1923	San Francisco	P.C.	OF-1B	112	325	54	120	30	4	3	39	.369	230	16	12	.953
1924	San Francisco	P.C.	OF	160	587	113	209	46	5	8	97	.356	284	28	10	.969
1925	San Francisco	P.C.	OF	174	699	167	280	75	7	11	130	.401	744	36	18	.977
1926	Pittsburgh	Nat.	OF	144	536	101	180	35	22	8	79	.336	307	21	8	.976
1927	Pittsburgh	Nat.	OF-1B	155	623	113	237	40	17	9	131	.380	430	25	10	.978
1928	Pittsburgh	Nat.	OF-1B	152	602	142	223	50	19	6	86	.370	533	22	12	.979
1929	Pittsburgh	Nat.	OF	151	596	131	200	43	15	15	100	.336	328	15	5	.986
1930	Pittsburgh	Nat.	OF	145	589	117	217	32	18	8	77	.368	344	9	15	.959
1931	Pittsburgh	Nat.	OF-1B	150	559	88	180	35	10	6	70	.322	441	31	9	.981
1932	Pittsburgh	Nat.	OF	154	630	107	215	62	10	7	82	.341	367	13	10	.974
1933	Pittsburgh	Nat.	OF	154	618	101	191	38	16	7	70	.309	346	16	7	.981
1934	Pittsburgh	Nat.	OF	146	599	122	217	32	16	14	90	.362	323	15	5	.985
1935	Pittsburgh	Nat.	OF	139	549	98	176	29	12	11	78	.321	283	13	5	.983
1936	Pittsburgh	Nat.	OF	148	585	107	218	53	9	5	94	.373	323	15	14	.960
1937	Pittsburgh	Nat.	OF	154	619	94	219	30	9	2	74	.354	271	16	9	.970
1938	Pittsburgh	Nat.	OF	148	625	77	175	31	6	6	69	.280	284	11	7	.977
1939	Pittsburgh	Nat.	OF	125	461	62	151	30	6	3	45	.328	206	12	5	.978
1940	Pittsburgh (a)	Nat.	OF-1B	89	238	32	69	16	1	1	32	.290	150	9	2	.988
1941	Brook (b)-Bost.	Nat.	OF	106	329	45	88	10	2	2	50	.267	160	8	8	.955
1942	Boston (c)	Nat.	OF	114	333	43	86	17	1	1	39	.258	150	6	5	.969
1943	Brooklyn	Nat.	OF	82	225	29	70	16	0	1	26	.311	116	4	5	.960
1944	Brooklyn (d)	Nat.	OF	83	136	16	39	4	1	0	16	.287	54	3	1	.983
1944	New York	Amer.	PH	9	7	1	1	0	0	0	1	.143	0	0	0	.000
1945	New York (e)	Amer.	PH	1	0	0	0	0	0	0	0	.000	0	0	0	.000
1946	Miami	Fla.Int.	PH-1	62	80	12	26	6	2	0	12	.325	102	4	6	.946

American League Totals				10	7	1	1	0	0	0	1	.143	0	0	0	.000
National League Totals				2539	9452	1625	3151	603	190	112	1308	.333	5416	264	142	.976
Major League Totals				2549	9459	1626	3152	603	190	112	1309	.333	5416	264	142	.976

a Unconditionally released by Pittsburgh, December 10, 1940, and signed by Brooklyn, January 31, 1941.
b Unconditionally released by Brooklyn, May 11, 1941; signed by Boston, May 24, 1941.
c Unconditionally released by Braves, January 9, 1943; signed with Brooklyn, January 21, 1943.
d Unconditionally released by Brooklyn, September, 1944 and signed with Yankees.
e Unconditionally released by New York Yankees, May 3, 1945.

WORLD SERIES RECORD

YEAR	CLUB	LEAGUE	POS.	G.	AB.	R.	H.	2B.	3B.	HR.	RBI.	B.A.	PO.	A.	E.	F.A.
1927	Pittsburgh	Nat.	OF	4	15	0	5	1	0	0	3	.333	8	0	0	1.000

THE KID: Teddy Ballgame, growing powerfully from a willowy young player called the Splendid Splinter as a .400 hitter, thought he was the best hitter. He just might have been.

TED WILLIAMS

As the last man to hit .400 in the major leagues a half century back, Ted Williams would be remembered even if he'd played just briefly and sweetly in the big leagues. Leaving aside all the color and controversy of the handsome, curly-haired, red-necked Red Socker, Williams rated a standing ovation for his most remarkable achievement. At 39, he batted .388 in 1957.

Managing the St. Louis Cardinals that season as Williams flirted with .400 after he'd gone over the top (.406) 16 years earlier, Fred Hutchinson, a rug-

ged former American League pitcher, explained why he'd never consider anything impossible when Boston's tall, temperamental No. 9 planted his feet in the batter's box.

Four years earlier, when Williams had returned as a Marine jet pilot from the Korean War—military service gouged nearly five gorgeous years out of his career—Hutchinson was managing the Detroit Tigers, who just had given $35,000 to a Baltimore schoolboy in whom Hutch immediately saw signs of future greatness. If he only could persuade Williams to talk to Al Kaline about two things—conditioning and hitting.

Williams, as kind to young players as he was crabby to nosey newspapermen, didn't know if he could help, but sure, he'd try. So early the next afternoon at Fenway Park, while the Red Sox were hitting and the stands were almost empty, Hutchinson brought the 18-year-old Kaline to the batting cage to meet the 35-year-old slugger.

As high-strung as a thoroughbred, Williams tossed his head in a nervous characteristic, laughed and said he'd been watching Kaline.

"You've got a good swing, kid," Ted told the righthanded-hitting rookie. "You can be a real good hitter if you want to be one hard enough."

Williams, on whom the cloying nickname "The Splendid Splinter" long time since had been misapplied, told Kaline that he'd broken into pro ball with only 146 pounds on his 6-3 frame, but that, an inch taller, he had filled out to 200 pounds over the years, partly as a result of a body-building program which had given him a powerful neck and bulging forearms like Popeye the Sailor's.

"For years," Ted said, "I've done 50 push-ups a day."

Kaline nodded, impressed, as he told Hutchinson later, but not astonished. Then he blinked as Williams added:

"And 50 more push-ups on my finger-tips."

Williams, continuing his seminar for Kaline's benefit, related how daily throughout the year he swung for 30 minutes a special 60-ounce bat, nearly double the weight of the bat he used in a game. Ted flexed his wrists as he spoke.

"They're sore," he said, frowning. "Just getting back from service, I'm having to recondition the wrists."

Now, both Hutchinson and Kaline would recall later, the pleasantness faded as, gripping a bat, Williams began to discuss hitting with the kid. As intently as though facing a pitcher in a crucial spot, Ted curled his lips in a snarl.

"Don't," he said, taking one hand off the bat and motioning toward himself, "don't let 'em jam you in here."

The hand came off the bat handle again to jab Kaline for emphasis. "Don't, I say," Williams snapped, "don't let 'em pitch in on your fists. Get out in front of the ball, boy! Hear me, get out in front of the ball! You've got to have fast hands, quick wrists. Practice! Practice!"

Williams, still facing that legendary monster on the mound, jabbed Kaline again, used his hand to simulate inside pitching, then repeated sharply:

"Don't let 'em jam you in here."

Kaline's eyes bugged out, Hutchinson said, as the affable professor of proper hitting became an angry combatant hating all toeplate talent. The lessons sank home, though, and, following the old master's suggestions, Kaline reported stronger and more powerful the following spring. At 20 he became the youngest batting champion in major league history with a .340 average.

If he couldn't sustain Williams' hitting pace over a career—who could?—Kaline maintained a consistency and conditioning that, despite the same kind of injury hex which handicapped Ted, enabled Al to become a better all-around player than his instructor and a Detroit landmark into the mid-1970s.

Williams, meanwhile, went on to post a .344 career average, one of the highest in baseball history, and came within debating distance of achieving his lofty boyhood ambition. "I want," he'd said in all seriousness and full confidence, "to be remembered as the greatest hitter who ever lived."

In evaluating Williams as a ballplayer, not as a person, observers often are as opinionated as the big boy himself. It's difficult to separate the white from the yolk of an egg with a toothpick or the quixotic nature of the man from his accomplishments. It's this view that Williams was neither as great as his most faithful followers thought nor as imperfect a player as his prejudiced critics tried to indicate.

As recurring passages in his excellent autobiography would indicate—*My Turn at Bat* by Ted as told to John Underwood is easy, interesting and informative reading—Williams was sensitive to suggestions that he was less than the best in any phase of play except hitting. Yet time and again he makes it plain that he fattened his wallet with his bat, not his glove. Particularly when he was younger, Williams had an immature view toward defensive play or any of the finer points except when he stood up there zeroing in on a pitcher.

"Hey, bush," manager Joe Cronin would yell from shortstop to catch his attention in those early days when The Kid was taking practice swings in the outfield.

"This," Joe would say, simulating fielding a ball, "and not that."

To one who tried to understand him, it was disturbing when Williams, as a White House favorite and as manager of the host Washington ball club, would pass up at the last minute baseball's centennial banquet at which all-time All-Star teams were disclosed in 1969. It's Ted's privilege to be annoyed that the conclusion he failed to show is because he'd learned that Joe DiMaggio would be named the outstanding living player. But he had no excuse, regardless of his reason, and his absence was rude and an affront to aged superstars who did show up and to baseball itself.

The answer, of course, is that Williams is an unpredictable man, one who defied all logic by ending a self-imposed exile from baseball to forsake fishing, his favorite diversion, for a return to the game as a successful manager. Even if he didn't plan to stay long in the Senators' dugout before moving into the front office, taking advantage of his authority and plush contract, Ted had proved definitely to his detractors that he could do what they thought impossible. The man they said couldn't even manage himself proved that he indeed could handle 25 others.

Chances are, Williams who could play the carom off Fenway Park's short left-field fence almost as well as he could find the distant seats in right, could

have accomplished anything to which he'd set the cap he stubbornly refused to tip to the fans.

Except for his double military jolt, a bitter irony because he once was called a draft dodger, Williams would have achieved well over 3,000 hits and in excess of 650 home runs. The part that injuries played, of course, is part of the game, but his wounds reduced his activity by the equivalent of another couple of seasons before he decided to quit at 42.

Even then, in 1960, Old Teddy Ballgame, as he'd called himself after a youngster once referred to him that way, finished with a flourish by hitting .316 and bowing out beautifully at Boston with a home run his last time up before the Hub fans with whom he'd had a stormier romance than his own personal life.

Twice divorced father of a grown daughter by his first wife, Ted sired a son when he was approaching 50, and it's just too bad that John Henry Williams, apple of the old slugger's eye, never saw the old slugger hit that apple. But the boy had the benefit of more warmth and interest than Ted received from his own father. Little John Henry didn't have to wait for a neighbor to take him fishing.

Although Williams hated crowds and often acted as if he didn't like people, delaying his exit from the Boston clubhouse until only the most persistent of the faithful remained outside, Williams showed a soft spot for kids. The Kid, as clubhouse man Johnny Orlando pegged him with a nickname that stuck for years, would line up the small fry and speak gruffly if they got out of line at autographing sessions, but he would sign often until, understandably, he ran out of time.

Williams' efforts on behalf of the Jimmy Fund, started by the Boston Braves and then picked up by the Red Sox, have been tireless and rewarding, particularly for the children's charity. And Ted at times would go to unusual lengths to please young admirers. Many Saturday mornings he would drive the indoor train which took the youngsters in their own beds to treatment areas.

The same man who was chided in the critical Boston press because he didn't visit his mother or was not at his first wife's bedside when their daughter was born—prematurely—once chartered a plane to visit a dying boy in a Carolina hospital. One of the small corps of veteran writers he felt he could trust, John Carmichael, long-time sports editor of the *Chicago Daily News*, told that one, years later, at the risk of offending Williams.

Williams, you see, is a public person who prizes his privacy. To some he's a bigger pain in the neck than the one that led to his only subpar season. (He batted just .254 in 1959 and was kissed off as through.) And unquestionably outspoken, forthright and tactless, he was called brash, cocky, aloof, antagonistic, stormy, fresh, surly, profane, indifferent, tempestuous and obviously—controversial.

But to those who won his confidence and knew him intimately, he was shy, sensitive, loyal, honest, generous, friendly and cooperative, hard only on phonies. His smile was—and is—charming and he's got the speaking voice that would make him a platform natural if he ever put a mind to it.

The speech Williams prepared in a motel hideaway at Oneonta, N. Y., and then delivered at Cooperstown when he was inducted into the Hall of Fame in July 1966, was exceptionally well-written and effectively presented.

Ted saluted his San Diego playground director, Rodney Luscomb, and his high school coach, Wes Caldwell, and his "patient" managers—Frank Shellenback, Donie Bush, Joe Cronin and Joe McCarthy—and the Hall of Famer who as Red Sox general manager had signed him, the late Eddie Collins.

Williams even saluted the baseball writers, with whom he had feuded, thanking them for his nearly unanimous election to the Hall of Fame in his first time around. "I know I didn't have 288 close friends among the writers," Ted said, wryly. "I know they voted for me because they felt in their minds and some in their hearts that I rated it, and I want to say to them: Thank you, from the bottom of my heart."

Ted paid tribute to sportsman Tom Yawkey, the Red Sox owner and his good friend as well as boss. He hailed Willie Mays for having passed his total 521 home runs and wished him well, expressing hope that "some day Satchel Paige and Josh Gibson will be voted into the Hall of Fame as symbols of the great Negro players who are not here only because they weren't given the chance." (Paige received Hall of Fame recognition in 1971, beginning a breakthrough for black league superstars.)

Williams, who often had said he felt that only possibly Ty Cobb could have hit more baseballs in practice than he did himself, emphasized the part hard work played in baseball success.

"I've never met a great player who didn't have to work harder at learning to play ball than anything else he ever did," said Williams. "To me, it was the greatest fun I ever had, which probably explains why today I feel both humility and pride, because God let me play the game and learn to be good at it."

Closing after a bow to fellow inductee Casey Stengel, with whom he formed a mutual admiration society, Williams said, "I am grateful and know how lucky I was to have been born an American and had a chance to play the game I loved, the GREATEST game."

When I stood on the green and listened at Cooperstown, it was difficult to match this wise, peace-with-the-world person with the one who had feuded with the press, spit at the fans, used obscene gestures and, among other things, castigated the Marine Corps, a leading Republican (Sen. Robert A. Taft) and a Democratic president (Harry S. Truman). Trouble is, when Ted talked, others listened and reported. And he didn't learn—or care enough—only to sound off in private.

Williams is, no doubt, the embodiment of the nonconformist, as witness his refusal to wear a necktie. This threatened to create a cataclysmic confrontation when Joe McCarthy, who had managed a dynasty of properly attired New York Yankees, took over as manager of the Bosox in 1948. The first morning at breakfast in spring training, McCarthy appeared in the dining room with an open-necked sport shirt.

"Any manager who can't get along with a .400 hitter is out of his mind," said McCarthy, to the delight of Williams, who said as manager that he hoped most to model himself after Marse Joe, a man for whom he had great admiration.

Williams is, too, a rugged individualist, as evidenced by his unwillingness as manager to relent on the 15-minute cooling-off period for players he first had pushed at Boston as a performer for McCarthy. He wished then he could have kept the press out an hour and 15 minutes, Ted said in his autobiography.

The rugged individualist surprised Los Angeles columnist Jim Murray, whose selected work appears in *The Sporting News* when, after acknowledging respect for President Richard Nixon, a Washington fan, he said in 1970 that the man he most admired was Herbert Hoover, the one-term president who bore the cross of the Great Depression that followed the stock market crash of 1929.

"You heard me," wrote Murray in typical amusedly outrageous exaggeration. "Not Lincoln, Washington, Alexander Graham Bell, Julius Caesar, Napoleon, Attila the Hun. Not Jefferson, Wilson, Churchill. Not even FDR, but Herbert, by God, Hoover."

"Look it up," roared Williams who, as Murray quipped, speaks in home runs, too. "Every cure for the Depression—the RFC, the SEC, labor legislation—was thought up by Hoover. Here is a man who is blamed for things that were not his fault, yet he never complained, and continued to help his country for the rest of his life…To me, that's a real man."

Murray, amused, wondered if Williams' all-time fighter was Tom Heeney, the rock-jawed New Zealand heavyweight who took more than he gave in the late '20s?

"Ezzard Charles," said Ted, naming a former heavy weight champion given little recognition, probably explaining himself as well as others when he said:

"I like underrated people. You look into them and you can see where they were more extraordinary than some of the heroes worshipped."

As a boy growing up too tall and too skinny in San Diego, Theodore Samuel Williams never idolized anyone, he insisted. The closest was Cotton Warburton, little Southern California quarterback and later a prominent Hollywood film editor. Ted's mother said he had in his room a picture of Babe Ruth, but Williams will insist tartly that he didn't idolize the Babe. If anyone in baseball 'way back East caught his fancy, he said, it was Bill Terry, first baseman of the New York Giants. That figured because Terry, like Williams, was an independent man. Bill helped lure Ted into becoming a Cooperstown attraction. There stands a handsome statue commissioned by Tom Yawkey's widow, Jean.

Ted is sensitive to suggestion that his father was a wanderer, but Sam Williams, a Spanish-American War veteran who dabbled in photography and politics, didn't provide well for his wife and two sons. Ted's younger brother, Danny, caused considerable trouble for the family, including Ted, before his death.

Ted's father was Welsh and English. His mother, the former May Venzer, was part French, part Mexican and all wrapped up in the Salvation Army. Mrs. Williams had considerably more time for the problems of others, but not enough for her family. As a boy, Ted often had to feed himself and not too well, particularly when, as reported, he'd given away his lunch money at times. From sunrise to sunset, when possible, he played ball.

One day he told playground instructor Rod Luscomb, "Lusk, some day I'm going to build myself a ballpark with cardboard fences and then I'm going to knock down every darn one of them with home runs."

When Williams looked self-consciously at his skinny arms, Luscomb started him on the push-ups that helped build the boy's body. Eat, man, he could eat, too, when he had the chance.

At Herbert Hoover High School—hey, you don't think school loyalty led to Ted's admiration for Mr. Hoover, do you?—the tall, skinny kid liked only history and sports, particularly baseball. His coach, Wes Caldwell, later a professor of architecture at the University of Florida, used to follow him around the bases with a switch whenever he felt Ted wasn't running fast enough. Truth is, Williams never did become fast and if he seemed conservative on the bases, there probably was a reason, as he'd explain in relating his most embarrassing moment.

One game at Washington early in his career, Ted tripled and was picked off third base by Jake Early, the Senators' catcher. Next time up, Williams tripled again and damned if Early didn't pick him off once more, a particularly red-faced result because the Red Sox lost, 1-0.

To get back to Ted's appetite, he played a high school doubleheader one day at Pomona and the boxscore on his eating was much more interesting than his hitting even though the pitcher-outfielder batted .430 for his three varsity seasons. He had a shortcake and malted milk, 13 ice cream bars and 11 bottles of soda before, during and after the double dip.

The Cardinals looked him over and hemmed and hawed about his lack of speed. The Yankees offered a $500 bonus, but Ted's parents, though apart on most things, including from each other most of the time, were agreed that he or they—should have a $1,000 bonus. So that's how, eventually, the Red Sox moved in when Collins personally came out from Boston to sign Bobby Doerr and decided he liked that lanky lefthanded-hitting Williams even more.

From a ballpark standpoint, Ted said he never missed going to New York because he didn't like the batting background at Yankee Stadium, where,

despite the short right field, he batted just .309 with 30 homers. Over his career, counting brief years in both Baltimore (.299) and Kansas City (.371), Williams batted this way:

St. Louis .400, Boston .360, Philadelphia .353, Detroit .332, Washington .326, Cleveland .301 and Chicago .298. The most homers he hit on the road were 55 at Detroit's Briggs Stadium, his favorite park because he could see the ball so well there. His king-sized clouts there included the dramatic blow that won the 1941 All-Star Game.

Actually, the Red Sox got Williams from San Diego, then an independently operated Pacific Coast League club when home ownership pressured the family to let Ted play with the Padres, which he did in 1936 when he was only 17 years old. His salary in the tough pre-war Pacific Coast League was $150 a month.

Veteran spitball pitcher Frank Shellenback, managing San Diego, became suspicious when the kid asked for so many old baseballs for extra batting practice on the neighborhood playground, but he found out that Williams was indeed using them, all right, not selling the balls.

Pinch-hitting his first time in pro ball, petrified, Ted took three straight strikes. Shortly thereafter at Los Angeles' Wrigley Field, the Padres trailed by a large margin midway through a game. Shellenback cast about for a pitcher because he had a doubleheader coming up the next day.

Williams told coach Eddie Mulligan, "Tell him to put me in, Eddie," said Ted. "I can get them out."

Shellenback, nodding, let Williams bat for the pitcher he would replace. Ted doubled and held L.A. an inning, then doubled again as San Diego once more rallied and closed the gap. Now, a good relief pitcher began to warm up and he was needed when the Angels shelled Williams in his second inning for two runs before he could get a man out.

"Skip," he told Shellenback as the manager came out to replace him, "I think you've got me playing the wrong position."

Playing left field in 42 games, Williams batted .271, but did not hit a home run. The next season, attracting Eddie Collins' attention, he batted .291 at San Diego, getting 23 homers and 98 RBIs in 138 games. He was barely 19 when the Red Sox bought him and offered a two-year contract, $3,000 and $4,500, but Ted's parents still insisted on the $1,000 bonus. Tom Yawkey, who had spent a fortune for established players, balked at first, but Collins was persuasive.

Considerable baseball history might have been written differently if Williams had gone to another club. With a less personal, less critical press—a competitive, crowded newspaper situation in Boston frequently leads to a deadly game of "Can You Top This?"—Ted Williams might have had a more peaceful and more pleasant career. Conceivably, he might have hit better, but he recognized that over the years the Red Sox fans were rabid. And Fenway Park was not the hitting disadvantage it might have seemed.

For a lefthanded pull-hitter, the depths of right field at Boston precluded cheap home runs. For hitting in general, however, the presence of the towering green monster in left field, the chummy fence, meant that if the pitchers didn't bring the ball into Williams, balls he didn't pull properly still would have enough heft to reach the barrier in left-center in the 340-375 area. Yet, though eventually hitting up the middle, he hit the left-field fence only a handful of times. Criminy, the guy couldn't have been much better anywhere, could he?

An 0-for-18 slump at San Diego in 1937 kept young Williams from hitting .300 and, as expected from a man who talked hitting with Lefty O'Doul, Rogers Hornsby and Ty Cobb, the young outfielder explained in his book, just what a slump is:

"A slump always follows a familiar pattern. When you first start going bad, you just try harder. Then you press, which means you do things unnaturally. Then you imagine you're getting all the tough breaks and you start feeling sorry for yourself."

Williams became "The Kid" to equipment man Orlando and then others who were around in 1938 when he reported to the Red Sox for spring training at Sarasota, Fla. The uniform shirt he was given was too small and when he trotted onto the field, a jut-jawed man in uniform growled, "Stick your shirt-tail in, busher, this is the big leagues."

Williams turned to Orlando and asked, "Who's that smart guy?"

"That," said Orlando, "is Joe Cronin—the manager."

Williams insists that when Doerr pointed out bulging-biceped Jimmie Foxx and said, "Wait'll you see Foxx hit," Ted did not reply, "Wait'll Foxx sees ME hit."

Old Teddy Ballgame would concede, though, that it sounded like him. He called everyone "Sport" in those days, including Cronin, which wasn't the most diplomatic thing to do. The veteran trio of .300-hitting outfielders—Doc Cramer, Joe Vosmik and Ben Chapman—needled the fresh kid and when he was shipped to farm club Minneapolis' training base at Daytona Beach after about a week, Ted told Orlando:

"Tell 'em I'll be back and tell them I'm going to wind up making more money in this frigging game than all three of them put together."

He did, too, but not before he first borrowed five bucks from Orlando.

At Minneapolis, the tall, carefree kid got into little manager Donie Bush's hair, doping off in the outfield, chasing flyballs by slapping his butt and, like radio's Lone Ranger, yelling, "Hi-yo, Silver."

Miffed when things didn't go right, usually at bat, Ted would scream in frustration. Once, in anger, he punched a water cooler in the dugout with his fist, broke the glass container and nearly crippled himself. But the elements of great hitting began to fall in place. Switching accidentally one night from his heavier bat to Stan Spence's light model, he choked up with two strikes against a lefthanded pitcher and hit a 410-foot home run over the center-field fence. Thereafter, he became a devotee of light bats usually from 31 to 34 ounces.

Williams insists that stories of his visual acuity are exaggerated. It's not true, he said, that he can read the label on a 78-RPM record when it's spinning. In fact, he had an injured eye for a time as a boy and he came out of the Korean War with permanent damage in one ear. But his senses were extraordinarily developed.

Over the years, working with his bats, honing and boning them, careful not to let them lie on the ground to gather moisture in cold, early-season weather, Williams became finicky about his bats and an authority on weight. Once, Bud Hillerich of the Louisville Slugger bat company put six bats on a hotel bed in Boston. One bat was a half-ounce heavier than the other five. With eyes closed, relying only on the feel of it, Ted twice in succession picked out the bat that was a fraction heavier than the others.

Another time, returning to Fenway Park from Korea, Williams stepped into the batter's box for batting practice and told Cronin he thought home plate was out of line.

"Gee, it couldn't be," said Cronin, then the Bosox general manager. To humor Ted, Joe had the plate surveyed with a transit. Sure enough, it was off a fraction.

At one point, if Donie Bush had had his way, weary of Williams' monkey shines in Minneapolis, Ted wouldn't have seen home plate at Boston, but who could shrug off a .366 average, 43 homers and 142 RBIs that year in the old American Association?

Ted was in right field, not left, for the Red Sox' rain-delayed opener in 1939 at Boston. Still short of 21, he was an inch taller and, at 175, about 30 pounds heavier than the kid who had turned pro three years previously at San Diego.

His first time up in the bigs, the Yankees' great righthander, Red Ruffing, struck him out. Next time up, same thing. The riled-up Red Sox rookie stormed back to the bench and, needled by pitcher Jack Wilson, snapped:

"If he throws me the same pitch again, I'll hit it out of here."

Almost did, too, with a drive high off the right-center field fence for a double, the first of his 2,654 major league hits.

Awed at first by teammate Foxx' long drives, Williams began to hit a few tape-measure shots, too. At Detroit, with a 3-and-0 count on Ted, Rudy York, catching for the Tigers, needled, "You're not hitting, are you, Kid?"

"I sure as hell am," said Williams, blasting a pitch against the facing of the right-field upper deck. Next time up, he became the first batter ever to hit a ball over the double-decked Detroit stands in right field. When he got to third base, Billy Rogell of the Tigers asked, "What the hell YOU been eating?"

Nothing but the best, of course, indulging himself in thick malted milks and thick steaks, too. Hailed by Babe Ruth as the Rookie of the Year, Williams batted .327 in 149 games and hit 31 homers, leading the American League in runs batted in with 145, a record for a first-year man.

He didn't smoke and in those days he didn't drink. He liked movies and to hunt and fish. He liked to walk, too, and did a lot of it on and off the field, setting a rookie record with 107 passes. But he struck out 90 times, which bothered him that he swung at too many bad balls.

Over the years, cutting down his strikeouts to fewer than 50 and about half of them called, he became as sharp-eyed as any umpire, as particular as a housewife at market, shopping for a good buy. Williams schooled himself not to hit a ball that was off the plate even though it cost him some RBIs, though obviously not too many. One year he reached base 16 consecutive times on hits and walks and he prided himself that his base-reaching percentage was higher than anybody's, including Babe Ruth's.

As a hitter, Williams put it all together after a sophomore season in which he batted .344, but saw his homers drop to 23 and his RBIs to 113. As a perfectionist who hit until his batting blisters bled, Ted was unhappy and, in an interview, remembering a happy uncle in suburban New York, he said, "Nuts to this baseball—I'd sooner be a fireman."

That did it. At Chicago, Jimmie Dykes and his bench jockeys were fitted out with fire helmets and piercing sirens. At New York, Lefty Gomez and Red Ruffing rang cow bells when Williams hit, and he sizzled all the more. Worse, when Ted and Tom Yawkey were shooting pigeons on an open date in Fenway Park, a writer called the Humane Society— or Ted thought he did, anyway—and there was another annoying headline about Williams.

When The Kid was booed for making an error and striking out at Boston that season, he vowed he'd never tip his hat again and no matter his heroics nor the fans' huzzahs thereafter, Williams wouldn't do it.

Although rabbit-eared and rednecked, always able to isolate the few boos from the many cheers in the cozy left-field corner at Fenway Park, Williams was at his best in 1941. By then, he was aware that, waiting to pull the trigger so that he wouldn't get out in front of the pitch too soon, he could reach the fence in left-center or straight-away if he swung a fraction late.

With a chipped bone in an ankle in spring training, he merely pinch-hit the first couple of weeks of the season, a cold period he never did like because of the chilling, adverse hitting winds in Boston. And when Joe Dobson came over from Cleveland and pitched only infrequently for the Red Sox, the burrheaded righthander began throwing batting practice regularly for Williams—hard and with good stuff.

Hitting over .400, Ted was heartened to find encouragement from many, including Harry Heilmann, who had batted .403 for Detroit in 1923 and was broadcasting at Detroit. Only Al Simmons, Philadelphia coach who had hit .390 one year, was disagreeable.

"How much do you want to bet you will hit .400?" sneered Simmons, steaming up the sensitive young slugger, who came down to the last day at Philadelphia with a .399955 average, which, rounded out, would be figured an even .400. The average had dipped from .413 in September, and Joe Cronin offered to sit him out the final doubleheader. Williams didn't want it that way.

Nervously, with Orlando for company, Williams estimated he walked 10 miles the night before the final games. The way Orlando tells it, Johnny made two stops for Scotch and Ted two for ice cream in their long prowl.

This one had to have a happy end because 1941 was The Kid's year. As mentioned, in the All-Star Game that summer at Detroit, he'd tagged the Chicago Cubs' Claude Passeau for a two-run, two-out homer in the ninth for a 6-5 American League victory, one of the most thrilling in All-Star competition and a shining highlight of Old Teddy Ballgame's career.

When Williams stepped up to bat in the first inning of the final day in 1941, a .400 season had become a novelty because no one had done it in the majors since Bill Terry in 1930. Heilmann's .403 in '23 had been the most recent in the American League.

Bill McGowan, calling balls and strikes, walked around the plate, bent over to dust it off and, without looking up, said, "To hit .400, a batter has got to be loose. He has got to be loose."

The Athletics' catcher, Frank Hayes, told Williams, "I wish you all the luck in the world, Ted, but we're not giving you a damn thing. Mr. Mack told us if we let up on you, he'll run us all out of baseball."

First time up against righthander Dick Fowler, Williams lined a single between first and second. Next, he hit a home run. Off Porter Vaughan, a lefthander he'd never seen before, he singled twice. In the second game, he hit one off the loudspeaker horn in right field for a double and wound up six for eight—.406.

Williams lost the Most Valuable Player award in

1941 because Joe DiMaggio had his incredible 56-game hitting streak with a .357 average and a league-leading 125 RBIs. Ted understood that, but, even though the Yankees again won in '42, he felt his .356, 36 homers and 137 RBIs outweighed clever-fielding Joe Gordon's best batting year, .322. Gordon got it, however, and Williams felt afterward that his draft difficulties figured in the MVP voting.

An early draft deferment as the support of his mother—Salvation May, they called her on the West Coast—caused no end of grief for Williams, who went into Navy aviation after the '42 season and, though he saw no combat, was a Marine pilot by the time he came back to baseball in 1946.

The Red Sox won their only pennant of Williams' career that year and he won the long-awaited MVP award with a .342 average, 38 homers and 123 RBIs. Cleveland's player-manager Lou Boudreau, squelched because Williams had beat the Indians with three homers in a game in which Boudreau belted four doubles and a home run, put into practice a shift in which everyone except the left fielder was on the right side of second base—and the left fielder was only 30 feet behind the skinned part of the infield.

Williams tried first to defy the shift, then refusing to adjust to hit to the opposite field because he crowded the plate and took a full swing. He did hit a pennant-winning homer to left, inside the park at Cleveland, in a 1-0 game for which the Red Sox finally broke out the champagne that had been on ice for days. But he was still troubled by the shift—and, worse, he just had been hit on the right elbow with a pitch by Mickey Haefner in a tune-up exhibition game—when the heavily favored Red Sox played the St. Louis Cardinals in the World Series.

The Redbirds' manager, Eddie Dyer, borrowed the Boudreau shift, altering it to leave one infielder on the third base side of second. Once in the Series, Williams beat out a bunt and a Boston paper bannered the news:

"TED BUNTS!"

But sharp control pitching by Harry Brecheen, Howard Pollet, Murry Dickson and others, keeping the ball tight on the ailing-elbowed slugger, limited Williams to just five singles and one RBI in 25 official trips in the seven games. A famous photograph showed the curly-haired slugger slumped over at his locker after the seventh game loss, crying. Williams gave his World Series share to Orlando.

If he could replay any part of his career, Old Teddy Ballgame said it would be only the years from 1946 to '50, seasons in which the Red Sox were engaged in close pennant races and he was freed of the physical miseries that began in earnest after he cracked his elbow on the left-field wall when making a catch in the first inning of the 1950 All-Star Game at Chicago's Comiskey Park. Williams felt he never had quite the same power or was really the same hitter thereafter.

Turning down a $300,000, three-year package from Mexico's Jorge Pasquel, The Kid stayed to become a $125,000-a-year man with Yawkey, for whom he won six batting championships and led four times each in homers and runs batted in. And in the '46 All-Star Game at Boston, going a perfect 4-for-4, Ted drove in five runs with two homers, one of which came colorfully on a high-arching blooper thrown by Pittsburgh's Rip Sewell. The eephus, they called it, a delivery which would float some 15 feet or more in the air and die of exhaustion in the strike zone.

"How'n hell do you hit that thing?" asked Williams beforehand, eyes wrinkled in an amused smile.

"By stepping up on it," volunteered the Yankees' Bill Dickey. Williams knew a tip when he saw one and, wading right into the eephus, Ted timed the pitch perfectly and, supplying all the power, lined the ball into the right-center field bullpen. Others might know how, but only Williams could do it.

In '47, facing more shifts, Williams found clubs throwing him tough sliders, down and in, trying to make him pull because they had so many people deployed defensively between first and second base and in short right field. Gradually, by moving away from the plate, Williams began to hit more through the middle. Eventually, meaning by 1957 when he almost hit .400 again, older and wiser and maybe not quite so quick, Ted was sending those sinking line drives to all fields.

"Loose" was the word for Williams at the plate. He looked like a marionette with the puppeteer's strings relaxed. Tall and gangly, he dipped his knees slightly, took a few nervous swishes with the bat, wrapped his fingers around the handle as if he were going to wring sawdust from it, but he became immobile as the pitcher prepared to deliver the ball.

Ted stood fairly deep in the batter's box, right foot somewhat closer to the plate than his left, which was about 15 inches behind the right. At one time he batted with his feet somewhat closer together and took a longer stride, but he widened his stance a bit and shortened his stride.

When Williams planted his left foot in the batter's box—taking a toehold, they call it—he did it deep and ceremoniously, apparently convinced the pitchers wouldn't dare throw at him. On inside pitches, he'd lean back almost casually. And when a catcher would throw the ball back to the pitcher, he would keep that back foot firmly planted, like someone marking a place in a book when looking up to answer an annoying question, and merely would turn his head sideways so he couldn't be hit by the return throw.

His swing was marvelously rhythmic and coordinated and his quick hips and rapid hands enabled him to take the ball out of the catcher's glove, as the saying goes. Ted's sharp eye and late commitment on a pitch were strong factors in his success.

In '47, despite a slow start against the shift, Williams came fast to win another batting title with a .343 average and then make it his second Triple Crown season with 32 homers and 114 RBIs. He lost the MVP award to DiMaggio by just one point, though Joe Dee's figures weren't comparable, and was incensed—properly—to learn that he'd lost only

because one Boston writer on the MVP committee hadn't even given him a 10th-place vote, which would have meant a point. Any vote higher would have been the difference.

In 1949, there was no doubt of the MVP even though, as usual, the Red Sox finished second. In '48, McCarthy's first year as manager, Williams had won another batting championship despite injuries, hitting 25 homers and driving in 127 runs. But the Bosox lost the pennant to Boudreau and his Cleveland Indians in an historic one-game playoff.

A year later, one game up with two to go, they blew it at Yankee Stadium in Casey Stengel's first season as boss of the Bombers. Williams' critics chided him unfairly for his lack of contribution that windup weekend, but they ignored big ball games just before and, for that matter, minimized his most productive season. Playing every game and hitting .343, Ted led the American League in runs scored (150), doubles (39), homers (43) and RBIs (159), a department in which he tied with teammate Vern Stephens.

The long, painful train ride back to Boston closed out the '40s and, albeit bittersweet, the happiest years of the batting perfectionist's tempestuous career.

Elbow surgery in mid-season, 1950, after Ted was hurt in the All-Star Game, limited Williams to 89 contests and reduced his average to .317, but he still had productive power totals, 28 homers and 97 RBIs.

The era of spitting at the pressbox, wagging donkeys' ears at the crowd and, unforgivably, obscene gestures, marred the man's efforts in this period, but Williams still could hit. He batted .318 in '51, with 30 homers and 126 RBIs, and then early in '52 received the jolting news that, as a Marine reservist close to 34 years old, he had been called to active duty.

Given a day, which included a Cadillac and a memory book with 400,000 signatures, Williams heard the crowd sing "Auld Lang Syne" in early May and, finishing his sixth game of the season batting .400, Ted belted a game-winning homer against Detroit and then threw a party at the Kenmore Hotel for the guys he liked—bellhops, cab drivers, bartenders, bat boys, cops, etc.

He thought his career was over and he nearly lost his life in Korea, belly-flopping a flaming jet skidding 2,000 feet along the runway, cussing and fuming, yet, as usual, coolly effective—this time with death as his co-pilot.

Cold, sick with pneumonia, his hearing impaired, Williams came back a war hero, urged to attend the 1953 All-Star Game at Cincinnati, where he threw out the first ball and received a standing ovation that touched him.

Uncertain whether to play, he bumped into Branch Rickey at the airport and had a cup of coffee. The Mahatma was encouraging. "Ted, you've got five or six more good years left," he said. "I think you should play."

Williams' business manager and good friend, Fred Corcoran, was more specific. He believed the slugger should forego the fishing and get back into baseball immediately so that, in effect, he'd have a head start for 1954.

Hell, as Joe Cronin suggested, Williams set back spring training 20 years. Out of baseball 15 months, he took batting practice for about 10 days, using golf gloves to cut down the blisters, and then popped up as a pinch-hitter at Washington. Back at Boston, where he'd left with a game-winning homer, Ted stepped up the next afternoon and blasted Cleveland's Mike Garcia for a pinch homer.

For the next 37 games, Williams hit .407, including 13 homers, an average of one every seven times at bat, for an incredible .901 slugging percentage.

So it was most unfortunate that on the opening day of spring practice, 1954, Ted fell chasing a line drive and broke his collarbone, requiring a pencil-thick, stainless-steel pin, about four inches long, which is still in there, a permanent souvenir of one of his more vexing injuries.

Out six weeks, his first marriage on the rocks and

discouraged, Williams wrote with the Associated Press' Joe Reichler a magazine story announcing that he would retire after the end of the season. But how could a guy quit while hitting like this? He went back into the lineup on May 7 in Detroit and went 8-for-9 in a doubleheader, springboard to a .345 season, which would have been enough for another title except that he was getting walked so much. Finally, in recognition of what bases on balls could do to a man's chances to win a batting championship, rules were changed to count total plate appearances, not only official times up.

Tom Yawkey, seconded by Joe Cronin, suggested that Williams become manager of the Red Sox after Lou Boudreau was fired, but Ted declined with thanks and didn't officially reconsider his retirement until May 13, 1955, four days after he was divorced and tapped for a sizable settlement and alimony.

Sure, once again the tall terror hit a homer his first time up, but, plagued by pneumonia, lumbago and an injury to the arch of one foot, the poor "cripple" hit .356 in 98 games, belting 28 homers and driving in 83 runs.

A year later, the Gold Sox gaffer hit well (.345-24-82), but no one could foresee the remarkable season at age 39 in 1957. Using a trifle heavier bat (34 ounces), choking his grip about a quarter-inch more and drilling to the left side of second base the hot smashes that formerly were mobbed by the right-side shift, Old Teddy Ballgame opened up the defenses. And when he wasn't hitting through 'em, he went over 'em. Twice during that fantastic .388 season he hit three homers in a game, tying a major league mark.

The grumpy geezer got better with the hot weather that year, too, hitting .453 over the last half of the season. At the finish, Williams was just five hits away from a .400 average.

Boss Yawkey called the voting "incompetent and unqualified" when the MVP went to Mickey Mantle, a .365 hitter with the champion Yankees, because two Chicago writers voted Williams way down, ninth and 10th. But Ted had the satisfaction of winning recognition in an annual AP poll as Athlete of the Year.

Armed with a two-year contract, which he figured to be his last, Williams collared teammate Pete Runnels in the 1958 batting race and then broke Pete's heart with a blistering windup at Washington, winning with a .328 average to .322.

Fishing, Ted hurt his neck in the off-season and was in traction almost as much as he was in misery in 1959 when he fell below .300 for the first time, dropping to .254 with just 10 homers and 43 runs batted in for 103 games. He was hurt even more when good friend Yawkey gently suggested it might be a good idea to call it a career.

Burned up, Ted quietly insisted that he'd like to wait until spring training to see, certain in his own mind that he'd been handicapped by the neck injury. This, he felt, wasn't the way to go and he volunteered to take a $35,000 pay cut to $90,000—almost a 30 percent bite.

He vindicated himself in 1960—and how!—as they'd say a generation ago. Williams, ahead of his time with open-neck sports shirts, forerunners of the turtleneck, didn't look old-fashioned at the plate in '60, the FOURTH calendar decade in which he'd appeared in big league baseball.

Passing the 500-homer milestone, he cracked 29 homers and drove in 72 runs in just 310 official times at bat as he played and pinch-hit in a total of 113 games with a .316 average. He had proved his point. What else was left? So it came to an end that raw late September afternoon at Fenway Park when there was a farewell ceremony at home plate. Ted received a silver bowl, a plaque and a $4,000 check for the Jimmy Fund, for the kids with cancer.

Williams wanted to give the 10,454 faithful at the Fens that day something to remember. Selfishly, he wanted to leave his calling card to future generations of hitters too. Hell, the guy just wanted to hit one. And against the wind whipping in briskly, he kissed one in the eighth inning off Jack Fisher, a hard-throwing Baltimore righthander. The line drive reached the right-center bullpen for a home run, No. 521 and final.

Circling the bases, Williams wanted to jump for joy. To blazes with that season-ending weekend series at New York, THIS would be it. And when the crowd roared louder and louder in a standing ovation, there was a moment when he admitted later, he almost tipped his cap for the first time in 20 years. But it wouldn't have been Old Teddy Ballgame if he had.

After all, Theodore Samuel Williams wore no man's collar, not even his own.

THEODORE SAMUEL (THE KID) WILLIAMS
Born August 30, 1918, at San Diego, Calif.
Height 6-4 Weight 198
Threw right and batted lefthanded.
Named to Hall of Fame, 1966.

YEAR	CLUB	LEAGUE	POS.	G.	AB.	R.	H.	2B.	3B.	HR.	RBI.	B.A.	PO.	A.	E.	F.A.
1936	San Diego	P.C.	OF	42	107	18	29	8	2	0	11	.271	64	5	2	.972
1937	San Diego	P.C.	OF	138	454	66	132	24	2	23	98	.291	213	10	7	.970
1938	Minneapolis	A.A.	OF	148	528	130	193	30	9	43	142	.366	269	17	11	.963
1939	Boston	Amer.	OF	149	565	131	185	44	11	31	145	.327	318	11	19	.945
1940	Boston	Amer.	OF	144	561	134	193	43	14	23	113	.344	302	15	13	.961
1941	Boston	Amer.	OF	143	456	135	185	33	3	37	120	.406	262	11	11	.961
1942	Boston	Amer.	OF	150	522	141	186	34	5	36	137	.356	313	15	4	.988
1943-44-45	Boston	Amer.						(In Military Service)								
1946	Boston	Amer.	OF	150	514	142	176	37	8	38	123	.342	325	7	10	.971
1947	Boston	Amer.	OF	156	528	125	181	40	9	32	114	.343	347	10	9	.975
1948	Boston	Amer.	OF	137	509	124	188	44	3	25	127	.369	289	9	5	.983
1949	Boston	Amer.	OF	155	566	150	194	39	3	43	159	.343	337	12	6	.983
1950	Boston (a)	Amer.	OF	89	334	82	106	24	1	28	97	.317	165	7	8	.956
1951	Boston	Amer.	OF	148	531	109	169	28	4	30	126	.318	315	12	4	.988
1952	Boston (b)	Amer.	OF	6	10	2	4	0	1	1	3	.400	4	0	0	1.000
1953	Boston (b)	Amer.	OF	37	91	17	37	6	0	13	34	.407	31	1	1	.970
1954	Boston	Amer.	OF	117	386	93	133	23	1	29	89	.345	213	5	4	.982
1955	Boston	Amer.	OF	98	320	77	114	21	3	28	83	.356	170	5	2	.989
1956	Boston	Amer.	OF	136	400	71	138	28	2	24	82	.345	174	7	5	.973
1957	Boston	Amer.	OF	132	420	96	163	28	1	38	87	.388	215	2	1	.995
1958	Boston	Amer.	OF	129	411	81	135	23	2	26	85	.328	154	3	7	.957
1959	Boston	Amer.	OF	103	272	32	69	15	0	10	43	.254	94	4	3	.970
1960	Boston	Amer.	OF	113	310	56	98	15	0	29	72	.316	131	6	1	.993
Major League Totals				2292	7706	1798	2654	525	71	521	1839	.344	4159	142	113	.974

a Suffered fractured left elbow when he crashed into the left field wall making catch in first inning of All-Star Game at Chicago, July 11, 1950; despite injury he stayed in game until ninth inning. Williams had played 70 American League games up to the All-Star affair—but appeared in only 19 more contests with the Red Sox for the rest of the season.
b In Military Service most of the season.

PITCHING RECORD

YEAR	CLUB	LEAGUE	G.	IP.	W.	L.	Pct.	H.	R.	ER.	SO.	BB.	ERA.
1936	San Diego	Pac. Coast	1	1 1/3	0	0	.000	2	2	2	0	1	13.50
1940	Boston	Amer.	1	2	0	0	.000	3	1	1	1	0	4.50

WORLD SERIES RECORD

YEAR	CLUB	LEAGUE	POS.	G.	AB.	R.	H.	2B.	3B.	HR.	RBI.	B.A.	PO.	A.	E.	F.A.
1946	Boston	Amer.	OF	7	25	2	5	0	0	0	1	.200	16	2	0	1.000

MIGHTY MIDGET: Hands down the shortest, heaviest hitter ever, Hack Wilson (left) was only 5'-6", six inches shorter than Lou Gehrig (right), eight smaller than slouching 6'-2" Babe Ruth, but the Cubs' power hitter had 56 homers one year and an unbelievable 190 RBIs.

HACK WILSON

Sardonic Westbrook Pegler, long-syndicated as a general columnist who could turn a phrase into a foe with a talented typewriter, was a cynical *Chicago Tribune* baseball writer when Rogers Hornsby was fired as manager of the Chicago Cubs in August 1932, joining in semi-oblivion the slugging center fielder who overnight had fallen as flat as warm, stale beer.

Lewis Robert (Hack) Wilson, one of the hardest-hitting and probably the most unusually tape-measured figure ever to hit tape-measure home runs,

was a colorful character who had faded overnight from perhaps the greatest all-around power season ANY batter ever muscled, 1930, to a journeyman on the way down in '32 when Hornsby was canned, and Pegler wrote:

"...Hornsby, a citizen who never fouled his lungs with the fumes of the noxious weed or put lip to a crock of ale, wine or hootch, has retired to his potato patch in Missouri. Hornsby is physically done for as a high-grade ballplayer...

"In Brooklyn, Hack Wilson is enjoying a bit of

revival. The victim of Hornsby's strict notions of hygiene and abstinence, Wilson pined and suffered all last year…

"Wilson liked beer, and Hornsby's aversion to beer was exceeded only by his aversion to ball players who drink it, so he made life socially and officially unpleasant for Wilson, who, a sensitive soul, was pulled temporarily out of joint.

"Hornsby contended that Wilson's indulgence in the high and low beers available in the beer dives of the National League cities was doing dirty tricks to his hitting and fielding and his eyes, legs and feet. Wilson tried to explain to sympathetic friends that his trouble was not too many beers, but too few…"

Uh-huh, Peg, but Hack didn't mention the bathtub gin he consumed by the quart, Prohibition poison that combined with dusk-to-dawn revelry, the unrelenting new manager's restrictions that were more "effective" on the field than off and a jackrabbit ball whose ears were snipped. They turned Wilson from a tiger at the plate into a tabby.

No hitter ever went from nowhere to somewhere—and back again—as fast and as fully—as the Chicago Cubs' sawed-off center fielder, author of a .356 average, a National League record 56 homers and major league mark 190 runs batted in one season (1930) and a .261-13-61 total the next.

Wilson, a printer's devil at 14, was a jolly good fellow—except when moved now and then to fling his fists at the enemy or to have his short, thick neck glow as fiercely as a mill furnace back home in Martinsburg, W. Va. when an umpire called a strike he didn't like or a fan called him a name he liked even less.

"Stouts," as they called Hack affectionately back there in West (By God) Virginia, might even vault into the stands to punish an offender or, without calling time to avoid an easy tag-out, he might even charge an opposing (Cincinnati) dugout to tee off on heckling pitcher Ray Kolp. And when the Cubs and Reds left town for the East on the same train that same July night, 1929, Wilson would continue

the fireworks against Cincinnati pitcher, Pete Donohue.

Heck, Hack had no quarrel with Donohue, but when Pete told him what would happen to Wilson if he dared invade the Reds' Pullmans, the red blood rushed to the slick-backed blond's round face and he wondered what 'n hell Donohue was doing sticking his nose in Wilson's and Kolp's business. Pow and plop! "Pow," Stouts swung and "plop," Pete hit the concrete at Chicago's Union Station.

For his Wrigley Field run-in, Wilson would receive a three-day suspension and $100 fine from National League president John Heydler, but Sherlock Heydler declined to penalize the homer hitter further for hitting Donohue. The league president just couldn't believe that anybody in his right mind, which he believed Donohue had, would dare to pick up his bags when arguing with Stouts.

Why, that would be as foolhardy as grooving a fat pitch for the fat man when Hack was hitting "cripples" so hard that, though he was a righthanded batter, master second baseman Frank Frisch of the rival St. Louis Cardinals played back on the grass 30 to 40 feet into right field for him. Wilson once hit the center-field scoreboard then BEYOND the fence at Wrigley Field, but his best shots there and elsewhere seemed to be to right-center.

Said Frisch, after finishing second to Wilson in the 1930 National League Most Valuable Player voting, "I go that deep for Hack, not because he can't run, but because he hits the ball so damned hard that he'd take my head off if I were at normal depth. Besides, back there, I still get the ball in time to throw him out."

For five seasons through 1930, Wilson was devastating anywhere and everywhere, but especially at Wrigley Field. In 1930, for instance, as determined by the statistical research of Dave Hewson of Eugene, Ore., Hack hit .381 at home compared with .324 away and drove in 115 of those 190 runs at Wrigley. He hit more homers at home, naturally, too.

"But when they deadened the ball a bit in 1931," said Al Lopez, who caught against the slugger and then played with him at Brooklyn, "I thought Hack was hurt more than most, especially on those drives that used to go up against or over the right-center field wall."

Wilson would acknowledge that the de-juiced ball of 1929 and '30—the entire National League AVERAGED .303 in '30—had hurt a bit, but he beefed even more because Hornsby, succeeding Joe McCarthy as manager late in 1930, had flashed the "take" sign frequently in 1931 on counts of 2-and-0 and 3-and-1.

"He took the bat right out of my hands," complained Stouts. "I feasted on 'cripples.'"

Although Hornsby himself was undoubtedly a 7-come-11 natural who needed only one swing, it's really hard to believe in a period when even the humpty-dumpty hitters get the "hit" privilege ahead on the ball-and-strike count, that The Rajah ever would have wished base on balls from a guy who so often could turn one base into four.

But Hornsby was hardheaded and Hack a hard drinker. Joe McCarthy, though he had tried to keep the pudgy long-ball hitter's drinking under control, handled Wilson gently and with understanding. "Mac," as Hack called him, could get a remorseful, painfully hungover Wilson crying like a baby with a reproach, but that's all it was.

After all, for one thing when managing Louisville to the American Association championship in 1925, McCarthy had been responsible in large measure for Chicago's drafting Wilson from Toledo at a time when the Cubs beckoned for Marse Joe. A clerical error in the New York Giants' office had exposed Wilson to the draft, and, after losing the final day of the season when Gabby Hartnett, of all people, committed two errors against the Cardinals, the Cubs finished last in '25 and, therefore, drafted first.

Another reason for McCarthy's indulgence—and the Yankees' great manager of the 1930s and early '40s lived until past 90 even though he had

more than just a nodding acquaintance with the stuff himself—was an error of judgment Mac had made his first year in the majors, 1926.

McCarthy didn't like Grover Cleveland Alexander's drinking habits and the occasional flippancy of the customarily quiet Old Pete when he'd had too much bug juice. So Joe opted for Alex' departure. St. Louis claimed the gallant gaffers in time for him to pitch the Cardinals to the world championship that fall, oddly under that milk-shake sipper at second base, Hornsby.

Rubbing it on Chicago further, Alexander was a 20-game winner in 1927 at 40 and contributed 16 more victories in another pennant season, 1928.

So McCarthy was interested more in production from Wilson than whether Hack burned the midnight oil or drank it. And, man, how that human fireplug delivered, delighting Chicago at a time the Toddlin' Town was the speakeasy citadel of the Roaring Twenties. If you think of Scarface Al Capone first in that period, you've got to put the heavy-hitting Cubs right up there and as best symbolized by the human fireplug in center field.

Stouts was a sight to behold. He was only 5 feet 6 inches tall, but his weight always hovered around 200 pounds or higher, as high—some say—as 230 pounds. He had an 18-inch neck, a big head that sat like a pumpkin on his torso, and his arms bulged with 16-inch biceps.

In the upper body, the hard work of his youth showed itself. Lewis Robert Wilson's father, Robert swung a hammer in a steel mill at Elwood City, Pa., where his wife died when son Lewis was just eight years old and the boy's two older sisters took care of him as they moved to Eddystone.

So when Hack was just 14 at the time royalty assasination at Sarajevo triggered World War I, the sixth-grade kid told Pop he thought it was time to go to work, and his German-American parent didn't object. Therefore, the kid progressed from print works' apprentice—"I'll bet in two years I carried a couple of million pounds of lead," he would reminisce—and the huskier lad went to work for the Baldwin Locomotive works. With a finishing gang, he swung a sledge hammer, drove rivets and did other jobs that required strength and made strong bodies ever stronger.

The bulky body with short legs on which the calves looked more like cows had one weakness—slender, delicate ankles supported by ridiculously small feet (shoe size $5\frac{1}{2}$). So when Stouts had a chance to get from behind hammering huge pieces of white-hot steel with a steam hammer, he jumped at the chance to swap his mill gear for a catcher's harness.

Historian Bob Soderman of Mt. Pleasant, Ill., and Chicago told it well after research for book entitled *Baseball's Unforgotten Man*, which Wilson most certainly was not. Not, it must be emphasized, when a generation born after his premature death at 48, only three years after V-J Day of World War II, campaigned actively for the national Baseball Hall of Fame's Committee on Veterans to elect Hack. They did in 1979, 31 years after Hack last sniffed life's sweet air.

Back there at the beginning, a former Philadelphia Athletics' player, Bris Lord, inspired the former printer's devil who had worked for $5 a week and caddied on weekends. Stouts did so well playing for the Chester (Pa.) A.C. that he attracted attention of the Viscoe Silk Mill team, which offered more money than young Wilson had been getting in the shipyards. So in 1921 he signed for $175 a month with the Blue Ridge League team at what would become his hometown—Martinsburg, W. Va.

As luck would have it, Hack's Achilles heel, those chorus girl ankles, betrayed him at the outset. He tripled first time up for Martinsburg and, eagerly trying to score on a play at the plate, he broke an ankle. Even when he was a big league star, squinting hungover in the clubhouse when quaffing a quart of milk to chase away the previous night's agony and ecstasy, the Cubs' equally colorful trainer, Andy Lotshaw, would use 10 yards of two-inch adhesive tape to bind up and protect the ankles.

By the time Wilson blossomed with a .388 season of 19 homers and 101 RBIs for long-time knowledgeable minor league operator, Frank Lawrence, at Portsmouth, Va., in 1923, a New York Giants' scout had filed a report to John McGraw, a report in which the ivory-hunter wound up that Wilson "looked as if he had his feet buried in wet cement."

But McGraw had been misled before and since. Hadn't that more famous scout, Jesse Burkett, told him that a kid catcher named Hartnett had hands that were "too small?" So Muggsy liked what he saw, even though by then Stouts Wilson had been moved to the outfield to save wear and tear behind the plate on those tiny feet and delicate ankles.

Still, McGraw was hesitant, but Lawrence was persuasive. The asking price of $25,000 was too high, Mac decided, but Lawrence had an intriguing counterproposal.

"I'll tell you what I'll do: Give me $5,000 down and if Wilson isn't hitting .300 for you next July 15, you don't owe me a cent more. Otherwise, give me $1,000 for every point over .300."

McGraw chuckled. "A sporting proposition, all right, Frank," he said, "but that wouldn't be fair to you. What if Wilson is hitting well—like .290—but not quite .300 on July 15?"

So McGraw countered with a deal in which he made considerably saving. For Stouts Wilson, he gave the Virginia League club $11,000 cash and a couple of warm bodies. My, if he'd taken up Lawrence's "sporting" proposition, he'd have owed the Portsmouth man $71,000. Wilson, you see, was hitting .371 for the Giants on July 15, 1924, though he tailed off to .295 in 107 games for the club that won its fourth straight National League pennant.

It was Billy Cunningham of the Giants who hung on L.R. Wilson the nickname that would become a byword for the future Babe Ruth of the National League.

"Why, you're the spitting image of Hack Miller," said Cunningham, referring to another big league ballplayer who, in turn, had been nicknamed because of a physique that reminded observers of the champion wrestler, George Hackenschmidt.

As "Hack," much more swashbuckling than "Stouts," 24-year-old Wilson included among his first 113 hits a total of 10 home runs. The first was a drive off Brooklyn's Burleigh Grimes and over the right-field wall at Ebbets Field into Bedford Avenue. Ten years later, No. 244 and last of his big league homers would clear the same barrier.

Although Wilson played all seven games of the '24 World Series, won by Washington on Earl McNeely's bad-hop single over Freddie Lindstrom's head at third base, McGraw thought he saw a simple way out of a dilema. Young Bill Terry had moved strongly into the first-base picture, though McGraw preferred at times to platoon Terry with versatile George Kelly, who could play center field and second base, too. And New York's outfielders included Billy Southworth, Irish Meusel and another future Hall of Famer, Ross Youngs.

It was the peppery Young who put things in proper perspective when interviewed by Bill Corum at a time the future columnist was a baseball writer.

"Bill, they just sent down the best outfielder I've been paired with," said the premier right fielder in testimony to Wilson's defensive ability. "I think it's a mistake they're going to regret."

Years later when the Hall of Fame old-timers were considering Wilson again, Bill Terry also spoke well of Wilson's defensive ability. "Yes," said the defense-minded, hard-hitting first baseman who managed the Giants to three later pennants himself, "Hack could have played center field for me."

In the old horseshoe-shaped Polo Grounds in New York, you know, the center-field clubhouse was a subway station's distance from home plate. Terry's high regard for Wilson could have been based partly on the fact that when Bill became the most recent National Leaguer to hit .400 (.401 in 1930), Hack beat him out of the MVP award. In fact, Terry finished third behind Wilson and another former teammate, Frank Frisch.

Wilson, not hitting when shipped down to To-

ledo in 1925, took the demotion hard. When he'd reported to the Giants and there wasn't a uniform built short enough, yet sufficiently ample to fill his bulging muscles, McGraw had dug up a uniform and said, "Here, kid, and don't digrace this one."

"Who wore it?"

"Me."

"Don't worry," the young athlete told the old manager, "I'll do all right by it, Mac."

He did, but not in that uniform or in the Big Apple because, as mentioned, after rebounding at Toledo, he'd become available when a pencil-pusher in the Giants' front office forgot to protect him from the draft. And Joe McCarthy and the Cubs, though unaccustomed to last place, snatched him quicker than Jack could down a bottle of Prohibition homebrew or shudder through a mouthful of that rot-gut booze.

Just think: If they'd only had the good bonded stuff in Hack's day...

At Chicago, where attendance had dropped to just above 600,000, the squatty slugger in center field became the toast of the town as Cubs' attendance rose immediately and then more than doubled to a 1,400,000-plus record that existed until past World War II.

With the Cubbies in 1926, Wilson clubbed his first home run at St. Louis off lefthander Art Rinehart, en route to a .321 season of 21 homers and 109 RBIs. In successive seasons, then, he tied New York's Mel Ott and St. Louis' Jim Bottomley for the league home run championship with 30 and 31, hitting .318 and .313 and driving in 129 runs, then 120.

Now, the year was 1929 and the Cubs, who faltered in the stretch the previous couple of seasons, kept coming with a hard-hitting team that had been supplemented by acquisition of Hornsby from the poorbox Boston Braves for five players AND $200,000. In a batting order of awesome righthanded hitting, including Riggs Stephenson, Wilson and Kiki Cuyler in the outfield and Hartnett catching when not laid up with mysterious arm ailment, The Rajah and The Hack vied for home run honors—Hornsby had 40, batting third, and Wilson, cleanup man, belted 39 in a .345 season in which he drove in what was then a National League record of 159 runs.

The Cubs' first World Series since 1918 was a debacle in which Hack Wilson wore the goat's horns. Yeah, even though he batted .471 in the five games.

Trouble was, in the pivotal fourth game when the Cubs held an obviously insurmountable 8-0 lead in the seventh inning, Wilson midjudged not one flyball, but two, prolonging an inning that will live in baseball infamy. The Athletics poured across 10 runs to win, 10-8. A day later they won the world championship.

Head up, Hack smiled his way from the chartered bus from Philadelphia's Shibe Park to the Cubs' hotel, but he was hurt, terribly hurt. Later, as first baseman Charley Grimm told it, Hack had broken his regular sunglasses and had switched to a kind too light for the sun that penetrated like fire into center field at the time Series games were played, a couple of hours earlier than customary in the regular season.

Curiously, though Rogers Hornsby hated Wilson's guts and vice-versa, The Rajah defended Hack years later in a book, explaining about the powerful sun field and putting the finger on Chicago third baseman Norm McMullen for having boxed a couple of plays that should have been handled, though not glaringly labeled as errors.

The Chicago management, though stunned at the time, was not unappreciative. For 1930, gum magnate William Wrigley increased to $22,500 the salary of the former West Virginia poor boy who had broken in with the Giants at $3,500. And the determined Wilson, especially because Hornsby was sidelined with a leg broken early in the season, put on that superb show highlighted by the 56 homers and those astonishing 190 runs batted in.

If only someone now could figure Hack's RBIs per opportunity during the one year he set the record, one that most impresses even ballplayers active nearly a half-century after he set it and 30 years after he became a name on a tombstone. Current kids admire Hornsby's .424 average in 1924 and George Sisler's 257 hits in 1920 and Babe Ruth's 60 homers in 1927 and Roger Maris' 61 in '61, but they whistle in respectful astonishment over the magic number: 190 RBIs.

Presumably, a man would have had to be better educated or at least more mature than Hack Wilson to withstand—and stand up under—the adulation everywhere, especially in Chicago, where he was the life of the party.

For a time, his son, Robert, born just before Hack took over the Toddlin' Town in 1926, was bitter at his father because of the parent's frailty, but, as a teacher, principal and then school superintendent, young Mr. Wilson later would remember fondly the Hack Wilson who loved to hunt, fish and to travel to ball games and to fights.

Shucks, Hack was willing to put on the gloves himself with the Chicago White Sox's first-base popoff, Art (Whataman!) Shires, after the 1929 season. Shrewdly, the Chicago Stadium was willing to offer a $10,000 purse, especially after Shires kayoed Boston Braves' catcher Al Spohrer. But Wrigley persuaded Wilson to stay out of the ring and then after the Chicago Bears' George Trafton beat The Great Shires, baseball commissioner Judge Landis stepped in and ordered ballplayers to use baseball mitts, not boxing gloves.

Still, it would have been something…

The stories about Hack Wilson are legend and legion. The best, probably, is when he was struggling for Brooklyn near the end, wincing as the Knight of Bustheads with a hangover and leaning against the corrugated right-field fence of Philly's chummy Baker Bowl. Manager Casey Stengel was changing Dodger pitchers and Hack, who had been running down Walter (Boom Boom) Beck's mistakes, needed a rest.

Just then—boom!—Hack heard the ball crash against the fence and, mortified, he hustled over, picked up the ball and fired to second base, certain he'd been embarrassed by lack of vigilance. Truth is, of course, Beck angrily had fired the ball from the mound to the nearby fence rather than hand it to Stengel.

Wryly, Stengel would observe, "Hack made his best throw of the season on that one…"

That was only a shell, the Wilson who got $33,000 in 1931 and, after he had been suspended when he either just stood by or goaded playmate pitcher Pat Malone into punching two Chicago baseball writers at the railroad station, he was sent home by Hornsby, some $8,500 short.

Traded to St. Louis with pitcher Bud Teachout for Burleigh Grimes, the Redbird pitching hero off whom he'd hit his first big league homer, Wilson expressed himself as happy, glad to be away from Hornsby's hyper bat control and the booing of fickle fans. But then Branch Rickey shocked him by offering only a $7,500 conditional contract for 1932 when Wilson expected only a 50 percent salary cut, not an amputation.

Hack balked, understandably, and was dealt to Brooklyn without ever pulling on a St. Louis uniform. The Dodgers gave him $15,000 and he had what would amount to a good year for many players since—.297 with 23 homers and 123 RBIs.

But by 1934, unconditionally released by Brooklyn in August and then cut adrift by the futile Phillies, Wilson was overweight and under-productive, completely washed up at 34.

After part of a season at Albany, he returned home to Martinsburg and opened a pool room and restaurant with a small bowling alley, but in 1937 long-suffering Virginia Mae Riddleberger, his wife since 1923, divorced Stouts. Three years later she was dead.

Wilson, meanwhile, had bummed from job to job, drinking heavily. In 1938, he made a triumphant return to Chicago where he played a semi-pro doubleheader before 8,000 at Mills Stadium, touched by the royal reception he was given.

"What a town," said the man who once owned it.

"What I wouldn't give to come back here in some capacity with the Cubs or Sox…"

He ducked back into Martinsburg for Virginia Mae's funeral, but Stouts was on the skids himself, winding up with a city swimming pool job at Baltimore, where in late 1948, debilitated from too many bouts with John Barleycorn, he died of pulmonary pneumonia. The National League and friends had to come to his rescue to keep one of the highest-salaried stars of his day from a pauper's grave.

The bittersweet story can't end so sadly, not when Hack Wilson loved to laugh so much. So how about the tried-and-true old one about an occasion with the contriviance of the Wrigley Field groundskeeper, Joe McCarthy sought to convince Stouts the evil of that bad blinding booze served up in the era of the hip flask. The Roaring Twenties in which the Volstead Act was not nearly so exciting—or respected—as Wilson swinging a thin-handled bat with those wide shoulders and small hands.

McCarthy called Hack into his clubhouse office one day and, motioning to two glasses of transparent liquid sitting before him, the great manager produced a wriggling worm the groundskeeper had acquired. McCarthy dropped the worm into a glass of water, and the wriggler swam happily.

Next, McCarthy gravely dropped the worm into a glass full of the same kind of gut-rotting, nerve-shattering gin with which the slugger had spent many a giggling, fast-paced night. The worm inhaled the perfumy gin vapors and dropped—kerplunk!—to the bottom of the glass: Deader than Stouts' baseball hopes had seemed when he'd broken that fragil ankle as a professional rookie.

"Do you get the point, Hack?" McCarthy inquired.

Lewis Robert (Hack) Wilson studied the scene, frowned, and then that round red face beamed with understanding.

"Sure, Joe," he said, "sure: If you drink gin, you won't get worms!"

LEWIS ROBERT (HACK) WILSON
Born April 26, 1900, at Ellwood City, Pa.
Died November 23, 1948, at Baltimore, Md.
Height 5-6 Weight 195
Threw and batted righthanded.
Named to Hall of Fame, 1979.

YEAR	CLUB	LEAGUE	POS.	G.	AB.	R.	H.	2B.	3B.	HR.	RBI.	B.A.	PO.	A.	E.	F.A.
1921	Martinsburg	B. Ridge	OF	30	101	17	36	8	0	5	-	.356	107	33	7	.952
1922	Martinsburg	B. Ridge	OF	84	322	66	118	17	3	30	-	.366	171	7	7	.962
1923	Portsmouth	Va.	OF	115	448	96	174	37	15	19	101	.388	304	15	12	.964
1923	New York	Nat.	OF	3	10	0	2	0	0	0	1	.200	6	0	1	.857
1924	New York	Nat.	OF	107	383	62	113	19	12	10	57	.295	230	8	8	.967
1925	New York	Nat.	OF	62	180	28	43	7	4	6	30	.239	75	3	2	.975
1925	Toledo (a)	Nat.	OF	55	210	42	72	15	6	4	36	.343	133	2	5	.964
1926	Chicago	Nat.	OF	142	529	97	170	36	8	21	109	.321	348	11	10	.973
1927	Chicago	Nat.	OF	146	551	119	175	30	12	30	129	.318	400	13	14	.967
1928	Chicago	Nat.	OF	145	520	89	163	32	9	31	120	.313	321	11	14	.960
1929	Chicago	Nat.	OF	150	574	135	198	30	5	39	159	.345	380	14	12	.970
1930	Chicago	Nat.	OF	155	585	146	208	35	6	56	190	.356	357	9	19	.951
1931	Chicago (b) (c)	Nat.	OF	112	395	66	103	22	4	13	61	.261	210	9	5	.978
1932	Brooklyn	Nat.	OF	135	481	77	143	37	5	23	123	.297	220	14	11	.955
1933	Brooklyn	Nat.	OF	117	360	41	96	13	2	9	54	.267	181	3	7	.963
1934	Brook (d)-Phila.	Nat.	OF	74	192	24	47	5	0	6	20	.245	82	3	2	.977
1935	Albany	Int.	OF	59	175	30	46	9	1	3	29	.263	71	3	5	.937
Major League Totals				1348	4760	884	1461	266	67	244	1063	.307	2810	98	105	.965

a Drafted by Chicago Cubs, October, 1925.
b Traded to St. Louis Cardinals with Pitcher Art Teachout for Pitcher Burleigh Grimes, December, 1931.
c Traded to Brooklyn Dodgers for Outfielder Robert Parham and $45,000, January 23, 1932.
d Unconditionally released by Brooklyn Dodgers, August, 1934; subsequently signed with Philadelphia Phillies.

WORLD SERIES RECORD

YEAR	CLUB	LEAGUE	POS.	G.	AB.	R.	H.	2B.	3B.	HR.	RBI.	B.A.	PO.	A.	E.	F.A.
1924	New York	Nat.	OF	7	30	1	7	1	0	0	5	.233	8	1	0	1.000
1929	Chicago	Nat.	OF	5	17	2	8	0	1	0	0	.471	14	0	1	.933
World Series Totals				12	47	3	15	1	1	0	5	.319	22	1	1	.958

EARLY WYNNER: Actually early and late, Early (Gus) Wynn was a dominating guy, an intimidating pitcher who hung on until he was 43 years old, perspiring here, as he achieved his 300th victory in his 23rd big league season.

EARLY WYNN

The ball was a blue blur as it screamed off the bat of Washington infielder Jose Valdivielso's bat in an early inning of a 1956 game at Griffith Stadium, the D.C. diamond where Early (Gus) Wynn had labored hard and long, losing more games than he won, but by now—in 1956—he had been a three-time winner of 20 or more for the Cleveland Indians.

As Al Lopez knew, the Indian chief of the Indians—one-eighth Cherokee or Siwash—was a game competitor, all wool and a yard wide through the

thick chest of a bulky body with legs as sturdy as an oak and jet black hair atop bronzed features.

Now, those fighting features were a mess because Valdivielso's line smash through the box had come off the Senator infielder's bat so squarely that Wynn had lost sight of it. The ball hit the pitcher squarely on the point of his rugged chin like a knockout punch.

As Gus staggered back, the ball rolled halfway toward first base. Righting himself, Wynn reeled after it, groping blindly as his head swam dizzily, seeking a handle on the spherical white lightning so that he could make a play at first base. He never found a handle and, resignedly, he straightened, chin buried into his barrel chest.

Lopez came out of the visiting club's dugout on a run to look at him. Wynn buried his chin in his chest and wouldn't talk.

"Let me see it," said the manager.

"I'm fine," said the pitcher.

"Come on, let me see the chin," Lopez insisted.

"No" was the muttered reply.

"Let me see the chin," insisted Lopez, "or I'll take you out without looking."

Wynn raised his head. What Lopez saw was a bloody mess. Early had a deep gash. His mouth was badly hurt, blood splattering his uniform. It would take 16 stitches to close the wound and he would lose seven of the lower teeth that were loosened by the staggering blow, but the man aptly named Wynn didn't want to come out.

"I want to pitch to him once more," bleary-eyed gritty Gus said of the guy who stood on first base, wearing a worried look with good reason.

Not only was Valdivielso concerned that he might have accidentally hurt the pitcher, but he probably also knew that if Wynn had a middle initial, it undoubtedly would have been "R." That's "R" as in "Revenge" or "Reprisal."

If an elephant doesn't forget, neither does an Indian, even with just a splash of red man in his veins. And if, like Burleigh Grimes of championship ball clubs a generation earlier, there was one kind of batter Early liked less than any other, it was the guy who hit through the middle. My, he'd have had a perpetual hate for such slashing sluggers as Rogers Hornsby and Joe Medwick, two of the most notorious for lining the ball at or near or through timid toeplate talent.

Early Wynn pitched long in the majors, all or part of 23 seasons until age 43, that he COULD have faced Medwick and, in fact, Hornsby just had laid down his still-quivering bat in 1937, a mere

two years before Gus' name first appeared in a big league boxscore for the Griffs at Washington.

"Why, do you know," the Early who stayed late said once, reminiscing, "that when I joined the Nats, Goose Goslin was still playing. Imagine, Goose Goslin!"

Yeah, the Goose, that waddling, big-honkered hitter who'd help bring a smile even to Calvin Coolidge's stony face when Washington—of all things!—won a world championship in 1924.

From Goslin to Yastrzemski, from Williams and DiMaggio to Wills and others who played from the '20s and-or to the '70s, Wynn covered a span from Coolidge to Kennedy. And in 1972, though no gimmick guy except for the gadgets he liked to drive, to fly or to fool with in his Florida retreat, Early was willing to listen at age 52 when his former boss, Calvin Griffith, proposed that Wynn pitch an inning to Ted Williams at Bloomington, Minn., the Twin Cities' compromise to which the Senators moved in 1961.

The idea was to enable both men to play into their fifth decade of big league ball, but Teddy Ballgame declined. When you've bowed out with a home run your last official time up, as Williams did at Boston in 1960, why risk a letdown as an anticlimax, especially when old Gus might decide to stick one in your ear?

In middle age as the '70s crept inexorably toward the '80s, Wynn might regard the foregoing, facetiously written, as a canard. In 1977, his first year behind a microphone as a member of the Toronto Blue Jays' broadcasting team, the former Cleveland moonlighting sports columnist said he'd really not been such a mean fellow, after all. Blame a lot of it on propaganda trumped up by Frank Lane, the frantic one, Wynn said with a straight face.

But in spring training, 1978, when Reggie Jackson was the resident World Series homer hitter, preening over a candy bar having been named for him, Jackson gave an oral brushoff to old Gus when Wynn sought a radio interview. The Wynn of old flared for an instant, overheard by a member of the Toronto press corps, when Early walked away, muttering:

"I'd like to get him in the batter's box just once…"

Not that the last of the major league's magic 300-game winners would have scared the bejabbers out of Jackson the way he did Valdivielso after that line drive parted Wynn's chin back in 1956, but Wynn had a way of working himself up into a king-sized hate for the foe. And he just MIGHT have pretended Jackson had hit one back that low-bridged Gus, in which case the codger might have transferred American League president Lee MacPhail's signature from a cowhide to a brand in Reggie's side.

You see, with cavalier courtesy and ethics, Wynn didn't believe in throwing at the head, making a definite distinction between a beanball and a brushback, but he learned early the value of the knockdown—(1) to keep the hitters from digging in and leaning over too familiarly into the strike zone and (2) to test their mettle to see whether they could be intimidated.

"Heck," Gus said in reflection, more profanely than that, "you weren't about to scare the great ones, like Williams or DiMag, for instance, but some of the others looked for your message and didn't like the ball high and tight any more than I did those shots through the box."

Pitching rhythmically from a three-quarter catapult, Wynn tried after his facial injury in '56 to follow through so that his glove and the right hand with which he threw were held up, palms facing the hitter. But, criminy, crusty Gus didn't let the mishap hurt or hinder as much as anger him. He was 20-and-9 that year and had a 2.72 earned-run average, one of the best of his career.

Still, he brooked no nonsense when it came to a batter's using him as a target far short of the 60 feet 6 inch pitching distance after Early had hurtled himself forward to throw that high, hard one. The rising fastball really was his only pitch until Mel Harder, the mound master at Cleveland, took the Washington refugee under his wing in 1948 and taught him the smarts.

Even, however, after Wynn, with a wrist almost as thick as his ankle, turned his wrinkle of a curve into a sharp one and added a slider and knuckler into a repertoire that was both good and versatile, he didn't like it one damned bit when friend or foe conked one back at him.

One time in Chicago when the White Sox were en route to a storybook pennant, one in which Wynn was the aging Prince Charming with a 22-10 record at age 39, first baseman-outfielder Joe Cunningham, who batted with a variety of stances, most of them closed, cuffed one that pinked old Gus up the middle as he pitched batting practice.

Years later, in charge of group sales for the St. Louis Cardinals, Cunningham could shake his head and smile. "That Wynn," he said, "glared at me, knocked me down twice and then nicked me with the third pitch."

Although Wynn might have been the meanest man of the mound in his lengthy era, a throwback to the days of Ty Cobb and other ask-no-quarter legends against whom Goslin and others of his big-league boyhood had competed, he certainly looked the toughest. His thin lips set in a virtual sneer and his dark eyes flashed a sinister glare.

Old Gus looked like anything except the hero, a shining knight on white horseback, which he was in 1959 when, en route to the Cy Young award as the American League's best, the gallant gaffer led the Chisox to their first pennant since the Pale Horse was soiled 40 years earlier in the Black Sox scandal.

After that '59 season, then just 29 victories short of the 300-game goal that had been his ambition since his peak seasons at Cleveland, Wynn could have had any promise short of an early round-trip reservation to the moon. But within a year, Bill Veeck had become ill and was forced out by illness. You know how it is: What have you done for me lately?

Wynn dipped to 13-12 in 1960 and after a bout with the gout, his quantity had dipped farther than his quality in '61, a year in which he was only 8-and-2. When the old boy slipped back to 7-15 in 1963 with a 4.46 earned-run average, he was still one devastating victory short at 299.

The wags suggested it would be even more newsworthy to stop at 299, but you didn't talk that kind of talk to one so competitive as the bristling geezer from the Nokomis-Venice area along Florida's West Coast. He wanted s-o-o much to join Lefty Grove and Warren Spahn as the only 300-game winners of his l-e-n-g-t-h-y era. And time and again, he'd come so frustratingly close.

The White Sox released him, but then invited him to spring training in 1963, unsigned. Double-chinned and with a paunch, old Gus drove himself relentlessly that spring at Sarasota's Payne Field, trying to sweat his way back into the starting rotation or, at least, the staff.

But then came the pink slip, which could have meant "The End," but a few clubs phoned, including Cleveland. For Wynn, the club with which he had spent the nine best center-cut seasons of his career offered the most, including the potential chance to become pitching coach. And for all his success outside of baseball, old Gus wanted to stay in the Grand Old Game.

So at Gabe Paul's invitation—Paul's first time around as chief of the Lake Erie Tribe—Early joined the Indians, managed by an old rival for whom he had considerable respect, Birdie Tebbetts, the Providence College psychology major and a former catcher who had delighted in exchanging oral barbs with Wynn the winner.

Time and again old Gus tried, pitching well, but, as the saying goes, unable to win for losing. Working in relief, more than starting, he had that year a 2.28 ERA that kind of tells it all. But then it was Saturday night, July 12, and time was running out on the geezer.

The gout murdered him that night. "I couldn't sleep," Wynn would recall. "Gout feels the like the drip-drip-drip of ice cold water on a cavity."

Back in the Wigwam since June, he'd just lost a 2-1 heartbreaker, but now—at least—the dice came "seven" for the old adventurous spirit. Setting off a big inning himself with a base hit, he built a 5-1 lead into the fifth at Kansas City, then saw the Athletics rough him up. He barely survived the fifth inning with a one-run lead.

"I was bushed," Wynn explained later. "Birdie had to take me out of there or I'd have fallen flat on my face."

Dutifully, the old team man sat on the bench, jacketed, as young teammate Jerry Walker took over in the sixth. But when Cleveland added a sixth run in the seventh, Early was asked to come up to the radio booth. He showered and got there in time to watch Walker wriggle off the hook in the eighth.

The Indians added a run in the ninth and when Walker breezed through the home half, the 7-4 Cleveland victory meant that Early Wynn, Jr., had made it. To show you how many foks were pulling for old Gus, Walker's mother rushed out of the stands to embrace Jerry on the mound for his game-saving excellence.

The Cleveland catcher, John Romano, leaped joyfully into the air and clutched the final ball certain to preserve it for Wynn. When old Gus came down to the clubhouse, his teammates gave him a rousing ovation. He stood there a moment, beaming, and then went from locker to locker, shaking hands.

To Walker, he said gleefully, "Attaboy, roomie. Thanks. We kept it in the room. Tomorrow we'll get a Cadillac and we'll both drive it."

Ironically, when the Indians' plane, immediately after the game the second half of a Sunday double-header, touched down at Minneapolis, Wynn found disappointedly that a party would have to be delayed because of Minnesota's Sunday drinking law. But Walker was the center of attraction.

For Wynn, No. 300 was it—period—victory No. 300 of a career that also included 244 defeats.

You might not win pennants regularly with Early's overall won-and-lost percentage, .551, but it's a fact that he was a Jekyll-and-Hyde in sweaty flannels, a thrower at Washington with a weak team and a pitcher at Cleveland with a good one. Ditto, to a degree, at Chicago.

Just 19 when he first joined Washington late in 1939, Wynn was 21 before he scored his first big league victory for the Senators, who figured in just one pennant race (1945) and, oddly, the year Early was off to war.

By the time Veeck obtained him with first baseman Mickey Vernon for pitchers Joe Haynes and Ed Kliemand and first baseman Eddie Robinson, shortly after Lou Boudreau and Gene Bearden had led the Indians to the world championship in 1948, Wynn owned a record of only 77-87 for six full big league seasons and a demitasse in each of two others.

So from then on until he staggered across the threshold of the exclusive 300-Victory Club, Gus grew athletically old while compiling 223 victories against 157 defeats, a percentage of about .570. And if you're wondering about that nickname, it was hung on him by that little infield pixy and later long-time scout, Ellis Clary, a fast-chattering Georgian who seemed to hiss it:

"Gu-s-s-s!"

Congratulated by Bill Veeck aboard his boat when charter-fishing in the Gulf of Mexico, Wynn gratefully thanked "Mr. Veeck," and The Sport Shirt chided him. "How come?" said Veeck, "I'm 'Mister' now when you used to call me 'Bill.'"

Said Wynn, brightly, "Because now you're the boss."

Don't get the notion, please, that Wynn was—or is—servile. Fact is, columning under the punny title "The Wynn Mill" for the late, departed *Cleveland News*, Early jousted with Boston Red Sox general manager Joe Cronin and J.G. Taylor Spink, long-time publisher of *The Sporting News*.

In retrospect, more than a dozen years later, it's apparent Wynn exercised faulty mental gymnastics, misreading more than really misunderstanding Cronin's comment about sideline commercialism hurting some players and baseball, too. Terrible-tempered Taylor, the soft-hearted Spink, got into the fire—and blasted back—because Wynn, resenting personal-life questions, wrote:

"... *The Sporting News* is beginning to look like a copy of a *Confidential* magazine..."

At that time (1955), *Confidential* magazine was a scandal sheet so that Spink—for once—was indeed properly indignant. But Wynn wouldn't apologize, nor would the *News*' executive sports editor, Regis McAuley, persuade the pitcher to stick to his toeplate rather than his typewriter.

Wynn had learned to spell—correctly, that is—and to punctuate big league from his second wife, the former Lorraine Follin, daughter of a Washington auto dealer. They were married in 1944 and Lorraine took over Early's 5-year-old son, Joe Early, and later presented him with a daughter, Shirley.

The pitcher's first marriage had ended tragically. In 1939, when he was pitching for Charlotte, N.C., he met a Carolina girl named Mabel Allman. Two years later, taking home a babysitter for the Wynns' infant son, Mabel was killed in an automobile accident. At 21, Early was left with a child and no wife.

Gu-s-s-s had learned about hardships back home in Hartford, Ala. Son of an auto mechanic who had played pro ball briefly, he was determined to follow in Early Sr.'s footsteps, but, between numerous odd jobs, which included farming peanuts, he played football with the same all-out effort he would give baseball. Running back a punt in high school, he suffered a broken leg.

Early never did finish school. His mother shipped him to her sister's in Sanford, Fla., to get the football notion out of his head. He drove a truck, reportedly barefooted and in overalls, 400 miles for a visit that became the turning point in his young life. The Washington ball club was holding a tryout camp there in 1937, and the hard-firing farm boy was signed for $100 a month.

By 1943 at Washington, he was an 18-game winner and, though his seasons in D.C. were more down than up, he was a raw commodity in a troublesome market. That one pitch was wicked, but just one. So, as mentioned, it took Harder's cunning and Wynn's willingness to learn to convert the thrower into a pitcher at Cleveland, where he followed an 8-19 season at Washington with 11-7, 18-8, 20-13, 23-12, 17-12, 23-11, 17-11, 20-9 and 14-17.

The deal that took him back to Lopez at Cleveland came at the December baseball meetings in 1957 and infielder-outfielder Al Smith also went along to the future (1959) pennant-winners in exchange for Chicago favorite Minnie Minoso, the outfielder, and infielder Fred Hatfield.

A switch-hitter who was all business the day he pitched, disdaining horsing around the batting cage to get in his licks, which helped him, Wynn was a stronger, more durable pitcher when fleshier, Veeck found after coaxing him to take off weight before his first season at Cleveland. Particularly in the later years, the sturdy six-footer would get up to a reported 235 pounds.

If necessary, Gus could and would fight, such as when he injured a finger on his pitching hand when dispatching an obnoxious patron at the steak house and bowling alleys that bore his name in Venice, Fla. He proved a ballplayer could be a business man and all business on the mound, too.

Off it, he got involved in heavy-duty construction down there between Sarasota and Ft. Myers. He had a handsome home with swimming pool at nearby Nokomis on the island canal from Venice to Tampa. He could pilot a boat and also a plane. He learned to wield a lariat so well—the Indian heritage maybe?—that teammates for a time called him "Wigwam Willie."

He fancied himself as a great outdoor cook, too, but even Wynn, whose proper sense of humor has not come through this kaleidoscopic look at a king of the hill, admitted he out-thought himself one time. Let Gus tell it:

"I went to a drug store and got a hypodermic syringe and injected my special sauce into the turkey. The sauce included wine, beer and brandy mixed in with vinegar, lemon and tomato base.

"The idea was that by injecting the sauce, the steam of the cooking turkey would permeate the entire bird."

Well?

"Well, we didn't get sick, but the turkey got awful drunk."

Not averse to the flowing bowl himself, Early Wynn never did like the guy who stayed late at the bar and then made a pest of himself, particularly with the private-person pitcher, as one chest-poking so-and-so did one evening at the bar of a restaurant, where the bore persisted to the point that he spoiled Wynn's appetite.

Old Gus looked down at his uneaten food later, looked at the table where the drunken so-and-so was slurping up the food as gustily as he had the booze. Disgusted that the aggressor should win, "victim" Wynn walked out and, as he did, he dropped his lighted cigarette into the unpleasant person's side coat pocket.

At the doorway, Early explained to a restaurant maitre 'd, a friend, what he had done and slipped the host extra money. "Now," said Wynn, leaving, "you'd better go over and tell that bleeping fool before he sets himself and the whole place on fire."

A mean trick, maybe, but a guy does have to live with himself and his image. That was Wynn's image. Mean. More recently heavy handed in trying to improve old players' pensions.

Once, when the Yankees' Gil McDougald crowded the plate, old Gus complained to the umpire. The man in blue shrugged, noting that the heel of Gil's sizable shoe still was on the chalkline at the front part of the box.

Wynn's point was that the batter still was crowding the plate, but the umpire, though sympathetic, was not moved to action.

"Okay," said old Gus, "if you won't move him, I will."

Up and in—zip!—and down went McDougald, to brush himself off up and to stand entirely within the batter's box.

One day when newspaperman Jimmy Breslin, the brilliant dead-end kid from Brooklyn, was bird-dogging Wynn for a lengthy magazine profile, Gu-s-s-s just had lost a tough game and Breslin sidled over to talk to Wynn where he sat at his locker, head down, expressionless.

"I wouldn't if I were you," warned Tony Cuccinello, the White Sox coach. "The mood he's in now, he might kill you."

Wynn and some of friends and admirers—press and public alike—thought he should have breezed into the national baseball Hall of Fame the first time he was eligible after five years out, 1969, but he needed four times around in voting by the Baseball Writers' Association of America.

The election still was impressive. And even though he'd won those 300 games, old Gus HAD lost 244, even if some were as tough as one veteran Chicago sportswriter Warren Brown remembered.

The score had been 1-0, a result of defensive boo-boos behind Wynn, who tried hard to be professional about it and walked into a plane to find some teammates laughing it up over beer in the rear. Early sat down and tried to read, but the slow burn still showed under the bronzed neck of his collar.

Finally, he arose, walked back toward the rear of the plane, picking up beer cans and, flinging them at the startled White Sox assembled, he said:

"Damnit, I'm trying to win a pennant. If you bleeping bleeps don't give a bleep, all right, but don't laugh your bleeping laughs where I can hear you."

That was Early (Gus) Wynn, all right, a guy known in the heat of a tough loss to walk in and tear up a clubhouse, which he did one night at Cleveland, where he then flung his uniform jacket toward the ceiling so that it caught on a rafter and hung limply, one arm dangling toward the floor.

Just then Hal Newhouser, a pitching veteran of no ordinary credentials himself, walked into the clubhouse and, feigning shock, Newhouser had 'em all laughing, including the Wynn who didn't like to lose, when he looked up at the ceiling and then blurted:

"My God, old Gus has hung himself!"

Old Gus thought that was funny, all right, but he saw no humor in it when young son Joe Early, barely in his teens, lit into a fat batting practice served up by the old man one day at Cleveland and hit the left-field fence. Park employees, witnesses, cheered.

Wynn pursed his lips and, the way the story is told, he immediately decked his own son, but Early's recollection is that he merely cut loose a high, hard one—high and outside—so that the pitch thudded against the backstop and merely shook up young Joe Early.

Regardless of apocryphal or actual, stories about Early's flaming embers of competitive fire will persist, such as when he was asked, facetiously, whether he'd loosen up his mother if she dug in against him at the plate.

"Sure," they quoted the deadpanned practitioner of intimidation and—winning—effort. "After all, Mom was a pretty good hitter."

EARLY (GUS) WYNN JR.
Born January 6, 1920, at Hartford, Ala.
Height 6-0 Weight 235
Threw right and batted right and lefthanded.
Named to Hall of Fame, 1972.

YEAR	CLUB	LEAGUE	G.	IP.	W.	L.	Pct.	H.	R.	ER.	SO.	BB.	ERA.
1937	Sanford	Florida St.	35	235	16	11	.593	224	113	89	106	81	3.41
1938	Charlotte	Piedmont	29	179	10	11	.476	195	124	105	94	73	5.28
1939	Charlotte	Piedmont	34	243	15	14	.517	254	132	107	150	98	3.96
1939	Washington	Amer.	3	20	0	2	.000	26	15	13	1	10	5.85
1940	Charlotte	Piedmont	31	144	9	7	.563	154	103	68	76	57	4.25
1941	Springfield	Eastern	34	257	16	12	.571	239	89	73	126	84	2.56
1941	Washington	Amer.	5	40	3	1	.750	35	14	7	15	10	1.58
1942	Washington	Amer.	30	190	10	16	.385	246	129	108	58	73	5.12
1943	Washington	Amer.	37	257	18	12	.600	232	97	83	89	83	2.91
1944	Washington	Amer.	33	208	8	17	.320	221	97	78	65	67	3.38
1945	Washington	Amer.					(In Military Service)						
1946	Washington	Amer.	17	107	8	5	.615	112	45	37	36	33	3.11
1947	Washington	Amer.	33	247	17	15	.531	251	114	100	73	90	3.64
1948	Washington (a)	Amer.	33	198	8	19	.296	236	144	128	49	94	5.82
1949	Cleveland	Amer.	26	165	11	7	.611	186	84	76	62	57	4.15
1950	Cleveland	Amer.	32	214	18	8	.692	166	88	76	143	101	3.20
1951	Cleveland	Amer.	37	274	20	13	.606	227	102	92	133	107	3.02
1952	Cleveland	Amer.	42	286	23	12	.657	239	103	92	153	132	2.90
1953	Cleveland	Amer.	36	252	17	12	.586	234	121	110	138	107	3.93
1954	Cleveland	Amer.	40	271	23	11	.676	225	93	82	155	83	2.72
1955	Cleveland	Amer.	32	230	17	11	.607	207	86	72	122	80	2.82
1956	Cleveland	Amer.	38	278	20	9	.690	233	93	84	158	91	2.72
1957	Cleveland (b)	Amer.	40	263	14	17	.452	270	139	126	184	104	4.31
1958	Chicago	Amer.	40	240	14	16	.467	214	115	110	179	104	4.13
1959	Chicago	Amer.	37	256	22	10	.688	202	106	90	179	119	3.16
1960	Chicago	Amer.	36	237	13	12	.520	220	105	92	158	112	3.49
1961	Chicago	Amer.	17	110	8	2	.800	88	43	43	64	47	3.52
1962	Chicago (c)	Amer.	27	168	7	15	.318	171	90	83	91	56	4.45
1963	Cleveland	Amer.	20	55	1	2	.333	50	14	14	29	15	2.29
Major League Totals - 23 Years			691	4566	300	244	.551	4291	2037	1796	2334	1775	3.54

a Traded to Cleveland Indians with First Baseman Mickey Vernon for Pitchers Joe Haynes and Ed Klieman and First Baseman Eddie Robinson, December 14, 1948.

b Traded to Chicago White Sox with Infielder-Outfielder Al Smith for Infielder Fred Hatfield and Outfielder Minnie Minoso, December 4, 1957.

c Released by Chicago White Sox, November 20, 1962; signed with Cleveland Indians, June 21, 1963.

WORLD SERIES RECORD

YEAR	CLUB	LEAGUE	G.	IP.	W.	L.	Pct.	H.	R.	ER.	SO.	BB.	ERA.
1954	Cleveland	Amer.	1	7	0	1	.000	4	3	3	5	2	3.86
1959	Chicago	Amer.	3	13	1	1	.500	19	9	8	10	4	5.54
World Series Totals - 2 Years			4	20	1	2	.333	23	12	11	15	6	4.95

511: *Denton (Cy) Young's incredible number of victories for 23 seasons boggles modern minds. The old Ohio sodbuster won so many games that as he told an inquiring young reporter before his death in 1955 at 88, "Son, I won more games than you'll ever see."*

CY YOUNG

A cub reporter approached a tall, strong-framed, pipe-smoking gaffer one day at a baseball clambake and inquired: "Did you ever pitch in the major leagues, Mr. Young?"

Denton True Young smiled and his watery old blue eyes twinkled. "Son," he said, "I won more games than you'll ever see."

That's a fact. Few average fans see 511 games, the total won by the Ohio sodbuster whose consistency and efficiency were almost as remarkable as his durability. These qualities are probably the outstanding characteristics of the pitching pioneer who was close to 89 years old when he died in 1955.

If the Young who lived quite old wasn't baseball's best pitcher ever, certainly he was its most successful and hardiest. He pitched 22 years in the big leagues and didn't have the hint of a sore arm until he was 44 and so paunchy that when the foe couldn't hit him, they bunted him into retirement.

Trying to keep up with Cy's accomplishments, much less comprehend them in the light of modern meaurements, is as difficult as trying to pry a ball

523

out of the old man's iron grip not too many years before he joined his beloved wife, Robba, in a cemetery high atop a hill overlooking the fertile Tuscarawas River Valley at Peoli, O.

What feats those ancient eyes had seen and tireless right arm achieved make Cy Young seem in the '90s as both its most amazing physical specimen and its link between the game's primitive infancy and its modern maturity. Imagine, with all the arm injuries now.

To grasp just how much of the sport's history the husky farmer touched, consider, please, that he played in the big leagues against the great Adrian (Cap) Anson, whose career had begun as early as 1871, and he performed against the flawless Tris Speaker, who didn't quit the game until 1930. That's 59 years.

When Young joined the Cleveland Spiders in 1890, the pitcher's box was just that, a flat, square area from which the boxman delivered the ball to a barehanded catcher just 50 feet away. By the time Cy delivered his last baseball competitively in 1911, pitchers were throwing as they are today from a rubber atop a mound, 60 feet, six inches from the plate, and to a catcher suited up in armor like a knight of old.

The increased pitching distance did not handicap the 6-2, 210-pound Young. Before the last change in the pitching distance in 1894, he posted seasons of 27, 36 and 32 victories. But after dipping to 25 in '94, he came back to win 35 and then 29 as he continued a string of 14 successive seasons in which he won 20 or more games. He was a 20-game winner for the 16th and last time in 1908, when he was 41 years old.

Five of those seasons in which he won 20 or more, Young gained more than 30 victories, including his first two years in the new American League when he had 33 and then 32 for the Red Sox. The endurance marvel wound up with 10 full seasons in both major leagues, so it was a fitting tribute when former baseball commissioner Ford Frick established the Cy Young award in 1956 as a pitching supplement to the time-honored Most Valuable Player awards in each league.

The Pitcher-of-the-Year presentation, at the request of the baseball writers, since has been made a dual award so that there is no unfair necessity, for instance, to try to compare a Denny McLain with a Bob Gibson. Or an Oral Hershisher with a Roger Clements. Or with the modern-day miracle like the old master, meaning Nolan Ryan. As a result, the memory of Cy Young is honored at least twice each year.

Well it should be, because he was a great one, you'll have to concede, even if you're a deep-dyed Democrat. Old Cy was an Ohio Republican, of whom there are none whomer, and he not only voted in the course of his career for Republican presidents William McKinley, Theodore Roosevelt and William Howard Taft, but he also pitched a no-hitter in each man's administration.

Young's first no-hitter came in 1897 against the Cincinnati Red Stockings at a time when Cleveland was in the National League. Cy walked one batter and three reached base in the course of a 6-0 contest.

The second one came seven years later when Rough Rider Roosevelt sat in the White House. Cy was positively perfect. A crowd of more than 10,000 sat in at Boston's Huntington Avenue grounds on May 5 to watch the pitching ace of their newly crowned world champions oppose the colorful lefthanded fireballer of the Philadelphia Athletics— Rube Waddell.

Connie Mack called Cy's performance that day the most impressive he ever saw. In the 3-0 game, he struck out eight, retired nine on grounders and 10 on pop flies and short outfield flies. There wasn't a tough defensive chance, and, in fact, only one loud foul by Dan Murphy in the fifth inning.

Young was concentrating so thoroughly on the job at hand that he said he didn't realize he had not permitted a baserunner until outfielder Chick Stahl caught a high lazy fly to end the game and then rushed into hand Cy the ball and swarm all over him.

The pitcher had been so intent on outpitching Waddell that he'd not heard it in the seventh when first baseman Candy LaChance passed him and said, "Ya know, nobody's been down here yet."

Four years later, in 1908, then 41 years old, Young came within a corner-missing pitch of achieving a second perfect game. Facing the High-landers at New York, the old man walked Harry Niles, the leadoff man, on a 3-and-2 pitch. Niles promptly was retired trying to steal, and Young breezed to an 8-0 triumph, retiring the next 26 bat-ters, aided by his own good play on Neal Ball's fifth-inning bunt and Cactus Cravath's fine ninth-inning catch of a long fly.

Since then, Bob Feller and Jim Maloney have pitched three no-hitters, Sandy Koufax four and Ryan seven. Feller, like Young, was elected to the Hall of Fame. Cy was named in 1937. Koufax, ergo, was a first-time choice. Ryan is also a Cooperstown certainty. Maybe closest to unanimity.

Young didn't live long enough to see Sandy or Ryan, but, despite his age, would drive often into Cleveland with friends to watch Feller pitch and was very much impressed by the Iowan who also had come from behind a plow to win fame and consider-ably more fortune than Young. Cy's highest salary was under $5,000, he would say without complaint.

He was a pliable old-timer who didn't live in the past, even though he had been born just two years after the Civil War and lived until past the Korean War. He was supremely confident in his own ability to win in any era, but he appreciated differences in times and conditions.

"I could throw a 'tobacco' ball, a pitch that was dirtied and a ball that wasn't so lively," he would say at the old-timers' reunions he attended regularly.

"Cripes," Toots Shor once said after a baseball bash at his bistro in New York, "the old man was the only guy in the joint who could drink more than I did."

Young would amplify the advantages he'd en-joyed, but he wasn't too modest to list the disadvan-tages, too.

"I had excellent control," he said, "throwing with four different deliveries and wheeling on the batter to hide the ball. I saw some fast ones—Amos Rusie, Walter Johnson, Lefty Grove and Feller, among others—but I was among them, too. My favorite pitch was a whistler right under the chin, and, as Ty Cobb said, I had a couple of good curveballs, an overhanded pitch that broke sharply down and a sweeping, sidearmed curve."

Young averaged fewer than two walks a game for the whopping 7,377 innings he pitched in 906 games. As a late-inning reliever, himself a physical freak, Hoyt Wilhelm has appeared in more games now, but, as Leo Durocher would say, there's no way—none—that any pitcher will approach old Cy's average of more than eight innings a game for 22 years on the firing line.

Cy pitched effortlessly and with absolutely no re-gard, he said, for whether he gripped the ball with the seams, across the seams or on the smooth part.

At one time he pitched 23 consecutive hitless in-nings, still a record, and another time the same year, 1904, he went 20 innings in a duel against Waddell and didn't issue a base on balls, but still lost. The man who won the most games, you see, also lost the most, 313, though his career won-and-lost percent-age, .620, would be a pennant pace. He was 222-141 in the American League for .612, 289-172 in the National for .627.

"I had the benefit of a larger strike zone—from the top of the shoulders to the bottom of the knees—and I admit some of my cut-plug tobacco would get on the ball," Young explained shortly be-fore his death, "but there were disadvantages other than the obvious financial ones.

"I'm thinking of the poorer fields, poorer equip-ment, bad food, bad traveling conditions, no shower baths, sooty trains, noisy rooming houses, some of them full of bedbugs that'd keep you up all night."

Even though the ball might have been juiced up outside, but not inside, meaning it wasn't nearly so lively, and even though ball clubs carried only four or five-man pitching staffs, rather than 10 or 11, how could a man work as frequently as Young? He pitched more than 300 innings a season 16 times, five of them working in excess of 400 rounds.

"My arm would get weak and tired at times, but never sore, even though I worked usually with just two days' rest and often with only one," Young said. "I credited it to my legs and my off-season conditioning.

"I ran regularly to keep my legs in shape. In the spring I'd run constantly for three weeks before I ever threw a ball. And I worked hard all winter on my farm, from sunup to sundown, doing chores that not only were good for my legs, but also for my arm and back. Swinging an axe hardens the hands and builds up the shoulders and back. I needed only a dozen pitches to warm up for a ball game."

If there's a clue to pitching longevity involved in off-season occupations, it might be mentioned that two extremely durable pitchers of much later vintage, Murry Dickson and Elroy Face, both were winter-time carpenters. They felt that the sawing and hammering motion preserved the strength, suppleness, flexibility and muscle tone of their right arms. They, too, were strangers to sore arms.

Dent Young, as they called him down on the farm, developed those good legs chasing squirrels as a kid, he said, reminding one of how Enos Slaughter, a hustling 20-year wonder of recent times, would outrun hunting dogs to fallen fowl in the duck-shooting season.

Deep in Ohio's fertile hill country, Denton True Young grew up as a powerful farmer and rail splitter. His father had given him as a middle name the surname of a soldier who'd saved the senior Young in the Civil War. Later, someone tried to romanticize it by saying the "T" that was Cy's middle initial stood for Tecumseh, but the Big Chief of pitchers would merely smile and say it just wasn't so.

It's hard to believe, considering how much ground he covered and how many games he won, that young Dent was all of 23 years old before he went from his home at Gilmore to play baseball professionally at Canton, 50 miles away.

Dent was making $10 a month and his keep on his father's farm. His parents were reluctant to see him leave, but when he talked the manager of Canton's Tri-State League club into upping the monthly ante from $40 to $60, the elder Youngs consented, reluctantly.

The big farm kid who checked in at Canton had hay shaker written all over. He shuffled hesitantly into the shabby office of the ball club, carrying a cheap cardboard suitcase. His jacket, sizes too small, barely reached below his waist. Its sleeves failed to conceal his brawny wrists. His shirt was stretched across a barrel chest.

City folks laughed and later that season when he was pitching for Cleveland in the National League, fabled Cap Anson called him "Rube," but the nickname, Cy, which seemed to fit, was not bestowed because of the pitcher's bucolic appearance or bumpkin background.

The Cy was short for Cyclone, which someone called him after he'd warmed up in blue coveralls and his pitches had battered the board fence of the Canton ballpark, which looked indeed as if a cyclone had struck it. A sportswriter picked up the nickname. Shortened, it stuck—and Dent Young had a new name the rest of his life.

After Cy divided 30 decisions at Canton, he was sold later that season to Cleveland. One story always has been that the financially harassed Canton club needed money and that Davis Hawley, a Cleveland banker and one of the Spiders' owners, got Young by buying the Canton club owner a suit of clothes. But Cy insisted he went for cash—$250.

Cy's debut in the majors was against Anson's Chicagos and is best told by Charles Mears, the Cleveland correspondent of *The Sporting News*, in that paper's issue of August 16, 1890. Mears wrote:

"Young gave the Chicagos only three puny singles. His curves were unsolvable and he was as cool as though he were back in Canton instead of pitching before a National League audience. Young pitches a speedy ball that gets to the hitter before he realizes it."

The 38-year-old Anson still was one of the best hitters in the game, but Cy remembered later that he wasn't scared or nervous. "All I can remember is that I was mad," he said, "because Anse had called me 'a big farmer' and 'Rube.' I wanted to show him up more than anything in my life."

He did. Without the effective curve that later helped make him a big winner, Young blazed the fastball past Anson, striking him out, and winning the first of the 511 by which he would average 23 victories a season for 22 years.

If a pitcher threw so hard, how could a man catch him barehanded?

Young knew a good question when he heard one. "You should have seen those amazing calloused hands," he explained. "Chief Zimmer didn't have a padded mitt when he first caught me. He wore an ordinary dress glove with sole-leather tips sewed on the fingers."

The first pitcher Young recalled seeing wear a glove was Nig Cuppy of the Spiders. Cy didn't try a glove himself until 1897, noting that Anson played first base barehanded and that the best second baseman of his early career, Biddy McPhee, never did wear a glove.

"The glove changed fielding a lot," Young stated the obvious. "We used to cup both hands and close them over the ball like a clam shell. When the glove came in, players began to depend on the gloved hand to stop the ball and the right hand to hold it. Naturally, their reach and range improved."

The era into which the gentle giant from the Ohio farm country came was a rough one in baseball. He always maintained that the Cleveland Spiders were as rough as the Baltimore Orioles of Hughie Jennings, John McGraw and Wilbert Robinson.

Young told a later Cleveland sports editor, Gordon Cobbledick, about the time, with only one umpire working the game, that McGraw cut across behind the man in blue on an infield out so that he, in effect, went from first to third across the pitcher's mound instead of touching second base, which was required then just as it is now. The Spiders screamed, but the umpire, Bob Emslie, though he could suspect he'd been had, couldn't declare McGraw out because he hadn't seen the play.

The Spiders' left fielder, Jesse Burkett, took matters into his own hands. While Cleveland was arguing, Burkett charged in, beckoning for the ball, and Young threw it to him. Jesse barged into McGraw, knocked him off third base, sat on him and, tagging out the runner, called to Emslie.

Turning, the umpire took one look and, relieved at seeing justice prevail by fair means or foul, jerked up his thumb and called to McGraw, 'Yer out!'

Young prided himself that he beat the famed Orioles five times in one season and never lost more to them than he won, though he always regarded Wee Willie Keeler, their hit-'em-where-they-ain't outfielder, as the best batter he ever faced.

"Better than Cobb, even though not as good a bunter, and not as good overall, but tougher for me to get out," Cy said. "With that little bat and his choppy swing, he could hit anything. You couldn't fool him with a curve. I always tried to keep the ball low and I always worked on him with my change of pace—fast, faster and fastest."

When the Temple Cup was inaugurated in 1894 as a forerunner of the World Series, Young was already a star and he proved it in '95 when Cleveland played Baltimore in the best-of-seven series between the National League's two top teams.

Young beat the Orioles three times in a five-game series marked by so much rowdiness that when the Spiders returned to their hotel after the fourth contest, the first at Baltimore, the regulars were forced to prostrate themselves on the floor of a carriage, with the reserves and newspapermen atop them. Police, en route, made 10 arrests, but the carriage still was bombarded with rocks and bottles.

The next day in the kind of sullen atmosphere in which the Spiders needed 40 policemen for protection, Cy beat the Orioles—the "Oysters," he called 'em—for a third time, 5-2, and set up a winning rally with a double.

That year Young had a 35-10 record, the first of four seasons in which he led a big league in victories.

As victory dulled Cleveland fans' appetite, Frank DeHaas Robison, owner of the Spiders, made them virtually a road team in 1898. The next year, after obtaining the St. Louis National League franchise, he switched his Cleveland stars to St. Louis. Included was Young, who was welcomed by a crowd of 11,000 which hiked out to the ballpark despite a transportation strike and saw Cy shut out Chicago, 8-0.

Although he pitched well enough in St. Louis, winning 26 games in 1899 and 20 in 1900, Young didn't like the city or its heat, and he missed his Ohio farm. He was in a receptive mood when Ban Johnson, forming the American League, offered him a $600-a-year raise to jump to the Boston Red Sox. Cy's St. Louis salary of $2,400 then was the individual limit in the tight-fisted National League.

The National League misjudged the pitching longevity of the strapping sodbuster, already 33 years old and potbellied. "Young is through," Robison sniffed. "In that bush league he may last another year, but we couldn't have used him."

There's little doubt that inferior competition did help Young at first, just as, for example, it aided Larry Lajoie, who also jumped leagues, to the highest average of his career. But within three years, when the first World Series was played, the Boston club on which Young teamed with Bill Dinneen, was good enough to upset the heavily favored Pittsburgh Pirates, five games to three.

The Pirates won three out of the first four games and the ho-hums and I-told-you-sos filled the air, but then Young won the fifth game, 11-2. Dinneen

took the sixth, 6-3. Young put the Red Sox ahead by beating the Pirates' ace, Deacon Phillippe, 7-3, and Dinneen closed it out with a four-hit shutout, 3-0.

Fittingly, therefore, Cy Young, the old master of both major leagues, pitched in the first official World Series. It was his first and last Series, but not his final distinction. Why, did you know that fair Harvard even asked the Ohio farmer to coach its baseball team in the winter?

"A testimonial," as Cobbledick wrote, "not only to his eminence as a craftsman, but also to his reputation as a gentleman in an era when that title was given to few professional ballplayers."

Old Tuscarawas preferred, as always, to spend the good rural life back home on the farm, though by continuing to pitch and to win, he couldn't escape further honors.

In 1908, an idea conceived by the *Boston Post*, a day was held at the old Huntington Avenue grounds for the grand gaffer who had rebounded from two losing seasons for 22-15 in 1907 and then, at 41, had turned in his third no-hitter en route to a 21-11 mark in '08.

A crowd of 20,000 crammed the grounds and about 10,000 were turned away. Young received cash gifts close to $7,500, considerably more than a season's salary, and other gifts of which at least one was unusual. The American League umpires showed their esteem by presenting him with a traveling bag.

Of several trophies, one particularly was unusual, too. It came from the old pitcher's rival players in the American League. Misty-eyed old Cy had no field microphone to help him thank his well-wishers without shouting.

He'd had big thrills in Boston, including the first World Series, which he could relive in later years, smiling.

"Brass bands were all over the place. Men came in long-tailed coats and high hats or derbies. The ladies were bedecked in their ankle-length skirts and picture hats. The bands played all the tunes of the times…'Dixie'…'Wait Till the Sun Shines, Nellie'…and all the rest. It was fine, just fine."

But the biggest thrill came the following year in his perfect game against Philadelphia, a club against which veteran writer Fred Lieb, then just a wide-eyed youngster, saw Cy perform one of the finest feats of mound magic. Lieb watched Young, protecting a one-run lead, yield a leadoff triple in the last inning against the Athletics and then strike out three batters on just nine pitches.

Cy liked to remember one considerably less significant. Back in '97, when Cleveland was playing the Philadelphia Phillies, Slidin' Billy Hamilton, the league's leading basestealer and foul-ball hitter, approached Young and bragged that the previous day he had fouled off 29 consecutive pitches against Sadie McMahon of the Baltimore Orioles.

Cy said nothing, but when Hamilton came up the first time that day and punched three pitches foul, the big righthander walked in toward the plate and said, "Look, Billy, I'm putting the next pitch right over the heart of the plate. If you foul it off, the next one goes right into your ear."

Grinning, the gaffer related, "Hamilton got the message. He sent the next pitch on a weak dribble to second base."

Essentially, of course, Cy did not believe in pitching over the heart of the plate. He knew, for instance, that Detroit's Sam Crawford murdered a ball inside, so he'd flirt with the ball down and away all day.

"But I defend pitchers who throw the ball into the strike zone at times with a count of two strikes and none," Young said in one of the numerous baseball bull sessions he enjoyed in later years. "I don't think a pitcher can permit the batter ever to type him or take him for granted. Every now and then, on an 0-and-2 count, I'd bring the ball right to the hitter, hoping to surprise him."

Looking at hits allowed in relation to innings pitched, Cy Young worked only 299 innings more than he yielded hits, but he was very stingy with

walks, especially after his first four full seasons in the majors, and he became sharp enough to yield just 28 passes in 380 rounds (1904) and strike out 203 men.

Although he pitched for five clubs, Young actually pitched in only three cities and, as mentioned, St. Louis merely was a short stop between long stints at Cleveland and Boston. He had two trips each into those cities, one in each league.

After the auld lang syne treatment at Boston in 1908, he was sold that fall for $12,500 to Cleveland, which by then was in the American League, too. At 42, he still had a 19-15 season in 1909, but then he dipped to 7-10 and finally to 3-4 in 1911 when he was released in August. He went back to Boston, this time with the National League he'd left 11 years earlier, and won four and lost five.

A sort of legend has grown up about Cy's last major league game. He himself used to recall that he lost his finale to a Philadelphia rookie, Grover Cleveland Alexander, 1-0.

The facts are that Young pitched six more times after that loss on September 7, 1911, when Alexander posted a one-hitter. Cy's last big league game was October 6, 1911, in the second game of a doubleheader at Brooklyn and two obscure hurlers, Eddie Dent and Wilbur Schardt, combined to beat him, 13-3. He was pounded for eight runs and eight straight hits with one out in the seventh inning before being relieved. Dent, who won only four games in his brief career, was the winner, with Schardt hurling the last two innings.

Young went south with Boston in the spring of 1912 but quit before the championship season opened.

So he went back to the farm country from where he'd left in 1890 with a long-armed buggywhip delivery which destroyed those six planks behind homeplate at the Canton ballpark. He'd gone away as Dent Young and he returned as Cyclone—no, as Cy Young.

A fairly prosperous man for his times, Cy turned to his Ohio farm, the white place with the big pillars. He farmed contentedly until his wife, the former Robba Miller, died in 1933. Shortly thereafter, he sold his holdings and moved in with friends and neighbors, the John Benedums, working the fields at Peoli until he was well past 80.

Between times, he went to many baseball reunions, including noteworthy ones at which he stood out as the link with the distant past. Included were the first Hall of Fame induction at Cooperstown in 1939, the National League's 75th birthday celebration in 1951 and the American League's half-century celebration the same season at Boston.

"You'd think they could give an old fella $75 or so," he said quietly at one reunion, indicating that he'd felt the financial pinch in his old age.

From the time he reached 80, the citizens of Tuscarawas County held a big annual birthday party on March 29 for their most famous neighbor. The indoor outing outgrew the high school gymnasium in Newcomerstown and threatened to tax the facilities of the largest gathering place in New Philadelphia, O.

A recreation park, complete with swimming pool and baseball field, was named for Cy Young in Newcomerstown in 1950. Five years later in November, rich with memories, Denton True (Cy) Young sat in his favorite arm chair at the Benedums, looking out the window, when the heart that had beat through doubleheader victories and incredible endurance effort beat its last.

Cy was something, all right. The dean of American sportswriters, Grantland Rice, introduced him to members of the press covering the 1940 World Series in Cincinnati. "Gentlemen," said Rice, "I'd like you to meet the greatest pitcher who ever lived—Cy Young. He won 511 games."

The old fellow shook his head. "Five hundred and twelve, Granny," he said. "I won one they didn't give me credit for."

DENTON TRUE (CY) YOUNG

Born March 29, 1867, at Gilmore, O.
Died November 4, 1955, at Peoli, O.
Height 6-2 Weight 210
Threw and batted righthanded.
Named to Hall of Fame, 1937.

YEAR	CLUB	LEAGUE	G.	IP.	W.	L.	Pct.	ShO.	H.	R.	SO.	BB.
1890	Canton	Tri-State	31	260	15	15	.500	0	253	165	201	33
1890	Cleveland	Nat.	17	150	9	7	.563	0	145	83	36	32
1891	Cleveland	Nat.	54	430	27	20	.574	0	436	239	146	132
1892	Cleveland	Nat.	53	455	36	11	.766	9	362	159	167	114
1893	Cleveland	Nat.	53	426	32	16	.667	1	441	229	102	104
1894	Cleveland	Nat.	52	409	25	22	.532	2	493	266	101	101
1895	Cleveland	Nat.	47	373	35	10	.778	4	371	176	120	77
1896	Cleveland	Nat.	51	414	29	16	.644	5	467	212	137	64
1897	Cleveland	Nat.	47	338	21	18	.538	2	389	195	87	50
1898	Cleveland (a)	Nat.	46	378	25	14	.641	1	394	174	107	40
1899	St. Louis	Nat.	44	369	26	15	.634	4	364	170	112	43
1900	St. Louis	Nat.	41	321	20	18	.526	4	337	146	119	38
1901	Boston	Amer.	43	371	33	10	.767	5	320	113	159	38
1902	Boston	Amer.	45	386	32	10	.762	3	337	137	166	51
1903	Boston	Amer.	40	342	28	10	.737	7	292	116	183	37
1904	Boston	Amer.	43	380	26	16	.619	10	326	104	203	28
1905	Boston	Amer.	38	321	18	19	.486	5	245	98	208	30
1906	Boston	Amer.	39	288	13	21	.382	0	289	135	146	27
1907	Boston	Amer.	43	343	22	15	.595	6	287	101	148	52
1908	Boston (b)	Amer.	36	299	21	11	.656	3	230	68	150	37
1909	Cleveland	Amer.	35	295	19	15	.559	3	267	110	109	59
1910	Cleveland	Amer.	21	163	7	10	.412	1	149	62	58	27
1911	Cleveland (c)	Amer.	7	46	3	4	.429	0	54	28	20	13
1911	Boston	Nat.	11	80	4	5	.444	2	83	47	35	15
American League Totals			390	3234	222	141	.612	43	2796	1072	1550	399
National League Totals			516	4143	289	172	.627	34	4282	2096	1269	810
Major League Totals			906	7377	511	313	.620	77	7078	3168	2819	1209

a Transferred with pick of team to St. Louis by Frank Robison, owner of both clubs.
b Sold to Cleveland for $12,500.
c Released, August, 1911, and signed with Boston, N.L.

TEMPLE CUP RECORD

YEAR	CLUB	LEAGUE	G.	IP.	W.	L.	Pct.	ShO.	H.	R.	SO.	BB.
1895	Cleveland	Nat.	3	27	3	0	1.000	0	27	7	2	4
1896	Cleveland	Nat.	1	9	0	1	.000	0	13	7	0	1
Temple Cup Totals			4	36	3	1	.750	0	40	14	2	5

WORLD SERIES RECORD

YEAR	CLUB	LEAGUE	G.	IP.	W.	L.	Pct.	ShO.	H.	R.	SO.	BB.
1903	Boston	Amer.	4	34	2	1	.667	0	31	13	17	4

531

Bob Broeg was born and raised in south St. Louis and is a 1941 graduate of the University of Missouri School of Journalism. His wit and wisdom have graced the sports pages of the *St. Louis Post-Dispatch* since 1945, as well as major sports publications such as *The Sporting News*. **SuperStars of Baseball** is his sixteenth book.

Broeg covered the St. Louis Cardinals—his passion, along with the University of Missouri Tigers—from 1945-1958. Broeg worked for the Associated Press before joining the U.S. Marines. After his military service, Broeg joined the *Post-Dispatch*. He served as the sports editor of the *Post-Dispatch* from 1958 until 1985, when he became that newspaper's contributing sports editor.

The Rockne Club of America presented Broeg with its Sportswriter of the Year Award in 1964 and in 1971 he was the recipient of the Journalism Medal from the University of Missouri, the first sportswriter to be honored.

One of the true giants of the sportswriting profession, Broeg's impressive credentials were recognized in 1980, when he received the Baseball Writers Association's most prestigious award at the Baseball Hall of Fame in Cooperstown, New York. He serves on the Board of Directors of the Baseball Hall of Fame and is also a member of the Hall of Fame's Veterans' Committee.

Broeg and his wife Lynette reside in St. Louis.